AMERICAN
LAW
YEARBOOK
1999

ISSN 1521-0901

AMERICAN LAW YEARBOOK 1999

AN ANNUAL SOURCE PUBLISHED
BY THE GALE GROUP AS A
SUPPLEMENT TO
WEST'S ENCYCLOPEDIA OF
AMERICAN LAW

GALE GROUP

Detroit
San Francisco
London
Boston
Woodbridge, CT

Allison McClintic Marion, *Editor*
Patrick Politano, Kathleen Romig, *Assistant Editors*
Linda S. Hubbard, *Managing Editor*

Maria Franklin, *Permissions Manager*
Keryl Stanley, *Permissions Assistant*

Mary Beth Trimper, *Production Director*
Evi Seoud, *Assistant Production Manager*

Cynthia Baldwin, *Product Design Manager*
Barbara J. Yarrow, *Imaging/Multimedia Content Manager*
Randy Bassett, *Image Database Supervisor*
Pamela A. Reed, *Imaging Coordinator*

CONTENTS

The need for a layperson's comprehensive, understandable guide to terms, concepts, and historical developments in U.S. law has been well met by *West's Encyclopedia of American Law* (*WEAL*). Published at the end of 1997 by the foremost legal professional publisher, *WEAL* has proved itself a valuable successor to *The Guide to American Law: Everyone's Legal Encyclopedia* from the same publisher, West Group, in 1983.

Now, in cooperation with West Group, Gale Group, a premier reference publisher, extends the value of *WEAL* with the publication of *American Law Yearbook*. The *Yearbook* both adds entries on emerging topics not covered in the main set and provides updates through May 1999, on cases, statutes, and issues documented there. A legal reference must be current to be authoritative, so the *Yearbook* is a vital companion to a key reference source. Uniform organization and cross-referencing make it easy to use the titles together, while inclusion of key definitions and summaries of earlier rulings in supplement entries, whether new or continuations, make it unnecessary to refer constantly to the main set.

Understanding the American Legal System

The legal system of the United States is admired around the world for the freedoms it allows the individual and the fairness with which it attempts to treat all persons. On the surface, it may seem simple. Yet, those who have delved into it know that this system of federal and state constitutions, statutes, regulations, and common law decisions is elaborate and complex. It derives from the English common law, but includes principles older than England, along with some principles from other lands. Many concepts are still phrased in Latin. The U.S. legal system, like many others, has a language all its own. Too often it is an unfamiliar language.

West's Encyclopedia of American Law (*WEAL*) explains legal terms and concepts in everyday language. It covers a wide variety of persons, entities, and events that have shaped the U.S. legal system and influenced public perceptions of the legal system.

FEATURES OF THIS SUPPLEMENT

Entries

This supplement contains 175 entries covering individuals, cases, laws, and concepts. Entries are arranged alphabetically and, for continuation entries, use the same entry title as in *WEAL*. There may be several cases discussed under a given topic. Entry headings refer to decisions of the U.S. Supreme Court by case name; other cases are identified by their subject matter.

Profiles of individuals cover interesting and influential people from the world of law, government, and public life, both historic and contemporary. All have played a part in creating or shaping U.S. law. Each profile includes a timeline highlighting important moments in the subject's life.

Definitions

Each entry on a legal term is preceded by a definition, which is easily distinguished by its sans serif typeface.

Cross References

To facilitate research, two types of cross-references are provided within and following entries. Within the entries, terms are set in small capital letters (e.g. DISCLAIMER) to indicate that they have their own entry in *WEAL*. Cross references at the end of an entry refer readers to additional relevant topics in *WEAL*.

In Focus Pieces

In Focus pieces present complex and controversial issues from different perspectives. These pieces, which are set apart from the main entries with boxed edges and their own logo, examine some of the difficult legal and social questions that confront attorneys, judges, juries, and legislatures. Stun belts and profiling are among the high-interest topics in this yearbook.

Appendix

The appendix to this volume features the full text of documents that complement the entries, such as the Articles of Impeachment for President Clinton, Child Online Protection Act, and Oregon's Death with Dignity Act.

Index of WEAL's Appendix and Milestones in the Law

This section indexes a number of primary documents included in the main set

Table of Cases Cited and Index

These features make it easy for users to quickly locate references to cases, people, statutes, events, and other subjects. The Table of Cases Cited traces the influences of legal precedents by identifying mentions of cases throughout the text. In a departure from *WEAL*, references to individuals have been folded into the general index to simplify searches. Litigants, justices, historical and contemporary figures, as well as topical references are included in the Index.

Citations

Wherever possible, *American Law Yearbook* includes citations to cases and statutes for readers wishing to do further research. The citation refers to one or more of the series called "reporters" that publish court opinions and related information. Each citation includes a volume number, an abbreviation for the reporter, and the starting page reference. Underscores in a citation indicate that a court opinion has not been officially reported as of publication. Two sample citations, with explanations, are presented below.

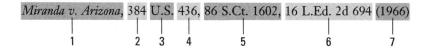

1. *Case title*. The title of the case is set in italics and indicates the names of the parties. The suit in this sample citation was between Ernesto A. Miranda and the state of Arizona.

2. *Reporter volume number*. The number preceding the reporter abbreviation indicates the reporter volume containing the case. (The volume number appears on the spine of the reporter, along with the reporter abbreviation.)

3. *Reporter abbreviation*. The suit in the sample citation is from the reporter, or series of books, called *U.S. Reports*, which contains cases from the U.S. Supreme Court. (Numerous reporters publish cases from the federal and state courts; consult the abbreviations list at the back of this volume for full titles.)

4. *Reporter page*. The number following the reporter abbreviation indicates the reporter page on which the case begins.

5. *Additional reporter citation*. Many cases may be found in more than one reporter. The suit in the sample citation also appears in volume 86 of the *Supreme Court Reporter*, beginning on page 1602.

6. *Additional reporter citation*. The suit in the sample citation is also reported in volume 16 of the *Lawyer's Edition*, second series, beginning on page 694.

7. *Year of decision*. The year the court issued its decision in the case appears in parentheses at the end of the cite.

Brady Handgun Violence Prevention Act, Pub. L. No. 103-159, 107 Stat. 1536 (18 U.S.C.A. § § 921-925A)

| 1 | 2 | 3 | 4 | 5 | 6 | 7 | 8 |

1. *Statute title.*

2. *Public law number.* In the sample citation, the number 103 indicates this law was passed by the 103d Congress, and the number 159 indicates it was the 159th law passed by that Congress.

3. *Reporter volume number.* The number preceding the reporter abbreviation indicates the reporter volume containing the statute.

4. *Reporter abbreviation.* The name of the reporter is abbreviated. The statute in the sample citation is from *Statutes at Large.*

5. *Reporter page.* The number following the reporter abbreviation indicates the reporter page on which the statute begins.

6. *Title number.* Federal laws are divided into major sections with specific titles. The number preceding a reference to the U.S. Code stands for the section called Crimes and Criminal Procedure.

7. *Additional reporter.* The statute in the sample citation may also be found in the *U.S. Code Annotated.*

8. *Section numbers.* The section numbers following a reference to the *U.S. Code Annotated* indicate where the statute appears in that reporter.

COMMENTS WELCOME

Considerable efforts were expended at the time of publication to ensure the accuracy of the information presented in *American Law Yearbook 1999.* The editors welcome your comments and suggestions for enhancing and improving future editions of this supplement to *West's Encyclope-* *dia of American Law.* Send comments and suggestions to:

American Law Yearbook
Gale Group
27500 Drake Rd.
Farmington Hills, MI 48331-3535

SPECIAL THANKS

The editor wishes to acknowledge the contributions of the writers who aided in the compilation of *American Law Yearbook.*. In particular, the editor gratefully thanks Geraldine Azzata, Joseph A. Bastianelli, Daniel E. Brannen, Jr., W. James Burns, Richard J. Cretan, Frederick Grittner, Lauri R. Harding, James Heiberg, Anne Kevlin, Paul S. Kobel, Melynda M. Neal, Kathryne O'Grady, Berna L. Rhodes-Ford, Mary J. Hertz Scarbrough, Robert E. Schnakenberg, Elizabeth Shostak, Scott D. Slick, Kelly Brown Willis, Richard R. Willis, and Lauren Zupnick for their writing contributions.

PHOTOGRAPHIC CREDITS

The editor wishes to thank the permission managers of the companies that assisted in securing reprint rights. The following list acknowledges the copyright holders who have granted us permission to reprint material in this edition of *American Law Yearbook*:

AP/Wide World Photos: pages 3, 4, 9, 17, 20, 26, 38, 39, 41, 48, 54, 58, 60, 61, 63, 73, 75, 77, 81, 85, 92, 104, 110, 112, 118, 120, 124, 127, 132, 134, 145, 147, 151, 156, 161, 166, 168, 177, 181, 185, 187, 190, 193, 197, 202, 203, 211, 217, 230, 232, 246, 248, 251, 262, 263, 265, 270, 277, 281, 285, 287, and 291; **Archive Photos**: pages 40, 137, 138, 149, 195, 200, 219, 258, and 275; **Corbis-Bettmann**: pages 42, 139, and 155.

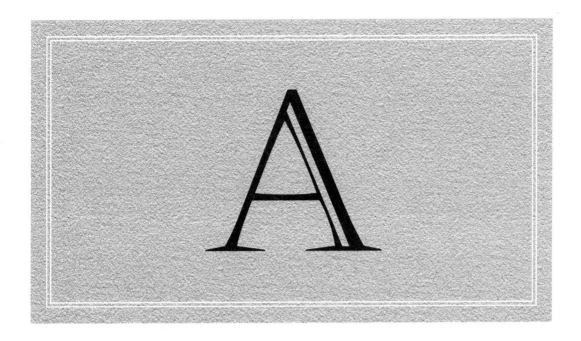

ABORTION

The spontaneous or artificially induced expulsion of an embryo or fetus. As used in legal context, usually refers to induced abortion.

Legislative Battles Continue Over Abortion

February 1998 was the twenty-fifth anniversary of the U.S. Supreme Court's decision in *Roe v. Wade*, 410 U.S. 113, 93 S. Ct. 705, 35 L. Ed. 2d 147 (1973), which made abortion a constitutionally protected medical procedure. In the years since *Roe*, most legislative initiatives have placed restrictions on women's access to abortion over the objections of abortion rights supporters. The fight continued in 1998 and 1999, with battles flaring up over discrete issues such as contraceptives, insurance coverage, and abortions by minors.

In October 1998, Congress considered a measure that would make health insurers of federal employees cover the costs of prescription contraceptives for women. Citing the rising costs of contraceptives for women, House and Senate negotiators agreed to cover Food and Drug Administration-approved female contraceptives: birth control pills, diaphragms, interuterine devices, Norplant, and Depo-Provera. The measure was given a chance for passage in the male-dominated Congress because it would make matters equal between men and women on insurance matters related to sex, as federal health insurance plans already cover Viagra, a drug for men with impotency.

State and federal courts declared several abortion laws to be unconstitutional. In December 1998, Federal District Judge Anne E. Thompson struck down a New Jersey law that barred late-term abortions. The law would have banned all abortions "in which the person performing the abortion partially vaginally delivers a fetus before killing the fetus and completing the delivery." Proponents of the law called the procedure "partial-birth abortion" and argued that the procedure was tantamount to murder. "Once the baby is out of the womb, it's no longer covered by Roe," said Marie Tasy, a legislative director for the New Jersey Right to Live organization. "To us, this is a human rights issue." Richard F. Collier, the attorney for the New Jersey legislature, called the procedure "infanticide."

Judge Thompson disagreed, emphasizing the health of the pregnant woman. According to Judge Thompson, the law threatened "a woman's constitutional right to terminate her pregnancy. It is in the public's interest to prevent the act from taking effect and thereby protect the woman's right to choose." New Jersey Governor Christine Todd Whitman had urged the legislature to adopt an exception in the law for cases in which the life or health of the mother is endangered. The majority of the legislature refused, claiming that such an exception could be abused and could render the law ineffective.

An abortion law similar to the New Jersey law was struck down in Iowa in January 1999. U.S. District Judge Robert Pratt declared the ban on late-term abortions unconstitutional because it was unclear and because it violated a woman's constitutional right to privacy in matters of pregnancy. "[P]hysicians are forced to guess at the act's meaning," wrote Judge Pratt, and uncertainty by doctors could put women's health in jeopardy. According to Judge Pratt, doctors would be "likely to 'steer far wider of the unlawful zone' than if the act were more clear." Despite these decisions, approximately twenty-eight states, as of December 1998, maintained laws banning late-term abortions. As of January 1999, seventeen federal and state courts had blocked legislative efforts designed to limit late-term abortions in other states.

Another front in the abortion debate was the topic of abortions by minors. In March 1998, an Alaskan parental notification law was struck down by a state court judge. The law would have required pregnant girls to obtain their parents' permission before receiving an abortion. Judge Sen Tan decided that the case involved "constitutional rights of all citizens of the state of Alaska to make decisions that are personal and intimate to their lives and to be treated equally."

In February 1999, the U.S. Supreme Court approved a Virginia law that required girls under the age of eighteen to notify a parent before having an abortion. Approximately twenty-two states have such laws, which supporters defend as constitutional because "parents have a right to know when their minor is undergoing a surgical procedure as serious as abortion," National Right to Life Committee member Louise D. Hartz told the *Washington Post*. Most states that have parental notification laws carve out some exceptions to the notification requirement. In Virginia, for example, a pregnant girl need not go through parental notification if the girl has been abused, if the girl could risk substantial physical injury through the pregnancy, or if the girl can convince a judge that she is mature enough to make an abortion decision on her own.

Abortion-rights supporters have found the most success in state courts, which are generally more liberal than federal courts. In November 1998, the New Mexico Supreme Court ruled that the state was required to pay for medically-necessary abortions for indigent women. That decision made New Mexico the sixteenth state to pay for medically necessary abortions for poor women. New Mexico has an Equal Rights Amendment that mandates equal treatment between men and women, and the state's highest court used that state constitutional provision as the basis for its decision.

In March 1999, a state court in Alaska struck down a law that would have denied public funding for poor women with medical problems. Judge Sen Tan ruled that the denial of public funding violated the state's protection of the right to privacy. Judge Tan disagreed with the state's decision to provide Medicaid funds to women who give birth while denying funding to Medicaid recipients who want to terminate their pregnancies. "A woman of financial means will have a real choice," Tan noted, "but an indigent woman will have no choice but to go forward with the pregnancy." Anna Franks, executive director of Planned Parenthood of Alaska, said the decision was "about equally covering medical expenses for all women…[and] not the morality of abortion."

Threats, intimidation, and violence against abortion clinic workers and their clients continued through 1999. Anti-abortion protesters continued their attempts to block persons from entering abortion clinics and to keep clients from aborting their pregnancies. In March 1999, the U.S. Supreme Court refused to hear an appeal of a Santa Barbara, California, ordinance that regulated how close protesters may get to abortion clinics and their clients. Under the Santa Barbara ordinance, demonstrators may not come within eight feet of an abortion clinic's entrances or driveways. The ordinance also created a "floating buffer zone" which required protesters to stay at least eight feet away from anyone who asked them to do so within one hundred feet of an abortion clinic. The Ninth Circuit Court of Appeals had struck down the floating buffer zone but had upheld the fixed buffer zone. The Supreme Court's refusal to hear the case meant that the appeals court's rulings were the last word on the topic.

Inmates Prohibited from Obtaining an Abortion

In 1997, Congress passed legislation that banned federal funding for abortions sought by federal inmates. However, the law for state jails are cloudy. State and federal courts have held that women in prison have the right to obtain an abortion. In *Monmouth County Correctional Institutional Inmates v. Lazaro*, 834 F.2d 326 (1987), a New Jersey federal court struck down Monmouth County regulations that interfered with a female prisoner's right to an abortion. However, at least two cases in 1998 involving pregnant inmates demonstrated how federal court decisions, such as the one in Monmouth County, do not always have the effect prochoice forces want.

In October 1998, Judge Patricia Cleary of the Common Pleas Court in Ohio ordered a pregnant woman to six months in jail to keep the woman from having an abortion. The woman, Yuriko Kawaguchi, a former student at the University of California at Berkeley, was charged with FORGERY of credit cards. For a defendant with no prior offenses, such as Kawaguchi, the crime typically carried a sentence of PROBATION. However, because Kawaguchi was pregnant and intended to have an abortion, Judge Cleary sentenced Kawaguchi to six months in jail.

At a court proceeding, Kawaguchi stated under questioning by Judge Cleary that she would "be trying to have a procedure done" if she were released on BAIL. Judge Cleary then asked Kawaguchi what she would do if she were not released on bail, Kawaguchi stated that she would put the child up for adoption. Judge Cleary sentenced Kawaguchi to six months in jail, but after the sentencing, Judge Cleary commented that she would "consider" her release if Kawaguchi stayed in the county and put the child up for adoption. Anthony Vegh, Kawaguchi's lawyer, asked Judge Cleary to explain and Judge Cleary responded "I'm saying that she is not having a second-term abortion."

Kawaguchi's lawyers filed motions to have Judge Cleary removed from the case. They also filed a motion to suspend the sentence imposed on Kawaguchi and an emergency motion for the posting of bail. They appealed the case to the Eighth District Court of Appeals in Ohio, and that case ruled on October 13, 1998, that Kawaguchi should be released after posting 10 percent of a $15,000 bond.

Upon her release, Kawaguchi was past twenty-two weeks into the pregnancy, making it illegal for her to secure an abortion. She filed suit against Judge Cleary, Sheriff Gerald McFaul, and other county officials.

Another case involving a pregnant inmate was in Pennsylvania. In 1998, Karen Ptaschnik, a single mother of three, was serving a sentence for selling cocaine and driving with a suspended license. The thirty-year-old Ptaschnik was also pregnant. When Ptaschnik told prison authorities that she was pregnant and that she wanted an abortion, the authorities refused her request for the abortion. Ptaschnik filed suit in federal court against the county and others, arguing that she was entitled to have an abortion and that, as a necessary medical procedure, the county was obliged to pay for the abortion. A federal court with jurisdiction over Pennsylvania had previously ruled that prison inmates had the right to publicly financed abortions. Nevertheless, officials at the Luzerne County jail denied Ptaschnik's request.

A judge sentenced Yuriko Kawaguchi to six months in jail, effectively preventing her from having an abortion.

TONY DEJAK/AP/WIDE WORLD PHOTOS

Ptaschnik was vilified by several persons in Luzerne County, a heavily Catholic area that has little tolerance for abortion. During her court battle, Ptaschnik and her children were harassed. At school, a child approached Ptaschnik's seven year-old daughter Jayme and told her that her mother was going to kill her unborn brother or sister and that Jayme might be next. "There was a baby doll with a knife in it left on our porch," Ptaschnik recounted to the *New York Times.* "And in my bunk, someone left a baby name book with a note saying 'Choose a name for your baby's grave.' People left me pictures of aborted fetuses." Bishop James C. Timlin publicly addressed the case, and prison officials and inmates told Ptaschnik that she was a "good excuse for court-ordered sterilization."

Ptaschnik became pregnant during her sentence while she was living at a halfway house. During that time, she was allowed to go home at dinner to feed her children, after which she was to return to the half-way house. One night, the father of Ptaschnik's youngest child came to the home. According to Ptaschnik, the man was intoxicated. Ptaschnik tried to keep the man out of the home because such visits were prohibited under the conditions of her supervised release, but the man and Ptaschnik eventually had sex, which led to Ptaschnik's jailhouse pregnancy. Judge Bernard Brominski ordered Ptaschnik's child-care leave revoked and Ptaschnik was returned to prison.

In November 1998, Ptaschnik won her battle when a federal judge ordered the county to pay for her abortion. The abortion was, said the court, a necessary medical procedure. Ptaschnik was given leave to go to the Allentown Women's

Center for the abortion, but she changed her mind as she waited for the procedure. She was, she told Lewin, worn down by all of the harassment. She also changed her mind because of the length of her pregnancy. She was sure of herself early in the pregnancy, but "when you feel the baby move, it's very real."

Thomas Makowski, the Luzerne County Commissioner, vowed to continue to oppose abortions for pregnant inmates. Other colleagues of Makowski, who describe themselves as "pretty adamant pro-life supporters," promised to continue to oppose abortions for incarcerated women. These intentions remain despite the federal judge's November order, which stated that requests from incarcerated inmates should be "honored as a necessary medical procedure." Although she had the baby, Ptaschnik says that she has been "left in a worse situation, and so [have] my kids." Ptaschnik said "[t]he kids need more attention from me, not less, and my mother is having to take care of them, at a time of life when she should be off doing whatever she wants." Ptaschnik's thoughts on the abortion debate have congealed over time. "I don't think abortion is right or wrong. It's whatever a woman can live with…you don't lose your constitutional rights just because you're in prison, but it all should have been private."

Murder of Dr. Barnett Slepian

The 1990s saw an increase in violence against doctors who perform abortions and their patients. On October 23, 1998, abortion provider Dr. Barnett Slepian was murdered as he stood in the kitchen of his Amherst, New York, home at 10:00 P.M., talking with his wife and four sons. A sniper fired into the home from approximately one hundred feet away and fatally shot Dr. Slepian, making him the third abortion provider and sixth abortion clinic employee to be killed since 1993.

Dr. Slepian worked at the only clinic in the Buffalo, New York, area that provided abortions. Shortly after Dr. Slepian's death, monitors of a web site called the "Nuremberg Files" crossed out Dr. Slepian's name from a list of abortion providers targeted by abortion-rights opponents. Dr. Slepian had spoken to the medical students at the State University of New York in the spring of 1998 and voiced his concern over the violence being used by abortion-rights protesters. According to Dr. Slepian, the fearful climate created by the protesters was causing medical students to stay away from providing abortion services for women. Furthermore, medical schools were excluding abortion services from their class requirements and even ignoring the topic altogether. The result, said Dr. Slepian, was a continuing reduction in the number of doctors willing to provide abortions.

Only 16 percent of the counties in the United States have abortion services. According to Stacey Blyth of *Free Inquiry*, the vast majority of current abortion providers are over the age

Mourners place flowers in front of the office of murdered abortion provider Dr. Barnett Slepian.

DON HEUPEL/AP/WIDE WORLD PHOTOS

of sixty-five years. Despite the fact that abortion is the most common surgical procedure practiced on women in the United States, the number of providers is dwindling, which Blyth says is leading to a "crisis of access."

The crisis of access stems from the persistent campaign of opposition that is being waged by abortion-rights opponents. Hospitals and clinics are being bought by entities that refuse to provide abortion services, and existing abortion clinics are being harassed, intimidated, bombed, and attacked. Well-trained protesters gather at abortion clinics every day in cities across the country to show their opposition to the procedures used inside the clinics. Sometimes the tactics used by the protesters include pushing and shoving and screaming in the faces of the employees and clients of abortion clinics.

Ostensibly to protect clients and employees of abortion clinics, Congress in 1997 passed the Federal Freedom of Access to Clinic Entrances Act, along with other statutes on racketeering to protect clients and employees of abortion clinics. These laws make it a federal crime for abortion protesters to make threats against the physical well-being of abortion providers and clients.

After the passage of the Freedom of Access Act, two health clinics and several doctors filed suit against a group of abortion activists in Oregon. The suit claimed, in part, that the abortion activists had issued threats of harm, and that the doctors and clinic employees were fearful for their lives. The abortion-rights opponents argued that they had not directly uttered any threats of harm against abortion clinic employers or employees, but the doctors did not argue that they had. Instead, the doctors emphasized the atmosphere of harassment and intimidation that, they argued, constituted threats of violence.

To support their claim of violent threats, the abortion providers presented a variety of evidence. In part, the abortion providers cited: public statements by abortion-rights opponents that the murder of abortion providers is justifiable homicide, the Nuremberg Files web site that had crossed out the names of murdered abortion providers, the necessity for protection from federal marshals; and the rising incidence of violence at clinics and against abortion providers. They also cited specific instances of harm suffered by abortion clinic clients and employees.

In their federal lawsuit, the abortion providers position clashed with the FIRST AMEND-MENT, which appeared to protect the speech of the abortion-rights opponents. Under First Amendment jurisprudence, a person cannot be held liable for controversial or offensive speech. A person may be held liable for speech that amounts to a threat of harm, and the question remained whether the abortion protesters had in fact threatened the abortion providers.

In early 1999, the federal jury hearing the case awarded the abortion providers $107 million in damages. In its brief to the court, the American Civil Liberties Union in Oregon (ACLU) argued for an extra element in the case. The abortion providers should have to prove, urged the ACLU, that the abortion protesters put the abortion providers in fear for their safety. Federal District Court Judge Robert Jones refused to require the extra element and the federal jury hearing the case decided that the abortion providers had in fact been threatened. The jury awarded the abortion providers $107 million in damages. The case will likely be appealed all the way to the U.S. Supreme Court for a ruling on the ACLU's argument.

State and federal police in New York have not been able to catch the killer of Dr. Slepian. In April 1999, law enforcement authorities found the rifle used to kill Dr. Slepian. The gun was found 200 feet from the Slepian home in an area that had been searched shortly after the killing. In May 1999, federal authorities charged James C. Kopp, a high-profile abortion opponent, with murder. In June he was indicted by a grand jury for "second-degree murder, reckless endangerment and criminal possession of a weapon." Kopp was seen jogging in Slepian's neighborhood just days before the murder; fibers and hairs at the scene of the crime also linked Kopp to the killing.

Early in 1999, New York lawmakers began to consider strengthening laws to protect abortion providers and their clients. New York Assembly Speaker Sheldon Silver co-sponsored the Reproductive Health Care Services Access and Anti-Violence Act of 1999, and Governor George Pataki promised that he would support such legislation. The New York law, if passed, would specifically address the violence against abortion providers and their clients. Critics of the proposed laws say they would unfairly target abortion protesters, but supporters note that legislatures have historically fashioned laws to resolve particular problems.

CROSS REFERENCES
Equal Protection; First Amendment; Internet; Prisoners' Rights; Privacy Rights

AFFIRMATIVE ACTION

Employment programs required by federal statutes and regulations designed to remedy discriminatory practices in hiring minority group members; i.e. continuing discrimination, to remedy lingering effects of past discrimination, and to create systems and procedures to prevent future discrimination; commonly based on population percentages of minority groups in a particular area. Factors considered are race, color, sex, creed, and age.

Dallas v. Dallas Fire Fighters

Proponents of affirmative action policies argue that such remedies are necessary to reverse long standing, often institutionalized, discriminatory practices. However opponents of affirmative action contend that such policies constitute "reverse discrimination" and are repugnant to the Constitution. Specifically, opponents argue that the Equal Protection Clause of the FOURTEENTH AMENDMENT, the Due Process Clause of the FIFTH AMENDMENT, and the Civil Rights Act of 1964 cannot be selectively applied; all citizens are entitled to protection against discrimination. In this case a policy intended to promote minorities and women over white males in the Dallas Fire Department was invalidated by a federal court and the U.S. Fifth Circuit Court of Appeals. City officials and the Dallas Fire Fighters Association asked the Supreme Court to review the appellate court's decision for different reasons. Both petitions (*Dallas v. Dallas Fire Fighters Association*, __ U.S. __, 119 S. Ct. 1333, 143 L. Ed. 2d 498, [1999] and *Dallas Fire Fighters Association v. Dallas*, __ U.S. __, 119 S. Ct. 1349, 143 L. Ed. 2d 511 [1999]) were denied. The Court did not offer an explanation for denying the latter appeal.

On March 29, 1999, the Supreme Court denied a petition for writ of CERTIORARI to review the decision handed down by the U.S. Fifth Circuit Court of Appeals in *City of Dallas v. Dallas Fire Fighters Association*, 150 F.3d 438 (1998). A writ of certiorari is the primary means by which the Supreme Court exercises its appellate jurisdiction, or its power to review decisions delivered by inferior courts. In order to review an appellate decision four affirmative votes are required by Supreme Court justices. Two justices, STEPHEN BREYER and RUTH BADER GINSBURG voted to review the case. The decision not to review the case is significant. It is suggestive of the Court's unwillingness to protect affirmative action programs. The Court

made its first significant retreat from minority assistance programs in *City of Richmond v. J.A. Croson Co.*, 488 U.S. 469, 109 S. Ct. 582, 102 L. Ed. 2d 601 (1989). Here, the Court invalidated a Virginia statute that privileged minority owned business in the allocation of contracts. In *Adarand Constructors, Inc. v. Pena*, 515 U.S. 200, 115 S. Ct. 2097, 132 L. Ed. 2d 158 (1995) a divided Court held that the hiring practices within the legislative and executive branches must be held to the same "strict scrutiny" standards as state and local governments.

The legal issue at the heart of most affirmative action cases since *Regents of the University of California v. Bakke*, 438 U.S. 265, 98 S. Ct. 2733, 57 L. Ed. 2d 750 (1978), in which the Court upheld an admissions policy that favored minorities, is strict scrutiny. In *Kramer v. Union Free School District*, 395 U.S. 621, 89 S. Ct. 1886, 23 L. Ed. 2d 583 (1969) the Court set the precedent insisting that in order for a legislative statute to justifiably violate a constitutional provision, such as the Equal Protection Clause of the Fourteenth Amendment or the Due Process Clause of the Fifth Amendment, there must be a "compelling state interest." The Court has subsequently labored over affirmative action cases that weigh the social value of rectifying historic discrimination against the broader application of equal protection and due process to all individuals. In recent decisions the Court has been gravitating toward the view that equal protection and due process for all individual citizens preempts remedial action for past discrimination. In other words, the arguments in favor of affirmative action programs have become less "compelling" in the view of the Court.

Dallas instituted an affirmative action plan in 1988 which favored the promotion of women and minorities over non-minorities, even if the non-minorities had earned higher scores on civil service promotion examinations. Having met the city's objective of increasing minority and female access to employment in the Dallas Fire Department, the policy was granted a five year extension in 1992. The program was subsequently challenged by a series of law suits from individuals and the Dallas Fire Fighters Association. The U.S. Fifth Circuit Court of Appeals invalidated the program on the basis that it failed to meet the somewhat subjective standards of a "compelling state interest."

Three plaintiffs claimed that the affirmative action plan had prevented them from receiving promotions to the positions of driver-engineer, lieutenant, and captain. A fourth plaintiff claimed that the fire chief, Dodd Miller, promoted Robert Bailey, a black male, exclusively on the basis of race which "trammeled" the rights of non-minorities. Chief Judge Politz, who presided over the appeal to the U.S. Fifth Circuit Court explained in his analysis of the case that there was insufficient evidence of past discrimination in Dallas to justify Dallas' Affirmative Action Plan. Politz noted that the only evidence of past discrimination was a 1976 consent decree between the Department of Justice and the city of Dallas in which violations of Title VII of the Civil Rights Act of 1964 were noted along with statistical disparities in the hiring of minorities and women. The court of appeals concluded that this did not suggest a historical pattern of "egregious and pervasive discrimination" required to justify the affirmative action plan. In the court's estimation the policy violated the Equal Protection Clause of the Fourteenth Amendment. The appeals court also found that there was even less evidence of gender discrimination that would warrant the promotion of women over men under the plan.

The court of appeals affirmed the decision. However, the U.S. Fifth Circuit Court of Appeals reversed the district court's effort to strike down the promotion of Robert Bailey who, in the opinion of the court of appeals, had been promoted largely on the basis of merit.

Justices Breyer and Ginsburg voted in favor of reviewing the appeals court's decision and offered a formal dissent to the Court's denial of certiorari. In their dissent, Justices Breyer and Ginsburg reviewed the evidence offered to support the claim that there had been past discrimination against minorities and women in Dallas which precipitated the affirmative action plan. They noted that in past cases the Court found that certain remedial actions designed to redress past discriminatory practices, when "narrowly tailored," do not violate the Equal Protection Clause of the Fourteenth Amendment: *Adarand Constructors, Inc. v. Pena*, 515 U.S. 200, 115 S. Ct. 2097, 132 L. Ed. 2d 158 (1995); *Richmond v. J.A. Croson Co.*, 488 U.S. 469, 109 S. Ct. 582, 102 L. Ed. 2d 607 (1989); *United States v. Paradise*, 480 U.S. 149, 107 S. Ct. 1053, 94 L. Ed. 2d 203 (1987). Breyer and Ginsburg also noted that past cases decided by appellate courts have upheld affirmative action plans that have been supported by statistical hiring disparities similar to the Dallas such as *McNamara v. Chicago*, 138 F. 3d 1219 (7th Cir. 1998) and *Stuart v. Roche*, 951 F. 2d 446 (1st Cir. 1991). The Supreme Court denied certiorari for both of these cases

as well. Breyer and Ginsburg concluded by pointing out that the decision handed down by the U.S. Fifth Circuit Court of Appeals deviated from the precedents that have been set regarding rulings on the constitutionality of affirmative action programs. Although the invalidation of the Dallas Affirmative Action Plan may be contrary to past decisions it may also signify a nation wide reversal of affirmative action policies.

FCC Requirements on Minority Hiring

In April 1998, a federal appeals court panel struck down an affirmative action policy that had governed the broadcasting industry for thirty years in *Lutheran Church-Missouri Synod v. FCC*, 141 F. 3d 344, 329 U.S.App. D.C. 381 (1998). The decision voided a longstanding policy of the Federal Communications Commission (FCC) that required radio and television stations to actively recruit minority and women employees in order to renew their federal licenses. Although the FCC argued that the policy existed solely to foster diversity in broadcasting content, the D.C. Circuit Court of Appeals panel ruled that the agency failed to show a compelling interest for the policy, which it characterized as a means of "pressuring" stations to make race and gender-based hiring decisions. That, the panel concluded, had improperly resulted in special breaks for some applicants. Criticizing the decision, civil rights groups noted that the policy had helped double minority hiring in the broadcasting industry since its enactment in the 1960s. But the plaintiff, the Lutheran Church-Missouri Synod, hailed the ruling as a blow for religious freedom.

As the federal commission in charge of regulating the radio, TV and cable industries, the FCC holds tremendous rule-making and licensing power over the nation's broadcast media. Broadcasters must meet FCC guidelines, or they will not get the federal license required to use the airwaves. Since 1968, the commission had used a two-part equal employment opportunity (EEO) policy to increase the numbers of women and minorities hired by broadcasters. First, the policy forbid discrimination in employment on the basis of race, color, religion, national origin, or sex. While that resembled most such federal policies, the second part of the FCC's policy was unique. The policy required each station to develop a plan for actively recruiting and promoting minority job applicants. And as part of the regular review of stations' licensing eligibility, the FCC evaluated how well they met this goal—specifically, by comparing the percentage of minorities hired to the percentage of minorities living in the communities where the stations operated.

Under a version of these rules developed in the late 1980s, the FCC required stations to demonstrate that they hired one half of the percentage of minorities living in their communities. The gender or race of a job applicant was not supposed to be an actual factor in the hiring decision. The station was instead expected to make a good faith effort to hire and promote qualified candidates who were women and minorities. And although the commission never turned down a station's license renewal on this basis, it had the power to do so.

Lutheran Church-Missouri Synod v. FCC arose from a licensing challenge brought in 1989 by the National Association for the Advancement of Colored People (NAACP). The civil rights group challenged the license renewal of two radio stations in Clayton, Missouri, on the ground that the stations had violated FCC rules by failing to hire black employees. The stations, which were owned by the Lutheran Church-Missouri Synod, broadcast classical music and religious programming. In its reply to the complaint, the church acknowledged not going out of its way to find black job applicants. But it argued that finding black applicants was difficult because employment at the station required knowledge of Lutheran doctrine and training in classical music.

The FCC ruled against the church. The commission found that the church violated FCC policy by not trying to recruit minorities and by requiring all job applicants to know Lutheran doctrine, even if they were merely secretaries. Although renewing the church stations' licenses, it ordered the stations to report at six-month intervals on its progress in finding minority employees. It also imposed a $25,000 fine.

In response, the church filed an appeal in federal court alleging violations of its constitutional rights. It alleged the FCC had violated the church's religious freedoms under the FIRST AMENDMENT, and its right to protection under the FIFTH AMENDMENT. The suit argued that the regulations amounted to an unconstitutional race-based hiring program.

On April 14 1998, a three-judge panel of the D.C. Circuit Court of Appeals ruled in favor of the church, finding that the $25,000 fine was an overreaction. The panel also found that the commission's equal employment opportunity regulations were unconstitutional. It reached this outcome after deciding that the

proper legal standard for reviewing the regulations was so-called "strict scrutiny"—a demanding level of legal analysis that the U.S. Supreme Court has applied when evaluating government use of racial classifications. To meet this standard, the government must show a compelling interest for the policy under review, or else the regulation is held unconstitutional under the Fifth Amendment. The commission's stated interest in its EEO policy was fostering diversity in broadcasting content.

Judge Laurence H. Silberman's opinion scathingly rejected the FCC's justification. He scorned the FCC's intention to foster diverse broadcasting content, concluding that the objective made no sense: "It clashes with the reality of the radio market," he wrote, "where each station targets a particular segment." In fact, the commission had never defined the term "diversity," Judge Silberman observed, but the court believed it had been "coined both as a permanent justification for policies seeking racial proportionality in all walks of life, and as a synonym for proportional representation itself." Although the FCC had avoided setting fixed quotas, the opinion concluded that its polices still unconstitutionally obliged stations to give some degree of preference to minority hires. Having reached this conclusion, the panel did not have to consider the religious freedom claims of the lawsuit.

The decision drew praise from the church, which called it a major victory for religious freedom. Proponents of affirmative action were less sanguine, criticizing the decision for dismantling what they said was thirty years of success increasing minority employment in the industry. In 1971, three years after the policy went into effect, only 9.1 percent of broadcasting jobs belonged to minorities, but by 1998 that figure had more than doubled to 19.9 percent. They also worried that the court's decision could be extended to the FCC's entire EEO policy and therefore affect women. In September 1998, the D.C. Circuit Court denied the FCC's request for a rehearing by the full appeals court. Thus in November, the commission announced proposed rule changes to satisfy the court's decision. Dropping the community-based percentages, FCC commissioners voted 5–0 to stop evaluating stations' hiring performance, and, instead, merely to encourage them to try to recruit women and minorities.

Hopwood v. Texas

On July 1, 1996, the Supreme Court denied a petition for writ of CERTIORARI to review an appellate court's ruling in *Hopwood v. Texas*, 78 F. 3d. 932 (5ᵗʰ Cir. 1996). A writ of certiorari is the primary means by which the Supreme Court exercises its appellate jurisdiction, or its power to review decisions delivered by inferior courts. In this case the U.S. Fifth Circuit Court of Appeals invalidated a University of Texas Law School admission policy that included race among its criteria for acceptance. By denying the petition for certiorari, the Court essentially endorsed the lower courts' rulings on the case which held that the practice of providing preferential treatment to minorities in a public university's admissions policy was repugnant to the Constitution. Interestingly, in the explanation for denying the petition, volunteered by Justices RUTH BADER GINSBURG and DAVID H. SOUTER, the Court did not pass judgment on affirmative action policies in particular. Ginsburg and Souter explained that the petitioner's challenge to the U.S. Fifth Circuit Court of Appeals decision was flawed in that it took issue with the reasoning used by the appellate court, rather than the actual judgment. The Court explained it is not their job to review the "opinions" of the lower courts; but rather, they are called upon to ascertain the constitutionality of judgments.

Proponents of affirmative action policies argue that such remedies are necessary to reverse long standing, often institutionalized, discriminatory practices. However opponents of affirmative action contend that such policies constitute "reverse discrimination" and violate civil liberties. Specifically, opponents argue that the Equal Protection Clause of the FOURTEENTH AMENDMENT, the Due Process Clause of the FIFTH AMENDMENT, and the Civil Rights Act of 1964 cannot be selectively applied; all citizens are entitled to protection against discrimination. The University of Texas Law School implemented an admissions policy in which the standards for admission were lowered for minorities. The school employed an index (called the "Texas Index," or "TI") that required minimum scores on standardized test that set the cut off for admission at 199 combined LSAT and GPA marks for whites and 189 for non-whites. The petitioners challenged that the difference in requirements put forth in the TI violated the Equal Protection Clause of the Fourteenth Amendment and Title VI of the Civil Rights Act of 1964. The central issue with which the Fifth Circuit Court took issue was the structure of the Texas Index. While minorities, specifically African Americans and Mexican Americans, earned scores sufficient to be categorized as "presumptive admits" (certain to be accepted),

David Rogers, a plaintiff in Hopwood v. Texas, *was denied admission to the University of Texas.*

AP/WIDE WORLD PHOTOS

whites who received the same scores were categorized as "presumptive denials" (certain to be rejected). Judge Jerry Smith, who presided over the *Hopwood* decision, invalidated the admissions policy arguing that using race as a criteria for admissions is as arbitrary as using one's blood type.

Advocates of affirmative action fear that the decision handed down by the appeals court is the beginning of the end of affirmative action programs. Samuel Issacharoff, the attorney for the University of Texas pointed out that it seemed ironic that the Fifth Circuit Court of Appeals, which includes states with track records restricting civil rights (Texas, Louisiana, and Mississippi) is forbidden from using remedial measures to redress past discrimination while the rest of the country is free to use affirmative action programs. Others believe that the *Hopwood* ruling and the Supreme Court's refusal to review the case will force universities, even beyond the deep South, to begin to explore alternative ways to diversify their student body. The decision also may have implications beyond higher education in that remedial discriminatory practices may be called into question in public and private employment sectors. The Supreme Court has already curtailed the federal government's ability to privilege minorities in the allocation of contracts (*Adarand Constructors, Inc. v. Pena* 515 U.S. 200, 115 S. Ct. 2097, 132 L. Ed. 2d 158 [1995]).

The *Hopwood* ruling was a departure from the 1978 benchmark decision in *Regents of the University of California v. Bakke*, 438 U.S. 265,

98 S. Ct. 2733, 57 L. Ed. 2d 750 (1978), in which the Court upheld an affirmative action admissions policy. Judge Smith avoided *Bakke* with little legal difficulty as Justice Powell's opinion in *Bakke* was open to radical modification. Powell held that employing remedial measures to rectify past discrimination was consistent with the Constitution. However, the standard of proof for historical discrimination was left undefined. Hence, determining whether an affirmative action program is justified under the Constitution is highly subjective.

Since the *Hopwood* decision California voters passed Proposition 209, a referendum that banned many of the affirmative action programs in California. The referendum was promoted by the nonprofit Center for Individual Rights, which was also instrumental in building opposition to the University of Texas admissions policy that was struck down in *Hopwood*. Another significant sign that affirmative action programs are in retreat is the elimination of race-based scholarship programs in Texas, Georgia, Florida, Colorado, and Arizona. The reaction of many universities to *Hopwood* is to take preemptive measures to potential law suits against their own programs. If affirmative action programs are to survive, an alternative approach, including a legal strategy capable of reconciling the application of constitutional provisions that address equal protection for individuals verses historically disadvantaged groups, is needed.

The Clinton administration has been somewhat reticent on the subject of recent court decisions that have undermined the institution. The administration has, however, issued a statement suggesting that *Bakke* is still the law of the land. According to recent decisions on the matter as well as the growing public sentiments in opposition to affirmative action programs, that *Bakke* may be overturned.

CROSS REFERENCES
Civil Rights; Colleges and Universities; Diversity; Federal Communications Commission; Minorities;

AIRLINES

Judge Orders Pilots to Return to Job

At a time when passenger dissatisfaction with airline service was at an all time low, American Airlines, the world's second largest airline, suffered an additional blow in February 1999 when its pilots staged an illegal strike. Approximately 2,500 pilots called in sick over a ten day period, resulting in the cancellation of about 6,700 flights and inconveniencing over 600,000 passengers over the busy President's Day weekend.

The actions of the pilots stemmed from a labor dispute between the Allied Pilots Association, the labor union that represents the pilots, and American Airlines, the pilots' employer. American Airlines purchased Reno Air, a small carrier in the West on December 23, 1998. Reno Air had approximately 300 pilots and 25 planes. It was from this purchase that the conflict between American Airlines and the Allied Pilots Association arose. Reno Air pilots were paid roughly half as much as American Airline pilots. The airline maintained that it was going to integrate the Reno Air pilots into the American salary structure within a year to eighteen months; however, this was not quick enough for the union as it argued that American was violating its contract with the union. The contract required all flying at the airline and any of its subsidiaries be done by members of the pilots' union. The union also feared an overall erosion of pay for its pilots if the integration did not proceed quickly. Therefore, the union demanded that American integrate Reno Air faster and pay pilots at both carriers as if the merger had been completed rather than wait and pay higher rates as the pilots were retrained to American standards. The two sides could not come to agreement and thus a labor dispute ensued.

Federal law prohibited the pilots from engaging in a strike, a method whereby employees represented by a union who have a grievance with their employer stop working to demonstrate those grievances and to facilitate negotiations. The pilots were allowed, however, to refuse overtime and to declare themselves "unfit to fly." Therefore, on February 6, 1999, hundreds of American Airline pilots began calling in sick over their dispute with the airline. What followed was a ten-day "sickout" by the pilots.

The airline and the union could not settle their dispute between themselves, and the public was being more seriously affected as the sickout continued. President BILL CLINTON even voiced concern over the impact on the travelling public and innocent bystanders involved. American Airlines ultimately sought a court order forcing the pilots back to work. On February 10, 1999, Judge Joe Kendall of the U.S. District Court in Dallas, Texas, held that the sickout was illegal and ordered the pilots to return to work. Kendall issued a temporary restraining order barring 9,200 pilots from calling in sick all at the same time. Kendall further warned that if the pilots did not return to work they would be held in contempt of court and would face serious fines. The union had maintained all along that they did not control the sickout, that it was a grass-roots protest. However, they agreed to abide by the court order and to encourage the pilots to return to work.

On February 12, 1999, the airline was back in court asking Kendall to find the union in contempt of court for disobeying his February 10, 1999, order to end the sickout. American stated to the court that it was still forced to cancel flights because pilots continued to call in sick despite Kendall's previous order. Kendall did find the union in contempt, but instead scheduled a hearing for the following week to allow evidence to be presented on the appropriate fine. He ordered the union to deposit $10 million into the court registry and noted that it was clear the DAMAGES from the canceled flights would be substantial. Kendall also imposed a $10,000 fine on the president of the union. After the hearing, the union urged its pilots to return to work; the president of the union even made a personal plea to the pilots to return to the cockpit. By February 15, 1999, a majority of the pilots had returned to work and the airline operated at close to 90 percent of its schedule. Overall, the sickout lasted approximately ten days.

On April 12, 1999, Kendall presided over a hearing on charges of damages for the contempt of court decision against the union. Kendall had to determine how much money the union owed to American Airlines due to the sickout and consequences thereof. At the hearing, lawyers for the union argued that only 233 pilots called in sick after the court order; therefore, only they should be considered when assessing damages. Kendall did not agree and also denied the union's request for a jury, stating that the case would remain before him. The airline presented evidence that it estimated the flight cancellations cost it approximately $58 million. However, expert witnesses for the union testified that depending on the time frame the judge set, the loss to the airline was $1.4 million to $4.7 million. The hearing lasted four days and Kendall ultimately ruled that the Allied Pilots Association was to pay American Airlines nearly $46 million in damages for defying his order for the pilots to return to work in February. It was one of the largest fines ever made against a union. The Allied Pilots Association only had an estimated $38 million in assets.

As an additional blow to the union, many passengers have filed lawsuits against them because their flights were canceled or disrupted by the sickout. All of the lawsuits have been moved to federal court in Dallas. The lawsuits seek more than $200 million in damages. The complaints are expected to be consolidated into one single class action lawsuit.

Despite the bleak period in February 1999 when passengers were expressing anger, frustration, and resentment toward American Airlines, it has been reported that few analysts expect the airline will suffer long-term damage. It is expected that fare reductions and other incentives will draw passengers back to the airline. The future of the Allied Pilots Union may not be as bright, depending on its ability to pay the fine issued against it, as well as to defend against the potential class action lawsuits being instituted in Dallas, Texas.

Passenger Rights

The 1990s saw an increase in the demand for airline passenger rights. Deficiencies in service left airline passengers frustrated and without recourse for their suffering. Passenger complaints against the airlines included lost baggage, rude service, high fares, strike-related cancellations, and false imprisonment. Northwest Airlines, for example, was accused of abusing a child in its care, and it kept a planeload of people on a runway in Detroit, Michigan, for eight hours.

In March 1999, the House Transportation and Infrastructure Committee invited airline customers to voice their complaints to the committee. The hearing was designed to help the committee in its consideration of airline passenger rights legislation proposed by Senators JOHN MCCAIN (R-AZ) and Ron Wyden (D-OR). Representative Bud Shuster (R-PA) and Representative John Dingell (D-MI) proposed similar legislation in the House of Representatives.

The idea of airline passenger rights legislation became a priority in CONGRESS. Senator Olympia Snowe (R-ME) told the Senate Commerce Committee that "[p]assengers have no recourse." The proposed legislation, said Snowe, "didn't just happen, it is a result of thousands of incidents." Robert Kingsley, a former executive at American Airlines, opined that the only way to remedy the poor service was through legislation. "If one carrier improves customer service, it must increase cost to the customer," said Kingsley. "Other carriers will offer lower fares, without much customer service. The only way to [improve service] is federal regulation." Representative Dick Armey (R-TX), the House Majority Leader, opposed the proposed legislation because "new regulations represent a one-way ticket to higher airfares. Low airfares are giving more people than ever access to affordable travel."

The House and Senate versions of passenger rights legislation contained various provisions. The House measures required airlines to: pay 200 percent of the ticket price to passengers whose flights are delayed for more than two hours; inform customers which flights are "codeshare" flights; and refrain from separating parents from children under two years old during the security screenings. The Senate proposal would require that carriers: refund ticket prices to passengers within 48 hours upon request; inform passengers of the availability of frequent-flyer seats; admit when they have overbooked a flight; return lost baggage within 24 hours of the flight; and provide access to fare information. Through its executive agencies, the White House weighed in with its own ideas, such as requiring airlines to: provide access to food, water, and restrooms during long delays and evacuations; provide a contact person for customer complaints; respond to complaints within sixty days; and pay damages for mishandled baggage and involuntary bumping. Vice President AL GORE announced that the Department of Transportation would propose that airlines give reasons for flight delays or cancellations and lost baggage.

The airline industry objected to the proposals. The industry argued that such measures would be costly, and the added costs would have to be passed on to consumers. According to a study by the Economic Strategy Institute, the measures proposed in Congress would cost airlines in the United States more than $6 billion. Carol Hallett, president and chief executive officer of the Air Transport Association, acknowledged to *Travel Agent* that the passenger rights bills were "offered with the best of intentions. But the fact is that its best provisions are unnecessary because they already reflect industry practice." The more onerous provisions, Hallett contended "would have unintended, adverse and worst of all, expensive consequences for the consumer."

Few airline industry observers believed that all of the proposals would find their way into a passenger rights law. Joe Galloway, president and chief executive officer of the American Society of Travel Agents, admitted to *Travel Agents* that he did not think that "everything suggested is 'fall-on-the-sword-for.'" However, many observers believed that the idea of a airline passen-

ger bill of rights was inevitable, and some airlines embraced it. US Airways chairman Stephen Wolf called for "a widespread effort to continue to improve all aspects of travel in the U.S." In testimony before the House Aviation Subcommittee, Richard Hirst, Northwest Airlines' senior vice president of corporate affairs, admitted that the airline does not "do everything perfectly. There are things we can do a lot better."

The issue of competition sprouted up at the same time as passenger rights legislation. Major airlines in the United States stood accused of quelling competition through unfair business practices. The U.S. Department of Justice, for example, began to investigate American Airlines for anti-competitive behavior. Specifically, American Airlines was suspected of targeting areas served by emerging airlines and offering extra-low fares in those areas until the emerging airlines were forced out of business. American Airlines allegedly raised fares beyond normal rates in other areas to pay for its lost revenues, all of which allowed it to eliminate competition while losing no profits.

While the politicians and airlines wrangled over the details of passenger rights legislation, consumers grew weary of the poor service. Northwest Airlines, based in Eagan, Minnesota, has become the target of much criticism. The airline's service has inspired the creation of Internet web sites for persons to vent their frustrations with the airline. Dirk McMahon, Northwest Airlines' vice president of ground operations, told *Knight-Ridder/Tribune Business News* that Northwest is working on its customer service problems. "This was an extremely well-run airline between 1991–96, and nearly all the people who made that possible are still with us. That's one of our greatest assets, our people."

CROSS REFERENCES
Transportation

ALIENS

Foreign-born persons who have not been naturalized to become U.S. citizens under federal law and the Constitution.

Miller v. Albright

The case of *Miller v. Albright*, 523 U.S. 420, 118 S. Ct. 1428, 140 L. Ed. 2d 575 (1989) is a struggle between two powerful legal interests. On one side is the concept of equal protection, written into the U.S. Constitution in the FIFTH AND FOURTEENTH AMENDMENTS. Essentially, equal protection describes the notions that persons should be treated equally under the law, and that treating people differently based on characteristics such as race, sex, and national origin is unacceptable. The government may, in some cases, treat people differently under the laws based on these classifications, but there must be a compelling governmental interest at stake to treat people differently based on those classifications.

Opposing the equal protection doctrine is the governmental interest in controlling immigration. Although the United States is almost entirely composed of immigrants, unchecked immigration is not viewed by many in the country's best interests. The United States began to pass federal laws on immigration toward the end of the nineteenth century, and the laws have only increased since then.

It is not easy for a foreigner, or "alien," to gain U.S. citizenship. One circumstance that can help an alien to gain U.S. citizenship is if one of the alien's parents is a citizen of the United States. However, under U.S. immigration laws, the sex of that parent can be a decisive factor.

Lorelyn Penero Miller was born in Angeles City, Republic of the Phillipines, on June 20, 1970. Miller's mother, Luz Penero, was a native Filipino, and Miller's father, Charlie Miller, was in the U.S. Air Force and was a United States citizen who had a home in Texas. Charlie met Luz during his tour of duty in the Phillipines, but he was not present during Miller's birth and apparently had never returned to the Phillipines after completing his tour of duty.

A few years after Miller was born, her mother married a man named Frank Raspotnik. Miller grew up in the Phillipines, attending high school and college there. In November 1991, when Miller was twenty-one years old, she filed an application with the U.S. State Department, seeking to register as a U.S. citizen. In March 1992, the State Department denied Miller's application. In July 1992, Charlie Miller obtained a paternity decree from a Texas court which declared him to be Miller's father. Miller reapplied for citizenship, but the application was again denied. According to the State Department, the declaration of Charlie Miller's paternity did not satisfy the requirements of § 309(a)(4) of the Immigration and Naturalization Act (8 U.S.C.A. § 1409(a)(4)). Under that section, a child born out of wedlock and outside the United States to an alien mother must be legitimated before the age of eighteen to acquire citizenship. Because Charlie Miller had not declared himself to be

the father of Miller until after she was eighteen years old, Miller could not attain U.S. citizenship based on her father's U.S. citizenship.

Miller and her father sued the U.S. secretary of state, MADELEINE K. ALBRIGHT, in federal district court in Texas. The Millers argued that Lorelyn Miller should be granted U.S. citizenship because the denial based on the sex of the parents violated the equal protection rights in the Constitution. Essentially, the laws made it more difficult for the illegitimate children of American citizen fathers to become U.S. citizens than for the illegitimate children of American citizen mothers. Under 8 U.S.C.A. § 1409(c), the child of an American mother and an alien father is considered a U.S. citizen at birth. This created an inequality in the treatment of citizenship matters, based on the sex of the parent. The Millers observed that the differences in the citizenship laws were based on sex, which is a "suspect classification," or a classification that deserves serious scrutiny by the courts. According to the Millers, the distinctions could not survive judicial scrutiny because there was not a sufficient governmental interest in creating the distinctions.

Charlie Miller was dismissed from the case because he lacked STANDING, or a sufficient interest, in the case. The case was transferred to the District of Columbia, and that court dismissed the suit because it did not have the power to grant citizenship. Miller appealed, and the appeals court ruled against Miller, holding that the government had sufficient interest in fostering a child's ties with the United States to create differences in citizenship requirements based on the sex of the citizen parent. Miller appealed to the U.S. Supreme Court, which agreed to hear the case.

In a splintered vote that seemed to support Miller, the Court ended up ruling against her. Two main issues faced the Court: (1) whether Miller had standing to sue; and (2) whether the challenged immigration laws violated the equal protection guarantees of the Fifth Amendment. Seven justices concluded that Miller had standing to sue, and five Justices concluded that the statute violated equal protection standards, but two of the five justices who concluded that the statutes violated equal protection principles happened to be the two justices who believed that Miller lacked standing.

Justice JOHN PAUL STEVENS, joined by Chief Justice WILLIAM H. REHNQUIST, wrote an opinion that constituted the plurality opinion. According to Justices Stevens and Rehnquist, there were sound biological reasons for the different treatment of illegitimate children. Mothers are always present at birth, and they are presumed to be the primary caretakers of children. Men, on the other hand, may come and go as they please, free of the burdens of childbirth, and that lack of attachment, for U.S. men who impregnate alien women, equals a lack of attachment to the United States. "The biological differences between single men and single women," wrote Stevens, "provide a relevant basis for differing rules governing their ability to confer citizenship on children born in foreign lands."

Justices SANDRA DAY O'CONNOR and ANTHONY M. KENNEDY voted to uphold the constitutionality of the disputed immigration laws, but they decided that Miller did not have standing to sue because the case attacked the sex-based classification of parents, and not their children. Justices ANTONIN SCALIA and CLARENCE THOMAS believed that only Congress had the power to grant U.S. citizenship to Miller, and that Miller thus did not have standing to sue. Justices RUTH BADER GINSBURG, STEPHEN BREYER, and DAVID H. SOUTER believed that Miller not only had standing, but that she should have won the case. According to Justices Ginsburg, Breyer, and Souter, the sex-based classifications of parents in the disputed immigration laws constituted a violation of the Equal Protection Clause of the Fifth Amendment.

The Supreme Court's vote the *Miller* case was remarkable because it was so splintered. Enough justices believed that the laws violated equal protection, but only three believed that Miller had standing to sue.

Reno v. American-Arab
Anti-Discrimination Committee

The Supreme Court, in *Reno v. American-Arab Anti-Discrimination Committee*, __U.S.__, 119 S. Ct. 936, 142 L. Ed. 2d 940 (1999), reversed a legal trend when it held that illegal immigrants cannot challenge their deportation by claiming they were selectively prosecuted because of their political beliefs and actions. The Court ruled that illegal immigrants do not have any constitutional rights because of their resident status. In addition, the Court ruled that a provision of a 1996 statute prevented the courts from reviewing the attorney general's administrative deportation decisions.

The controversy began in 1987, when the Immigration and Naturalization Service (INS), a division of the DEPARTMENT OF JUSTICE,

started deportation proceedings against Bashar Amer, Aiad Barakat, Julie Mungai, Amjad Obeid, Ayman Obeid, Naim Sharif, Khader Hamide, and Michel Shehadeh. The eight individuals belonged to the Popular Front for the Liberation of Palestine (PFLP), a group that the U.S. government characterized as an international terrorist and communist organization. The INS charged all them under the McCarran-Walter Act, a now-repealed law that provided for the deportation of aliens who "advocate...world communism." After the eight aliens filed suit, challenging the constitutionality of the McCarran-Walter Act advocacy-of-communism provision, the INS dropped those charges.

However, the INS charged six of the eight aliens with technical violations of the immigration laws, and charged the other two with violating another provision of the McCarran-Walter Act that dealt with advocating the death of government officials. The eight aliens argued that the INS targeted them for deportation because they were affiliated with a politically unpopular group. They pointed out that the INS had not accused them of carrying out any terroristic acts. Thus, the eight argued that the government had restricted their FIRST AMENDMENT right to freedom of political expression.

The federal district court issued an injunction that prohibited the INS from carrying out the deportation proceedings. Attorney General JANET RENO appealed this ruling, but while it was pending Congress enacted the Illegal Immigration Reform and Immigrant Responsibility Act of 1996 (IIRIRA). 110 Stat. 3009–546. This act repealed a judicial review process in the Immigration and Nationality Act, replacing it with a new provision that restricted judicial review of the attorney general's deportation orders. 8 U.S.C.A. § 1252(g). Congress sought to streamline a deportation process that led to lengthy court battles over administrative decisions, such as occurred in this case. Reno then filed motions in federal court arguing that the courts did not have jurisdiction under the new law to hear the cases brought by the eight aliens. The Ninth Circuit Court of Appeals rejected her argument and ruled that the district court had properly stopped the deportation proceedings.

The Supreme Court, on an 8–1 vote, upheld the 1996 law. On a 6–3 vote, the Court also held that illegal immigrants do not have the right to assert constitutional rights in an effort to avoid deportation. The second ruling surprised the parties and legal observers because when it agreed to hear the case, the Court specifically excluded the First Amendment issue and stated that it would only review the 1996 law. Therefore, neither side discussed this issue in their legal briefs.

Justice ANTONIN SCALIA, writing for the Court, noted that a general provision of the IIRIRA stated that the revised procedures for removing aliens would not apply in deportation proceedings pending on the day the new law became effective. However, another section of the statute specifically directed that § 1252(g) should apply "without limitation to claims arising from all past, pending, or future exclusion, deportation, or removal proceedings." § 306(c)(1).

Turning to § 1252(g), Justice Scalia found that it applied to three types of actions the attorney general may take: her decision or action to "commence proceedings, adjudicate cases, or execute removal orders." Scalia believed that the provision sought to protect some of the attorney general's "discretionary determinations." If an illegal immigrant sought to have a court review a determination by the attorney general, the provision made clear that judicial review was to be reviewable by a court only after all administrative proceedings had been exhausted. The eight aliens' challenge to the attorney general's decision to "commence proceedings" against them fell squarely within § 1252(g). Therefore, the courts did not have jurisdiction to hear their challenge.

Justice Scalia then examined the aliens' claim that they were selectively prosecuted for asserting their First Amendment rights. He stated that as both a "general matter" and in the present case, "an alien unlawfully in this country has no constitutional right to assert selective enforcement as a defense against his deportation." Scalia concluded that the government "does not offend the Constitution" by deporting an illegal immigrant for the additional reason that it believes him to be a member of an organization that supports terrorist activity."

Justice RUTH BADER GINSBURG, in a separate opinion joined by Justice STEPHEN BREYER, agreed with Justice Scalia that § 1252(g) deprived the federal courts of jurisdiction over the case. However, she concluded that the Court should not have decided the selective enforcement issue. Because the parties had not briefed the issue, the Court should have left the question open.

Organizations such as the American Civil Liberties Union (ACLU) decried the decision as an infringement of First Amendment principles and argued that the ruling relegated immigrants to a second-class status. According to Lucas Guttentag, director of the ACLU's Immigrant's Rights Project, the decision gave the "government free rein to target immigrants for deportation based on their lawful political activities." However, other legal commentators saw the decision upholding a legitimate government right to determine who is lawfully or unlawfully in the country.

Immigration experts concluded that the decision would not have much practical effect. Of the thousands of illegal immigrants who are subject to deportation annually, few are subjected to deportation because of their political views.

CROSS REFERENCES
Equal Protection; First Amendment; Standing

ANTI-DEFAMATION LEAGUE

The Anti-Defamation League (ADL) is an agency of B'nai B'rith, an international Jewish service organization. The ADL combats anti-Semitism, religious and racial intolerance and all forms of organized discrimination based on stereotypical beliefs. The ADL also is a strong advocate of the state of Israel, lobbying Congress in support of legislation that benefits the Jewish State. It has its headquarters in New York City and has regional and satellite offices throughout the United States. The ADL also has offices in Jerusalem and Vienna.

Sigmound Livingston founded the ADL in 1913 with the support of B'nai B'rith. Livingston, a Chicago attorney, stated that the mission of the league was "to stop, by appeals to reason and conscience, and if necessary, by appeals to law, the defamation of the Jewish people...to secure justice and fair treatment to all citizens alike...[and] put an end forever to unjust and unfair discrimination against and ridicule of any sect or body of citizens."

The ADL first gained recognition by taking steps to eradicate negative stereotypes of Jews in print and their stereotyping on stage and in film. By the early 1920s, objectionable references to Jews in the national press had virtually disappeared. However, popular culture was filled with negative stereotypes of Jews. The rise of the Ku Klux Klan in the 1920s was based as much on anti-Semitism as racial intolerance. The ADL responded by circulating pamphlets that challenged hatred of Jews and demanding apologies from prominent citizens, such as automobile manufacturer Henry Ford, for endorsing anti-Semitic views.

With the rise of Nazism in the 1930s, the ADL fought U.S. supporters of Hitler who endorsed his anti-Semitic policies. During this decade, the ADL began to collect information on extremist individuals and organizations and to monitor and investigate fascist groups in the United States. These fact-finding and monitoring activities have remained a central part of the ADL's work.

From the 1940s to the 1990s, the ADL has lobbied for civil rights legislation, filed briefs in courts supporting the separation of church and state, and educated succeeding generations in religious tolerance. Since the creation of Israel in 1948, the ADL has also defended Israel's right to exist and has fought against anti-Zionism. In the 1990s, the organization began monitoring the Internet for evidence of anti-Semitism and right-wing extremism.

The ADL is divided into numerous divisions and departments. The Civil Rights Division is the most prominent wing of the organization, as it has investigated and exposed anti-Semitism and bigotry. The division's research department has become a central source of information on organized bigotry, collecting and analyzing racist, anti-Semitic, terrorist and extremist literature. The department issues an annual *Audit of Anti-Semitic Incidents* that serves as a reliable measurement tool of anti-Semitic trends. The Civil Rights Division's fact finding department uses investigative journalists to track the activities of extremist groups. For example, this department tracked neo-Nazi skinhead activity in thirty-three countries and issued the first major survey on this movement.

The Civil Rights Division's legal affairs department serves as the ADL's advocates in court and before legislatures. The department's attorneys file briefs, analyze proposed bills and regulations, draft model laws, and prepare testimony and legal reports for ADL staff. The department's model hate crimes law has been adopted by almost four-fifths of the states and has been upheld as constitutional by the U.S. Supreme Court in *State v. Mitchell,* 508 U.S. 476, 113 S.Ct. 2194, 124 L.Ed.2d 436 (1993). In addition, the department works with local attorneys in the ADL's thirty regional offices.

The ADL's Braun Holocaust Institute, established in 1977, serves as a centralized information center on the Holocaust. The institute encourages public and religious schools to teach about the Holocaust by providing curricula for elementary and high school students. It has also organized teacher-training workshops and seminars to help teachers incorporate Holocaust studies into mainstream disciplines. The institute's collection of Holocaust-related materials is recognized as one of the best in the world. In addition, the institute publishes *Dimensions: A Journal of Holocaust Studies,* a general interest magazine on the Holocaust, and resource guides, catalogs, and background primers.

The Government and National Affairs Office in Washington, D.C., serves as the ADL's lobbyist, promoting the legislative agenda of the organization. The office worked with Congress to establish a congressional task force against anti-Semitism. The ADL has also led a broad coalition of civil rights, religious and law enforcement groups in support of federal hate crime initiatives. In addition, the ADL has fought against federal school voucher programs and has sought to increase workplace protection for employees who wish to observe their religious duties.

The ADL's commitment to the state of Israel includes maintaining an office in Jerusalem. This office provides information on current issues to ADL staff and members, and it communicates the U.S. Jewish community's concerns to the Israeli government. The Jerusalem office also introduces visiting Americans, such as members of Congress and journalists, to the people and politics of Israel. The ADL has endorsed the need for a just peace between Israelis and Palestinians but has been an adamant defender of Israel and opponent of terrorism.

CROSS REFERENCES
Discrimination; Hate Crime

ANTITRUST LAW

Legislation enacted by the federal and various state governments to regulate trade and commerce by preventing unlawful restraints, price-fixing, monopolies, to promote competition, and to encourage the production of quality goods and services a the lowest prices, with the primary goal of safeguarding public welfare by ensuring that consumer demands will be met by the manufacture and sale of goods at reasonable prices.

Archer Daniels Trials

In September 1998, a jury convicted three former top executives of the Archer Daniels

Midland (ADM) Corporation of price-fixing. In antitrust law, which seeks to make business compete fairly, price-fixing is the crime of conspiring with competitors to set prices for the detriment of consumers or other competitors. Price-fixing charges had beset the agribusiness giant since the mid-1990s, when federal investigators completed a four-year long undercover probe. In October 1996, the company pleaded guilty to price-fixing in two markets and paid what was then the highest antitrust fine in history, $100 million. Later that year, a GRAND JURY handed down indictments against the three executives, all of whom pleaded innocent. With evidence in the form of undercover audio and video tapes made by one of the defendants for the Federal Bureau of Investigation (FBI), prosecutors won convictions in all three cases.

The ADM investigation first became public in June 1995, following a federal raid of the company's Decatur, Illinois, headquarters. A month later, the *Wall Street Journal* announced that federal agents were probing price-fixing allegations at the $4 billion agribusiness. According to federal sources, ADM had engaged in a year-long price-fixing conspiracy with Asian competitors. The corporations had allegedly discussed ways to fix prices in the markets for three products: lysine, citric acid, and high fructose corn syrup (HFCS). Lysine is an amino acid used by farmers in livestock feed, citric acid is a flavor additive and preservative, HFCS is a sugar substitute. Unlike some other kinds of antitrust activity, which courts evaluate for legality in light of a variety of circumstances, price-fixing is PER SE illegal. Among antitrust violations it is considered one of the most harmful to consumers, since it defeats the purpose of competition in the free market and allows crass manipulation of consumer spending.

From the outset, ADM officials denied the charges, but investigators had strong evidence. Unbeknownst to the corporation, starting in 1992, the FBI had planted a mole at meetings between ADM and foreign competitors—one of ADM's own executives. Mark E. Whitacre, forty-one, who headed ADM bioproducts division in the early 1990s, had secretly made audio and video recordings as he and his fellow executives talked prices with the competition. Made in 1993, one videotape showed executives from ADM and Ajinimoto of Japan divvying up sales in a California hotel room. And an audio recording captured James Randall, then company president, at ADM's headquarters telling Japanese executives, "We have a saying at this company.

Michael Andreas was convicted on charges of price-fixing.
AP/WIDE WORLD PHOTOS

Our competitors are our friends and our customers are our enemies."

After repeated denials, ADM stunned the business world with its guilty plea in October 1996. Even more dramatic was the criminal fine it agreed to pay—a record-setting $100 million, along with an additional $90 million to settle civil lawsuits. Attorney General JANET RENO hailed the plea as a major victory for the Justice Department's antitrust division that put the worldwide business community on watch—it would not allow consumers to be robbed. "If you engage in collusive behavior that robs U.S. consumers," Reno warned, "there will be vigorous investigation and tough, tough penalties." ADM admitted to price-fixing only in the lysine and citric acid markets while; the JUSTICE DEPARTMENT dropped its probe into high fructose corn syrup. Two months earlier, the department had also won more than $20 million in criminal fines in agreements with executives of two Japanese and one U.S.-based Korean firms.

In December 1996, a Chicago GRAND JURY issued criminal indictments against ADM executives for their role in the lysine price-fixing scam. The FBI stopped cooperating with Whitacre after learning that he was EMBEZZLING from ADM, a crime for which he was convicted and sentenced to nine years in prison. The indictment accused him of engaging in price-fixing for a year before 1992, whereas the other two men were accused of the crime through 1995. They were Terrance Wilson, sixty years old, the now-retired head of ADM's corn-processing unit, and Michael Andreas, forty-nine years old, ADM's executive vice president. At the time of the indictment, Andreas was supposed to succeed his aging father, seventy-eight-year old company chairman and CEO Dwayne Andreas. All three men pleaded innocent.

During the seven-week long trial in August and September 1998, prosecutors relied heavily upon the undercover tapes. They played the material for the jury, and then supported it with corporate documents and testimony by nine witnesses. Among their star witnesses was Japanese executive Masaur Yamamoto, a mid-level executive with Japan's Kyowa Hakko Kogyo Company. Yamamoto testified that he attended meetings with the defendants in cities all over the world at which they set prices and split up sales. Andreas, prosecutors said, approved all the price-fixing schemes.

In closing arguments on September 9, federal prosecutor Scott Lassar told jurors, "This was a crime of greed—a crime by an extremely large corporation that wanted to make even more money at the expense of their customers." Lassar said the jury had ten or twenty times the amount of evidence needed to convict.

By contrast, the defense pursued a surprisingly low-key strategy. It called only one witness to testify for an hour on a relatively insignificant issue. Primarily, defense attorneys for Andreas and Wilson tried to convince jurors that the government had misunderstood the real nature of the executive meetings. Neither man was a price-fixer, the attorneys said. Indeed, the executives had only pretended to engage in price-fixing so that they could fool their competitors—pulling off what Andreas' lead attorney Reid Weingarten characterized as "an unorthodox mission" in corporate trickery. This argument met with mockery from prosecutor Lassar, who asked jurors, "When was he pretending? When wasn't he?"

When the defense went on the attack in closing arguments, it tried to destroy the credibility of the government's mole, Whitacre. Defense attorneys contended that Whitacre was an embittered felon who sought to deflect attention from his embezzling. Defense attorney Mark Hulkower called him a "master manipulator" who had succeeded in running the FBI's investigation for it.

On September 17, after five days of deliberation, the jury returned guilty verdicts for all three men, who vowed to appeal. Following the

trial, jurors said the prosecution's undercover evidence as well as the defense's odd low-key style had swayed them. Sentencing was set for early 1999, but subsequently delayed when the court sought additional information on the price-fixing in order to determine an appropriate penalty. Each convicted man faces up to three years in prison and fines that could mount into the millions of dollars.

FTC v. Intel

On March 8, 1999, the Federal Trade Commission (FTC) entered into a consent judgment (a legally enforceable agreement in which a defendant consents to stop allegedly illegal practices) with Intel Corp., the world's largest maker of personal computer (PC) chips. The decree prohibits Intel from withholding technical information, assistance, and product samples from customers with whom it is having a dispute concerning intellectual property rights to microprocessor technology. Often called the "brains" of a computer system, microprocessors are a PC's central processing unit (CPU). The decree resolved the legal issues raised in the FTC's June 1998 complaint, which accused Intel of violating federal antitrust laws by suspending its relationships with three computer manufacturers (also know as original equipment manufacturers or OEMs) as a means of coercing the OEMs into licensing their technological innovations to the chipmaker.

The three OEMs identified in the complaint were Digital Equipment Corp., Intergraph Corp., and Compaq Computer Corp. The FTC alleged that Intel's actions hampered the competitiveness of the three OEMs, whose ability to introduce new computer systems depended largely upon incorporating the latest technology from the chipmaker's family of microprocessors known by the trade names Pentium, Pentium with MMX, Pentium Pro, Pentium II, and Pentium III. According to the FTC, Intel had no rival that could have provided the three OEMs with a microprocessor of substantially similar speed and quality. Although the FTC linked Intel's business relations with the three OEM's for the purposes of its complaint, each commercial relationship was in fact separate and distinct.

Digital is a Massachusetts corporation that manufactures and sells computer hardware and software, including PCs, workstations (powerful computers programmed to run demanding scientific, engineering, and design-intensive applications), and servers (huge network computers). Digital generated approximately $2 billion in revenue from Intel-based computers during 1997, having invested $250 million in the company's chips. But when Digital sued Intel for infringing on Digital's Alpha microprocessor technology, Intel demanded return of the technical data it had earlier supplied and withheld assistance that Digital needed to make Pentium-based computer systems.

Intergraph is an Alabama corporation that manufactures and sells computer hardware and software, including workstations with sophisticated graphics and animation. Intergraph was the first computer-systems manufacturer to offer a workstation with a Pentium Pro microprocessor, and by 1995 Intel-based systems represented over 75 percent of Intergraph's hardware unit sales. In 1996 Intel demanded a royalty-free license to Intergraph's Clipper microprocessor as a condition for providing further technical assistance that Intergraph needed to continue timely development of Pentium-driven work stations. When Intergraph refused, Intel cut off technical assistance, demanded return of its Pentium prototypes, and allegedly failed to inform Intergraph of a known bug in a computer chip.

Compaq is the largest manufacturer of PCs in the world. Headquartered in Texas, Compaq designs, develops, and sells a full line of computer system products, including workstations and servers. Compaq is Intel's largest dollar and volume customer for microprocessors, purchasing more than $2 billion worth of Pentium chips in 1997. In 1994 Compaq sued Packard Bell Electronics, Inc., (now Packard Bell NEC, Inc.) for infringing on certain patented computer technology. Having supplied the allegedly infringing components, Intel intervened in the suit on behalf of Packard Bell and began cutting off technical information that Compaq needed to design Pentium-based products.

In each case the FTC accused Intel of suspending commercial relations in retaliation for the customer's assertions of intellectual property rights. The FTC complained that Intel made the same type of technical assistance widely available to other customers who had succumbed to chipmaker's bullying tactics. As a result certain computer manufacturers favored by Intel were able introduce new computer systems in an efficient manner, while the three OEMs disfavored by Intel were delayed in bringing their products to market. Because the life cycle of a computer system may be as short as six months, any delay in introducing new products can have a significant adverse affect on an OEM's profit

margin. Thus, the FTC concluded that Intel was using its dominant market share in a monopolistic fashion to impede competition and hinder the profitability of its rivals.

Intel never denied that it attempted to dictate the outcomes of its intellectual property disputes by withholding technical support and product samples. However, Intel maintained that its behavior was an aggressive, but lawful way of protecting its own intellectual property rights. As the proprietor of the popular Pentium line of microprocessors, Intel argued that it could choose to do business with whomever it pleased and cease doing business whenever it pleased. Intel also argued that it was vindicated on this point by the consent judgment, which attributed no wrongdoing to the chip's maker. Nor did the consent judgment brand the defendant a monopoly, a label that Intel has fought despite enjoying a 75 percent share of the CPU market.

But the consent judgment was not a one-sided victory for Intel. Hammered out just two days before the trial was scheduled to begin, a ten-year agreement required Intel to provide all of its customers with necessary technical data at least six months prior to a microprocessor's official release date. Access to technical information, support, and prototypes may not be withheld or even restricted by Intel during intellectual property disputes with customers. If a customer asserts its intellectual property rights against Intel, it may sue the customer to resolve the issue or negotiate a license in an arms–length transaction. But Intel may not extort a licensing agreement with threats of suspending business relations.

The consent judgment permits Intel to ask customers for written assurance that they will not attempt to block the company from selling, making, or importing microprocessors. Intel may also ask its customers to sign a nondisclosure agreement that protects the chipmaker's trade secrets and other valuable proprietary information. If a customer refuses to give such assurances or sign such an agreement, the decree authorizes Intel to then cease providing support. Additionally, the decree allows Intel to end commercial relations with customers who fail to pay their bills, go into direct competition with a Pentium product, or provide other legitimate business reasons for termination. Finally, Intel may end commercial relations with customers who seek an injunction (an order compelling a party to take or refrain from taking certain actions) preventing Intel from designing, developing, manufacturing, importing, or selling new computer chips.

Approved by a 3–0 vote of FTC Commissioners (one commissioner did not participate due to medical reasons), the consent judgment was subject to a sixty-day public comment period that ended May 24, 1999. The FTC is required to give consideration to any bona fide concerns raised by the public during this period before finalizing the terms of the decree.

United States v. Microsoft

On May 18, 1998, nineteen state attorney generals joined the U.S. Department of Justice (DOJ) in filing an antitrust lawsuit against Microsoft Corporation. The suit alleges that the software company forces computer manufacturers (known as original equipment manufacturers or OEMs) to license and distribute Microsoft's Internet Explorer (IE) in exchange for the right to pre-install Microsoft's Windows 95 operating system on new personal computers (PCs). IE is a program known as a web browser that is used for accessing the World Wide Web, e-mail, and other Internet media. Microsoft contends that IE is an integral part of Windows 95 and cannot be separated without causing the operating system as a whole to malfunction. The plaintiffs argue that Microsoft is engaging in an illegal TYING ARRANGEMENT, by conditioning the purchase of a popular product (Windows 95) on the purchase of an additional, unrelated product (IE).

The lawsuit represents the culmination of an ongoing legal battle between Microsoft and the federal government. The Federal Trade Commission (FTC) began investigating Microsoft in 1990. But when four FTC commissioners deadlocked over whether to commence formal proceedings against Microsoft in 1993, the DOJ

One of Microsoft's attorneys, John Warden, arrives at federal court.

assumed control of the investigation. A year later Microsoft and the DOJ entered into a consent judgment (a legally enforceable agreement in which a defendant consents to stop allegedly illegal practices) that prohibited the software manufacturer from entering tying arrangements. However, the decree contained a clause permitting Microsoft to bundle products that are so integrated as to offer "technological advantages" to PC owners. In October of 1997 the DOJ asked a federal district court to hold Microsoft in contempt for violating the anti-tying provision of the consent decree. The district court declined to do so in light of the ambiguous nature of "integrated product clause." Nonetheless, the court did issue an injunction (an order compelling a party to take or refrain from taking certain action) prohibiting Microsoft from bundling IE with Windows 95.

The government suffered two setbacks during 1998. In May, a federal appeals court held that the injunction did not prohibit Microsoft from bundling IE with its new Windows 98 operating system. In July the same federal court of appeals overturned the injunction altogether on procedural and substantive grounds. Both decisions addressed the integrated product clause. The July decision found that the clause was consistent with federal antitrust law. It also found that Microsoft had introduced a "facially plausible" explanation as to how IE's interpenetrating design and graphic functionality had been integrated with the Windows operating system. The May decision held that the DOJ had failed to present any evidence that Windows 98 was not an integrated system. To present such evidence the DOJ and the state attorneys general pushed forward with a lawsuit that would resolve the issues raised by the consent decree.

The nonjury trial began on October 19, 1998, in the U.S. District Court for the District of Columbia, with Judge Thomas Penfield Jackson presiding. The trial rules limited each side to presenting twelve primary witnesses and three rebuttal witnesses. The government took approximately three months to present its case-in-chief, while Microsoft took approximately six weeks. Before hearing from the rebuttal witnesses, the court took an indefinite recess in February 1999 to facilitate settlement discussions.

The trial posed four central questions: (1) does Microsoft have monopolistic power?; (2) did Microsoft employ predatory practices to prevent OEM's from marketing Netscape Communications Corp.'s Navigator web browser?;

(3) has Microsoft engaged in illegal tying arrangements that bundle nonintegrated products?; (4) has Microsoft tried to split markets with competitors?

The trial court must first decide whether Microsoft is a MONOPOLY. None of Microsoft's alleged predatory practices would violate antitrust law if the software company were deemed to have meaningful competition. In other words, the government must prove that the operating-system market is completely dominated by Windows. Federal courts will presume that monopoly power exists if the market share enjoyed by a particular defendant exceeds 70 to 80 percent. Conversely, federal courts will presume no monopoly power exists if a defendant's market share is below 50 to 60 percent.

The government attempted to establish that Microsoft has monopolistic power by the testimony of two economists, who told the court that the defendant owns a 90-percent share of the operating-system market. Economist Frederick Warren-Boulton testified that Microsoft records "astonishing" profit margins due to its ability to maintain software prices above market levels. Economist Franklin Fisher said that he considers Microsoft a monopoly, forecasting that unless the government prevails in its antitrust lawsuit "we're going to live in a Microsoft world." Microsoft offered the testimony of Richard Schmalensee, dean at the Sloan School of Business, Massachusetts Institute of Technology (MIT), who told the court that the software industry is intensely competitive despite Window's prominence.

Antitrust law prohibits monopolies from counseling their distributors against offering competitors' products. The government alleges that Microsoft bullies OEMs into not distributing Netscape's Navigator by leveraging the power of its dominant Windows operating system. David Colburn, senior vice president of business affairs at America Online Inc. (AOL), testified that he was forced to sign an exclusive deal with Microsoft for the right to give PC owners easy access to AOL on the Windows desktop via a clickable button. An Intel Corporation executive testified that Microsoft pressured his company to stay out of the software field and threatened to withdraw support for future Intel computer chips if the company developed software that Microsoft viewed as a threat. The government also introduced evidence that Compaq Computer Corp., had to feature the IE web browser if it wanted to get Windows preinstalled on its new PCs.

Paul Maritz, Microsoft's vice president for platforms and applications, admitted during cross-examination that his company offered financial incentives to persuade Netscape to support Microsoft's Internet technologies rather than offer a competing web-browsing product. Other defense witnesses contended that there are still plenty of ways for Netscape to distribute its product, including distributing Navigator through thousands of Internet service providers who do not have deals with Microsoft. The defendant's position was bolstered by a witness for the government, William Harris, Jr., president of Intuit Inc. Harris testified that he considers IE the best browser for his company's Quicken personal finance software, regardless of whether Microsoft may have agreed to bundle some Intuit software with Windows.

To establish an illegal tying arrangement, the government has to prove that Microsoft customers receive virtually no benefits from the company's bundling of Windows with its IE web browser. The government's allegation that Windows and IE are not one integrated product relies in part on the fact that when Microsoft first began marketing Windows 95 the company sold its web browser separately. The government also relies on two witnesses who testified that neither Windows 95 nor Windows 98 depend on IE for optimal functionality. Edward Felten, director of the Secure Internet Programming Laboratory, Princeton University, testified that it is possible to remove web-browsing functions from Windows without harming the rest of the operating system. David Farber, director of distributed computing at the University of Pennsylvania, testified that that a browser is really a separate application from an operating system, and that there is no technical necessity for Microsoft to bundle its browser with Windows.

James Allchin, Microsoft senior vice president for personal and business systems and the executive in charge of Windows, testified that integrating IE's graphic functionality with Windows is good for consumers because it reduces confusion and is more efficient. But during cross-examination Allchin admitted to discrepancies in a Microsoft videotaped demonstration that the defense had offered to support arguments about the benefits of browser integration. The government's lawyers repeatedly attacked the credibility of Microsoft's witnesses. Daniel Rosen, Microsoft's general manager of new technology, contradicted his previous assertions and those of Microsoft Chairman Bill Gates, when he testified that his company did not view other Internet browsers as a competitive threat. Robert Muglia, Microsoft's senior vice president of tools, testified that Microsoft had not tried to undermine Sun Microsystems Inc.'s rival Java technology, even though a memo from Gates indicated to the contrary.

The government charges that Microsoft made a number of overtures to split the web-browsing market with several businesses, instead of allowing competition to weed out the good from the bad. Netscape CEO James L. Barksdale testified that Microsoft discussed separating the two companies' markets, with Microsoft providing browsers for Windows 95 and Netscape getting everything else. Executives from Apple Corporation and Intel strengthened Barksdale's testimony, telling the court that Microsoft made similar offers to their companies. The defense offered testimony that Microsoft's meetings with its competitors consisted of routine discussions between application developers and nothing more. The government provided no "smoking gun" in support of its allegations, and Microsoft was quick to point out that the only evidence against it was the self-serving and sometimes murky testimony of it competitors. Thus, many legal experts have questioned whether the government has marshaled convincing proof on this issue.

As settlement talks continued in May 1999, the two sides began preparing for the rebuttal phase of trial. Microsoft announced its plan to recall AOL executive David Colburn to the stand, and question him about his company's $10 million acquisition of Netscape and its side agreement to buy and jointly develop software with Sun Microsystems. Microsoft contends that the deal will enable AOL to offer a product that directly competes with IE and possibly with Windows itself, and that competition between the two businesses will likely become fierce. Even Judge Jackson suggested that the deal might result in a "very significant change" in the industry.

Meanwhile, the government has been exploring remedies it might seek should it prevail in the liability phase when the trial resumes. The state attorneys general said that they would not be satisfied with any remedy that does not completely revamp Microsoft. One remedy receiving favor by the government would compel Microsoft to license the source code for Windows to several other companies that could then market rival operating systems. Federal courts have long upheld the validity of compulsory licensing in antitrust suits, and such remedies usually require little judicial monitoring to implement. While some monopoly busters have advocated a remedy that would require Microsoft to divest itself of Windows or its web-browsing products, divestiture is rarely invoked in antitrust suits outside the context of a MERGER involving two conglomerates.

NYNEX Corporation v. Discon, Inc.

In *NYNEX Corporation v. Discon, Inc.*, 525 U.S. 128, 119 S. Ct. 493, 142 L. Ed. 2d 510 (1998), the U.S. Supreme Court was asked to determine whether the antitrust rule making group BOYCOTTS illegal per se (inherently illegal without regard to justification or factual context) applies to a single buyer's decision to purchase telephone-equipment-removal services from one supplier rather than another. In a unanimous opinion written by Justice STEPHEN BREYER the Court ruled that a buyer's decision in this situation is not subject to a per se rule of illegality, even when that decision does not further ordinary competitive objectives and may result in harm to both a competitor and consumers. The Court concluded that persons or entities alleging injury from a buyer's decision to switch suppliers may prevail under antitrust law only if they prove that harm actually resulted to the competitive process, and not just to one competitor.

Discon was a company that supplied services for the removal, salvaging, and disposal of obsolete telephone equipment. Its largest customer was Material Enterprises Company (MECo), a subsidiary of the NYNEX holding company. MECo acted as the purchasing agent for another NYNEX subsidiary, New York Telephone Company (NYTel), which provided local telephone service for much of New York State and parts of Connecticut. MECo terminated its relationship with Discon after two years, switching to a competing provider of removal services, AT&T Technologies (AT&T).

Discon alleged that MECo purchased removal services from AT&T for an inflated price that NYTel passed on to its customers. NYTel was accused of relying on these inflated costs to gain regulatory approval for charging higher rates to its customers. At the end of each year Discon claimed that AT&T would secretly rebate some or all of the overcharge to MECo and NYTel in the form of a KICKBACK. Discon argued that this alleged scheme not only DEFRAUDED customers, but also excluded Discon from the removal-service market and drove it out of business in violation of the SHERMAN AN-

TITRUST ACT's prohibition against group boycotts. 15 U.S.C.A. 1.

The U.S. District Court for the Western District of New York disagreed, dismissing Discon's suit for failure to state a claim upon which relief could be granted. However, the U.S. Court of Appeals for the Second Circuit partially reinstated the suit. It ruled that Discon could go to trial and offer evidence demonstrating that the defendants' actions constituted an illegal group boycott and a CONSPIRACY to monopolize, despite the fact that the alleged unlawful transaction involved only one buyer and one seller. *Discon, Inc. v. NYNEX Corporation*, 93 F. 3d 1055 (2nd Cir. 1996). NYNEX then appealed.

The Supreme Court agreed that certain kinds of agreements will often prove so harmful to competition and so rarely prove justified that antitrust laws do not require evidence of their anticompetitive effects. The Court said that such agreements are presumed to be unlawful in and of themselves, or illegal per se. The Court noted that some group boycotts fall into this category of presumptively illegal agreements. An agreement by clothing designers, manufacturers, and suppliers not to sell their goods to retailers who buy their apparel from competitors, the Court said, is an example of a group boycott that is per se illegal. No evidence may be offered by the defendants in this situation to explain why the boycott was reasonable or necessary. Injury is inferred to the competitive process as a whole from the nature of the boycott agreement.

The Court drew a distinction between two kinds of boycott agreements, horizontal and vertical. A horizontal agreement is one between competitors at the same level of distribution, such as an agreement between wholesalers. A vertical agreement is one between parties at different levels of distribution, such as an agreement between a wholesaler and a retailer. The Court held that the per se rule of illegality in antitrust suits applies to horizontal agreements among direct competitors, but does not generally apply to vertical agreements (unless they involve PRICE-FIXING). The legality of vertical agreements is analyzed under the so-called rule of reason, which requires the party asserting an antitrust violation to prove both that anticompetitive behavior actually took place and that the behavior produced measurable anticompetitive results.

The deal between NYNEX and AT&T, the Court said, was a vertical agreement because it represented a single buyer's decision to purchase telephone-equipment-removal services from one seller rather than another. It was not an agreement between a tier of buyers, sellers, or suppliers. The Court wrote that the "freedom to switch suppliers lies close to the heart of the competitive process that antitrust laws seek to encourage." To apply the per se rule of illegality against vertical boycott agreements that do not involve price-fixing would discourage firms from changing suppliers, the court opined, even in cases where the competitive process itself is not harmed.

Although the case was remanded to allow Discon the opportunity to establish that the competitive process was in fact harmed by NYNEX's deal with AT&T, the Supreme Court openly questioned whether the deal had any anti-competitive effects whatsoever. The Court observed that Discon's own description of the telephone-equipment-removal business suggested that entry into the field by other firms was easy, perhaps to the point where competitors might enter the field almost at will. For example, Discon's complaint stated that even NYTel was a potential competitor that had already performed removal services on a few occasions in the past. The Court reasoned that such competition should provide effective checks on prices in the equipment-removal market with or without Discon's participation.

At the same time, the Court recognized that NYNEX'S behavior hurt consumers by raising telephone service rates. But both NYNEX's competitors and its customers, the Court emphasized, could have pursued a host of remedies available outside of antitrust law. For example, state and federal law provide a number of remedies for predatory and injurious business practices, including injunctions, fines, penalties, and orders for restitution. In fact, the government successfully obtained some of these remedies against NYNEX. The New York State Public Service Commission (PSC) assessed $72 million in penalties against NYNEX for its role in the rate scam, while the Federal Trade Commission (FTC) required NYNEX to refund $35 million to the customers. The Court said that any remaining uncompensated victims could have pursued additional remedies in private civil actions asserting claims for damages under business tort law.

CROSS REFERENCES
Internet; Tying Arrangement

ARBITRATION

The submission of a dispute to an unbiased third person designated by the parties to the controversy, who agreed in advance to comply with the AWARD—a decision to be issued after a hearing at which both parties have an opportunity to be heard.

Duffield v. Robertson Stephens & Co.

National securities exchanges, such as the New York Stock Exchange, have required persons who wish to be stockbrokers to waive, as a condition of their employment, the right to sue in a court of law to resolve all employment related disputes. Instead, brokers must agree to arbitrate any such disputes under the exchanges' rules. Prospective employees must satisfy this compulsory arbitration condition by signing the industry's Uniform Application for Securities Industry Registration of Transfer, commonly known as Form U-4, which registers them with all of the securities exchanges with which their employers are members. However, questions have arisen whether this waiver applies to employment discrimination actions under Title VII of the CIVIL RIGHTS ACT OF 1964.

The Ninth Circuit Court of Appeals, in *Duffield v. Robertson Stephens & Co.*, 144 F. 3d 1182 (9th Cir. 1998), addressed this issue, holding that under the Civil Rights Act of 1991 (Pub.L. 102–166, 105 Stat. 1071), employers within the securities industry may not require their employees to waive their right to bring a Title VII claim in court. Therefore, employees do not have to agree in advance to submit all such related disputes to binding arbitration. However, the court also held that employers may require employees to agree in advance to arbitrate state law TORT and contract claims, other than for violation of state civil rights law.

Tonyja Duffield signed her Form U-4 in 1988, before starting her job as a broker-dealer for Robertson Stephens & Company. In 1995, Duffield filed a lawsuit in federal court, alleging SEX DISCRIMINATION and SEXUAL HARASSMENT in violation of Title VII. She also alleged state law claims that included breach of CONTRACT, deceit, and intentional and negligent infliction of emotional distress. She asked the federal district court to issue a DECLARATORY JUDGMENT stating that securities industry employees cannot be compelled to arbitrate their employment disputes under the arbitration provision in Form U-4. A declaratory judgment is a statutory remedy in which the plaintiff asks the court to resolve his or her legal rights. In this case, Duffield realized that if the court upheld compulsory arbitration, the court would dismiss her lawsuit. A declaratory judgment can resolve a threshold legal issue before the plaintiff spends time and money on the fact-finding part of litigation. The district court refused to declare the compulsory arbitration invalid and later granted Robertson Stephens' motion to compel arbitration of all her substantive claims. Duffield then appealed to the Ninth Circuit.

The Ninth Circuit, in striking down the compulsory arbitration agreement, relied heavily on Supreme Court precedent and the legislative history of the Civil Rights Act of 1991. The appeals court first looked at *Alexander v. Gardner-Denver Co.*, 415 U.S. 36, 94 S. Ct. 1011, 39 L. Ed. 2d 147 (1974). The Supreme Court held that an arbitration clause contained in a COLLECTIVE BARGAINING AGREEMENT could not prohibit a plaintiff from seeking Title VII remedies in federal court. However, in 1991, the Supreme Court, in *Gilmer v. Interstate/Johnson Lane Corp.*, 500 U.S. 20, 111 S. Ct. 1647, 114 L. Ed. 2d 26 (1991), ruled that employees could be required under Form U-4 to arbitrate age discrimination claims brought under the Age Discrimination in Employment Act of 1967. 29 U.S.C.A. 621 et seq.

Although the two decisions appeared to be contradictory, the Supreme Court distinguished the *Alexander* decision on the ground that it involved a collective bargaining agreement rather than an individual agreement to arbitrate.

At almost the same time the Supreme Court released its *Gilmer* decision, Congress enacted the Civil Rights Act of 1991. This act was primarily designed to overturn Supreme Court decisions in order to make discrimination claims easier to bring and to prove in federal court. It also addressed, for the first time, the arbitration of Title VII claims. Section 118 of the act stated that the parties could, "where appropriate and to the extent authorized by law," choose to pursue alternative dispute resolution, including arbitration, to resolve their Title VII disputes.

The Ninth Circuit pointed out that Congress explicitly directed courts "that when the statutory terms in [Title VII] are susceptible to alternative interpretations, the Courts are to select the construction which most effectively advances the underlying congressional purpose" of the act. The court interpreted this to mean that the purpose of the act was to expand employees' rights and "to increase the possible remedies available to civil rights plaintiffs."

The appeals court analyzed what it considered to be the critical statutory language: the phrase "[w]here appropriate and to the extent authorized by law." It held that the phrase "where appropriate" meant where arbitration furthers the purpose and objective of the act. It was appropriate if victims of discrimination wished to use compulsory arbitration, but inappropriate if it was forced upon them by the securities industry.

The court read the phrase "to the extent authorized by law" in light of the other qualifying phrase and the objectives and purposes of the act. It concluded that it was far more likely that Congress was referring to the 1974 *Alexander* decision than to the 1991 *Gilmer* decision that allowed compulsory arbitration. The Ninth Circuit believed that Congress was not in favor of all forms of arbitration, regardless of the desires and interests of the persons whose rights the Civil Rights Act of 1991 was designed to protect.

In addition, the appeals court concluded that the legislative history confirmed that Congress sought to codify the law as it stood at the time the section was drafted. Therefore, Congress did not intend either to write the *Gilmer* decision into Title VII law or to leave the question of which forms of arbitration were permissible to future court decisions. The court emphasized that workers should not be forced to choose between their jobs and their civil rights.

The Ninth Circuit declared that Congress' expressed intent in drafting § 118 was to codify its position that "compulsory arbitration" of Title VII claims was not authorized by law. In addition, Congress did not want to compel employees to forego their rights to litigate future Title VII claims as a condition of employment; this was not "appropriate." Based on this interpretation of the legislative history, the court held that Form U-4 is unenforceable as applied to Title VII claims.

However, the court ruled that Duffield had to pursue her state TORT and contract claims through compulsory arbitration. As a practical matter, a plaintiff will have to file Title VII and state claims separately, unless the parties agree to adjudicate the claims in one court.

CROSS REFERENCES
Securities; Sexual Harassment

ATTORNEY-CLIENT PRIVILEGE

In the law of EVIDENCE client's privilege to refuse to disclose and to prevent any other person from disclosing confidential communications between the client and his or her attorney under the doctrine of client's privilege. Such privilege protects communications between attorney and client made for the purpose of furnishing or obtaining professional legal advice or assistance. That privilege that permits an attorney to refuse to testify as to communications from the client though it belongs to the client, not the attorney, and hence the client may waive it. In federal courts, state law is applied with respect to such privilege.

Swidler & Berlin v. United States

In a widely-publicized decision, the U.S. Supreme Court upheld the protection of privileged communications between attorneys and their clients, even after the death of the client in *Swidler & Berlin v. United States*, 524 U.S. 399, 118 S. Ct. 2081, 141 L. Ed. 2d 379 (1998). The Court declined to adopt a balancing test created by the court of appeals, thus reversing the appellate court and reaffirming the long-standing language and intent of common law and tradition.

What brought the case to the attention of those far removed from the parameters of legal circles was the general familiarity of the names

Vincent Foster's confidentiality with his attorneys was protected even after his death.

AP/WIDE WORLD PHOTOS

and faces of the parties involved. The alleged privileged communications belonged to then-Deputy White House Counsel Vincent W. Foster. The party seeking disclosure of those communications was Independent Counsel KENNETH W. STARR, on behalf of the U.S. government.

On July 11, 1993, Foster had consulted with Washington attorney James Hamilton about being a potential subject of congressional and federal criminal inquiry over the dismissal of seven White House Travel Office employees during the WHITEWATER investigations. A former White House aide had given the investigators a memo stating that HILLARY RODHAM CLINTON was behind the firings, and that she had consulted with Foster about the matter. Investigators were attempting to find out whether any of the presidential aides had lied about Mrs. Clinton's involvement in the employees' dismissals. Hamilton took three pages of handwritten notes during the consultation with Foster. Near the beginning of the first note, he wrote the word "Privileged."

Nine days after the consultation, Foster committed suicide. The Office of the Independent Counsel continued its investigation into whether various individuals had obstructed justice, made false statements, or had committed other crimes during investigations of the 1993 dismissal of the Travel Office employees. In December 1995, a federal GRAND JURY (at the request of the independent counsel) subpoenaed Hamilton's handwritten notes and other items from Hamilton and his law firm, Swidler & Berlin. The law firm filed a motion to quash the SUBPOENA, arguing that the notes constituted attorney work product and were also protected by the attorney-client privilege. (The privilege actually belongs to the client, but the attorney may invoke the privilege on behalf of the client, whether or not the client is absent or present, living or deceased.)

The federal district court conducted an IN-CAMERA review of the notes, then granted the motion to QUASH, concluding that the notes were protected from disclosure. In the government's subsequent appeal, it acknowledged that the attorney-client privilege would have been applicable had Foster still been alive and it also conceded that the use of the privilege was applicable to federal grand jury proceedings. But the government argued that an exception should be made when the information sought is needed for criminal investigations and the privilege-holder has since become deceased. In those circumstances, whether a crime has been committed should "trump" any continued confidentiality, in the interest of ultimate justice and truth finding.

A divided Circuit Court of Appeals for the District of Columbia agreed, *In re Sealed Case*, 124 F. 3d 230 (D.C. Cir. 1997). The court considered, among other things, Federal Rule of Evidence 501, which provides that "the privilege of a witness…shall be governed by the principles of common law…as interpreted…in the light of reason and experience." It went on to discuss the original intent of the attorney-client privilege, which is to encourage free and open communications between the two parties. Inversely proportional to the degree of frank disclosure and openness on the part of the client is the extent to which his/her attorney might caution that the communications might not be privileged. Of key importance was the consideration as to whether anticipation of loss of privilege at some later point might inhibit a client's full disclosure of facts to his/her attorney, referred to as a "chilling effect." The court of appeals went on to note that this was already the case in the one widely-recognized exception to post-death confidentiality of communications,—that of determining testamentary intent in will-contesting cases. However, a majority of the Court agreed that, as an abstract principle, an attorney-client privilege generally survives the death of the client.

The appellate court also considered academic arguments of several commentators that privileges should not expect infinite lives, as well as the general principle that uncertain privileges are disfavored. Concluding that clients would not commonly be concerned about post-death disclosures, the court reasoned that permitting disclosure under the circumstances outlined (criminal investigations) would not undermine the general policy of promoting free and open communications. (The government had argued that the only clients "chilled" by the possibility of future disclosure of their communications would be those intent on committing perjury, not truthful clients or those who might assert the Fifth Amendment.)

The court of appeals decided to create a new, narrow exception to post-death privileged communications, applicable only in a criminal context, and which would neither undermine the general policy of intent, nor create a chilling effect on general client communications. It articulated a balancing test to be used when considering whether, in the interest of justice, the sought information was so relevant to a criminal proceeding that it should outweigh the otherwise extended privilege of the communications after the death of the privilege-holder. In such limited criminal cases, the risk of posthumous disclosure would have little or no chilling effect, as opposed to the high cost of protecting communications after death. By applying this balancing test, the court held, the incremental uncertainty of whether or not communications would be infinitely privileged would be "hardly devastating."

The decision prompted immediate appeal by Hamilton and his law firm, and several AMICUS CURIAE briefs, all urging the rejection of a balancing test. The U.S. Supreme Court, on writ of CERTIORARI to the court of appeals, decided the matter on June 25, 1998. Chief Justice WILLIAM H. REHNQUIST delivered the unanimous opinion of the Court. It reversed the court of appeals, holding that Hamilton's handwritten notes, taken during his meeting with Foster, were protected by the attorney-client privilege, even after Foster's death.

While acknowledging that the arguments made by independent counsel, on behalf of the government, were by no means lacking in merit, the Supreme Court found the arguments had "simply not made a sufficient showing" to overturn the common law rule, embodied in case law, that attorney-client privilege would prevent disclosure of the notes at issue.

Contrary to the court below, the Supreme Court concluded that a post-death exception to the attorney-client privilege would in fact prevent complete candor and full disclosure in communications during the life of a client. Moreover, the Court reiterated that the reason for a privilege is to protect the interests of a client. When the privilege is compromised under the testamentary exception, it is done so only to fulfill the client's testamentary intent. That is not true with the government's proposed exception: there is no reason to conclude that a criminal federal grand jury inquiry into the confidential communications of a client would further his intent or interest.

Thus, in conclusion, the Supreme Court has left intact the common law rule, previously upheld in case law, that attorney-client privileges survive the death of the client, with narrow exceptions for testamentary intent cases involving "those claiming under the client." For trusts and estates attorneys, this is a mere confirmation of what has already been understood. But for all else, the decision has enormous impact, providing reasonable certainty that communications between clients and their attorneys will remain confidential, even after death of the client.

CROSS REFERENCES
Independent Counsel; Whitewater

AUTOMOBILE SEARCHES

Florida v. White

The Supreme Court ruled in *Florida v. White*, __U.S.__, 119 S. Ct. 1555, 143 L. Ed. 2d 748 (1999), that police do not need to obtain a WARRANT before seizing an automobile from a public place under laws that require FORFEITURE of property tied to crime. The ruling meant that the illegal narcotics police found after seizing the car could be used against the owner of the car in a criminal prosecution. The ruling continued a series of decisions that give police more discretion to search and seize without violating the FOURTH AMENDMENT's warrant requirement.

Three times during July and August of 1993, Bay County, Florida, police officers observed Tyvessel White delivering cocaine while using his car. The police developed probable cause that White's car was subject to forfeiture under the Florida Contraband Forfeiture Act, Fla. Stat. § 932.701 et seq. This law requires criminals to forfeit property that they used in connection with a crime. However, the police did not immediately act on the probable cause. Over two months later, the police arrested White at his place of employment on charges unrelated to the drug transactions. The arresting officers also seized White's automobile from his workplace parking lot without a warrant, based on the forfeiture law. The police later conducted an inventory of the auto and found two pieces of crack cocaine in the ashtray. Based on this evidence, White was charged under state law with possession of a controlled substance.

White asked the trial court to suppress the cocaine as evidence because the warrantless search violated the Fourth Amendment. The judge denied the request and White was convicted of the charge by a jury. The Florida Court of Appeals asked the Florida Supreme Court to decide whether White's Fourth Amendment rights were violated by the failure of police to obtain a warrant before seizing the car.

The Florida Supreme Court ruled that absent "exigent circumstances," police must obtain a warrant before seizing property that has been used in violation of the state forfeiture act. 710 So. 2d 949 (Fla. 1998). Although the majority of federal circuit courts of appeal had found no violation, three circuits agreed with the Florida court. Therefore, the Supreme Court granted review to resolve the issue.

The Court, on a 7–2 vote, held that police do not need a warrant to seize property governed by forfeiture acts. Justice CLARENCE THOMAS, writing for the majority, cited *Carroll v. United States*, 267 U.S. 132, 45 S. Ct. 280, 69 L. Ed 543 (1925). The Court ruled that when police believe a vehicle contains contraband they do not need to obtain a warrant before searching the car and seizing the contraband. The Court based the ruling on the movable nature of a vehicle, which made it more difficult to apprehend if a warrant was needed. However, the Florida Supreme Court rejected the argument that the warrantless seizure of the vehicle itself was appropriate under *Carroll*. The court found a "vast difference" between an immediate search of movable vehicle that is based on actual knowledge that it contains contraband and the "discretionary seizure of a citizen's automobile based upon a belief that it may have been used at some time in the past to assist in illegal activity."

Justice Thomas found no merit in this distinction. The principles underlying the rule in *Carroll* "support the conclusion that the warrantless seizure" did not violate the Fourth Amendment. Although the police lacked probable cause to believe White's car contained narcotics, "they certainly had probable cause to believe that the vehicle itself" was contraband under the Florida forfeiture law. The need to secure a readily movable item is "equally weighty when the *automobile*, as opposed to its contents, is the contraband that the police seek to secure."

The Supreme Court also referred to its tradition of allowing "law enforcement officials greater latitude in exercising their duties in a public place." Although a warrant is generally required for a felony arrest in a suspect's home, the Fourth Amendment permits warrantless arrests in public places where police have probable cause to believe that a felony has occurred. Justice Thomas reemphasized this distinction between a warrantless seizure in open area and a seizure on private premises.

Justice Thomas noted that a previous case had found that seizing vehicles that are on "public streets, parking lots, or other open places" did not "involve any invasion of privacy." In

White's case, his car was parked in his employer's lot, a public space. Therefore, the seizure of White's car did not invade his privacy and the Fourth Amendment did not require that police obtain a warrant to seize it.

Justice JOHN PAUL STEVENS wrote a dissent in which Justice RUTH BADER GINSBURG joined. Justice Stevens criticized the conduct of the police, specifically the two-month period between the observation of allegedly criminal behavior and the seizure of the car. He noted the "basic constitutional rule" that searches and seizures are presumptively unreasonable under the Fourth Amendment unless they fall within certain carefully drawn exceptions. He argued that the Court's decision "suggests that the exceptions have all but swallowed the general rule." It made no sense to claim an exception when the seizure occurred months after the alleged drug trade and White was "safely in police custody."

Justice Stevens found "particularly troubling" the fact that the police gave no reason why they did not seek a warrant before or after White's arrest. He assumed that "the officers who seized White's car simply preferred to avoid the hassle of seeking approval from a judicial officer." It was unwise, he concluded, to allow "bare convenience" to overcome traditional Fourth Amendment principles.

Knowles v. Iowa

Though the FOURTH AMENDMENT requires a police officer to have a WARRANT before conducting a search, the Supreme Court has recognized a number of exceptions to this rule. The Court allows the police in certain situations to legally conduct a search without a warrant. One of these exceptions is for automobile searches. Since the automobile search exception was first announced in *Carroll v. United States*, 267 U.S. 132, 45 S. Ct. 280, 69 L. Ed. 543 (1925), the Court has been called on to determine the limits of this exception.

In *Delaware v. Prouse*, 440 U.S. 648, 99 S. Ct. 1391, 59 L. Ed. 2d 660 (1979), the Court held for an officer to search an automobile, he must have more than a suspicion that a motorist has violated the law. The officer must believe that the driver is driving without a license, the car is unregistered, or the passengers or vehicle are otherwise subject to seizure. Such issues were again challenged in *Knowles v. Iowa*.

In *Knowles v. Iowa*, 525 U.S.113, 119 S. Ct. 484, 142 L. Ed. 2d 492 (1998), the Supreme Court reviewed an Iowa law that gave police of-

ficers the right to conduct a search of an automobile and the driver where they issue a citation instead of making an arrest and taking the driver into custody. The Court concluded that the Iowa law violated the Fourth Amendment because it did not come within any of the allowable exceptions to warrantless search and seizure.

The case arose when an Iowa police officer stopped Patrick Knowles for driving almost twenty miles per hour over the speed limit. The police officer issued a citation to Knowles, although under Iowa law he had the option of arresting him. The officer then conducted a full search of the car, and under the driver's seat he found a bag of marijuana and a "pot pipe." Knowles was then arrested and charged with violation of state laws dealing with controlled substances.

Knowles sought to suppress the evidence found in his car, so it could not be used at his criminal trial. He argued that the search could not be justifed under the "search incident to arrest" exception recognized in *United States v. Robinson*, 414 U.S. 218, 94 S. Ct. 467, 38 L. Ed. 2d 427 (1973), because he had been cited and had not been placed under arrest. At the hearing on the motion to suppress the evidence, the police officer acknowledged that he had neither Knowles' consent nor PROBABLE CAUSE to conduct the search. He relied on Iowa law when dealing with automobile searches.

The Iowa statute, Iowa Code Ann. § 321.485(1)(a), provides that Iowa police officers who have cause to believe that a person has violated any traffic or motor vehicle equipment law may arrest the person and immediately take the person before a MAGISTRATE. Iowa law also authorizes the more typical practice of issuing a citation instead of arrest or in lieu of continued custody after an initial arrest. Iowa Code Ann. § 805.1(1). Section 805.1(4) provides that the issuance of a citation in lieu of an arrest "does not affect the officer's authority to conduct an otherwise lawful search."

The Iowa Supreme Court had interpreted this provision as giving officers the authority to conduct a complete search of an automobile and driver in those cases where police elect not to make a custodial arrest and instead issue a citation. In short, the Iowa court had created a "search incident to citation" exception to the Fourth Amendment.

Based on this exception, the trial court denied the motion to suppress and found Knowles

SHOULD POLICE
PRACTICE PROFILING?

The 1998 shooting death of three young minority men by state troopers during a traffic stop on the New Jersey Turnpike helped spark a national debate on the issue of so-called "racial profiling" by law enforcement officials. Critics of profiling charge that the practice is inherently racist, because law enforcement officials tend to stop and search African Americans and other minorities more often than whites. Critics also charge that aggressive stop-and-search tactics erode public confidence in law enforcement and violate the civil rights of all citizens. In 1999, they led the charge for federal legislation to determine the extent to which racial profiling is practiced. Defenders of profiling concede that some law enforcement officials may stop and search blacks and other minorities at a disproportionately high rate. However, they ascribe this to overzealous police work and believe it can be addressed through training. Furthermore, they credit profiling, in part, with a significant decrease in America's crime rate and oppose efforts to collect data on stop-and-search tactics.

Critics of profiling acknowledge that law enforcement officials have broad discretion when it comes to stopping and searching citizens. On the highway, evidence of a traffic infraction alone is justification for stopping a motorist. Off the highway, a police officer must have a "reasonable suspicion" that a person is armed and presents a danger, and must be able to articulate why he or she felt that way. This "reasonable suspicion" standard evolved from a landmark 1968 Supreme Court decision, *Terry v. Ohio*, and it is significantly lower than the "probable cause" standard that police must meet to make an arrest or to obtain a search WARRANT. Just how much lower has been the subject of much debate and considerable litigation. The courts have consistently held that simply being of a certain race or fitting a certain type or loitering in a high-crime area does not constitute sufficient grounds for frisking. Making a furtive gesture or having a bulge in your pocket, on the other hand, does.

The extent to which racial stereotyping is used in identifying "suspicious"

individuals is a key point of contention in the debate over profiling. Critics of profiling point to statistics that indicate that African American and other minority drivers are stopped and searched at a disproportionately high rate in comparison with white motorists. In Maryland, for example, a study revealed that 70 percent of those stopped and searched on a stretch of I–95 were African American—despite the fact that they represented only 17 percent of drivers on the road. A demographic expert who examined the data described the odds of this disparity's occurring by chance as "less than one in one quintillion." A similar study conducted in New Jersey in 1994–95 showed that on the southern section of the New Jersey Turnpike cars with black occupants represented only 15 percent of those violating the speed limit, yet they accounted for 46 percent of the drivers pulled over.

Profiling's detractors renounce efforts to defend profiling on the grounds that tendency toward criminality, not race or ethnicity, is being profiled as reflecting a pattern of stereotyping by police. When police look for minorities, these critics say, it is minorities they

guilty. The Supreme Court of Iowa affirmed the conviction. It upheld the constitutionality of the search under a lucid "search incident to citation" exception to the Fourth Amendment's warrant requirement, concluding that so long as the arresting officer had probable cause to make a custodial arrest, there need not in fact have been a custodial arrest. 569 N. W. 2d 601 (Iowa 1997).

Chief Justice WILLIAM H. REHNQUIST, writing for a unanimous Court, ruled that the Iowa law and the Iowa Supreme Court's interpretation of the law violated the Fourth Amendment. Rehnquist began his analysis by revisiting the *Robinson* decision and its "search incident to arrest" exception. He noted that there were two historical reasons for the "search incident to arrest" exception: (1) the need to disarm the suspect in order to take him into custody, and (2) the need to preserve evidence for later use at

trial. In Knowles' case neither of these underlying justifications for the search incident to arrest exception was sufficient to justify the search.

Justice Rehnquist acknowledged that the first reason, officer safety, is a legitimate and serious one. But he found that the threat to officer safety from issuing a traffic citation "is a good deal less than in the case of a custodial arrest." In *Robinson* the Court stated that a custodial arrest involves "danger to an officer" because of "the extended exposure which follows the taking of a suspect into custody and transporting him to the police station." The Court also recognized that the danger to the police officer "flows from the fact of the arrest, and its attendant proximity, stress, and uncertainty, and not from the grounds for arrest. Rehnquist found a significant difference between an arrest and a routine traffic stop. A traffic stop is a rel-

will arrest. While acknowledging the role of aggressive policing in the recent drop in crime, they decry the deleterious effect of profiling on public confidence in law enforcement, particularly in minority communities. How many innocent citizens have to be inconvenienced, these critics ask, in order to keep the streets free of criminals?

The lack of national data on profiling has led critics of the practice to call for national legislation to study the problem. The "Traffic Stops Statistics Study Act of 1999," introduced by Representative John Conyers, Jr. (D-MI), would require the attorney general to conduct a study of stops for routine traffic violations by law enforcement officers. It would require officers to record the following types of information: the number of individuals stopped for routine traffic violations; and identifying characteristics of each individual stopped, including race and/or ethnicity, approximate age, and gender, among other requirements.

Defenders of profiling are quick to deny or deemphasize its racial component. They condemn profiling solely on the basis of race, but defend profiling by looking for signs that a person might be a lawbreaker as good police work. If blacks are being stopped and search at a disproportionately high rate as compared to whites, they charge, it is be-

cause they commit a disproportionately high number of crimes. Defenders of profiling point to statistics that show, for example, that while blacks comprise only about 13 percent of the population, they make up 35 percent of all drug arrests and 55 percent of all drug convictions.

Where there is unreasonable racial stereotyping, these defenders assert, the problem is easily solved by training and discipline. Police academy graduates in New York City, for example, are drilled insistently on what does and does not constitute reasonable grounds for a frisk. Members of the city's elite Street Crimes Unit receive a copy of the department's training manual, "Street Encounters," which expressly stipulates that if an officer's reason for approaching someone "is a personal prejudice or bias, such as the person's race or hair length, the encounter is unlawful."

Furthermore, defenders of profiling argue that it has proven to be an effective tactic in the fight against crime. Profiling, they say, allows law enforcement officials to focus their attention on those thought most likely to commit crimes. If this sometimes results in law-abiding citizens being inconvenienced when police aggressively enforce the laws and investigate crimes, this should not cause those stopped and searched to

believe that their rights were violated. As the nation's violent crime rate continues to plummet, profiling advocates ask, is it an acceptable time to change police practices that have contributed to this drop in crime?

Law enforcement groups have been almost universal in their opposition to the Traffic Stops Statistics Study Act of 1999, claiming it would be costly and could lead to lawsuits against police. The bill, they say, would place an unfair burden on the police and lengthen traffic stops. In addition, collecting information on personal characteristics would likely be considered highly offensive by many individuals. If an officer is uncertain of someone's ethnic background, for example, the officer would often have to ask for this information and an uncomfortable situation could result.

However, in June 1999, the Massachusetts Supreme Judicial Court ruled in a 5–2 decision that police in Massachusetts cannot order people out of their cars unless they pose a threat, which is a stricter standard than the U.S. Supreme Court handed down in its decision that police may order people out of their cars on routine traffic stops. The majority opinion cited concerns of racial discrimination by police in its ruling, taking note of allegations that police stop African Americans disproportionately.

atively brief encounter in which a person is likely to be less hostile to the police and less likely to take immediate steps to destroy incriminating evidence.

A concern for officer safety in the Knowles situation might justify ordering a driver and passengers out of the car, but Rehnquist concluded that it did not by itself justify the a full search. Moreover, officers have other, independent bases to search for weapons and protect themselves from danger. For example, they may order out of a vehicle both the driver and any passenger, "patdown" a driver and any passengers upon reasonable suspicion that they may be armed and dangerous, and conduct an inspection of the passenger compartment of a vehicle upon reasonable suspicion that an occupant is dangerous and may gain immediate control of a weapon.

Iowa also failed to show the second justification for the authority to search incident to arrest: the need to discover and preserve evidence. Justice Rehnquist stated that "once Knowles was stopped for speeding and issued a citation, all the evidence necessary to prosecute that offense had been obtained. No further evidence of excessive speed was going to be found either on the person of the offender or in the passenger compartment of the car." He rejected Iowa's nevertheless contention that a "search incident to citation" is justified because a suspect who is subject to a routine traffic stop may attempt to (1) hide or destroy his driver's license or vehicle registration so as to conceal his identity, or (2) to conceal evidence of an undetected crime. Rehnquist pointed out that if a police officer is not satisfied with the identification furnished by the driver, this may be a basis for arresting him rather than merely issuing a citation. As for destroying evidence of other crimes, he found that "the possibility that an officer would stumble onto evidence wholly unrelated to the speeding offense seems remote."

Chief Justice Rehnquist concluded that there was no compelling reason to extend the "bright-line rule" of *Robinson* to a situation "where the concern for officer safety is not present to the same extent and the concern for destruction or loss of evidence is not present at all."

Minnesota v. Carter

The Supreme Court, in *Minnesota v. Carter*, 525 U.S. 83, 199 S. Ct. 469, 142 L. Ed. 2d 373(1998), balanced law enforcement and privacy interests in assessing the reasonableness of a drug search and seizure. The key issue was whether a police officer who looked in an apartment window through a gap in a closed window blind violated the privacy of the drug dealers in the apartment because they had an expectation of privacy that is protected by the FOURTH AMENDMENT. The Supreme Court held that the police officer did not violate the Fourth Amendment because the occupants of the apartment did not have an expectation of privacy.

The case began when an Eagan, Minnesota, police officer went to an apartment building to investigate a tip from a confidential informant. The informant said that he had walked by the window of a ground-floor apartment and had seen people putting a white powder into bags. The officer looked in the same window through a gap in the closed blind and observed the bagging operation. He then notified headquarters, which began preparing affidavits for a search warrant while he returned to the apartment building. When two men left the building in a previously identified car, the police stopped the vehicle. Inside were Wayne Thomas Carter and Melvin Johns. As the police opened the door of the car to let Johns out, they observed a black zippered pouch and a handgun on the vehicle's floor. Carter and Johns were arrested, and a later police search of the vehicle the next day discovered pagers, a scale, and 47 grams of cocaine in plastic sandwich bags.

The police returned to the apartment, where the woman who rented it told officers that Carter and Johns lived in Chicago and had come to the apartment for the sole purpose of packaging the cocaine. Carter and Johns had never been to the apartment before and were only in the apartment for approximately 2 1/2 hours. In return for the use of the apartment, Carter and Johns had given the woman one-eighth of an ounce of the cocaine.

Carter and Johns were charged in state court with conspiracy to commit controlled substance crime in the first degree and aiding and abetting in a controlled substance crime in the first degree. They moved to suppress all evidence obtained from the apartment and the car, as well as to suppress several post-arrest incriminating statements they had made. They argued that the police officer's initial observation of their drug packaging activities was an unreasonable search in violation of the Fourth Amendment and that all evidence obtained as a result of this unreasonable search should be inadmissible at trial. The Minnesota trial court held that since Carter and Johns were not overnight social guests but temporary out-of-state visitors, they were not entitled to claim the protection of the Fourth Amendment against the government intrusion into the apartment. Carter and Johns were each convicted of both offenses.

The Minnesota Court of Appeals upheld the convictions of Carter and Johns, but the Minnesota Supreme Court reversed, holding that they had "standing" to claim the protection of the Fourth Amendment because they had, quoting *Rakas v. Illinois*, 439 U.S. 128, 99 S. Ct. 421, 58 L. Ed. 2d 387 (1978), "a legitimate expectation of privacy in the invaded place." The court concluded that society recognizes "as valuable the right of property owners or leaseholders to invite persons into the privacy of their homes to conduct a common task, be it legal or illegal activity." Therefore, Carter and Johns had standing to bring their motion to suppress the evidence and the police officers observation constituted an unreasonable search of the apartment under the Fourth Amendment.

The U.S. Supreme Court overruled the Minnesota Supreme Court, holding, on a 6–3 vote, that any search that may have occurred did not violate Carter and John's Fourth Amendment rights. Chief Justice WILLIAM H. REHNQUIST, writing for the majority, concluded that the state supreme court had improperly based its decision on the standing of Carter and Johns to claim Fourth Amendment protection. To claim the protection of the Fourth Amendment, Rehnquist stated that a defendant must demonstrate that he personally has an expectation of privacy in the place searched, and that his expectation is reasonable.

Rehnquist noted that the Fourth Amendment protects persons against unreasonable searches of "their persons [and] houses." This suggested that the amendment's protections extend only to people in "their" houses. However, he acknowledged that the Court had held that in some circumstances a person may have a legitimate expectation of privacy in the house of someone else. In *Minnesota v. Olson*, 495 U.S. 91, 110 S. Ct. 1684, 109 L. Ed. 2d 85 (1990), the Court ruled that an overnight guest in a house had the sort of expectation of privacy that the Fourth Amendment protects.

Chief Justice Rehnquist, building on prior case law that examined the "legitimate expectation of privacy," held that "an overnight guest in a home may claim the protection of the Fourth Amendment, but one who is merely present with the consent of the householder may not." Carter and Johns were not overnight guests, but were present for a business transaction and were only in the home a matter of hours. They did not have a previous relationship with the woman who rented the apartment nor did they have any other purpose for their visit. While the apartment was a dwelling place for the woman, it was for Carter and Johns only a place to do business. Moreover, property used for commercial purposes is treated differently for Fourth Amendment purposes than residential property and persons are regarded as having a lower expectation of privacy.

The Court viewed the facts in this case as being in between the overnight guest who may claim the protection of the Fourth Amendment in the home of another, and those persons who are merely on the premises as typifying those who may not do so. Justice Rehnquist was persuaded that the "purely commercial nature of the transaction engaged in here, the relatively short period of time on the premises, and the lack of any previous connection between respondents and the householder" put Carter and Johns closer to that of someone simply permitted on the premises. Therefore, the Court held that any search that may have occurred did not violate their Fourth Amendment rights.

Justice RUTH BADER GINSBURG, in a dissenting opinion joined by Justices JOHN PAUL STEVENS and DAVID H. SOUTER expressed concern that the majority's decision undermined personal privacy. "The Court's decision undermines not only the security of short-term guests, but also the security of the home resident herself. In my view, when a homeowner or lessor personally invites a guest into her home to share in a common endeavor, whether it be for conversation, to engage in leisure activities, or for business purposes licit or illicit, that guest should share his host's shelter against unreasonable searches and seizure."

Wyoming v. Houghton

The FOURTH AMENDMENT to the U.S. CONSTITUTION protects "A[t]he right of the people to be secure in their persons, houses, papers, and effects, against unreasonable searches and seizures." In determining whether a particular governmental action violates this provision, the U.S. Supreme Court has developed a two part inquiry. The Court first determines whether the framers of the Constitution would consider it an unlawful search and seizure under COMMON LAW (See *Wilson v. Arkansas*, 514 U.S. 927, 115 S. Ct. 1914, 131 L. Ed. 2d 976 [1995]; *California v. Hodari D.*, 499 U.S. 621, 111 S. Ct. 1547, 113 L. Ed. 2d 690 [1991]). If no answer is provided, the Court must then evaluate the search and seizure under traditional standards of reasonableness, which balance the intrusion upon the individual's PRIVACY against the governments need to promote its legitimate interests. (See, e.g. *Vernonia School District 47J v. Acton*, 515 U.S. 646, 115 S. Ct. 2386, 132 L. Ed. 2d 564 [1995]).

In applying this inquiry, the U.S. Supreme Court, in *Wyoming v. Houghton* __ U.S. __, 119 S. Ct. 31, 141 L. Ed. 2d 791 (1999) determined that police can search the personal belongings of all passengers inside a car when lawfully seeking criminal evidence against the driver. The case arose out of a routine traffic stop on Interstate 26 in Natrona County, Wyoming. In the early morning hours of July 23, 1995, the Wyoming Highway Patrol stopped an automobile for speeding and driving with a faulty brake light. While the driver, David Young, was being questioned, the officer noticed a hypodermic syringe in Young's shirt pocket. In response to the officer's question as to why he had a syringe, Young candidly said he used it to take drugs. The other two passengers were ordered out of the car and asked for identification. One passenger indicated she did not have identification and falsely identified herself as Sandra James instead of Sandra Houghton.

Due to Young's statements and the officer's observations, the car was searched. On the backseat was a purse containing Houghton's wallet with her driver's license, a pouch, and a black wallet-type container. The pouch, which she denied was hers, contained drug paraphanelia and a syringe with methamphetemaine. The black container, to which she admitted ownership, also contained paraphenelaia and a syringe, but with a smaller amount of methamphetamnie. The officer also observed fresh needle marks on Houghton's arms. She was placed under arrest and charged with felony possession of methamphetamine.

Houghton filed a motion to SUPPRESS the evidence prior to trial, which the trial court denied and admitted the evidence, indicating that the officer had PROBABLE CAUSE to search the vehicle for contraband and therefore any containers that could hold the contraband, including Houghton's purse. Based upon the evidence, Houghton was convicted by a jury.

The conviction was reversed by the Wyoming Supreme Court, which held that the search was illegal because the officer "knew or should have known" that the purse did not belong to the driver, but to one of the passengers, "and because 'there was no probable cause to search the passengers' personal effects and no reason to believe that contraband had been placed within the purse." It was noted that the officer did not, prior to the search, have probable cause to believe that Houghton was involved in any wrongdoing (*Wyoming v. Houghton*, 956 P.2d 363 [Wyo. 1998]).

Disagreeing with the Wyoming Supreme Court's decision, the state of Wyoming petitioned for a writ of CERTIORARI to the U.S. Supreme Court. The Supreme Court has long held that automobiles deserve considerably less FOURTH AMENDMENT protection than dwellings and other buildings. The question on appeal, however, was whether passengers' belongings in automobiles are also entitled to less protection when a police officer has probable cause to search the vehicle for contraband based on the driver's conduct.

Citing to a long list of prior cases that allow the police to extensively search a driver's car and compartments without a WARRANT, provided there is probable cause that the driver has committed a crime, The U.S. Supreme Court, on April 5, 1999, decided by a 6–3 vote that police officers with probable cause to search a car, may inspect passengers' belongings found in a car that are capable of concealing the object of the search. The Court determined that pursuant to COMMON LAW at the time the Fourth Amendment was framed, the warrantless search of the automobile, as well as the warrantless search of containers within the automoblie, was reasonable (*Carroll v. United States*, 267 U.S. 132, 45 S. Ct. 280, 69 L. Ed. 2d 543

[1925], *United States v. Ross*, 456 U.S. 798, 102 S. Ct. 2157, 72 L. Ed. 2d 572 [1982]). The Court further indicated that passengers as well as drivers have a "reduced expectation of privacy with regard to the property they transport in cars" and further distinguished the search of packages from more intrusive body searches.

Justice ANTONIN SCALIA, writing for the majority and joined by Chief Justice WILLIAM H. REHNQUIST and Justices SANDRA DAY O'CONNOR, ANTHONY M. KENNEDY, CLARENCE THOMAS, and STEPHEN BREYER, stated "Effective law enforcement would be appreciably impaired without the ability to search a passenger's personal belongings when there is reason to believe contraband or evidence of criminal wrongdoing is hidden in the car." Justice Scalia pointed out that a "car passenger will often be engaged in a common enterprise with the driver, and have the same interest concerning the fruits or evidence of their wrongdoing." Justice Scalia further stressed the stakes of law enforcement and noted that a rule protecting passengers' belongings could lead criminals to hide contraband in those items.

Justice Breyer, in a separate concurring opinion, noted that although he agreed with the majority, he felt that if Houghton's purse had been "attached to her person" in the car, it may have amounted to a kind of "outer clothing" requiring greater protection from search.

Justices RUTH BADER GINSBURG, JOHN PAUL STEVENS, and DAVID H. SOUTER dissented. Writing for the dissent, Justice Stevens stated that the Court's newly minted test "would allow serious intrusions on privacy." Justice Stevens noted that prior case law does not justify searching an entire taxi cab if contraband is found in the trunk. However, the rule of *Wyoming v Houghton* "would apparently permit a warrantless search of a passenger's briefcase if there is cause to believe the taxi driver had a syringe somewhere in his vehicle."

Wyoming v. Houghton has not only created a split of opinion in the Supreme Court, but has caused a refueled debate over the rights of individuals versus the rights of the government. Steven R. Shapiro, legal director of the American Civil Liberties Union told the *Washington Post*. "I don't think the court's opinion corresponds to how people live their lives. It shouldn't be true that whenever you get into a car as a passenger, you forfeit all your privacy rights because of suspicion raised by the driver." Donna Domonokos, the attorney who represented Houghton in the appeal agreed, complaining that the decision "presumes guilt by association."

Those in support of a stronger law enforcement presence, however, have expressed agreement with the decision. The National Association of Police Organizations and the state of Wyoming attorney general's office have praised the Court's ruling, since it assists the police in doing their job because it does not require them to separate items in a vehicle by ownership and wrongdoing by passengers.

CROSS REFERENCES
Criminal Procedure; Forfeiture; Fourth Amendment; Search and Seizure

BANKRUPTCY

A federally authorized procedure by which a DEBTOR—an individual, CORPORATION, or municipality—is relieved of total LIABILITY for its DEBTS by making court-approved arrangements for their partial repayment.

Livent, Inc.

In late 1998, the financial collapse of a major theatrical production company rocked the entertainment world. Livent, Inc., known for such major Broadway musicals as "Show Boat" and "Ragtime," became the target of a federal criminal probe and a civil lawsuit after the Canadian-based company was purchased by American investors, who discovered that the company had hidden substantial losses. Subsequently, in early 1999, a federal indictment charged former Livent executives Garth H. Drabinsky and Myron I. Gottlieb with sixteen FELONY counts each, ranging from falsifying accounts and financial statements to paying themselves kickbacks. As federal authorities filed charges against six other former employees of the stage producer, Drabinsky and Gottlieb refused to leave Canada, prompting the Manhattan district attorney to threaten them with EXTRADITION. Meanwhile, as the once-profitable Livent underwent bankruptcy proceedings, the case produced accounts of mismanagement, FRAUD, and abuse.

Livent was the brainchild of Drabinsky, a Canadian impresario known for his flamboyant style. In the 1980s, Drabinsky built the Cineplex Odeon company into an 1,800-screen chain of movie theaters in the United States and Canada. However, he was forced out of the company by one of its investors, MCA, amid accusations of accounting improprieties. Drabinsky then co-founded Livent with his partner, Gottlieb, as a theatrical production company specializing in musicals. By the mid-to-late 1990s, a string of critical and financial successes had pushed the publicly-traded company to the top of its field, with major plays touring the nation as well as running in its own theaters in Toronto, Vancouver and New York. Musical theater was enjoying a resurgence in the United States, and, according to a May 19, 1997, *Time* Magazine article that praised Drabinsky for "his achievements, his guts and his undeniable passion," the impresario was "flying high".

The glamour began to fade in 1998. Although Livent had sales of $224 million for the preceding year, it lost $31 million. Nonetheless, in June, the company attracted high-stakes investors led by former talent agent Michael Ovitz, once widely regarded as the most powerful man in Hollywood, who invested $20 million as part of the takeover. But only two months later, the new management team announced the dramatic discovery that serious accounting irregularities existed in the company's books, and Livent would have to reissue financial statements for past years. Underscoring this announcement, Drabinsky and Gottlieb were demoted and public trading of Livent stock was temporarily halted.

In November Ovitz's management team was forced to reissue financial statements for 1996, 1997, and the first two quarters of 1998. Livent also had no equity left: its debts exceeded the value of its assets, and it was forced to file

Former Livent executive Garth Drabinsky was charged with sixteen felony counts.

KEVIN FRAYER/AP/WIDE WORLD PHOTOS

for Chapter 11 bankruptcy protection and reorganization.

At the same time, the management team formally fired Drabinsky and Gottlieb and filed suit against them alleging fraud. According to the lawsuit, the pair concealed from Ovitz the fact that the company had been hemorrhaging millions of dollars. They also allegedly manipulated its financial books: one set of real financial records was kept in order to track the flow of money, while false set was kept to show a company with financial health. On the orders of Drabinsky and Gottlieb, company accountants allegedly hid extravagant expenditures in order to report $60 million in false profits.

Additionally, the lawsuit accused the pair of paying themselves kickbacks and attempting to cover up their improprieties. It said they asked an engineering company to inflate its bills, then had that company pass the money back to them, and ultimately funneled up to $7.5 million into another company owned by Gottlieb, King Commodity Services Ltd. To hide their misdeeds, said the lawsuit, the men tried to enlist the company's senior financial executive, Gordon Eckstein, with offers of higher pay.

By the end of 1998, Drabinsky and Gottlieb's legal position grew worse. Denying the allegations in the lawsuit, they accused Ovitz of blaming them for his own managerial failures and filed a countersuit against him. Simultaneously, however, the civil case had attracted government investigators. Throughout the fall,

U.S. and Canadian officials separately probed the company's records. Although the Canadian inquiry remained ongoing, both the U.S. JUSTICE DEPARTMENT and the Securities and Exchange Commission (SEC) announced results of a their probes in the new year. On January 13, 1999, the New York U.S. attorney's office indicted Drabinsky and Gottlieb on sixteen felony counts each, while the SEC filed civil charges against the pair and six other former Livent employees.

The federal agencies repeated many of the charges found in Ovitz's civil lawsuit. In the criminal indictments, the U.S. attorney's office described the same scenario of losses hidden, financial records falsified, and sleight of hand used to conceal expenses, while also accusing Drabinsky and Gottlieb of misleading outside auditors. Federal officials announced that two Livent executives had already plead guilty to one felony count each of violating securities laws.

For its part, the SEC's civil lawsuits accused Drabinsky, Gottlieb, and former Livent accountants of perpetuating "a multifaceted and pervasive eight-year fraudulent accounting scheme." Simultaneously, it was announced that the existing management of Livent had reached a settlement with the commission in which it agreed to end any securities law violations that had been set in motion by its predecessors. The SEC also reached settlements with some former Livent employees, including Eckstein, former senior corporate controller Diane Winkfein, and former senior production controller D. Grant Malcolm, but its suit was going ahead against others.

While the various cases wound through the justice system in 1999, the Livent saga continued to produce drama. In March, Livent's executive vice president Robert Webster chronicled a long saga of financial deceit that he pinned on Drabinsky, whom he accused of personally bullying accountants into committing violations. In March, an AFFIDAVIT from In May, Drabinsky and Gottlieb's refusal to leave Canada to face charges brought threats from the New York attorney's office to arrest and extradite them to the United States. Livent's curtain call, meanwhile, took place on the auction block when in early June it announced a $115-million deal to sell most of its assets to New York-based SFX Entertainment, pending approval by a federal bankruptcy court.

CROSS REFERENCES
Fraud; Securities and Exchange Commission

BENNETT, ROBERT S.

Robert S. Bennett was hired in 1994 to defend President BILL CLINTON in the SEXUAL HARASSMENT lawsuit brought by former Arkansas state employee Paula Jones. In the suit Jones alleged that Clinton made unwanted sexual advances to her while he was governor of Arkansas. Bennett specializes in white-collar criminal defense as a successful partner in a large Washington, D.C., firm.

Robert S. Bennett was born in Brooklyn in 1939. He went to Washington, D.C., in 1957 to attend Georgetown University planning to study pre-med, but soon became engrossed in criminal trials. Bennett graduated from Georgetown University Law Center in 1964 and then obtained an advanced legal degree from Harvard the following year. After clerking for a federal district judge in Washington, D.C., for two years, he prosecuted cases in Washington, D.C., for the Office of the U.S. Attorney from 1967 until 1970. In 1970, he entered private practice in Washington, focusing on white-collar criminal defense work. Throughout his private career, he has worked at three law firms, one as a founding member. In 1990, Bennett joined Skadden, Arps, Slate, Meagher and Flom in Washington. His brother is William Bennett, former U.S. education secretary, drug czar, editor of *The Book of Virtues*, and outspoken critic of the Clinton administration. Although Bill Bennett's political views are widely known, his brother has been extremely adept at maintaining an apolitical appearance.

Through the years, Bennett has periodically served as special counsel to the Senate Select Committee on Ethics. He gained national prominence for this representation during and after the 1989 Lincoln Savings and Loan affair involving the so-called Keating Five. The five were senators who had allegedly improperly intervened on behalf of Lincoln owner Charles Keating with federal regulators. He has had a string of well-known clients including former defense secretary Caspar Weinberger, Cincinnati Reds owner Marge Schott, former U.S. Representative Dan Rostenkowski, former Clinton deputy chief of staff Harold Ickes, and Clark Clifford, the late chairman of the First American Bank in Washington. His rumpled appearance belies a remarkable ability to settle cases, negotiate plea bargains, and head off indictments. One of Paula Jones's former attorneys, Joseph Cammarata, characterized Bennett as "a zealous advocate and a formidable opponent."

Bennett was instrumental in delaying the Jones case until after the 1996 presidential election. He initially argued that the president was immune from the lawsuit, or alternatively that the case had to be delayed until after the president left office. The U.S. Supreme Court disagreed in a May 1997 decision and ordered the case to proceed. Bennett scored a victory on April 1, 1998, when Federal District Judge SUSAN WEBBER WRIGHT dismissed the sexual harassment lawsuit, ruling that Jones had failed to make out a case for LIABILITY against President Clinton.

Settlement negotiations came and went during the course of the lawsuit, breaking down at one point over Jones's demand that any settlement include an apology. The settlement deal as ultimately agreed to did not include an apology or admission of wrongdoing by the president. Although Bennett once called the Jones case "tabloid trash with a legal caption," the case was settled on November 13, 1998 for $850,000, while the case was on appeal to the court of appeals. Bennett has been criticized in some circles for not settling the case earlier, although his authority to settle earlier remains unclear. Clinton's deposition in the Jones case in January 1998 and allegations of his relationship with former White House intern Monica Lewinsky led to Clinton's investigation by KENNETH STARR and subsequent impeachment on the grounds of perjury and obstruction of justice.

In April 1999, Judge Wright held that the president was in CONTEMPT for TESTIMONY

Robert S. Bennett
DENIS PAQUIN/AP/WIDE WORLD PHOTOS

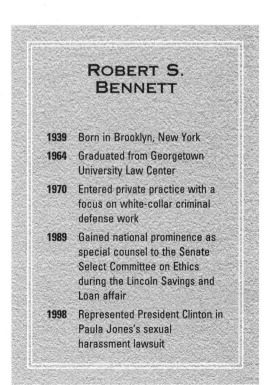

ROBERT S. BENNETT

1939   Born in Brooklyn, New York

1964   Graduated from Georgetown University Law Center

1970   Entered private practice with a focus on white-collar criminal defense work

1989   Gained national prominence as special counsel to the Senate Select Committee on Ethics during the Lincoln Savings and Loan affair

1998   Represented President Clinton in Paula Jones's sexual harassment lawsuit

given in the Jones case in January 1998 regarding questions about his relationship with former White House intern Monica Lewinsky. The judge ruled that the president gave "false, misleading, and evasive answers" about that relationship. Wright also ordered to Clinton pay Jones's attorneys for their work related to his answers to questions about Lewinsky. Judge Wright gave the president thirty days to appeal her contempt order or to ask for a hearing, but warned that if he appealed, she would permit a wide-ranging inquiry into his conduct.

Although Clinton did not appeal the judge's order or ask for a hearing, his lawyers continue to wrangle over parts of the order. The lawyers for Paula Jones sought nearly $500,000 for legal expenses. When Bennett rejected this figure as "grossly excessive," Jones's attorneys sought to see Clinton's billing records to determine how much his lawyers had charged for the same work. Bennett characterized the request as "frivolous" and "an unjustified fishing expedition." The president argued that his liability for legal fees should not exceed $33,734.

CROSS REFERENCES
Impeachment

BLACKMUN, HARRY

Obituary notice
Born on November 12, 1908, in Nashville, Illinois; died March 4, 1999 in Washington, D.C. Blackmun was appointed to the U.S. Supreme Court by President Nixon, and became a highly regarded justice, usually taking a middle-of-the-road position. Blackmun's most famous and controversial ruling was his opinion in *Roe v. Wade* (1973), declaring that the right of privacy included a woman's right to terminate her pregnancy by means of an abortion.

Harry Blackmun
ARCHIVE PHOTOS, INC.

BRIBERY

The offering, giving, receiving, or soliciting of something of value for the purpose of influencing the action of an official in the discharge of his or her public or legal duties.

Mike Espy Found Not Guilty
The Supreme Court set important standards for government bribery cases. In *United States v. Sun Diamond Growers* __ U.S. __, 119 S. Ct. 1402, 143 L. Ed. 2d 576 (1999). The Court held that prosecutors face a high burden proving that gifts to government officials are bribes. Prosecutors must show a "specific connection" between gifts to officials and the specific "official act" for which the gift was made. The case grew out of the long ordeal of former Secretary of Agriculture Mike Espy, who was investigated by an independent counsel appointed by the Department of Justice. Though Espy resigned amid scandal that year, he was acquitted of all charges in December 1998. In finding that Sun Diamond Growers had not violated federal law governing the giving of gifts to public officials, the Court handed another defeat to the independent counsel's office which had spent more than four years and $17.5 million prosecuting Espy, Sun Diamond, and others.

In 1993, Espy, a former Mississippi congressman, became the first African American to hold the post of agriculture secretary. One year later, however, his tenure ended abruptly. As charges mounted that he had illegally accepted gifts from the people and companies that his office regulated, Attorney General JANET RENO appointed an INDEPENDENT COUNSEL to investigate the allegations, and Espy promptly resigned. Independent Counsel Donald Smaltz opened his probe in September 1994. From the start, critics accused Smaltz of overzealousness, lavish spending, and lax prosecutorial standards. But in late August 1997, with his probe having grown to include Espy, Espy's brother, and several important agribusinesses, Smaltz obtained what he had been seeking when a federal GRAND JURY indicted Espy on a thirty-nine counts of illegally accepting gifts and favors while in office. Though the indictment was later trimmed to thirty counts, none of the charges stuck. In December 1998, Espy was acquitted on all counts.

The Sun Diamond case was a by-product of Smaltz's wide-ranging investigation, which ultimately netted fifteen convictions and guilty pleas as well as more than $6 million in fines. Smaltz accused Sun Diamond of violating the federal GRATUITIES statute, 18 U.S.C. § 201(c)(1)(A), which is part of a number of federal laws and regulations that are intended to prevent bribery. Under the statute, gratuities are "anything of value"—gifts, favors, and so on. It prohibits giving gratuities to present, past, or future public officials "for or because of any official act performed or to be performed by such public official." Sun Diamond, a trade association for a five-thousand-member agricultural cooperative, was accused of giving Espy nearly $6,000 worth of gifts that included luggage and tickets to the 1993 U.S. Open Tennis Tournament while matters concerning the cooperative were pending Espy's review. The cooperative also faced charges for donating $4,000 to Espy's brother's failed congressional campaign.

Although Sun Diamond lost at trial before a jury and was fined $1.5 million, it won on appeal. At issue in the appeal was how the federal gratuities statute should be interpreted: does the 1960s-era statute ban all gifts given to an official because of his position, as the district court believed and instructed the jury? Or does the law require a connection to an "official act" by the public official for a gift to be considered illegal? The court of appeals said the latter scenario was necessary, and reversed the conviction. The independent counsel appealed, arguing that the law should be read more broadly, and the Supreme Court granted review in order to settle the matter of how much prosecutors must prove to obtain a conviction.

The justices' skepticism was apparent during oral arguments in March 1999. As an attorney from the independent counsel's office argued for the government's broad interpretation, the Court hurled questions that appeared to be almost hostile and, in some respects, echoed the long-standing criticisms of Smaltz's office. Justice STEPHEN BREYER asked why "such an extensive reading" of the law was necessary if it led to "prosecut[ing] trivial things" that would be better handled in the non-criminal forum of an ethics investigation. Justice ANTHONY M. KENNEDY asked whether the counsel's office was aware of the "huge gap" between the general understanding of the law and the independent counsel's interpretation. For its part during oral arguments, Sun Diamond insisted that the law required that prosecutors show specific proof of a tie between gifts and actions by a public official.

On April 27, the Court unanimously ruled in Sun Diamond's favor. Writing for the Court, Justice ANTONIN SCALIA stated that the law requires the government to show a link between a gift and a specific "official act," either in the past or in the future, for which the gift was given. The independent counsel's broad reading would produce "peculiar" results, Justice Scalia wrote, by criminalizing token gifts to officials such as the gift of a sports jersey that championship teams give to the president. He acknowledged the possibility that the Court's narrow reading might lead to peculiar results as well. But he emphasized that this could be avoided by properly understanding the law's definition of an "official act" —an "action on [a] matter…before any public official, in [his] official capacity, or in [his]

place of trust or profit." That definition would not include the examples of sports teams, he wrote, unlike the independent counsel's flawed reading.

Justice Scalia cited support for the holding in Congress' own language. In other federal statutes, lawmakers have drafted very broad criminal prohibitions on gift giving, he noted; but in this case, they had not done so. Moreover, the statute in question was "merely one strand of an intricate web" of laws and regulations in this area, and as such, the Court was wary of reading too much into it: "a statute that can linguistically be interpreted to be either a meat axe or a scalpel should reasonably be taken to be the latter," he concluded.

The decision did not surprise legal observers, many of whom had long criticized the independent counsel's interpretation of the law. Nor did it necessarily make gratuity convictions harder to obtain as the original Sun Diamond conviction had seemed like an anomaly in light of the fact that federal lawmakers routinely accept the sort of gifts for which Espy was prosecuted. While the Supreme Court returned the case to district court for a possible new trial, further prosecution of Sun Diamond seemed unlikely, and, along with Espy's acquittal some four months earlier, the case appeared to mark the last chapter of the independent counsel's probe.

CROSS REFERENCES
Independent Counsel

George Walker Bush
REUTERS/CORBIS-BETTMANN

BUSH, GEORGE WALKER

For years, George W. Bush's public identity was inextricably tied to his famous father, the former president, George Herbert Walker Bush. But in 1994, the son of the former Republican president established an identity of his own when he defeated incumbent Ann Richards in a hotly contested political race to become the forty-sixth governor of Texas. Convincing Texas voters that he was a strong politician in his own right, Bush claimed a victory that he could call his own.

Born in Connecticut on July 6, 1946, and raised in Texas, George Walker Bush's lineage is well-documented. His grandfather, Prescott Bush, a Connecticut resident who worked on Wall Street, was elected to the Senate. His father, George Herbert Walker Bush, earned his fortune as an oilman in Texas, entered politics, became director of the Central Intelligence Agency, and eventually achieved the country's highest office as president. George W. Bush., the oldest of five Bush children, retraced his father's early career. Like his father, he attended Phillips Academy in Andover, Massachusetts, and Yale University.

After graduating from Yale, the young Bush continued to be his father's shadow. He learned how to fly a combat aircraft and then became an oilman. He completed a 53-week program with the Texas Air National Guard, learning to fly F-102s and earning the rank of lieutenant, he returned home looking for a new challenge when he was not called to fight in Vietnam. He spent time in Houston holding various short-term jobs, including a stint at a program called Pull for Youth for underprivileged kids. Pos-

GEORGE W. BUSH

1946	Born in New Haven, Connecticut
1968	Graduated from Yale University
1975	Received an MBA from Harvard University
1994	Elected governor of Texas
1998	Elected to a second term as governor of Texas
1999	Entered 2000 presidential race

sessing his father's drive and fierce determination to make something of himself, Bush attended Harvard Business School, returned to Texas with an M.B.A., became an oilman, and ventured into politics. At age thirty-two, he ran for Congress in west Texas, but was defeated by six points. He was successful in the oil business, however, and within ten years of working in the industry earned his first million dollars.

Bush's biggest oil venture, however, proved controversial. During the late 1970s, he built a small, thriving company called Bush Exploration. When the energy market turned soft in the early 1980s, Bush Exploration, like many oil enterprises, foundered. In 1983, Bush merged his outfit with Spectrum 7; three years later Spectrum 7 was bought by Harken Energy. Bush's supporters said the sale was the work of a shrewd dealmaker, while others—including journalists from conservative and liberal publications—suspected that the deal came about because of Bush's father's political contacts. "Many oil companies went belly-up during that time," reported Stephen Pizzo of Mother Jones. "But Spectrum 7 had one asset the others lacked— the son of the vice-president. Rescue came in 1986 in the form of Harken Energy. Harken absorbed Spectrum, and, in the process, Bush got $600,000 worth of Harken stock in return for his Spectrum shares. He also won a lucrative consulting contract and stock options. In all, the deal would put well more than $1 million in his pocket over the next few years—even though Harken itself lost millions." Bush came under fire again in 1990. *Time* reported, "About a month before Iraq invaded Kuwait, young Bush sold 66 percent of his Harken stake (or 212,140 shares) at the top of the market for nearly $850,000, which represented a 200 percent profit on his original stake." President Bush balked at the allegations of impropriety. "The media ought to be ashamed of itself for what they're doing," he said. Meanwhile, the younger Bush dismissed the criticism "claiming something close to penury," according to *Newsweek*.

While speculation swirled in the media about his oil dealings, Bush left business for politics. He helped manage his father's 1988 presidential campaign, moving with his wife and twin daughters to Washington, where he worked closely with Lee Atwater. By all accounts, Bush did not enjoy the experience. "He remembers finding Washington a 'hostile environment,'" reported *Time*. "The campaign operation was often a mud wrestle among contending egos." Confessed the young Bush, "I was the loyalty thermometer." But he gained respect for handling volatile diplomatic matters, such as the firing of chief of staff John Sununu, and for swiftly taking care of business.

After the election, Bush wasted no time getting back to Texas, where he promptly found a new venture—baseball. The sport offered Bush the first honest chance at independence. In a matter of months, he successfully organized a coalition of wealthy investors to purchase American League's Texas Rangers, and he assumed a role as managing partner. Not only did Bush rally support to bring major league baseball to Dallas, but he helped to promote the team and boost attendance. Riding the wave of popularity that arose from his success with the Rangers, Bush decided it was an ideal time to try his hand at local politics.

For most of his life, Bush had been discouraged from entering politics as a full-time career by his parents, who believed that their son should first secure his financial future. Even after Bush earned a small fortune in the oil industry, and with the promise of more to come from his baseball investments, his mother remained wary of his chances in the 1994 gubernatorial race. Like other political observers, Barbara Bush believed that Texans were not ready to retire their quick-witted Democratic Governor Ann Richards. Nevertheless, Bush jumped into the race, while his younger brother, Jeb, did the same in Florida. The brothers were, of course, highly skilled campaigners, having served as aides to their father since the age of eighteen.

Bush's strategy was to run an intensely focused and positive, issue-oriented campaign.

When Richards attacked his credibility with barbs like "If he didn't have his daddy's name, he wouldn't amount to anything," Bush countered with pleasantries. "I don't have to erode her likability," he told the *New York Times.* "I have to erode her electability." And when Richards called him "some jerk," Bush replied, "The last time I was called a jerk was at Sam Houston Elementary School in Midland, Texas. I'm not going to call the Governor names. I'm going to elevate this debate to a level where Texans want it." That debate focused on welfare reform, a crackdown on crime (especially concerning juveniles), increased autonomy and state financing for local school districts, and personal responsibility. As he campaigned, it was clear to observers that he was not the spitting political image of his father. As he told local audiences, "Let Texans run Texas." It was a message that appealed to the proud Texans. And despite the popularity Ann Richards had enjoyed during her reign as governor, Bush, to the surprise of many, won with 53.5 percent of the vote. Twenty thousand people attended Bush's inauguration in Austin, including the famous preacher Billy Graham, legendary baseball pitcher Nolan Ryan, movie star Chuck Norris, and, of course, George and Barbara Bush.

After only a year in office, Bush was hailed as the most popular big-state governor in the country. In 1998 he won reelection in a landslide. His vote-getting among minorities impressed national Republicans. Bush entered the 2000 presidential election race in 1999 and quickly amassed $40 million in funds, making him the frontrunner.

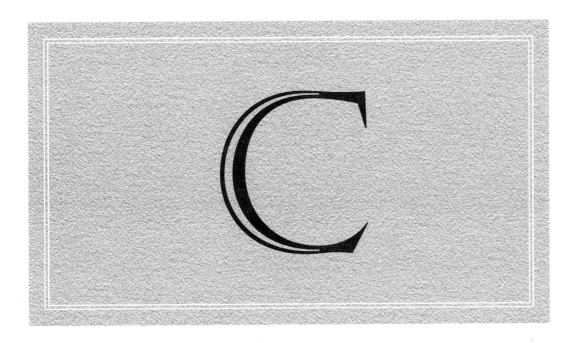

CAPITAL PUNISHMENT

The lawful infliction of death as a punishment; the death penalty.

Calderon v. Coleman

HABEAS CORPUS is the last opportunity for the federal courts to review state court convictions and sentences to determine whether serious violations of the U.S. Constitution have occurred. If so, the federal court must reverse the state court and direct that the prisoner be retried or resentenced. Habeas corpus is used frequently in capital punishment cases.

The Supreme Court, in *Calderon v. Coleman*, 525 U.S.141, 119 S. Ct. 500, __ L. Ed. 2d __(1998), ruled that the lower federal courts had erred in granting habeas corpus to a death row inmate, despite the fact that the JURY at his trial had been improperly instructed about the possibility of him receiving clemency from the governor if the jury sentenced him to death. The Supreme Court ruled that even if a mistake has been made, a court must apply the harmless error rule to see if the mistake had done any serious harm. If no serious harm has occurred, the writ of habeas corpus must be denied.

In 1981 a California jury convicted Russell Coleman of RAPE, SODOMY, and MURDER. At the penalty phase of Coleman's trial, the trial judge gave the jury a so-called Briggs instruction, which was then required by California law. This instruction informed the jury of the governor's power to commute a sentence of life without possibility of parole to some lesser sentence that might include the possibility of parole. After giving the standard Briggs instruction, the state trial court instructed the jury that

it was not to consider the governor's commutation power in reaching its verdict.

Following his conviction, Coleman appealed his conviction to the California Supreme Court. He argued that giving the Briggs instruction in his case was a reversible error under the California Supreme Court's decision in *California v. Ramos*, 37 Cal. 3d 136, 689 P. 2d 430 (1984). There the California Supreme Court held that the Briggs instruction violated the California Constitution because it was misleading, invited the jury to consider irrelevant and speculative matters, and diverted the jury from its proper function.

The California Supreme Court rejected Coleman's argument and upheld his death sentence. While the court found that the giving of the Briggs instruction was error under California law, it held that the error was not prejudicial because the additional instruction told the jury it should not consider the possibility of commutation in determining Coleman's sentence. *People v. Coleman*, 46 Cal. 3d 749, 759 P. 2d 1260 (1988).

Coleman then sought a federal writ of habeas corpus. The district court granted the writ for Coleman's death sentence. It found the Briggs instruction was inaccurate as applied to Coleman because it did not mention a limitation on the governor's power to commute Coleman's sentence. Under the California Constitution, the governor may not commute the sentence of a prisoner who, like Coleman, is a twice-convicted felon without the approval of four judges of the California Supreme Court. (Cal. Const., Art. 5, § 8.) The district court found that, because the

ARE COMMUTED DEATH SENTENCES EXACERBATING PRISON OVERPOPULATION?

A 1998 report released by the U.S. JUSTICE DEPARTMENT revealed a steady increase in the nation's prison population (state and federal), growing by 5.2 percent in 1997 alone. That percentage equated to approximately 97,900 more individuals in jails and prisons for 1997 than in the previous year, or roughly 445 inmates per 100,000 Americans.

The report was updated in early 1999, indicating that by June 1998, the inmate population had grown to 668 per 100,000 residents, increasing the overall prison population to 1.8 million. This was the highest level ever, according to the same report, (although the increase from June 1997 to June 1998 was 4.4 percent, compared to the 1997 annual rate of 5.2 percent). According to Darrell Gilliard, author of the Justice Department report, prison populations had grown an average 6.2 percent between late 1990 and mid-1998. Overall, the imprisonment rate has doubled since latter 1985. For purposes of comparison, the prison population is growing at a rate 13 times faster than that of the general population. By June 1998, the

nation's prisons were filled to 97 percent capacity, even after adding more than 26,000 beds the previous year. Twenty-five years ago, Americans spent $4 billion on construction of new prisons; in 1996, it was $31 billion.

In addition, as of 1998 there were more than 3,500 inmates on death row, most of them exhausting a series of appeals that typically could last for more than ten years. Each inmate costs taxpayers between $25,000 and $30,000 per year for sustenance, not including the cost of the appeals, which can run into the millions of dollars. When appeals fail, there are gubernatorial clemencies which may result in commuted sentences, either through direct appeal or political pressure. The commuted sentence is most often life imprisonment, with or without PAROLE.

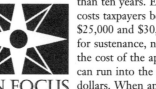

IN FOCUS

Even though a thirty-eight states have the death penalty, very few prisoners are actually executed. In the last twenty-five years, there have been 500 executions nationwide, which, when averaged out, means approximately one execution every two years for each of the thirty-eight states, federal and mili-

tary systems. In practice, states vary in their executions. New York has not executed anyone in thirty years, whereas Texas executed 16 in 1998. Both states have had the death penalty for a number of years.

Critics of the death penalty are quick to point out that a mere 3,500 inmates on death row hardly make a dent in a prison population which grows by nearly 100,000 annually. Moreover, a 1998 study revealed that one in every eight death row inmates has been wrongfully convicted, a statistic so shocking that even proponents are taken aback. Added to this are accusations of unfairness, arbitrariness, and alleged racial bias in the use of capital punishment, including those articulated in a 1998 report from the United Nations' Commission on Human Rights. The American Bar Association joined the U.N. in calling for a worldwide moratorium on executions. (At least four states have raised legal challenges to death penalty laws, arguing arbitrary application and geographic imbalance. None were successful.)

Finally, academics argue that any potential deterrence that the threat of execution is intended to have on would-

Briggs instruction did not mention this limitation on the governor's commutation power, it violated the EIGHTH AND FOURTEENTH AMENDMENTS. The instruction gave the jury inaccurate information and potentially diverted its attention from evidence that might have dissuaded them from sentencing Coleman to death.

The Court of Appeals for the Ninth Circuit affirmed the district court's grant of the writ as to Coleman's sentence. 150 F. 3d 1105 (1998). The appeals court agreed with the district court's finding that the instruction, as applied to Coleman, gave the jury inaccurate information about the governor's commutation power. The court also declared, "[a] commutation instruction is unconstitutional when it is inaccurate." The instruction at issue was fatally flawed, the

court held, because it "dramatically overstate[d] the possibility of commuting the life sentence of a person such as Coleman" and thus prevented the jurors from understanding the choice they were asked to make. The instruction also invited the jurors to speculate that Coleman could be effectively isolated from the community only through a sentence of death.

The state of California had argued that even if the instruction was unconstitutional, it did not have a substantial and injurious effect or influence on the jury's sentence of death, as required by the U.S. Supreme Court's decision in *Brecht v. Abrahamson*, 507 U.S. 619, 113 S. Ct. 1710, 123 L. Ed. 2d 353 (1993). The appellate court rejected this approach, preferring to apply another Supreme Court case, *Boyde v. California*,

be criminals is, in fact, nebulous at best: the imminence of execution is lost in the time span between the conviction and the last midnight-hour petition, — usually several years. Many capital defendants do not actually believe they will ever be executed.

Still, the fear of death-row inmates being paroled, or released on a technicality, is a disturbing thought to many citizens. Recidivism (repeat or recurrent crimes by the same criminal) remains consistently high. A 1996 report showed that as many as 80 percent of those released from jail return within one year. One in three *violent* crimes is committed by someone on parole, probation or pretrial release. The actual time served for violent crimes in state prisons averages to less than four years.

Many states have gubernatorial CLEMENCY laws which permit governors to commute even life sentences without possibility of parole to some lesser sentence, including parole. The U.S. Supreme Court has upheld a jury instruction which informs jurors of a governor's powers to commute life sentences in capital cases. See *California v. Ramos*, 463 U.S. 992, 103 S. Ct. 3446, 77 L. Ed. 2d 1171 (1983). The Court has agreed to review two cases for the 1999–2000 term which will greatly impact the appellate process for death row inmates. One (*Jones v. United States*) involves the issue of when state defendants may challenge their convictions in federal courts, challenging a 1996 law passed by Congress which limited second or successive habeas corpus petitions to federal judges. Another (*Slack v. McDaniel*) will clarify whether jurors should be told that if they fail to agree on whether a defendant should receive a death penalty or life imprisonment, the judge will automatically sentence the defendant to life in prison without parole.

While prison populations have risen, crime rates have appreciably declined, continuing a trend started in the early 1990s. (The crime rate had peaked in 1991 to 758 per 100,000 population.) The consensus of opinion among experts is that no singular event, policy, or attitude accounts for this decline, but clearly, keeping prisoners locked up greatly contributes to the decrease. The American public is willing to pay for prisons in order to curtail violence. State laws have imposed tougher sentences on repeat offenders, many adopting "three strikes, you're out" laws which severely limit or remove the possibility of parole. Other states have toughened appeals processes, especially for capital defendants, which will nonetheless withstand due process challenges that the death penalty is administered or used unfairly.

The schism remains deep. Lawmakers want to speed up executions, tired of newspaper headlines filled with stories of seemingly frivolous and costly last-minute appeals by capital defendants. They also argue that the true deterrent effect of the death penalty is difficult to gauge because of the lengthy appeals at multiple levels, and that the true effect of capital punishment will not be appreciated until criminals have some palpable sense of the reality of execution. Others argue to tighten laws so that only the truly guilty will actually be executed—a task easily articulated but not simply accomplished. Still others want total abolition of capital punishment, calling it barbaric or outdated. They argue that there should be increasing use of life imprisonment without parole. But they concede that rehabilitative efforts to "correct" deviant or criminal behavior have failed miserably since the 1970s; psychologists and psychiatrists have been slow to admit that they do not know how to cure a criminal from "doing it again." Therefore, some say, keeping the worst criminals alive at Alcatraz indefinitely negates the message of justice and fairness, when compared to the harm suffered by victims and families of victims.

The Supreme Court has repeatedly upheld the constitutionality of the state to deprive one of life. However, the Court strives, through its decisions, to ensure that the death penalty is administered fairly and justly. Meanwhile, prison walls continue to bulge at the seams with criminals not fit to be released back into society.

494 U.S. 370, 110 S. Ct.1190, 108 L. Ed. 2d 316 (1990). This decision states that when the inaccuracy undermines the jury's understanding of sentencing options, there is a reasonable likelihood that the jury has applied the challenged instruction in a way that prevents the consideration of constitutionally relevant evidence. Therefore, the Ninth Circuit ruled that Coleman's death sentence must be vacated.

On appeal, the Supreme Court rejected the approach taken by both the district and appellate courts. On a 5–4 vote, the Court reversed the lower courts and denied Coleman a writ of habeas corpus. The Court assumed for the sake of argument that the jury instruction was unconstitutional. It then turned to the key question: must a court apply *Brecht* or *Boyde?*

The Supreme Court held in *Brecht* that a federal court may grant habeas relief based on trial error only when that error "had substantial and injurious effect or influence in determining the jury's verdict." This standard reflects the "presumption of finality and legality" that attaches to a conviction at the conclusion of direct review. It protects the state's interest in punishing offenders and its "good-faith attempts to honor constitutional rights," while ensuring that the extraordinary remedy of habeas corpus is available to those "whom society has grievously wronged."

The Supreme Court stated that a federal court should not set aside a state court conviction or sentence "without first determining that the error had a substantial and injurious effect on the jury's verdict." It noted the significant social costs of retrial or resentencing, which are "acute in cases such as this one, where the original sentencing hearing took place in November 1981, some 17 years ago." Therefore, once the court of appeals determined that the giving of the Briggs instruction was a constitutional error, it was bound to apply the harmless-error analysis mandated by *Brecht*.

The Supreme Court dismissed the application of *Boyde*, as it is not a harmless error case. Its test is only for determining, in the first instance, whether constitutional error occurred when the jury was given an ambiguous instruction. It does not examine the actual effect of the error on the jury's verdict; it merely asks whether constitutional error has occurred.

Therefore, the majority concluded that the writ must be vacated and the matter remanded for further proceedings. The lower court must find that the error, in the whole context of the particular case, had a substantial and injurious effect or influence on the jury's verdict.

Justice JOHN PAUL STEVENS, in a dissenting opinion joined by Justices DAVID H. SOUTER, RUTH BADER GINSBURG, and STEPHEN BREYER, admitted that the Ninth Circuit's decision could have offered a more detailed analysis. Nevertheless, the result was correct, especially when viewed in the context of the district court's 117-page opinion. Justice Stevens also suggested that the Ninth Circuit's

opinion contained evidence that it had performed the necessary harmless error analysis. Specifically, the court of appeals cited to the portion of its earlier decision in *McDowell v. Calderon*, 130 F.3d 833 (9th Cir. 1997), finding a similar claim was not harmless under *Brecht*. Finally, in support of his conclusion that the lower courts reached the correct result, Justice Stevens referred to the affidavit of a sentencing juror. The juror stated that the question of parole was central to the jury's decision to sentence Coleman to death.

Death Row's Wrongly Convicted

In opinion polls conducted across the country, most Americans support the death penalty, particularly for heinous crimes. By May 1999, thirty-eight states, as well as the federal government and the military, had laws providing for death sentences.

Of course this support presumes that those convicted on death row are guilty. Unfortunately, that is not always the case. In November 1998, more than thirty persons, once death-row inmates but later acquitted because of wrongful convictions, gathered as guest speakers for the first National Conference on Wrongful Convictions and the Death Penalty, held at Northwestern University Law School in Chicago. The well-publicized event was attended by more than one thousand anti-death penalty advocates including several lawyers, academics and family members of the acquitted.

After having his murder conviction overturned, Anthony Porter was released from death row two days before his execution.

STEPHEN J. CARRERA/AP/WIDE WORLD PHOTOS

The conference organizers identified seventy-three persons whose death sentences had been overturned since 1976, the year in which the U.S. Supreme Court ruled that a state may constitutionally deprive a person of life. There had been a brief abolishment of the death penalty from 1972–76, following a fact-specific ruling by the Court in *Furman v. Georgia*, 408 U.S. 238, 92 S. Ct. 2726, 33 L. Ed. 2d 346 (1972). Between 1976 and May 1999, more than 500 persons have been put to death nationwide, and there are more than 3,500 on death row.

Capital punishment advocates stress that there has not been a single uncontroverted case of an *innocent* person being executed since 1976. And they point out that many convictions have been overturned because of technical error, not because of the innocence of the accused. "Only the guilty are being executed," Robert Pambianco of the Washington Legal Foundation has said. "This is an attempt on the part of people with agendas to weaken public support for the death penalty." Moreover, the APPELLATE, which is multi-tiered and can take several years to exhaust, seemingly provides more than adequate recourse for those who believe they have been wrongly accused and/or convicted. When all else fails, state governors may still grant clemency in questionable cases.

Still, it remains unthinkable to many Americans to mistakenly execute a person for a conviction which later appears to have been based on perjured testimony, mistaken identity, or some other error. The issue becomes more palpable when a name or face is attached to the person. One such person who came very close to losing his life, but was saved by a last-minute discovery of an error in his conviction is Anthony Porter.

In March 1999, Cook County Circuit Court Judge Thomas R. Fitzgerald overturned two 1983 MURDER convictions which had kept forty-three-year old Porter on death row for sixteen years. He was two days from execution. Porter was convicted in 1982 even though there had been no physical evidence linking him to the murder of a Chicago couple during an armed robbery. In addition, testimony from a prosecution witness had been equivocal at best, and other evidence had cast doubts on Porter's motives. In 1999, the state's witness recanted the incriminating statements against Porter, and another person implicated her estranged husband. The husband, a Milwaukee laborer named Alstory Simon, later admitted to killing the couple in a statement videotaped by a private investigator. Following assessment of the tape and other evidence, Porter was released from prison. Simon was charged with the murders.

What made Porter's case so remarkable was that neither prosecutors nor his defense counsel discovered the error. In fact, Porter owes his freedom to a group of journalism students and their professor, David Protess, at Northwestern University. Each semester, Protess assigns murder cases to his students for reinvestigation. In this case, the students were able to locate witnesses and develop leads which eventually led to Simon's wife. She implicated him when told that the mother of one of the victims last saw her daughter with the Simons shortly before the murders.

Statistics show that one out of eight prisoners on death row has been wrongfully convicted. Formal studies have implicated a variety of causes for these startling numbers. Results show that the leading cause is poor legal representation. Court-appointed counsel are often less skilled than those retained by private-paying citizens, and this is reflected in their low pay. Additionally, public defenders are often assigned cases with little advance notice or preparation.

Another recurring problem is perjured TESTIMONY. Sociologist Michael Radelet of the University of Florida and philosopher Hugo Bedau of Tufts University studied four hundred wrongful murder and rape convictions and found that prisoners are often all too eager to contrive testimony implicating a fellow prisoner in return for favors for themselves. "Overheard" confessions or claims that a fellow prisoner bragged about a murder, are common backdrops for perjured testimony by inmates hoping to get a break by testifying. (The statements are not considered "hearsay" testimony if they constitute statements of "admission" on the part of the person implicated.)

Mistaken identity by eyewitnesses also contributes to errors in convictions, as do faulty confessions obtained from children, mentally impaired individuals, or persons susceptible to suggestion. All of these problems are exacerbated by prosecutors who are under internal pressure to indict and external pressure to win. To a much lesser degree is the concealment of mitigating evidence by prosecutors, and in some instances, fabricated testimony by police officers and other prosecution witnesses. However reprehensible, this most often occurs when police believe they have the right person, but are fearful that they might not have substantial evidence to bring about a conviction. In January 1999, seven police officers and prosecutors were brought to trial in Illinois for conspiracy to conceal and fabricate evidence, following the reversal of two death sentence convictions which were premised on false evidence.

Finally, a contributing factor is the lack of appellate lawyers willing and available to take up a convicted death row inmates's cause. This is apparently of more concern since 1996 when Congress funding to death penalty resource centers in twenty states.

Perhaps the most significant development in the continued efforts to discover and correct wrongful convictions has been in the area of DNA profiling and testing. Despite accuracy and admissibility in trial proceedings, DNA profiling is often thwarted by the fact that hair, semen, blood, and other evidence has already been discarded by the time the possibility of a wrongful conviction is realized. Nonetheless, in the last ten years, no less than ten persons have won release from death row because of DNA testing clearing their involvement in the crime at issue.

Other suggested means for minimizing the risk of wrongful convictions include increasing legal aid monies, limiting the use of "jailhouse snitches," preserving evidence for longer periods, and recording all police interrogations. In the end, one simple statistic brings the issue home: for every wrongful conviction on death row, there is a guilty person who has gone free.

Stewart v. LaGrand

In a succinct three-page opinion, the U.S. Supreme Court put an end to a series of sequential appeals and challenges filed by death-row prisoner Walter LaGrand. The Court ruled, in *Stewart v. LaGrand*, ___U.S.___, 119 S. Ct.1018, 143 L. Ed. 2d 196 (1999), that LaGrand had waived his right to challenge the constitutionality of execution by lethal gas, because LaGrand had selected that form of execution over others, when given his choice. He was executed on March 3, 1999, hours after release of the Court's opinion. Thus ended a fourteen-year period during which LaGrand had effectively stayed his execution several times by filing protracted challenges at the state, federal district, circuit, and Supreme Court levels.

Brothers Walter LaGrand and Karl LaGrand were each convicted in 1984 of first-degree murder, attempted murder, armed robbery, and kidnapping. Each was sentenced to death. At the time, Arizona had in force a law which mandated lethal gas as the method of execution for all capital defendants. Both LaGrands filed numerous appeals regarding their convictions and meted punishments. However, throughout their appeals, neither one of them raised any challenge of EIGHTH AMENDMENT constitutionality (cruel and unusual punishment) regarding execution by lethal gas. The Arizona Supreme Court affirmed their convictions on all charges, and their sentences. See *State v. LaGrand*, 734 P. 2d 563 (1987) (Walter LaGrand); *State v. LaGrand*, 733 P. 2d 1066 (1987) (Karl LaGrand). The Arizona Superior Court denied their post-conviction relief petitions, as did the Arizona Supreme Court. Both LaGrands' petitions for CERTIORARI were denied by the U.S. Supreme Court, 484 U.S. 872, 108 S. Ct. 207, 98 L. Ed. 2d 158 (1987). Following denial of certiorari, each filed a petition for writ of HABEAS CORPUS under 28 U.S.C.§ 2254.

In the interim, Arizona had changed its law regarding the method of execution for capital defendants, from lethal gas to lethal injection. The law went into effect in January 1993. Because there were still several capital defendants awaiting execution under the old law, the new statute contained an express provision that any such defendant who was sentenced to death for offenses committed prior to November 23, 1992, "shall choose either lethal injection or lethal gas at least twenty days before the execution date." In the event the capital defendant failed to choose, a default rule of execution by lethal injection would be affected. This legislative change followed the U.S. Court of Appeals for the Ninth Circuit's finding that execution by lethal gas was unconstitutional under the Eighth Amendment.

In the LaGrands' habeas corpus writs, their claims included juror bias, lack of competency to be executed, denial of fair hearings, denial that their crimes were "cruel, heinous or depraved," and denial of aggravating circumstances in their underlying cases. Of importance is that in Walter LeGrand's petition, he raised the claim of cruel and unusual punishment by lethal gas execution. The U.S. federal district court found his claim to be procedurally defaulted for having failed to raise this new claim at any prior time in direct appeal or state post-conviction relief petitions. On appeal, the Ninth Circuit never reached the issue of procedural default, finding the issue not yet ripe until and unless LaGrand chose lethal gas as the method of execution, (133 F. 3d 1253 [1998]). The writ was denied.

Subsequently, Karl LaGrand filed a successive state petition, also raising the issue of cruel and unusual punishment for lethal gas. The trial court found his claim MOOT by reason of default for having failed to raise this issue earlier in prior state court proceedings. The Arizona Supreme Court denied review. In Karl's second federal petition for habeas corpus, he again raised this issue. The federal district court again found the claim procedurally defaulted, and further, found no established cause or prejudice to set aside default. (A petitioner must establish cause and prejudice or a fundamental miscarriage of justice in order to have default excused.) The court again denied the writ and Karl appealed to the Ninth Circuit.

However, this time the Ninth Circuit (while agreeing on the procedural default) reversed on the matter of excuse, finding cause and prejudice. They reasoned that Karl LaGrand's failure to raise the Eighth Amendment claim was excused because, at the time, there was no factual or legal basis for the claim. He was now prejudiced by having to face execution by means which had since been found unconstitutional, though not unconstitutional at the time of his sentencing in 1984. With respect to any issue over whether Karl had waived his current claim, the Ninth Circuit quoted its own precedent that "Eighth Amendment protections may not be waived, at least in the areas of capital punishment." *LaGrand v. Stewart,* (No.99–99004 [1999]). It stayed his execution and enjoined Arizona from executing him with lethal gas. The state filed an application with the U.S. Supreme Court to vacate the stay of execution. This was granted. At the last moment, however, Karl agreed to lethal injection instead of lethal gas, and the appellate matter was never tested on the merits.

Walter then filed a petition for a writ of habeas corpus which challenged execution by lethal gas as a cruel and unusual punishment. The district court, declining to follow the Ninth Circuit's previous opinion in Karl's case because the Supreme Court had lifted the stay of execution. It denied Walter's writ and also denied a certificate of appealability, holding that the issue of procedural default of Walter's lethal gas challenge "is not debatable among jurists of reason."

The Ninth Circuit again overruled, concluding that notwithstanding the Supreme Court's lifting of the stay of execution, the Court had not addressed the merits of their previous decision. Deeming the previous opinion as sound, it stayed Walter's execution and enjoined Arizona from executing him with lethal gas. The

state then filed an application for writ of certiorari and application to lift the Ninth Circuit's injunction.

The Supreme Court was brief and to the point. Spending little time on procedural or criminal history, it ruled that Walter LaGrand had waived his Eighth Amendment claim that lethal gas was unconstitutional. LaGrand had been given a choice, and he chose lethal gas. Moreover, two days before execution, on March 1, 1999, Arizona's Governor Jane Dee Hull had again offered LaGrand an opportunity to rescind his previous choice and select lethal injection, but he again insisted on lethal gas. The Court held that LaGrand's affirmative declaration of choice, over the state's default form of execution by injection, constituted a waiver of objection he might have had. The Court found the Ninth Circuit's holding that a capital defendant could not waive Eighth Amendment protections as violative of *Teague v. Lane,* 489 U.S. 288, 109 S. Ct. 1060, 103 L. Ed. 2d 334 (1989).

The Court further held that LaGrand's claims were procedurally defaulted, as a factual and legal basis (for cause and prejudice) did in fact exist at the time he was originally sentenced. The Court cited several arguments and legal controversies over the constitutionality of execution by lethal gas since 1921.

LaGrand had argued in the alternative that he was prejudiced by ineffective assistance of counsel. The Court held that this argument failed as well, since LaGrand had previously advised the district court that there was no basis for such a claim. (The district court was attempting to address all actual and potential issues on the first writ, requiring LaGrand to discuss all possible claims of ineffective assistance with his attorney and to affirmatively file a report with the district court. LaGrand insisted that he did not desire new counsel and that he wanted his present counsel to continue representing him.) Therefore, LaGrand had failed to show cause or prejudice as to why he had not raised these claims on direct review.

Justice DAVID H. SOUTER, joined by Justices RUTH BADER GINSBURG and STEPHEN BREYER, concurred in part and concurred in the judgment, on the understanding "that petitioner makes no claim that death by lethal injection would be cruel and unusual punishment…" They did not reach the applicability of the *Teague* case.

Justice Souter filed a two-sentence dissent, declaring that he would not decide the issue of whether a capital defendant may consent to be executed by unacceptable means "without full briefing and argument."

CROSS REFERENCES
DNA Evidence; Habeas Corpus; Harmless Error

CENSORSHIP

The suppression or proscription of speech or writing that is deemed OBSCENE, indecent, or unduly controversial.

Monteiro v. Tempe High Union High School District

Although federal and state laws prohibit acts of racial discrimination and harassment, the FIRST AMENDMENT protects the free expression of ideas, even racist ideas. The Ninth Circuit Court of Appeals, in *Monteiro v. Tempe High Union High School District*, 158 F. 3d 1022 (9th Cir. 1998), examined the border between protected expression and prohibited conduct in the public schools. The court ruled that an African American woman could not sue to remove Mark Twain's *The Adventures of Huckleberry Finn* and a short story by William Faulkner from the required-reading list at her daughter's Tempe, Arizona, high school. However, the court ruled that the woman could pursue her claim against the school district that it failed to respond to complaints that white students were harassing African American students with racial slurs and graffiti.

Kathy Monteiro's daughter was a student in a freshman English class at McClintock High School in Tempe. The class required-reading list included *The Adventures of Huckleberry Finn* and Faulkner's *A Rose for Emily*. Monteiro filed a federal civil rights lawsuit on her daughter's behalf, alleging that both of these literary works "contains repeated use of the profane, insulting and racially derogatory term 'nigger.' "She also alleged that neither work was a necessary component of a freshman English class and that none of the assignments in the curriculum referred to Caucasians in a derogatory manner. Monteiro claimed that her daughter and other African American students suffered psychological injuries and lost educational opportunities due to the required reading of the literary works. She alleged that the school district was notified that her daughter suffered these injuries, but refused to offer a remedy other than to allow her to study alone in the library while the works were being discussed in class.

Monteiro asserted that the assignment of the literary works "created and contributed to a racially hostile educational environment," including increased racial harassment by other students. Finally, she alleged that by its conduct the school district intentionally discriminated against her daughter.

Monteiro asked the court to declare that the school district's conduct violated her daughter's rights under the EQUAL PROTECTION CLAUSE of the FOURTEENTH AMENDMENT and Title VI of the Civil Rights Act of 1964. In addition, she requested the court to issue an injunction that would prohibit the school district from assigning these or other racially offensive works in the future. However, Monteiro did not seek the exclusion of the literary works from a voluntary reading list. Monteiro also asked for compensatory damages.

The federal district court dismissed the complaint because Monteiro had failed to state specific allegations of fact required to establish discriminatory intent under either Title VI or the Equal Protection Clause. Monteiro then appealed to the Ninth Circuit.

Judge Stephen Reinhardt, writing for the three-judge panel, noted that the court had to balance competing constitutional rights. Monteiro's daughter had the right to receive a public education that did not foster or allow a racially hostile environment. The other students in the class had a right, under the First Amendment, to receive information or ideas, even when contained in literary works that may appear to have racist overtones.

Judge Reinhardt also noted that school boards are given broad authority "to establish curricula they believe to be appropriate to the educational needs of their students." He acknowledged that "words can hurt," and that "words of a racist nature can hurt especially severely." Moreover, the court was aware that the "historic prejudice" against African Americans that "has existed in this nation since its inception has not yet been eradicated—by any means."

The court did not find it surprising that the lawsuit involved *Huckleberry Finn*. It pointed out that, according to the American Library Association, the book is the most frequently banned book in the United States, as well as one of the most respected literary works. African American parents throughout the United States have asserted, as did Monteiro, that the book's use of the word "nigger" 215 times hurts the self-esteem of young African American students. Parents have sought to remove the book from libraries and reading lists in school districts in a number of states, including Pennsylvania, Ohio, and California. Although some districts have retained the book, many others have removed it from the curriculum due to concerns about the use of racial stereotypes and epithets.

However, the court concluded that the two literary works could not be removed because of First Amendment concerns. Reinhardt stated that if schools must bar racially offensive books from the curriculum, this "could have a significant chilling effect on a school district's willingness to assign books with themes, characters, snippets of dialogue, or words that might offend the sensibilities of any number of persons or groups." This would be detrimental to education, as books containing pedagogical value could be removed from the classroom. In addition, he rejected the idea that the courts could "serve as literary censors." It was not the role of the courts to "make judgments as to whether reading particular books does students more harm than good."

The court also noted that if it granted Monteiro's demand, school districts that removed books for such reasons would themselves be open to First Amendment suits. Other students and teachers who wished to study those books could assert that the school district violated their rights. This would leave the districts in a dilemma between warring litigants. Moreover, the court did not want to limit a school board's discretion in overseeing school matters, including establishing challenging and appropriate curriculum. However, Reinhardt stated that this discretion did not immunize teachers and school districts from repercussions from deliberate discriminatory conduct.

Although the court dismissed the book claim, it did revive Monteiro's claim that the school officials did not respond to her complaints about racial harassment. Judge Reinhardt applied a three-part test contained in Title VI of the Civil Rights Act of 1964. He determined that a racially hostile environment existed, and that the school district was adequately notified of the problem. However, he found that the school district's response was "deliberately indifferent" and therefore inadequate. As such, the school district could be liable for damages under Title VI when the case went to trial. Therefore, the court of appeals remanded this portion of he case to the district court so Monteiro could pursue this claim.

CROSS REFERENCES
First Amendment

CENSUS

The official count of the population of a particular area, such as a district, state, or nation.

Sampling and the Decennial Census for 2000

After months of lower-court action and political sparring, the U.S. Supreme Court ruled in January 1999 that the U.S. Department of Commerce could not use statistical "sampling" in lieu of actual head counts to calculate population for the 2000 census. In the case of *Department of Commerce v. United States House of Representatives*, __ U.S.__, 119 S. Ct.765, 142 L. Ed. 2d 797 (1999), the Court ruled that the 1976 Census Act prohibits the use of statistical sampling for purposes of population head counts, which would ultimately be used for apportionment (the allocation of 435 Congressional House of Representative seats among the states). (The Court's decision also applied to a pending corollary case, *Clinton v. Glavin*, which contained essentially the same issues.)

The controversial "sampling" is a form of statistically estimating the number and characteristics (race/ethnicity, political party alignment, etc.) of certain identifiable groups of persons, particularly in the two extremes of either dense urban or very rural areas, which are often undercounted during regular census-taking. Sampling is generally accomplished by counting everyone in 90 percent of the households, and using those figures to estimate the number and characteristics of the remaining 10 percent. The Department of Commerce's Census Bureau wanted to use sampling to ensure that the final figures reflected those often missed in census-taking, e.g., renters, children, illegal aliens, poor persons, etc. Since, historically, minorities tended to constitute a majority of such populations in very dense urban and/or rural areas, it had been alleged that actual head-counting disproportionately affected minorities, because these persons were often missed in the head-count. Some believe that sampling could correct actual census counts by allowing a margin for the estimated sample populations.

But the sensitive political underpinnings of the case evolved around the fact that most of the at-issue geographic areas—and persons, were more likely to be aligned with the Democratic party, particularly in the dense urban areas of large cities. Potentially millions of uncounted persons were at stake. If sampling were allowed, the "sample" would automatically be characteristically aligned with the surrounding area,

U.S. Census Bureau Director Kenneth Prewitt meets with reports to discuss the 2000 census.

LINDA SPILLERS/AP/WIDE WORLD PHOTOS

translating into millions of potential Democratic party members. The quintessential issue thus became whether sampling could be used for apportionment, which is officially the only function of census under the Constitution.

At the lower court levels, the arguments were legal rather than factual, i.e., it was argued by the Clinton administration's Department of Commerce that the plaintiffs lacked legal STANDING to sue. According to the administration, the plaintiffs' "injuries" were too remote and speculative to give them standing to bring suit alleging that they had been wronged or harmed. Conversely, the plaintiffs argued that their's was a question of law. The 1976 Census Act expressly prohibited sampling for purposes of apportionment. SUMMARY JUDGMENT was granted to the plaintiffs. Both lower courts agreed with the plaintiffs that the Census Act prohibited the use of sampling in allocating congressional House seats. Since this finding was dispositive to warrant summary judgment, there was no need for the lower courts to address the corollary constitutional issue of whether the Constitution's language of "actual enumeration" dispositively ruled out statistical sampling.

In a narrow 5–4 opinion, the Supreme Court ruled first, that the appellees (original plaintiffs) had legal standing to bring suit. Losing a House seat "satisfies the injury-in-fact requirement for standing," the Court noted.

As to the second, and critical issue, the Court began its holding by stating that the Cen-

sus Act expressly prohibited the use of sampling to determine populations for congressional apportionment purposes. The Court juxtaposed two specific provisions of the act. Although the first provision of the act grants broad powers to the secretary of Commerce to "take a decennial census in such form and content as he may determine," the Court quoted a further, limiting provision in the 1976 amendments which provides that "[e]xcept for the determination of population for purposes of [congressional] apportionment…the Secretary shall, if he considers it feasible, authorize the use of…statistical…'sampling' in carrying out the provisions of this title." Ruling that this limiting provision must be interpreted in context with the broader-authority language of the first provision, the Court opined that the express prohibition of the second provision was controlling, and dispositive of the issue.

Justice SANDRA DAY O'CONNOR, in writing the opinion for the majority, further noted that there has been over two hundred years of history "during which federal census statutes have uniformly prohibited using statistical sampling for congressional apportionment." (The first census in 1790, was delivered by THOMAS JEFFERSON to President GEORGE WASHINGTON. The head-counted population was 3,929,000. In the 1990 census two hundred years later, 248,718,301 persons were counted.) The Court's opinion then pointedly noted that the Executive Branch had accepted and "even advocated" this interpretation of the act until 1994.

Justice JOHN PAUL STEVENS was joined in dissent by Justices DAVID H. SOUTER, RUTH BADER GINSBURG, and STEPHEN BREYER. The dissent interpreted the 1976 amendments to the Census Act as leaving a possibility open for statistical sampling for purposes of House seat allocation.

Notwithstanding, the majority opinion did not end the controversy. First, it left open the possibility that statistical sampling could be used for other purposes, such as federal funding for roads, education, and public housing, as well as redistricting within a state, resulting in redrawn political boundaries affecting state legislative, congressional and local electoral seats. Moreover, Congress might then be required to fund two separate sets of population numbers: one for apportionment, and another adjusted one for "other purposes." The Clinton administration made it clear, after the ruling, that it intended to pursue funding for a "two-number" census. The Republicans' answer to the problem of census inaccuracy is to hire an additional 100,000 census-takers and increase the budget for publicizing the census. That way, the census-taking stays true to the letter of the law, but makes a good faith effort to correct any undercounting. Otherwise, they argue, statistical "adjustments" invite political manipulation and maneuvering.

CROSS REFERENCES
Standing

CIVIL RIGHTS

Personal liberties that belong to an individual owing to his or her status as a CITIZEN or resident of a particular country or community.

At-will Contracts

Individuals who have suffered employment discrimination based on race can use two federal statutes to vindicate their rights: Title VII of the CIVIL RIGHTS ACT OF 1964, 42 U.S.C.A. § 2000e et seq., and 42 U.S.C.A. § 1981. Although Title VII is used more, it applies only to employers with fifteen or more employees. Therefore, § 1981 provides the only opportunity under federal law to remedy race-based employment discrimination by those who employ fewer than fifteen employees.

Section 1981, which Congress enacted shortly after the Civil War, states that all persons have the right to "make and enforce contracts...as is enjoyed by white citizens." In two recent court of appeals cases, the courts examined whether at-will employees have a "contract" for employment that would allow them to sue their employer for racial discrimination under § 1981. Both the Fourth Circuit, in *Springs v. Diamond Auto Glass*, 165 F. 3d 1015 (4th Cir. 1999), and the Fifth Circuit, in *Fadeyi v. Planned Parenthood Association of Lubbock, Inc.*, 160 F. 3d 1048 (5th Cir. 1998), ruled that the statute did apply to at-will employees.

In the Fifth Circuit case, Lamarilyn Fadeyi sued the Lubbock, Texas, Planned Parenthood office where she worked for seven years. Fadeyi, an African American, claimed that the office had committed various acts of racial discrimination during the years of she was employed. She filed complaints with the Equal Employment Opportunity Commission (EEOC) and the Texas Commission on Human Rights, but both dismissed her complaints because Planned Parenthood had fewer than fifteen employees. The commissions did not have jurisdiction under Title VII to investigate her complaints. Two days

after the EEOC notified Planned Parenthood that it had dismissed Fadeyi's complaint, Planned Parenthood fired her.

Fadeyi then filed a lawsuit in federal district court under § 1981, alleging discrimination in her employment and termination. The district court dismissed her case, ruling that she could not show the existence of an employment contract, which is an essential part of a § 1981 action.

Fadeyi appealed to the Fifth Circuit. The court acknowledged that the sole issue was whether an employment-at-will relationship is a contract for § 1981 purposes. Employment at will is a COMMON LAW rule that either the employer or the employee can end an employment contract of indefinite duration at any time for any reason. The appeals court noted that Texas had adopted this definition, but concluded that this does not mean that the "employment-at-will relationship is not contractual one for the purposes of § 1981."

Though more than forty states recognize the employment-at-will relationship, the court found that the case law addressing this issue was sparse. Therefore, it used two main sources for its decision: *Patterson v. McLean Credit Union*, 491 U.S. 164, 109 S. Ct. 2363, 105 L. Ed. 2d 132 (1989), and the Civil Rights Act of 1991. In *Patterson*, the Supreme Court held that § 1981 did not apply in the case of an at-will employee who alleged she had been harassed and denied a promotion based upon her race. The Court held that § 1981 only applied to the formation and enforcement of contracts, as distinguished from employment situations.

Congress overturned this decision when it passed the Civil Rights Act of 1991. It amended § 1981 to clarify that "to make and enforce contracts" included "performance, modification and termination," as well as "enjoyment of all benefits, privileges, terms and conditions of the contractual relationship." Thus, racial harassment, racially based compensation, racially motivated discharges, as well as racial discrimination in hiring, transfers, and promotions were within the scope of § 1981.

The Fifth Circuit pointed out that although the *Patterson* Court refused to recognize work place racial harassment as actionable under § 1981, "it acknowledged that Patterson, an at-will employee, might have a cause of action" based on her employer's failure to promote her because of her race. Thus, the Supreme Court "considered the employee's relationship with her employer to be a contractual one."

The court also concluded that Congress intended to protect "minorities in their employment relationships when it overruled *Patterson* in 1991. To hold that at-will employees had no right of action under § 1981 would "effectively eviscerate the very protection Congress expressly intended to install for minority employees," especially those not protected by Title VII.

The Fifth Circuit also referred to Texas law to support its view that at-will employment relationships are contracts. Based on all of these sources, the appeals court stated that "though an at-will employee can be fired for good cause, bad cause, or no cause at all, he or she cannot be fired for an illicit cause." Therefore, the appeals court remanded the case to the district court to allow Fadeyi to pursue her claim.

In the Fourth Circuit case, James Spriggs alleged that he had been subjected to racial discrimination and retaliation in connection with his at-will employee relationship with Diamond Auto Glass in Forrestville, Maryland. Spriggs, an African American, worked as a customer service representative. He alleged that his supervisor used racial slurs in his presence and several times directed these remarks at Spriggs. Spriggs quit after enduring two years of these incidents. A year later a manager at the glass company asked him to return and promised to control the supervisor. Spriggs returned, but the supervisor's racist comments and actions continued. Spriggs left again after six months. He was persuaded to return one month later, with further assurances that the supervisor would be kept in check. However, the supervisor presented Spriggs with new job duties that Spriggs considered unreasonable and racially motivated. He permanently left the company soon after his return.

Spriggs filed a § 1981 in federal court, but as in the *Fadeyi* case, the court dismissed the action because it believed at-will employees were not protected by the statute. The Fourth Circuit acknowledged that Spriggs had "never entered into a written employment agreement with Diamond." Nevertheless, the court concluded that there had been an employment contract between Spriggs and the company. Diamond had offered to pay Spriggs if he would perform the duties of customer service representative and Spriggs had accepted the offer by beginning work. Spriggs' performance of his assigned job duties was "consideration exchanged for Diamond's promise to pay." Therefore, the actions of Spriggs and Diamond created a contractual relationship. The fact that either party could terminate the contract at-will did not "invalidate the underlying contract itself."

The appeals court adopted the analysis of the Fifth Circuit's decision in *Fadeyi*, concluding that Spriggs could bring a § 1981 action.

Crawford-El v. Britton

The federal civil rights statute 42 U.S.C.A. SECTION 1983 allows individuals to sue public officials for DAMAGES for violations of their civil rights. Since the Supreme Court broadened the application of the law in the 1960s, prisoners have used its provisions against prison guards and prison officials. The explosion in prisoner litigation ultimately led to the Prison Litigation Reform Act of 1995, 28 U.S.C.A. § 1932, which requires inmates to pay filing fees in civil suits and restricts the amount of money inmates may recover.

Litigious prisoners have drawn attention from some federal courts, to the point that these courts have tried to impose evidentiary rules that make it easier to quickly dismiss prisoner lawsuits. However, the Supreme Court, in *Crawford-El v. Britton*, 523 U.S. 574, 118 S.Ct. 1584, 140 L.Ed.2d 759 (1998), struck down an appellate court decision that imposed a higher BURDEN OF PERSUASION on an inmate's claim. The Court found that the higher burden of proof would have to apply to all § 1983 lawsuits, not just those brought by prisoners. The higher burden could not be justified by the Court's prior rulings or any congressional statute.

Leonard Crawford-El, a convicted murderer, was sentenced to life in prison. During the course of his confinement he filed several lawsuits and assisted other inmates with their cases. In addition, he gave interviews to reporters that described prison conditions as extremely poor. In 1988, Crawford-El was transferred because of prison overcrowding from a prison in Lorton, Virginia, to Washington D.C. During 1988 and 1989, he was transferred five times, ultimately being assigned to a Florida prison.

During the multiple transfers, three boxes of Crawford-El's personal belongings, including legal materials, moved as well. When he was transferred from the Washington prison, Patricia Britton, a D.C. correctional officer, gave the boxes to Crawford's brother-in-law, also a D.C. correctional officer. Typically, the boxes would have been shipped by the correction system to his next destination. Crawford-El's mother ultimately mailed him the boxes, but he did not receive them until he had spent several months at the Florida prison. Crawford-El then filed a § 1983 against Britton, alleging that she had deliberately misdirected the boxes to punish him for exercising his FIRST AMENDMENT rights and to deter similar conduct in the future. He alleged that her actions were in retaliation for him talking to reporters about the conditions at Lorton. Crawford-El asserted that his constitutional right to access to the courts had been violated. He asked for damages caused by the delay in receiving his boxes and for emotional and mental distress.

Britton moved the federal district court to dismiss the action, claiming a qualified IMMUNITY from § 1983 liability. An official will qualify for immunity if she can show that she has not violated an individual's clearly established statutory or constitutional rights of which a reasonable person would have known. The district court granted Britton qualified immunity and dismissed the case. Crawford-El appealed to the Circuit Court of Appeals for the D.C. Circuit.

The appeals court ruled that the case should not have been dismissed and remanded it to the district court. It concluded, however, that in an "unconstitutional motive" case such as this, Crawford-El had to establish the illegal motive by "clear and convincing evidence" to defeat the qualified immunity defense of Britton. In civil rights lawsuits the plaintiff's burden of proof is usually a "preponderance of the evidence," a lesser standard than clear and convincing. The court justified the heightened evidentiary burden as a way to protect defendants from the costs of litigation. 93 F.3d 813 (D.C. Cir.1996).

The Supreme Court voted 5–4 to reverse the court of appeals, ruling that courts could not require clear and convincing evidence of improper motive. Justice JOHN PAUL STEVENS, writing for the majority, acknowledged that the appeals court sought to remedy a potentially serious problem. Because the state of mind of an official is "easy to allege and hard to disprove," frivolous claims that turn on improper intent are more difficult to dismiss right away. The PLAINTIFF can argue that the case should go to trial to determine motivation, thus forcing the public official to endure the social and economic costs of discovery and trial.

Justice Stevens pointed out that the appeals court rule was not limited to prisoner lawsuits but applied to any plaintiff who sought damages from a public official for violation of civil rights. Such a sweeping rule would have a substantial impact on many categories of civil rights litigation involving the motives of officials.

The court of appeals had based its rule on the Court's landmark case of official immunity, *Harlow v. Fitzgerald*, 457 U.S. 731, 102 S. Ct. 2690, 73 L. Ed. 2d 349 (1982). In this case, the Court announced a single objective standard for judging whether an executive branch official qualified for immunity. In this ruling, the Court abandoned a subjective standard that allowed plaintiffs to defeat immunity by alleging malice. Thus, an official could obtain immunity by showing that he or she did not violate a clearly established statutory or constitutional right.

Justice Stevens agreed that Britton's subjective intent about why she transferred the boxes was irrelevant for the qualified immunity defense. However, her intent was an essential component of Crawford-El's underlying case. Because *Harlow* only related to the scope of Britton's affirmative defense, it provided no support for changing Crawford-El's burden of proof for the constitutional violation.

The Supreme Court concluded that officials may have a case dismissed if there is doubt about the illegality of the official's conduct. Nevertheless, the improper motive element of "various causes of action should not ordinarily preclude" dismissal of "insubstantial claims."

Having found that there were no case precedents to support the appeals court rule, Justice Stevens examined federal statutes for support. He found nothing in § 1983, other civil rights laws, and the Federal Rules of CIVIL PROCEDURE to justify a clear and convincing burden of proof. The appeals court's "unprecedented change" lacked any independent support and undermined § 1983's main purpose: providing a remedy for the violation of federal rights. If such a change in the burden of proof was necessary, Congress needed to legislate it.

Chief Justice WILLIAM H. REHNQUIST filed a dissenting opinion, which Justice SANDRA DAY O'CONNOR joined. Rehnquist contended that a government official who is a defendant in a motive-based TORT action "is entitled to immunity from suit so long as he can offer a legitimate reason for the action being challenged," and the plaintiff cannot show that the offered reason is a pretext. Justice ANTONIN SCALIA also wrote a dissent, which Justice CLARENCE THOMAS joined. Scalia argued that the objective reasonableness test of *Harlow* should be extended to motive-based constitutional torts.

Department of Agriculture Settles Lawsuit with Black Farmers

Racial discrimination has touched virtually every part of U.S. society, including American agriculture. This fact was illustrated in 1997 when a group of African American farmers filed a lawsuit against the U.S. Department of Agriculture (USDA), alleging that their loan applications had been treated unfairly because of their race. A political and legal battle ensued, ending in 1999 when the USDA and the farmers reached a settlement that may result in up to $2 billion being paid to the black farmers.

The frustration of black farmers, who are primarily located in southern states, over the actions of the USDA's Farmers Home Administration (FmHA) went back decades. Congress established the FmHA in the 1930s, during the Great Depression, as a lender of last resort to small farmers. By the mid-1960s, the U.S. Civil Rights Commission had concluded that FmHA had discriminated against black staff members and black farmers. In 1970, an internal USDA study found that FmHA's lending practices were "callous" toward blacks. In 1982 a commission scrutinized the USDA and found its practices discriminatory, calling it "the last plantation." The commission concluded that if things did not change within the agency, there would be no black farmers by the year 2000.

The USDA, unlike most other federal agencies, has relied on locally administered offices. Therefore, black farmers seeking farm loans had to seek them from county FmHA committees that prominent white farmers and businessmen controlled. With 2,700 county USDA offices, decisions were made at the local rather than at the federal level. The USDA's inspector general's office found that black farmers' loan applications were consistently denied, delayed, reduced or foreclosed sooner than their white counterparts'. One study disclosed that in North Carolina a black farmer had to wait an average of 222 days for a loan decision, while a white farmer had to wait only 84 days.

The problem of racial discrimination within the USDA became more difficult to address in the early 1980s, when the Reagan administration dismantled the department's civil rights office. This meant that the USDA did not promptly investigate discrimination complaints. In 1984, black farmers testified before a House Judiciary Committee investigating USDA loan practices. By the mid-1990s, there was a large backlog of uninvestigated complaints. In November 1996 the director of the Farm Service Agency, the former FmHA, admitted publicly that the agency still discriminated in its lending. By the spring of 1997, the USDA offered a token settlement to some of the farmers that had filed complaints.

Faced with this administrative inertia, in 1997 a group of black farmers, on behalf of the National Black Farmers and Agriculturists Association, filed a CLASS ACTION federal lawsuit

Members from the National Black Farmers Association hold a press conference after meeting with President Clinton.

against the USDA. The farmers alleged that the USDA had not investigated hundreds of complaints between 1987 and 1997. They asked for over $2.5 billion in DAMAGES to be distributed to black farmers nationwide. The farmers also sought the intervention of the U.S. Department of Justice to help press their case.

In May 1998, the Department of Justice announced that it would not participate in the lawsuit, concluding that a two-year STATUTE OF LIMITATIONS prohibited the farmers from seeking financial compensation for past discrimination. Most of the alleged discriminatory acts had taken place many years before.

The National Black Farmers and Agriculturists Association then turned to the political arena. It worked with the Congressional Black Caucus and other leaders in Congress to have a law passed that would extend the time for the filing of discrimination lawsuits against the USDA. In addition, association members met with President BILL CLINTON at the White House to air their concerns. The political lobbying paid off, as Congress in 1998 passed a bill waiving the statute of limitations.

After the congressional action, the USDA and Secretary of Agriculture Dan Glickman sought to settle the lawsuit. Glickman openly admitted that department managers had not been committed to, or accountable for, their actions on civil rights. He noted that a review panel he appointed had found that "minority farmers have lost significant amounts of land and potential farm income as a result of discrimination."

In January 1999, a proposed settlement was announced that would give farmers who had little documentary evidence $50,000 each and erase their federal debts. Farmers with more evidence could seek to obtain a higher amount of compensation through arbitration. In March 1999, members of the National Black Farmers and Agriculturists Association appeared in the District of Columbia courtroom of U.S. District Court Judge Paul L. Friedman and attacked the settlement. Other members of the association held protests outside the courthouse, arguing that the $50,000 figure was inadequate. One protester said the amount would not even buy a medium-sized tractor. Some farmers expressed concern that there were no review mechanisms for examining arbitrators' rulings, while other farmers demanded that USDA officials in counties where discrimination occurred be fired. Judge Friedman informed the members that he had no authority to dictate a modified settlement but he could bring pressure to bear on both sides.

Finally, in May 1999 Judge Friedman approved a settlement that may amount to $2 billion for thousands of black farmers. By that date over 18,000 farmers had signed up for the settlement. Farmers with less documented evidence would receive $50,000 as compensation, $12,500 to cover taxes, and would have their farm loans forgiven. Farmers with more evidence could seek greater compensation by appearing before an independent arbitrator. Both sides agreed to adopt Judge Friedman's suggestion that he be allowed to appoint a monitor to oversee the settlement. Responding to the concerns of the farmers at the March hearing, the parties also agreed to have a group of retired judges review the decisions made by an arbitrator as to whether farmers qualify for compensation.

Despite the settlement, many farmers were disappointed, believing it would not stem the loss of black farmers. The number of black-owned farms has fallen from 925,000 in 1920 to 18,000 by 1992. This decline means that black farmers now make up only 1 percent of the farmers in the United States.

CROSS REFERENCES
Agriculture Department; Burden of Persuasion; Class Action; Contracts; Employment Law; Prisoners' Rights; Statute of Limitations

CLASS ACTION

A lawsuit that allows a large number of people with a common interest in a matter to sue or be sued as a group.

Breast Implant Litigation

An important legal issue was resolved in 1998 with Dow Corning's settlement of its protracted silicone breast implant litigation which had spanned at least eight years. On November 9, 1998, in the U.S. Bankruptcy Court, Eastern District of Michigan, Dow filed its Joint Plan of Reorganization (disclosure statement), labeled "joint" because it represented the collaborative and cooperative efforts of both sides. The plan included details of a $3.2 billion fund to settle an estimated 170,000 pending silicone implant claims in various class-action suits around the world. Dow Corning had filed for BANKRUPTCY in 1995, when more than nineteen thousand cases were pending.

Dow had tried twice previously to submit reorganization plans, but they had been rejected by both the court and the plaintiffs. Essentially, and as is usually the case in structured mass tort

Barbra Houser, center, holds up an example of the document package that will be mailed out to thousands of claimants in the breast implant suit.

settlements, the plaintiffs had wanted more money, and wanted it sooner rather than later. The reorganization plan had to be approved, first by the court in which the actions were pending, then by at least two-thirds of the plaintiffs, then approved by the bankruptcy court. The plaintiffs' position had been organized and presented under the auspices of the Tort Claimants Committee.

After the court had accepted the plan, the two sides launched a sixty-day court-ordered open voting period from March 15 through May 15, 1999, for the class-action claimants to accept or reject it. As of May 16, 1999, the plan had been overwhelmingly accepted by plaintiff-claimants. A confirmation meeting was scheduled for June 28, 1999, and if all went well, the plan would still need approval by the bankruptcy court prior to becoming effective. Acceptance of the plan would also allow the company to emerge from bankruptcy status.

Essentially, the fund plan provided for $3.17 to $3.2 billion in payments over 16 years to settle all global tort-related claims (the largest group of which was the breast implant group). Express provisions addressed the *Spitzfaden* and Canadian class-actions. Another $1.3 billion would be set aside for other creditor/commercial claims (approximately 60,000). Even though the silicone breast implant product had never constituted more than one percent of the company's total revenues, the massive costs of the implant litigation had crippled all other product and service operations.

Highlights of the plan included provisions to allow women up to fifteen years to file dis-

ease claims and up to ten years to file claims for removal of implants. Additionally, women had two years to file claims for ruptured implants and three years to file claims of expedited settlements. Pay-out settlements ranged from approximately $2000 for simple expedited claims up to more than $300,000 for women with alleged disease. An emergency fund would also be established for women whose disease or medical condition changes after initial compensation under the plan. Separate provisions addressed women whose implants were made by other manufacturers using Dow materials. With respect to tort claims for other products covered under the plan (such as artificial joints using silicone), claimants could choose either expedited payments or medical condition payments. All claimants could choose not to settle, and instead maintain their rights to a jury trial.

However, settling their claims could not have come at a more opportune time for many of the plaintiffs. Since the U.S. Supreme Court's decision in *Daubert v. Merrell Dow Pharmaceuticals, Inc.*, 509 U.S. 579, 173 S. Ct. 2783, 125 L. Ed. 2d 469 (1993), many silicone implant cases had fallen by the wayside for failure to produce admissible evidence from their expert witnesses. *Daubert* requires a showing of "sufficient scientific basis" for expert opinions. In June 1998, the U.S. District Court for the District of Colorado, relying in part on *Daubert*, excluded all the "causation" evidence by plaintiffs' expert witnesses in two separate silicone cases,—an exclusion which was fatal to such a case. At the appellate court level, in January 1998, the U.S. Court of Appeals for the Ninth Circuit similarly upheld a lower court's exclusion of plaintiff's expert testimony for failure to meet the *Daubert* standard.

Even more damaging to the plaintiffs was the November 1998 reliance, by a federal judge in one of the major implant class-actions, on an independent panel of experts' review of "causation" in the implant cases, which concluded that there was no scientific basis supporting such a causative relation between silicone and the alleged medical conditions. The National Science Panel, comprised of an immunologist, an epidemiologist, a toxicologist, and a rheumatologist, was independently retained by the judge (empowered under the auspices of the *Daubert* decision), to provide objective and non-biased assessment of the experts' technical evidence. The panel's findings, originally due in September, were delayed while the parties worked out their differences for the joint settlement plan. In this case, the panel's findings were released in late November 1998, a few weeks after the settlement plan had been entered with the court.

An important distinction between the breast implant class-actions and other mass-tort litigation (such as asbestos cases) is that in the implant cases, the lawsuits preceded the supportive evidence which linked the silicone to any of the alleged illnesses or diseases claimed by the thousands of litigants. In the 1980s a few medical reports hypothesized a causal relationship between silicone implants and serious autoimmune disease such as lupus and scleroderma. Once released to the press, the anecdotal reports resulted in literally thousands of lawsuits being filed by implant recipients. Later, in the 1990s, more than twenty-five independent studies by such top institutions as Harvard, University of Michigan, and the Mayo Clinic, all concluded that breast implants do not cause disease.

Notwithstanding its continued claim of innocence and non-liability, seemingly supported by a pool of authoritative evidence, Dow proceeded with the $3.2 billion settlement. In speaking to the Economic Club of Detroit in October 1998, Dow Corning Corporation's Chairman and CEO Richard A. Hazleton addressed this matter. He advised the group that each individual lawsuit was costing Dow approximately $1 million to defend, whether it won or lost. Mathematically, the settlement made sense. Moreover, the settlement would end litigation against its two shareholders, The Dow Chemical Company, and Corning, Inc.

But Dow was not the only breast implant entity to gain media coverage in 1998. In June 1998, two courts had approved terms of a revised settlement program offered by defendant implant manufacturers Bristol-Meyer, Baxter Healthcare and 3M. It was accepted by plaintiffs, and by April 1999, the Claims Office had already processed more than 80,000 payments to current claimants and other registrants who had filed proof of having at least one implant covered by the defendants plan. In that plan, claimants could choose a Fixed Amount Benefit Schedule, or a Long Term Benefit Schedule. Also in June 1998, preliminary approval was given to a class-action settlement plan in the cases involving INAMED/McGhan/CUI breast implants.

Y2K Litigation

As the clock ticked closer to January 1, 2000, an expected flood of class-action lawsuits caused by Year 2000 (Y2K) computer failures began. Most of the problems were caused by computers' traditional long-time reliance on the last two digits of a four-digit year. Some computers, upon attempting to read "00" in the year 2000, may revert back to the year 1900, causing havoc in everything from airplane schedules to bank balances. The issue first appeared in 1995 at a Warren, Michigan, gourmet market known as Produce Palace. When cashiers began processing purchases from credit cards with expiration dates ending in "00," eleven cash registers broke down. The company, in the first known Y2K lawsuit, settled for $260,000.

In May 1999, the U.S. House of Representatives, in a vote of 23–190, passed a bill to limit liability in Y2K lawsuits. Under the bill's provisions, PUNITIVE DAMAGES against companies responsible for computer breakdowns would be limited to $250,000 or three times the pecuniary loss, whichever was greater. The proposal was defeated in the Senate in early June 1999 by a 57–41 vote. However, alternative Senate proposals were expected to move ahead, despite threats of being vetoed by the White House.

The reason party politics have entered the picture is that trial lawyers, longtime supporters of the Democratic party, along with consumer groups, do not want upper limits to damages awards. Conversely, the Republican party, historically aligned with big business, has argued that without limits or ceilings to damage awards, litigation costs could reach $1 trillion—more than all tobacco, asbestos, breast implant and toxic waste damages combined. In addition, this

Mark Yarsike initiated the first Y2K lawsuit when the credit card machines at his store failed to read "00".

CARLOS OSORIO/AP/WIDE WORLD PHOTOS

type of litigation is complex because companies who are sued for not taking preventive action often draw in cross-claims and third-party defendant-manufacturers of software products, who in turn may bring in software designers, etc., ultimately dragging in customers and shareholders.

The year 1998 also saw its share of Y2K lawsuit protection devices and products flooding the market. Techno-jargon such as "Y2K readiness" became commonplace, as did products bearing labels of "Y2K compliant" warranties. In February 1998, the proposed "Examination Parity and Year 2000 Readiness for Financial Institutions Act" was introduced in the Senate. By July 1998, the Securities and Exchange Commission (SEC) had released a document providing guidance for companies filing with the SEC regarding required disclosures to the SEC of Year 2000 issues. But none of this stopped the onslaught of new class-actions being filed.

Generally, the Y2K allegations in the filed actions varied only slightly. Most alleged claims of negligence or passive negligence for failing to undertake corrective or preventive measures. Others, like the class-action suit filed in February 1998 against Symantec Corporation (*Capellan v. Symantec Corp.*), alleged that software companies were making consumers "*purchase upgrades to remedy latent product defects.*" Most claims were couched in terms of breaches of IMPLIED WARRANTIES of merchantability, violations of the Magnuson-Moss Consumer Product Warranty Act, FRAUD, and unfair business practices in addition to the NEGLIGENCE.

One of the Y2K cases which was settled in 1999—and therefore watched closely by litigation analysts, was the New York dispute between Andersen Consulting and the retailer J.Baker. The central issue of the case was Baker's demand for reimbursement of costs associated with its need to bring its computerized merchandising system into Y2K compliance. Andersen, which installed the system in 1991, filed suit for DECLATORY JUDGMENT that it had met all its obligations under the 1991 contract. Following mediation, Baker agreed that the CONTRACT terms had been met, and the suit was dropped. But an issue potentially applicable to many Y2K suits was brought into focus in this case: whether companies in 1991 should have known or even anticipated year 2000 problems, since most systems are designed with a life expectancy of five to seven years.

Another settled class-action suit was the Florida case of Tampa software maker Medical Manager Corporation., who agreed to provide Y2K compatible upgrades to its customers in return for insulation from future lawsuits.

In December, 1998, the highly-profiled company Intuit, Inc., maker of the software QUICKEN, was dismissed from a class-action suit because the judge found that the plaintiffs had not yet suffered any damages, but had only anticipated them. The company had also offered free upgrades to its customers. Similarly, in March 1999, the software giant Microsoft won a federal class-action case in Illinois, where the suit was dismissed with prejudice (*Kaczmarek v. Microsoft Corporation*). The presiding federal judge had found that the "default setting" (reading "00" as the twentieth century) had been disclosed to consumers along with the product literature. Therefore, there was no defect *per se* in the product.

One of the early 1999 Y2K class-actions involving big business was filed against Lucent Technologies, Inc. and AT&T in a New York state court. The lawsuit alleged that at least eleven product categories were affected, including "Merlin" and other call-accounting and in-house management products, various video conferencing systems, voice response and the DEFINITY wireless system. The suit also alleged that the companies had made no effort to offer repairs or upgrades.

Otherwise, the April 1999 status of some of the more majors Y2K suits was as follows. In the 1998 case of *SPC, Inc. v. Neural Tech, Inc.*, involving one of the nation's largest credit card processors against the supplier of its processing system, the parties reached an agreement on 4 November 1998, terms not being disclosed publicly.

In the July 1998 case of *Sunquest Information Systems v. Dean Witter Reynolds, Inc.*, partial dismissal was granted to defendants in March 1999 as to claims against it for breach of implied warranty, fraudulent misrepresentation and negligence. However, Sunquest was allowed to go forward with claims for IDEMNITY, breach of contract, and breach of express WARRANTY. Those claims were also pending against defendant Compucare.

The class-action lawsuit of *Qual-Craft Industries, Inc. v. RealWorld Corp.* was settled when RealWorld agreed to provide Y2K compliant modules to its clients, in addition to licensee discounts on Versions 6.0 to 7.2 of the Classic Accounting software.

CROSS REFERENCES
Bankruptcy; Scientific Evidence

CLEAVER, ELDRIDGE

Obituary notice

Born on August 31, 1935, in Wabbaseka, Arkansas; died May 1, 1998, in Pomana, California. Cleaver was an American writer and a leader of the Black Panther party, noted for advocating violent revolution within the United States. Cleaver's colorful and controversial life included a nine-year prison sentence, (during which he wrote *Soul on Ice*), a time with the Nation of Islam, an exile in Cuba, and a conversion to Christianity.

CLEMENCY

Leniency or mercy. A power given to a public official, such as a governor or the PRESIDENT, to in some way lower or moderate the harshness of punishment imposed on a prisoner.

Ohio Adult Parole Authority v. Woodard

A person who has been convicted of a crime has the right to appeal the decision through the courts. If the conviction is affirmed, the individual may request clemency from the state governor (or in the case of a federal crime, the president), seeking either a pardon or a commutation of the sentence. The governor has complete discretion to grant or deny clemency, and the decision cannot be contested in a court of law. Questions have arisen, however, as to whether a convict sentenced to death is entitled to certain constitutional protections during clemency proceedings.

The U.S. Supreme Court, in *Ohio Adult Parole Authority v. Woodard*, 523 U.S. 272, 118 S. Ct. 1244, 140 L. Ed. 2d 387 (1998), ruled that an inmate does not have a protected life or liberty interest in clemency proceedings. The Court also held that giving an inmate the option of voluntarily participating in an interview as part of the clemency process does not violate the inmate's FIFTH AMENDMENT rights. However, four members of the Court designated that there might be circumstances where a court must review clemency proceedings to insure minimal procedural safeguards have been applied.

Eugene Woodard was sentenced to death by the state of Ohio for aggravated murder committed in the course of a car jacking. The Ohio courts upheld his conviction and sentence, and forty-five days before his scheduled execution date, the state's clemency review began. The Ohio Adult Parole Authority carried out the review, which is conducted according to the

terms of Ohio law. (Ohio Revised Code Ann. § 2967.07 [1993].) The procedure for inmates under death sentence requires the authority to conduct a clemency hearing within forty-five days of the scheduled date of execution. Prior to the hearing, the inmate may request an interview with one or more parole board members. Legal counsel for the inmate is not allowed at this interview. The authority must hold the hearing, complete its clemency review, and make a recommendation to the governor, even if the inmate subsequently obtains a stay of execution. If additional information later becomes available, the Authority may in its discretion hold another hearing or alter its recommendation.

Woodard did not request an interview, objecting to the short notice of the interview and the fact that his attorney could not attend and participate in the interview and hearing. He filed suit in federal court, alleging that Ohio's clemency process violated his FOURTEENTH AMENDMENT right to due process and his Fifth Amendment right to remain silent. The district court dismissed his case, but the Sixth Circuit Court of Appeals affirmed in part and reversed in part this ruling. 107 F. 3d 1178 (6th Cir. 1997).

The appeals court agreed with the state that there was no liberty interest in clemency that gave Woodard a due process claim. However, the court held that using a due process analysis centered on the "role of clemency in the entire punitive scheme" demonstrated that Woodard's "original" life and liberty interests that he possessed before trial remained with him during the clemency process.

The court did note that the amount of due process could be minimal at the clemency stage. Finally, the court agreed with Woodard that the voluntary interview procedure was unconstitutional, because it forced him to make a choice between asserting his Fifth Amendment rights and participating in the clemency review process. Woodard had a strong interest in avoiding incrimination in ongoing postconviction proceedings, as well as with respect to possible charges for other crimes revealed during the interview.

The Supreme Court rejected the Sixth Circuit decision. Chief Justice WILLIAM H. REHNQUIST noted that a "death row inmate's petition for clemency is...a 'unilateral hope.' The defendant in effect accepts the finality of the death sentence for purposes of adjudication, and appeals for clemency as a matter of grace." There was no life or liberty interest implicated in this

Eldridge Cleaver
PAUL SAKUMA/AP/WIDE WORLD PHOTOS

process because clemency was completely dependent on the discretion of the governor. Justice Rehnquist reemphasized prior rulings of the Court that PARDON and commutation proceedings have not traditionally been the business of courts and are rarely, if ever, appropriate subjects for judicial review.

Turning to the Ohio clemency process, Rehnquist concluded that it did not violate due process. He rejected the Sixth Circuit's holding that clemency is an integral part of Ohio's system of adjudicating the guilt or innocence of a defendant, and therefore subject to due process protection. Rehnquist stated that clemency proceedings "are not part of the trial—or even of the adjudicatory process." Instead the executive branch conducted clemency proceedings "independent of direct appeal and collateral relief proceedings."

Finally, Chief Justice Rehnquist concluded that giving the inmate the option of voluntarily participating in an interview did not violate the Fifth Amendment. The Fifth Amendment protects a person against compelled self-incrimination, but nothing in the clemency process grants inmates immunity for what they might say. Woodard faced a choice similar to one made by a criminal defendant in the course of a criminal proceeding. For example, a defendant who chooses to testify in his own defense "abandons the privilege against self-incrimination when the prosecution seeks to cross-examine him." In the Ohio clemency process, Woodard had a choice of providing information—at the risk of damaging his case for clemency or for post conviction relief—or of remaining silent. The pressure on him to speak did not, however, make the interview compelled.

Justice SANDRA DAY O'CONNOR wrote a dissenting opinion, which was joined by Justices DAVID H. SOUTER, RUTH BADER GINSBURG, and STEPHEN BREYER. Justice O'Connor agreed that in Woodard's case he had failed to allege any constitutional violations, but concluded that in some circumstances the Due Process Clause of the Fourteenth Amendment could provide constitutional safeguards. Judicial intervention might be warranted, for example, "in the face of a scheme whereby a state official flipped a coin to determine whether to grant clemency, or in a case where the State arbitrarily denied a prisoner any access to its clemency process."

CROSS REFERENCES
Due Process Clause; Fourteenth Amendment; Prisoners' Rights; Testimony

COMMERCE CLAUSE

The provision of the U.S. Constitution that gives Congress exclusive power over trade activities between states and with foreign countries and Indian tribes.

Violence Against Women Act Held Unconstitutional

The Violence Against Women Act of 1994 (VAWA) (Pub. L. No. 103–322, § 40001–40703, 108 Stat. 1796, 1902–55) continued a string of victories, but suffered one major defeat, in federal courts in 1998 and 1999. Congress enacted VAWA after four years of investigation which revealed that three out of four women will be victims of violent crime in their lifetimes. From this and other statistics, CONGRESS concluded that gender motivated violence is rampant in the United States. Equally disturbing was Congress' finding that states treat crimes against women less seriously than comparable crimes against men. (S. Rep. No. 102–197 [1991]).

To fill the perceived gap in state law, one of VAWA's many sections declares, "All persons within the United States shall have the right to be free from crimes of violence motivated by gender." (42 U.S.C. § 13981(b)). A crime of violence is motivated by gender if the perpetrator commits it because of "an animus based on the victim's gender." (42 U.S.C. § 13981(d)(1)). Under VAWA, victims have the right to sue their assailants to recover both COMPENSATORY DAMAGES and PUNITIVE DAMAGES. Eleanor Smeal, president of the Feminist Majority Foundation, described VAWA as "the first major advance for women since Congress banned sex discrimination in federally funded schools in 1975."

When Congress enacts a statute, it must do so pursuant to its powers under the U.S. CONSTITUTION. Powers not specifically granted to the federal government are reserved for the states. To enact VAWA, Congress relied on article one, section 8 of the Constitution, which says, "Congress shall have Power…To regulate Commerce…among the several states." Commonly called the COMMERCE CLAUSE, it allows Congress to regulate activities that substantially affect interstate commerce, which is business that crosses state lines. Congress determined that gender-based violence has such an effect because it bars women from full participation in the national economy and deters them from engaging in employment and travel required by interstate business. This determination has been the focal point of LITIGATION concerning VAWA's constitutionality.

Defendants claim VAWA is unconstitutional because gender-based violence has nothing to do with commerce. Defendants say instead that VAWA is an exercise of the general POLICE POWER, which states use to legislate for the health, safety, and welfare of their citizens. To support this argument, defendants have relied on *United States v. Lopez*, 514 U.S. 549, 115 S. Ct. 1624, 131 L. Ed. 2d 626 (1995), in which the U.S. Supreme Court declared the Gun-Free School Zone Act of 1990 to be unconstitutional under the Commerce Clause. The Gun-Free School Zone Act of 1990 made it a federal crime to possess a gun in school areas. In *Lopez*, the United States argued that the act was constitutional because the legal and medical costs of violent crime, and the victims' reduced productivity, affect interstate commerce. The Supreme Court explained that if it accepted that argument,

> Congress could regulate any activity that it found was related to the economic productivity of individual citizens: family law (including marriage, divorce, and child custody), for example. Under the theories that the Government presents in support of [the Gun-Free School Zone Act], it is difficult to perceive any limitation on federal power, even in areas such as criminal law enforcement or education where States historically have been sovereign. Thus, if we were to accept the Government's arguments, we are hard pressed to posit any activity by an individual that Congress is without power to regulate.

The Supreme Court concluded that because the mere possession of a gun in a school zone is not economic activity and does not substantially affect interstate commerce, the Gun-Free School Zone Act of 1990 was unconstitutional.

From 1996–99, VAWA withstood similar arguments in federal district courts across the country, including in Connecticut (*Doe v. Doe*, 929 F.Supp. 608 [D. Conn. 1996]), Illinois (*Anisimov v. Lake*, 982 F.Supp. 531 [N.D.Ill. 1997]), Iowa (*Doe v. Hartz*, 970 F.Supp. 1375 [N.D. Iowa 1997]), New York (*Crisonino v. New York City Housing Authority*, 985 F.Supp. 385 [S.D.N.Y. 1997]), Tennessee (*Seaton v. Seaton*, 971 F.Supp. 1188 [E.D.Tenn. 1997]), and Washington (*Ziergler v. Ziergler*, 28 F.Supp. 2d 601 [E.D.Wash. 1998]). These courts decided that VAWA is constitutional because gender motivated violent crimes have legal and medical costs and deter participation by women in the national economy, all of which substantially affect interstate commerce.

The string of victories ended, however, in March 1999, when the U.S. Court of Appeals for the Fourth Circuit declared VAWA to be unconstitutional. (*Brzonkala v. Virginia Polytechnic Institute and State University*, 169 F. 3d 820 [4th Cir. 1999]). The plaintiff, Christy Brzonkala, was a freshman at Virginia Tech University who attended a beer party on the evening of September 21, 1994. On her way home to her dormitory with a friend, Brzonkala heard guys whistling at them from the third floor. The two young women sought their admirers, Antonio J. "Tony" Morrison and James L. Crawford, members of the school's nationally ranked football team. When small talk turned into sexual innuendo, Brzonkala's friend left. According to Brzonkala, Morrison then forced her onto his bed and the two men raped her. Afterward, Morrison told Brzonkala, "You better not have any f****** diseases." Later in the dormitory's dining hall, Morrison announced publicly, "I like to get girls drunk and f*** the s*** out of them."

Brzonkala sued her assailants under VAWA, alleging that Morrison's statements were evidence that animus against women motivated his attack. The Federal District Court for the Western District of Virginia dismissed the case on the ground that VAWA was unconstitutional. On appeal, a panel of three judges from the Fourth Circuit reversed and reinstated the case. After rehearing, however, by the entire court of eleven judges (a procedure called EN BLANC), the Fourth Circuit found VAWA to be unconstitutional in a 7–4 decision. Writing for the majority, Judge J. Michael Luttig explained that the case was a matter of FEDERALISM, the foundation of American government by which the Constitution reserves to the states any power not specifically given to the federal government:

> We the People, distrustful of power, and believing that government limited and dispersed protects freedom best, provided that our federal government would be one of enumerated powers, and that all power unenumerated would be reserved to the several States and to ourselves. Thus, though the authority conferred upon the federal government be broad, it is an authority constrained by no less a power than that of the People themselves. 'That these limits may not be mistaken, or forgotten, the constitution is written.' *Marbury v. Madison*, 5 U.S. 137, 2 L. Ed. 60

(1803). These simple truths of power bestowed and power withheld under the Constitution have never been more relevant than in this day, when accretion, if not actual accession, of power to the federal government seems not only unavoidable, but even expedient.

Relying on *Lopez*, Judge Luttig declared that under the Commerce Clause, Congress only has the power to regulate activities that substantially affect the economic or commercial activity of interstate commerce. "Not only is violent crime motivated by gender animus not itself even arguably commercial or economic, it also lacks a meaningful connection with any particular, identifiable economic enterprise or transaction." Like the Court in *Lopez*, Judge Luttig rejected the argument that the medical, legal, transportation, and productivity effects of violent crime substantially affect interstate commerce. According to Judge Luttig, accepting that argument would "eliminate all limits on federal power" and "would arrogate to the federal government control of every area of activity that matters, reserving to the States authority over only the trivial and the insignificant."

Writing for the dissent, Judge Diana Gribbon Motz accused the majority of ignoring overwhelming congressional evidence, particularly testimony that domestic violence alone costs $8 to $15 billion annually in health care, law enforcement, and lost wages.

Pending appeal to the U.S. Supreme Court, which is likely, *Brzonkala* is binding in Virginia, West Virginia, Maryland, North Carolina, and South Carolina, the area covered by the Fourth Circuit. VAWA, however, remains in force elsewhere. A federal court in New York, the first federal district court to consider VAWA after *Brzonkala* rejected the Fourth Circuit's holding. In *Ericson v. Syracuse University*, No. 98 Civ 3435-JSR (S.D.N.Y. April 13, 1999), a case that settled out of court, Judge Jed S. Rakoff explained his pre-settlement ruling that VAWA is constitutional:

> Unlike the mere threat of violence involved in the Gun-Free School Zones Act overturned in *Lopez*, [VAWA] deals with actual acts of gender-based violence, whose impact on interstate commerce, though indirect, is far from remote or speculative…Where the states fail to exercise their police power to combat a form of antisocial activity—violence against women—that also

negatively impacts interstate commerce, the federal government need not likewise default but may instead seek to remedy these indirect but substantial injuries to the functioning of the national economy.

CROSS REFERENCES
Sex Discrimination; Women's Rights

CONTEMPT

An act of deliberate disobedience or disregard for the laws, regulations, or decorum of a public authority, such as a court of legislative body.

President Clinton Held In Contempt Of Court

In April 1999, a federal judge found President BILL CLINTON in contempt of court for lying about his relationship with White House intern Monica S. Lewinsky during his deposition in the SEXUAL HARASSMENT lawsuit brought by Paula C. Jones. *Jones v. Clinton*, 36 F.Supp. 2d 1118 (E.D.Ark. 1999).

In her lawsuit, Jones alleged that Clinton made unwanted sexual advances in a hotel room in Little Rock, Arkansas, in 1991, while he was governor of Arkansas and she was a state employee. Prior to Clinton's DEPOSITION in January 1998, U.S. District Judge SUSAN WEBBER WRIGHT ruled that Jones had a right to know about every state or federal employee with whom Clinton had sexual relations while governor of Arkansas or president of the United States. In an interrogatory response in December 1997, Clinton denied having any such relations. In affidavits filed shortly thereafter, Monica Lewinsky denied having sexual relations with the president.

At Clinton's deposition, which Judge Wright attended at Clinton's request, Jones's lawyers asked about his relationship with Lewinsky. For purposes of the deposition, Judge Wright approved the following definition: "a person engages in 'sexual relations' when the person knowingly engages in or causes … contact with the genitalia, anus, groin, breast, inner thigh, or buttocks of any person with an intent to arouse or gratify the sexual desire of any person. … 'Contact' means intentional touching, either directly or through clothing." Clinton testified under OATH that he did not remember being alone with Lewinsky except for a few moments on one or two occasions when she brought papers and a pizza to him in the White House.

Clinton also testified that he did not have an "extramarital sexual affair," "sexual relations," or a "sexual relationship" with Lewinsky.

Shortly after the deposition, Judge Wright dismissed Jones's lawsuit on the ground that even if Clinton did what Jones alleged, it did not amount to sexual harassment under the law. *Jones v. Clinton*, 990 F.Supp. 657 (E.D.Ark. 1998). Jones filed an appeal. Meanwhile, Independent Counsel KENNETH W. STARR began investigating whether Clinton lied during his January 1998 deposition in *Jones*. Clinton maintained his innocence, declaring to reporters and the American public, "I did not have sexual relations with that woman, Miss Lewinsky." Lewinsky, however, ultimately testified before Starr's GRAND JURY that she did have a sexual relationship with Clinton.

Under pressure to come forward with the truth, Clinton testified before the grand jury on August 17, 1998. There he admitted to being alone with Lewinsky on as many as five to ten occasions. He also admitted to having "inappropriate intimate contact" with Lewinsky a few times in early 1996 and once in early 1997. While he would not give details, Clinton testified that he tried to hide the activity from others because he would have been an "exhibitionist" not to have concealed the activity. Clinton insisted that his answers at his January 1998 deposition had been legally accurate under Judge Wright's definition of sexual relations. In a television appearance after his TESTIMONY, however, Clinton admitted that he misled people about his relationship with Lewinsky because he believed Starr and others were using his personal conduct for political gain.

Amid IMPEACHMENT proceedings in November 1998, Jones dropped her appeal after Clinton agreed to settle the case for $850,000. After the impeachment trial in the Senate ended in Clinton's favor, Judge Wright issued an order on April 12, 1999, holding Clinton in contempt of court for "giving false, misleading and evasive answers that were designed to obstruct the judicial process" during his January 1998 deposition. In her thirty-two page opinion, Judge Wright recognized that no court had ever found a president to be in contempt, but decided there was no constitutional impediment to doing so. In *Jones*, the U.S. Supreme Court ruled that a sitting president can be sued in a civil action for his unofficial conduct. *Jones v. Clinton*, 520 U.S. 681, 117 S. Ct. 1636, 137 L. Ed. 2d 945 (1997). Judge Wright reasoned that "the power to determine the legality of the President's unofficial conduct includes with it the power to issue civil contempt citations and impose sanctions for his unofficial conduct which abuses the judicial process."

To find Clinton in contempt, Judge Wright needed clear and convincing evidence that Clinton violated an order that was clear and reasonably specific. On two occasions, once in December 1997 and once at the January 1998 deposition, Judge Wright ruled that Jones was entitled to all information about state or federal employees with whom Clinton had sexual relations while governor of Arkansas or president of the United States. Judge Wright found that Clinton violated these orders during his deposition by claiming to be alone with Lewinsky only twice, and by denying that he had sexual relations with Lewinsky. Judge Wright rejected Clinton's use of "tortured definitions and interpretations of the term 'sexual relations'" to claim that his answers were legally accurate.

Judge Wright decided that sanctions against Clinton were necessary "to deter others who might themselves consider emulating the President of the United States by engaging in misconduct that undermines the integrity of the judicial system." She ordered Clinton to pay Jones's reasonable legal expenses caused by his false testimony. She also ordered Clinton to reimburse the court for its travel expenses to attend the January 1998 deposition as a referee. Finally, Judge Wright referred the matter to the Arkansas Supreme Court's Committee on Professional Conduct, which could revoke Clinton's license to practice law in Arkansas.

While legal experts questioned Judge Wright's power to issue a contempt citation in a case that is settled and over, President Clinton decided not to appeal the decision unless he is ordered to pay an unreasonable amount to cover Jones's legal expenses. Although they originally estimated those expenses to amount to tens of thousands of dollars, on May 8, 1999, Jones's lawyers asked Clinton to pay over $496,000. ROBERT S. BENNETT, Clinton's lawyer, called the request "unreasonable, greedy, and contrary to law." Clinton instead offered to pay $33,737. Judge Wright resolved the dispute in July 1999 by ordering Clinton to pay $90,686, which included $1,202 for court expenses and the remainder for Jones's legal representation. Clinton paid the fines from his legal defense fund and decided not to appeal.

CROSS REFERENCES

Clinton, William J.; Impeachment; Starr, Kenneth W.; Wright, Susan Webber

COPYRIGHT

An intangible right granted by statute to the author or originator of certain literary or artistic productions, whereby, for a limited perod, the exclusive privilege is given to the person to make copies of the same for publication or sale.

Digital Millennium Copyright Act

On October 28, 1998, President BILL CLINTON signed the Digital Millennium Copyright Act (DMCA), (§ 2037) into law following a 99–0 vote in the U.S. Senate. This legislation was the focus of intense lobbying efforts on the part of a wide range of interest groups because it was the most significant copyright update in twenty years. These groups included telecommunications companies and online service providers, consumer electronics manufacturers, library, museum and university groups, and the publishing, recording, film, and software industries. The primary goal of this legislation was to adapt U.S. copyright laws for the digital age.

Passage of the DMCA was also required for the United States to keep pace with changes in international copyright treaties. In December 1996, the World Intellectual Property Organization (WIPO), an agency of the United Nations, negotiated the Copyright Treaty and the Performances and Phonograms Treaty at a meeting in Geneva, Switzerland. The WIPO is responsible for the advancement and safeguarding of intellectual property throughout the world, and it has 170 member countries.

Once ratified by a consensus of member organizations, these treaties will provide increased protection for copyrighted materials in the digital world. By signing, each country agrees to put into place laws, based on their own legal system, to enforce the treaties. The DMCA serves that purpose for the United States.

The DMCA has five main sections: WIPO Treaties Implementation, Online Copyright Infringement Liability Limitation, Computer Maintenance or Repair Copyright Exemption, Miscellaneous Provisions, and Protection of Certain Original Designs. Title I, WIPO Treaties Implementation, contains an "anti-circumvention" provision making it illegal to "manufacture, import, offer to the public, provide, or otherwise traffic in any technology, product, service, device, component, or part thereof," for the primary purpose of "circumventing a technological measure that effectively controls access to" a copyrighted work. Thus,

technologies designed to protect digital material are safeguarded.

Moreover, this provision makes the act of circumventing a "technological measure that effectively controls access to a work protected" by copyright illegal. There is a two-year grace period through October 28, 2000, before this portion of the provision takes effect. At the end of the two years, and every three years after that, the librarian of Congress, the register of Copyrights and the assistant secretary for Communications and Information of the Department of Commerce must determine if people with legitimate noninfringing uses of copyrighted materials are being unfavorably affected by the law. The law does state that fair use is not affected, but this nevertheless proved to be a controversial provision. Libraries, museums and scholars were concerned about digital materials only being available on a pay-per-use basis. An exemption was included for nonprofit libraries, archives, and educational institutions allowing them to circumvent for the purpose of determining whether or not to purchase the copyrighted work.

Title I of the DMCA also contains another addition to U.S. copyright law required by the WIPO treaties. This section prohibits the deletion or alteration of information associated with copyrighted material. Organizations will benefit from this provision because it will help protect information and images on their websites. Furthermore, it prohibits the distribution of false copyright management information (author, title, owner, copyright notice, identifying numbers, etc.). The DMCA provides for civil and criminal enforcement. However, archives, schools, nonprofit libraries and public broadcasting stations are exempt from criminal prosecution.

The DMCA also limits the liability for copyright infringement by providing safe harbors for online service providers. The definition of an online service provider for the purposes of the law is generous. Other organizations may qualify for protection, which could be useful if they provide Internet access, have a company bulletin board or intracompany email, or chat rooms. Prior to the DMCA, online service providers could have been liable if infringing materials were posted on their site even if they were unaware of the problem. The DMCA explains the responsibilities of copyright owners and service providers. Under specific conditions service providers are exempt from having to pay monetary damages as long as they are not benefiting financially from the infringing activity and they remove the material promptly from the Internet.

Limitations have also been set on exclusive rights for computer programs. This provision allows computer owners to copy programs needed to maintain and repair the machine. Any such copies must be destroyed as soon as the machine is repaired.

A "miscellaneous provisions" section of the law sets limitations on exclusive rights for distance education, as well as furnishing an exemption for libraries and archives and defining exclusive rights for sound and ephemeral recordings. The register of Copyrights was required to consult with "representatives of copyright owners, nonprofit educational institutions, and nonprofit libraries and archives" by April 28, 1999. Recommendations were submitted to Congress "on how to promote distance education through digital technologies, including interactive digital networks, while maintaining an appropriate balance between the rights of copyright owners and the needs of users of copyrighted works."

A significant exemption for libraries and archives was included in Title IV of the DMCA. Up to three copies can now be made of a copyrighted work without the permission of the copyright owner for research use in other libraries or archives through interlibrary loan. The word "facsimile" has been struck from the former copyright law allowing for digital formats. Libraries and archives can now loan digital copies of works to other libraries and archives by electronic means. This is important because digital formats are increasingly utilized to store our cultural heritage. Copies for preservation and security purposes are also permitted when the existing format the material is stored in becomes outdated, or if the work is lost, stolen, damaged or deteriorating.

Title IV also established guidelines for licensing and royalties in regard to copyrighted music transmitted over the internet and in other digital forms. Transmissions are not subject to licensing if transmitted with encoded copyright information and with permission from the copyright owner of the sound recording.

The final section of the DMCA is known as the "Vessel Hull Design Protection Act". This provides copyright protection to the owners of original boat hull designs for a term of ten years. Protection is lost if the owner does not apply for registration of the design within two years of the date it is made public.

Passage of the DMCA made it possible for the U.S. Senate to ratify the WIPO Copyright Treaty and the Performances and Phonograms Treaty. This is expected to pave the way for other countries to follow suit. Interested groups will continue to monitor the anti-circumvention provision closely. Computer technology is evolving so quickly that it is conceivable that devices prohibited by this provision will eventually be necessary to gain access to material in order to preserve it in new formats.

Sonny Bono Copyright Term Extension Act

The most significant revision in U.S. copyright law in twenty years occurred on October 27, 1998, when President BILL CLINTON signed into law the Sonny Bono Copyright Term Extension Act, (PL 105–298). The law essentially adds twenty years of copyright protection to existing and newly copyrighted materials. Title I defines the terms of copyright extension while Title II of the law provides a "music licensing exemption for food service or drinking establishments." This portion of the law is also known as the "Fairness In Music Licensing Act of 1998."

The duration of copyright has been extended for all currently copyrighted materials. Works created on January 1, 1978, or after are protected from the time the work was "fixed in a tangible medium of expression." The term is for life of the creator plus 70 years. If the creator is a corporation then the term is 95 years from publication or 120 years from the date of creation, whichever is shorter.

Works published from 1923–63 are protected if they were published with notice. If published with notice, the works are protected for 28 years and can be renewed for 67 years. If not renewed, they are in the PUBLIC DOMAIN. Materials published during this period without notice went in to the public domain upon publication.

Items published from 1964–77 are protected if they were published with notice. They are protected for 28 years and the copyright is now automatically extended for 67 years. Works created before January 1, 1978, but not published, are protected for the life of the creator plus 70 years or until December 31, 2002, whichever is greater. Materials created before January 1, 1978, but published between then and December 31, 2002, are protected for the life of the creator plus 70 years or until December 31, 2047, whichever is greater.

Materials published prior to 1923 are still in the public domain, which means that anyone

ARE STUN BELTS CRUEL AND UNUSUAL PUNISHMENT?

Should prisoners be forced to wear belts that can zap them with 50,000 volts of electricity if they misbehave? That question lies at the heart of the debate over electro-shock stun belts, the controversial high-tech restraining devices increasingly used in U.S. prisons and courtrooms during the late 1990s. Operated by remote control, the belts stun, and can temporarily paralyze, their wearer with an excruciatingly painful electric discharge. Proponents within industry and law enforcement say the technology helps prison, court and police officers do their job more effectively and safely. But civil liberties groups call the devices barbaric, warn that they can be used for torture, and argue that their use by authorities violates the U.S. Constitution's ban on cruel and unusual punishment as well as international human rights treaties. In 1999, these arguments came to a head in a much-covered federal lawsuit that produced a temporary ban on the belts in Los Angeles County.

Although seemingly lifted from the pages of science fiction, stun belts first appeared in the late 1980s. They were the technological descendants of stun guns and tasers—the high-voltage electric guns developed earlier in that decade to allow police to subdue suspects without firing bullets. Using a taser, an officer can temporarily paralyze a suspect with electric current.

Stun belts work on the same principle, but are worn by a prisoner and operated by an official via remote control. A leading stun belt, the R.E.A.C.T. (Remote Electronically Activated Control Technology), manufactured by Cleveland, Ohio-based Stun Tech, is attached around a prisoner's waist and connected to a portable battery. Once activated, it sends a 50,000-volt, 4-milliamp charge through the wearer's body for up to eight seconds. Prisoners typically scream in pain, collapse, convulse, and can remain incapacitated for as long as fifteen minutes. Describing the experience in court documents, one prisoner said it was "as if a long needle had been inserted up through [my] spine and into the base of [my] skull."

IN FOCUS

Law enforcement officials have embraced the technology. Since its introduction, the number of facilities using belts has increased dramatically as officials have recognized how effectively it works. Not only does the technology reliably achieve the desired physical results, they say, but it also reportedly has sharp psychological effects on prisoners, who resist misbehavior out of fear of being zapped. In 1994, recognizing this usefulness, the federal Bureau of Prisons placed large orders for stun belts in order to protect its personnel from violent prisoners and help ensure against escapes. Proponents even praise the belt for protecting prisoners. Police officers

told the NBC news program *Dateline* in June 1999 that the belt prevents them from having to resort to shooting with their guns. By that summer, an estimated 130 jurisdictions in all but three states used stun belts, and while originally they were employed only in medium and high-security prisons, they now commonly appeared on prison chain gangs of low-risk inmates and on prisoners in courtrooms.

Critics denounce the belt for a number of reasons. Their case against the technology ranges from the reliability of stun belts to their physical dangers, their capability for abuse, and the deprivation of civil liberties which wearers undergo. In a 1996 article, *The Progressive* noted the propensity of stun belts to go off accidentally despite their manufacturer's claim that the chance of a misfire due to radio interference was one in twenty-six million. The magazine cited criminal trials in 1994 and 1996 in which prisoners forced to wear stun belts were accidentally shocked a total of three times. Although the manufacturer insisted the misfirings were due to operator error, critics say no one should be subject to mistaken electrocution.

Both sides dispute the health risks of stunning. According to a 1990 study by the British Forensic Science Service, the devices can cause heart disease or even failure. Proponents are quick to point out that nobody has died from wearing a stun belt, and that guards themselves

is free to utilize them. Nobody can claim exclusive rights to works in the public domain, of which there are three types: "works on which the copyright has expired, works on which there was no claim of copyright and works published by the federal government." There are no use restrictions on works in the public domain, and no permission is required. Therefore, they are very useful to the scholarly and research communities.

Libraries, archives, museums, and scholars expressed concerns about the twenty-year extension. Items created in 1923 would have passed into the public domain on January 1, 1999, if the law had not been changed. At the beginning of the year 2000 works created in 1924 would have fallen under the pubic domain and so on and so forth. Members of the above mentioned groups argued that original scholarly research would be hampered by the extension.

In answer to those concerns, a special clause was included in the Copyright Term Extension Act for libraries, archives, and nonprofit educational institutions. Such institutions are permit-

regularly undergo voluntary shocks as part of their training. A promotional video from Stun Tech shows guards yelping and thrashing as they are zapped. In reply, critics point to the 1995 death of Texas corrections officer Harry Landis, who died will being shocked with 45,000 volts during training with a related technology, the stun shield. And even though manufacturers worn against using the devices on prisoners who have heart problems, doctors note that arrhythmia—a potentially dangerous irregular heartbeat that is caused when the electrical system cells of the heart malfunction—often occurs in people with healthy hearts. Moreover, there are no scientific, peer-reviewed studies of stun belt safety, the only assurance available is from the manufacturer, which had a similar stun technology tested on anesthetized pigs.

Civil liberties groups have decried the belt's capacity for abuse. In particular, Amnesty International and the American Civil Liberties Union (ACLU) have argued that the belt can be used not merely for deterrence but as punishment. The former issued a scathing report in June 1999 entitled "Cruelty in Control? The Stun Belt and Other Electro-Shock Equipment in Law Enforcement," placing the belt in the context of a quarter century of electric torture in world prisons and urging an immediate ban on its use. "The USA's growing use of high-tech stun weapons dangerously blurs the line between torture and legitimate prisoner control techniques," the human rights group concluded. Agreeing with the report, Elizabeth Alexander, director of the

ACLU's National Prison Project, called the belt "a clear opening for abuse" in prison settings.

In defense of the belt, proponents argue that it was never intended to be used punitively. "The belt is not to be used for punishment," Dennis Kaufman, president of Stun Tech, Inc., told the *New York Times*, in June 1999. "If it is, consequently it is clearly a violation of civil rights as well as a violation of what the belt was designed for." The American Correctional Association, a trade organization for corrections employees, asserted that there was no evidence of the devices being used abusively.

In mid-1998, in Long Beach, California, these arguments crystallized in the disturbing case of Ronnie Hawkins. While acting as his own attorney at a sentencing hearing in municipal court, Hawkins, a forty-eight-year old felon who had been forced to wear a stun belt, angered Judge Joan Comparet-Cassani by making repeated interruptions. After being warned, Hawkins protested that stunning him would be unconstitutional. Judge Comparet-Cassani then ordered the device activated, and Hawkins was zapped. Later, he filed a federal lawsuit against the judge, Los Angeles municipal and Superior Courts, and the County of Los Angeles, which sought, among other things, a CLASS ACTION INJUNCTION against the county to prevent it from using the stun belt against its prisoners. The lawsuit alleged that merely being forced to wear the belt amounted to an unconstitutional form of cruel and unusual punishment. Essentially any form of torture, barbarity or degradation

meted out by government employees, cruel and unusual punishment is barred by the EIGHTH AND FOURTEENTH AMENDMENTS as well as most state constitutions.

Although the judge was dismissed as a defendant, Hawkins won an early round in the rest of his suit in January 1999. Federal Judge Dean Pregerson of the Central District of California issued a preliminary order banning use of the belt in Los Angeles courtrooms. Judge Pregerson's ruling held that the belt, "even if not activated, has the potential of compromising the defense." Its mere presence on a defendant's body could keep the wearer from exercising his or her rights in court out of fear, the ruling said. Even worse was the impact on a defendant who was shocked. It would be unreasonable to expect such a defendant to meaningfully participate in the preceding after the shock, for fear that even appropriate conduct could lead to more shocks.

Expected to be decided some time in 1999, Hawkins' case brought greater national attention to stun belts. The legal future of the technology remained uncertain, but moral debate over its usage was waged in many quarters. As proponents continued to hail the utilitarian advantages of stun belts while minimizing the potential for abuse, civil libertarians observed that only one other country in the world was currently using the devices—South Africa, a nation with a long history of prison torture.

CROSS REFERENCES
Eighth Amendment; Prisons

---

ted to "reproduce, distribute, display, or perform in facsimile or digital form" a copy of any copyrighted, published work during the last 20 years of its term "for purposes of preservation, scholarship, or research. However, the work cannot be used in such a manner if it "can be obtained at a reasonable price".

These changes in the copyright law were made partly to keep pace with the evolution of European copyright laws. In 1995, Europe extended its copyright protection to life of the creator plus 70 years, but in the United States it

remained life of the creator plus 50 years. The United States and other member nations adhere to an 1886 international treaty, which requires them to "honor the copyright protections of foreign works sold and used commercially in their countries." Without the act, materials created in the United States would have passed into the public domain earlier than similar works created in foreign nations at the same time.

The term of copyright has substantially increased since the first U.S. copyright law was enacted in 1790. At that time copyright was granted for 14 years with an optional 14-year renewal. In 1909 copyright was extended to 28 years with an optional 28-year renewal. Finally, in 1976, in response to changes in European copyright law, the United States extended copyright to life of the creator plus 50 years.

Copyright and licensing issues relating to musical performances were addressed by the "Fairness In Music Licensing Act", the second portion of the law. Concerns expressed by individual proprietors about the licensing practices of performing rights societies such as the American Society of Composers, Authors and Publishers and Broadcast Music, Inc. prompted this legislation. The law grants an exemption for individual proprietors who own seven or less establishments that wish to have public performances of non-dramatic musical works. Proprietors who have a complaint about a licensing fee charged by a performing rights society can now dispute the fee and apply for a reduction. The judge has the option to appoint a special master to hear the complaint, and during this process, the individual proprietor pays an interim licensing fee based on the industry rate. This fee is placed in an interest bearing escrow account and may be adjusted later depending on the judgement.

Additional exemptions are provided for business owners, and the "Fairness In Music Licensing Act" includes businesses other than food and drinking establishments. The exemptions apply only for businesses with less than 2,000 square feet or those that have six or less speakers and four or less televisions. Moreover, there cannot be more than one television or four speakers in any given room or outdoor area. Food and drinking establishments may also qualify for the exemption if they meet the same restrictions or have less than 3,750 square feet. None of the televisions may have a screen larger than 55 inches diagonally, and the establishment may not charge a fee or retransmit the performance to another facility.

CROSS REFERENCES
International Law

CROCKETT, GEORGE W., JR.

Obituary notice

Born on August 10, 1909, in Jacksonville, Florida; died September 7, 1997, in Washington, D.C. Crockett compiled a long and often controversial record as a defender of civil liberties, personal rights, and unpopular causes. Crockett went to Washington, D.C., in 1939 as the first African American lawyer to work for the U.S. Department of Labor. He quickly rose to become the highest ranking black lawyer in the federal government. Crockett was considered the finest expert on the Constitution to serve on the Detroit bench. He served ten years in the U.S. House of Representatives, representing Michigan's Thirteenth Congressional District.

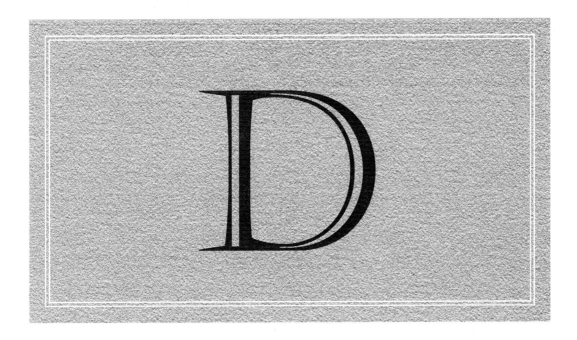

DALEY, RICHARD M.

Richard M. Daley is the mayor of Chicago, Illinois. The oldest of seven children, Daley's father was the controversial Richard J. Daley, who was Chicago's mayor from 1955 until his death in 1976. Throughout his public life, Daley struggled to separate himself from his father's identity and legacy and establish himself. In the 1990s, even Daley's detractors had to admit that Daley had accomplished the task through hard work and perseverance.

Daley was raised in the working-class Chicago neighborhood of Bridgeport by his father and his mother, Eleanor. After a stint in the Marine reserves from 1960 to 1964, Daley attended De Paul University law school, the same law school that his father attended. Daley did not pass the bar exam until his third attempt. After obtaining his license to practice law, Daley entered public life.

Daley's first public position came in 1970 when he was elected to the Illinois Constitutional Convention, which set about the task of re-writing the state constitution. In 1972, Daley was elected to the Illinois legislature as a state senator. Daley stayed in the state senate until 1980, when he ran for state's attorney general for Cook County (which encompasses the city of Chicago) and won. Daley served as the top prosecutor in Cook County until 1989, when he won the mayor's seat in a special election after the death of Harold Washington, who had beaten Daley in the previous mayoral election.

Although is father was the most influential man in Chicago for many years, the young Da-

ley was by no means predestined for the mayor's office. Daley tried to unseat Washington in 1983, but he finished behind Washington and incumbent mayor Jane Byrne in the Democratic primaries. Only after several years in office as mayor of Chicago has Daley earned city-wide respect and a national reputation for his accomplishments.

Daley has lived much of his political life in the shadow of his father. The senior Daley was a powerful figure who controlled Chicago politics with an iron fist. The senior Daley played an important part in the election of JOHN F. KENNEDY to the presidency in 1960 when he backed Kennedy, which helped Kennedy to win the sizable number of electoral votes in Illinois. Ever hungry for political power, the senior Daley lured the Democratic party to Chicago for its 1968 presidential nomination convention. What resulted still haunts the city. During the convention, anti-war protesters converged on Chicago by the thousands, and the Chicago police department responded with force that left hundreds of protesters beaten and bloody. The senior Daley spent much of his remaining time in office trying to live down the violence that occurred during the convention.

The young Richard Daley also wanted to escape the legacy left by the bloody convention. In 1996 Chicago again played host to the Democratic presidential nomination convention, this time without incident. *American City & County*, reported that Daley, at a press conference after the convention, became emotional and seemed to be saying "Dad, I did it right." In 1997, Daley was named Municipal Leader of the Year by *American City & Country*.

Richard M. Daley
OLIVER FANTITSCH/AP/WIDE WORLD PHOTOS

RICHARD M. DALEY

1942 Born in Chicago, Illinois

1972 Elected Illinois state senator

1980 Elected state's attorney general for Cook County

1989 Elected mayor of Chicago

1996 Hosted Democratic national convention in Chicago

Daley's success is by no means defined by a violence-free presidential nomination convention. Daley has gained his favorable reputation by running a practical, hands-on mayor's office. Daley does not run Chicago in the same way that his father did. While his father enjoyed hoarding political power, the younger Daley is more flexible, opting to spread power around the city as a way of solidifying his own position as mayor.

Daley has placed tremendous emphasis on the physical appearance of Chicago. He is credited with beautifying Chicago by planting half a million trees around the city during his first seven years as mayor. On his regular walks through Chicago neighborhoods, Daley points out potholes, stray garbage bags, and dirty windows and personally orders city workers to remedy the problems. Daley once sent his personal security guards to arrest a person spraying graffiti.

Restoring Chicago's beauty is only one of Daley's missions. Daley is concerned about the plight of the urban poor and discrimination against minorities. Although he does not enjoy overwhelming support in Chicago's African American communities, respect for Daley's work is increasing. Daley has brought many minorities into the city government, rehabilitated many public housing projects, and he has been instrumental in balancing the financial budgets of the public schools. Daley has bulked up the city's police force and promoted aggressive policing in an attempt to thwart the city's violent gangs. Daley also began a campaign in 1997 to make Chicago an economically attractive home for computer industry companies. Library users applaud Daley's efforts to improve Chicago's library system by infusing it with increased funds. Daley has supported the opening of li-braries on Sundays. "On Sunday afternoon, instead of watching football games," Daley told *Library Journal*, "maybe some people will venture to a library to read to their child."

Daley's stint as mayor has not been without controversy. In 1993, Daley and his wife Maggie moved from their house in Daley's home neighborhood of Bridgeport to a town house on Lake Michigan, near the Loop in downtown Chicago. To some political observers, the move seemed to be symbolically hypocritical because Daley was trying to revitalize ailing Chicago neighborhoods such as Bridgeport. A less symbolic, more immediate problem emerged a few years later, when the Federal Bureau of Investigation and the U.S. Department of Justice began a probe into the mayor's office on suspicion of illegal favoritism. Investigators probed allegations that the mayor's office directed too much city business to the law firm of Daley and George, Ltd., which is headed by Daley's younger brother Michael and by John George, a close friend.

Daley met his wife Maggie at a Christmas party in 1970 and married her in spring of 1972. Maggie is credited by many for softening Daley's rough edges and taming his abrasive personality. They have three children: Nora, born in 1973, who works in the insurance field; Patrick, born in 1975, who studied at the University of San Diego, and Elizabeth, born in 1984. A fourth child, Kevin, died in 1981 at the age of 2 from spina bifida. Daley enjoys riding horses and bikes, watching movies, and country western-style line dancing. He is also a die-hard, long-suffering fan of the White Sox.

Daley was raised Catholic and was an altar boy at the Nativity of Our Lord Catholic Church. Daley has, according to Steven R. Strahler of *Crain's Chicago Business*, "A guy-next-door persona" who "sputter[s] away with a fractured language that resonates in bungalows and boardrooms alike." Walter Jacobson, a political commentator in Chicago, told *People Weekly* that the elder Daley was "an old-time pol, the ultimate Windy City brawler," while the younger Daley "is more into government than politics. The city works."

CROSS REFERENCES
Due Process

DEFAMATION

Any intentional false communication, either written or spoken, that harms a person's reputation; decreases the respect, regard or confidence in which a person is held; or induces disparaging, hostile, or disagreeable opinions or feelings against a person.

Tawana Brawley Case

The Tawana Brawley case began on November 24, 1987. That day, Brawley, a fifteen year-old African-American girl, disappeared from her home in Wappingers Falls, New York. Four days later, Brawley emerged from a large plastic bag near an apartment complex where she once lived. She was smeared with dog feces and she had "KKK" and "NIGGER" written on her stomach. Brawley claimed to have been abducted and held for four days in the woods by a gang of white law enforcement officers, all of whom took turns raping her repeatedly. However, a witness at the apartment complex reported seeing Brawley stuff herself inside the plastic bag. The incident quickly went from a minor incident to a legal and political cottage industry.

According to *Time* magazine Lance Morrow said, "[a]s lies go, it wasn't a very good one. To anyone who ever raised a child, Tawana's story had the unmistakable ring of a whopper." After investigating and hearing TESTIMONY on the incident, a GRAND JURY in New York agreed, concluding in 1988 that Brawley had simply made up the story to explain her long absence to her stepfather. The facts indicated that Brawley was not injured or malnourished when she was found, she was not suffering from exposure, and that there were no signs of RAPE. Brawley apparently had recently brushed her teeth and washed her jean jacket in the laundry room of the apartment complex.

The matter attracted three social activists, Reverend Al Sharpton, Alton H. Maddox, Jr., and C. Vernon Mason. The three became Brawley's most vocal supporters and, as her "advisers," they railed against what they saw as a cover-up by police and prosecutors. One person they singled out for especially harsh criticism was a white Dutchess County assistant district attorney, Steven Pagones. Brawley's advisers publicly insisted that Pagones might have had some involvement in the attack on Brawley. Reverend Sharpton, for example, appeared on Richard Bey's television talk show and said "[w]e stated openly that Steven Pagones, the assistant district attorney, did it. His lawyers say he may or may not sue us. If we're lying, sue us, so we can go into court with you and prove you did it."

Pagones found his life in a shambles. His reputation was damaged, he developed an ulcer,

Steven Pagones won his defamation suit against Tawana Brawley, Reverend Al Sharpton, Alton H. Maddox, Jr., and C. Vernon Mason.

RICHARD HARBUS/AP/WIDE WORLD PHOTOS

and he had to hire security guards for his wedding. Pagones eventually filed a defamation suit against Brawley, Sharpton, Maddox, and Mason on October 31, 1988, asking for $395 million. Pagones accused Sharpton, Maddox, and Mason of uttering twenty-two defamatory statements. Brawley never appeared for the case, and she lost by default in May 1991. The case against Sharpton, Maddox, and Mason went to trial.

Sharpton, who maintained aspirations for political office, argued that he reasonably believed his statements to be true. Maddox and Mason were less yielding, arguing as they did that it was actually true that Pagones had raped Brawley. Jackson and Mason felt that Pagones should have answered the charges and submitted to an investigation. Mason's lawyer, Stephen Jackson, declared to the jury that "[i]t is incredible in this day and age, people can get away with things like that. And what is more incredible is that he actually sued. He's lucky he is not in jail. Don't let him get away with it." Attorneys for Pagones compared the three advisers to Joseph Goebbels, the Nazi propagandist who advocated the notion that a lie can become true if it is repeated often enough.

On July 13, 1998, after nearly ten years of legal wrangling, the jury came back with a partial victory for Pagones. By a vote of 5–1, the jury, comprised of four whites and two blacks, found that Sharpton, Maddox, and Mason were liable for ten of the twenty-two statements that Pagones had claimed were defamatory. Pagones was upbeat after the verdict. "What Mason, Maddox, and Sharpton did hurt a lot of people," Pagones said. "They hurt race relations." Sharpton declared the verdict a victory and vowed that the verdict would be turned around faster than "James Brown on the stage at the Apollo." Maddox maintained that the verdict showed that "[t]he main thing here, was that [Brawley's abduction] was not a hoax." Sharpton agreed, saying "I didn't believe it to be a hoax then, and I don't believe it to be a hoax now."

One matter remained in the case, and that was the amount of DAMAGES due to Pagones. William E. Stanton, a lawyer for Pagones, had asked the jury for a large award to "shut them up," but Pagones had testified that he did not want to destroy the defendants, and the jurors took him at his word. The jurors, who were never told exactly how much Pagones was asking for, ordered Brawley's advisers to pay $345,000, the amount that Pagones spent to take the three to court. A subdued Pagones said that "[t]he jury put this case to rest." Mason ended up hugging Pagones and declaring that "[w]e have fought the good fight." Maddox displayed no such largesse and proclaimed that "[t]his was the greatest comeback in American jurisprudence. Pagones was looking for $395 million and we ended up getting only a slap on the wrist."

Jurors later expressed surprise at the amount of damages originally sought by Pagones. But, as one juror put it, "Steve said it himself: he didn't want to hurt these guys." The jurors tried to keep their focus on the defamation case. "Steve Pagones did not do it," said juror Glen Heinsohn. "That was the overriding fact here. Was Tawana abducted? We don't know." In October 1998, Justice S. Barrett Hickman ordered Brawley to pay $185,000 in damages to Pagones for "perpetuating a lie." In his opinion, Justice Hickman wrote that "[i]t is probable that in the history of this state, never has a teenager turned the prosecutorial and judicial systems literally upside down with such false claims."

DISABLED PERSONS

Dentist Refuses to Treat HIV Patient in Office

Since the Americans with Disabilities Act (ADA) was enacted in 1990, more than 100,000 lawsuits have been filed under its auspices around the nation. The act is essentially a civil rights law which prohibits discrimination of any individual on the basis of disability, primarily in the enjoyment or use of services of any public place of accommodation or in an employment setting. According to the EEOC, 50 percent of the cases filed are dismissed or rejected for fail-

ure to establish cause or grounds for suit. On review of these statistics, it would appear that persons alleging protection under the act were either not qualifiedly disabled, or, if they were disabled and had experienced adverse action, it was not premised upon their disability.

But the high rejection rate probably has less to do with frivolous claims than it does with inconsistencies in rulings and interpretations of the act from jurisdiction to jurisdiction. One of the biggest and most important issues of concern under the act—and central to its primary focus—is the definition and scope of the term, "disabled."

In its first ruling under this federal law, the U.S. Supreme Court held, albeit with a narrow 5–4 margin, that HIV-infected persons were protected under the act, —even if they were asymptomatic and they could still work and perform other life activities normally. The disease usually becomes symptomatic when the body attempts to immunologically respond to the disease—a more acute condition referred to as "AIDS" (acquired immunodeficiency syndrome). Persons who are HIV-positive may or may not become symptomatic with the disease.

Bragdon v. Abbott, 524 U.S. 624, 118 S. Ct. 2196, 141 L. Ed. 2d 540 (1998), was decided in June 1998, and the scope and potential implication of its holdings surprised even liberal activists. The Court ruled that even if the individual is able, by all outward appearances, to appear and function normally, that individual is still "disabled" under the law because HIV prevents that person from having children (at least it is medically inadvisable), which makes him or her "disabled" and protected under the law. The Court's ruling in this case pales in comparison to the very major impact that the ruling's logic might have on a much broader and multiple class of persons who might now be deemed disabled under the act.

On a visit to the Bangor, Maine, office of dentist Randon Bragdon, plaintiff Sidney Abbott disclosed on her patient registration form that she had the HIV virus. Upon finding a cavity in one tooth, Bragdon advised Abbott that his policy was to treat cavities in HIV-positive persons only at a hospital, and not in his office. He further advised that there would be no additional charge for his services, but that the patient would be responsible for hospital facility charges. Abbott sued under the ADA's "public accommodation" provisions in the federal district court in Maine. The professional office of

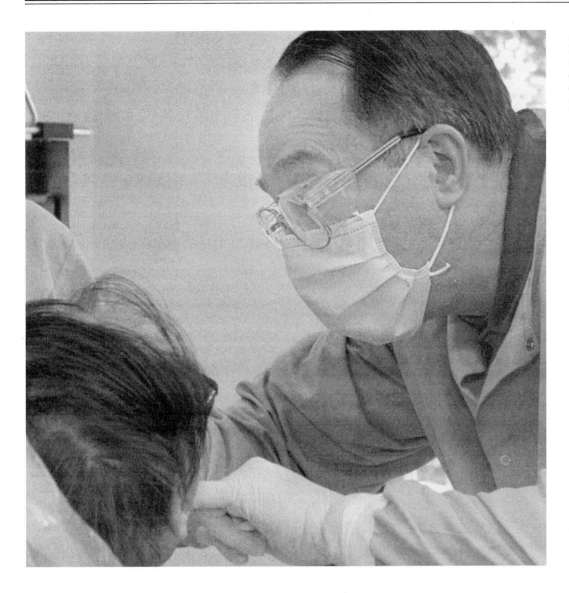

Dr. Bragdon was taken to court for insisting on treating a patient with HIV at the hospital.

a health care provider is specifically included as a place of public accommodation under the act.

Next, the plaintiff needed to establish that her HIV infection qualified as a disability under the act. Since her disease was asymptomatic, there were no external signs or symptoms of her status. It had been generally accepted that full-blown AIDS was a disability under ADA (and the 1974 Rehabilitation Act that preceded it). But whether HIV infection could be considered a disability prior to its progressing to a symptomatic phase was undecided. Abbott argued that her disease prevented her from having children, so as not to pass on the disease, and that this, in and of itself, was a disability "affecting a major life activity," a necessary element to establish a *prima facie* case.

The federal district court, as well as the U.S. Court of Appeals for the First Circuit, ruled in favor of the plaintiff Abbott. Many lower courts around the country had previously ruled (in other cases) that reproduction was not a "major life activity" within the meaning of the act. Further, many courts had also ruled that asymptomatic illness, with no apparent interference with normal life activities, was not a "disability" within the meaning of the act. Finally, Bragdon had a meritorious defense—his fear of risk and harm to himself and his other patients, i.e. the risk of transmission of the disease. It is to be emphasized that he did not refuse to treat her. He simply refused to treat her in his office, offering instead to provide comparable services to her, at the same fee, under the auspices of a hospital facility.

A divided Supreme Court affirmed the lower and appellate courts' decisions in favor of Abbott. First, the Court concluded that HIV-positive persons were to be considered "disabled" under the act, even if their symptoms were not apparent. As to whether such disability interfered with her ability to perform a major life activity, the Court again found that her HIV status substantially limited the major life activity of reproduction. (This is also an important ruling, as her ability to procreate is not in any way related to her receiving of dental services.) Finally, and significantly, the Court held that anyone engaging in adverse action against an individual based upon the individual's disability (and often, adverse action is legally justified, even when based upon the disability) must have objective scientific evidence to back up the reasons for the adverse action. In direct response to Bragdon's defense, the Court ruled that fear of contracting disease or fear of exposure was insufficient to warrant discrimination. The Court emphasized that whether or not a risk existed was not the issue. Rather, the risk must be significant. It would not tolerate "fear" alone, without scientific evidence justifying the fear, and even if the fear was in good faith, as in Bragdon's case. The Court found the evidentiary record incomplete on this issue, remanding the case for more consideration and development. However, the Court stated that in reviewing such evidence, courts should "assess the objective reasonableness of the views of healthcare professionals rather than defer to individual judgments."

Justice ANTHONY M. KENNEDY, joined by Justices JOHN PAUL STEVENS, DAVID H. SOUTER, RUTH BADER GINSBURG, and STEPHEN BREYER, delivered the opinion of the Court. Dissent was pointedly shared by Justices SANDRA DAY O'CONNOR, ANTONIN SCALIA, CLARENCE THOMAS and Chief Justice WILLIAM H. REHNQUIST on the issue of "major life activity." The dissent expressed the fact that millions of persons lived perfectly normal lives without ever having reproduced. But not breathing or walking or seeing or speaking clearly would impair a person's ability to live a perfectly normal life. Therefore, the dissent argued, according reproduction the status of "major life activity" could result in a very expansive reading of the act and its intent.

Clearly, the impact of the decision is expansive. It leaves to be resolved in future cases whether all infertile persons are to be considered "disabled" under the act, as well as other persons with asymptomatic conditions, such as certain types of diabetes, low or high blood pressure, certain forms of cancer, mental illness or side effects from medication. Secondly, it leaves open whether a "medically advisable" limitation upon a life's activity will suffice, rather than a *per se* limitation in fact. Third, although this was a case of public service/accommodation, the same language applies to the act's provisions regarding employment, which could cause major changes in employer policies and employment benefits. Fourth, future cases will need to delineate the parameters of any scientifically substantiated fear (e.g., of transmission of disease) raised as a defense.

Cleveland v. Policy Management Systems Corp.

The Americans with Disabilities Act of 1990 (ADA), 42 U.S.C.A. § 12101 et seq., is a major U.S. civil rights law. It seeks to ensure that disabled persons are not discriminated against in employment or in public accommodations. The ADA's key principle in employment is that an employer must make "reasonable accommodation" for a disabled person who is qualified and able to work. In contrast to the ADA, the Social Security Disability Insurance (SSDI) program provides benefits to persons with severe disabilities who are unable to do their present work and cannot engage "in any other kind of substantial gainful work which exists in the national economy." 42 U.S.C.A. § 423(d)(2)(A).

The differing purposes of the ADA and SSDI have led to disputes over whether a person classified as disabled under SSDI should be barred from pursuing an ADA claim against an employer. The federal circuit courts of appeal split over this issue, leaving it to the Supreme Court, in *Cleveland v. Policy Management Systems Corp.*, ___ U.S.___, 119 S. Ct. 1597, 143 L. Ed. 2d 966 (1999), to resolve the question. The Court held that receipt of SSDI benefits does not automatically prohibit a recipient from pursuing an ADA claim. However, the Court made clear that an ADA plaintiff must offer a reasonable explanation for receiving SSDI benefits while at the same time claiming to be ready to perform work. If the explanation is not persuasive, the court may dismiss the ADA lawsuit.

Carolyn C. Cleveland began work at Policy Management Systems (PMS) in 1993, where she performed background checks on prospective employees of PMS's clients. In January 1994 she suffered a stroke that damaged her concentration, memory, and language skills. That month she filed for SSDI in which she stated she was disabled and unable to work. However, by April Cleveland's condition improved enough for her to return to work. She reported this information to the Social Security Administration (SSA) two weeks later. Based on this information, the SSA denied her SSDI application on July 11. Four days later PMS fired Cleveland.

Cleveland asked the SSA in September to reconsider its denial. In her request she stated that she was fired because she "could no longer do the job" in light of her "condition." After the SSA denied reconsideration, Cleveland asked for an SSA hearing. She presented new evidence about her injuries. On September 29, 1995, the SSA awarded her SSDI benefits retroactively to the day of her stroke in January 1994.

However, on September 22, 1995, one week before receiving the SSDI award, Cleveland filed a civil lawsuit against PMS under the ADA. She alleged that PMS fired her without making a reasonable accommodation for her disability. She also alleged that she had requested but was denied accommodations such as training and additional time to complete her work. Cleveland submitted an AFFIDAVIT from her doctor to support her claims.

The federal district court granted PMS's request for SUMMARY JUDGMENT, dismissing Cleveland's action. The court believed that Cleveland, by applying for and receiving SSDI benefits, had admitted she was totally disabled. That fact prevented Cleveland from proving an essential element of her ADA claim—that she could perform the essential functions of her job with reasonable accommodation. Cleveland appealed but the Fifth Circuit Court of Appeals affirmed the district court. The appeals court concluded that "the application for or the receipt of social security disability benefits creates a rebuttable presumption that the claimant or recipient of such benefits is judicially estopped from asserting that he is a 'qualified individual with a disability.'" 120 F. 3d. 513 (5th Cir. 1997). In essence, the court created a legal presumption that Cleveland would find difficult to rebut.

The Supreme Court accepted Cleveland's appeal to resolve the split in the circuits over this issue. Three circuits agreed with the Fifth Circuit, while three others held that receiving SSDI benefits did not automatically bar an ADA action. The Supreme Court, in a unanimous decision, agreed with the latter view. Justice STEPHEN BREYER, writing for the Court, pointed out that SSDI and ADA "both help individuals with disabilities, but in different ways." SSDI provides needed benefits to severely disabled persons, while the ADA seeks to eliminate "unwarranted discrimination against disabled individuals."

In Breyer's view, the Fifth Circuit had concluded that claims under both acts would "incorporate two directly conflicting propositions, namely, 'I am too disabled to work,' and 'I am not too disabled to work.'" The appeals court, to prevent two claims with this type of "factual conflict," used a "special judicial presumption" which it believed would ordinarily prevent a plaintiff like Cleveland from successfully making an ADA claim.

Although there might be an "appearance of conflict" between the two statutes, Breyer held that the two claims "do not inherently conflict to the point where courts should apply a special negative presumption." In his view, there were too many situations in which an SSDI claim and an ADA claim "can comfortably exist side by side."

Justice Breyer pointed out that the SSA does not take into account the possibility of reasonable accommodation in determining SSDI eligibility. Therefore, an ADA plaintiff's claim that "she can perform her job *with* reasonable accommodation may well prove consistent with an SSDI claim that she could not perform her job *without* it." Justice Breyer posited other fact situations that might explain both an SSDI claim and an ADA claim. Faced with these real possibilities, the Court refused to impose a "special legal presumption" that would allow a person to bring an ADA claim "only in some limited and highly unusual set of circumstances."

However, the Court did not ignore the possibility that an SSDI claim may conflict with an ADA claim. A trial court could dismiss an ADA case on summary judgment if the plaintiff fails to provide an explanation for why she applied for disability benefits. The explanation must be sufficient to persuade a reasonable juror that despite the plaintiff's earlier statement, the plaintiff "could nonetheless perform the essential functions of her job, with or without reasonable accommodation."

In Cleveland's case, the trial court had not given her an opportunity to present her explanation for the discrepancy between the SSDI statement of total disability and the ADA claim. Therefore, the Court remanded the case to the trial court to give her the chance to reconcile the apparent contradictions.

School Required to Pay for Disabled Student's Care While at School

A major U.S. Supreme Court ruling, impacting education and disabled persons, was decided in March 1999. In *Cedar Rapids Commu-*

nity School District v. Garret F., __ U.S. __, 119 S.Ct. 992, 143 L.Ed.2d 154 (1999), the Court ruled, by a 7–2 majority, that under provisions of the Individuals with Disabilities Education Act (IDEA), a school district must pay for nursing services required by a disabled student during school hours.

Student Garret Frey was injured in a motorcycle accident at the age of four. He is quadriplegic,—paralyzed from the neck down, and needs a ventilator to breathe. In the course of a school day, he also has health care needs such as having someone suction his tracheotomy, provide urinary catheterization, monitor his blood pressure, reposition him in his wheelchair, and assist him with food and drink. Until 1993, most of the costs for a licensed practical nurse who provided these services were paid under the terms of an insurance policy, or from the proceeds of a lawsuit settlement following the accident. In 1993, his mother asked the school district to pay for an attendant, but the district declined, taking the position that it was not required under IDEA to provide medical services that are excluded under the act, but it would, however, provide an education assistant. (The IDEA requires school districts to provide children with disabilities "a free appropriate public education which emphasizes special education and related services designed to meet their unique needs.")

The matter was first brought before the Iowa Department of Education, where an administrative law judge (ALJ) ruled in favor of the student. Ultimately, after appeal by the school district, a federal district court and the U.S. Court of Appeals for the Eighth Circuit upheld the original ruling of the ALJ. In fact, the court of appeals found nothing new about the issue, having found that the issue had been previously ruled upon by the U.S. Supreme Court in *Irving Independent School District v. Tatro*, 468 U.S. 883, 104 S. Ct. 3375, 82 L. Ed. 2d 664 (1984). In *Tatro*, the Court had provided a two-step analysis to resolve whether the services in question were "related services" under the IDEA, thus requiring schools to pay for them. As applied, "related services" encompasses those *supportive services* that "may be required to assist a child with a disability to benefit from special education." A "medical services" exclusion exempted schools from paying for services provided by a licensed physician or requiring "the special training, knowledge, and judgment of a physician to carry out" (excepting diagnostic or evaluatory services).

Importantly, the district did not raise the argument that a licensed physician was required to provide the services that Garret needed. Nor did the district, in its petition for CERTIORARI, challenge the court of appeals' finding that the services at issue were "supportive services." In fact, the district did not contend that any of the required services for Garret should have been excluded from that scope. Instead, the district argued that the law did not require that it provide Garret with "continuous one-on-one nursing services." Because the requested services were continuous in nature, the district instead proposed a test which would depend upon a series of factors, including (1) whether the requested services were continuous or intermittent, (2) the associated costs of the service, (3) whether existing school health personnel could provide the service, and (4) the potential consequences if the service was not properly performed, i.e., the technical skill needed to perform the service. To support its proposed test, the district cited several federal court cases which employed similar tests, focusing on the nature and extent of the services, and not whether the services required the performance by a physician. Because two of the cited favorable federal cases were actually denied certiorari by the Supreme Court, the Court accepted the district's petition for certiorari to resolve the seeming conflict.

But the Supreme Court found no reason to depart from established law. Writing for the majority, Justice JOHN PAUL STEVENS went back to the Court's 1984 decision in *Tatro* to rearticulate the established criteria for exclusion of "medical services" from the "supportive services" for which school districts were required to pay under IDEA.

In *Tatro*, the Court had previously held that a requested service must be analyzed under two-part criteria to determine whether it was a "related service," and whether, if a related service, it was or was not excluded as a "medical service." The Court further held in that case that specific forms of health care (such as clean intermittent catheterization for bladder drainage), which are often performed by a nurse, are not excluded "medical services."

In the present case, the Court ruled that since Garret's requested services were essential to his ability to attend school, they were related services which were supportive. Since they did not require a physician to perform them, they could not be excluded as "medical services." Therefore, the school district was required under the IDEA to pay for Garret's requested services.

The Court also addressed the district's proposed substitute test, which, according to the Court, was "a kind of undue-burden exemption primarily based on the cost of the requested services." While recognizing that the district may have legitimate financial concerns about providing the requested services, the Court made clear that its role was "to interpret existing law." To take into consideration the cost of providing the service, when cost was not included as a determinative factor in the language of the act, "would require [the Court] to engage in judicial lawmaking without any guidance from Congress." (Federal IDEA funds are distributed to states based upon the number of disabled students enrolled in their respective school districts. While helpful in defraying costs, they only cover a fraction of the total expense.)

Justice CLARENCE THOMAS, joined by Justice ANTHONY M. KENNEDY, filed a dissenting opinion. They expressed their concern that the majority's interpretation of the law turned its focus into a mandate for medical care rather than a law designed to boost educational opportunities, as Congress had intended.

CROSS REFERENCES
Administrative Law; Civil Rights; Education Law; Presumption; Social Security

DOLE, ELIZABETH

Elizabeth Hanford Dole's career in public service has encompassed more than three decades, and includes service on two cabinets under two presidents. Dole was appointed secretary of transportation under RONALD REAGAN in 1983. She also served as labor secretary under President GEORGE BUSH. Dole become president of the American Red Cross in 1991, where she served until January 1999 when she left to form an exploratory committee to consider a Republican bid for the U.S. presidency in 2000.

Mary Elizabeth Hanford was born on July 29, 1936, in Salisbury, North Carolina, to John Van Hanford, a flower wholesaler, and Mary Ella (Cathey) Hanford, a homemaker. Liddy, as she was known when she was young, and her older brother John, Jr., enjoyed a privileged childhood in a devout Methodist home. Dole's perfectionism and scholarly abilities were evident from her earliest years, and her friends teased her about becoming the first woman president. Dole attended Duke University, earning a bachelor of arts degree with honors in political science. At Duke, she was inducted into Phi Beta Kappa, served as student body president, and was chosen as May Queen. She obtained an master of arts degree from Harvard in 1960, and also studied at Oxford University in England.

Dole decided to enter law school in 1962. After graduating in 1965, she moved to Washington, D.C., and briefly practiced law, before joining the Department of Health, Education, and Welfare in 1967. Dole was then a Democrat, and in 1968 she went to work for President Lyndon Johnson's Committee for Consumer Interests. When Republican RICHARD NIXON became president the following year, Dole became an Independent and managed to keep her job in the renamed Office of Consumer Affairs. In 1973 Nixon appointed Dole to the Federal Trade Commission, where she served until 1979.

Through her position in the Office of Consumer Affairs, Dole met Kansas Republican Senator Bob Dole. The two were wed on December 6, 1975, and Dole switched her party affiliation to Rebpublican. Just months after the wedding, Dole took a leave of absence from the FTC to campaign for President GERALD FORD and his vice-presidential running mate, BOB DOLE. Senator Dole called his wife his "Southern strategy," for her winning ways and tireless campaigning, but despite her efforts, Democrat JIMMY CARTER won the election.

Bob Dole launched a short-lived bid for the presidency in 1980, and Elizabeth Dole left the FTC to campaign for him. When Ronald Reagan captured the Republican nomination, she went on the campaign trail for him, and was rewarded with a spot on his transition team. In January 1983 Reagan appointed Dole as secretary of transportation, and she was approved a month later with a vote of 97–0. Dole's tenure as transportation secretary encompassed the installation of the third brake light in the rear window of cars, a crusade to raise the drinking age across the United States to twenty-one, and the beginning of air bag installation (although Dole and her detractors differ on her influence on the implementation of air bags). She also oversaw the $2 billion sale of Conrail (Consolidated Rail Corporation), the government-owned freight railroad, to private interests. She had the delicate task of supervising the Federal Aviation Administration following the 1981 strike by air-traffic controllers, when Reagan fired thousands of strikers. Dole's charming yet persuasive style earned her the nickname "Sugar Lips" among Hill staffers.

Elizabeth Dole
STEVE C.WILSON/AP/WIDE WORLD PHOTOS

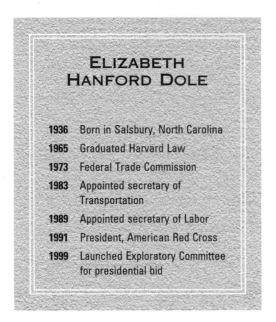

ELIZABETH HANFORD DOLE

1936 Born in Salsbury, North Carolina

1965 Graduated Harvard Law

1973 Federal Trade Commission

1983 Appointed secretary of Transportation

1989 Appointed secretary of Labor

1991 President, American Red Cross

1999 Launched Exploratory Committee for presidential bid

Dole served as labor secretary under President Bush from 1989–91. She intervened in a bitter coal workers' strike and brought in a prominent mediator to broker a settlement. In 1991 Dole left the government to become president of the American Red Cross, where she promptly donated her first year's salary back to the organization. A successful fund raiser, she also worked to ensure the safety of the blood supply. Critics charged that although her efforts to increase safety were successful, they were tardy in coming. Dole took a leave of absence to campaign for her husband's presidential bid in 1996, then returned until January 1999, when she launched her own committee to explore the possibility of a run for the presidency.

A recurring criticism of Dole's fledgling candidacy has been her reluctance to define her stance on election issues, coupled with a hesitancy to face the media or public without a carefully scripted performance. Key issues for Dole include high taxes, low defense spending, and downsizing of the military at a time when "rogue nations and terrorists" threaten the United States. She also contends that the federal government must take a much more active role in combating drug abuse. Moreover, Dole favors less federal involvement in education, and supports school vouchers.

Dole quickly declared her support for the 1999 NATO air strikes in Kosovo. Regarding ABORTION, Dole wrote in April 1999, "...I am pro-life, with exceptions in cases of rape or incest, or to save the life of the mother." She would support a constitutional amendment banning abortion, but does not believe such an amendment is viable in the face of significant opposition by many Americans. Following the school shooting in Littleton, Colorado, in April 1999, Dole risked alienating National Rifle Association members when she called for stiffer gun regulation and endorsed gun safety locks to protect children. Dole commented, " I don't think you need an AK-47 to defend your family."

Dole has stated that her spiritual life seemed out of balance in the early 1980s, commenting that God was lost somewhere between gardening and government. She reorganized her priorities, now reads the Bible at least thirty minutes a day, and has spoken frequently about the power of faith. Her active faith has not immunized her from criticism from religious conservatives, who contend that the ideological leanings of some of her staff members are too liberal.

DRUGS AND NARCOTICS

Drugs are articles intended for use in the diagnosis, cure, mitigation, treatment, or prevention of disease in humans or animals, and any articles other than food inteded to affect the mental or body function of humans or animals. *Narcotics* are any drugs that dull the senses and commonly become addictive after prolonged use.

Campaign to Legalize Marijuana

In a dramatic victory for drug law reformers, voters approved referenda legalizing marijuana for medicinal use in five states in November 1998. The initiatives brought the total number of states where voters have allowed doctors to recommend marijuana use to certain patients to six. The campaigns in each of the states were hard-fought, and the popular success of the measures reached margins of victory as high as 59 percent. While demonstrating growing national support for medicinal marijuana, the ballots also pointed out the growing tension between the states and the federal government, which continues to regard marijuana as one of the most serious illegal drugs. Since the first state initiatives passed in 1996, reformers and anti-drug forces have squared off in bitter public arguments, and federal authorities have threatened doctors with drastic legal consequences if they prescribe the drug. The new state laws set the stage for greater confrontation even as a White House-commissioned medical report appeared in March 1999 with positive findings about pot's medicinal benefits.

The medicinal use campaigns are a recent development in the legal history of marijuana. Marijuana has been illegal in the United States since the 1930s, but its increase in popularity in the 1960s led to several ongoing efforts to decriminalize and even legalize its use by groups such as the National Organization for the Reform of Marijuana Laws (NORML). Built largely on claims that recreational use of pot was on a par with drinking alcohol, such campaigns failed to move voters, who continued to view pot suspiciously. Since the 1980s, Congress has only strengthened criminal penalties for possession and distribution as part of the war on drugs. In fact, federal law regards marijuana as one of the Schedule 1 drugs—the top tier of illegal substances, along with heroin and cocaine, which carry the harshest prison sentences for violators.

But as advocates began promoting the medicinal benefits of marijuana, legal reform gained ground in the mid-1990s. Patients enduring such excruciatingly painful and debilitating diseases as glaucoma, multiple sclerosis, and Acquired Immune Deficiency Syndrome (AIDS)-related conditions reported that smoking pot eased their suffering, allowed them to function productively, and gave them hope. AIDS patients, in particular, said pot curbed appetite loss and nausea. In order to help these patients procure pot, so-called "cannabis clubs" sprung up on the West coast in the mid-1990s as non-profit centers where the ill could receive free or inexpensive pot. This movement, supported by a number of sympathetic physicians and politicians, produced a new reason for legal reform of drug laws. In 1996, voters passed referenda in California and Arizona, the first two states to legalize marijuana for medicinal use.

Not eager to see its multi-billion dollar war on drugs undermined, the federal government reacted with alarm. From the office of National Drug Control Policy, drug czar General Barry McCaffrey argued that no evidence existed showing positive health benefits from pot smoking, denounced the ballots for sending "a disastrous message to young Americans that marijuana is good for you," and blamed the state measures on "libertarians" and "elitists." The White House warned that prescribing pot would cause physicians to lose their prescription-writing power and revoke their participation in the federal Medicare and Medicaid programs. Similarly, the federal Drug Enforcement Agency (DEA) threatened to revoke doctors' licenses to prescribe certain drugs, including cocaine, morphine, Demerol and Percodan. In

this context, the defeat of a ballot measure in 1997 in Washington State seemed attributable to an imminent federal crackdown. But it never came. Apart from scattered federal raids on a few cannabis clubs, federal officials largely engaged in threats. Significantly, not one physician recommending or prescribing pot has yet faced federal prosecution.

However, as the 1998 campaign showed, the battle is far from over. In debate prior to the elections, opponents of legalization campaigned vociferously. Drug czar McCaffrey and former First Lady Barbara Bush stumped against the vote in Washington State, warning against a decline in moral decency if patients were allowed to use marijuana. In Arizona, opponents put a measure on the ballot to reverse the 1996 law. And in Washington, D.C., which is under the legal control of Congress, federal lawmakers were angered when a pro-pot measure appeared on the November ballot. Congress swiftly voted to disallow the use of federal funds to conduct the ballot, although voting proceeded, anyway. Afterwards, with exit polls showing up to 80 percent support for the measure, District of Columbia authorities refused to count the votes for fear of being found in violation of Congress. The American Civil Liberties Union filed suit to compel tabulation of the votes.

In other states, the measures passed. Majorities of 59 percent in Alaska, Nevada, and Washington approved measure, and Oregon passed its measure with a 55 percent majority. While all of the laws had the same general purpose and each specified particular illnesses for which pot is a legal treatment, they varied slightly in approach. In Alaska, for example, patients will not be allowed to possess or grow limited amounts of pot, ranging from one ounce to three plants, while in Washington State they will be allowed to maintain a sixty-day supply. Other laws were less specific: Nevada's permits usage under a doctor's supervision, and Oregon's simply states that medical usage is legal. Oregonians also soundly defeated a measure that would have raised penalties for simple possession. Only in one state did medical use proponents suffer a setback: voters in Colorado approved legalization by 57 percent, but the secretary of state invalidated the vote because allegedly not enough signatures had been collected to place the measure on the ballot. Voters there also filed suit to validate the election.

Then, in March 1999, a federally-sponsored medical report surprised opponents. Two years earlier, in 1997, amid public battles with reform forces, drug czar McCaffrey had commissioned a report on the health benefits of pot from the federal Institute of Medicine (IOM), a branch of the National Institutes of Health. Anti-drug forces hoped scientific evidence could silence the reform movement. But the opposite occurred: offering the most detailed analysis to date, the report concluded that cannabinoids—the drug's active components—can be useful in treating symptoms of AIDS and cancer, and even recommended short-term usage for some patients. Not completely favorable, the report warned specifically about health risks from marijuana smoke. As an alternative, it recommended the development of smokeless cannabinoids in the form of nose inhalers. The report pleased reform advocates, who predicted that opponents would have a harder time fighting them. Opponents, however, denounced parts of the report for concluding that marijuana usage does not necessarily lead to harder drug use. McCaffrey told reporters he was uncertain what the report meant for the future.

For several reasons, the future of medicinal usage laws is uncertain as well. Although the votes showed that the medicinal usage movement is obviously growing, patients reported in 1999 that finding marijuana still remained difficult—largely because doctors, clinics and pharmacies remained fearful of prosecution. The medical community took a wait-and-see approach to gage the forthcoming response from Washington, D.C. That response was easy to predict: with an election year coming and drugs traditionally serving as a hot-button issue for politicians, no one expected to hear dozens of congressmen and senators calling for more pot for sick people. For that reason, with reform advocates vowing to bring referenda in more states, an ongoing battle between federal and state authorities looked unavoidable.

DUE PROCESS OF LAW

A fundamental constitutional guarantee that all legal proceedings will be fair and that one will be given notice of the proceedings and an opportunity to be heard before government acts to take away one's life, liberty, or property. Also, a constitutional guarantee that a law shall not be unreasonable, arbitrary, or capricious.

Chicago's Anti-Loitering Law

The growth of crime-oriented gangs in the United States has become a national crisis. To deal with the problem, lawmakers passed aggressive laws that have pushed the boundaries of acceptable low enforcement policies.

In the early 1990s, the Rocksprings neighborhood in San Jose, California, was besieged by a gang that had claimed the area as its "turf." Residents were intimidated by loud music, loud and vulgar speech, occasional gunfire, drug dealing, vandalism, harassment, and public urination. The residents of the neighborhood felt that were being held hostage by the gang.

In 1993, the city of San Jose sought an IN-JUNCTION against the gang in state court. The injunction was remarkable because, among other things, it specifically identified members of a Latino gang by name and forbid them from appearing together in public. The injunction also forbid the named persons from intimidating or harassing persons who complained about them to the police. The court granted the injunction, and the California Supreme Court upheld the injunction on appeal. Justice Janice Brown, writing for the majority, opined that "[t]o hold that the liberty of the peaceful, industrious residents of Rocksprings must be forfeited to preserve the illusion of freedom for those whose ill conduct is deleterious to the community as a whole is to ignore half the political promise of the Constitution and the whole of its sense." Justice Stanley Mosk dissented, arguing that the injunction penalized minorities for non-criminal behavior. According to Mosk, the injunction permitted cities "to close off entire neighborhoods to Latino youths who have done nothing more than dress in blue or black clothing or associate with others who do so; they would authorize criminal penalties for ordinary, nondisruptive acts of walking or driving through a residential neighborhood with a relative or friend." The U.S. Supreme Court declined to hear the case. *People v. Acuna*, 929 P. 2d 596 (Cal 1997), cert. denied, 521 U.S. 1121, 117 S. Ct. 2518, 138 L. Ed. 2d 1016 (1997).

In 1992, the city of Chicago, Illinois, passed an ordinance that allowed police officers to break up any group of two or more persons whom they believed to be loitering in a public place, provided the officer also believes that at least one of the persons is a member of a gang. A state appeals court struck down the law in 1995, but not until Chicago police had made approximately 43,000 arrests under the ordinance. The law was used to prosecute only seventy cases. Six defendants were found guilty and sentenced to jail. The other sixty-four defendants had their cases dismissed by judges who ruled that the ordinance was unconstitutional. The six defendants who were convicted later had their convictions reversed by appeals courts.

The Illinois Supreme Court heard the case in 1997 and approved the appeals court's decision to strike down the ordinance. According to the court, the law gave police officers "absolute discretion" in deciding whether a person is a gang member and whether a person is loitering. To the Illinois Supreme Court, the law was so vague that it constituted a violation of the due process rights of persons in Chicago. *City of Chicago v. Morales*, 687 N.E. 2d 53 (Ill. 1997).

The city of Chicago appealed the ruling to the U.S. Supreme Court, and the case sparked a national debate. A group of Chicago-area community organizations filed a brief with the Court, stating in it that "[t]he kids the police can't order off the streets today are the same ones who will be taken off to jail tomorrow, if they are not taken to the emergency room or the morgue first." Catherine Coles of Harvard University's Kennedy School of Government suggested to *Insight on the News* that the ordinance was not misplaced. "Things like graffiti, panhandling, loud music or broken windows" in a community can have an insidious effect on quality of life, said Coles. "As disorderly behavior increases, law-abiding people withdraw from the streets; informal social control breaks down." Harvey Grossman, legal director of the American Civil Liberties Union in Chicago, noted that the U.S. Supreme Court has held for

years that vague statutes leading to arbitrary law enforcement are unconstitutional. Grossman called the Chicago ordinance "a broad, omnibus, dragnet law that sweeps up innocent people."

At oral arguments, some of the U.S. Supreme Court justices seemed uncomfortable with the Chicago ordinance. Justice SANDRA DAY O'CONNOR stated that there was "a concern here about the arbitrariness of police" and Justice DAVID H. SOUTER suggested that there may be a "purpose for most of what is called loitering." Many persons, said Souter, just "like to watch cars go by." Chief Justice WILLIAM H. REHNQUIST and Justice ANTONIN SCALIA seemed more sympathetic to the ordinance. Scalia noted that "[g]angs perpetuate themselves by showing off. That's how gang violence occurs." Scalia wondered aloud whether Chicago did not have "the right to stop that activity."

On June 10, 1999, the High Court, by a vote of 6–3, struck down the Chicago anti-gang ordinance and affirmed the decision of the Illinois Supreme Court. The case fractured the court, with three different opinions constituting the majority. According to the majority, the ordinance was unconstitutional because it did not draw a line between innocent and guilty behavior and failed to give guidance to police on the matter. Justice JOHN PAUL STEVENS, writing for the plurality, noted that under the ordinance it did not matter "whether the reason that a gang member and his father…might loiter near

Harvey Grossman, lead attorney representing sixty-six people arrested under the Chicago anti-loitering law, speaks in front of the Supreme Court.

Wrigley Field is to rob an unsuspecting fan or just to get a glimpse of Sammy Sosa leaving the ballpark." Such indiscriminate policing was a violation of the FIRST AMENDMENT right to freedom of assembly. "It allows and even encourages arbitrary police enforcement."

Justice CLARENCE THOMAS authored a dissent and declared in it that minorities would suffer from the Court's decision to favor gang members over law-abiding citizens. The Court could afford to do so, Thomas slyly wrote, because "the people who will have to live with the consequences of today's opinion do not live in our neighborhoods." In his own dissent, Justice Scalia, stated that "I would trade my right to loiter in the company of a gang member for the liberation of my neighborhood in an instant."

High-Speed Police Chases

High-speed police chases have often resulted in deaths and injuries, especially to innocent victims who are in the wrong place at the wrong time. In the 1990s, criticism of this police practice mounted, with victims seeking DAMAGES from cities and counties for the damages inflicted during these pursuits. Police argue that chases are necessary to apprehend fleeing criminals, but critics charge that poor judgment is often used in chasing persons for trivial offenses. Police now contend that these lawsuits might inhibit them from carrying out their duties, as they now fear that they will be sued if invloved in an accident during a chase.

The Supreme Court, in *County of Sacramento v. Lewis*, 523 U.S. 833, 118 S. Ct. 1708, 140 L. Ed. 2d 1043 (1998), ruled that high-speed police chases do not violate the FOURTEENTH AMENDMENT's DUE PROCESS CLAUSE, which prohibits states from depriving a person of life, liberty, or property without due process of law. The Court emphatically rejected the claim that police pursuits violate "substantive due process."

James Everett Smith, a Sacramento County, California sheriff's deputy, and another officer, Murray Stapp, were leaving the scene of a police call in separate squad cars when they saw a motorcycle approach at high speed. It was operated by eighteen-year-old Brian Willard and carried sixteen-year-old Philip Lewis as a passenger. Stapp turned on his overhead lights, yelled to the boys to stop, and pulled his patrol car closer to Smith's, attempting to pen the motorcycle in. Instead of pulling over, Willard maneuvered the cycle between the two police cars and spcd off. Smith then switched on his own emergency lights and siren and began pursuit at

high speed. For over a minute Smith pursued the motorcycle through a residential neighborhood, as the motorcycle wove in and out of oncoming traffic, forcing two cars and a bicycle to swerve off the road. The motorcycle and patrol car reached speeds up to one hundred miles an hour, with Smith following at a distance as short as one hundred feet.

The chase ended after the motorcycle tipped over as Willard tried a sharp left turn. Smith slammed on his brakes, but the patrol car skidded into Lewis at forty miles an hour, propelling him some seventy feet down the road and inflicting massive injuries. Lewis was pronounced dead at the scene. Willard escaped serious injury.

The mother and father of Phillip Lewis sued, on behalf of his estate, Sacramento County, the Sacramento County Sheriff's Department and Deputy Smith under the federal civil rights statute 42 U.S.C.A. § 1983. The parents alleged that the county and Smith had deprived Lewis of his FOURTEENTH AMENDMENT substantive due process right to life. The federal district court dismissed the action against Smith, concluding that even if he violated the CONSTITUTION, he was entitled to qualified immunity. The Lewis family could not show that there were any court decisions issued before the alleged misconduct took place that supported their view that their son had a "Fourteenth Amendment substantive due process right in the context of high speed police pursuits;" therefore, Smith was entitled to qualified immunity. The court also dismissed the lawsuit against the county and the sheriff's department, finding that they had not failed to properly train Smith on how to conduct a high-speed chase.

The Ninth Circuit Court of Appeals reversed the district court as to the dismissal of the case against Smith. It did affirm the lower court's decision that the county and the sheriff's department were not LIABLE. (98 F. 3d 434 [9th Cir. 1996]). The appeals court found that "the law regarding police liability for death or injury caused by an officer during the course of a high-speed chase was clearly established" at the time of Lewis's death. The court noted that Smith had apparently disregarded the sheriff's department's general order on police pursuits. Therefore, the case should be sent back for a trial on the issues. The Ninth Circuit also ruled that Smith could be held liable for damages if his conduct during the chase amounted to deliberate indifference to, or reckless disregard for, a person's right to life and personal security.

The Supreme Court, in a unanimous decision, overruled the Ninth Circuit's conclusions on substantive due process and deliberate or reckless indifference to life. Justice DAVID H. SOUTER, writing for the Court, concluded that the allegations were insufficient to state a substantive due process violation.

Substantive due process is an ambiguous and often controversial concept. The Supreme Court developed the concept during the late 1800s in a series of cases involving state regulation of business and the scope of the Fourteenth Amendment's Due Process Clause. A conservative Court used it to strike down government regulation of business until the 1930s when it was largely disregarded for business and commerce cases. Yet the concept has proved to be durable in other fields. By the 1960s the Court had extended its interpretation of substantive due process to include rights and freedoms that are not specifically mentioned in the Constitution, but that, according to the Court, extend or derive from existing rights. These rights and freedoms include the freedoms of association and non-association and the right to PRIVACY.

In this case, Justice Souter found that the Lewis estate could not show "governmental arbitrariness," which the Due Process Clause guards against. He noted that only the most egregious actions by government officials could be said to be arbitrary in the constitutional sense. Prior Supreme Court decisions had used the SHOCK THE CONSCIENCE test to assess whether government conduct violated substantive due process. The Court established the "shock the conscience test" in *Rochin v. California*, 342 U.S. 165, 72 S. Ct. 205, 96 L. Ed. 183 (1952), stating it prohibits conduct by state agents that falls outside the standards of civilized decency. In that case the Court found that pumping the stomach of a criminal suspect in a search for drugs violated substantive due process.

Justice Souter found the circumstances of a high-speed chase much different than pumping the stomach of a custodial suspect. In the case of a high-speed chase aimed at apprehending a suspected offender, the police officer is confronted with unforeseen circumstances that "demand an instant judgment on the part of an officer who feels the pull of competing obligations." Souter concluded that a police officer would only be liable for the consequences of a high-speed chase if the officer's only purpose was to "cause harm unrelated to the legitimate object of arrest." Such a purpose would shock the conscience. Absent this purpose, "chases

with no intent to harm suspects physically or to worsen their legal plight do not give rise to substantive due process liability."

Applying this analysis to the facts of the case, Justice Souter ruled that Deputy Smith's conduct did not shock the conscience. Smith and the other officer saw Willard's lawless behavior and responded. They were not to blame for the actions Willard took in trying to evade capture. In the Court's view, Willard's "outrageous behavior" was "instantaneous" and so was Smith's. Therefore, Smith was not liable under the Fourteenth Amendment and the case would be dismissed.

Recovering Personal Property After a Search

When police seize personal property for a criminal investigation, DUE PROCESS does not require them to provide the owner with detailed information regarding the procedures that must be followed to have that property returned. This was the unanimous decision of the U.S. Supreme Court in *City of West Covina v. Perkins*, 525 U.S. 234, 119 S. Ct. 678, 142 L. Ed. 2d 636 (1999).

On May 18, 1993, Julio Alberto Clark was murdered in West Covina, California. When the murder scene was searched, police found evidence that incriminated Marcus Marsh. Other items found at the scene included cocaine, $99,400 in cash, and gang-related evidence. The investigators traced Marsh's last known telephone number to the address of Lawrence, Clara, and April Perkins in LaPuente, California. They confirmed that address and obtained a search warrant which allowed for the search of any evidence of street gang membership or affiliation and certain firearms. When the police came to search the Perkins' residence on May 21, 1993, no one was at home. Not knowing which room belonged to Marsh, they searched the entire residence and seized gang photographs, some of which included Marsh, an address book belonging to Lawrence Perkins, a shotgun and ammunition, a pistol, and $2,469 in cash. The officers left a "Search Warrant Notice of Service" which read:

To Whom it May Concern:

1. These premises have been searched by peace officers of the West Covina Police Department pursuant to a search warrant issued on 5–20–93, by the Honorable Dan Oki, Judge of the Municipal Court, Citrus Judicial District.

2. The search was conducted on 5–21–93. A list of the property seized

pursuant to the search warrant is attached.

3. If you wish further information, you may contact: Det. Ferrari or Det. Melnyk at [telephone number].

The form also listed the name "Lt. Schimanski" and his telephone number. It did not include the SEARCH WARRANT number, but an itemized list of the seized property was included. *Perkins v. City of West Covina*, 113 F. 3d 1004 (9th Cir. 1997).

The officers explain that they did not leave the search warrant number because it was under seal and could have jeopardized the current investigation. According to Lawrence Perkins, the homeowner, he and his wife returned home to find their doors damaged, their personal property out of order, and their cash savings taken from a locked closet. After reading the posted notice, Perkins called Detective Ferrari. Detective Ferrari told Perkins a few days later that he would return the property, but that Perkins had to get a court order before he could do this. In his complaint, Perkins claimed that the detectives asked him for help in finding Marsh, and when Perkins declined to help, the detectives told him they could not return the property, only the court could do that. This claim was denied by Detective Ferrari. Approximately a month after the search took place, Perkins went to see the judge who signed the search warrant. However, the judge was on vacation for a month. When he tried to see if another judge could authorize the release of his property, he was informed that there was nothing under his name and that he would need the warrant number. Perkins' lawyer, Patrick S. Smith, described this as being worse than a "run around," as it required his client to give information that he did not have in order to get his own money back.

Instead of continuing to inquire about the return of his property, Perkins filed a § 42 U.S.C. 1983 civil rights claim in U.S. district court against the city of West Covina for having a policy which allowed unlawful searches, and the officers for violating their FOURTH AMENDMENT rights when they performed the search. The district court granted SUMMARY JUDGEMENT for both the city of West Covina and the officers. On remand, the district court held that California law for return of seized property satisfied due process and that the notice provided by the city regarding remedies to obtain seized property was sufficient.

On Appeal, the Ninth Circuit Court of Appeals affirmed in part and reversed in part the district court's decision. The court of appeals affirmed the decision that the officers were protected by qualified IMMUNITY. However, they reversed the decision for summary judgement in favor of the city of West Covina and found in favor of Perkins based on their opinion that the notice given to him violated their due process rights.

The FOURTEENTH AMENDMENT of the U.S. Constitution, often referred to as the "DUE PROCESS CLAUSE," clearly states that no state shall "deprive any person of life, liberty, or property, without due process of law." This has been interpreted to mean that a property owner shall be given notice of a seizure of property and an opportunity for a hearing. *Schneider v. County of San Diego*, 28 F. 3d 89 (9th Cir. 1995). The notice required by due process must reasonably convey the required information for remedy. *Mullane v. Central Hanover Bank and Trust Co.*, 339 U.S. 306, 70 S. Ct. 652, 94 L. Ed. 865 (1950). The court of appeals compared the circumstances in Perkins to *Memphis Light, Gas and Water Division v. Craft*, 436 U.S. 1, 98 S. Ct. 1554, 56 L. Ed. 2d 30 (1978), where due process was held to have been violated. In that case, the gas company provided plaintiffs with notice of termination, but did not explain a procedure to dispute a claim. Such a procedure did exist in a document that was not readily available to the public. The Ninth Circuit found that the plaintiff in the *Memphis Light* case, like Perkins, did make an effort to determine the proper procedures to seek a remedy to the seizure. Further, the plaintiff in the *Memphis Light* case, like Perkins, was not accused of breaking any laws, yet was in need of details explaining how to retrieve his property, which could only be found in a document not readily accessible to the public. While the attorney for the city of West Covina argued that due process was not violated because Perkins could merely hire a lawyer to find out the proper procedures for reclaiming his property, the Ninth Circuit believed that such a solution is not financially possible, or fair, for everyone who may be in that situation. Therefore, the Ninth Circuit Court of Appeals found, largely by analogy to the *Memphis Light* case, that the notice given to the Perkins by the city of West Covina Police Department was constitutionally inadequate under the Due Process Clause. In so finding, they recommended that notice sufficient to satisfy "due process" would include the information provided by the city of West Covina and, in addition, information on the procedure and proper forum for obtaining one's property plus the necessary information required to initiate this process, such as the search warrant number in this case.

The city of West Covina was joined by city attorneys for Los Angeles and San Diego, along with sixty-five other California municipalities, when they appealed the Ninth Circuit's broad decision to the U.S. Supreme Court. The Supreme Court reversed the court of appeals' decision finding that there was no precedent for the expansive notice requirement. Furthermore, it noted that neither the federal government nor any of the fifty states had such stringent requirements. The Federal Rule of Criminal Procedure § 41(d) only requires that when a federal agency obtains a warrant to seize property, they must give the property owner a copy of the warrant and a list of the property that was taken.

The Court went further to distinguish the present case from the *Memphis Light* case, in that the administrative procedures necessary for the plaintiff in *Memphis Light* were not available in any public publication. In contrast, the post-deprivation state-law remedies were readily available to Perkins, as any state law or procedure would be. The fact that Perkins did not exhaust his remedies before filing this suit in the U.S. district court did not go unnoticed by the Supreme Court, as they did comment on the fact that he failed to file a motion with the municipal court or, at the very least, make any additional inquiries into the matter before filing this lawsuit. In the end, the Supreme Court's decision was that the Due Process Clause does not require the police to provide the owner with notice of state law remedies for the property's return.

As a final attempt to have the court of appeals' decision affirmed, Perkins argued that the notice was insufficient because the warrant number was witheld from him. However, the Supreme Court cited the district court's finding that Perkins was unable to prove that he needed the search warrant to file a motion for a hearing on the return of his property.

CROSS REFERENCES
Due Process; Daley, Richard M.; Fourteenth Amendment; *Rochin v. California*

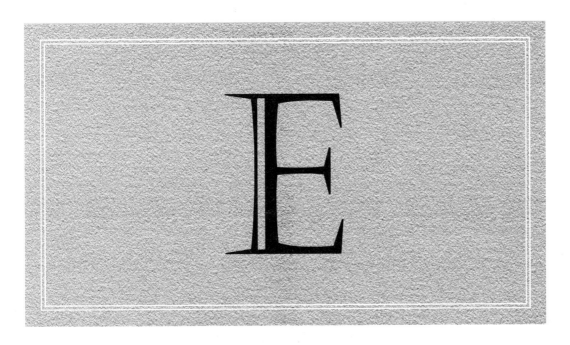

EDUCATION LAW

The body of state and federal constitutional provisions; local, state, and federal statutes; court opinions; and government regulations that provide the legal framework for educational institutions.

Bilingual Education

A sensitive and controversial issue in 1998 which continues to face resistance in some circles was California's Proposition 227, mandating the termination of California's bilingual education program for school-aged children who are "limited English proficient." Although passed into law by California voters with a resounding 61–39 percent victory in June 1998, the new law was immediately challenged in a CLASS ACTION suit filed in federal district court by the Mexican-American Legal Defense and Education Fund, The Southern Christian Leadership Conference of Los Angeles, and several other parties. But within the first eight weeks of the election, legal challenges in both northern and southern federal district courts were resolved in favor of Proposition 227, and on July 31, 1998, the U.S. Circuit Court of Appeals for the Ninth Circuit upheld the Northern District's opinion. The new law also succeeded over political resistance from President BILL CLINTON, the chairmen of the state Democratic and Republican parties, all four candidates for governor, and a barrage of negative publicity in newspaper editorials. But the voters prevailed, and Proposition 227 became law in August 1998, being implemented for the 1998–99 school year. However, internal resistance in several of the school districts tended to disrupt the smooth transition from old to new programs.

Bilingual education purports to make use of both the English language and the child's native language for educational instruction. It is premised upon the belief that this approach enables children to grasp the tenets of basic mathematics, science and social studies in their own language, while simultaneously being exposed to English instruction. In theory it works, but in reality, children have reverted to their native language or resisted communicating in English, much to the growing frustration of both educators and taxpayers saddled with the financial burdens brought to them by poor academic performance in the school systems. After sinking millions of taxpayer dollars into bilingual education, many taxpayers decided to express their opinions at the voting booths. It had been estimated by the Department of Finance that for the 1997–98 school year, California had spend as much as 70 percent of its $385 million funds for economically disadvantaged children in bilingual programs.

Proposition 227 was the brainchild of Ron Unz, a software entrepreneur from Silicon Valley who sponsored the legislation. It was the cumulative result of the public's growing impatience and dissatisfaction with the poor acquisition and use of English language skills in many of California's ethnic school districts (a trend echoed across the nation, although California accounts for 40 percent of the students nationally who need English language skills). On the national level, 3.2 million students speak little if any English, approximately 73 percent of them Hispanic-speaking, followed by approximately 4 percent Vietnamese, and less than 2 percent each for Hmong, Cantonese, and Cam-

bodian. In California alone, non-English speaking students account for one-fourth of the total student population, and 80 percent of that one-fourth is Hispanic. Proposition 227 mandated that students be placed in structured English language programs, without native language support, for one year. Upon successful immersion into the program and demonstration of sufficient English language skills, the students would then be mainstreamed into regular classrooms.

The concept of bilingual education began in the 1960s. In 1974, the U.S. Supreme Court ruled in *Lau v. Nichols*, 414 U.S. 563, 94 S. Ct. 786, 39 L. Ed. 2d 1 (1974) that both the CIVIL RIGHTS ACT OF 1964 and the Bilingual Education Act of 1968 required schools to take "affirmative steps" to overcome educational barriers caused by language difficulties in non-English speaking students (but the Court has never mandated or required bilingual education as a matter of law). The Court ruled out both extremes at either end of the definitive spectrum of bilingual education: on the one end was the "sink or swim" mainstreaming philosophy (a civil rights violation), and on the other, the "separate but identical education programs" for non-English-speaking students (an equal protection violation). But it has been the gray area in the middle which has caused the most controversy: programs which survive constitutional muster, but are in reality ineffectual or lackluster in their results. Proposition 227 was the first major initiative to compel change in the bilingual education system and still pass legal challenge. It was deemed as compliant with legal precedent in that it afforded a one-year transition ("immersion period") for students to acquire basic English language skills, thereby circumventing the "sink or swim" prohibition. Secondly, it incorporated a "mainstreaming" objective, thereby avoiding the "identical but separate" prohibition articulated in *Lau*.

Additionally, "waivers" have been granted to school districts that can demonstrate an adverse effect caused by the law's requirements. This has proven to be a bigger menace to the law's effectiveness than litigation. Thousands of California parents have requested waivers for the 1998–99 school year, and the number of charter schools, exempt from the law, is also significantly on the rise.

In September 1998, the U.S. House of Representatives passed a bill (HR3892) to limit federal support for bilingual education, but the bill did not have a chance to make it through the Senate prior to the year's adjournment. The bill would have converted existing funding for bilingual and immigrant education to block grants, limited enrollment in bilingual education to three years, and changed the name of the education department's Office of Bilingual Education to the "Office of English-Language Acquisition." When Congress began the next session, the Senate passed a bill (SB1001) to *bolster* bilingual education programs, but in March 1999, the bill was defeated by a House committee. It was also anticipated that the Senate would again kill a new House bill (HB2387) and leave the issue until the 2000 session.

CROSS REFERENCES
English-Only Laws

ELECTION CAMPAIGN FINANCING

Federal Elections Commission v. Akins

Since the 1960s, the financing of U.S. political campaigns has been a controversial subject. Concerns about political corruption that flows from campaign contributions have been juxtaposed with concerns about preserving every citizen's FIRST AMENDMENT right to freely support political views and candidates. The Federal Election Campaign Act (FECA) of 1971, 2 U.S.C.A. 431 et seq, which sets rules on political contributions for federal elections, has become part of the political landscape. The Federal Election Commission (FEC), an independent agency, acts as both a clearinghouse of information on federal campaign law and as the enforcer of these campaign laws.

The U.S. Supreme Court, in *Buckley v. Valeo*, 424 U.S. 1, 96 S. Ct. 612, 46 L. Ed. 2d 659 (1976), ruled that the act's limitation on campaign expenditures was unconstitutional. The Court did uphold the limit of $1000 for individual contributions, but ruled that a candidate could spend as much of his or her personal fortune on a political campaign as they wanted.

Because of loopholes in the law and the *Buckley* decision, there has been a tremendous growth in "political action committees" (PACs) as vehicles for major campaign spending. PACs are special organizations formed by labor, industry, the professions and other interest groups that are not identified with individual candidates. PACs are not bound by the individual contribution restriction; therefore their political influence has risen with their large contributions. Under the campaign act, any political committee that receives more than $1000 in contributions or makes expenditures in any given year must submit to extensive record-keeping and disclosure requirements.

In *Federal Elections Commission v. Akins*, 524 U.S. 11, 118 S. Ct. 1777, 141 L. Ed. 2d 10 (1998), the Supreme Court was called upon to examine whether an organization was a PAC and therefore subject to public disclosure. In the end the Court declined to rule on the organization's status under the law, but the case illustrates the legal and political complexities that typify campaign finance in the 1990s.

A group of voters filed a complaint with the FEC, alleging that the American Israel Public Affairs Committee (AIPAC) was a "political committee" as defined by the Federal Election Campaign Act of 1971. AIPAC described itself as an issue-oriented organization that seeks to maintain friendship and promote goodwill between the United States and Israel. However, AIPAC also conceded that it lobbied elected officials and disseminated information about candidates for public office. The FEC ruled that although AIPAC had spent more than $1000 it was not a political committee because, as an issue-oriented lobbying group, its major purpose was not the nomination or election of candidates. Therefore, AIPAC did not have to make disclosures regarding its membership, contributions, and expenditures that FECA would otherwise require. The group of voters appealed this decision to the federal district court, but it affirmed the FEC's decision. However, the Circuit Court of Appeals for the District of Columbia reversed the district court, ruling that the FEC's "major purpose" test improperly interpreted FECA's definition of a political committee.

The Supreme Court, on a 6–3 vote, ruled that the complainants had legal standing to bring an action against the FEC, but concluded that because of the "unusual and complex circumstances" surrounding the case, the matter should be sent back to the FEC for a review based on the commission's new regulations. Justice STEPHEN BREYER, writing for the majority, first addressed the standing issue.

In this case the FEC alleged that the voters who filed the complaint did not have standing to bring the lawsuit. Justice Breyer disagreed, ruling that voters who seek information to which they believe the FECA entitles them, have standing to challenge the FEC's decision not to bring an enforcement action. Justice Breyer, in reviewing the FECA, concluded that Congress meant to "cast the standing net broadly," allowing persons to pursue their complaints through th FEC and the judicial system. In addition, the voters group asserted an injury—their failure to obtain information about AIPAC—that was the kind that the FECA seeks to address. Justice Breyer also found that Congress, in enacting the FECA, intended to alter the traditional view that agency enforcement decisions are not subject to judicial review.

Though the case was properly before the Supreme Court, Justice Breyer concluded that the Court could not rule on its merits. He cited another court of appeals case that overturned the FEC's regulations defining "members," in part because the appeals court thought the regulations defined membership organizations too narrowly in light of an organization's First Amendment right to communicate with its members. *Chamber of Commerce v. Federal Election Commission*, 69 F. 3d 600 (D.C.1995). The FEC then issued proposed rules redefining "members." Justice Breyer concluded that under these rules, "it is quite possible that many of the persons who belong to AIPAC would be considered 'members.' " If that happened, the expenditures "apparently would not count as the kind" of 'expenditures' that can turn an organization into a "political committee," and AIPAC would fall outside the definition for that reason.

Because these new rules could change the answer as to whether the AIPAC was a political committee under the FECA, the Court directed the FEC to determine whether or not the political expenditures of the AIPAC were subject to the new rules. If the expenditures fell outside the new rules, then the AIPAC would not qualify as a political committee and it would not have to make the disclosures requested by the complainants in this case. If they did qualify as a political committee, then the AIPAC would have to comply with the FECA and the case would become moot.

Justice ANTONIN SCALIA, in a dissenting joined by Justices SANDRA DAY O'CONNOR and CLARENCE THOMAS, argued that the complainants should not have been allowed to bring the lawsuit against the FEC in the first place. Scalia was troubled by the prospect of private parties using the courts to compel an agency to enforce its laws against a third party. Executive agencies should be allowed to make administrative decisions without the fear that court action will follow.

CROSS REFERENCES
Federal Election Commission; Standing

ELECTIONS

The processes of voting to decide a public question or to select one person from a designated group to perform certain obligations in a government, corporation, or society.

Buckley v. American Constitutional Law Foundation, Inc.

Twenty-four states, most of them in the West and Midwest, allow their citizens to vote on INITIATIVES and REFERENDUMS that have been placed on the ballot through a petition process. This process gives people the power to propose legislation and to enact or reject the laws at the polls independent of the lawmaking power of the governing legislative body. Although many people laud this method of participatory democracy, there has been increasing concern that special interest groups have manipulated the process to accomplish ends they cannot achieve in state legislatures. Some states have attempted to limit the influence of these groups by enacting regulations that govern how PETITIONS for initiative and referendum are obtained, but these attempts at limitations have been attacked in court as violations of the FIRST AMENDMENT.

The Supreme Court, in *Buckley v. American Constitutional Law Foundation, Inc.*, 525 U.S. 182, 119 S. Ct. 636, 142 L. Ed. 2d 599 (1999), reviewed Colorado's efforts to regulate the way petitions get on the ballot and concluded that they were unconstitutional. The Court embraced the First Amendment arguments of those who opposed the Colorado regulations, but the decision provoked strong dissents from two members of the Court who worried that states had lost control of the electoral process.

In the early 1990s, Colorado enacted a series of controls on the petition process for placing initiatives on the ballot. The American Constitutional Law Foundation, Inc., a Denver-based organization that promotes initiative and referendum as a means of promoting direct democracy, and other groups filed suit in federal court. They challenged the constitutionality of six of the controls as violating the First Amendment's freedom of speech guarantee.

The six controls included (1) requiring petition circulators be at least eighteen years old; (2) requiring that the circulators be registered voters; (3) limiting the petition circulation period to six months; (4) requiring petition circulators to wear identification badges stating their names, their status as "volunteer" or "paid," and if the latter, the name and telephone number of their employer; (5) requiring circulators to attach to each petition section an AFFIDAVIT containing the circulator's name and address; and (6) requiring initiative proponents to disclose (a) at the time they file their petition, the name, address, and county of voter registration of all paid circulators, the amount of money proponents paid per petition signature, and the total amount paid to each circulator, and (b) on a monthly basis, the names of the proponents, the name and address of each paid circulator, the name of the proposed ballot measure, and the amount of money paid and owed to each circulator during the month.

The district court struck down the badge requirement and portions of the disclosure requirements, but upheld the age, affidavit, and registration requirements, and the six-month limit on petition circulation. The Court of Appeals for the Tenth Circuit upheld, as reasonable regulations of the ballot-initiative process, the age restriction, the six-month limit on petition circulation, and the affidavit requirement. The court struck down the requirement that petition circulators be registered voters, and also held portions of the badge and disclosure requirements invalid as intruding unnecessarily and improperly on political expression. 120 F.3d 1092 (1997).

The Supreme Court, on a 6–3 vote, upheld the Tenth Circuit's decision. Justice RUTH BADER GINSBURG, writing for the majority, noted that a previous attempt by Colorado to regulate initiative petitions had been struck down by the Court. In *Meyer v. Grant*, 486 U.S. 414, 108 S. Ct. 1886, 100 L. Ed. 2d 425 (1988), the Court had ruled unconstitutional Colorado's prohibition against paid petition circulators, concluding that petition circulation is "core political speech" deserving the highest form of First Amendment protection.

Turning to the three disputed regulations, Justice Ginsburg acknowledged that states have considerable latitude to protect the integrity and reliability of the ballot-initiative process. In addition, she restated prior Court precedent that there is no "litmus-paper test" for separating valid ballot-access provisions from invalid provisions that restrict speech. Therefore, the Court was guided by the knowledge that the protection offered by the First Amendment requires "vigilance" to guard against "undue hindrances to political conversations and the exchange of ideas." The three regulations significantly inhibited communications with voters about proposed political change and could not be justified by the state's interests.

The registration requirement failed First Amendment review because it would "drastically reduce" the number of paid and volunteer persons available to circulate petitions. Justice Ginsburg held that the requirement would di-minish speech in the same way Colorado had sought to ban paid circulators at issue in *Meyer*. Limiting the number of petition circulators would result in a reduction in the size of the audience that initiative supporters could reach.

Colorado argued that registering to vote was a simple process that did not unfairly burden potential petition circulators. Justice Ginsburg dismissed this argument, stating that for some individuals the choice not to register "implicates thought and expression." Moreover, other Colorado regulations could address the state's desire to police circulators who violate the law. Circulators were required to submit an affidavit that included his or her address. In addition, Colorado's requirement that all circulators be residents helped protect the state's interests. The registration requirement, therefore, was not warranted.

Justice Ginsburg agreed with the Tenth Circuit that forcing circulators to wear a badge with their names on it would inhibit people from participating as circulators. Ginsburg noted that when circulators solicit signatures, they might encounter reactions that are "intense, emotional, and unreasoned." The badge requirement "compels personal name identification at the precise moment when the circulator's interest in anonymity is greatest." The state's interest in identifying circulators guilty of misconduct could be accomplished by relying on circulators to disclose their names and addresses on affidavits submitted with each section of the petition.

The Supreme Court also found unconstitutional the regulation requiring monthly reports and a final report containing information on the amount paid to circulators, along with their names and addresses. Justice Ginsburg endorsed the Tenth Circuit's ruling that Colorado could require this information from those who pay the circulators. Disclosure of the names of initiative sponsors, and the amounts they spend to gather petitions, "responds to Colorado's substantial interest in controlling domination of the initiative process by affluent special interest groups." As for releasing the names of paid circulators, Ginsburg concluded that there was no perceived benefit to the electoral process from the release of this information.

Justice Ginsburg sought to make clear that Colorado had other means of regulating the ballot-initiative process that do not violate the First Amendment. To deter FRAUD and diminish corruption, the state had an "arsenal of safeguards," including a number of regulations not challenged in the lawsuit.

Justice SANDRA DAY O'CONNOR, in a dissenting opinion joined by Justice STEPHEN BREYER, agreed with the majority that the badge requirement was unconstitutional, but argued that the voter registration and financial disclosure regulations were reasonable and necessary. The registration requirement was a "neutral qualification for participation in the petitioning process" and one that was easily met. The financial disclosure requirement was a legitimate means of combating fraud and "providing the public with information." Overall she saw the Court's decision as a blow to the efforts of states to maintain the "integrity of the political process."

Chief Justice WILLIAM H. REHNQUIST, in a rare dissent, agreed with the other dissenters, but emphasized that requiring circulators to be registered voters was a legitimate state regulation.

CROSS REFERENCES
Initiative; Referendum

EMPLOYMENT LAW

The body of law that governs the employer-employee relationship, including individual employment contracts, the application of TORT and CONTRACT doctrines, and a large group of statutory regulation on issues such as the right to organize and negotiate COLLECTIVE BARGAINING AGREEMENTS, protection from DISCRIMINATION, wages and hours, and health and safety.

EEOC Issues Guidance on Right to Protection Against Retaliation

In 1998, the U.S. Equal Employment Opportunity Commission (EEOC) issued comprehensive written guidance that clarifies the prohibition against retaliation aimed at individuals who file charges of employment discrimination or who participate in an investigation of an discrimination charge. The policy tells employers what they cannot do and informs employees or former employees when it is appropriate to file a complaint based on retaliation. It applies to a number of federal civil rights laws, including Title VII of the Civil Rights Act of 1964, the Age Discrimination in Employment Act, the Equal Pay Act, Title I of the Americans with Disabilities Act, the Rehabilitation Act, and sections of the Civil Rights Act of 1991.

The EEOC implements the provisions of these laws and also investigates complaints that allege violations of the laws and EEOC regulations. During the 1990s the number of charges received by the EEOC alleging retaliation more than doubled, rising from 7,900 in 1991 to 18,110 in 1997.

The legal issues surrounding employer retaliation became confused in the 1990s as the federal circuit courts of appeal developed contradictory holdings over whether Title VII prohibited retaliation against former employees as well as current employees. The Fourth Circuit ruled that Title VII did not apply to retaliation of former employees, while six other circuits (the Second, Third, Seventh, Ninth, Tenth, and Eleventh) held that the term "employees" in Title VII included former employees.

The Supreme Court resolved this issue in *Robinson v. Shell Oil Company*, 519 U.S. 337, 117 S. Ct. 843, 136 L. Ed. 2d 808 (1997). In a unanimous decision, the Court ruled that a former employee could sue an employer for illegal retaliation based on conduct that occurred after the employee was discharged. The Court was persuaded that to exclude former employees from the statue's protection would undermine the effectiveness to Title VII, "allowing the threat of post-employment retaliation to deter victims of discrimination from complaining to EEOC, and would provide a perverse incentive for employers to fire employees who might bring Title VII claims." The Court viewed it as important to provide victims of illegal discrimination with "unfettered access" to the provisions of Title VII.

The EEOC's policies on retaliation are contained in a new chapter of the commission's Compliance Manual. The chapter states that federal CIVIL RIGHTS laws prohibit retaliation by an employer, employment agency, or labor organization because an individual "engaged in a protected activity." A protected activity includes "opposing a practice made unlawful by one of the employment discrimination statutes" and "filing a charge, testifying, assisting, or participating in any manner in a investigation, proceeding, or hearing under the applicable statute."

A person who files a retaliation charge with the EEOC does not have to allege that he or she was treated differently because of race, religion, sex, national origin, age or disability. For example, a white employee who is fired because she testified on behalf of a person of color in an EEOC investigation could file a charge of employer retaliation.

The EEOC chapter describes three essential elements of a retaliation claim: (1) opposition to discrimination or participation in a employment discrimination proceeding, (2) adverse action by the employer, and (3) a causal connection between the protected activity and the adverse action.

Opposition to discrimination occurs if the individual "explicitly or implicitly" communicates to the employer a "belief that its activity constitutes a form of employment discrimination" that is covered by the laws the EEOC enforces. Opposition may also be nonverbal, such as picketing or engaging in a production slowdown. Even "broad or ambiguous complaints of unfair treatment" will qualify as opposition.

Participation, rather than opposition, may be an essential element of a retaliation claim. A person who participates in the challenge of employment discrimination in EEOC proceedings, state administrative or court proceedings, or federal court proceedings, falls within the definition of participant. The EEOC emphasizes in the chapter that participation is protected "regardless of whether the allegations in the original charge were valid or reasonable." The retaliation provisions of the statutes also prohibit retaliation against "someone so closely related to or associated with the person exercising his or her statutory rights that it would discourage or prevent the person from pursuing those rights." For example, it would be unlawful for an employer to retaliate against an employee because his or her spouse, who is also an employee, filed an EEOC charge. Both spouses could bring retaliation claims.

The most common types of retaliation include denial of promotion, refusal to hire, denial of job benefits, demotion, suspension, and discharge. Other types of adverse actions include threats, reprimands, negative evaluations, and harassment. Adverse actions can occur after the employee no longer works for the employer. In *Robinson*, for example, the employer responded by giving the former employee a negative job reference that was based on a retaliatory motive. The EEOC made clear that the retaliation statutes "prohibit any adverse treatment that is based on a retaliatory motive and is reasonably likely to deter the charging party or others from engaging in the protected activity." However, "petty slights and annoyances are not actionable."

The third essential element of a retaliation charge is proof of the causal connection. There must be proof that the employer took an adverse action because the person filing the retaliation charge engaged in a protected activity. Proof of this retaliatory motive can be made through direct or circumstantial evidence.

Direct evidence is any "written or verbal statement" by the employer that he or she took the challenged action because the person filing the charge engaged in a protected activity. Direct evidence of retaliation is rare, but when it is found the EEOC states that cause should be found. More common is circumstantial evidence, where facts raise an inference of retaliation. If the employer fails to produce evidence of a "legitimate, non-retaliatory reason" for the action, or if the reason advanced by the employer is merely a pretext to hide a retaliatory motive, the causal connection will be proved.

If retaliation is proven, the person filing the charge may receive compensatory and PUNITIVE DAMAGES. Retaliation claims are particularly well suited for the recovery of punitive damages because retaliation is often undertaken with malice or with reckless indifference. These elements are fit within the framework for recovery of punitive damages.

Hughes Aircraft Co. v. Jacobson

In the U.S. Supreme Court case of *Hughes Aircraft Co. v. Jacobson*, ___ U.S.___, 119 S. Ct. 755, 142 L. Ed. 2d 881 (1999), the Court reclarified the rule that there is no violation of the Employee Retirement Income Security Act of 1974 (ERISA) where a company uses the surplus money in a pension plan to fund retirement benefits for workers other than those who contributed to the fund. In the unanimous decision reached in January 1999, the Court remarked that plaintiff retirees "proceed[ed] on the erroneous assumption that they had an interest in the plan's surplus."

In the unanimous opinion written by Justice CLARENCE THOMAS, the Court held that the retired workers had not bought a share of the pension plan's investment gains with their contributions, but rather, they bought a guarantee of a specific pension benefit based upon their salaries and years of service. Any surplus monies gained by the pension plan in excess of that guaranteed benefit belonged to the company to do with as it deemed best.

The CLASS ACTION suit involved five original plaintiffs, retired workers of Hughes who filed suit in federal district court in 1992. The suit named Hughes Aircraft and its corporate successors Hughes Electronics, a subsidiary of the General Motors Corporation, and the Raytheon Company. At issue was a traditional, defined-benefit pension plan, started in 1955, in which both company and employees contributed funds. Employee contributions were mandatory for several years. In 1986, the plan's assets exceeded the value of accrued benefits payable under the plan by over one billion dollars, so the company stopped contributing to the plan. In 1989, Hughes established an early-retirement program providing for enhanced benefits to certain eligible employees, and following this, Hughes again amended the plan with respect to new participants/new employees effective in January 1991. Under this new amendment, new participants to the plan could not contribute, and therefore, would receive commensurately-reduced benefits upon retirement. Existing members could either continue with their contributions, or cease contributions and be treated under the plan as the new participants, i.e., receive a reduced benefit.

Under ERISA, where a plan with a surplus is terminated, existing participants are entitled to a share of the surplus. The five plaintiffs believed that they stood to gain approximately 25 percent on their vested benefits due to what they deemed was a terminated plan. (They argued that the amendments and changes to the existing plan were so extensive in nature and had substantively altered benefits to such a degree, as to constitute a "terminated" plan under ERISA.) When the workers subsequently retired and received only their guaranteed defined benefit, they sued.

The complaint alleged six causes of action: that Hughes had violated ERISA's prohibition against using employees' vested benefits to meet its obligations (by using the funds to support the non-contributory part of the plan); that Hughes violated ERISA's anti-inurement prohibition by benefiting itself at the expense of the plan's surplus fund; that the termination of Hughes' previous plan violated ERISA's requirement that the terminated plan's residual assets be distributed to plan beneficiaries; and three separate counts alleging violations of Hughes' fiduciary duties, including funding a program outside of the plan's purpose and using the surplus to benefit non-contributing participants.

The federal district dismissed the case, for failure to state a claim. The U.S. Court of Appeals for the Ninth Circuit reversed, finding that indeed, plaintiffs' causes of action were viable. Interestingly, the Ninth Circuit made special note of the U.S. Supreme Court's previous decision in a similar case, *Lockheed Corporation v. Spink*, 517 U.S. 882, 116 S. Ct. 1783, 135 L. Ed. 2d 153 (1996), wherein the High Court found

no ERISA violation. The Ninth Circuit distinguished the *Spink* case, reasoning that it concerned a plan funded solely by employer contributions, whereas in the present case, plan participants had contributed to the plan's fund and therefore had a vested interest in the surplus money. The appellate court thus concluded that the addition of a noncontributory benefit structure, which made use of previously contributed funds, constituted a termination of the old plan and the creation of two new plans under ERISA.

The Supreme Court unanimously reversed the Ninth Circuit and agreed with the federal district court. In essence, the plaintiffs got what they bargained for: their pre-existing plan benefits were not adversely affected by any subsequent changes or alterations to benefits. They retired with the exact guaranteed benefit that they had purchased with their contributions. By terms of their guaranteed benefit, the company risked having to pay benefits to them even if the company had lost money: plaintiff members had earned a nonforfeitable "accrued benefit," which by statute cannot be reduced below their contribution amount. But as members of a defined benefit plan, they had no vested interest in the plan's surplus money created by the company's investment savvy or good fortune, even if their contributions helped increase the surplus. Further, since the only use of the surplus money was to fund other components of the benefit plan, the surplus did not "inure" to the benefit of Hughes, i.e., Hughes did not stand to benefit itself with the surplus.

Moreover, the amendments and changes to the plan, specifically the addition of a non-contributory structure, did not constitute a "termination" of the old plan under ERISA, so as to warrant distribution of surplus funds. Nor does it constitute a "wasting trust" under common law. Because the plan at issue continues to operate as before with respect to the thousands of participants in the contributory structure, it can not be said that the plan has, by function, terminated.

Finally, with respect to the alleged breaches in FIDUCIARY DUTIES, the Court held that *Spink* dispositively foreclosed them. *Spink*'s reasoning applies, irrespective of whether the plan at issue is contributory, non-contributory or other, as the language makes no such distinction when defining "fiduciary." Further, *Spink* held that, without exception, plan sponsors who altered the terms of a plan "do not fall into the category of fiduciaries."

The decision was hailed as a victory by employers who enjoy the latitude of amending retirement programs to provide a new or better benefit formula, without the risk of causing a "termination" of the old plan under ERISA. Additionally, employers do not compromise fiduciary duties by using surplus funds to finance other plan benefits, which may or may not enhance the benefit of any sub-class of plan participants. What is owed to employees is the fulfillment of the contracted-for benefit.

Haddle v. Garrison

It has long been established that at-will employees (which the law presumes all employees to be, unless contract, statute or other case laws apply) can be discharged from employment, with or without good cause, at any time by the employer. Employees are conversely presumed to have the same right to terminate their employment, with or without cause, at any time. At-will employment means, literally, at the will of the parties to the employment agreement. The few exceptions carved out in case law from this general rule include terminations for discriminatory purposes, or terminations which are "retaliatory" in nature, particularly in response to an employee having exercised a constitutional or statutory right. One of the most familiar and viable, causes of action for "retaliatory discharge" of an at-will employee is, for example, under the Whistleblower's Act. Employees who are discharged after having exposed company wrongdoing under the act may file lawsuits alleging retaliatory discharge (the burden remains upon the employees to prove that the reason for their discharge was retaliation).

In *Haddle v. Garrison*, 525 U.S. 121, 119 S. Ct. 489, 142 L. Ed. 2d 502 (1998), the plaintiff, an at-will employee, alleged that he had been fired in retaliation for obeying a federal GRAND JURY subpoena in an upcoming Medicare fraud trial against his employer. Since the employee had not yet testified, he could not take advantage of the Whistleblower's Act. As an at-will employee, he had no protected interest in continued employment. Therefore, he sued under 42 U.S.C.§ 1985, which protects persons from conspiracies to:

> deter, by force, intimidation, or threat, any…person in any [federal] court…from attending such court, or from testifying in any matter pending therein,…or to injure [him] in his person or property on account of his having so attended or testified.

Therefore the relevant issue in *Haddle* was whether a discharged at-will employee suffered an actual legal injury cognizable under this statute to give him a viable cause of action.

Michael Haddle (an at-will employee under Georgia law) was employed in a middle-management position at Healthcare, Inc., an healthcare company which mostly serviced patients covered by Medicare. The company made most of its money from Medicare reimbursements. In 1994, the federal government began investigating the company, and in 1995, company owner and president Jeannette Garrison was indicted, along with other company officials, for Medicare fraud. Haddle had cooperated with the investigators, and he was subsequently subpoenaed to testify before the federal grand jury. At about the same time, the company had filed for BANKRUPTCY, and a TRUSTEE was appointed by the bankruptcy court to run the company. The former in-house lawyer became the company president, and he recommended to the trustee that Haddle be fired. Haddle was fired in 1995.

Haddle alleged in his complaint that the trustee fired him at Garrison's direction, in retaliation for his threat to testify against her and other company officials. Since Haddle had no recourse or protection from firing under employment law, he sued in federal district court under an old 1871 federal CIVIL RIGHTS statute, 42 U.S.C. § 1985(2), which is not an employment statute. Section 1985 protects persons from injuries caused by deterrence, "by force, intimidation or threat," such as that alleged in this case.

Both the federal district court and the U.S. Court of Appeals for the Eleventh Circuit dismissed the case for failure to state a claim. Again, they reiterated that at-will employees do not enjoy constitutionally-protected interests in continued employment and can be dismissed, at any time, for good, bad, or no cause at all. Further, the Eleventh Circuit held that Haddle did not suffer an "injury" to his "person or property" as required under the statute.

Inconsistency existed at the appellate level on this issue. The Ninth Circuit had previously held that an at-will employee could sue after losing his job. So the U.S. Supreme Court ordered a writ of CERTIORARI to the Court of Appeals for the Eleventh Circuit. It unanimously reversed the Eleventh Circuit.

It first found error in the Eleventh Circuit's conclusion that Haddle needed to suffer an injury to a "constitutionally-protected property interest" in order to state a viable cause of action. The Court noted that nothing in the clear language of § 1985 supported that conclusion. As the Court explained, the gist of the statutory provision is that it protects a person from "intimidation or retaliation." The term, "injured in his person or property" only describes the type of harm that the victim may suffer as a result of the violations of § 1985. The Court noted that loss of employment has long been considered a compensable injury under TORT law, and there was no reason why that should not apply here. The Court then went through a careful explanation to support its holding that the term "injured in his person or property' referred to or incorporated tort principles.

The significance of this case is that at-will employees who are precluded from suing their employers following termination from employment may still have viable causes of action under other areas of the law, particularly, as in this case, federal civil rights statutes. The lawsuits are essentially the same, but couched in different terms. At-will employees have always had the protections of other statutes that may only collaterally apply to employment. Some of these viable causes of action include retaliatory discharges for having filed a workers compensation claim or for having exposed company wrongdoing under the Whistleblower's Act. Virtually all discrimination laws are available to the at-will employee as well.

CROSS REFERENCES
Civil Rights; Equal Employment Opportunity Commission

ENVIRONMENTAL LAW

An amalgam of state and federal statutes, regulations, and common-law principles covering air pollution, water pollution, hazardous waste, the wilderness, and endangered wildlife.

Liability for Parent Corporations

In *United States v. Bestfoods*, 524 U.S. 51, 118 S. Ct. 1876, 141 L. Ed. 2d 43 (1996), a unanimous Supreme Court clarified the circumstances under which parent corporations may be held liable under the Comprehensive Environmental Response, Compensation and Liability Act of 1980 (CERCLA, § 101 et seq., 42 U.S.C.A. § 9601 et seq.) for "operating" facilities owned by their subsidiaries.

CERCLA is a statute that was enacted by the U.S. Congress in 1980 as a response to the serious environmental and health risks posed by industrial pollution. It grants the president broad power to require both government agencies and private parties to clean up hazardous waste sites. Suits brought by the United States to recover cleanup or remediation costs—which often can run into the tens of millions of dollars—may be brought against, among others, "any person who at the time of disposal of any hazardous substance owned or operated any facilities." 42 U.S.C. § 9607(a)(2).

CERCLA's ability to impose liability upon any person or entity that has "owned or operated" a polluting facility is the focus of much controversy and is the focus of the *Bestfoods* decision. In particular, the concept of an "operator" has been troubling for courts because CERCLA does not clearly define what it means to be an "operator." Accordingly, considerable disagreement characterizes the case law over the instances where a "parent" corporation—so called because of its control of another corporation through its ownership of that corporation's stock—can be deemed to be an "operator" and, therefore, be held liable for the cleanup costs of hazardous waste sites that it does not own, but that are owned by its subsidiary. This issue is particularly important because under the doctrine of limited liability, the law generally treats a parent corporation and its subsidiary corporation as distinct and separate entities, with neither liable or responsible for the debts or obligations of the other.

The controversy in *Bestfoods* began in 1957, when Ott Chemical Co. began manufacturing chemicals for pharmaceutical, veterinary, and agricultural uses at a plant in western Michigan. At the same time, Ott began dumping hazardous substances at that site. In 1965, a wholly-owned subsidiary of CPC International Inc. (which later changed its name to "Bestfoods") purchased Ott, and that subsidiary continued to produce chemicals at the facility and continued to contaminate the site. Finally, in 1972, the subsidiary sold this operation to another company which continued operations at the site until 1986.

Prior to and during the time that this facility was owned by Bestfoods' subsidiary, chemical and other hazardous waste disposal was widespread. This included discharging chemical waste into lagoons, burying hundreds of drums of waste, and dumping gallons of hazardous chemicals in the woods on the site. In addition to this purposeful disposal of hazardous waste and other toxic chemicals, the site was plagued by numerous unintentional chemical spills and discharges. This led to heavy contamination of the soil, surface water, and ground water.

Following the enactment of CERCLA in 1980, the Environmental Protection Agency (EPA) investigated the facility and determined that an intensive, sustained clean-up effort was necessary—an effort that would cost tens of millions of dollars. Accordingly, in 1989, the EPA sued several former "owners and operators," including Bestfoods, as the parent of the company that had owned the site, to recover the cleanup costs.

At the district court level, in deciding only the question of whether Bestfoods and the other defendants were liable under CERCLA, the district court argued that CERCLA broadened the potential for liability of parent corporations without discarding entirely the traditional concept of limited liability. (*CPC Int'l, Inc. v. Aerojet General Corp.*, 777 F.Supp. 549 [W.D. Mich. 1991]) CERCLA did so, the court reasoned, by creating a new "middle ground" in which a parent corporation may be directly liable as an "operator" of a site that it does not own when it exerts power or influence over the subsidiary that owns the facility by actively participating in, and exercising control over, the subsidiary's business. Using this logic, the district court held Bestfoods directly liable under CERCLA as the "operator" of the facilities owned by its subsidiary by virtue of its control over the subsidiary's functions and decision making. In this way, the district court held that because Bestfoods owned and controlled the subsidiary, which in turn owned and controlled the facility, Bestfoods was deemed an "operator" of the facility within CERCLA.

On appeal, the Court of Appeals for the Sixth Circuit reversed the district court, essentially finding that a parent corporation should not be liable for a facility owned by its subsidiary merely because the parent owns and controls the subsidiary. (*United States v. Cordova/Michigan*, 113 F. 3d 572 [1997]). Rather, the court held that under such circumstances, and absent direct involvement by the parent corporation in operating the facility, a parent corporation should incur liability as an "operator" under CERCLA for the facility owned by its subsidiary only when the requirements necessary to "pierce the corporate veil" are met. (The concept of "piercing the corporate veil" is an instance where a court will disregard the general rule of limited liability. It is used by courts to impose liability upon a parent corporation for the acts of its subsidiary in instances where the parent corporation exer-

cises so much control over its subsidiary that there is no separateness of the two corporate entities, and where allowing the parent corporation to escape liability for its subsidiary's acts would perpetuate a fraud.) In this instance, the district court did not find that the "corporate veil" should be "pierced," but, instead, relied on this "middle ground" under CERCLA. The Court of Appeals for the Sixth Circuit was not similarly convinced, and noted that the factors the district court used in finding Bestfoods as an "operator" of its subsidiary—which included 100 percent ownership of its subsidiary, officers that held dual positions both at the parent and the subsidiary level, participation in environmental matters, and financial control—were not, by themselves, sufficient to "pierce the corporate veil." Accordingly, those factors were not sufficient to impose direct liability upon Bestfoods as an "operator" under CERCLA.

The Supreme Court granted CERTIORARI to resolve the conflict. The Supreme Court affirmed the reasoning of the court of appeals, indicating that a parent corporation may have derivative liability under CERCLA for its subsidiary's actions, and with respect to a facility owned by its subsidiary, "but only when" the corporate veil may be pierced. In clarifying CERCLA and direct liability as an "operator," however, the Supreme Court went on to indicate that "nothing in the statute's terms bars a parent corporation from direct liability for its own actions in 'operating' a facility," even if that facility is owned by its subsidiary. That is, parent corporations may be directly liable for wrongs committed by their directors, officers, employees and other agents with respect to any polluting facility, regardless of who owns the facility. Whereas "veil piercing" is a form of derivative or indirect liability whereby a parent corporation may be held liable for the actions of its subsidiary, CERCLA's "operator" provision is concerned primarily with direct liability for the parent's own actions.

In determining direct "operator" liability, the Supreme Court focused not on the relationship between the parent and its subsidiary (which are relevant to a veil-piercing analysis), but rather on the parent's relationship with the subsidiary's facility. "The question is not whether the parent corporation operates the subsidiary, but rather whether it operates the facility, and that operation is evidenced by participation in the activities of the facility, not the subsidiary."

Bestfoods thus clarifies the long-confused standard for operator liability by separating the test for indirect liability from the test for direct liability in circumstances where a parent corporation's subsidiary owns a polluting facility. Under the CERCLA theory of direct liability, a parent corporation may be liable as an "operator" of a facility even if that facility is owned by its subsidiary. This liability is determined by examining the parent's role in managing, directing, or conducting "operations having to do with the leakage or disposal of hazardous waste, or decisions about compliance with environmental regulations."

By focusing attention on the acts of the parent corporation at the subsidiary's facility, *Bestfoods* has narrowed the circumstances under which a corporate parent may be held directly liable as an "operator" under CERCLA, and preserves a parent corporation's ability to avoid liability for a polluting facility owned by its subsidiary.

Private Title VI Lawsuits and Environmental Racism

On August 17, 1998, the U.S. Supreme Court dismissed an appeal in the case of *Seif v. Chester Residents Concern for Quality Living*, __ U.S. __, 119 S. Ct. 22, 141 L. Ed. 2d 783 (1988). The Court had agreed to hear the case on June 8, 1998, but later dismissed it as MOOT without ruling on the merits of the case. This dismissal leaves open a question in the area of law known as "environmental racism." This is racism which manifests itself through environmental policies with disproportionate effects on minorities. Specifically, the U.S. Supreme Court was to decide whether private parties (e.g., citizens), as opposed to government agencies, can seek enforcement of federal regulations governing Title VI of the CIVIL RIGHTS ACT OF 1964.

Seif was a case brought by residents of Chester, Pennsylvania, whose population is largely African American. The residents claimed that the state of Pennsylvania had allowed a disproportionate number of waste treatment facilities to be built in Chester. The residents of Chester argued that Pennsylvania had allowed five such facilities in their city and only two in the rest of the county in which Chester was located (Delaware County), which was predominantly inhabited by white citizens. Specifically, the city of Chester had, at the time of the suit, a population of approximately 42,000, of which 65 percent were African American and 32 percent were white. In contrast, the remainder of Delaware County (excluding Chester) had a population of approximately 502,000, of which 6.2 percent were African American and 91 per-

cent were white. In addition, the five Chester waste treatment facilities had a total permit capacity of 2.1 million tons of waste per year, while the two non-Chester facilities located elsewhere in Delaware County had total permit capacity of only 1,400 tons of waste per year. In light of this, the residents of the city of Chester fought to block the Pennsylvania Department of Environmental Protection (DEP) from granting a permit for yet another waste treatment facility proposed to be located in Chester.

The legal approach of the residents was novel. Specifically, the residents relied on regulations relating to Title VI of the Civil Rights Act of 1964, which bars racial bias in federally financed projects. 41 U.S.C. § 2000d et. seq. The residents relied on two parts of Title IV in asserting their claim against DEP. The first was Section 601 of Title VI, which provides:

"No person in the United States shall, on the ground of race, color, or national origin, be excluded from participation in, be denied the benefits of, or be subjected to discrimination under any program or activity receiving Federal financial assistance."

The Chester residents also relied on Section 602 of Title VI, which provides:

Each Federal department and agency which is empowered to extend Federal financial assistance to any program or activity, by way of grant, loan, or contract other than a contract of insurance or guaranty, is authorized and directed to effectuate the provisions of [Title VI] with respect to such program or activity by issuing rules, regulations, or orders of general applicability which shall be consistent with the objectives of the statute authorizing the financial assistance in connection with which the action is taken.

In essence, Section 602 authorizes federal government agencies, like the Environmental Protection Agency, to issue regulations to implement Title VI.

In attempting to rely on both Sections 601 and 602 of Title VI, the Chester residents noted that DEP issued or denied applications to operate waste processing facilities, and also received funding from the Environmental Protection Agency to operate Pennsylvania's waste programs. Title VI, and the EPA civil rights regulations implementing Title VI (which the EPA is authorized to issue pursuant to Section 602 of Title VI), condition the receipt by DEP of federal funding on its assurance that it will comply with Title VI and the EPA regulations. 40 C.F.R. § 7.80(a) (1997). These EPA regulations, in part, prohibit recipients of federal funds from using "criteria or methods...which have the effect of subjecting individuals to discrimination because of their race, color, national origin, or sex..." Therefore, the Chester residents argued that DEP's issuance of yet another permit for a waste treatment facility violated their civil rights and the EPA regulations implementing Title VI.

The district court dismissed the Title VI claim based on Section 601, holding that the section applied only to "intentional discrimination," which was not being alleged in this instance. Instead of alleging that DEP was intentionally discriminating against them on the basis of race (which is very difficult to prove), the residents of Chester were arguing that the effect of DEP's actions was discriminatory and, as such, violated the EPA regulations.

The district court, however, without ruling on whether DEP's actions had a discriminatory effect, dismissed the claim on the grounds that no private right of action exists under which the residents of Chester could sue the enforce EPA regulations. In other words, while the EPA could bring a lawsuit to enforce its own regulations (it could have, for instance, sued DEP directly), the district court concluded that private citizens did not have a similar right. This was in contrast to Section 601 of Title IV, with respect to which a private right of action does exist, as held by the U.S. Supreme Court in *Guardians Association v. Civil Service Commission of the New York*, 463 U.S. 582, 103 S. Ct. 3221, 77 L. Ed. 2d 866 (1983).

On appeal, the Court of Appeals for the Third Circuit reversed the district court's decision. *Chester Residents Concerned for Quality Living v. Seif*, 132 F. 3d 925 (3rd Cir. 1997). In so doing, the court of appeals held that a private right of action did exist under Section 602 and the EPA regulations implementing them. Specifically, the court of appeals found that "the statute under which the rule was promulgated properly permits the implication of a private right of action."

The DEP appealed the court of appeals' decision to the U.S. Supreme Court, arguing that the Third Circuit improperly made it possible for private citizens to enforce in federal court EPA regulations that, in its view, should only be enforced by the agency itself. On June 8, 1998, the U.S. Supreme Court agreed to hear the case. The stage was set for the Supreme Court to decide whether private parties alleging discriminatory effect could seek enforcement of federal regulations governing Title VI. While the U.S. Supreme Court had earlier determined, in *Guardian*, that a private right of action was available in cases alleging intentional discrimination, the question remained whether a similar private right of action existed in claims of "discriminatory effect," such as those asserted by the Chester residents.

However, after the Supreme Court agreed to hear the case, the proposed operator for the waste treatment plant in Chester, Pennsylvania, abandoned its plans for the facility. As a result, in a summary order announced in August 1998, the U.S. Supreme Court dismissed the case and vacated the ruling of the court of appeals. This dismissal was not a reflection of the merits of the case; rather, the U.S. Supreme Court routinely dismisses cases, even those where parties have filed briefs and presented oral arguments, when circumstances change to make the issues moot, or where its decision will not have any practical effect on the controversy.

In doing so, the U.S. Supreme Court overturned the court of appeals' decision, eliminating it as a binding legal precedent and failing to resolve the important question of whether private litigants can sue under Title VI alleging discriminatory effect.

CROSS REFERENCES
Civil Rights; Corporations; Liability; Moot

ESPIONAGE

The act of securing information of a military or political nature that a competing nation holds secret. It can involve the analysis of diplomatic reports, publications, statistics, and broadcasts, as well as spying, a clandestine activity carried out by an individual or individuals working under a secret identity for the benefit of a nation's information gathering techniques. In the United States, the organization that heads most activities dedicated to espionage is the CENTRAL INTELLIGENCE AGENCY.

Jonathan Pollard

A spy scandal of the 1980s entered the news again in 1999. At the heart of the story was Jonathan Pollard, who was an intelligence-research specialist in the Navy's Field Operational Intelligence Office during the 1980s. In 1985, Pollard, an American Jew, was arrested on charges of spying for Israel. Pollard was accused

of turning over more than 360 cubic feet of documentation containing top-secret technical and human information belonging to the United States.

Israel paid Pollard approximately $50,000 for his espionage. The secret information, or "intelligence," revealed by Pollard included: the identity of many sensitive and expensive sources of intelligence used by the United States; secret codes, manuals, and communication methods; methods used by the United States to obtain its intelligence; and secret military plans, weapons systems, and military operations of the United States. The intelligence also revealed classified information about chemical weapons manufacturing sites in Iraq and Syria.

Pollard insisted that he had turned over information only to help Israel with its own defense and its own survival. According to Pollard, it was proper for the United States to give the secret information to Israel because Israel was an ally. Pollard further argued that he was giving the information to an Israeli intelligence operative who already was receiving classified information from the United States.

However, the turning over of intelligence is not a matter for researchers such as Pollard, and Pollard's intentions made no difference to the U.S. government. Nobody knew for sure what Israel would do with the information, and some officials feared that Israel could use the information in its relationships with other countries. It is known how secure Israel's own intelligence was, and intelligence officials feared that

spies for other countries could gain access to the intelligence through Israel. Intelligence operatives also believed that they would find it more difficult to do their jobs because of the trade secrets that were revealed. Espionage is a federal felony and carries with it a possible sentence of life in prison. Pollard pleaded guilty to spying on March 4, 1987, and he received a sentence of life in prison.

The U.S. intelligence community struggled to come to grips with the fallout. Caspar Weinberger, secretary of defense under President RONALD REAGAN, called the effects of the espionage catastrophic. Senator Richard Shelby (R-AL) said that "Pollard betrayed our country on a grand scale (the extent of the damage is not yet fully known) and he deserves every day of his life sentence."

Supporters of Pollard argue that Pollard did not actually place any lives in danger. They further argue that Pollard was not guided by malice toward the United States or motivated by profit. Rather, Pollard was motivated by, as lawyer Alan Dershowitz said "misguided ideology." Dershowitz charges the United States with its own double dealing. According to Dershowitz, the United States broke a plea bargain agreement with Pollard in which it agreed not to seek life in prison as a sentence for Pollard if he pleaded guilty.

In the early 1990s, pressure for Pollard's release began to mount. Pollard supporters in Israel and the United States convinced President Bill Clinton to review Pollard's case and decide whether to grant clemency to Pollard. Clinton reviewed the case in 1993 and 1996 and rejected clemency both times.

In 1995, Pollard, sitting in a U.S. federal prison, was granted citizenship by Israel. Benjamin Netanyahu was elected Prime Minister of Israel in 1996 and began to press for Pollard's release. Netanyahu went so far as to connect Pollard's release to peace negotiations with the Palestinians. At a meeting in Wye River, Maryland, in October 1998 with President Clinton and Palestinian Authority President Yasser Arafat, Netanyahu requested Pollard's release. Clinton promised Netanyahu that he would review the case again.

President Clinton's promise sparked a heated debate. Constitutional expert Bruce Fein, called Netanyahu's request "chutzpah at its best" and noted that "Pollard has voiced no contrition for his betrayal of the United States." Fein compared the Pollard case to a case involving

Mordechai Vanunu, an Israeli who worked as a nuclear technician at the Israeli Atomic Research Reactor at Dimono in the Negev. Vanunu eventually converted to Christianity and, seeking to alert the world to Israel's nuclear arsenal, Vanunu went to London and gave details of Israel's nuclear program to *The London Sunday Times*. Vanunu was then lured to Italy by Israel's spy agency, the Mossad. Vanunu was kidnapped in Italy, taken to Israel, and tried on spying charges. After a secretive trial, Vanunu was found guilty and sentenced to eighteen years in prison. Fein argued that if anyone deserved clemency on spying charges it was Vanunu. "He was not a spy, acted from conscience, did not enlist his loyalties on behalf of a foreign country and his release would pose no danger of further injury to Israel's security," said Fein. The *New York Times* opined that "[j]ustice was served by Mr. Pollard's conviction and imprisonment and should not be upended to placate his sympathizers in Israel."

For years after the espionage revelations, Israel denied any connection to Pollard. Israel has consistently refused to return the documents that Pollard delivered. The matter of clemency for Pollard created a dilemma for President Clinton, but in May 1999 Clinton learned that he may be able to avoid the issue entirely. That month, Israel ousted Netanyahu from office by electing a new Prime Minister, Ehud Barak.

CROSS REFERENCES
Clemency; Rosenberg, Julius and Ethel

EVIDENCE

Any MATTER OF FACT that a party to a lawsuit offers to prove or disprove an isse in the case. A system of rules and standards used to determine which facts may be admitted, and to what extent a JUDGE or JURY may consider those facts, as proof of a particular issue in a lawsuit.

American Medical Association Votes on Expert Testimony

In the wake of rising incidences of "junk science" and persons willing to hold themselves out as "experts" for a fee, the American Medical Association (AMA) voted in early 1998 to consider the offering of medical "expert testimony" in litigation as constituting the "practice of medicine." Such an adopted provision could enable the AMA to subject members who hold themselves out as experts in private litigation, and their TESTIMONY, to peer review and potential

discipline if the proffered testimony was false or misleading to a jury. Affecting these policies, as well as sharing data, would be a joint effort with state and county medical societies.

During early 1999, AMA subcommittees and affiliates continued to discuss provisions to include in proposed policies. Opposition to the proposed policies primarily focused upon disagreement that the proffering of medical opinion testimony constituted "the practice of medicine." Several medical and legal consequences attach to such a proposition, delaying final adoption of any particular national plan. Some of the state medical societies, notably those in California and Florida, have nonetheless forged ahead in their efforts to contain and control any abuse of medical expert testimony in their states. They have proposed sanctions against offenders who have offered false, exaggerated, or misleading testimony at trial, ranging from written reprimands to full expulsion from the state medical association. However, the right to practice medicine is governed by state licensing boards, not medical societies, so most proposed sanctions would not affect a physician's ability to practice medicine.

It has long been lamented that the "expert witness" industry has developed into a self-policing litigation enterprise, flooded with persons willing to hold themselves out as experts in various specialized areas of medicine or science, and available to testify in litigation for an appropriate fee. Until the AMA initiative, there was little effort made to universally track, monitor, or refute medical expert testimony outside the parameters of the courtroom. Both retired and actively-practicing physicians with equally-credentialed backgrounds seemed perfectly willing to offer wholly inconsistent, diametrically-opposed, and mutually exclusive evidence on the very same subject. Worse yet, the proffering of medical expert testimony, tailored to the needs of the particular claim or defense, is often premised upon the respective financial resources of the parties, i.e., who was willing to pay, and how much, for the testimony. The controversy is not limited to medical expert testimony, but pervades the entire realm of technical knowledge, whether scientific or not. It is commonly referred to as "junk science."

Another way in which ostensibly-authoritative expert testimony has thus far evaded discipline is that it is often offered in the form of "opinion" testimony, rather than scientific or dogmatic principle. The potential harm of such evidence getting into courtrooms is that it often confuses jurors, who become stalemated in their deliberations. Trial tactics are then directed toward discrediting or rehabilitating one or both of the witnesses' testimony, sometimes even reaching the level of personal attacks against the witnesses, rather than against the articulated opinions. Ultimately, unable to decide which to accept because of equally-plausible expert testimony, the jury unfortunately turns to personal likes or dislikes of the witness, or worse, the parties or their counsel, in determining their verdict.

In *Daubert v. Merrell Dow Pharmaceuticals, Inc.*, 509 U.S. 579, 113 S. Ct. 2786, 125 L. Ed. 2d 469 (1993), the U.S. Supreme Court developed criteria for federal judges to use when ruling on the admissibility of expert witness testimony used when presenting scientific evidence in a courtroom. The factors relied upon in *Daubert* were whether the expert's theory or technique had been tested; whether it had been subjected to peer review and publication; whether there was a high "known or potential rate of error; and whether the theory or technique enjoyed general acceptance within a "relevant scientific community." The 1999 case of *Kumho Tire Company v. Carmichael*, ___U.S.___, 119 S. Ct. 1167, 143 L. Ed. 2d 238 (1999) expanded the applicability of the *Daubert* standards to other areas of expert testimony.

The gross abuse of "expert witness" status in the medical community has thus prompted the AMA to speak out on the issue and propose measures to contain it. Perhaps one of the most egregious examples of "junk science" was in the medical testimony proffered by plaintiffs' medical experts in the lucrative CLASS ACTION breast implant cases. In that situation, the lawsuits preceded the evidence which could link the silicone to any of the alleged illnesses or diseases claimed by the thousands of litigants. In the 1980s a few medical reports hypothesized a causal relationship between silicone implants and serious autoimmune disease such as lupus and scleroderma. Once released to the press, the anecdotal reports resulted in literally thousands of lawsuits being filed by implant recipients. Each of these litigants had retained a medical "expert witness" who would ostensibly testify as to the causal relationship between the plaintiff's alleged medical condition and the breast implant. (Most civil litigation, particularly PRODUCT LIABILITY cases, require that plaintiffs prove their cases by a mere "preponderance" of evidence—meaning as little as 51 percent—conversely, prosecutors in criminal matters must prove the defendant's guilt "beyond a reasonable doubt.") Later, in the

1990s, more than twenty-five independent studies by such top institutions as Harvard, University of Michigan, and the Mayo Clinic, all concluded that breast implants do not cause disease. While the causal relationship between implants and disease has not been negated dispositively as a matter of law, exaggerated, misleading or speculative evidence had stirred up the controversy and confused both litigants and juries for nearly a decade. Similarly, it has been argued that hundreds of beneficial drugs and therapies have been taken off the market because of medical "expert" testimony which either exaggerated or wrongfully incriminated adverse reactions or effects of the medicine.

The AMA has also taken the position of supporting full disclosure of backgrounds involving prospective recipients of medical grant awards or the authors of published medical studies and research. Full disclosure of financial interests, alliances, stock ownership, consultancies, and/or other indicia of actual or potential conflicts of interest has been proposed. What has not been universally agreed upon is whether conflicts of interest should merely be disclosed, or should be prohibited.

Another vehicle increasingly utilized to help control "junk science" and unreliable expert testimony has been through the updating and revising of both state and federal rules of evidence. Many evidentiary rules allow parties to query experts about the actual amount of the fees charged for the testimony, such evidence often reaching the jury. The use of prior deposition testimony in other cases can also often be used to discredit an expert, who might have offered conflicting evidence in a previous case. The proposed revision of Federal Rule of Evidence 702 would permit the admission of expert testimony only if the testimony is sufficiently based on reliable facts or data, the testimony is the product of reliable principles and methods, and the witness has applied the principles and methods faithfully to the facts of the case. As of early 1999, the proposed rule was making its way through several committees and Congress and was said to have elicited wide support.

Expert Testimony

In *Daubert v. Merrell Dow Pharmaceuticals, Inc.*, 509 U.S. 579, 113 S. Ct. 2786, 125 L. Ed. 2d 469 (1993), the U.S. Supreme Court developed criteria for federal judges to use when ruling on the admissibility of expert witness testimony used when presenting scientific evidence in a courtroom. The 1999 case of *Kumho Tire Company, Ltd. v. Carmichael*, ___U.S.___, 119 S.

Ct. 1167, 143 L. Ed. 2d 238 (1999) expands the applicability of the *Daubert* standards to other areas of expert testimony.

The unanimous opinion reached in *Kumho* was released on March 23, 1999. Its clear intent was to assist federal judges in keeping expert witness testimony of questionable reliability away from the jury. The increase in the number of "professional consultants" and persons claiming to be "experts" in many fields has given rise to a new evidentiary tool in litigation, often referred to as "junk science." Such evidence often confuses jurors—sometimes even judges—and tends to distort the other evidence and the real issues. Trial tactics then tend to be directed toward discrediting or rehabilitating one or both of the witnesses' testimony, sometimes even reaching the level of personal attacks against the witness, rather than against the articulated opinion.

Although under federal (and most states') rules of evidence, it is within the province of the jury to decide which expert's opinion to rely upon, the judge has great latitude in deciding what evidence or testimony even gets to the jury. The *Daubert* decision referred to this power as a "gatekeeping" judicial duty to limit testimony to that which was based "on the application of scientific principles."

In *Kuhmo*, suit was brought by the victims and survivors of an automobile crash which was allegedly caused by a defective tire manufactured by defendant Kuhmo. The accident occurred on Interstate 65 in Alabama's Baldwin County during 1993. The plaintiffs' Ford Minivan overturned after the right rear tire blew out. One passenger was killed and the other seven passengers were injured in the accident. No other vehicles were involved. The Carmichael family then sued Kuhmo.

In the federal district court case filed in Mobile, Alabama, Kuhmo's defense was that the tire was badly worn (bald in spots) and ill-maintained (it had imperfect repairs of two previous punctures). Plaintiffs sought to admit as evidence the deposition testimony of their "expert witness" who testified that the accident was caused by some defect in design or manufacture of the tire. The opinion was challenged by Kuhmo, particularly since the expert could not identify exactly what the defect was. The expert, Carlson, was a former tire-testing engineer for Michelin North America who had examined the tire one hour before his deposition. Carlson testified that his opinion was premised upon a process-of-elimination method. He testified that after ruling out "minor" signs of abuse and

wear on the tire, he concluded that the tire was therefore defective. Because the jury could be impressed with Carlson's prior employment with Michelin and/or his years of experience, weighing more heavily than the substance of his opinion, Kuhmo sought to have his testimony excluded.

The federal district court in Alabama agreed with defendant Kuhmo. The federal judge concluded that the proposed testimony was more technical than scientific, but still capable of being assessed by utilizing the *Daubert* approach. The court ruled that Carlson's analytical methods used in assessing the tire were not sufficiently reliable under *Daubert*, and excluded the testimony. As Carlson was the only one testifying in plaintiffs' behalf on the matter of defect, the court then granted SUMMARY JUDGMENT to Kuhmo.

But the Eleventh Circuit Court of Appeals reversed. The most significant part of its decision was in finding that the *Daubert* standards did not apply to non-scientific witnesses, and that judges' gatekeeping roles were limited to testimony based on "the application of scientific principles."

Accompanying Kuhmo's appeal to the Supreme Court were several amicus briefs, urging the Court to allow for an expansive interpretation of a judge's gatekeeping powers. On the other hand, other amicus groups argued to not change the traditional role of juries when evaluating evidence. In unanimously reversing the court of appeals and reinstating the federal court's original opinion, the Court ruled, in clear, unambiguous language, that the *Daubert* factors may apply to other experts who are not scientists. The factors relied upon in *Daubert* were whether the expert's theory or technique had been tested; whether it had been subjected to peer review and publication; whether there was a high "known or potential rate of error; and whether the theory or technique enjoyed general acceptance within a "relevant scientific community." The Court also referred to the express language of Federal Rule of Evidence 702, which made no distinction between scientific and technical or "other" specialized knowledge in its provisions that a witness must be "qualified as an expert" before being permitted to "testify thereto in the form of an opinion."

The Court further emphasized that *Daubert*'s application of Rule 702 was a "flexible" one, and that a trial judge may use any or all of the *Daubert* factors in undertaking its gatekeeping responsibilities. Since Rule 702 made no distinction between "scientific," "technical," or "other specialized" knowledge, there was no reason for the Court to.

Moreover, the Court found the appellate court's reversal to be in error. The court of appeals may only reverse a lower court's decision under an "abuse of discretion" standard. The trial court had broad latitude to determine whether any or all of *Daubert*'s factors were reasonable means to assess the reliability of an expert's proposed testimony in any particular case, and the court of appeals had no power to reverse that determination in the absence of an abuse of discretion.

Kuhmo was a product liability case. But the Court's expanded ruling now makes the *Daubert* criteria applicable to the screening of all expert testimony, whether scientific or otherwise, whether in PRODUCT LIABILITY, medical MALPRACTICE or other PERSONAL INJURY cases.

Polygragh Tests

The POLYGRAPH, also known as a "lie detector," is an instrument that is used to measure physiological responses in humans when they are questioned in order to determine if their answers are truthful. Although supporters of the polygraph claim that the results of the machine are overwhelmingly accurate, polygraph evidence is generally not admissible in criminal trials because it is considered unreliable. The Supreme Court reviewed this blanket denial of polygraph evidence in *United States v. Scheffer*, 523 U.S. 303, 118 S. Ct. 1261, 140 L. Ed. 2d 413 (1998), affirming its inadmissibility in military court-martials. The decision gave all state and federal jurisdictions the right to exclude outright all polygraph evidence.

The Air Force administered a polygraph examination to Edward G. Scheffer, an airman stationed in California. Scheffer had volunteered to work as an informant on drug investigations for the Air Force Office of Special Investigations (OSI). His supervisors informed him when he began his assignment that he would be subject to random drug testing and polygraph examinations. Scheffer agreed to these requirements. Soon after he began his work the OSI administered a urine test, but before the results were known the OSI also conducted a polygraph examination of Scheffer. The OSI examiner concluded that the test "indicated no deception" when Scheffer denied using drugs since joining the Air Force. Following the examination, Scheffer left the base and went absent without leave. Police finally arrested him in Iowa and re-

turned him to the military authorities. During Scheffer's absence the ISO discovered that the urinalysis revealed the presence of methamphetamine.

Scheffer was tried by a general court-martial on charges that included using methamphetamine, failing to report for duty, and wrongfully leaving the air force base. A court-martial is a criminal legal proceeding conducted by the military, with a jury made up of military officers. The Military Rules of Evidence govern what types of facts may be admitted.

Scheffer testified that he had "innocently ingested" the drugs and sought to buttress this claim by introducing the polygraph evidence. The military judge denied Scheffer's motion, citing Military Rule of Evidence 707 (a), which states that "the results of a polygraph examination, the opinion of a polygraph examiner, or any reference to an offer to take, failure to take, or taking of a polygraph examination, shall not be admitted into evidence."

The military court convicted Scheffer on all charges. The Air Force Court of Criminal Appeals affirmed Scheffer's conviction and found that Rule 707 did not "arbitrarily limit" Scheffer's ability to present "reliable evidence." 41 M.J. 683(1995). However, the U.S. Court of Appeals for the Armed Forces, the military's highest court, reversed his conviction. 44 M.J. 442 (1996). The appeals court held that a "per se" exclusion—a categorical prohibition that prevents the judge from using any discretion in admitting the evidence—of polygraph evidence violated Scheffer's SIXTH AMENDMENT right to present a defense.

The Supreme Court, on an 8–1 vote, reversed the military appeals court. Justice CLARENCE THOMAS, writing for the Court, concluded that Rule 707's exclusion of polygraph evidence did not abridge Scheffer's Sixth Amendment right to present a defense. Justice Thomas grounded his analysis on prior rulings that state that a defendant's right to present relevant evidence is subject to reasonable restrictions. He noted that there are other legitimate interests in the criminal trial process besides a defendant's right to present evidence. In addition, the CONSTITUTION gives state and federal governments broad authority to establish rules excluding evidence. As long as these rules are not arbitrary or disproportionate to the purposes they are designed to serve, they do not abridge the accused's right to mount a defense. The Supreme Court has struck down rules as arbitrary only when they "infringed upon a weighty interest of the accused." Moreover, state and federal governments have a legitimate interest in seeing that only reliable evidence is introduced at a trial.

Turning to Rule 707, Justice Thomas found that it served a number of legitimate interests. These interests included "ensuring that only reliable evidence is introduced at trial, preserving the jury's role in determining credibility, and avoiding litigation that is collateral to the primary purpose of the trial."

The interest in ensuring the introduction of only reliable evidence went to the heart of the argument about polygraph evidence. Justice Thomas noted that there is no consensus that polygraph evidence is reliable, with the scientific community "extremely polarized" about the reliability of polygraph techniques. A review of the scientific literature disclosed that while some studies concluded that polygraph tests are accurate and reliable, far more studies found them unreliable. Thomas concluded that there was no way to determine whether a polygraph examiner's conclusions were correct "because certain doubts and uncertainties plague even the best polygraph exams." Therefore, the military had a legitimate interest in keeping out unreliable evidence.

Rule 707 also served another interest: reserving the jury's role in determining credibility. Allowing a polygraph examiner to testify might shift the role to the examiner, as this person is in a unique position for an expert. Unlike forensic scientists who testify about fingerprints or DNA evidence, a polygraph examiner can only offer the jury his or her opinion as to whether the accused is telling the truth. Justice Thomas believed that jurisdictions have a legitimate concern in restricting polygraph information out of fear that the jury will simply adopt the conclusion of the examiner.

A third legitimate interest served by Rule 707 was avoiding litigation over issues other than the guilt or innocence of the accused. Justice Thomas concluded that allowing polygraph evidence would inevitably complicate and lengthen a criminal trial, as there would be debates over the type of questions asked and the credentials of the examiner. These three legitimate interests were not arbitrary or disproportionate. Moreover, they did not violate the Sixth Amendment.

Justice Thomas also rejected Scheffer's argument that prior case law supported the introduction of polygraph evidence. The exclusions of evidence that the Court declared unconstitutional in prior cases "significantly undermined fundamental elements" of the accused's defense. In these cases the Court struck down prohibitions against the introduction of evidence obtained through hypnosis, against the introduction of testimony by a co-defendant, and against allowing a party to discredit the testimony of the party's own witness. In Scheffer's case, he was able to mount a credible defense. The court heard all the relevant details from Scheffer's perspective, and Rule 707 did not prevent him from introducing any factual evidence. Justice Thomas concluded that Scheffer "was barred merely from introducing expert opinion testimony to bolster his own credibility." This limitation did not significantly impair his defense.

The Court made clear that jurisdictions may either allow polygraph evidence, allow it into evidence at the discretion of the judge, or may, as in this case, exclude it entirely. It acknowledged the debate within the legal and scientific community over the reliability of polygraph evidence but refused to strike down per se exclusions. Had it ruled in Scheffer's favor, its decision would have invalidated per se exclusion rules in state and federal courts.

CROSS REFERENCES
Military Law; Polygraph; Witnesses

EXECUTIVE PRIVILEGE

The right of the PRESIDENT of the United States to withhold information from CONGRESS or the courts.

Federal Courts Reject Privilege For Secret Service Agents Protecting President

Secret Service agents unsuccessfully asserted that a "protective function" privilege prevents GRAND JURY investigators from questioning them about what they observe when protecting the president. The issue arose during Independent Counsel KENNETH W. STARR's investigation of whether President BILL CLINTON lied in a deposition when he denied having sexual relations with White House intern Monica S. Lewinsky. At the January 1998 deposition, which occurred in the sexual harassment lawsuit brought against Clinton by Paula C. Jones, Clinton insisted he was alone with Lewinsky only for a few moments on one or two occasions when she brought papers and a pizza to him at the White House.

During his investigation, Starr SUBPOENAED Secret Service agents to testify before a

grand jury about Clinton's relationship with Lewinsky. Retired agent Lewis Fox testified that one weekend afternoon in autumn 1995, he and a uniformed officer were outside the Oval Office when Clinton opened the door and said he was expecting a young aide from the legislative affairs office. Fox told the other officer that Clinton meant Monica Lewinsky, whom Fox described with a curvaceous hand gesture. After Lewinsky arrived and Clinton greeted her at the door, he said to the agents, "Close the door. She'll be in here for a while." Fox testified that when his shift ended forty minutes later, Lewinsky was still with the president.

When Starr subpoenaed other Secret Service agents to appear before the grand jury, they refused to testify to what they observed while protecting the president. This forced Starr to file a motion in the U.S. District Court for the District of Columbia to compel their TESTIMONY.

In court papers, the Secret Service claimed that a never before recognized "protective function" privilege allows them to conceal what they observe while protecting the president unless their observations would reveal that a felony has been, is being, or is about to be committed. The Secret Service explained that the relationship between a president and his protectors is as important as that between an attorney and her client, a priest and his penitent, and a husband and his wife. Just as the law protects those relationships by preventing disclosure of their private communications, so should it protect the president by preventing secret service agents from testifying against him. Without such a privilege, presidents would push agents away to maintain privacy, increasing the risk of assassination.

Opposing the privilege, Starr argued that Secret Service officers are law enforcement agents who are duty bound to report wrongdoing, even by the president. According to Starr, recognizing a protective function privilege would make the president above the law.

U.S. District Chief Judge Norma Holloway Johnson declined to recognize the privilege, holding that there was no support for it in either the U.S. Constitution, federal statutes, or COMMON LAW, as required by Federal Rule of Evidence 501 to recognize a privilege. Judge Johnson cited federal statutes that require the president to accept Secret Service protection, and require executive branch personnel, which includes Secret Service agents, to report criminal activity that they observe. The absence of a protective function privilege in those statutes suggested that Congress did not intend to create one. Judge Johnson rejected the argument that without the privilege, presidents will push away their protectors:

> When people act within the law, they do not ordinarily push away those they trust or rely upon for fear that their actions will be reported to a grand jury. It is not at all clear that a President would push Secret Service protection away if he were acting legally or even if he were engaged in personally embarrassing acts. Such actions are extremely unlikely to become the subject of a grand jury investigation.

The U.S. Department of Justice appealed for the Secret Service. In support of the appeal, an association of former secret service agents filed a brief saying, "[i]t is the unanimous view of these [former agents] that, if not reversed, the decision of the district court in refusing to recognize a protective function privilege will lead inexorably to the successful assassination of another American president in our lifetime." An opposing brief filed by a former U.S. attorneys general, however, said, "Secret Service agents are law enforcement professionals, not members of a personal household guard. ... This proposed privilege was suddenly crafted to meet the immediate demands of a criminal investigation." Former presidents also commented about the privilege, GEORGE BUSH in favor of it and JIMMY CARTER and GERALD FORD against it. President Clinton declined to get involved, but he refused Starr's request to ask the Secret Service to waive the privilege.

On July 7, 1998, the U.S. Court of Appeals for the District of Columbia affirmed Judge Johnson's rejection of the privilege. *In re Sealed Case*, 148 F. 3d 1073 (D.C.Cir. 1998). While the Court agreed that the president's safety is "a

public good of the utmost importance," it held that the Secret Service failed to prove that rejecting the privilege would jeopardize that safety. Without such proof, there was no reason to override "the primary assumption that there is a general duty to give what testimony one is capable of giving." The Court supported its decision with reference to the same federal statutes cited by Judge Johnson, and with the same confidence that "the President has a profound personal interest in being well protected" and "knows that effective protection depends upon the proximity to his protectors."

While the JUSTICE DEPARTMENT applied for CERTIORARI, or review, by the U.S. Supreme Court, Starr was allowed to subpoena and examine Secret Service agents. In his final report to Congress recommending Clinton's impeachment, Starr cited six current or former agents who said Clinton spent time alone with Lewinsky in or around the Oval office, and twenty other agents who supported Lewinsky's version of when and where she visited Clinton. Officer John Muskett testified that he and White House chief of staff Harold M. Ickes once came upon Clinton and Lewinsky in a private study attached to the Oval Office. Officer Gary Byrne testified that Muskett told him Clinton and Lewinsky had been in an intimate situation. Two other officers testified that White House steward Bayani Nelvis complained about having to clean up tissues and towels soiled with lipstick and other substances after Lewinsky's visits with Clinton. Officer Steve Pape testified that, referring to Lewinsky, he once told a new officer, "This is probably the president's mistress, so treat her, you know, decent, but again, don't break the rules for her."

On November 9, 1998, the U.S. Supreme Court declined to review the decision by the District of Columbia Circuit, leaving intact the latter's rejection of the protective function privilege.

CROSS REFERENCES
Contempt; Impeachment; Starr, Kenneth

EXTRADITION

The transfer of an ACCUSED from one state or country to another state or country that seeks to place the accused on TRIAL.

Ira S. Einhorn

In 1998, a long-running, international extradition case moved closer to completion as a high French court removed obstacles to the return of murder fugitive Ira S. Einhorn. Popu-

larly known as the "Unicorn killer," Einhorn, fifty-eight years old, a one-time hippie guru and university lecturer, has been on the run since fleeing on BAIL nearly sixteen years earlier. In 1993, a Philadelphia court convicted him in absentia—without his being present—of murdering his girlfriend, Holly Maddux. He surfaced in France four years later, but a French court blocked U.S. efforts to extradite him. For the next two years, the case became an international cause celebre that pitted contrasting visions of Gallic and American justice against each other, while Maddux's surviving family members watched helplessly. But in February 1999, following passage of special legislation by Philadelphia lawmakers, a high French court finally granted extradition. However, Einhorn, who remained free pending appeal, vowed never to be taken home.

Einhorn made a name for himself in the 1960s. Calling himself "the Unicorn" at times and, at others, a "planetary enzyme," he organized hippie events called "Be Ins" in Philadelphia, protested the war, and organized the first Earth Day celebration. A friend to famous hippies such as the poet Allen Ginsburg and the counterculture leader Abbie Hoffman, he parlayed his reputation for futurism and earth-worship into a New Age consultancy that commanded high fees from corporate clients. In the 1970s, he was awarded a teaching fellowship at Harvard. In 1972, he met Maddux, a Bryn Mawr graduate, with whom he had a relationship until 1977, when she ended it.

Following the break-up, Maddux disappeared. It was known that Einhorn, who was furious about her decision, had summoned her to his apartment. Questioned by police, he said that they had talked and she had left. Her disappearance remained a mystery for another year and a half until Maddux's family hired a private detective. The detective found a building occupant who related stories about seeing a dark liquid oozing from the ceiling of Einhorn's apartment, and smelling an awful stench. In March 1979, police returned to Einhorn's apartment, searched the closet, and in a steamer trunk, under newspapers and styrofoam packing, found the woman's mummified remains. Her skull had been crushed.

Einhorn claimed he was framed by an international conspiracy out to get him for his advanced investigations into weapons and psychic research. He suspected the international intelligence community. Supporters believed him, and influential character witnesses, including an attorney, executive, and minister, testified in his behalf at his bail hearing. Their support helped his attorney—future U.S. senator Arlen Specter—win him release on a mere $40,000 in bail. But others soon came forward with grim allegations. His friends told police that he had asked them to help him get rid of the trunk, and former girlfriends alleged that he beat them when they tried to end relationships. Before his January 1981 trial could start, Einhorn skipped bail.

Twelve years later, in 1993, Philadelphia tried him in absentia out of concern that witnesses' memories were fading. He was convicted of first degree murder and sentenced to life in prison.

Only after sixteen years of searching by U.S. and international authorities was Einhorn found, thanks largely to the determination of a Philadelphia investigator. Former Philadelphia district attorney's office investigator Richard DiBenedetto chased the fugitive across several countries before a lead pointed to France. On June 13, 1997, French police found him living under the alias Eugene Mallon and pretending to be a British writer. He was married to a beautiful woman and lived in a converted mill near the village of Champagne-Mouton, in the heart of the Bordeaux wine country.

Einhorn next won a stunning reprieve. Extradition proceedings had begun in the customary way, with U.S. authorities asking a French appeals court to remand the prisoner into their custody. Although the pace of such proceedings is typically slow, no one was prepared for Einhorn's rapid success in convincing the French court to deny the request. His rambling testimony at the September 1997 extradition hearing covered everything from "Star Trek," international spies, and assassination conspiracies to how he secretly discovered the Internet. But in December, the French court ruled in his favor because of a key difference between the French and U.S. justice systems: French law requires a new trial for anyone convicted in absentia, while many U.S. jurisdictions, including Philadelphia, do not. Additionally, the court, observing that France had abolished the death penalty, was not satisfied that Philadelphia would not seek the death penalty if it retried Einhorn.

The case set off international fireworks. Exacerbating feelings in the United States were statements by Einhorn's defense attorney Dominique Delthil told reporters, "The United States has learned today to its distress that it still has lessons to learn from old Europe in matters of human rights." In an interview with the French media, Einhorn denounced the U.S. justice system as primitively "wild." Newspaper editorialists fumed, Philadelphia District Attorney Lynne Abraham said she was incensed over the French court system, and the Maddux family vowed to fight.

In January 1998, hoping to remove roadblocks to extradition, Philadelphia lawmakers intervened. Clearly intending to meet the objections of the French court, they passed a law providing Einhorn with a new trial upon his return to the United States. "What we're trying to do is clear away the obvious obstacle that stands in the way of bringing this brutal murderer to justice," the sponsor of the bill, state Representative Dennis M. O'Brien, told the *Philadelphia Inquirer.*

In September 1998, French authorities rearrested Einhorn, and the same French court of appeals heard new legal arguments in December. Then, in February 1999, the court reversed its earlier decision and ruled that he may be extradited. Both the Philadelphia legislature's guarantee of a new trial and assurances from U.S. authorities that Einhorn would not face the death penalty had swayed the French justices. However, the court released Einhorn again pending the completion of the full extradition process, which may take up to two years. Mindful of Einhorn's vow never to be taken back to his country, Philadelphia officials and the Maddux family worried that he might try to escape again. Meanwhile, he remained in Champagne-

Mouton, where the mayor told French reporters that he was welcome to stay.

In the interim, the Maddux family filed a civil suit against Einhorn in order to prevent him from profiting from any book or film deals regarding his case. In July 1999, a jury awarded the Maddux family $907 million—$752 million in punitive damages and $155 million in compensatory damages. Though the family is unlikely to see any of the money, they were pleased with the ruling, both because it prevents Einhorn from profiting and because of the "psychological blow" it delivered him.

New Mexico, ex rel. Ortiz v. Reed

When a person charged with a crime in one state flees the state and is captured in another state, the person may be returned to the prosecuting state using the process of extradition. The governor of the prosecuting state makes a formal request to the asylum state (the state where the accused is located) to return the person. The asylum state must hold an extradition hearing before a judge, unless the accused waives it and agrees to be returned.

Most extradition hearings are routine matters and are limited to a review of the extradition documents to makes sure they are in order. Once the court is satisfied that the person either has been accused of a crime or is a FUGITIVE, the governor of the asylum state is authorized to order the person returned. However, in some cases the courts may go beyond the procedural formalities and look at the merits of the criminal charge or at allegations by the accused that extradition will lead to harmful consequences beyond a prison term. These cases are rare because under the U.S. Constitution, states are not given the power to review the underlying charges. This problem occurred in *New Mexico, ex rel. Ortiz v. Reed,* 524 U.S. 151, 118 S. Ct. 1860 141 L. Ed. 2d 131 (1998), where the state of New Mexico refused to return a fugitive to the state of Ohio. The Supreme Court overturned the decision of the New Mexico Supreme Court and directed New Mexico to return the fugitive. The Court made clear that the New Mexico courts had overstepped their authority in handling the extradition in this case.

The state of Ohio sentenced Manuel Ortiz to twenty-five years in prison following his conviction for armed robbery and theft of drugs. He was paroled from prison in 1992, but the following year Ohio correctional officials told him that they planned to revoke his parole and return him to prison. A date was set for Ortiz to meet with his parole officer to discuss the revocation but Ortiz fled the state before the meeting. He eventually was located in the state of New Mexico.

The governor of Ohio asked that Ortiz be extradited and the governor of New Mexico issued a warrant directing Ortiz's extradition. Ortiz was arrested in 1994 and soon after he requested a writ of HABEAS CORPUS from the New Mexico district court. Typically, a person will claim that the original criminal conviction was tainted by prosecutorial and judicial errors. Ortiz claimed he was not a fugitive for purposes of extradition because he fled under duress. He claimed that Ohio authorities intended to revoke his parole without due process and to cause him physical harm once they put him behind prison walls again. In early 1995, the district court ruled in Ortiz's favor and ordered him released from custody. The state of New Mexico appealed this decision to the New Mexico Supreme Court but the court upheld the grant of habeas corpus. 124 N.M. 129, 947 P. 2d 86 (1997).

The state appealed to the U.S. Supreme Court, which unanimously agreed that the decision must be reversed and the grant of habeas corpus be revoked. In a *per curiam* opinion, in which no judge signs the opinion, the Court noted that Article IV of the U.S. Constitution contains the Extradition Clause. The Extradition Clause provides that a person charged with a crime who flees to another state 'shall on Demand of the Executive Authority of the State from which he fled, be delivered up, to be removed to the State having Jurisdiction of the Crime." Art. IV, § 2. The Court also cited the Extradition Act, 18 U.S.C.A. § 3182, which sets out procedures on how this constitutional provision is carried out.

The Court, citing its opinion in *Michigan v. Doran*, 439 U.S. 282, 99 S. Ct. 530, 58 L. Ed. 2d 521 (1978), stated that a court considering release on habeas corpus can only decide four issues: (1) whether the extradition documents on their face are in order, (2) whether the petitioner has been charged with a crime in the demanding state, (3) whether the petitioner is the person named in the request for extradition, and (4) whether the petitioner is a fugitive.

The New Mexico Supreme Court found that the first three requirements had been met but concluded that Ortiz was not a "fugitive" from justice. It held that Ortiz was a "refugee from injustice," agreeing with his arguments that he would not receive due process in a parole revocation hearing and that he would have been physically harmed in prison. This "duress" meant that he could not be classified as a fugitive under Article IV.

The U.S. Supreme Court noted that Ortiz's charges were not challenged at the trial court hearing. However, the state of Ohio was not a party at the hearing and the state of New Mexico was placed "at a considerable disadvantage in producing testimony, even in affidavit form, of occurrences in the state of Ohio." The Court also surmised that Ohio did not participate because all substantive issues, such as those raised by Ortiz, are typically heard by the prosecuting state, not the asylum state.

Despite the New Mexico Supreme Court's determination that Ortiz's testimony was credible, the Supreme Court ruled that New Mexico courts had no right to consider this issue. The Court cited cases reaching back eighty-five years for the conclusion that claims relating to what actually happened in the prosecuting state, the laws of the prosecuting state, and what may be expected to happen in the prosecuting state, are issues for the courts of the prosecuting state to resolve.

The Court saw serious problems with New Mexico's approach. Allowing the asylum state to litigate issues that "can be fully litigated in the charging state would defeat the plain purposes of the summary and mandatory procedures authorized by Title IV, § 2." In addition, it pointed to an AMICUS CURIAE brief signed by forty states that discussed the high volume of prisoners extradited every year. The Court worried that if asylum states could litigate issues, then the states demanding extradition would have to produce witnesses and records in asylum states to counter allegations such as Ortiz made. This would add expense and time to the extradition process.

Therefore, the Court ruled that New Mexico courts "went beyond the permissible inquiry in an extradition case."

CROSS REFERENCES
Prisoners' Rights

FAMILY LAW

Statutes, court decisions, and provisions of the federal and state constitutions that relate to family relationships, rights, duties, and finances.

Foster Care Reform

Although public policy dictates that children should be kept with their biological parents whenever possible, occasionally children are subjected to maltreatment that requires state intervention and removal of the children from their parents' home. Many of these children are placed into foster care. According to a report issued by the National Center for Policy Analysis, more than 650,000 children, mostly due to substantiated cases of abuse and neglect, spent all or part of 1997 in state funded foster care. At approximately the same time this report was released, several states and the federal government were reviewing the foster care system for improvements.

The Adoption and Safe Families Act of 1997, 105 Pub L. 89, 111 Stat 1115, signed into law November 19, 1997, reformed the nation's foster care and adoption system. The intent of the act is to shorten the time children spend in foster care and prevent them from being reunited with parents who abuse them. The act clarifies that a child's health and safety is the paramount consideration. "Reasonable efforts" to reunite a child with his or her biological parents are not required if the child or a sibling has been subjected to "aggravated circumstances" including abandonment, torture, chronic physical or sexual abuse, or if a parent's rights have been previously involuntarily terminated with regard to other children.

The act also implements a fast-track permanent placement plan that requires states to begin permanent placement within twelve months of a child's entrance into foster care, as opposed to eighteen months under previous rules, and use reasonable efforts to place a child for ADOPTION or with a legal guardian. The act also requires courts to terminate parental rights if a child has been in non-relative foster homes fifteen out of the previous twenty-two months; if there is evidence of severe abuse, including abandonment, torture, or physical or sexual abuse; or if the parent has caused the death of a sibling.

Several states, including Michigan, have also begun to revamp their foster care system in compliance with the federal law and other recommendations. In a study conducted by the Institute for Children in Boston, Massachusetts, it was found that at the close of fiscal 1996, Michigan ranked eighth nationally in the number of children in foster care with a population of 17,003. Equally alarming was Michigan's failure to find permanent homes for almost two-thirds of the foster children available for adoption.

In response to this situation, Governor John Engler of Michigan, formed a commission headed by Lieutenant Governor Connie Binsfeld. Its mission was to conduct hearings throughout the state to elicit testimony from social workers, attorneys, judges, psychologists, foster parents, and others involved with the foster care system to determine the system's short comings and then suggest improvements. After a year of hearings, the Binsfeld Commission issued a report containing several recommendations, which were codified into proposed legislation. All of the bills, which are collectively

SHOULD MORE CRIMES BE MADE FEDERAL OFFENSES?

Enforcement of criminal laws in the United States has traditionally been a matter handled by the states. The federal government, conversely, has typically limited itself to policing only crimes against the federal government and interstate crime. This is just one expression of the U.S. system of "federalism," the notion that the federal government exists in tandem with the states and does not, without necessity, deprive states of their powers. The TENTH AMENDMENT to the U.S. Constitution is an example of federalism at work. That amendment states that "[t]he powers not delegated to the United States by the Constitution, nor prohibited by it to the States, are reserved to the States respectively, or to the people."

Near the end of the twentieth century, Congress disregarded the concept of federalism in the area of criminal law. Over the last two decades of the twentieth century, Congress passed a host of federal laws that overlap with already existing state criminal laws, such as: the Anti-Car Theft Act of 1992, the Child Support Recovery Act of 1992, the Animal Enterprise Protection Act of 1992, and new criminal laws on arson, narcotics and dangerous drugs, guns, money laundering and reporting, domestic violence, environmental transgressions, career criminals, and repeat offenders.

In 1998, the number of criminal prosecutions in federal courts increased by 15 percent. That increase was nearly three times the increase in federal criminal prosecutions in 1997. In a Report of the Federal Judiciary issued at the end of 1998, U.S. Supreme Court Chief Justice WILLIAM H. REHNQUIST criticized the congressional trend toward federalizing the criminal justice system. "Federal courts were not created to adjudicate local crimes," Rehnquist instructed, "no matter how sensational or heinous the crimes may be." Rehnquist noted the tremendous toll that federalization of crime was exacting on the federal judiciary, and he decried the damage it was doing to the concept of federalism. "The trend to federalize crimes that traditionally have been handled in state courts not only is taxing the judiciary's resources and affecting its budget needs, but it also threatens to change entirely the nature of our federal system." According to Rehnquist, the problem is political in nature; Senators and Representatives in Congress were using the act of lawmaking to win or keep their seats. "The pressure in Congress to appear responsive to every highly publicized societal ill or sensational crime needs to be balanced with an inquiry into whether states are doing an adequate job in this particular area and, ultimately, whether we want most of our legal relationships decided at the national rather than local level."

In his 1998 Report of the Federal Judiciary, Rehnquist cited a report on federal courts issued by the 1995 Judicial Conference of the United States. The Judicial Conference recommended that federal courts be used for only five types of cases: 1) offenses against the government or its inherent interests; 2) criminal activity with substantial multi-state or international aspects; 3) criminal activity involving complex commercial or institutional enterprises most

known as the Binsfeld legislation, passed unanimously and, in 1997, the Michigan legislature adopted significant reforms to the child protection statutes involving cases of abuse and neglect (1997 PA 163–172). These reforms, which initially took effect in March and June 1998, make it easier to remove children who have been abused or neglected by their parents and make them available for adoption.

In Michigan, children normally come into the foster care system through the courts. Child protection proceedings are commenced when a person reports a suspected instance of child abuse or neglect to the Family Independence Agency (FIA). Abuse and neglect reports are referred to a protective services worker, who is responsible for investigating the allegations. If the case involves certain enumerated factors, such as sexual or serious physical abuse, the FIA must obtain the assistance of law enforcement [*MCLA* 722.623; 722.628(1)]. If the allegations are substantiated, a formal petition is filed with the court requesting that the court take jurisdiction over the children.

If the court determines that the allegations are true and the statutory basis is met, the court can take jurisdiction. This allows for a treatment plan to be developed and if necessary for the children to remain in state funded foster care until the parents are ready to have the children returned to their care. The treatment plan is developed to address the needs of the family and to rectify the conditions that initially brought the children before the court. If the parents do not successfully complete the treatment plan within a reasonable period of time, the parent's rights can be permanently terminated and the children placed up for adoption.

This process, although appearing to move the child through the system timely, could actu-

effectively prosecuted under federal resources or expertise; 4) serious high level or widespread state or local government corruption; and 5) criminal cases raising highly sensitive local issues. "Although Congress need not follow the recommendations of the Judicial Conference, this long-range plan is based not simply on the preference of federal judges," Rehnquist wrote, "but on the traditional principle of federalism that has guided the country throughout its existence."

The criticism of the federalization trend began to mount in the late 1990s. The American Bar Association's (ABA) Criminal Justice Section organized a task force to look into the matter. The ABA's Task Force on the Federalization of Criminal Law issued a report in 1998 in which it criticized the trend. Victor S. (Torry) Johnson, a representative of the National District Attorneys Association on the Task Force, declared in *Highlight* that "[b]y trying to fight street crime through federal legislation, Congress misleads the public into believing that a national response will be effective and that the problem will be solved with federal intervention." Congress then fails to provide enough federal funding to prosecute all the new laws, creating a situation in which the efforts of local law enforcement "are undermined by the unrealistic expectations created by Congress's well-publicized enactments." In his article for *Corrections Today*, James A. Gondles, Jr., Executive Director of the American Correctional Association, lamented the introduction of low-level, local criminals into the federal system. Mixing such prisoners with big-time federal criminals blurs the jurisdictional line and makes it "more difficult for those at the state and local levels to do their jobs."

Not all persons are troubled by the federalization of criminal law enforcement. Proponents of federal criminal laws argue that they are necessary in an increasingly mobile society. Crime tends to span more than one state, and even local crime can have effects that cross state boundaries. In his article for the *Hastings Law Journal*, Rory K. Little, a professor of law at the University of California, Hastings College of Law, defended the increase in federal crimes as a protection against the inability of states to catch and prosecute all criminals. "If the quality of justice is better in the federal courts," Little opines, "then problems of crime cannot be ignored federally while state criminal justice systems slowly sink and justice fails."

A U.S. Supreme Court decision in March 1999 constituted an approval of increased federal authority over crime.

In *United States v. Rodriguez-Moreno*, __ U.S.__, 119 S. Ct. 1239, 143 L. Ed. 2d 388 (1999), Jacinto Rodriguez-Moreno kidnapped a drug associate and took him from Texas to New Jersey, then to New York, and finally to Maryland. Rodriguez-Moreno was charged with, among other crimes, kidnapping and using and carrying a firearm in relation to a kidnapping, an act that violated 18 U.S.C.A. § 924(c)(1). Section 924(c)(1) makes it a crime to use or carry a firearm "during and in relation to any crime of violence." Rodriguez-Moreno was tried in New Jersey on the charges, even though he did not have a gun in New Jersey. Rodriguez-Moreno, who did not want to be tried in New Jersey, argued that the statute did not allow the federal government to prosecute him for the § 924 crime in New Jersey because he did not commit the crime in that state. The Court rejected the argument, holding that because the crime of violence (kidnapping) continued through several states, prosecution was proper in any district where the crime of violence was committed, even if the firearm was used or carried in only one state. The decision made it easier for federal prosecutors to pick and choose the venues for their cases.

CROSS REFERENCES
Criminal Law; Federal Courts

ally take several years, while the child languishes in foster care. The Binsfeld legislation was designed to prevent this. The most notable reforms accelerate the time frames in which each stage of the proceedings take place and under certain circumstances require mandatory filing of permanent custody to terminate parental rights.

For instance, prior to the Binsfeld legislation, a hearing known as a permanency planning hearing was to be held 364 days after the initial disposition. The permanency planning hearing determines whether FIA is to file a request for permanent custody to terminate the parent's rights or whether the child may remain in foster care for a short period of time for the parent to complete the treatment plan. The initial disposition, strictly adhering to the time frames under the previous statute, could take place 98 days from the date the child was initially placed. Under the new time frames created, the permanency planning hearing must take place 364 days from the day the child is placed, which effectively cuts short the process by over three months.

As for the mandatory permanent custody filing provision, which took effect April 1, 1998, FIA was mandated to file for termination of parental rights if one of the following circumstances was present: (1) a parent, guardian, custodian, or person eighteen years of age or older, who resides in the house, has abused the child through abandonment, criminal sexual conduct (CSC) involving penetration, attempted CSC involving penetration, battering, torture, severe physical abuse, loss or serious impairment of an organ or limb, life-threatening injury, or murder or attempted murder; (2) the parent's rights in another child have been terminated, or (3) the parent released his or her rights to a child after a termination petition was filed (*MCLA*.638).

Although few would dispute the legitimacy of mandatory filing due to the reasons listed in the first provision, the statute created a flood of cases requesting termination due to prior history. For example, under the statute as it was originally written, a sixteen-year-old girl who neglected her child due to immaturity; realized that she could not care for her child; and then voluntarily released her rights after the court was involved, was subject to permanently losing another child born to her until she was twenty-five, due to her prior history. Or a mother who had previously used crack cocaine and as a result had her rights terminated by the court, could have a permanent custody petition filed against her, even if she had not used any drugs in ten years and the baby was born healthy and substance free.

The mandatory filing provision and a provision that required visitation to be stopped once the initial hearing on the permanent custody petition was conducted created the most controversy. The legislature reconvened to clean up some of the difficulties in the law. Although the amended legislation, which took effect March 1, 1999, gave FIA more discretion in filing for termination of parental rights. The "no visitation requirement" was actually made more stringent in that visitation would now stop at the time the permanent custody petition was filed rather than at the first hearing.

These changes are not the only adopted as a result of the federal regulations and recommendations from the Binsfeld Commision. The latest legislation coming out of the work of the Binsfeld Commission took effect July 1, 1999, and the legislature still has before it drafts of several more bills that could affect the child protection and foster care systems in Michigan.

FEINSTEIN, DIANNE

For more than two decades, U.S. Senator Dianne Feinstein (D-Ca.) has been one of the most highly visible women in American politics. Feinstein first gained national attention with her appointment as mayor of San Francisco in 1978 following a pair of tragic assassinations. Her two-and-a half terms in office made her popular with voters, earned her wide recognition as a vanguard liberal, and set the stage for a successful Senate campaign in a special election in 1992. In 1994, she and her opponent, Republican candidate Michael Huffington, fought the most expensive senatorial race in U.S. history, which Feinstein narrowly won. As a senator dur-

Dianne Feinstein

J.SCOTT APPLEWHITE/AP/WIDE WORLD PHOTOS

ing the last half of the 1990s, she has developed a reputation as a hard bargainer in her drives for legislation promoting GUN CONTROL and tough crime solutions, while sometimes drawing criticism from her liberal supporters for her positions on environmental and civil liberties issues.

Born on June 22, 1933, in San Francisco, Feinstein, the daughter of a prominent surgeon and medical professor, set her sights as a young woman on public service. While an undergraduate studying history at Stanford University, she won election as student body vice president, and after graduating in 1955, looked for a way into city government. In 1960, Governor Pat Brown recognized her interest in criminal justice by appointing her to the California Women's Parole Board; for the next six years, Feinstein, the youngest parole board member in the nation, set sentences and granted parole in some five thousand cases. In 1968, she served on the San Francisco Committee on Crime, and the following year, made her first run for political office. She was elected the first woman president of the city's legislative body, the San Francisco Board of Supervisors, and served on it for nearly a decade.

On November 27, 1978, two political assassinations rocked San Francisco. City supervisors Harvey Milk and Mayor George Moscone died when they were gunned down by their conservative political rival, city supervisor Dan White. Feinstein, as president of the Board of Supervisors, became acting mayor for the remainder of Moscone's term. Deep divisions existed in the city in the wake of the tragedy, particularly since Milk, the first openly gay city supervisor, was one of the nation's pioneering gay politicians. Feinstein set about mending wounds, and a year later, when her temporary term expired, ran for office and was elected to the first of two four-year terms.

During nine years as mayor, Feinstein's mixture of liberal social positions and pragmatic fiscal management proved immensely popular with voters. Liberals liked her easy rapport with the city's diverse communities, while conservatives warmed to her balanced budgets and promotion of the city's business sector. In addressing neighborhood problems, she showed a pragmatic hand and created the nation's first City Conservation Corps to fight joblessness. She also led clean-up operations to scour graffiti, and hired greater numbers of police officers, all of which she credited for reducing crime by 27 percent over a six year period.

With an 81 percent majority vote in her last elected term, Feinstein began eyeing higher office. She narrowly lost a bid for the state governor's office in 1987, the same year that *City and State Magazine* named her the nation's most effective mayor. Leaving office the following year, she served as director of the Bank of California from 1988 to 1989, but politics beckoned again in 1992. When then-U.S. Senator Pete Wilson won election as governor of California and vacated his senate seat with two years remaining in his term, Feinstein won a special election held to fill the seat.

Two years later, in 1994, she was heavily favored to walk away with reelection, but faced a stiff challenge from upstart Republican hopeful Michael Huffington. A first-term congressman and heir to a family oil fortune, Huffington spent over $17 million on his campaign—making it the costliest senatorial battle in history. Huffington hammered Feinstein for what he called her failure to stop illegal immigration in California. But then, in a surprise twist, he was discovered to have employed an illegal alien as a servant in his home. He had to recant allegations that Feinstein had done the same thing, and, after a neck-and-neck battle that hinged on a count of absentee ballots, Feinstein narrowly won reelection.

In the Senate, Feinstein served on the Appropriations, Rules and Administration, and Judiciary Committees, making a name for herself on the latter by writing high-profile anti-crime bills. Notably, the Gun Free Schools Act of 1994 requires officials to expel students who bring guns to school, and the Hate Crimes Sentencing Enhancement Act stiffened penalties for HATE CRIMES—those committed against persons because of their ethnicity, religion, gender, or sexual orientation. A proponent of the war on drugs, she sponsored other measures targeting gang violence and establishing new criminal penalties for the sale and possession of metamphetamines. Along with Senator Jon Kyl (R-Az.), she proposed the Crime Victims' Bill of Rights, a constitutional amendment to increase the legal rights of victims. Her best known legislative accomplishment was the federal ban on the manufacture, sale and possession of nineteen different assault weapons. Opposed by the gun industry yet widely endorsed by law enforcement groups, the bill became law in September 1994 as part of the omnibus crime bill.

Feinstein has earned praise from women's organizations for her work on behalf of women's health issues. In 1997, she wrote legislation creating the Breast Cancer Research Stamp, a first class postage stamp issued to raise funds for re-

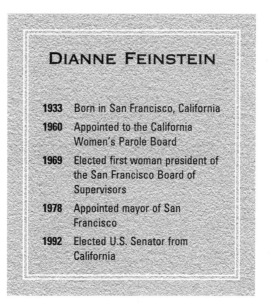

DIANNE FEINSTEIN

1933 Born in San Francisco, California

1960 Appointed to the California Women's Parole Board

1969 Elected first woman president of the San Francisco Board of Supervisors

1978 Appointed mayor of San Francisco

1992 Elected U.S. Senator from California

search that generated $6 million for research. And in late 1998, as part of an omnibus appropriations bill, Congress approved Feinstein's measure to require health insurance plans nationwide to pay for breast reconstruction following mastectomies.

But the senator has not shied away from unpopular stands. Her positions on censorship have drawn heat from civil liberties groups, as in the case of her support for a constitutional amendment to prohibit flag burning and calls for criminalizing the behavior of the celebrity photographers known as paparazzi. Her calls to regulate the INTERNET also proved controversial when she was one of few Democrats to support the ill-fated Communications Decency Act of 1996, the anti-obscenity law which federal courts later held unconstitutional, and has also proposed censoring the dissemination of bomb-making material. At the same time, however, she has called for regulating the access that Internet businesses have to personal data, such as social security numbers, in order to protect citizen PRIVACY. A similar mixed approach has characterized her stand on environmental issues. She wrote the California Desert Protection Act to preserve desert land, but in late 1997, her permissive position on the logging of ancient trees in California's Headwaters Forest drew more than 8,000 environmental protesters.

Feinstein, who is married to real estate mogul Richard C. Blum, has received numerous honors. These include awards from the Women's International Center, Mothers Against Drunk Driving, and Physicians for Human Rights. She is the recipient of the first annual Paul E. Tsongas Memorial Award, along with recognition honoring her work in behalf of gun control from Handgun Control, Inc. and the National Association of Police Organizations.

CROSS REFERENCES
Freedom of Speech; Gun Control; Immigration

FOOD AND DRUG ADMINISTRATION

Dietary Supplement Labels

Under the 1990 Nutrition Labeling and Education Act (NLEA) (21 U.S.C.A. § 301), the federal Food and Drug Administration (FDA) is authorized to review health claims made on the labels for dietary supplements such as medicinal herbs and vitamins. After a party petitions the FDA to allow it to make a claim, the FDA has a set time period to approve or reject the claim, after determining whether or not there is "significant scientific agreement" to support it.

This procedure was challenged in federal court as an unconstitutional restraint on FREE-DOM OF SPEECH by the National Health Alliance (NHA), a coalition of dietary supplement manufacturers, retailers, and consumer groups. After the challenge was rejected by a district court in New York and the appellate court for the Second Circuit (*Nutritional Health Alliance v. Shalala*, 144 F. 3d 220 [2nd Cir. 1998]), the coalition appealed to the U.S. Supreme Court.

NHA, in its Supreme Court appeal, again argued that the labeling restriction was an unconstitutional restraint on commercial free speech. Attorneys for the JUSTICE DEPARTMENT, on the other hand, defended the labeling regulations' constitutionality against the free speech challenge, and also argued that the NHA and other parties opposing the circuit court decision had not even asked the FDA to review any specific health claim, so that any challenge to the regulations was not ripe.

In *Nutritional Health Alliance v. Shalala*, __ U.S. __ 119 S. Ct. 589, 142 L. Ed. 2d 532 (1998), the Supreme Court refused to consider the free speech claim. This left in effect the Second Circuit's finding that "[g]iven the need to protect consumers before any harm occurs, we conclude that the...prior restraint is sufficiently narrowly tailored...It grants a limited, but reasonable, time within which the FDA can evaluate the evidence in support of the labeling claims." However, one key element in the Supreme Court's decision was that the NHA had not actually submitted a claim to the FDA for review.

NHA's attorney, Milton Bass, lamented the Supreme Court's action. As he told the trade newsletter *Nutraceuticals International*, in his opinion the Court's decision was, "unfortunate for every American business with a stake in freedom of commercial speech. What's the use of going through the rigmarole of seeking FDA approval when the agency already has indicated it will not give that approval?"

NHA v. Shalala is part of an ongoing controversy about the regulation of dietary supplements. When Congress passed the NLEA, it gave the FDA authority to regulate health claims made for dietary supplement products. The NLEA required health claims for many products (drugs, food, and supplements included) to be based on "the totality of publicly available scientific evidence" (21 U.S.C.A. § 343[r][3]). The FDA also was allowed to review and approve claims made on labels before the products were sold.

Not surprisingly, soon after passage of the NLEA, momentum grew among both supplement manufacturers and some consumers for less demanding regulation of supplements. In 1994, Congress passed the Dietary Supplement Health and Education Act (DSHEA) (21 U.S.C.A. § 343). Under the DSHEA, dietary supplements are placed in a special category. They are not subject to the much more rigid testing requirements for drugs that hope to en-

Secretary of Health and Human Services Donna Shalala

JIM BOURG/AP/WIDE WORLD PHOTOS

ter the market. Instead, they are considered akin to a type of food.

Since the passage of the DSHEA, dietary supplements do not have to pass FDA safety tests required for new drugs before they can be marketed. Drugs must go through a prolonged process of animal testing, review of the manufacturer's application, and research following the drug's introduction to the market. If a supplement was already in use before the passage of the DSHEA, or had been used safely before, it had few hurdles to surmount before sale. Newer products were to be considered safe if the manufacturer could point to a single favorable study, even one conducted by the manufacturer itself. If the FDA wanted to remove a supplement from the market, it had to show that it posed a "significant or unreasonable risk of illness or injury," a very difficult task.

Similarly, the DSHEA gave more leeway to advertising claims for supplements than those for drugs. The NLEA had imposed a high standard on health claims. They had to be "based on the totality of publicly available scientific evidence," and scientists had to be in "significant agreement" about the claims' validity. Even the products' names could be scrutinized to make sure they did not make implied claims. Under the DSHEA, claims could not be misleading or deceptive, but they did not have to be substantiated any more solidly than the product's safety. As a result, many substances that are more like drugs, such as ephedrine, were being marketed as supplements.

The FDA, restricted by the DSHEA from applying more stringent requirements on supplements before they reached the market, decided to establish regulations to determine if health claims made by supplement labels were valid. It set up a procedure by which manufacturers must petition the FDA before making a health claim on a supplement's label. The FDA then had a set time period in which to decide whether there was "significant scientific agreement" about the claim. It was this set of regulations, challenged by the NHA as a free speech restriction, that eventually reached the Supreme Court in *NHA v. Shalala*.

In addition to the FDA's attempts to regulate dietary supplements, challenges to the supplement industry are coming from other directions, especially given its tremendous growth in the later 1990s. According to Marlys Mason the supplement industry has grown between 25 and 30 percent annually since the passage of DSHEA in 1994, with industry sales predicted

to reach $12 billion by 2001. Along with this freer commercial environment have come added concerns about consumer safety.

On the national level, the Federal Trade Commission (FTC), which enforces general regulations on deceptive advertising, uses a more rigorous standard than the FDA in evaluating supplement claims. It has ordered several supplement manufacturers to stop making claims that it considers deceptive or unsubstantiated.

Others stepping into the supplement controversy are state governments and private organizations. The attorneys general of seven states (Arizona, California, Illinois, Minnesota, Pennsylvania, Texas, and Wisconsin) joined forces in 1997 to seek a ban in their states on the advertising and sale of "Herbal Ecstasy," an ephedra supplement. (The FDA and FTC had already reached separate agreements with the manufacturer.) The American Medical Association (AMA), on the same day that the Supreme Court rejected Nutritional Health Alliance's appeal, announced the launching of efforts to amend the DSHEA, so that the FDA would be authorized to test supplements and herbal remedies for safety and effectiveness. And supplement manufacturers are fighting among themselves, in private lawsuits based on claims of TRADEMARK infringement, deceptive advertising, and anticompetitive acts.

CROSS REFERENCES
Administrative Law; Constitutional Law; Freedom of Speech

FREEDOM OF INFORMATION ACT

A federal law (5 U.S.C.A. § et seq.) Providing for the disclosure of information held by ADMINISTRATIVE AGENCIES to the public, unless the documents requested fall into one of the specific exemptions set forth in the statute.

The Assassination Records Review Board

The assassination of President JOHN F. KENNEDY on November 22, 1963, traumatized the United States and changed the way many people viewed government. From the first hours of the shooting of the president in Dallas, Texas, people raised suspicions that there had been a conspiracy to kill Kennedy. President LYNDON B. JOHNSON responded by appointing Supreme Court Chief Justice EARL WARREN to head a commission of distinguished public servants to investigate assassination evidence. The Warren Commission released its report in 1964, concluding that Lee Harvey Oswald had killed the president and that he had acted alone.

Many people were skeptical of the report's conclusions and that skepticism grew over time. Thousands of articles and books have been written that challenge the commission's findings and allege that agencies of the federal government withheld information from the commission and that the commission itself concealed evidence that contradicted its conclusions. In 1978 and 1979, the House Select Committee on Assassinations reexamined the evidence and concluded that President Kennedy "was probably assassinated as a result of a conspiracy."

Director Oliver Stone's popular 1991 movie, *JFK*, renewed the charge that a vast government-inspired conspiracy orchestrated the assassination. Congress, in an effort to restore government credibility, enacted the President John F. Kennedy Assassination Records Collection Act of 1992, 44 U.S.C.A. § 2107. The act created the Assassination Records Review Board, an independent federal agency whose mission was to identify and release as many records related to the assassination as possible.

The board, whose members were appointed by President BILL CLINTON, consisted of lawyers, historians, and scholars, all from outside the federal government. The board hired a professional staff skilled in document collection and review. During the course of the review board's work, its chair, John R. Tunheim, was appointed a federal district court judge for Minnesota. From 1994 to the publication of its final report in 1998, the board made exhaustive efforts to find, declassify and release assassination documents.

The board's final report made clear that its mission was not to reinvestigate the assassination and make conclusions about the accuracy of the WARREN COMMISSION's report. Nevertheless, the report disclosed that new sources of information had been found that might aid investigators and historians.

Congress had defined the term "assassination record" broadly, including any record from the investigating agencies, and records in possession of the federal government, and any local or state government that assisted in the inquiry into the assassination. Congress empowered the board to determine whether a document was an assassination record and to, in the words of the final report, "cast a broad net for such records."

The board's most important job was reviewing the information federal agencies that wished not to release. During its four years of existence, the board's review process went through three stages. During the first stage the five board members "scrutinized each document with infinite care," making decisions on a document-by-document basis. By doing so, the board developed a body of information and found ways to balance the requirements of the act with the ongoing needs of federal agencies. In the second stage, the board delegated some routine decision-making to its staff. The last stage shifted the decision-making from the board to government agencies. Once the agencies saw how the board voted on various types of documents, they began bypassing the review process and released on their own initiative records under the board's guidelines.

The board established a "stringent standard for postponing the opening of a record. The board's bias toward disclosure and the limited number of documents that were not released demonstrated that it was more liberal than the Freedom of Information Act. Because the act authorizing the review board presumed that documents should be immediately disclosed, a document could be postponed only through "clear and convincing evidence." The board developed a detailed set of principles that helped it make decisions concerning names, dates, pseudonyms, file numbers, sources of information and the methods by which it was obtained.

Although the board's work centered on government records, it encouraged private citizens and organizations that had records of their own to donate them to the board's collection. The board received personal documents from Warren Commission members, notes taken during interviews with Lee Harvey Oswald by a Dallas police detective and a former FBI agent. The board also received the diary of Clay Shaw, the only person tried and later acquitted, for the murder of President Kennedy.

The board sought records from the governments of Russia, Cuba, and Mexico, but these attempts were "fruitless owing to political and diplomatic constraints." It also held seven public hearings and twice called together groups of "experts" in the Kennedy assassination research. These experts helped target possible sources of additional documents.

Finally, the board established a program that ensured that government agencies complied with the act, requiring each agency to execute, under oath, a compliance statement. This statement described "the record searches that the agency completed, records that it located, and other actions it took to comply with the law."

In the end, the review board located and declassified over four million pages of records, which are now in the National Archives and available for public inspection. These records include "critical documentation on the events in Dallas, Lee Harvey Oswald, and the reactions of government agencies to the assassination." It sought to clarify the controversy over the autopsy records of President Kennedy by deposing numerous participants in the autopsy and the treating physicians in Dallas. The board also reviewed records relating to New Orleans District Attorney Jim Garrison's prosecution of Clay Shaw. The board made available all FBI and CIA documents from previous official investigations, acquired film footage depicting events surrounding the assassination, and sponsored ballistics and forensic testing of a bullet fragment found in the front seat of the presidential limousine.

As the board prepared to disband, it recommended to Congress that short time frames should not hinder future declassification efforts. The board had to carry out its duties in four years, which it believed limited its effectiveness. The board also recommended that Congress strengthen the Freedom of Information Act by adding independent oversight to the review process when agency heads exclude records from public release. Most importantly, the board recommended the adoption of federal classification policy that would (1) substantially limit the number of people in government who can classify documents, (2) reduce the categories of documents that can be classified, (3) reduce the time for which documents can be classified, (4) encourage efforts to open material that might otherwise be classified, and (5) provide for money to agencies for the declassifying of records.

CROSS REFERENCES
Warren Commission

FREEDOM OF SPEECH

The right, guaranteed by the FIRST AMENDMENT to the U.S. Constitution, to express beliefs and ideas without unwarranted government restriction.

"Decency" Standard Upheld For National Endowment For The Arts Grants

A contentious issue in the 1990s has been federal funding of the arts. Various politicians have attracted funding of controversial shows, while others have defended the artist's FIRST

AMENDMENT right to expression. The Supreme Court, in *National Endowment for the Arts v. Finley*, 524 U.S. 569, 118 S. Ct. 2168, 141 L. Ed. 2d 500 (1998), entered the controversy.

Since its creation by the federal government in 1965, the National Endowment for the Arts has provided monetary grants to artists. The NEA's creation evidenced a "broadly-conceived national policy of support for the arts in the United States," pledging federal funds to "help create and sustain not only a climate encouraging freedom of thought, imagination and inquiry but also the material conditions facilitating the release of...creative talent." (National Foundation on the Arts and the Humanities Act of 1965, 20 U.S.C.A. § 953(b), § 951(7).) Since its creation, the NEA has dispersed over $3 billion to both individuals and organizations. Many argue that it serves an important role in the artistic community as well as in the development of artistic talent in this country. Indeed, one commentator has argued that, in the list of roughly 5,000 NEA grants awarded to individual artists since its inception, there is hardly a significant American artist who did not, at one time or another, receive some support.

The federal statute that created the NEA gives it substantial discretion in awarding funds, clarifying only the broadest funding priorities, including "artistic and cultural significance, giving emphasis to American creativity and cultural diversity," "professional excellence," and the encouragement of "public knowledge education, understanding, and appreciation of the arts." Within these wide, subjective and discretionary guidelines, the NEA, through its advisory panels, its twenty-six-member National Council on the Arts, and its chairperson, awards public funds to support the arts.

In 1990, the NEA statute was amended to direct the chairperson of the NEA, in establishing procedures to judge the artistic merit of grant applications, to consider "general standards of decency and respect for the diverse beliefs and values of the American public." This amendment, which established what is sometimes referred to as the "decency test," is at the heart of the *Finley* controversy.

The 1990 amendment and its focus upon "decency" were a reaction to the work of NEA-funded artists of the late 1980s, including Robert Mapplethorpe, Andres Serrano, and others. Mapplethorpe's work consisted of explicit photographs of gay men in poses that members of the Congress condemned as pornographic,

while one of Serrano's most noted, and controversial, works was a photograph of a crucifix immersed in urine. Mapplethorpe's work was funded by the Institute of Contemporary Art at the University of Pennsylvania, which had used $30,000 of the visual arts grant received from the NEA, while Serrano had been awarded a $15,000 grant from the Southeast Center for Contemporary Arts, another organization that received NEA support. Performance artist Karen Finley was another controversial NEA grant recipient. At her performances, Finley appeared nude on stage, smeared with chocolate, in an effort to symbolize a woman covered in excrement as a statement upon women's role in American society.

The public reaction to these artists was hostile, especially when it was revealed that federal tax dollars were being used to fund their work. The "decency test" was added to the statute largely in response to the uproar surrounding the NEA's funding of the work of these artists.

Subsequently, Finley and three other artists whose NEA grant applications were rejected brought suit, claiming that the amendment creating the "decency test" violated their constitutional right to free speech and due process. The district court agreed and found that the "decency test," as added to the NEA guidelines, was unconstitutional. 795 F.Supp 1457 (C.D. Cal. 1992). The U.S. Court of Appeals for the Ninth Circuit upheld the district court decision in 1996 100 F. 3d 671 (9th Cir.).

The Supreme Court, however, reversed the court of appeals' decision, concluding that the amendment creating the "decency test" was facially valid, as it neither interfered with FIRST AMENDMENT rights nor violated constitutional vagueness principles. In so holding, the Supreme Court found that the government can consider "general standards of decency" when awarding an NEA grant. In writing the opinion of the Court, Justice SANDRA DAY O'CONNOR argued that the entire NEA grant process was subjective, and since the NEA was not required, but merely allowed or advised, to consider decency, doing so did not make the amendment unconstitutional.

The artists claimed that the "decency test," on its face and in practice, discriminated against controversial ideas, making it far more difficult for those ideas to be funded. Because "decency" has no precise legal definition and can be measured only subjectively, Finley and others argued that such a consideration would have a harmful effect on artistic expression and free speech in violation of the First Amendment. The Supreme Court disagreed, holding that when the government acts as a "patron," deciding to fund expression through the consideration of subjective criteria, it "may advise" one of its funding agencies to include "decency" among those subjective criteria. The funding agency (in this instance, the NEA) is then free to follow or reject that advice. The Supreme Court noted that while the NEA may consider "decency," the amendment did not preclude awards to projects that might be deemed "indecent" or "disrespectful," and did not otherwise categorically require that "decency" be considered. Focusing on the subjective nature of the grant process itself, the Supreme Court commented that "it seems unlikely that this provision will introduce any greater element of selectivity than the determination of 'artistic excellence' itself."

Wisconsin Statute Forbidding Defiling of U.S. Flag Found Unconstitutional

The Wisconsin Supreme Court recently found to be unconstitutional a Wisconsin statute that made it illegal to "defile" the U.S. flag. *State v. Janssen*, 219 Wis. 2d 362, 580 N.W. 2d 260 (1998). In doing so, that court continued a line of cases which show that governmental attempts to criminalize flag desecration (e.g. flag burning) often prove to be unconstitutional when challenged.

In May or June of 1996, the defendant, Matthew Janssen, together with several of his friends, began stealing U.S. flags from various locations in Appleton, Wisconsin. One such theft occurred at a golf course, where Janssen and his friends stole and discarded the flag. On approximately June 9, 1996, Janssen and his friends returned to the same golf course and noticed that a new flag had been hung on the flag pole. Janssen lowered and removed the flag, then defecated upon it, leaving it on the steps of the golf course clubhouse.

Janssen and his friends returned to the golf course once again on June 26 to find that the flag had been cleaned and was flying once more. Again they stole the flag, this time leaving a handwritten note at the scene:

> Golf Course Rich F***s: When are you dumb f***s going to learn? We stole you're first flag and burnt it, then we used your second flag for a s***-rag and left it on your doorstep with a peice of s***. The ANARCHIST PLATOON HAS INVADED Appleton and as long as you put flags up were going to burn them you yuppie f***s. Shove you're club up your a**.

Approximately one month later, Janssen was arrested by the Appleton Police Department and confessed to stealing and desecrating the flags. In addition to theft, Janssen was charged with one count of "intentionally and publicly defiling the United States flag." Janssen was charged pursuant to the Wisconsin flag desecration statute which provides, in relevant part: "Whoever intentionally and publicly mutilates, defiles, or casts contempt upon the flag is guilty of a Class E felony...Wis. Stat. § 946.05(1)." At the circuit court level, the flag desecration count was dismissed on grounds that the statute was unconstitutionally vague and overbroad on its face.

On appeal, the court of appeals affirmed the circuit court's decision, concluding that Wisconsin's statute was overbroad because it made illegal acts which are protected expression within the meaning of the FIRST AMENDMENT. *Janssen*, 213 Wis. 2d 471, 570 N.W. 2d 746 (1997). The court of appeals determined that the statute covered too many types of expression, including some types of expression that were meant to be protected by the First Amendment.

With these two lower court decisions as a backdrop, the Wisconsin Supreme Court affirmed the court of appeals' determination of the statute's unconstitutionality on the grounds of overbreadth. While sickened and outraged by Janssen's behavior, the Wisconsin Supreme Court essentially agreed with his assertion that the Wisconsin statute was unconstitutional. However, the Supreme Court found the statute to be unconstitutional *not* because the act of defecating on the flag was protected expression within the meaning of the First Amendment (an issue which the Court declined to rule upon), but rather, because the statute conceivably could be applied unconstitutionally to others. That result, the Court noted, could undesirably cause persons to refrain from exercising their constitutionally guaranteed First Amendment rights by "chilling" protected speech or expression.

A statute is overbroad, and therefore unconstitutional, "when its language, given its normal meaning, is so sweeping that its sanctions may be applied to constitutionally protected conduct which the state is not permitted to regulate." For example, the Wisconsin statute was worded in a way such that clearly protected expression—such as painting a flag for artistic purposes or affixing a peace symbol to a flag with removable black tape in protest of government foreign policy—would be criminalized. Indeed, the statute's prohibition against behavior that "casts contempt" upon the flag could be used to prevent not just physical desecration or destruction, but speech that is protected by the First Amendment. For example, a person protesting foreign policy by standing on a street corner, exclaiming that the U.S. flag is a symbol of war and hate could be held to "cast contempt" upon the flag. Yet free speech of that sort is precisely what the First Amendment is intended to protect.

While the Wisconsin Supreme Court was compelled to reach the decision that it did in *Janssen*, it did so with considerable anguish:

> The hard fact is that sometimes we must make decisions we do not like. We make them because they are right, right in the sense that the law and the Constitution, as we see them, compel the result...Our final assessment of Janssen's behavior is no different from our initial, instinctive reaction to the facts of this case: we are deeply offended. Janssen's conduct is repugnant and completely devoid of any social value. To many, particularly those who have fought for our country, it is a slap in the face.

The Wisconsin Supreme Court decision in *Janssen* can be compared and contrasted with U.S. Supreme Court decisions that reached similar results.

For example, *Street v. New York*, 394 U.S. 576, 89 S.Ct. 1354, 22 L.Ed.2d 572 (1969) involved a New York law which made it a crime to "publicly mutilate, deface, defile, or defy, trample upon or cast contempt upon either by words or act" any U.S. flag. In *Street*, the defendant was convicted for burning a flag on a street corner, in reaction to the news that civil rights leader James Meredith had been shot by a sniper, while shouting, "we don't need no damn flag" and, "if they let that happen to Meredith we don't need an American flag." In holding the New York statute unconstitutional as applied to the defendant, the U.S. Supreme Court noted that it impermissibly permitted Mr. Street to be punished merely for speaking defiant or contemptuous words about the flag—speech that is protected by the First Amendment.

More recently, a 1989 U.S. Supreme Court decision struck down the conviction of a Texas man for burning a flag in a political protest. *Texas v. Johnson*, 491 U.S. 397, 109 S.Ct. 2533, 105 L.Ed.2d 342 (1989). There, the Court addressed the question of whether the act of burning the flag is "sufficiently imbued with elements of communication" so as to warrant First Amendment protection—in other words, whether burning the U.S. flag could be deemed to be protected "speech." In upholding the reversal of the defendant's conviction, the Supreme Court concluded that his flag burning constituted expressive communication within the protection of the First Amendment, stating, "We do not consecrate the flag by punishing its desecrators, for in doing so we dilute the freedom that this cherished emblem represents."

Accordingly, while the *Janssen*, *Street*, and *Johnson* cases each allowed a defendant to go unpunished for what many consider disturbing acts (particularly with respect to Janssen), each did so for different reasons. In *Janssen*, it was because the statute was overbroad and could restrict speech and protected expression which is protected by the First Amendment. In *Street*, it was because the statute, as applied to the defendant, prohibited protected speech. In *Johnson*, it was because the act of flag burning, under the facts presented, was *itself* protected expression. In each instance, the Court ignored the sheer offensiveness of the conduct in question, instead focusing on the important issue of protecting freedom of speech and expression under the First Amendment.

Steve Forbes Denied Participation in Debate

In connection with a 1992 Arkansas congressional election, the Arkansas Educational Television Commission (AETC), a state-owned public television broadcaster, sponsored a debate. AETC invited only the Democratic and Republican nominees for the congressional seat to participate. Ralph Forbes, who was a minor party candidate with little public support, formally requested that he also be allowed to participate in the debate. The AETC denied this request, making the determination that, in their journalistic judgment, the station's viewers would best be served by limiting the debate to the two candidates that had already been invited. Forbes then sued the AETC, claiming that this exclusion violated the FIRST AMENDMENT.

The U.S. Supreme Court disagreed and ruled against Forbes in a 6–3 decision (*Arkansas Educ. Television Commission v. Forbes*, 523 U.S. 666, 118 S.Ct. 1633, 140 L.Ed.2d 875 [1998]), holding that the station's exclusion of Forbes from the debate was consistent with the First Amendment. Specifically, the Court found that Forbes was not excluded because of his views or beliefs, but rather because of permissible, non-viewpoint oriented, criteria. Because the station's decision to exclude Forbes from the debate was reasonable and not based upon Forbes' viewpoint, it was upheld as constitutional.

The issue ultimately decided by the Supreme Court in *Forbes* was whether, by reason of its state ownership, the television station had a constitutional obligation to allow every candidate access to the debate. The resolution of this issue turned on whether the debate was a "public forum" to which all candidates, legally qualified to appear on the ballot, had a presumptive right of access. If the debate were held to be a public forum, any decision by the AETC to exclude Forbes would be subject to "strict scrutiny," meaning that it would require a "compelling" and "narrowly-tailored" reason in order to be permissible under the First Amendment. This is precisely what Forbes argued, and, prior to this case reaching the Supreme Court, the court of appeals agreed (*Forbes v. Arkansas Ed. Television Network Foundation*, 93 F.3d 497 [8th Cir. 1996]), holding that the debate was a public forum to which Forbes had a First Amendment right of access. The Supreme Court, however, did not agree, and reversed the court of appeals decision, holding that the debate was a "non-public forum."

In deciding free speech issues under the First Amendment, the Supreme Court has long separated government-controlled and government-owned areas and property into three distinct categories. "Public fora" are governmental properties that the government must make available for speech and dissemination of ideas; a city park or town square are two classic examples. Traditional public fora are defined by the objective characteristics of the property, such as whether, "by long tradition or government fiat,"

Steve Forbes brought suit against the Arkansas Education Television Commission for not allowing him to participate in a televised presidential debate.

SCOTTY MORRIS/AP/WIDE WORLD PHOTOS

the property has been "devoted to assembly and debate." The government can exclude a speaker from a public forum only when the exclusion is necessary to serve a compelling state interest and is narrowly drawn to achieve that interest.

The second class of forum is a "designated public forum," where a purposeful governmental action opens a non-traditional forum for expressive use by the general public or a particular class of speakers. An example of this is a state-owned university which makes a classroom generally available for student group meetings. In this example, where such an action has been taken, and a particular student group is specifically excluded from using the classroom for a meeting, the decision to exclude is subject to strict scrutiny. Therefore, absent a "compelling" and "narrowly-tailored" reason for the exclusion, such action would violate the First Amendment.

The final, and least protected, type of forum is a "non-public forum." Government-controlled restrictions upon access to this type of forum are permissible so long as they are reasonable and are not an attempt to suppress expression. For example, because the government has not made the interior of the White House generally available for public meetings, it clearly is a "non-public forum," and restrictions upon its use are not only permissible, but obviously necessary.

With this background, the Supreme Court concluded that the Arkansas congressional debate was a non-public forum. Acknowledging that "the almost unfiltered access of a traditional public forum would be incompatible with the programming dictates a television broadcaster must follow," the Supreme Court quickly concluded that the debate was not a public forum. Further, the Court reasoned it was not a "designated public forum," because the AETC did not intend to make access to the debate generally available to a particular class of speakers (in this case, all candidates for the congressional seat). Rather, AETC, in the exercise of its journalistic judgment, intended to allow selective access to specific speakers—the major party candidates. Accordingly, the Supreme Court concluded that the debate was a non-public forum and, as such, AETC could exclude Forbes from the debate so long as its decision to do so was based on restrictions that were reasonable and viewpoint-neutral.

In writing for the majority, Justice ANTHONY M. KENNEDY expressed the Supreme Court's conclusion that AETC's decision to exclude Forbes was viewpoint-neutral, not based on "objections or oppositions to his views," and, accordingly, did not violate the First Amendment. The Supreme Court stated, "There is no substance to Forbes' suggestion that he was excluded because his views were unpopular or out of the mainstream. His own objective lack of support, not his platform, was the criteria." As such, the decision by AETC to exclude Forbes "was a reasonable, viewpoint-neutral exercise of journalistic discretion consistent with the First Amendment."

Critics of this decision believe that it represents a narrowing of First Amendment rights and protections. Some believe that the Court's conclusion that AETC's decision to exclude Ralph Forbes was misguided. For instance, noted law Professor Erwin Chemerinsky has argued that the station's classification of Forbes as a "minor party" candidate was, in and of itself, a decision based on viewpoint. Chemerinsky wrote in *Trial*:

> But what causes a candidate to be from a minor, rather than a major, party? The answer, of course, is that the views of a minor party candidate are favored by a much smaller percentage of the population than the views of a major party candidate. From this prospective, choosing whom to include in a debate based on whether the candidate is from a minor or major party is all about viewpoint.

A Lawyer's Public Statements To The Press Can Be Restricted Within The First Amendment

A U.S. court of appeals held in the case of *In re Morrissey*, 168 F.3d 134 (4th Cir. 1999) that lawyers, under certain circumstances, may be constitutionally prohibited from making pre-trial statements to the press in criminal cases if there is a "reasonable likelihood" that those statements would interfere with a fair trial. The appeals court continued a line of cases holding that similar restrictions upon a lawyer's speech are constitutional in the appropriate circumstances.

Morrissey involved the criminal contempt conviction of Joseph Morrissey, a criminal trial lawyer, for violating a local court rule restricting lawyers' extrajudicial comments—comments made outside the courtroom—about pending litigation. (A recent example of extrajudicial comments are the comments made to the press, almost daily, by the criminal defense lawyers for O.J. Simpson during his murder trial.) The case presented the question of whether the rule was unconstitutional as a violation of the attorney's FIRST AMENDMENT right to free speech.

Morrissey was a trial lawyer hired to represent Joel Harris, who had been indicted on drug distribution charges in Virginia. Because Harris was a long-time political "insider" and former mayoral aide in Richmond, his indictment attracted substantial media attention throughout the area. Because of Harris' political connections and accusations that the case was being influenced by political considerations, the case was moved to federal court.

In connection with his trial preparation, Morrissey interviewed a witness whose TESTIMONY was heard by the GRAND JURY that indicted Harris. Morrissey knew that this WITNESS was going to be called as a government witness at trial. During that interview, which was videotaped, the witness recanted his grand jury testimony. Subsequently, Morrissey held a press conference during which he made some remarks, presented a press release, and played the videotape of the witness' recantation. Morrissey held the press conference even though the assistant U.S. attorney general assigned to the case had reminded him, in writing, of the applicability of local Rule 57, a local court rule. Rule 57 provides, in part, as follows:

> *Potential or Imminent Criminal Litigation:* In connection with pending or imminent criminal litigation with which a lawyer or a law firm is associated, it is the duty of that lawyer or firm

not to release or authorize the release of information or opinion (1) if a reasonable person would expect such information or opinion to be further disseminated by any means of public communication, and (2) if there is a *reasonable likelihood* that such dissemination would interfere with a fair trial or otherwise prejudice the due administration of justice. *(emphasis added.)*

Approximately three weeks later, two weeks before the trial, Morrissey again made public statements about the case in a newspaper interview. Morrissey characterized the charges against Harris as vicious and vindictive, and went on to remark that if the charges had been filed when he was a prosecutor (Morrissey was a former Commonwealth of Virginia prosecutor), they would have been laughed out of court. Morrissey was again charged with willfully violating Rule 57 by making comments to the media regarding the merits of a pending case.

At trial for these charges, the district court found that Morrissey had knowingly violated Rule 57, that his actions were reasonably likely to taint the jury pool, make jury selection more difficult, and interfere with prospective witnesses. In so doing, the district court found that Rule 57 did not violate the First Amendment.

Morrissey claimed that Rule 57 was unconstitutional because it required only a "reasonable likelihood" that extrajudicial statements would interfere with a fair trial. In contrast, the U.S. Supreme Court decision of *Gentile v. State Bar of Nevada*, 501 U.S. 1030, 111 S.Ct. 2720, 115 L.Ed.2d 888 (1991), upheld a similar rule that required there be a "substantial likelihood" of prejudicing a court proceeding. Accordingly, Morrissey argued that the *Gentile* case stood for the proposition that the "substantial likelihood" standard was the only constitutionally permitted standard for restrictions on lawyer speech under the First Amendment. Morrissey argued that the difference between the "reasonable likelihood" standard of Rule 57, and the Supreme Court

standard of "substantial likelihood," as cited in *Gentile*, was meaningful and rendered Rule 57 unconstitutional.

The Fourth Circuit disagreed. While acknowledging the "substantial likelihood" standard articulated in *Gentile*, the Fourth Circuit noted that the Supreme Court did not hold in that case that it was the only constitutionally permissible standard for restrictions on a lawyer's speech under the First Amendment. Further, the court of appeals found Rule 57 permissible as a restriction on a lawyer's free speech by applying the test established in *Procunier v. Martinez*, 416 U.S. 396, 94 S.Ct. 1800, 40 L.Ed.2d 224 (1974). In *Procunier*, the Supreme Court established that for a regulation proscribing lawyer speech to be constitutional, it must "further an important or substantial government interest unrelated to the suppression of expression … [and] the limitation on First Amendment freedoms must be no greater than is necessary or essential to the protection of the particular governmental interest involved."

Applying the *Procunier* analysis to Rule 57, and citing *Gentile* and other similar cases, the court of appeals found that "Local Rule 57, like the rule evaluated in *Gentile*, satisfies each of the elements required for constitutionally adequate protection and therefore does not impermissibly infringe on a lawyer's First Amendment rights."

Nevertheless, the issue remained open to debate. The Second Circuit upheld the constitutionality of a local rule identical to Rule 57 in *United States v. Cutler*, 58 F.2d 825 (2d Cir. 1995). However, the Seventh Circuit reached a contrary result in *Chicago Council of Lawyers v. Bauer*, 522 F.2d 242 (7th Cir. 1975). Accordingly, the permissible bounds for the restriction of a lawyer's speech remain somewhat vague, notwithstanding the guidance provided to date by the Supreme Court in decisions such as *Gentile*, and *Procunier*.

CROSS REFERENCES
Ethics; First Amendment; Freedom of Speech

GAY AND LESBIAN RIGHTS

The goal of full legal and social equality for gay men and lesbians sought by the gay movement in the United States and other Western countries.

Anti-Sodomy Laws

In 1986, the U.S. Supreme Court ruled in *Bowers v. Hardwick*, that Georgia's SODOMY law did not violate the U.S. Constitution, leaving states free to have such laws if they choose. As with other issues held not to violate the Constitution, advocacy groups have challenged those laws under state constitutions. In November 1998, civil liberties groups gained a major victory when the Supreme Court of Georgia struck down, under the Georgia State Constitution, the very law upheld in *Bowers*. In March 1999, Louisiana followed suit at the trial court level. And a suit filed in Texas in late 1998 will, if successful, invalidate that state's sodomy law as well.

Sodomy laws were once on the books in all fifty states as well as the District of Columbia and Puerto Rico. By late 1998, however, sodomy laws had been repealed or struck down by courts in thirty-two states. Legislative repeal defeated sodomy statutes in twenty-five states and the District of Columbia, while courts invalidated the statutes in seven states.

Sodomy laws, which prohibit acts of oral and anal sex, have been harshly criticized for their inconsistent application and enforcement. As of late 1998, five states had sodomy laws targeting only same-sex acts, while fourteen states and Puerto Rico had laws prohibiting sodomy between both same-sex and opposite-sex partners. Even in states where sodomy bans included heterosexual acts, the laws have most often been invoked specifically against gay and lesbian couples, and have been used to deprive them of rights such as child custody or employment. A proposed bill in Texas, for example, would prohibit the state from placing children in adoptive or foster homes that could be sites of "deviate sexual intercourse." Heterosexuals, however, are exempted from the proposed legislation. In 1991, lesbian lawyer Robin Shahar had a job offer in the office of Georgia attorney general Michael Bowers rescinded after Bowers, who won the Supreme Court case upholding states' rights to enact and enforce sodomy laws, found out that Shahar and her partner had celebrated a private commitment ceremony. He withdrew the job offer because Georgia's sodomy law implied that Shahar was a felon. A federal appeals court ruled 8–4 that Bowers did not violate Shahar's rights. The U.S. Supreme Court refused to hear the case.

The case that invalidated the nation's most infamous sodomy law, however—the Georgia statute that made consensual oral or anal sex a with a maximum prison term of twenty years—did not involve homosexual activity. In *State v. Anthony Powell*, the Georgia Supreme Court ruled 6–1 to overturn Powell's sodomy conviction, which had resulted from an act of oral sex with his seventeen-year-old niece. Powell, originally charged with RAPE, testified that the sex had been consensual. He was convicted of sodomy and served fourteen months of a jail sentence before making bail pending his appeal. "We cannot think of any other activity that reasonable persons would rank as more private and more deserving of protection from governmen-

tal interference than consensual, private, adult sexual activity," wrote Chief Justice Robert Benham in the majority opinion. Though the Georgia sodomy law had withstood a legal challenge as late as 1996, when its use by undercover police at highway rest stops was upheld in a 5–2 vote, the court in *Powell* ruled that Georgia's sodomy law "manifestly infringes upon a constitutional provision...which guarantees to the citizens of Georgia the right of privacy."

The *Powell* decision prompted the threat of legislative backlash. "I can't imagine how they can make such a ruling..." commented former attorney general Mike Bowers, who predicted "a legislative move to the altar." And Georgia state senate minority leader Eric Johnson and other conservative legislators began considering a move to amend the state constitution. "I think we ought to be able to ban gay sex," Johnson told the *Savannah Morning News*. Civil liberties

lawyers and advocates, however, stressed the positive impact of the *Powell* decision and predicted that remaining sodomy laws throughout the country will soon be invalidated.

Gay civil rights lawyer John D. Rawls has urged the defeat of sodomy laws even where they are rarely enforced. There is "no chance of real gay civil rights at a federal level," he emphasized in an interview quoted in *The Advocate*, "until we get rid of every last sodomy law." Rawls challenged Louisiana's statute, which deemed "unnatural carnal copulation" a FELONY punishable by a maximum of five years in prison and applied to both same-sex and opposite-sex partners, in a suit brought in October 1998. Rawls contended that Louisiana's sodomy law was religious in nature, was devoid of any scientific basis, and deprived individuals of constitutionally guaranteed rights. Rawls presented evidence showing that at least 460 species of mammals are known to engage in some type of homosexual behavior, and called witnesses who testified that Louisiana's sodomy law had been used to discriminate against them. Rawls further argued that present day "crime against nature" laws date back to twelfth century ecclesiastical laws. Charles Braud, who defended the case for the Louisiana attorney general's office, said in a statement quoted in the *New York Times*, "I believe all we have to do is show that the legislators had a rational reason for enacting the law." On March 18, 1999, Judge Carolyn Gill-Jefferson rejected that argument. "The state has presented no evidence, much less the required compelling state interest, to justify its intrusion on plaintiffs' constitutionally protected right of privacy," she wrote.

Texas' sodomy law is also being challenged. In 1998, John Lawrence and Tyrone Garner were arrested after Harris County police entered their apartment in response to a false report that a man there had a gun. The officers found the couple engaged in sexual activity and arrested them on sodomy charges. The Texas sodomy statute makes same-gender oral and anal sex a misdemeanor with a fine of up to $500. Lawrence and Garner spent a night in jail before being released on $200 bail. They pleaded no contest and then appealed the case to a county criminal court. "There is a zone of privacy that's been recognized by the U.S. Supreme Court," said the defendants' lawyer, David Jones, in a *CNN* report. "It's in their interest that we fight the sodomy laws." Legal analysts believe this may be the first sodomy case in Texas to involve consenting adults engaged in private conduct. District Attorney John B. Holmes, Jr., said that only two or three sodomy cases have been prosecuted in Harris County in the past thirty years, and all of these involved homosexual activity witnessed by others in prison.

Legal analysts believe the Georgia decision, issued just three days after the Houston men's arrest, could affect the outcome of their appeal. Neil McCabe, a constitutional law professor at South Texas College of Law, told the *San Antonio Express-News* "There's no reason why Texas can't rely on Georgia for its reasoning." He further noted that the Georgia Supreme Court "expressly relies" on a 1992 Texas appeals court decision (*Morales v. Texas*), later overturned by the Texas Supreme Court, which found Texas's sodomy law unconstitutional. Prosecutors in the Houston case, however, commented in the *San Antonio Express-News* that the *Powell* decision is "not binding on state law, and it's not binding on the Texas Court of Crimi-

nal Appeals. It doesn't mean anything." Analysts believe the Houston case could eventually reach the Texas Court of Criminal Appeals and possibly the U.S. Supreme Court.

Same-sex Marriages

The issue of same-sex MARRIAGE continues to provoke controversy throughout the country. The U.S. Supreme Court has consistently refused to find that state laws preventing same-sex marriage violate the federal Constitution, holding that states have the right to make laws that either prevent or allow such unions. But to date, no state legislature has legalized same-sex marriage. While the courts have increasingly ruled that restrictions on same-sex marriage violate state constitutional provisions, legislatures have reacted by drafting stricter laws governing the definition of marriage.

In 1993, the Hawaii Supreme Court in *Baehr v. Lewin*, 852 P. 2d 44 (Hawaii 1993) found that the denial of marriage licenses to same-sex couples violated the EQUAL PROTECTION guarantee of the state's CONSTITUTION. The court ruled that Hawaii's marriage law "regulates access to the marital status 'on the basis of the applicants' sex" and further noted that a compelling state interest must be demonstrated in order for a classification based on sex to be upheld. In December 1996, a lower court found that the state failed to meet this standard, but stayed its decision pending the higher court's review. The *Baehr* decision polarized Hawaii voters and prompted a campaign to amend the state constitution. In November 1998, the Hawaii electorate ratified an AMENDMENT that authorized the legislature to define marriage as only a union between a man and a woman, thereby excluding same-sex couples. After the vote, the Hawaii Supreme Court asked lawyers for both sides in the case to submit additional arguments to determine whether the election results affected the impending ruling.

Events in Alaska followed an almost identical pattern. In February 1998, an Alaska trial court ruled in *Brause v. Bureau of Vital Statistics*, (Case No. 3AN–95–6562 Cl) that the state's ban on marriage between same-sex couples violated Alaska's constitutional guarantee of privacy. The court held that "the right to choose one's life partner is quintessentially the kind of decision which our culture recognizes as personal and important." The Supreme Court is expected to review this decision, which prompted legislative initiatives, similar to Hawaii's, to amend the Alaska constitution. On the same day that Hawaii voted to allow its legislature to restrict

*Same-sex couples
continue the legal
battle to have their
marriages legally
recognized.*

the legal definition of marriage, Alaska voted by a 2–1 margin in favor of a similar amendment. In addition, a measure was proposed to require that appointees to Alaska's Supreme Court, court of appeals, and judicial council be subject to legislative approval. This was seen as an attempt to bar the confirmation of judges sympathetic to same-sex marriages.

By 1998, several states had adopted legislation that banned marriages between couples of the same sex. The federal government has also dealt with the matter. In September 1996, the U.S. Congress passed the Defense of Marriage Act (DOMA). This law gives states the right to refuse to recognize same-sex marriages performed in other states, a move that legal analysts have argued violates the FULL FAITH AND CREDIT CLAUSE of the U.S. Constitution, which requires states to recognize certain "acts, records and proceedings" of other states, including civil marriage. In addition, DOMA creates for the first time a federal definition of "marriage" and "spouse." DOMA specifies that marriage is "a legal union between one man and one woman as husband and wife." It defines a spouse as "a person of the opposite sex who is a husband or a wife." It specifies that, even if individual states decide to recognize same-sex marriages, the federal government would not do so, and would deny individuals in such unions federal benefits usually awarded to spouses, such as SOCIAL SECURITY survivor benefits, INHERITANCE RIGHTS, and veterans' benefits.

Though many states and municipalities have recognized domestic partnerships and have extended limited benefits to individuals in such relationships, domestic partnership status does not

guarantee many of the rights and responsibilities conferred by civil marriage, such as hospital visitation or inheritance rights. In fact, civil marriage bestows more than 300 protections, supports, and obligations at the state level and 1049 at the federal level. Insisting on the right to the legal status of civil marriage, same-sex couples have continued to press their claims in the courts. In 1997, Stan Baker and Peter Harrigan, Stacy Jolles and Nina Beck, and Lois Farnham and Holly Puterbaugh, brought suit against the state of Vermont as well as the towns of Shelburne, South Burlington, and Milton, respectively because the clerks in those towns refused to issue them marriage licenses (*Baker v. State*). Their attorneys, Susan Murray and Beth Robinson of Langrock, Sperry & Wool in Middlebury, argued that "the refusal to allow our clients to marry violates both state marriage laws and the state Constitution, which require that all citizens and families have the same access to the legal protections and obligations of civil marriage."

Judge Linda Levitt dismissed the case. The judge rejected the state's argument that the question of same-sex marriages should be resolved in the legislature, noting that it was the court's proper role to interpret the constitutionality of marriage statutes. Judge Levitt further found, however, that Vermont's marriage laws do not violate constitutional rights. But plaintiffs were heartened by the judge's rejection of six of the state's arguments claiming that legitimate public policy objectives should allow Vermont's marriage statutes to stand.

Judge Levitt found that, although Vermont marriage laws do not explicitly refer to gender, they are based on the traditional definition of marriage as the union between a man and a woman and therefore "do not allow civil marriages between partners of the same gender." In her analysis of the statutes' constitutionality, Judge Levitt relied on the U.S. Supreme Court's decision in *Zablocki v. Redhail*, 434 U.S. 374, 98 S. Ct. 673, 54 L. Ed. 2d 618 (1978), in which the right to marry is linked to the fundamental rights to procreation, childbirth, child rearing, and family relationships. Because Vermont standards also link marriage with sexual intercourse and procreation, Judge Levitt determined that Vermont laws do not give "a fundamental constitutional right to same-sex marriage." Judge Levitt then considered whether Vermont laws discriminated against members of a suspect class. Agreeing that homosexuals have suffered historic discrimination, the judge noted that they cannot claim obvious distinguishing characteristics that define them as a unique group nor claim to be a politically powerless minority, thus failing to meet two of the three standards that define a suspect class. She cited several U.S. Circuit Courts of Appeals cases, including *Thomasson v. Perry*, 80 F. 3d 915 (4th Cir.), cert. denied, 519 U.S. 948, 117 S. Ct. 358, 136 L. Ed. 2d 250 (1996), to support this analysis. Judge Levitt further found that Vermont marriage laws do not unconstitutionally discriminate on the basis of gender.

In her analysis of whether any legitimate public policy objective existed to support the state's marriage statutes, Judge Levitt rejected six arguments: the state's purported interest in promoting a setting for both male and female role models; in preserving marriage as a "time honored" institution; in ensuring that Vermont marriages are recognized in other states; in preserving the legislature's authority "to channel behavior and make normative statements;" and in "minimizing the use of modern fertility treatments in order to avoid increased child custody and visitation disputes." Judge Levitt did, however, agree that a rational basis analysis required that "distinctions will be found unconstitutional only if similar persons are treated differently on wholly arbitrary and capricious grounds," a standard not demonstrated in this case. Judge Levitt concluded that the state's interest in furthering the link between marriage and procreation and child rearing justified the statutes' implied prohibition of same-sex unions, and dismissed the case. The plaintiffs filed an appeal in January 1998. "No trial judge has ever ruled in favor of a same-gender couple seeking to be free from discrimination at [the trial court] stage of the proceedings" noted plaintiffs' lawyers. "Now we're one step closer and we look forward to engaging the Justices in a full airing of the issues." The case has been argued to the Vermont Supreme Court and a decision is expected soon.

The *Baker* decision did not cause a legislative backlash in Vermont, where a REFERENDUM movement failed to gain widespread support. But voters in California began a petition drive to put the issue on the state ballot in March 2000. While analysts cannot predict the outcome of a ballot issue in California, they are optimistic that the Vermont Supreme Court decision will be favorable. Regardless of the outcome of the appeal, however, the question of whether the U.S. Constitution's Full Faith and Credit Clause will compel individual states to recognize same-sex marriages considered legal in other states remains problematic.

CROSS REFERENCES
Family Law; Privacy

GERRYMANDER

The process of dividing a particular state or territory into election districts in such a manner as to accomplish an unlawful purpose, such as to give one party a greater advantage.

Racial Gerrymandering

The Supreme Court has reviewed a North Carolina congressional voting district case three times in the 1990s over the question of racial gerrymandering. White voters argued that the North Carolina legislature created a district with a majority of black voters, thereby insuring the election of an African American to Congress. In the first case, the Supreme Court established that racial gerrymandering violated the FOURTEENTH AMENDMENT. Three years later it struck down the legislature's first attempt. A three-judge federal court panel threw out the legislature's second attempt, but the Court, in *Hunt v. Cromartie*, __U.S.__, 119 S. Ct. 1545, 143 L. Ed. 2d 731 (1999), reversed the three-judge panel. The Court held that the panel should have conducted a full hearing to determine whether the legislature based the redistricting plan on an impermissible racial motive.

In 1992, the North Carolina legislature created two black-majority districts, the First and the Twelfth. In November 1992, Eva Clayton and Mel Watt were elected from these districts, the first African Americans to represent North Carolina since 1901. However, the Republican party and five white voters challenged the two election districts in federal court. The white plaintiffs argued that the two districts amounted to unlawful racial gerrymandering.

The Twelfth District was worm-shaped, stretching 160 miles from Gastonia to Durham, hugging the thin line of Interstate 85. The district was so narrow at one point that drivers in the northbound lane were in the district, while drivers in the southbound lane were in another district. Of the ten counties through which the district passed, five cut into three different districts, with some towns divided.

A three-judge panel reviewed the claims of the plaintiffs and dismissed the case. However, the Supreme Court, in *Shaw v. Reno*, 509 U.S. 630, 113 S. Ct. 2816, 125 L. Ed. 2d 511 (1993), on a 5–4 vote, reversed the three-judge panel. The Court reinstated the lawsuit, ruling that the plaintiffs did have a cause of action under the

FOURTEENTH AMENDMENT'S EQUAL PROTECTION CLAUSE. It held that race-based districts will be considered suspect if they disregard traditional districting principles "such as compactness, contiguity, and respect for political subdivisions."

The three-judge panel reviewed the plan again but reiterated that the Twelfth District plan was constitutional. The Supreme Court, in *Shaw v. Hunt*, 517 U.S. 899, 116 S. Ct. 1894, 135 L. Ed. 2d 207 (1996), disagreed. It ruled that the redrawing of the district into a bizarre-looking shape so as to include a majority of African-Americans violated the Equal Protection Clause. The Court sent the matter back to the North Carolina legislature for another attempt at redistricting.

The legislature then created a district that was seventy-one miles long in which African Americans comprised 47 percent of the registered voters. This contrasted with the original plan's 57 percent black majority. Nevertheless, white plaintiffs again challenged the plan as racially motivated.

The three-judge panel granted SUMMARY JUDGMENT to the plaintiffs, agreeing that the legislature unconstitutionally used race as a major factor in drawing the district. When the facts in a civil action are not in dispute, one or both of the parties may ask the court to make a summary judgment decision. Summary judgment is purely a matter of law, as the court takes the facts as given and renders a decision based on the applicable legal principles. In this case, the three-judge panel found that "uncontroversial material facts" led to the conclusion that the legislature violated the Fourteenth Amendment.

The Supreme Court unanimously reversed the three-judge panel. Justice CLARENCE THOMAS, writing for the Court, noted that the motivation of the legislature was in dispute. The white plaintiffs were required to prove that the Twelfth District was drawn "with an impermissible racial motive." Moreover, the plaintiffs had to prove that race was the "predominant factor" motivating the legislature. The plaintiffs had the burden of showing, through direct and circumstantial evidence, this racial motivation.

Justice Thomas found that the plaintiffs had offered only circumstantial evidence to support their claim. Their evidence consisted of maps of the district and some statistical and demographic evidence. Thomas agreed that the evidence "tends to support an inference that the State drew its distinct lines with an impermissible racial mo-

tive." However, he concluded that summary judgment is only appropriate "where there is no genuine issue of material fact and the moving party is entitled to judgment as a matter of law."

Despite the three-judge panel's conclusion that the facts were uncontroverted, Justice Thomas found evidence that put the motivation of the legislature in doubt. The two members of the legislature that had been responsible for developing the redistricting plan had submitted affidavits to the court. The legislators stated that in creating the districting plan for all the congressional districts they had sought to protect incumbents, to adhere to traditional redistricting criteria, and to preserve the existing partisan balance in the state congressional delegation. In 1997, the state's delegation was composed of six Republicans and six Democrats.

The state also introduced an affidavit from an expert on redistricting. He concluded that the legislature had drawn the Twelfth District to create a strong Democratic district. African Americans were more likely to vote for Democratic candidates, but he concluded that the redistricting data "supported a political explanation at least as well as, and somewhat better than, a racial explanation."

Though Justice Thomas expressed some skepticism at the state's evidence, he pointed out that when a party moves for summary judgment, the court must treat the nonmoving party's evidence in the most favorable light. With the record presented to the Supreme Court, Thomas concluded that "motivation was in dispute." Reasonable inferences could be drawn that the legislature redistricted either based on racial motivation or political motivation. The three-judge panel, however, had concluded that race was the "predominant factor" in the drawing of the district. It had credited the plaintiffs' inferences over those advanced and supported by the state. This was in error because a court cannot resolve "the disputed fact of motivation at the summary judgment stage."

Justice Thomas found that summary judgment was inappropriate "where the evidence is susceptible of different interpretations or inferences." Moreover, even if the three-judge panel believed that there was no dispute of material fact, the "sensitive nature of redistricting" suggested that a full hearing should be held. Therefore, the Court reversed the panel and returned the case for a full hearing on the merits.

CROSS REFERENCES
Civil Rights; Fourteenth Amendment; Summary Judgment; Voting

GIULIANI, RUDOLPH

Rudolph Giuliani, mayor of New York City and former U.S. attorney for the Southern District of New York, is widely known for his "zero tolerance" for criminal and social misconduct. His zero tolerance policy has resulted in unprecedented changes in New York City since he became its mayor in 1994. Now in his second term, Giuliani announced a run for the U.S. Senate in 2000, and many observers believe he has national political aspirations as well.

Rudy Giuliani was born in Brooklyn in 1944 and attended school in both the Bronx and Manhattan. After graduation from New York University Law School, he clerked for a federal district court judge, then launched a legal career that foreshadowed the prosecutorial bent so visible in his mayoral governing style. He joined the office of the U.S. attorney in New York after his clerkship, where he was soon named chief of the narcotics unit. He caught the attention of DEPARTMENT OF JUSTICE officials, and from 1975–77, he held high-ranking positions with the department. After four years of private practice in New York from 1977–81, he returned to the Justice Department as associate attorney general, the third-ranking position in the department. In 1983 he was appointed as the U.S. Attorney for the Southern District of New York (encompassing New York City). In 1993, Giuliani ran for mayor against incumbent David Dinkins, defeating the city's first African American mayor in a highly antagonistic contest. Giuliani easily won a second term in 1997, against Ruth W. Messinger, a Democrat and the president of the city's Manhattan borough. Giuliani enjoyed a sixteen-point win in a city where registered Democrats outnumber Republican by a ratio of five to one.

Under Dinkins, the city lost about 300,000 private sector jobs while accumulating a $2 billion deficit. Giuliani turned the deficit into a $2 billion surplus, and used tax cuts to lure back private sector jobs. In 1998 the city's economy grew faster than the national economy. Harlem is experiencing a renaissance, with a huge retail and entertainment complex going up on 125th Street.

Perhaps more amazing is the turnaround in crime in New York City under Giuliani's watch, hitting a thirty-year low. Murders have dropped 70 percent during his tenure. In Central Harlem, overall crime dropped 61 per cent since 1994. East New York, a high minority area, reported 110 murders in 1993. In 1998, 37 murders were reported in the area, and through the first three months of 1999, no murders had been committed.

Giuliani employed a message of "zero tolerance" against minor examples of antisocial behavior to achieve the startling turnaround in crime statistics. The zero-tolerance method was first employed in New York's grafitti-laden, crime-beleaguered subway system by transit-police chief William Bratton in the early 1990s. Giuliani incorporated the program city-wide, employing it to combat graffiti, panhandlers, public drunkenness, jaywalkers, and other seemingly minor problems that combined to make life in New York City one confrontation after another. In his 1997 mayoral campaign, Giuliani rallied against the "squeegee men," men who extorted money form drivers during traffic jams in return for pretending to clean the windshield.

Giuliani's zero-tolerance police policy came under attack after the brutal assault of a Haitian immigrant, Abner Louima, by police officers in 1997. However, Giuliani immediately condemned the beating, helping to quickly quell racial tensions. The mayor did not condemn the police as promptly in 1999, when officers shot forty-one bullets at Amadou Diallo, an unarmed Guinean immigrant, hitting him nineteen times. Giuliani's initial reluctance to criticize the four police officers involved in the killing inflamed his critics. Giuliani ordered the arrest of those protesting the killing, further fanning the flames and ensuring that the protests would not end quickly. Former Mayor David Dinkins was one of those arrested, as was the Reverend Jesse Jackson and actress Susan Sarandon. The Reverend Al Sharpton, an African-American activist, head

Rudolph Giuliani
ARCHIVE PHOTO/MALAFRONTE

RUDOLPH GIULIANI

1944	Born in Brooklyn, New York
1970	Joined office of U.S. attorney
1975	Department of Justice
1977	Entered private practice
1981	Appointed associate attorney general
1983	U.S. attorney
1993	Elected mayor of New York City

of the National Action Network, and a perpetual critic of Giuliani, was instrumental in organizing the protests. Giuliani's approval rating dropped by twenty points in the weeks following the shooting.

Cleaning up the streets has taken its toll in other ways, as the number of civilian complaints against the police has soared as a result of an increased number of random traffic stops and street frisks. The increased number of complaints in turn resulted in a doubling of the amount the city has paid to settle charges of police brutality. Giuliani's efforts to get drunk drivers off the road has come under fire as well. The program permits the seizure of the cars driven by those accused of a first-time drinking and driving offense, even when the driver is not convicted. Drivers can only seek reclamation of their cars by bringing a civil lawsuit.

Giuliani has drastically reduced the city's welfare rolls, but some have charged that the mayor has done so at great social and economic expense to the former recipients. Many of Giuliani's critics also charge that the public school system remains woefully inadequate. A reported third of the city's elementary schools do not have playgrounds, and more than half of the high schools are not connected to the Internet. In 1999, to the dismay of the New York schools chancellor, Giuliani touted a pilot plan to use vouchers to allow poor students in a certain district to attend private schools for three years. Giuliani has also announced his intention to reform the special education system in New York, by privatizing certain segments of the systems.

In April 1999, Giuliani made a long-anticipated announcement that he had filed formal papers to explore a run for the U.S. Senate, for the seat being vacated by Daniel Patrick Moynihan. The race may be the most closely watched in the nation, as First Lady HILLARY CLINTON is also seriously exploring a Democratic run for Moynihan's seat.

CROSS REFERENCES
Police Brutality; Pornography

GOLDWATER, BARRY

Obituary notice

Born on January 1, 1909, in Phoenix, Arizona; died May 29, 1998, in Paradise Valley, Arizona. Goldwater was elected as a Republican to the U.S. Senate five times between 1952 and 1980, leaving temporarily to run unsuccessfully for president in 1964. His outspoken conservatism gained him the label "Mr. Conservative" in American politics. He was considered the most important American conservative between Senator Robert Taft's death in 1953 and Ronald Reagan's election as governor of California in 1966.

GORE, ALBERT, JR.

Albert Gore, Jr., was born in Washington, D.C., on March 31, 1948. His father, Albert Gore, Sr., was serving as a Democratic member of the U.S. House of Representatives from Tennessee. The senior Gore was to serve in the House and the Senate for nearly three decades. His mother was Pauline LaFon Gore. She had the distinction of being one of the first women to graduate from the law school at Vanderbilt University.

Gore attended St. Alban's Episcopal School for Boys in Washington, D.C., where he was an honor student and captain of the football team. In 1969 he received a B.A. with honors in government from Harvard University. He was interested in becoming a writer, rather than following his father's footsteps as a politician. After graduation he enlisted in the army, although he opposed the United States' intervention in the Vietnam War.

While stationed in Vietnam, Gore served as an army reporter. After Gore left the military service in 1971, the *Nashville Tennessean* hired him as an investigative reporter and, later, as an editorial writer. In addition to his journalism career, Gore was a home builder, a land developer, and a livestock and tobacco farmer.

Interested in religion and philosophy, Gore enrolled in the Graduate School of Religion at Vanderbilt University during the 1971–72 academic year. In 1974 he entered Vanderbilt's law school but left to enter elective office two years later.

In 1976 Gore ran for a seat in the U.S. House of Representatives. He won the primary election against eight other candidates and went on to win in the general election. He ran successfully in the three following elections. Gore claimed some early attention in 1980 when he was assigned to the House Intelligence Committee studying nuclear arms. Gore researched and eventually published a comprehensive manifesto on arms restructuring for future security, which was published in the February 1982 issue of Congressional Quarterly. In 1984 Gore campaigned for a seat in the U.S. Senate that had

Barry Goldwater

just become vacant. He won that office with a large margin of votes.

While in Congress, Gore was interested in several issues. He focused attention on health-related matters and on cleaning up the environment. He worked for nuclear arms control and disarmament, as well as other strategic defense issues. He stressed the potential of new technologies, such as biotechnology and computer development.

The race for the 1988 presidential election attracted Gore. He was only thirty-nine years old at the time. He ran on traditional domestic Democratic views and was tough on foreign policy issues. He failed, however, to develop a national theme for his campaign and was criticized for changing positions and issues. He was successful in gaining public support in the primaries during the early spring and won more votes than any other candidate in southern states. However, he obtained only small percentages of votes in other states and withdrew from the presidential nomination campaigns in mid-April. Two years later he won election to a second term in the U.S. Senate. He chose not to seek the presidency in 1992, citing family concerns (his son Albert had been hit by an automobile and was seriously injured). It was during this time that Gore wrote the book *Earth in the Balance: Ecology and the Human Spirit*, which expressed his concern, ideas, and recommendations on conservation and the global environment. In the book he wrote about his own personal and political experiences and legislative actions on the environmental issue. One of Gore's statements in the book that sums up his philosophy regarding the environment and human interaction was, "We must make the rescue of the environment the central organizing principle for civilization."

In the summer of 1992 Bill Clinton selected Gore as his vice-presidential nominee. The choice startled many people because it ended a long-standing pattern of a candidate choosing a vice presidential nominee to "balance the ticket." Both men were of the same age, region, and reputation and moderate in political outlook. Clinton's idea was to project a new generation of leadership as a campaign theme. Gore did balance Clinton's strength by bringing to the ticket his experience in foreign and defense policy, expertise in environmental and new technology matters, and an image as an unwavering family man.

Clinton and Gore won the election in 1992. Gore was inaugurated as the forty-fifth vice president on January 20, 1993. At the age of

forty-four years, he became one of the youngest people to hold the position. Clinton and Gore were re-elected in 1996, running against Republicans Bob Dole and Jack Kemp.

During his time as vice-president, Gore continued to stress environmental concerns. In 1997 the White House launched an effort to start producing a report card on the health of the nation's ecosystems. This project was carried out by an environmental think tank and initiated by Gore.

Also in 1997, Gore's reputation was somewhat tarnished when he was accused of and admitted to making fund-raising telephone calls from the White House during the 1996 presidential campaign. Gore held a press conference on March 3, 1997, to defend his actions, saying there was nothing illegal about what he had done, although he admitted it may not have been a wise choice. Gore was also criticized for toasting Li Peng, initiator of the Tiananmen Square Massacre, during a trip to China. In September 1997, Buddhist nuns testified before the Senate panel investigating the abuses of campaign fund-raising. The nuns admitted that donors were illegally reimbursed by their temple after a fund-raiser attended by Gore, and that they had destroyed and/or altered records to avoid embarrassing their temple. Some believe these incidents have further damaged Gore's reputation.

Gore married his college sweetheart, Mary Elizabeth "Tipper" Aitcheson, in 1970. Tipper holds a B.A. degree from Boston University and an M.A. in psychology from George Peabody College. She was an active mother and politician's spouse, while working to forward her own

Albert Gore, Jr.
CORBIS-BETTMANN

AL GORE

1948 Born in Washington, D.C.

1969 Graduated from Harvard

1970 Married Mary Elizabeth "Tipper" Aitcheson

1976 Elected to U.S. House of Representatives from Tennessee

1984 Elected to U.S. Senate

1992 Elected Vice President on Bill Clinton's ticket

issues. She gained attention through her efforts to influence the record industry to rate and label obscene and violent lyrics. She was cofounder of the Parents Music Resource Center, which monitors musical and video presentations that glorify casual sex and violence. The Gores have four children: Karenna, Kristin, Sarah, and Albert III.

GUN CONTROL

Government regulation of the manufacture, sale, and possession of firearms.

Cities Across the United States Sue Gun Manufacturers

The debate over gun control entered a new phase when, in late 1998 and continuing through early 1999, major U.S. cities brought lawsuits against the gun industry. Frustrated by decades of meager progress in gun control, as well as mounting costs in law enforcement and health care, mayors from New Orleans, Miami, Atlanta, Chicago, and Bridgeport looked beyond traditional regulation and tried litigation as a means to recoup the millions of dollars the cities spend each year coping with gun violence. The cities hoped to emulate the success of U.S. states in winning record settlements from the tobacco industry. In February 1999, they were encouraged when a federal jury returned the first-ever verdict holding gun makers liable for DAMAGES caused by the use of their products in a crime. But as many more cities considered filing suits, the gun industry fought back with lobbying and launched preemptive strikes in state legislatures against future lawsuits.

The lawsuits marked a new chapter in a legal saga that is over three decades old. Since the 1960s—when gun control began to be debated with earnest—federal, state and local governments have periodically tried to regulate the purchase and carrying of handguns. From its origin in registration requirements and bans on carrying guns within city limits to more recent devices like background checks on gun buyers, the focus of most gun control has been on the gun buyer—and especially on preventing criminals from legally obtaining guns. But while advocates and opponents of gun control have hotly argued its merits for years, no form of gun control has ever affected the market for illegal guns, stopped gun violence, or ended tragic accidents caused by misfiring weapons.

The innovation behind the lawsuits came from another quarter. Inspiring the cities was a recent celebrated example of PRODUCT LIABILITY litigation. During the mid-1990s forty state attorneys general sued tobacco manufacturers for the billions of dollars that the states spent annually on health care for treating tobacco-related illnesses. The states argued that cigarettes and chewing tobacco cost society at large—and state treasuries in particular—a vast amount of money while the tobacco industry reaped profits from a lethal substance. Early observers expected the industry to win, just as it had prevailed in most lawsuits against it. But when the industry agreed to a settlement in early 1999, the result for the states was a spectacular success. They won $246 billion over twenty-five years.

Building upon this example of government suing industry for reimbursement of costs due to the use of its products, the cities devised two main legal strategies. Both invoked the legal concept of NEGLIGENCE—the idea that the manufacturer knew, or should have known, that its products would cause harm. The first approach, which has been taken by New Orleans, Miami, and Atlanta, is a common form of product liability lawsuit. The cities allege that gun makers were negligent in failing to build adequate safety devices into their guns. They take note of the fact that some guns are made and sold without any safety devices at all, while others come without warnings that they still may contain a single bullet even after the magazine is removed. Over 1,100 people were killed in accidents in 1996.

As illustrated by the lawsuits of Chicago and Bridgeport, the second approach is a more novel claim. Both cities have restrictive laws governing the sale of guns within city limits, but both say that guns continue to flow into the city where they are used by criminals. Their suits argue that this is the fault of negligent marketing by gun makers. They contend that gun makers negligently oversupply gun stores in outlying suburban areas where the laws are more lax, intentionally flooding these shops with guns that criminals buy and then take back into the city. Under this theory, the negligence of the gun manufacturers circumvents the cities' laws, supplies criminals with guns, and ends up costing taxpayers millions of dollars spent on law enforcement and hospital costs.

Chicago filed its lawsuit in November 1998, after police conducted a three-month long undercover operation. Posing as mercenaries and gang members, they bought 171 handguns in suburban gun shops without having required state gun permits, and even while boasting about planning to use the guns in crimes. The suit, naming twenty-two manufacturers, twelve stores, and four distributors, seeks $433 million in damages. Commenting on the collusion between gun makers and dealers, Mayor RICHARD M. DALEY said at a press conference, "Gun manufacturers and retailers know exactly what they're doing. They knowingly market and distribute their deadly weapons to criminals in Chicago and refuse to impose even the most basic controls." Bolstering the city's argument was new federal data released in late 1998 that dispelled a long-standing belief that criminals steal their weapons. According to the new findings by the Bureau of Alcohol, Tobacco, and Firearms, nearly two out of five handguns used in crimes were purchased from legitimate gun dealers only three years earlier.

Although the gun industry has faced product liability lawsuits before, it had never lost one until 1999. On February 12, a federal district court jury in Brooklyn, New York, held nine gun makers liable for shootings caused by illegally obtained handguns. The jury in *Hamilton v. Accu-Tek*, a civil lawsuit brought by family members of gun victims, decided that the marketing and distribution practices of the gun makers helped to foster the illegal gun market generally— much in the manner that is alleged in the lawsuits by Chicago and Bridgeport—and, in specific, led to criminals illegally obtaining the handguns used in shootings in the case. One surviving victim was awarded $560,000 in damages, but in an apparent compromise, no damages were awarded to the survivors of two victims who died. Overall, however, the verdict was ambiguous: the jury found negligent marketing and distributing in fifteen of the twenty-five manufacturers named in the suit, but it said that only three of the seven shootings in the case were the result of that negligence. Afterwards, both sides claimed victory.

As expected, the gun industry fought the cities' lawsuits vigorously. Noting that guns are commonly viewed as dangerous, it denied having any liability for how they are used. And it denounced the cities' lawsuits as greed by product liability attorneys, whose fees are percentages of awards and settlement amounts. "We're going to do whatever we can to expose these rich trial lawyers for what they are," vowed Bob Ricker, a representative of the American Shooting Sports Council. The industry quickly organized a new lobbying body, the Hunting and Shooting Sports Heritage Fund, and tried to thwart the lawsuits through legislation. In Geor-

gia, it succeeded in convincing the state legislature to pass a law making it illegal for any of the state's cities to sue the gun industry. Similar attempts to protect the industry through antilitigation laws were underway in other states and in Congress, although many observers doubted the laws would hold up in court.

No one could predict whether the cities' lawsuits would succeed. While many comparisons were made to the state tobacco litigation, significant differences exist between the two: big tobacco had few political allies, could point to no benefits for its products, faced the concerted efforts of the vast majority of states, and was an attractive target for litigation because its annual billions in sales. On the other hand, the gun industry has enjoyed widespread support for decades, can point to a constitutionally-protected product that many owners believe makes them safer, and has much smaller annual sales. Even so, there was wide agreement that the lawsuits represented the most radical development to date in the history of gun control. Beyond the novelty of the suits, there was also the goal, acknowledged by some cities, that winning monetary awards would not be the only victory: short of reimbursement for their gun-related costs, they hoped to force the gun industry to accept new regulation and change its marketing practices.

What Does "To Carry a Gun" mean?

In a June 1998 decision, the Supreme Court explored the linguistic roots of what it means to carry a gun in the context of a decade-old anti-drug policy. In *Muscarello v. United States*, 524 U.S. 125, 118 S.Ct. 1911, 14 L.Ed.2d 111 (1998), the Court held that transporting a gun in a locked trunk or glove compartment of a vehicle meets the definition of carrying a gun under federal law, even though the gun is not immediately accessible. As a result, the 5–4 majority upheld the convictions of three defendants under a 1984 provision that adds heftier sentences to drug trafficking convictions when firearms were used or carried. The case, which has potentially deep implications for future drug prosecutions, sharply divided the justices. It also reflected an unusual approach by the Court, which spent considerable time on linguistic debate over the meaning of the word "carry," utilized computer databases in a new way, and drew its research from such different sources as the novel *Robinson Cruesoe* and the television show *M*A*S*H*.

The case marked a second time that the Court dealt with controversies under a 1980s-era amendment to federal firearms law. In 1984, during a wave of anti-drug sentiment in Congress, lawmakers seeking additional means to punish drug dealers enacted a variety of tougher penalties. One of these was meant to deter gun violence in drug deals. Dealers convicted of trafficking drugs faced an extra five-year prison term—which is added to the trafficking sentence—if they used or carried a gun during the deal. Thus, a section of the federal firearms code first enacted in the late 1960s to penalize the use of guns in felonies was strengthened. Touted by politicians as a new salvo in the so-called war on drugs, the law later gave headaches to the courts which had to interpret it. By the mid-1990s, there was wide disagreement among the federal circuits over what constituted "using" a gun under the law. The Supreme Court cleared up that matter in the 1995 case of *Bailey v. United States,* 516 U. S. 137, 116 S.Ct. 501, 133 L.Ed.2d 472 (1995), ruling unanimously that prosecutors must prove that defendants "actively employed" a gun in a drug deal—not merely that they had it nearby or available to them. That decision insisted that the law be interpreted narrowly.

In fact, the decision led to appeals of two separate cases that involved convictions under the law, which the Supreme Court consolidated into the *Muscarello* case. In the first case, Frank Muscarello was a court bailiff and former police chief of a Louisiana town who pleaded guilty to several felonies stemming from delivering eight pounds of marijuana to an undercover federal agent. Muscarello had a loaded .38 caliber revolver in the locked glove compartment of his truck, and he also pleaded guilty to using or carrying a gun in a drug deal. The second case involved two defendants, Donald Cleveland and Enrique Gray-Santana, who were arrested while en route to rob their cocaine suppliers in Boston, Massachusetts. When police found three loaded handguns in the trunk of their car, the two men pleaded guilty to violating the firearms law. Muscarello, Cleveland, and Gray-Santana all filed appeals following the decision on "use" in *Bailey.* Although each was unsuccessful in federal appeals court, the Supreme Court agreed to hear the case in order to determine what precisely constitutes "carrying" a gun under the law.

But the Court did not have as easy a time answering the question. Justice STEPHEN BREYER's majority opinion framed the problem before the Court in simple terms: "The question before us is whether the phrase 'carries a firearm' is limited to the carrying of firearms on the person." Because the defendants had vigorously contested the meaning of the phrase and

argued the point at length, Justice Breyer explained that the Court, too, had "looked into the matter in more than usual depth." Indeed, the majority undertook a linguistic analysis of historical and contemporary uses of the word "carry" not only by consulting dictionaries but also by searching electronic databases to compare its use by "the greatest of writers," including Biblical authors and the novelists Daniel Defoe and Herman Melville, as well as recent journalism in the *New York Times.* This marked the first time a Supreme Court opinion had turned to online search methods in order to settle a dispute over semantics.

For the majority, only two of the many meanings of "carry" were relevant. The first was the word's most basic definition, which is to convey an item in a vehicle. The second meaning was the idea of supporting or bearing an item on one's person. There was no linguistic reason, the majority concluded, to believe that Congress meant to limit the law to the second meaning when it is the first meaning which formed the origin of the word and which is still prevalent today. "The generally accepted contemporary meaning of the word 'carry' includes the carrying of a firearm in a vehicle," wrote Justice Breyer.

The majority opinion next turned to the legislative history and basic purpose of the statute. As the *Congressional Record* for 1968 revealed, the provision's chief sponsor in Congress had said at the time that it was intended "to persuade the man who is tempted to commit a Federal felony to leave his gun at home." Later, in 1993, in light of the subsequent anti-drug amendments to the statute, the Supreme Court itself had observed that another basic purpose of the law was to combat the "dangerous combination" of drugs and guns in *Smith v. United States,* 508 U. S. 223, 113 S.Ct. 2050, 124 L.Ed.2d 138 (1993). Justice Breyer concluded that nothing in the law's legislative history or intent suggested that the word "carry" should be interpreted only as meaning "on the person."

The opinion concluded by rejecting four other arguments by the defendants. First, although the defendants argued that a broad reading of the word "carry" would eliminate the distinction between "carry" and "transport" that Congress had drawn elsewhere in the firearms statute, the majority emphasized that it was not attempting to equate the two terms. Second, the Court was not contradicting itself by narrowly reading the statute's definition of "use a gun" while broadly reading its definition of "carry a gun": in other words, the *Muscarello* decision was not at odds with the earlier *Bailey* decision. Third, the Court's reading was not so overbroad that it would unfairly extend the statute to cover passengers on buses, trains, or ships who placed a firearm in their luggage, since the statute was already specifically limited to drug deals. Fourth, the majority refused to apply the so-called Lenity Rule, which sometimes helps defendants in disputes over meaning in a statute: it holds that, when the intent of the legislature is not clear from the law itself, courts should adopt the less harsh meaning. But the majority held that the intent of Congress was far from being so unclear as to permit the defendants to use the rule.

The decision is likely to produce greater numbers of convictions under the firearms statute, thus increasing the length of sentences in drug trafficking convictions. And yet this very point divided the Court and created an unusual majority. Usually, liberals and conservatives split along ideological lines. But in *Muscarello*, Justice Stephen Breyer's opinion was joined by a cross-section of liberals and conservatives. The dissent was written by Justice RUTH BADER GINS-BURG, a liberal, who was joined by two conservatives, Chief Justice WILLIAM H. REHNQUIST and Justice ANTONIN SCALIA, well as Justice DAVID H. SOUTER. Justice Ginsburg's dissent contended that the Court "should leave it to Congress to speak in language that is clear and definite if the Legislature wishes to impose the sterner penalty." The dissent also rebutted the majority's methodology. Justice Ginsburg surveyed a wide range of literature and published material to illustrate that there are many meanings of the word "carry," even taking to the Internet to find a quote from the TV series *M*A*S*H*, in which Alan Alda (as the character Hawkeye Pierce) proclaims: "I will not carry a gun...I'll carry your books, I'll carry a torch, I'll carry a tune, I'll carry on, carry over, carry forward, Cary Grant, cash and carry, carry me back to Old Virginia, I'll even 'harikari' if you show me how, but I will not carry a gun!" Such examples, Justice Ginsburg concluded, demonstrated that linguistic analysis is an unreliable tool to determine what Congress meant by the word.

CROSS REFERENCES

Crime; Product Liability; Tobacco

HASTERT, DENNIS

After seven terms in Congress, J. Dennis Hastert (R-Il.) emerged from relative political obscurity to become Speaker of the House in January 1999. First elected to the House in 1986, Hastert built a reputation as a reliable behind-the-scenes lieutenant to the Republican party leadership. His low-key style seldom brought him to attention outside of Washington or his home state of Illinois, where he was regarded as a tax-cutting, anti-regulatory fiscal conservative with a hard-right stand on social issues. In fact, the fifty-seven-year old Hastert expected to continue serving as House Deputy Whip, a position he had held since the One Hundred and Fourth Congress. But the complicated succession battle to replace outgoing House Speaker NEWT GINGRICH (R-Ga.), who resigned in November 1998, catapulted the former high school teacher into the limelight after a sex scandal forced the party's first choice to resign.

Born on January 2, 1942, Hastert graduated from Wheaton College, an evangelical Christian school in Illinois, in 1964, and added a master's degree from Northern Illinois University at Dekalb in 1967. For sixteen years, he taught government and history at Yorkville High School in northern Illinois. After school, he coached the wrestling team. Entering politics in the 1980s, he served for three terms in the Illinois General Assembly, where he promoted economic development, property tax reform, and higher educational standards.

In 1986, Hastert won his first election to the U.S. House of Representatives from the sub-urban Chicago Fourteenth Congressional district. A plain spoken and low-key campaigner, he won reelection six more times on a staunchly conservative platform—handily beating his Democratic opponent in 1998 by a greater than 2–1 margin. Fiscally, he favored lowering taxes and opposed regulation of business. Socially, his positions typified the social conservatism of the religious right: he opposed abortion, gay and lesbian rights, and the separation of church and state, once introducing a so-called "Religious Freedom Amendment" that would have curtailed First Amendment limits on state-sponsored religion. He earned a 100 percent approval rating in 1998 from the Christian Coalition, a conservative political organization.

Hastert's prominence increased after 1993, when he was the GOP liaison to the Clinton administration's health care reform task force. He ultimately wrote the compromise reform bill that rose from the wreckage of that effort and which was signed into law in 1996. During the mid-1990s he helped increase federal spending on anti-drug efforts through his chairmanship of the House Government Reform and Oversight Committee's National Security, International Affairs and Criminal Justice Subcommittee. Most importantly, from 1994 on, Hastert served as Chief Deputy under House Whip Tom DeLay (R-Tex.), a key behind-the-scenes position in which he helped secure party votes on legislation and earned respect for grasping issues and personalities equally well.

Hastert's election as House Speaker marked his highest ascent in national politics, but he was not his party's first choice. In fact, his election was the product of two crises. A succession bat-

Dennis Hastert

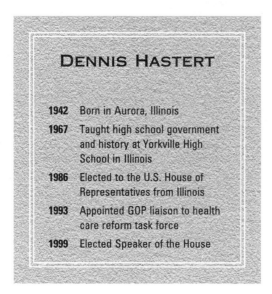

DENNIS HASTERT

1942   Born in Aurora, Illinois

1967   Taught high school government and history at Yorkville High School in Illinois

1986   Elected to the U.S. House of Representatives from Illinois

1993   Appointed GOP liaison to health care reform task force

1999   Elected Speaker of the House

tle had been brewing for months as Republican party leaders vied to replace House Speaker Newton Gingrich, the Georgia congressman who had held the position since 1995. Gingrich's enormously influential reign as Speaker gave prominence to the so-called "Contract With America," the wide-ranging Republican legislative agenda which dominated domestic politics through the mid-1990s. But by 1998, he was reprimanded and fined $300,000 by the House Ethics Committee in 1997, his influence had steadily declined. Upstart party members tried but failed to oust him that summer. Following his party's poor showing in the November mid-term elections in 1998, which left it with only a six-seat majority, he faced sharp criticism and swiftly announced his resignation. In December, the GOP chose Robert Livingston (R-La.) as his successor.

But the second crisis involved Livingston before he could even take the office. For most of 1998, Republican lawmakers had been inching toward impeachment of President Bill Clinton for his affair with White House aide Monica Lewinsky and subsequent lying under oath. A socially conservative Republican, Livingston had earnestly condemned the president's sexual infidelity. But in late December, the tables were turned. As word leaked out that the pornographic magazine *Hustler* would publish an expose revealing Livingston's own record of infidelity, he admitted to having cheated occasionally on his wife during their thirty-three-year marriage. On December 19, facing accusations of hypocrisy, Livingston dramatically resigned from Congress in the midst of the floor debate on impeachment.

Embarrassed by this ironic chain of events, GOP leaders looked for a more stable replacement. They quickly turned to Hastert, who had more than his loyalty and squeaky clean image to offer. Known for his ability to gently persuade colleagues, Hastert looked like an appealing Speaker for the difficult period ahead: the impeachment battle was going to shape how Republicans and Democrats worked together—or did not—for years to come. Hanging on to the slightest of majorities, the GOP knew it needed someone capable of reconciliation, and Hastert is well-respected by many Democrats.

To a large extent, the specter of impeachment defined the first few months of Hastert's service. On January 6, 1999, his acceptance speech acknowledged the deep wounds it had created between the parties as well as between lawmakers and the White House. "Solutions to problems cannot be found in a pool of bitterness," he warned. "They can be found in an environment in which we trust one another's word; where we generate heat and passion, but where we recognize that each member is equally important to our overall mission of improving the life of the American people." The message of bipartisanship was not lost on Democrats. That February, Clinton, Hastert and other Republican leaders held their first post-impeachment meeting, a session widely reported as cooperative and productive.

By early summer, it was still too early to judge Hastert's performance. Critics mockingly contended that Delay was actually in charge of the House, and that Hastert was merely a figurehead. In May, a GOP aide told *Time*, "Hastert is Speaker in title only. DeLay is running rings around him." Yet others saw in Hastert a dedicated leader. They noted that the new Speaker had devoted himself not only to forging bipartisan reconciliation but actual productivity, too, with Hastert warning legislators they must finalize a budget by summer—or stay in session longer.

CROSS REFERENCES
Gingrich, Newt; Impeachment

HATE CRIME

A crime motivated by racial, religious, gender, sexual orientation, or other PREJUDICE.

The Burning of Macedonia Baptist Church

In 1995, church services at the Macedonia Baptist Church in Bloomville, South Carolina,

were plagued by loud KU KLUX KLAN rallies. In spring of 1995, Reverend Jonathan Mouzon was forced to call police to complain about the rallies, which were conducted less than two hundred feet from the church and disturbed his parishioners. Members of Rev. Mouzon's congregation could hear racial slurs during quiet moments in the services. On June 21, 1995, approximately three weeks after Rev. Mouzon asked the Clarendon County sheriff to speak to the Klan leaders about the noise, the Macedonia Baptist Church in Bloomville, South Carolina, was burned to the ground.

A short time after the fire, Timothy A. Welch, twenty-three years old, and Gary C. Cox, twenty-two years old, tried to pawn a public address sound system that they had stolen from Mt. Zion African Methodist Episcopal Church. Mt. Zion, situated near Macedonia Baptist, had been destroyed by a fire the day be-

fore the Macedonia Baptist Church was torched. Welch and Cox were arrested and charged with ARSON and BURGLARY.

The burning of the one hundred year-old Macedonia Baptist Church was just one in a series of African American church burnings in the southern United States. Between 1993 and April 1996, more than two dozen churches with large African-American congregations or integrated congregations were damaged or ruined by fire. Federal authorities have been unable to piece together an organized CONSPIRACY, and many of the fires have gone unsolved.

Welch openly admitted that he and Cox urinated in the Mt. Zion church and that they had used hymnals to start the fire. One of the men had a Ku Klux Klan membership card in his wallet and the other had a white hooded robe in his trailer home. As prosecutors investigated the men, they discovered that they were members of the Christian Knights of the Ku Klux Klan and that Welch had been among the group that had been disturbing the Macedonia Baptist congregation.

Welch and Cox eventually pleaded guilty to violating federal CIVIL RIGHTS and arson statutes. A federal judge sentenced Cox to nineteen and one-half years in prison and Welch to eighteen years. Rene Josey, a U.S. attorney in South Carolina, announced that the sentences "should serve as a wake-up call to those individuals who may consider the unlawful use of force and violence to intimidate persons based on their race and religious beliefs." Prosecutors also charged two other men in connection with the Macedonia Baptist fire. Arthur Haley, fifty-one years old, and Hubert Rowell, fifty years old, were charged with, among other crimes, conspiring with Cox and Welch in the Macedonia Baptist fire. Welch and Cox also were charged with ASSAULT AND BATTERY with intent to kill for stabbing a mentally disabled black man to death a few days prior to the Macedonia Baptist and Mt. Zion fires.

After the fire destroyed their church, the members of the Macedonia Baptist congregation decided to file suit against the Christian Knights of the Ku Klux Klan—Invisible Empire, Inc., Horace King (the grand dragon of the Ku Klux Klan), Welch, Cox, Haley, and Rowell. The plaintiffs argued that the Ku Klux Klan created a climate of antipathy toward predominantly black churches that caused the arson of the churches. Klan leaders allegedly told their members that African Americans were plotting against white persons, and that they were doing the plotting in the predominantly African American churches. King argued that his speech was protected by the FIRST AMENDMENT guarantee of free speech, and he denied that he exhorted Klansmen to violence. However, the plaintiffs produced video evidence in which King, among other things, said to a crowd in Washington, D.C., "[i]f we had this garbage in South Carolina, we would burn the bastards out or run them out of town."

The South Carolina jury did not believe King when he denied encouraging violence. In a stunning verdict, the jury ordered the defendants to pay $37.8 million in damages to the Macedonia Baptist congregation, with King responsible for $15 million. Joe Roy, director of the Intelligence Project at the Southern Poverty Law Center in Montgomery, Alabama, told *Trial* magazine that Clarendon County, South Carolina, "really took offense at this group of Klansmen coming in like snake-oil salesmen and spewing their hate." Rev. Mouzon commented to the *New York Times* that the verdict was "a verdict for Clarendon County," and that the suit was not "a monetary thing. This was about taking a stand for your rights." Morris Dees, the lawyer from the Southern Poverty Law Center who represented the plaintiffs, declared that "[t]here are always going to be people who hate. And lawsuits like this make it harder for them to operate."

The plaintiffs had little hope of collecting all of the money, but Dees promised to acquire the title to the Klan's South Carolina headquarters: a plot of land and a shed owned by Horace King. Richard Welch, the younger brother of Timothy Welch, beseeched "every Klan member to stay away from our town. We don't put up with this. We're not going to put up with this."

James Byrd, Jr., and Mathew Shepard

In 1997 the federal government documented 9,861 hate crimes based on the victim's religion, ethnicity, gender, sexual orientation, and disability. More than half of these crimes were motivated by racial bias and over 1,000 were based on sexual orientation.

According to the ANTI-DEFAMATION LEAGUE (ADL), which has been instrumental in the development of hate crime legislation, an act is considered a hate crime if the defendant intentionally selects the victim based upon his/her perception of the victim's race, religion, national origin, or sexual orientation. At present, forty states have enacted hate crime laws based on or similar to model legislation developed by the ADL.

One state that has not adopted the model ADL language is Texas. Rather the Texas law protects victims selected "because of the defendant's bias or prejudice against a person or group." Although there is a criminal penalty for violation of Texas' hate crime law, neither the language nor risk of sanction could protect James Byrd, Jr., an African American who was subjected to a brutal death due to his race.

Byrd was walking along Martin Luther King, Jr., Boulevard at approximately 2:30 A.M. on June 7, 1998, when he was given a ride by three white men in a pick-up truck: Shawn Berry, John William King, and Lawrence Russell Brewer. The men beat him and chained him by his ankles with a towing chain to the back of their truck and dragged him for nearly three miles. Byrd was decapitated and dismembered as he was dragged behind the truck. Byrd was alive and conscious when it all began. According to the testimony at King's trial, Byrd's elbows were ground down to the bone while he desperately tried to hold himself off the road surface before he died from overwhelming trauma.

All three men were on parole and had extensive criminal records. It is alleged that at least two of the men had affiliations with racist groups, such as the Aryan Nation and the Ku Klux Klan, and displayed white supremacist tattoos. John William King has was tried and convicted of the murder. On February 25,1999, he was sentenced to die by lethal injection. The other two defendants are awaiting trial.

Since 1998, two other states have also been the sites of particularly heinous hate crimes that have garnered national attention. Both of these hate crimes involved homosexuals.

Mathew Shepard was a twenty-one-year old, five foot two inch, 105 pound college freshman majoring in political science at the University of Wyoming in Laramie. On October 12, 1998 he died, in part, because he was a homosexual. On October 6, 1998, Russell Henderson and Aaron McKinney, also both in their early twenties, entered a local bar where Shepard was already drinking. The men, pretending to be gay, approached Shepard who eventually left with them. The men then drove him to a deserted area where they tied him to a fence and pistol whipped him with a .357 magnum until his skull collapsed. They took his wallet and shoes and obtained his address so that they could rob his apartment. Shepard was discovered eighteen hours later still tied to the fence. He never regained consciousness.

Henderson and McKinney were charged with first degree murder, kidnapping, and aggravated robbery. Although separate trials were ordered, Henderson pled guilty to the charges and has been sentenced to serve two consecutive life sentences, escaping a possible death sentence. It is virtually certain that he will die in prison, absent a governor's PARDON. McKinney is still awaiting trial, which is scheduled for late summer 1999. It is expected that Henderson will testify against McKinney at his trial.

An equally violent story surrounds the death of Billy Jack Gaither, a computer operator from Alabama who was abducted and beaten to death on February 19, 1999. According to the Coosa County, Alabama, sheriff's report, two acquaintances of Gaither, Charles Monroe Butler, Jr., and Steven Eric Mullins, met him at a local nightclub. Investigators believe that the two men planned for two weeks to attack Gaither, claiming that he had earlier made unwanted sexual advances towards them. Butler and Mullins locked Gaither in the trunk of his own car, drove to a deserted boat dock, bludgeoned him to death with an ax handle, and then threw his body onto a pile of burning tires. His remains and his charred vehicle were found the next day. Each defendant, is awaiting trial on $500,000 bond.

Aaron Mckinney, right, stands with his lawyers during the murder trial for killing Mathew Shepard.

ED ANDRIESKI/ARCHIVE PHOTOS, INC.

Gaither's tragic death has perplexed the entire community. Gaither lived with his disabled parents and was their primary caretaker. Unlike Mathew Shepard, who belonged to gay organizations and was more open with his homosexuality, Gaither was extremely private, revealing his sexual orientation only to close friends and meeting men by driving several miles to Birmingham to go dancing at a gay bar. Although by description Mullins appeared to be a skinhead with racist philosophies, there were no reported instances of violence committed by him or Butler against the homosexual community. Like the assailants in the Mathew Shepard case, however, although facing the death penalty if convicted of capital murder, none of these men could be charged with a hate crime. Alabama's hate crime statute does not include sexual orientation and Wyoming does not have a hate crime law.

In the wake of these murders, the Anti-Defamation League has renewed the call for penalty enhancement for bias motivated crimes, on both the federal and state levels. Ten states still do not have hate crime legislation and of those that do, most do not protect individuals on the basis of sexual orientation. Even the two states with the closest connection to the Mathew Shepard case, Wyoming and Colorado, have failed to support initiatives to pass hate crime laws, even after Shepard's murder.

Federal law also does not include homosexuals as a protected class. However, on March 12, 1999, a bipartisan congressional group reintroduced the Hate Crimes Prevention Act, which would give federal authorities the power to investigate and prosecute crimes that are based on sexual orientation. Current law limits prosecution of hate crimes to instances where the victim is targeted for engaging in certain federally protected activities, such as serving on a jury, voting, or attending public school. The Hate Crimes Prevention Act would expand the area of protected activity and make federal prosecution of hate crimes easier.

The act has not yet passed and stiff opposition is expected. On a smaller scale, however, the JUSTICE DEPARTMENT, with assistance from the Lawyer's Committee for Civil Rights (LCCR), is attempting to make some inroads. Funded with $200,000 from the Ford Foundation, the LCCR is working through eight national offices. The Washington-based committee will advocate for hate crime victims with law enforcement and file civil suits on behalf of the victims.

CROSS REFERENCES
Anti-Defamation League; Civil Rights

HEALTH CARE LAW

Criminalization of Spreading HIV

The AIDS crisis took on new character in October 1997. In Jamestown, New York, a young drifter by the name of Nushawn Williams directly infected thirteen women with human immunodeficienus virus (HIV), the virus that causes acquired immunodeficiency syndrome (AIDS), by having sex with them. Williams had at least forty-eight sexual partners during the one year that he stayed in Jamestown; one as young as thirteen years old. Nushawn Williams, who grew up in the Bronx, first found out that he was HIV positive in September 1996, after he moved to Jamestown. However, this did not stop him from continuing to have unprotected sex with women and teens, in exchange for drugs or what some naive victims thought was love. Authorities in Chautauqua County were first alerted in the summer of 1997 when several young women showed up at the local health department for AIDS tests. After a thorough investigation (Williams has many aliases, including "Face" and "JoJo"), it was discovered that many of these people listed Williams as a sexual partner. What is disturbing to officials is that these victims have had subsequent sexual partners, therefore increasing the number of people possibly infected with HIV by this one person...this "monster," as some have called him.

"He's not a monster—this guy is worse. He is the epitome of someone who is a sociopath. He has damaged hundreds and hundreds of lives. We have the devil here," said Robert Berke, the Chautauqua County Health Commissioner in *People Weekly*. After the Chautauqua County Department of Health discovered that Williams had infected all of these people, they went to court and won approval to make Williams' identity public. The Health Department posted a photograph of Williams, a list of aliases and his HIV status. This was the first exception to be made for New York State's strict confidentiality law. However, Williams had moved out of Jamestown long before his status was made public. It only took days before Williams' face and HIV status were made known throughout the world via national television, CNN and newspapers.

The wake-up call was heard in New York City where Williams had returned. It was again received too late for many more of Williams' sexual conquests. In fact, at the time this news became public, he was already in jail at Rikers Island awaiting a sentence for selling crack cocaine to a New York City undercover cop. Williams has told health officials that he had 50–75 sexual partners in New York City.

When this news first broke out, Chautauqua County District Attorney, James Subjack, said he was going to pursue charges of reckless endangerment and first degree assault for each person that Williams had infected with the HIV virus. However, many of Williams' victims would not come forward to testify. Instead, Nushawn Williams plead guilty in February 1999 to one count of reckless endangerment for having unprotected sex with a woman without disclosing his HIV status, and two counts of second-degree rape for having sex with a thirteen-year-old girl in Chautauqua County. According to Chautauqua County Assistant District Attorney William Caughlin, those were the only two victims who were willing to testify in court. In April 1999, Williams was sentenced to 4–12 years in prison for the above offenses. Williams also has been charged with one count of reckless endangerment in Bronx County for having unprotected sex with a fifteen-year-old girl. The sentence for the Bronx charge will run concurrently with the Chautauqua County sentence. Williams is already serving a 1–3 year sentence for selling crack cocaine in the Bronx. According to William Cember, Williams' attorney, the 4–12 year sentence will run retroactive to the time that the defendant first became eligible for parole for his drug conviction. Therefore, he could be released as early as 2002.

One can only hope that if Williams is released in 2002, he will no longer be a threat to the young female population since his HIV status has been revealed to the world. As Sue Genco, a Jamestown mother of three, told *Time* (November 10, 1997), "The Williams case has been our wake-up call."

Unfortunately, the entire United States is in need of a wake-up call. Many still believe that only homosexual males and drug users get HIV. Although no national figures exist for HIV infection, the Center for Disease Control (CDC) has been able to compile statistics based on information that they get from the twenty-five states that report to them. The statistics, as reported in *Harper's Magazine* show that, between 1994 and 1997, 44 percent of thirteen to twenty-four year olds who tested positive for HIV were women, a majority of which did not use protection during sex with a man. Additionally, in recent years, the number of gay men and intravenous drug users with full-blown AIDS declined, but the number of men who reported

having AIDS from heterosexual sex increased 11 percent and women increased 7 percent.

These statistics and the few known cases like that of Nushawn Williams has rekindled the motion to mandate the reporting of individuals infected with HIV. As of April 6, 1998, thirty-two states required that the names of those with HIV be made public. Many feel that there are several benefits that can come from this mandate. The first and most important would be to trace partners who in the past had sexual contact with the person who is reported to have HIV. This information will also provide invaluable data to assist in detecting both emerging trends in infection and behavioral risk factors. However, this new mandate also has many critics, including many AIDS advocacy groups and civil rights organizations. These critics fear that it jeopardizes the confidentiality and privacy of the individuals. Most importantly, they fear it will inhibit possible HIV carriers from being tested at all.

The CDC has given weight to both camps as it creates guidelines for carrying out HIV surveillance. Although they have not come up with an alternative to name reporting, John Ward, M.D., chief of the Surveillance Branch for the Division of HIV at CDC's National Center for HIV, STD and TB Prevention says that their guidelines will recommend that surveillance be conducted to provide reliable, accurate information and also maximize confidentiality. Some states, including Texas and Maryland, have experimented with patient codes, instead of names.

However, this has proven to be less effective. The reports were not always complete. This resulted in false data, and it was more difficult to notify previous contacts. However, many states are developing methods to ensure confidentiality in name reporting. For example, in Ohio, HIV reports are stored in a computer database where information is entered but can only be accessed by a few authorized staff members of the HIV/AIDS Surveillance Program for the Ohio Department of Health.

In the aftermath of Nushawn Williams, how is the state of New York, the state with the highest number of AIDS cases, dealing with the wake-up call that Williams delivered? As recent as April 1998, health officials were not requiring name reporting for adults. The state only requires every newborn baby to be tested for HIV, which often can be informative for many of the mothers who did not even know they carried the HIV virus. New York state does try to keep track of HIV and AIDS through blind tests of blood samples taken from various groups including those in the hospital, those in drug treatment centers, and those who get tested for sexually transmitted diseases.

U.S. Supreme Court Allows Patients To Sue Hospitals Under Federal Law

In January 1999, the U.S. Supreme Court ruled that patients with an emergency medical condition who are transferred from a hospital before being stabilized may sue the hospital under the Emergency Medical Treatment and Active Labor Act (EMTALA). (*Roberts v. Galen of Virginia, Inc.*, 525 U.S. 249, 119 S. Ct. 685, 142 L. Ed. 2d 648 [1999]).

Congress passed EMTALA in 1986 in reaction to "patient dumping," a practice by which some hospitals refuse to admit or treat emergency room patients who lack health insurance to pay their medical bills. EMTALA protects such patients in two ways. Under the screening requirement, hospitals must give emergency room patients and women in labor "appropriate" screening for emergency medical conditions regardless of the patient's ability to pay. (42 U.S.C. §1395dd(a)). Under the stabilization requirement, hospitals must stabilize patients with emergency medical conditions before transferring them to another facility, also regardless of ability to pay. (42 U.S.C. § 1395dd(b)(1)(A)). EMTALA allows patients to sue to recover personal injury damages from hospitals that violate the act. (42 U.S.C. §1395dd(d)(2)(A)).

In *Roberts*, the U.S. Supreme Court interpreted EMTALA to allow any patient to sue under the stabilization requirement, even those who are not emergency room victims of "patient dumping." The plaintiff in *Roberts*, Wanda Johnson, was run over by a truck on May 19, 1992, and rushed to Humana Hospital-University of Louisville. Humana treated Johnson for six weeks for severe injuries to her brain, spine, right leg, and pelvis. On July 24, 1992, Humana transferred Johnson to Crestview, a long-term health care facility. When Johnson's condition deteriorated severely one day later, Crestview transferred her to Midwest Medical Center, where she received treatment for many months costing almost $390,000. After Medicaid refused to cover the expenses, Johnson's guardian, Jane Roberts, sued Humana under EMTALA for transferring Johnson to Crestview before stabilizing her condition.

While there was evidence that Humana transferred Johnson because she lacked health insurance, the doctor who signed her transfer order was unaware of this fact. The Federal District Court for the Western District of Kentucky thus granted summary judgment for Humana on the ground that there was no evidence that the doctor acted from an "improper motive." The U.S. Court of Appeals for the Sixth Circuit affirmed. Although EMTALA does not specifically require a plaintiff to prove an "improper motive," the Sixth Circuit ruled that such proof is consistent with the act's requirement that a hospital's screening of emergency room patients be "appropriate." The Sixth Circuit refused, however, to limit "improper motive" to cases where the patient could not afford to pay. "Rather, other improper reasons include race, sex, politics, occupation, education, personal prejudice, drunkenness, or spite."

The U.S. Supreme Court reversed with an unsigned opinion (called a PER CURIUM opinion). The Supreme Court decided that the lower courts had mixed up EMTALA's screening and stabilization requirements. While the act requires a hospital to give "appropriate" screening to emergency room patients, it does not contain an "appropriateness" element for the stabilization requirement. Johnson, therefore, could recover if Humana transferred her to Crestview before stabilizing her condition regardless of whether the doctor who signed the transfer order did so because Johnson lacked health insurance, or for any other improper purpose.

Because the case did not involve EMTALA's screening requirement, the Supreme Court declined to decide whether a plaintiff must prove an "improper motive" when a hospital fails to screen an emergency room patient. In a footnote, however, the Supreme Court noted a conflict among the circuit courts of appeals on the issue, which suggests it may decide the issue in a future case that involves the screening requirement.

Your Home Visiting Nurse Services v. Shalala

In February 1999, the U.S. Supreme Court resolved a MEDICARE issue on which the lower courts had been in conflict for a decade. In *Your Home Visiting Nurse Services v. Shalala*, __ U.S. __, 119 S. Ct. 930, 142 L. Ed. 2d 919 (1999), the Court unanimously held that health care providers that receive Medicare funding cannot appeal when a government-designated intermediary refuses to reopen its payment decision for a previous year.

The Medicare Act, (Title XVIII of the Social Security Act, 79 Stat. 290 [42 U.S.C.A. § 1395]) established a procedure by which a health care provider that seeks Medicare reimbursement must submit an annual cost report to an intermediary selected by the Department of Health and Human Services (HHS). Often this intermediary is a private insurance company, such as a Blue Cross affiliate. If the provider disagrees with the reimbursement set by the intermediary, it can appeal within 180 days to the Provider Reimbursement Review Board (PRRB); the PRRB's decision in turn can be appealed within sixty days to a federal district court. A second way in which a provider can have a reimbursement decision reexamined, created in the Medicare regulations, is to ask the intermediary to reopen a previous year's funding decision, within three years after the original decision. Reasons for reopening include grounds such as the discovery of "new and material evidence." But the Medicare regulations (42 C.F.R. § 405.1885 [1997]) do not require an appeal process if the intermediary refuses to reopen its decision.

The reopening process became the subject of several federal cases, resulting in different reimbursement appeal processes depending on where the provider did business. For the northwestern states within the Ninth Circuit, the standard set in *Oregon v. Bowen*, 854 F. 2d 346 (9th Cir. 1988), applied. *Bowen* held that a provider could seek review of an intermediary's refusal to reopen a decision, first before the PRRB and then in federal court. Other circuit courts decided that the Medicare Act and its regulations did not require an intermediary to reopen a decision. Instead, the intermediary could act within its discretion, and no appeal was possible. Among this second line of cases was *Your Home Visiting Nurse Services v. Shalala*, 132 F. 3d 1135 (6th Cir. 1997).

Your Home Visiting Nurse Services, a Tennessee-based health provider, had submitted its cost report for fiscal year 1989 to its designated intermediary, Blue Cross and Blue Shield of South Carolina. It did not appeal Blue Cross' decision within 180 days, which would have triggered the PRRB and court appeal process. However, before three years had passed Your Home asked Blue Cross to reopen its decision for 1989, claiming that it had discovered "new and material evidence" that would result in a higher reimbursement. Your Home alleged that another intermediary had miscalculated its 1987 reimbursement and so had incorrectly reduced its later reimbursements. It also alleged that other local providers had received higher reimbursements. But Blue Cross refused to reopen its 1989 decision. Your Home turned to the PRRB and then to federal district and circuit courts, all three of which decided that they lacked jurisdiction to review the intermediary's refusal to reopen the decision.

The Court of Appeals for the Sixth Circuit, in finding that there was no valid argument for reopening the reimbursement decision, rejected three arguments made by Your Home. Relying on the Medicaid statute and regulations, as well as the Medicare Provider Reimbursement Manual created by HHS, the court found that the PRRB lacked jurisdiction to reopen the reimbursement decision. It further ruled that the district court had neither FEDERAL QUESTION jurisdiction nor MANDAMUS jurisdiction to hear an appeal. In its findings, the court strongly relied on an earlier Supreme Court opinion, *Heckler v. Ringer*, 466 U.S. 602, 104 S. Ct. 2013, 80 L. Ed. 2d 622 (1984), which involved denial of Medicare coverage for a certain surgical procedure, and *Good Samaritan Hospital Regional Medical Center v. Shalala*, 894 F. Supp. 683 (S.D.N.Y. 1995), *affirmed on other grounds*, 85 F. 3d 1057 (2nd Cir. 1996), which found that reopening an intermediary's reimbursement decision was discretionary, not mandatory.

Following the Sixth Circuit's decision, Your Home petitioned the U.S. Supreme Court for a rehearing of the case. Speaking for the unanimous Court, Justice ANTONIN SCALIA issued an opinion that followed the Sixth Circuit's reasoning. The opinion focused on what the Court considered the primary issue in the case, the PRRB's refusal to reopen its reimbursement decision. It concluded that the HHS secretary's construction of the Medicare statute and regulations, leaving the final reimbursement decision in the hands of the PRRB, was reasonable.

> The Secretary construes the regulation to mean that where, as here, the intermediary is the body that rendered the last determination with respect to the cost reports at issue, review by the board of the intermediary's refusal to reopen would divest the intermediary of its exclusive' jurisdiction for reopening a determination...The Secretary's reading of [the regulation] frankly seems to us the more natural—but it is in any event well within the bounds of reasonable interpretation, and hence entitled to deference.

The Court also refused to buy into Your Home's argument that the reimbursement procedure was "grossly unfair." Your Home's reasoning was that it could not appeal an incorrect reimbursement underpayment beyond the PRRB level after 180 days, while the PRRB could recover erroneous overpayments for three years. Justice Scalia noted that the designated intermediaries granted between 30 and 40 percent of providers' requests to reopen reimbursement decisions. He also pointed out that 180 days was sufficient time for a provider to identify an underpayment, while the intermediaries needed additional time given the volume of reimbursement decisions they handled.

The Supreme Court's reimbursement ruling came in the midst of massive public concern and debate about the future of the Medicare system. According to *Business Week*, by 1999 Medicare involved $207 billion annually, and accounted for 12 percent of the national budget. With rising medical costs and the aging of 77 million "baby boomers," the system was projected to increase to 30 percent of the national budget by 2030. Without a major overhaul, it also was predicted to become insolvent within the first fifteen years of the twenty-first century. Given this crisis, it is possible that the courts hearing Your Home's arguments were reluctant to open the doors further for reexamination of past reimbursements.

CROSS REFERENCES
Administrative Law; Health Insurance; Jurisdiction; Privacy

HEALTH INSURANCE

Health Insurance Company Sued Under RICO

A unanimous U.S. Supreme Court ruling granted insurance policyholders in Nevada the right to bring a lawsuit against their health insurer based on the federal Racketeer Influenced Corrupt Organizations Act (RICO), 18 U.S.C.A. § 1961 et. seq. The decision, *Humana v. Forsyth*, __U.S.__, 119 S. Ct. 710, 142 L. Ed. 2d 753 (1999), afforded plaintiffs in the case the opportunity to pursue treble damages, and opened the door to possible RICO and other federal law claims against insurance companies nationwide.

The plaintiffs in the case held health insurance policies with Humana Health Insurance of Nevada, Inc. and received medical care between 1985 and 1988 at a Humana-owned hospital. The health insurance policies specified that Humana would pay 80 percent of the hospital bills over a specified deductible, with the policyholders remaining liable for the remaining 20 percent.

In their lawsuit, the plaintiffs alleged that the hospital entered into a concealed agreement with Humana whereby the hospital would significantly discount Humana's portion of the bills without the plaintiffs' knowledge or consent, while the plaintiffs' portions of the bills were not reduced. Consequently, the plaintiffs paid more than 20 percent of the actual hospital charges while Humana paid less than its 80 percent share of the actual charges.

Bringing their lawsuit in federal court, the plaintiffs claimed that Humana had engaged in a pattern of racketeering activity through mail, wire, radio and television fraud. Humana cited as its defense the McCarran-Ferguson Act, and moved for summary judgment. The McCarran-Ferguson Act, 15 U.S.C.A. § 1011 et. seq, provides that "No act of Congress shall be construed to invalidate, impair, or supersede any law enacted by any State for the purpose of regulating the business of insurance, or which imposes a fee or tax upon such business, unless such Act specifically relates to the business of insurance." Although RICO does not prohibit conduct that Nevada insurance laws allows, the remedies under the state and federal laws differs: RICO allows for the recovery of treble damages, while Nevada law allows for recovery of compensatory and punitive damages only. Because of this difference in the federal and state laws, the defendants argued, the McCarran-Ferguson Act applied and precluded the plaintiffs from continuing the lawsuit.

After the district court granted summary judgment for the defendants, the Ninth Circuit Court of Appeals reversed, citing its decision in *Merchants Home Delivery Serv., Inc. v. Frank B. Hall & Co.*, 50 F. 3d 1486 (9th Cir. 1995). In the *Merchants Home* decision, the Ninth Circuit adopted a "direct conflict" test to determine whether a federal law invalidated, impaired, or superseded a state law, as prohibited by the Mc-Carran-Ferguson Act. The McCarran-Ferguson Act, according to the Ninth Circuit, does not preclude federal legislation such as RICO that prohibits acts also prohibited by Nevada state legislation. Without direct conflict between RICO and the state insurance laws, the plaintiff's suit was not barred by the McCarran-Ferguson act and the Ninth Circuit reversed the lower court's summary judgment.

Humana appealed to the U.S. Supreme Court to determine the issue of whether the Mc-Carran Ferguson Act precluded the application of RICO in this case, and specifically whether applying RICO to the plaintiff's case would invalidate, impair, or supersede Nevada's insurance laws. The Court used standard definitions in finding that RICO neither invalidated nor superseded the state's laws regulating insurance. The Court then determined whether RICO's application in this case would impair Nevada insurance laws.

Humana argued that by using the word "impair," Congress intended to leave the regulation of insurance completely to the states. The Court disagreed. Reciting the standard dictionary definitions of "impair" to include weakening, reducing in power, diminishing, making worse, or relaxing, the justices found that the intent behind the McCarran-Ferguson Act was not to permit every federal regulation that does not completely contradict state regulation. Nor did Congress intend to completely disallow federal laws in favor of state regulation of insurance. If that were the case, federal tax laws could not coexist with a state's taxation of insurance companies—under the federal system of dual taxation, nothing prevents an insurance company from paying both state and federal taxes. Striking a balance, the Court held that the Mc-Carran-Ferguson Act does not preclude the application of a federal law when the federal law does not directly conflict with state regulation and when applying the federal law would not frustrate or interfere with a state policy or administrative regime.

The unanimous Court went on to apply that standard to the facts of the Humana case. It concluded that a lawsuit under RICO would not impair Nevada insurance regulation. The law governing insurance in Nevada prohibits insurance fraud and misrepresentation. It allows victims of insurance fraud to pursue private actions for unfair insurance practices. It allows the state insurance commissioner to issue charges, administer fees, or issue cease and desist orders against violators of the law. Insured may receive PUNITIVE DAMAGES from insurers guilty of FRAUD, oppression, or malice, and it is conceivable that punitive damages under the Nevada regime could exceed treble damages under RICO. Moreover, the state insurance law does not exclude the application of laws of other states. Therefore, the Court held, the RICO lawsuit did nothing to frustrate Nevada's regulation of insurance; rather, RICO's private right of action and treble damages provision complemented the state's insurance laws.

Insurance industry observers have anticipated that the Supreme Court's decision in Humana will increase RICO lawsuits against insurers, and could subject insurers to other federal claims such as federal anti-discrimination lawsuits, mail fraud charges, lawsuits under the federal Truth in Lending Act (15 U.S.C.A. § 1601 et seq), as well as the jurisdiction of the federal bankruptcy courts. Insurers expect to see a jump in class action lawsuits invoking RICO, and a potential rise in insurance premiums as a result of increased litigation exposure.

CROSS REFERENCES
Federalism; Health Care Law

HIGGINBOTHAM, A. LEON, JR.

Obituary notice

Born on February 25, 1928, in Trenton, New Jersey; died December 14, 1998, in Boston, Massachusetts. Higginbotham was appointed as the youngest ever and first African American commissioner with the Federal Trade Commission in 1962. From there, he won several other prominent political posts, culminating in his appointment as chief judge of the U.S. Court of Appeals for the Third Circuit in 1989. Higginbotham also earned distinction as a writer, speaker, and activist, and was elected the first black trustee of Yale University in 1969.

A. Leon Higginbotham, Jr.
CORBIS-BETTMANN

HYDE, HENRY

Henry J. Hyde, (R-Ill.), chairman of the House Judiciary Committee, attracted attention in 1998 and 1999 for his key role in IMPEACH-

Henry J. Hyde
JOE MARQUETTE/AP/WIDE WORLD
PHOTOS

MENT proceedings involving President BILL CLINTON. Hyde led the investigation into the Starr Report in the House of Representatives, then became the chief prosecutor after two articles of impeachment were approved and sent to the Senate for trial.

Hyde was born in Chicago on April 18, 1924 and grew up during the Depression in a Catholic, Democratic home. He served in the U.S. Navy during World War II. He attended Loyola University School of Law, obtaining his J.D. degree in 1949 and was admitted to the Illinois bar the next year. He served as a representative in the Illinois General Assembly from 1967–74, including a period as majority leader in 1971–1972. He was elected to the Ninety-fourth Congress on November 5, 1974, representing a portion of suburban Chicago. In his years in Congress, he has also garnered the respect of the opposing party. Opponents routinely speak of him with respect and note his gift of oratory.

Hyde credits Eleanor Roosevelt for turning him into a Republican. Consistently conservative in his politics, he has proposed or supported constitutional AMENDMENTS on a variety of issues including ABORTION, flag desecration, a balanced budget, victims' rights, and religious equality. Hyde has called flag burning "a hate crime." He also has commented that a school prayer amendment is necessary because of "judicial amendments to the Constitution," referring to court rulings that go beyond the intended meaning of the Constitution. Hyde has long been an outspoken critic of abortion; in 1976 Hyde made his mark when he managed to get a

ban on Medicaid funding of abortion enacted in legislation known as the Hyde amendment. He also served on the Iran-Contra committee, where he was an outspoken supporter of Oliver North and the Reagan administration. He has deviated from Republican stances on gun control and term limits. He sided with Clinton on the ban on assault weapons and the 1993 Family and Medical Leave Act. He was selected in 1994 to head the House Judiciary Committee.

In late 1998, Hyde had to confront charges that he had engaged in an adulterous affair many years ago. He quickly admitted the affair, but could not escape criticism for his characterization of it. Hyde called it a "youthful indiscretion," but in actuality it was a long-term affair when Hyde was in his forties.

As chairman of the House Judiciary committee, Hyde shepherded the articles of impeachment through the House, beginning in early September 1998 when INDEPENDENT COUNSEL KENNETH STARR's report and thirty-six boxes of supporting evidence were delivered to the House. The Starr Report contended that the office of independent counsel had found "substantial and credible information...that may constitute grounds for impeachment." Information in the Starr Report focused on the president's sexual relationship with former White House intern Monica S. Lewinsky, and the president's denial of such a relationship in a January 1998 deposition in the *Jones v. Clinton* lawsuit, in grand jury testimony in August 1998, and elsewhere.

On October 8, 1998, the House voted to hold an impeachment inquiry, conducted by the House Judiciary Committee. Hyde, on behalf of the committee, submitted questions to the president, in which the president denied in late November that his testimony regarding Lewinsky had been "false and misleading." On December 11, 1998, the Judiciary Committee approved three impeachment articles, accusing the president of perjury in his deposition the Jones case and in his grand jury case, and for obstruction of justice in the Jones case. The following day, the committee approved a final article of perjury, and rejected a Democratic resolution to censure Clinton for his "reprehensible conduct." The full House approved articles I and III on December 19, 1998, charging Clinton had committed perjury and obstruction of justice. The House did not approve the other two articles of impeachment.

Hyde led the team of thirteen House managers who unsuccessfully prosecuted the im-

HENRY HYDE

1924	Born in Chicago, Illinois
1949	J.D. from Loyola
1967	Elected representative to Illinois General Assembly
1974	Elected to House of Representatives
1996	Chairman, House Judiciary Committee
1999	Led House managers in Clinton impeachment trial

peachment case in the Senate. Hyde clearly did not relish his role, quipping at one point "I'd trade it for a Hershey bar." He chafed under certain Senate procedures which he believed impeded the House managers from presenting their best case for impeachment, and called the House managers an "annoyance," a "constitutional annoyance." Hyde knew that the House managers faced an uphill battle from the start of the January trial, but doggedly pursued his goal.

He beseeched his Senate counterparts to "never tolerate one law for the ruler and another for the ruled," but his efforts failed to convince a two-thirds majority to convict President Clinton. Although his opinion on the propriety of impeachment was clearly at odds with that of much of the country, Hyde appeared to share a sense of relief with the general public that the ordeal was over, remarking that "We are blessedly coming to the end of this melancholy procedure." In an interview in March 1999, Hyde stated that he did not believe Ken Starr should indict the president, despite his belief that Clinton should have been convicted in the impeachment trial.

IMMUNITY

Exemption from performing duties that the law generally requires other citizens to perform, or from a penalty or burden that the law generally places on other citizens.

Conn v. Gabbert

The Supreme Court has granted immunity from civil lawsuits to many types of public officials, thereby preventing citizens from suing officials for DAMAGES resulting from public conduct. The Court has made it clear that when criminal prosecutors perform the traditional functions of an advocate, they are absolutely immune from money damage lawsuits. Absolute prosecutorial immunity, however, does not extend to functions that are not associated with advocacy. A prosecutor may still escape litigation by claiming a qualified immunity if the constitutional right which allegedly has been violated was not clearly established and the defendant's conduct was not "objectively reasonable" in light of the information which the official possessed at the time of the alleged violation.

In *Conn v. Gabbert*, __U.S.__, 119 S. Ct. 1292, 143 L. Ed. 2d 394 (1999), the Supreme Court ruled that prosecutors cannot be sued for having lawyers searched and interfering with their ability to advise a client appearing before a GRAND JURY. The Court found that the actions taken by prosecutors did not violate a lawyer's constitutional right to practice law.

The case arose out of the high-profile California trials of Lyle and Erik Menendez, for the murder of their parents. In 1994, after the first Menendez trial ended in a hung jury, the Los Angeles County District Attorney's Office assigned Deputy District Attorneys David Conn and Carol Najera to prosecute the retrial. Conn and Najera learned that Lyle Menendez had written a letter to Traci Baker, his former girlfriend, in which he may have instructed her to TESTIFY falsely at trial. Paul Gabbert, a criminal defense attorney, represented Baker, who had testified as a defense witness in the first TRIAL.

Conn obtained and served Baker with a SUBPOENA directing her to testify before the Los Angeles County grand jury and directing her to produce at that time any correspondence that she had received from Lyle Menendez. However, Baker told the police that she had given all her letters from Menendez to Gabbert. When Baker arrived to appear before the grand jury, accompanied by Gabbert, Conn had a police officer secure a WARRANT to have Gabbert searched for the letter. California law provides that a warrant to search an attorney must be executed by a court-appointed special master. When the special master arrived, Gabbert requested that the search take place in a private room, but did not request that Baker's grand jury testimony be postponed. The search yielded two pages of a three-page letter from Lyle Menendez to Baker.

At about the same time that the search of Gabbert was taking place, Najera called Baker before the grand jury and began to question her. After being sworn, Najera asked Baker whether she was acquainted with Lyle Menendez. Baker replied that she had been unable to speak with her attorney because he was "still with the special master." After a short recess, Gabbert still was unavailable to consult with his client. Baker then declined to answer questions from the grand jury based on her FIFTH AMENDMENT privilege against self-incrimination. The grand jury then recessed.

Believing that the actions of the prosecutors were illegal, Gabbert brought suit against Conn, Najera and other officials in federal court under 42 U.S.C. § 1983, a federal civil rights law that permits individuals to sue government officials for violating their constitutional rights. Gabbert argued that his FOURTEENTH AMENDMENT right to practice his profession without unreasonable government interference was violated when the prosecutors executed a search warrant at the same time his client was testifying before the grand jury. Conn and Najera moved to dismiss the case on the basis of qualified immunity and the district court granted the motion.

The Court of Appeals for the Ninth Circuit reversed the dismissal, holding that Conn and Najera were not entitled to qualified immunity on Gabbert's Fourteenth Amendment claim. 131 F. 3d 793 (9th 1997). The appeals court relied on *Board of Regents of State Colleges v. Roth*, 408 U.S. 564, 92 S. Ct. 2701, 33 L. Ed. 2d 548 (1972), a Supreme Court case that recognized a right to choose one's vocation. The appeals court held that Gabbert had a right to practice his profession without undue and unreasonable government interference. The court of appeals also held that based upon notions of "common sense," the right allegedly violated was clearly established. Therefore, Conn and Najera were not entitled to qualified immunity.

The Supreme Court, in a unanimous decision, reversed the Ninth Circuit. Chief Justice WILLIAM H. REHNQUIST, writing for the Court, restated the PRECEDENT that obtaining qualified immunity requires the official to show that she has not violated clearly established statutory or constitutional rights of which a reasonable person would have known. The first task of a court examining a qualified immunity claim is to determine whether the plaintiff has "alleged the deprivation of an actual constitutional right at all, and if so, proceed to determine whether that right was clearly established at the time of the alleged violation."

Rehnquist found no support in prior Supreme Court cases for the conclusion of the Ninth Circuit that Gabbert had a Fourteenth Amendment right which was violated in this case. He dismissed the applicability of the *Roth* case, which the appeals court had relied on, stating that *Roth* did not "even came close to identifying the asserted 'right' violated by the prosecutors in

this case." Rehnquist was equally dismissive of other cases offered by Gabbert. He concluded that none of these cases "provide any more than scant metaphysical support for the idea that the use of a search warrant by government actors violates an attorney's right to practice his profession." The cases relied upon by the Ninth Circuit and Gabbert had a common flaw: they dealt with the complete prohibition of the right to engage in a calling, not the brief interruption that Gabbert encountered that day in the courthouse.

Chief Justice Rehnquist also rejected Gabbert's claim that the improper search interfered with his client's right to have him outside the grand jury for consultations. Rehnquist noted that a grand jury witness has no constitutional right to have counsel present during the grand jury proceeding. Moreover, the Court had never ruled that a grand jury witness has a right to have her attorney present outside the jury room. In the present case, there was no need to decide whether such a right existed, because Gabbert had no STANDING to raise the issue on behalf of Baker. The general rule is that a plaintiff must assert his own legal rights and interests, and cannot rest his claim to relief on the legal rights or interests of third parties.

Gabbert did have standing to complain of the allegedly unreasonable timing of the execution of the search warrant to prevent him from advising Baker. However, Chief Justice Rehnquist held that challenges to the reasonableness of a search by government agents clearly fall under the FOURTH AMENDMENT, and not the Fourteenth Amendment. Because Gabbert had based his constitutional argument on the Fourteenth Amendment, Gabbert's argument failed.

Therefore, the Court concluded that the Fourteenth Amendment right to practice one's calling is not violated by the execution of a search warrant, "whether calculated to annoy or even to prevent consultation with a grand jury witness." Gabbert's lawsuit was dismissed because of prosecutorial immunity.

CROSS REFERENCES
Fourteenth Amendment; Search and Seizure

IMPEACHMENT

A process used to charge, try, and remove public officials for misconduct while in office.

President Clinton Impeached by House, Acquitted by Senate

President BILL CLINTON became only the second president to be impeached by the House of Representatives on December 19, 1998. After holding a trial, however, the Senate acquitted Clinton of PERJURY and obstruction of justice, the charges made by the House, on February 12, 1999. The votes in both houses mostly followed party lines, reflecting the partisan nature of the entire process.

The roots of Clinton's impeachment went back to 1994, when Independent Counsel KENNETH W. STARR was appointed to investigate the president's involvement in a complicated series of land and loan transactions known as WHITEWATER. That same year, Paula C. Jones filed a sexual harassment lawsuit against Clinton, alleging that he made unwanted sexual advances in a hotel room in Little Rock, Arkansas, in 1991, when he was governor of Arkansas and she was a state employee. Meanwhile, as early as 1995, Clinton began an adulterous affair with White House intern Monica S. Lewinsky that lasted into 1997.

In December 1997, Jones's lawyers named Lewinsky as a potential witness in the sexual harassment lawsuit. (They wished to use Lewinsky to support their theory that Clinton rewarded women who accepted his sexual advances, and punished those who did not.) Soon thereafter, Vernon E. Jordan, Jr., Clinton's close friend, increased his efforts to get Lewinsky a job in New York City, which the president had requested months earlier. Then, after Lewinsky received a SUBPOENA to testify and to turn over gifts from Clinton, she met with him on December 28 and asked whether she instead should give the gifts to Clinton's personal secretary, Betty Currie. Clinton said he would think about it. Shortly after Lewinsky left, Currie called Lewinsky at her Watergate apartment, retrieved the gifts, and hid them under her bed. Lewinsky soon filed an AFFIDAVIT in the *Jones* case denying that she ever had sexual relations with the president.

On January 12, 1998, Linda Tripp, a coworker of Lewinsky who recorded their telephone conversations about Lewinsky's affair and Jordan's job search, turned the tapes over to Independent Counsel KENNETH STARR. Four days later, Attorney General JANET RENO approved Starr's expansion of his Whitewater investigation to include whether Clinton and Jordan encouraged Lewinsky to lie in her affidavit. On January 17, 1998, at a deposition in *Jones*, Clinton testified under oath that he did not have an "extramarital sexual affair," "sexual relations," or a "sexual relationship" with Lewinsky. Starr proceeded to investigate whether Clinton lied under oath and if he encouraged others to lie too.

After months of securing testimony from minor witnesses and wrangling over testimonial privileges, Starr granted Lewinsky immunity for her testimony. Appearing before the grand jury on August 6, 1998, Lewinsky described eleven sexual encounters with President Clinton, including oral sex but not sexual intercourse, and ten to fifteen sexually graphic telephone conversations. Under intense pressure to come forward with the truth, Clinton testified before Starr's grand jury on August 17. There he admitted to having "inappropriate intimate contact" with Lewinsky a few times in early 1996 and once in early 1997. While he would not give details, Clinton insisted that, even accepting Lewinsky's testimony that she had performed oral sex on him, his answers at his January 1998 deposition had been legally accurate under the Court's definition of sexual relations.

On September 9, 1998, Starr delivered to the House of Representatives a report outlining eleven grounds for impeaching President Clinton. Starr accused Clinton of committing perjury in his January 1998 deposition, obstructing justice in *Jones* and the grand jury investigation, committing perjury in his August 1998 grand jury testimony, and abusing his power by agreeing to cooperate with the grand jury investigation and then lying about his relationship while refusing to testify for seven months.

Clinton's conduct offended House Republicans and Democrats alike. Two days after receiving Starr's report, which contained vivid, graphic details of Clinton's sexual relationship with Lewinsky, the House voted 363–63 to release it to the public. It was the last House vote to command a substantial majority. Especially

Senators are sworn in as jurors for the impeachment trial of President Clinton.

OFFICIAL SENATE PHOTO/
CNP/AP/WIDE WORLD PHOTOS

HOW WILL THE TRIAL AFFECT FUTURE IMPEACHMENTS?

Impeachment, the constitutional method for removing presidents, judges, and other federal officers who commit "Treason, Bribery, or other high Crimes and Misdemeanors," requires a majority vote by the House of Representatives, and then conviction by a two-thirds vote in the Senate. President BILL CLINTON's impeachment trial was the fifteenth in U.S. history, and the second of a president. ANDREW JOHNSON, the other president to be impeached by the House of Representatives, was acquitted by the Senate in 1868 in a vote that mostly followed party lines. Especially in light of prior impeachments, seven of which ended with the removal of federal judges, Clinton's case will affect the future use of impeachment, the process of impeachment, and the definition of "high Crimes and Misdemeanors."

IN FOCUS

Clinton's experience, like Johnson's, shows that impeachment can be a tool of political warfare. Although the U.S. Constitution only requires a House majority for impeachment, scholars and politicians say it should be a bipartisan effort to remove a president who is dangerous to the nation. However, the world of academia differs from that of politics. In contrast, House Republicans pursued Clinton by disregarding polls that said two-thirds of the nation opposed impeachment. The vote in the House then fell mostly along party lines. Future House majorities could use this precedent and to impeach a political opponent without substantial public support.

The price of the impeachment, however, was high for House Republicans. Speaker NEWT GINGRICH (R-Ga.) resigned after mid-term elections in November 1998, trimmed the Republican House majority to six votes. Then, upon exposure of his own extramarital affair, Speaker-Elect Robert L. Livingston (R-La.) resigned on the day of impeachment, urging Clinton to follow his example. Republicans and Democrats alike might hesitate to pursue another unpopular impeachment with so much at risk. However, when Democrats someday control the House of Representatives with a Republican in the White House, the human temptation for revenge will be great. As historian Benjamin Ginsberg observed, "[t]he history of American politics over the last few decades is that the victims of a political attack denounce it as an ille-gitimate endeavor—but within a few years adopt it themselves. It's like an arms race."

As for the process of impeachment, Clinton's experience may affect the future use of witnesses and the viability of censure. The House Judiciary Committee declined to call a single witness to any of Clinton's misconduct, relying instead in the investigation by Independent Counsel KENNETH W. STARR. Democrats criticized this procedure, asking how the House could vote on impeachment without an independent investigation. (In fact, the only other time the House failed to conduct an investigation was when it impeached President Johnson, suggesting that such an approach is political.) During Clinton's trial in the Senate, however, Democrats themselves opposed calling witnesses, a political move motivated by fear that witnesses would reveal something leading to conviction. House managers running the prosecution, who now wanted fifteen witnesses after calling none in the House, had to settle for just three. Everyone will remember that lesson next time.

As an alternative to impeachment, Democrats tried to introduce censure resolutions in both the House and Senate. Republicans defeated these efforts.

after the September 21, 1998, broadcast of Clinton's videotaped grand jury testimony humanized his plight, and after the Republican majority in the House slipped to six votes after mid-term elections in November, Democrats lined up behind polls which said two-thirds of the nation opposed impeachment.

On October 5, 1998, the House Judiciary Committee, headed by Chairman HENRY J. HYDE (R-Ill.), voted 21–16, along party lines, to recommend that the House begin formal impeachment proceedings. The House passed such a resolution three days later with a vote of 258–176, including only 31 yes votes by Democrats. On November 5, 1998, Hyde sent Clinton a letter asking him to admit or deny 81 assertions in Starr's report. Then on November 19, the Judiciary Committee called its only witness, Independent Counsel Starr, who explained his report and recommendations. Critics said the committee should have called actual witnesses, not the man who conducted the investigation.

After the Judiciary Committee took detours investigating matters not covered by Starr's report and then held hearings on the importance of punishing perjury, Clinton's defense team made its presentation on December 9 and 10, 1998. Panels of experts testified that perjury and obstruction of justice in a civil lawsuit concerning consensual sexual conduct are not impeachable offenses because they do not harm the nation. Clinton's lead attorney, White House

Some said CENSURE was not a legal option, as the U.S. Constitution provides for censure of congressmen but not presidents. Democrats, however, pointed to past censures of Presidents ANDREW JACKSON, JOHN TYLER, and JAMES BUCHANAN, and suggested that Republican opposition stemmed from a desire to brand Democrats as supporting Clinton's misconduct during upcoming elections.

Any future impeachment, whether of a president, judge, or other civil officer, will revisit the question of what constitutes "high Crimes and Misdemeanors," which is undefined in the U.S. Constitution. Those in favor of impeaching Clinton argued that perjury and obstruction of justice of any kind are impeachable because they subvert the rule of law, making it impossible to expect lawful behavior from ordinary citizens and even future presidents, who are charged by the Constitution with taking "Care that the Laws be faithfully executed." Those who opposed impeachment said that while perjury and obstruction of justice are wrong, they are not impeachable offenses unless they concern the president's official duties and present a danger to the nation.

Clinton's impeachment by the House and acquittal by the Senate thus will affect future interpretation of "high Crimes and Misdemeanors" in many ways. The House Judiciary Committee recommended impeachment for perjury in Clinton's deposition in a civil lawsuit, and for perjury in his criminal grand jury testimony. The House voted to impeach only for the latter, suggesting that perjury in a criminal matter is impeachable, while perjury in a civil matter is not.

The Senate, however, voted to acquit Clinton of perjury and obstruction of justice even though most Republicans and Democrats believed Clinton lied under oath and tried to influence the testimony of other witnesses. As explained by Senator Richard H. Bryan (D-Nev.), "[t]he president's conduct is boorish, indefensible, even reprehensible. It does not threaten the republic." This suggests that misconduct, even perjury, that is unrelated to the president's official duties and does not present a danger to the nation is not impeachable.

As such, Clinton's acquittal creates a double standard for impeachment of presidents and judges. In 1986, the House impeached and the Senate convicted Judge Harry E. Claiborne for filing false income tax returns. In 1989, the House impeached and the Senate convicted Judge Walter L. Nixon, Jr., for lying under oath about conduct unrelated to his official duties. In neither case did anyone suggest that lying about personal conduct is not an impeachable offense. In fact, the House managers' report concerning Judge Nixon said, "It is difficult to imagine an act more subversive to the legal process than lying from the witness stand. A judge who violates his testimonial oath and misleads a grand jury is clearly unfit to remain on the bench. If a judge's truthfulness cannot be guaranteed, if he sets less than the highest standard for candor, how can ordinary citizens who appear in court be expected to abide by their testimonial oath." The Senate's acquittal of Clinton suggested that lying about private matters is an impeachable offense for judges, but not for presidents.

Finally, the most significant effect of Clinton's impeachment and acquittal may be to define "high Crimes and Misdemeanors" to mean whatever the public wants. Scholars and politicians argued that the term purposefully is vague and undefined to allow Congress to handle each instance in the best interests of the nation. According to constitutional scholar Laurence H. Tribe, "[u]nless the rights of individuals or minority groups are threatened, our governing institutions are structured to make the sustained will of a significant majority all but impossible to topple—as the failure of the effort to remove President Clinton will dramatically illustrate." Even Senator Orrin G. Hatch (R-Utah), who voted to convict Clinton, said "[i]t's not just law. It's politics...And you have to combine those two and say—and this ought to be the prevailing question—what is in the best interest of our country, of our nation, of our people."

Counsel Charles F.C. Ruff, then dissected the particular allegations. He said Clinton did not commit perjury in his grand jury testimony because he admitted to the affair. Ruff asked the committee if they were prepared to impeach the president simply because he got some of the details wrong. As for obstruction of justice, Ruff said Lewinsky's grand jury testimony that nobody told her to lie or promised her a job for her silence disproved Starr's circumstantial case against the president.

On December 11 and 12, 1998, the Judiciary Committee voted along party lines to recommend four articles of impeachment accusing Clinton of perjury in his August 1998 grand jury testimony, perjury in his January 1998 deposition, obstruction of justice in both proceedings, and abuse of power by giving evasive answers to the eighty-one questions posed by the Judiciary Committee. On December 19, the House approved the first article by a vote of 228–206, with only five Republicans against and five Democrats in favor. The House also approved article three, by a vote of 221–212, with twelve Republicans against and five Democrats in favor. House Democrats objected to the partisan vote by traveling to the White House to stand by Clinton as he announced his intention to serve until "the last hour of the last day" of his term.

Clinton's trial on perjury and obstruction of justice moved to the Senate, where Chief Justice WILLIAM H. REHNQUIST presided as the Senators listened in silence to presentations by Clinton's defense team and thirteen Republican

House managers, led by Hyde, from the Judiciary Committee. The Senate strove to conduct the proceedings in a dignified, bipartisan manner, reaching a unanimous agreement behind closed doors on January 9, 1999, to proceed with the trial while postponing the controversial question of whether to call witnesses. In opening statements, House manager Bill McCollum (R-Fla.) outlined the evidence on perjury and obstruction of justice, highlighting Lewinsky's grand jury testimony that "[i]t was a pattern of the relationship to sort of conceal it." In opening statements for the president, however, David E. Kendall, Clinton's personal lawyer, emphasized other Lewinsky testimony: "No one ever asked me to lie, and I was never promised a job for my silence." Senators were allowed to question the lawyers only through written interrogatories to Chief Justice Rehnquist.

On January 27, 1999, Senator Robert C. Byrd (D-W.Va.) made a motion to dismiss the case on the ground that Clinton was not charged with impeachable offenses. The motion failed, but the 54–46 vote signaled that the House managers would not have the two-thirds vote necessary to convict the president and remove him from office. In this environment, the managers capitulated to pressure from Senate Republicans to present videotaped deposition testimony of only three witnesses. The managers chose Lewinsky, Jordan, and White House aide Sidney Blumenthal. There were no surprises in their testimony. Lewinsky repeated that the president neither told her to lie nor to tell the truth. Jordan admitted that he was conducting the job search for Lewinsky on behalf of Clinton, and that he telephoned Clinton to say "mission accomplished" after succeeding, but that it had nothing to do with Lewinsky's testimony in *Jones*. Blumenthal testified that days after Clinton's January 1998 deposition, Clinton "said that [Lewinsky] had come on to him and made a demand for sex, that he had rebuffed her, turned her down, and that she, uh, threatened him. And ... that she was called 'the stalker' by her peers."

On February 9, 1999, both sides presented closing arguments. After deliberating behind closed doors for three days, the Senators emerged to cast their votes on February 12. On Article I, charging Clinton with perjury, ten Republicans joined all Democrats to defeat the article 45–55. On obstruction of justice, five Republicans joined all Democrats to defeat the article 50–50. Comments from the Senators suggested that most believed Clinton had lied under oath, but that it was not serious enough to warrant the drastic measure of removal from office.

Shortly after the trial adjourned, Republicans blocked an effort by Senator DIANNE FEINSTEIN (D-Calif.) to offer a censure resolution condemning Clinton for "shameful, reckless and indefensible" behavior. (Walsh, "Senate Puts Censure Resolution on Hold—Indefinitely," *The Washington Post*, February 13, 1999.) Some Republicans said censure was unconstitutional, that impeachment was their only option. Others said censure was a Democratic effort to avoid being accused of supporting Clinton's conduct in upcoming elections. Democrats claimed censure could have been a unifying statement that Clinton's conduct, while not impeachable, was reprehensible.

In a brief statement after his acquittal, Clinton said he was "profoundly sorry" for his actions and words that led Congress and the nation into an impeachment trial. "Now I ask all Americans, and I hope all Americans here in Washington and throughout our land, will rededicate ourselves to the work of serving our nation and building our future together." When asked whether he could forgive his accusers, Clinton said, "I believe any person who asks for forgiveness has to be prepared to give it."

The Role of Chief Justice Rehnquist at the Impeachment Trial

Chief Justice WILLIAM H. REHNQUIST presided over the Senate impeachment trial of President BILL CLINTON during January and February 1999. The U.S. Constitution (Art. I, Sec. 3) provides "[w]hen the President of the United States is tried, the Chief Justice shall preside," but provides no guidance for what the chief justice's role should be. The Constitution also gives the Senate the "sole power" to try impeachments, suggesting that the chief justice's role is fairly circumscribed during the proceedings.

Clinton's impeachment trial marked only the second time in U.S. history that a chief justice has presided over an impeachment trial of a president. Rehnquist shares this distinction with his predecessor, SALMON P. CHASE, who presided over the 1868 trial and subsequent acquittal of President ANDREW JOHNSON. Rehnquist studied the Johnson trial and in 1992 published *Grand Inquests*, a history of the Johnson trial and the trial of Samuel Chase, a justice of the Supreme Court who was impeached and acquitted in the early nineteenth century. In the book, Rehnquist used a cautionary tone in the book regarding the perils of politically driven impeachments.

The rules governing Clinton's impeachment trial were modeled upon those enacted for the 1868 impeachment. The impeachment trial little resembled a typical courtroom trial, because the chief justice's authority was rigidly circumscribed. The rules mandated that senators sit mute through the trial. Only Rehnquist could ask questions, upon the written request of the senators. He had the authority to decide questions of procedure and admissibility of EVIDENCE, but the Senate had the power to overturn any ruling by a simple majority vote. Rehnquist was not called upon to rule on any evidentiary issues, nor was he asked to decide what questions a witness could be asked. Unlike a judge in a normal case, Rehnquist had no power to dismiss the charges against Clinton.

Rehnquist earned a reputation for impartiality during the impeachment trial. Attired in a Gilbert and Sullivan inspired robe with four gold stripes on each sleeve, he governed the impeachment with order and decorum, bringing his brisk and businesslike Supreme Court reputation to the Senate chambers. Rehnquist's rulings during the impeachment trial underscored the supreme role of the Senate with its "sole power" to try the impeachment. For example, he ruled that he would not block House managers from interviewing Monica Lewinsky or other potential WITNESSES. Rehnquist stated he was "by no means certain" whether Senate rules gave him the authority to block the questioning. Rehnquist's first ruling during the trial was an objection by a senator to the "continued use of the word 'jurors'" to describe senators, because the Constitution refers to senators in impeachment trials as "triers" and avoids the use of the word "juror." Rehnquist agreed, stating that "[t]he Senate is not simply a jury, but a court."

Prior to the impeachment hearing, legal scholars examined Rehnquist's Supreme Court decisions for clues to determine how the chief justice might rule at Clinton's trial. In a 1995 case, *United States v. Aguilar*, 515 U.S. 593, 115 S.Ct. 2357, 132 L.Ed.2d 520 (1995), the chief justice wrote the opinion overturning the criminal conviction of a federal district judge on an obstruction of justice charge, the same federal law cited in Clinton's impeachment articles. Rehnquist's opinion limited the reach of a broadly-worded statute. Article II charged that Clinton obstructed justice by relating "a false and misleading account of events...to a potential witness" (in this case secretary Betty

Currie and other White House staff members). This "potential witness" language was viewed as too speculative in the *Aguilar* decision. Because of the Rehnquist's limited role in the impeachment process, he was never called upon to rule on the wording used in the article of impeachment. Even if he had ventured in an opinion, the Senate would not have been bound by his interpretation.

Rehnquist also wrote the decision in *Nixon v. United States*, 506 U.S. 224, 113 S.Ct. 732, 122 L.Ed.2d 1 (1993), involving the impeachment of a federal judge. The decision underscored the point that the sole power for impeachment lies in the legislature, without judicial involvement. The High Court ruled that it did not have the authority to review the Senate's impeachment.

In a sense, a ruling made with Rehnquist's acquiescence helped land him in his impeachment role. In 1997, the Supreme Court unanimously ruled that a sexual harassment case brought by Paula Corbin Jones should proceed during the president's tenure. In addition, Rehnquist was responsible for appointing the three-judge panel that selected KENNETH STARR as INDEPENDENT COUNSEL in 1994.

CROSS REFERENCES
Appendix: Articles of Impeachment; Clinton, William J.; Contempt; Independent Counsel; Sexual Harassment; Starr, Kenneth W.

INTERNAL REVENUE SERVICE

The federal agency responsible for administering and enforcing all internal revenue laws in the United States, except those relating to alcohol, tobacco, firearms, and explosives, which are the responsibility of the Bureau of Alcohol, Tobacco and Firearms.

Law Reorganizes IRS And Increases Taxpayers' Rights

In July 1998, President BILL CLINTON signed into law the Internal Revenue Service Restructuring and Reform Act of 1998 (IRSRRA) (P.L. 105–206, H.R. 2676). Stories of taxpayer abuse by the Internal Revenue Service (IRS) were the catalyst for IRSRRA.

In 1996, for example, the IRS seized, without warning, the bank account of Bernice Flemming, widow of Arthur S. Flemming, who served under Presidents FRANKLIN ROOSEVELT, HARRY TRUMAN, DWIGHT EISENHOWER, and

RICHARD NIXON and received the Medal of Freedom, the nation's highest civilian honor. Flemming, who faithfully filled out his tax returns well into his ninety-first year of life, apparently missed a payment during his final month of life, when he was bedridden with a broken leg.

In March 1995, armed IRS agents raided the tax preparation business of Richard Gardner and seized the computers. The U.S. Department of Justice then indicted Gardner on twenty-one counts of tax and bankruptcy FRAUD. Gardner claimed it was retaliation for his business's lawful declaration of bankruptcy in 1994 to postpone certain tax payments until funds became available. After the JUSTICE DEPARTMENT ultimately withdrew the charges in January 1998, it paid $75,000 in February 1999 to cover Gardner's legal fees under a 1997 law designed to reduce prosecutions that are "vexatious, frivolous or in bad faith."

To investigate taxpayer abuse, Congress held hearings and heard testimony from IRS agents and taxpayers in autumn 1997. The investigation revealed that some IRS agents operated under collection quotas when auditing tax returns. Jennifer Long, the only agent not to testify behind a curtain with a voice distortion mask, said that to meet the quotas, agents targeted weak taxpayers who would be unable to fight an audit. Long also claimed that agents ignored cheating by friends and by those with resources to fight an audit. Indeed, statistics show that the audit rate for people with annual incomes over $100,000 declined from 11.41 percent to 2.79 percent from 1988 to 1995. During that same period, the audit rate for people with annual incomes less than $25,000 nearly doubled, from 1.03 percent to 1.96 percent.

After concluding its investigation, Congress issued committee reports and passed IRSRRA to overhaul operations within the IRS. Title I reorganizes the structure and management of the IRS with three sections that should improve taxpayer treatment. (H.R. 2676, § 1001–1205.) First, IRSRRA directed the commissioner of Internal Revenue to discard the IRS' organizational structure, which was based on local, regional, and national offices. In its place the commissioner must substitute organizational units serving taxpayers with similar tax obligations, such as individuals, small businesses, large businesses, and nonprofit organizations. (H.R. 2676, § 1001.) Congress believes this structure will promote a customer service environment at the IRS.

Second, IRSRRA created the Internal Revenue Service Oversight Board, which will operate within the Department of the Treasury. (H.R. 2676, § 1101.) The Oversight Board will contain nine members, including the secretary of the treasury, the commissioner of Internal Revenue, plus six civilians and one federal government employee appointed by the president with the advice and consent of the Senate. The board's general responsibility is to oversee the IRS "in its administration, management, conduct, direction, and supervision of the execution and application of the internal revenue laws." (H.R. 2676, § 7802(c)(1).) Although the board may not view the tax returns of individual taxpayers, and therefore cannot rectify individual taxpayer abuse, IRSRRA commands the board "to ensure the proper treatment of taxpayers by the employees of the Internal Revenue Service." (H.R. 2676, § 7802(d)(5).)

Third, IRSRRA directs the commissioner of Internal Revenue to terminate IRS employees who engage in a list of forbidden conduct that includes: failing to obtain required signatures before seizing homes, personal belongings, and business assets to satisfy tax deficiencies; making a false statement under oath concerning a taxpayer's case; violating a taxpayer's constitutional or civil rights; falsifying or destroying documents to conceal IRS mistakes; committing assault or battery on a taxpayer; violating the tax laws or regulations for the purpose of retaliating against or harassing a taxpayer; and threatening to audit a taxpayer to extract a personal benefit. (H.R. 2676, § 1203.) Although a loophole allows the commissioner to take personnel action other than termination in his sole discretion, he may not delegate that authority to any other officer.

Title III of IRSRRA contains a Taxpayer Bill of Rights, also designed to reduce taxpayer abuse. (H.R. 2676, § 3000–3804.) Most notably, it shifts the burden of proof in most tax cases to the IRS. (H.R. 2676, § 3001.) Previously, taxpayers sued by the IRS had the burden of proving that their tax calculation was correct. Under IRSRRA, if a taxpayer keeps the appropriate records, cooperates during IRS investigations, and presents "credible evidence" to support his tax calculation, the IRS has the burden of proving the calculation is wrong. While supporters hailed this as an important change, critics noted that it only affects the one out of every 4,500 tax returns that the IRS challenges in court. Some tax experts even said the change will be a detriment to taxpayers. Audits could take longer because the IRS will need to amass evidence to satisfy the burden of proof. Tax cases also could last longer, and thus be more expensive, because the court must decide whether a taxpayer satisfied the record keeping, cooperation, and "credible evidence" prerequisites to shifting the burden of proof to the IRS.

The Taxpayer Bill of Rights also regulates the IRS's collection efforts. A section called "Fair Tax Collection Practices" prohibits harassment and abuse of taxpayers, including the use or threat of violence, obscene language, and repeated telephone calls. (H.R. 2676, § 6304.) Another section requires the IRS to provide taxpayers with notice and a hearing before seizing and selling property to satisfy a tax deficiency. (H.R. 2676, § 6330.) The act prohibits the IRS from seizing a residence to satisfy a tax deficiency less than $5,000. (H.R. 2676, § 3445(a).) To seize a taxpayer's primary residence, the IRS must obtain written approval from a federal judge. (H.R. 2676, § 3445(b).)

The Taxpayer Bill of Rights also helps specific groups of taxpayers who might lack power to protect themselves. It allows the secretary of the TREASURY DEPARTMENT to increase funding to clinics that help low income taxpayers prepare returns and handle disputes with the IRS. (H.R. 2676, § 3601.) It suspends the time limit (called the statute of limitations) for filing refund claims during periods when a taxpayer is disabled. (H.R. 2676, § 3202.) It also allows persons who are divorced, separated, or living apart for more than one year to avoid liability for their spouse's understatement of tax liability on a joint return if they were unaware of the understatement. (H.R. 2676, § 3201.)

There is evidence that IRSRRA has reduced taxpayer abuse already. As of March 1999, property seizures were down 98 percent from levels two years earlier, garnishment of paychecks and bank accounts were down 75 percent, and liens, which ensure that a tax is paid when property is sold, were down 66 percent. Critics, however, say these figures reflect reduced, not better, enforcement efforts caused by IRS employees' fear of losing their jobs for violating IRSRRA. According to one IRS agent, "With this new law, if somebody says 'I'm not paying,' then we just say 'thank you' and leave." Indeed, some tax experts are concerned that IRSRRA will encourage and reward tax evasion. Lee A. Sheppard, a tax policy critic for *Tax Notes*, said IRSRRA would so hamper IRS collection efforts that it "should be called the mobsters and drug dealers tax relief act."

The IRS, however, has not yet cleaned up its act entirely. In September 1998, Commissioner of Internal Revenue Charles O. Rossotti disciplined twelve agents for using prohibited dollar collection quotas. Then on April 15, 1999, Jennifer Long, the agent who testified before Congress without hiding her identity, received a sixty-day termination notice. Following fifteen years of "fully successful" employment reviews for Long, the notice said she would be fired in sixty days for poor performance if she did not straighten up. Long claimed the notice was retaliation for her congressional testimony. After she returned from giving her testimony, managers became very picky about her performance and accused her of not being a team player. The IRS withdrew the termination notice only after Senate Finance Committee Chair William V. Roth (R-Del.) protested to Commissioner Rossotti.

CROSS REFERENCES
Taxpayer Bill of Rights

INTERNET

A worldwide telecommunications network of business, government, and personal computers.

Anti-Abortion Web Site

ABORTION is legal under U.S. law. A pregnant woman in the United States has had the right to abort her pregnancy since 1973, when the Supreme Court made its decision in *Roe v. Wade*, 410 U.S. 113, 93 S. Ct. 705, 35 L. Ed. 2d

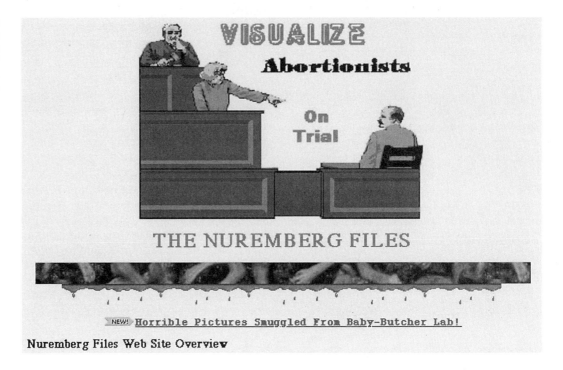

Nuremberg Files Web Site Overview

147 (1973). In the 1990s, an organized opposition to abortion escalated into sporadic violence, as a few abortion opponents killed abortion providers. In 1999, the case of the abortion web site seemed to capture all the anger and fear that surrounded the topic of abortion.

Called "The Nuremberg Files: Visualize Abortionists on Trial," the web site was created by abortion rights opponent Neal Horsley. In the 1990s, Horsley and other abortion rights opponents placed the web site on the Internet and began to use it as a tool to fight abortion rights. "A coalition of concerned citizens throughout the U.S.A. is cooperating in collecting dossiers on abortionists in anticipation that one day we may be able to hold them on trial for crimes against humanity," the web site proclaimed. "We anticipate the day when these people will be charged in perfectly legal courts once the tide of this nation's opinion turns against the wanton slaughter of God's children." The web site listed the names of abortion providers around the country along with their photographs, vehicle license plate numbers, addresses, and the names of their spouses and children. Above this list was a legend that explained the status of each doctor, whom the web site described as "baby butchers." The doctor was still healthy if the doctor's name was in bold print; if the doctor had been attacked and wounded, the doctor's name appeared in grey; doctors that had been murdered had their names crossed out. Two murdered doctors were listed on the web site with their names crossed out. The web site also contained a link to a letter from Paul J. Hill, murderer of an abortion provider in Pensacola, Florida. In the letter, Hill described the "joy" he felt (and still feels) after killing his victim.

In October 1998, Dr. Barnett A. Slepian, an abortion provider in the Buffalo, New York area, was shot to death by a sniper as he talked in his kitchen with his wife and sons. Shortly after the murder, the Nuremberg Files web site crossed out Dr. Slepian's name. Shortly thereafter, Planned Parenthood and several abortion providers filed suit in an Oregon federal court against twelve individuals and two anti-abortion groups, the American Coalition of Life Activists and Advocates for Life Ministries, alleging that the web site operated by the defendants constituted a threat to their lives. The plaintiffs asked for up to $200 million in DAMAGES. The defendants argued that the web site was protected by the FIRST AMENDMENT guarantee of free speech.

The defendants moved the court to dismiss the case several times, but trial judge Robert E. Jones rejected all of the motions. At trial, lawyers for the plaintiffs cited the recent trend of violence against abortion providers. In the twenty years preceding the trial, abortion providers had been subjected to 7 killings, 15 attempted murders, 99 attacks with acid, 154 arsons, and 39 bombings. Dr. Warren Hern, an abortion provider in Boulder, Colorado, testified that he felt "a great sense of personal isolation" because of the web site. Hern was also the subject of a homemade "Wanted" poster distributed by anti-abortion protesters which declared that he and others doctors were "Guilty of Crimes Against Humanity." Maria Vullo, a lawyer for the plaintiffs, compared the defendants to "bounty hunters of the Old West" and called their actions "terrorism." Martin London, another lawyer for the plaintiffs, pleaded that the abortion doctors just wanted their freedom. "They want the freedom to hug their child in front of a window."

The defendants argued that they were providing nothing more than public information on the Nuremberg Files web site. Furthermore, they argued, the web site did not specifically advocate violence against any doctor or abortion clinic. "This is a case about the threat to kill or injure, which is simply not there," argued Chris Ferrara, a lawyer for the defendants. "Opinions? Yes, sometimes harsh. But no violence."

While the case was presented and the jurors deliberated, scholars debated the question and concluded that it was problematic. The web site did not specifically advocate murder or other violence, but, within the context of the violent campaign against abortion providers, the question was, according to law professor Jonathan Entin of Case Western Reserve University in Cleveland, "to what extent will people take seriously the implicit message on this Web site, which is that all right-thinking people should use whatever means necessary to stop people from performing abortions?" David J. Fidanque of the American Civil Liberties Union of Oregon admitted to the *New York Times* that "[t]he issues in this case are very tricky."

On February 2, 1999, the federal jury in Oregon, apparently not as stumped by the case as the experts, found for the plaintiffs and ordered the defendants to pay them $107 million in damages. The defendant vowed to appeal and openly admitted that they had no intention of ever paying the judgment. "I could not in good conscience give money to an industry that thrives on killing children," said defendant Catherine Ramey. "That would be like asking Martin Luther King to pay money to the Ku Klux Klan." Advocates of abortion rights hailed the decision as important for the safety of abortion providers. "Whether these threats are posted on trees or on the Internet, their intent and impact is the same: to threaten the lives of doctors who courageously serve women seeking to exercise their right to choose abortion," said Gloria Feldt, president of the Planned Parent-

hood Federation of America. On February 5, 1999, the Internet service provider for the Nuremberg Files web site removed the web site from the Internet.

Child Online Protection Act

The dramatic growth of the Internet has raised concerns about children gaining easy access to pornographic materials that are found on thousands of web sites. Congress responded in 1998 by enacting the Child Online Protection Act (COPA), 47 U.S.C. § 231, but a federal district issued a preliminary injunction that prohibits its implementation while a lawsuit on the constitutionality of the law is pending. The court's order suggested that COPA infringes on the First Amendment and might be struck down. *American Civil Liberties Union v. Reno*, 31 F.Supp. 2d 473 (E.D.Penn. 1999).

The Child Online Protection Act makes it a federal crime to "knowingly" communicate "for commercial purposes" material considered "harmful to minors." Penalties include fines of up to $50,000 for each day of violation, and up to six months in prison if convicted of a crime. The government also has the option to bring a civil suit against individuals under a lower standard of proof, with the same financial penalty of up to $50,000 per violation. Material considered harmful to minors includes any "communication, picture, image, graphic image file, article, recording,[or] writing" that "depicts, describes, or represents, in a manner patently offensive with respect to minors, an actual or simulated sexual act or sexual contact, an actual or simulated normal or perverted sexual act, or a lewd exhibition of the genitals or post-pubescent female breast."

The act provided an affirmative defense to web site operators. Operators would not be prosecuted if they made a good faith effort to restrict access to minors by (1) requiring use of a credit card, debit account, adult access code, adult personal identification number, (2) accepting a digital certificate that verifies age, or (3) using any other reasonable measures that are feasible under available technology.

Before COPA could become effective, the American Civil Liberties Union, the Electronic Privacy Information Center, the Electronic Frontier Foundation and a group of news media and web site operators filed suit in Philadelphia, Pennsylvania, alleging that the law was unconstitutional. Federal District Court Judge Lowell A. Reed, Jr., granted the plaintiffs a temporary restraining order, thereby preventing the

TAXING THE INTERNET: FAIR SHARE OR GOVERNMENT GREED?

The growth in popularity of the Internet during the 1990s has been fueled by technological advances in personal computers, software, and telecommunications. With millions of new subscribers going online each year, political and legal issues have arisen concerning a myriad of Internet issues: personal privacy, pornography, gambling, computer viruses, and the bootlegging of software and musical recordings. However, by 1998 the issue of Internet commerce drew increasing attention, as software developers provided businesses with secure means of selling products and services over the Net.

Though consumers and businesses have embraced "e-commerce," state and local government officials have expressed concerns about the loss of sales tax revenues from these online sales. A few states enacted laws that tax the access charge subscribers pay each month to their Internet Service Provider (ISP), such as America Online, but many more states began exploring the feasibility of charging sales tax for online sales made by subscribers in their states. A coalition of ISPs, electronic retailers, and catalog sales companies responded by lobbying Congress for a law that would prohibit the states from imposing sales taxes on Internet transactions. This in turn led to the lobbying of Congress by the National Association of Counties and the National Governors Associa-

tion, which urged Congress to enact a law that would make it easy for the states to collect sales taxes on e-commerce.

In October 1998, Congress passed the Internet Tax Freedom Act (Pub. L. 105–277), which imposed a three year moratorium on the ability of state and local governments to tax electronic transactions. The act also established a commission to investigate the issues surrounding the taxation of electronic commerce and catalog sellers and to report to Congress by October 2001 its recommendations for future legislation. Therefore, the advocates on both sides of the issue will continue to make their cases before the commission and the public.

Opponents of Internet sales taxes contend that this new form of commerce is in its infancy and should be given a chance to become mature before taxes are imposed. Even the threat of taxation could impede the growth of electronic commerce, which promises to be a major force in both the national and international economy.

Opponents also note that the Internet provides consumers with more opportunities, information, and choices, while often lowering the prices of goods and services. In addition, Internet companies have demonstrated the ability to provide good customer service.

These changes have forced U.S. businesses to rethink their business practices to remain competitive. The imposition of sales taxes on e-commerce risks derailing this competitive dynamic, which is a fundamental part of the capitalist system.

There are also practical objections to the collection of an Internet sales tax. Opponents of taxation point out that forty-five states impose sales taxes (and many cities do as well), making it time-consuming, confusing, and expensive for Internet businesses to collect and distribute sales taxes. Typically, a business collects sales taxes at the time of purchase and pays government revenue departments on a quarterly basis. However, a purchaser may live in a jurisdiction where both the state and the municipality collect sales taxes. Opponents contend that it would be a bookkeeping nightmare to determine the right amount of tax to charge and then to distribute it to the correct government units. It is estimated that a company active in every state and local jurisdiction would have to file over 2,600 sales tax returns a year. Moreover, such a process would drive up business costs, thereby depriving consumers of the lowest prices.

Opponents of taxation also argue that some companies would try to evade taxation by locating Web servers in jurisdictions that have lower taxes or in foreign countries, where the collection

IN FOCUS

act from going into effect until he ruled on the merits of the case.

The court conducted a six-day hearing in January 1999. The ACLU presented testimony from web site operators who provide information for artists, lesbians and gay men, and disabled persons, who all feared that COPA would force them to shut down their web sites. For example, one web site provided graphic information on sexual pleasure for people with disabilities or illnesses. Because COPA contained no exception for material that has educational or medical value for minors, the operator believed

he might have to censor his site for all visitors, including adults.

The plaintiffs argued that COPA was vague, overbroad, and a direct ban on speech. Although the law provided affirmative defenses to prosecution, the plaintiffs contended that the available defenses burdened speech. Implementation of identification verification imposed an economic and technological burden on web site operators, which would result in loss of anonymity to users and the loss of users to their sites. The plaintiffs also alleged that COPA was neither narrowly tailored to meet a compelling govern-

of taxes would be difficult, if not impossible. Such evasion would create inequities in e-commerce and prevent a level playing field for businesses on the Internet.

Finally, opponents contend that imposing taxes on e-commerce would be unfair because catalogue retailers currently do not charge sales taxes on purchases made by out of state customers. If states were allowed to collect sales taxes on Internet sales, catalogue companies would be able to price their goods lower and therefore enjoy a competitive advantage. In addition, the Supreme Court, in *Quill Corp. v. North Dakota*, 504 U.S. 298, 112 S. Ct. 1904, 119 L. Ed. 2d 91 (1992), ruled that an out of state mail order supplier of office products with no physical presence in North Dakota did not have to collect and remit taxes on purchases made by North Dakota residents. The Court made clear that a business had to have a physical presence in the state for it to collect sales taxes. Opponents of Internet taxation argue that this ruling should apply to e-commerce transactions as well.

Proponents of taxation on Internet commerce acknowledge that the *Quill* ruling restricts the ability of states to tax catalogue retailers. However, the Court also made clear in that case that Congress was free to overturn its ruling by enacting a law that requires catalogue seller to collect sales taxes. State and local governments point out that the impact of *Quill* on state revenue collection has been substantial, as catalog sales have reached $48 billion annually.

For example, the state of Utah estimates it loses $30 million of sales tax through catalogue transactions. Allowing e-commerce the same status would be devastating to tax collections, as it is estimated that e-commerce will continue to grow rapidly.

Proponents of taxation also note that most e-commerce sales are currently business-to-business transactions. Therefore, the argument that no taxes benefit consumer buying rings hollow. It is estimated that business-to-business sales will reach $1.3 trillion by 2002, sales that ten years before would have been subject to state and local taxation. The impact on tax collections will only grow worse as e-commerce expands.

State and local government officials worry that a substantial part of their revenue will dry up as e-commerce becomes more accepted. These shortfalls will require reductions in government programs and services, and may force state and local governments to look at other ways of collecting taxes on purchased items. Most states currently have use taxes, which require the individual purchaser to pay the state the sales tax instead of the catalogue or e-commerce seller. However, most consumers are unfamiliar with this requirement and government collection efforts are costly. Proponents of Internet taxation contend that states will be required to spend more money on collecting use taxes for high priced goods sold over the Net. In addition, states may have to raise income and property taxes to make up for the loss of sales tax revenues.

To overcome the charge that an e-commerce business would have to file over 2,600 sales tax returns, the National Governors Association has proposed that Internet tax collection be made more efficient by having states establish a single statewide sales tax rate. In addition, the association has recommended that a network of private businesses develop a system of tax collection. E-commerce firms could use software provided by these companies to collect the tax and then forward these tax payments to the collection companies. In turn, the collection companies would charge a fee for their services to the states and remit the rest of the tax payments to the states. Proponents of this approach argue that it would be efficient, fair, and would not unduly burden e-commerce. In addition, many state officials believe this same approach should be used with catalog businesses.

Apart from the loss of tax revenue, state officials have expressed concern that the failure to tax e-commerce will drive out of business "Main Street" retail stores that are required to charge sales taxes. Local retailers are already at a competitive disadvantage because e-commerce firms have lower overhead. If local retail businesses fail, local economies may go into decline and unemployment may rise. A sales tax should be collected on the purchase of an item, regardless of whether the person bought it in a local store, through a catalog from an out of state company, or over the Internet from a firm two thousand miles away.

---

ment interest nor the least restrictive means to accomplish its ends. Finally, the plaintiffs argued that COPA was vague and overbroad, which would result in a chilling effect on Internet free speech.

The government argued that COPA was constitutional because it was narrowly tailored to meet the government's compelling interest in protecting minors from harmful materials. It contended that the statute did not inhibit the ability of adults to access the type of speech covered by the act. The government pointed to the affirmative defenses as a technologically and economically feasible method for speakers on the Web to restrict the access of minors to harmful materials. It also rejected the argument that COPA was overbroad, contending that the definition of "harmful to minors" did not apply to any of the material on the plaintiffs' web sites. The law only targeted commercial pornographers who distribute material that is harmful to minors "as a regular course" of their business.

In his order granting a preliminary INJUNCTION to the plaintiffs, Judge Reed examined what the parties would likely be able to prove at a trial for a permanent injunction. He admitted that a majority of Americans "would like to see the efforts of Congress to protect children from harmful materials on the Internet to ultimately succeed." However, the courts are "not to protect the majoritarian will at the expense of stifling the rights embodied in the Constitution."

Judge Reed applied the strict scrutiny test to the statute. Under STRICT SCRUTINY, the content of protected speech may be regulated in order to promote a compelling governmental interest. However, the regulation must be narrowly tailored and it must be the least restrictive means to further the articulated interest, without unnecessarily interfering with FIRST AMENDMENT freedoms. Therefore, the burden imposed on speech must be outweighed by the benefits gained by the challenged statute. Judge Reed noted that the U.S. Supreme Court has "repeatedly stated that the free speech rights of adults may not be reduced to allow them to read only what is acceptable for children."

Applying strict scrutiny, Judge Reed found that COPA would place a restraint on free expression. Although the economic costs associated with compliance with COPA were relevant to the determination of the burden imposed by the statute, he noted that "the relevant inquiry is determining the burden imposed on the *protected speech* regulated by COPA, not the pressure placed on the *pocketbooks or bottom lines* of the plaintiffs." However, the web site operators and content providers may feel an economic disincentive to engage in communications that may be considered harmful to minors. This could lead them to self-censor the content of their sites. Therefore, Reed concluded that the plaintiffs could show that the law burdened the free speech of adults.

Judge Reed found that Congress had a compelling interest to protect minors, but he expressed concerns about the tailoring of the legislation to meet this compelling interest. He pointed out that minors might still be able to access materials on foreign web sites, noncommercial sites, and online via chat rooms. There was also the possibility that minors might be able to legitimately possess a credit or debit card, thereby gaining entry to sites with material deemed harmful to them. He concluded that it was not apparent "that the defendant can meet its burden to prove that COPA is the least restrictive means available to achieve the goal of restricting the access of minors to this material." Therefore, he issued the preliminary injunction.

E-mail

The Communications Decency Act of 1996 (CDA), 47 U.S.C.A. § 223, sought to prohibit the use of the Internet for transmission of obscenity. In 1997, the U.S. Supreme Court, in *Reno v. American Civil Liberties Union*, 521 U.S. 844, 117 S. Ct. 2329, 138 L. Ed. 2d 874 (1997) ruled unconstitutional the part of the act that prohibited the "knowing" dissemination of obscene and indecent material to persons under eighteen through computer networks or other telecommunications media.

Another part of the CDA makes it a crime to send obscene e-mail as a way to annoy other people. A three-judge panel upheld the constitutionality of this provision in *Apollomedia Corp. v. Reno*, 19 F. Supp. 2d 1081 (1998). In its decision the court found that both Supreme Court precedent and legislative history supported its conclusion that the provision outlaws obscene material but not indecent material.

Apollomedia is a multimedia company with headquarters in San Francisco, California. One of its business activities is a web site entitled "annoy.com," which is used by Apollomedia and visitors to the site to communicate strong views using expression that Apollomedia believed might be considered indecent in some communities. Apollomedia organized annoy.com into four sections. The "heckle" section contains articles by authors who take strong, provocative positions on various issues. Drop-down menus allow web site visitors to construct, from a preselected list of options, anonymous e-mail to public officials or figures named in the articles. Another section, entitled "gibe," is a threaded message board that allows visitors to read previously posted messages and to add messages of their own. Apollomedia does not censor messages left by visitors in the "gibe" section.

The "censure" section enables visitors to send digital postcards through the Internet. The visitor selects a postcard and enters the e-mail address of the intended recipient, the desired message text, and the visitor's name and e-mail address. Annoy.com automatically generates an e-mail to the intended recipient which informs him or her that a postcard has been created and provides instructions on how to retrieve the postcard. Finally, the "CDA" (Created and Designed to Annoy) section consists of several pages of commentary and visual images.

In 1997, Apollomedia filed a lawsuit in federal court, challenging the provision of the CDA that prohibited "indecent" communications "made with an intent to annoy." 47 U.S.C.A § 223(a). Apollomedia argued that this provision violated the corporation's First Amendment right to send annoying and indecent e-mails from its web site. The three-judge panel stayed consideration of the case until the Supreme Court issued its ruling in *Reno v American Civil Liberties Union.*

The central question for the court was whether the CDA prohibited indecent e-mails or only obscene ones. The statute prohibits telecommunication 'which is obscene, lewd, lascivious, filthy or indecent, with intent to annoy, abuse, threaten, or harass another person." The U.S. government argued that this provision only proscribed obscene speech, which is not protected by the First Amendment. Apollomedia contended that the word "indecent" was not synonymous with obscene and that indecent speech is protected by the First Amendment. Therefore, the Court should strike down the provision in terms of indecent communications.

The Court noted that the government relied on cases in which the Supreme Court had construed the "string of words" found in the CDA as referring solely to obscenity. The 1957 obscenity decision in *Roth v. United States,* 354 U.S. 476, 77 S. Ct. 1304, 1 L. Ed. 2d 1498, first used a similar string of words to refer to obscenity. In later Supreme Court obscenity decisions, the Court recited the words "obscene, lewd, lascivious, indecent," suggesting that the words were synonymous. The three-judge panel found that these cases demonstrated that in the context of print and film, the string of words were almost identical to the CDA language. Moreover, the Supreme Court had used them to proscribe only obscene materials.

However, the panel agreed with Apollomedia that several Supreme Court decisions construed "indecent" to bear a distinct meaning. In *FCC v. Pacifica Foundation,* 438 U.S. 726, 98 S. Ct. 3026, 57 L. Ed. 2d 1073 (1978), the Supreme Court ruled that Congress intended to restrict speech which is "indecent" as separate from "obscene." Pacifica used the string of words argument, but the Court rejected it, ruling that each term bore a separate meaning. The Court found it "unrealistic" to assume Congress would have made obscene and indecent synonymous.

In the more recent case of *Sable Communications of California, Inc. v. FCC,* 492 U.S. 115, 109 S. Ct. 2829, 106 L. Ed. 2d 93 (1989), the Court looked at a "dial-a-porn" statute which prohibited any "obscene or indecent" telephone communication "for commercial purposes to any person." The Court held the statute unconstitutional to the extent it sought to proscribe communications that were indecent as opposed to obscene.

The three-judge panel concluded, however, that the CDA language was intended to regulate only obscene communications. The string of words employed in the act more closely resembled "in both length and syntax" the string of words used in the statute as interpreted in *Roth* and later cases "than the words at issue in *Pacifica* and *Sable.*"

The court also examined the legislative history of the CDA provision. The provision was first enacted in 1968 to prohibit obscene telephone calls. A review of the 1968 legislative record gave no indication that the provision was intended to proscribe indecent speech that is not obscene. The Court noted that the legislative record for the CDA provision was sparse on this issue. However, the court drew from this silence the inference that Congress had not sought to change the nature of the proscribed speech contained in this section.

The floor debates over the CDA were not illuminating either. The court admitted that some senators expressed the view that the CDA provision would prohibit the transmission of indecent material over the Internet. Nevertheless, the Court put more weight on the conference report that the CDA amendments were intended to "simply clarify" that the current obscenity laws did not prohibit using a computer to transmit and receive obscene materials. Therefore, the court concluded that Congress "intended to merely update those provisions to address new technology."

The court ruled that the provisions were constitutional because they only applied to obscene material. The Department of Justice reiterated that it would not prosecute indecent material. Apollomedia appealed to the Supreme Court, but it denied review, thus making the decision the final word on the constitutionality of the provisions in question.

Gambling

The growth of the Internet in the 1990s has touched virtually all facets of life, including gambling. In the 1990s, Internet entrepreneurs began to use Internet web sites as forums for gambling, offering casino games and other gambling fare. In December 1997, Senator Jon L. Kyl (R-AZ) sponsored a bill in the U.S. Senate that would make online betting illegal.

Under the Internet Gambling Prohibition Act of 1997 proposed by Senator Kyl, a person found guilty of betting online could be jailed for six months and fined up to $2,500. Online casino operators, for their part, could be imprisoned for four years and fined up to $20,000. The bill was supported by many casino operators and was opposed by the horse racing industry, Indian tribes engaged in their own gambling enterprises, and participants in sports leagues such as "fantasy football." Internet service providers opposed the bill because it made them criminally liable for web sites created by their users. Regulating the content of, and activity on, the Internet is no easy task because it is difficult to track down its users.

Even the U.S. Department of Justice questioned the wisdom of creating criminal laws to thwart online betting. In June 1998, Deputy Assistant Attorney General Kevin DiGregory acknowledged to the House Judiciary Crime Subcommittee that enforcement of the proposed law would be fraught with obstacles. DiGregory also announced that the Justice Department opposed the prosecution of "mere bettors." Members of Congress were perplexed by DiGregory's report. Bob Barr (R-GA), a Representative from Georgia, said he did not "quite understand the hesitancy of the [Justice] Department to move into this area." Despite their confusion, the Senate committee members did not ask to hear from persons and businesses opposed to the bill.

Despite the misgivings of the JUSTICE DEPARTMENT, the U.S. Senate in July 1998 approved the bill by a vote of 90–10. The final bill had been modified since its inception: online gamblers would be fined $550 or three times what they bet through the Internet, and they could be jailed for up to three months. The bill would allow state lotteries and off-track betting, but only under closed, subscriber-based systems. The bill also provided an exemption for fee-based fantasy sports leagues, provided the fees are not pooled and distributed as prizes. In support of his bill, Kyl proclaimed that the bill was designed to protect children. According to Senator Kyl, children had the capacity to access more than 140 different web sites that offered gambling, and the Senate was forced to act to protect the children from those sites. "More than a million dollars will be gambled over the Internet this year," said Kyl. "Children can access Internet gambling sites on the family computer, wager with mom's credit card, click the mouse and bet the house."

After the Senate vote, the bill was tacked onto an appropriations bill, but the bill never passed. In 1999, Kyl sponsored another Internet gambling bill, this time with the bipartisan support of Senator DIANNE FEINSTEIN (D-CA). The new bill gave some protection to Internet service providers by exempting from criminal liability those providers who do not know that they are providing gambling web sites. Internet service providers must remove an Internet gambling web site at the request of law enforcement personnel, unless there is a technological or economic reason that the web site cannot be removed. One issue that vexed the Senate was whether to exempt Indian tribes from the proposed law's reach. State officials testified at Senate committee hearings against such an exemption.

Just as it had in 1998, the Senate committee refused to hear from witnesses who opposed the legislation. The witnesses who did testify included representatives of the National Football League, the National Collegiate Athletic Association, the Major League Baseball player's union, a New Jersey casino regulator, and state attorneys general. Betty Montgomery, the Ohio attorney general, described the online gambling as a "cyberdrain," and James Doyle, attorney general from Wisconsin and also the president of the National Association of Attorneys General, said that a rejection of the bill would be like "asking for a national policy permitting gambling." Senator Kyl reminded all concerned that gambling has been illegal on the federal level since 1961, when Congress passed the Wire Act, which banned gambling over the telephone. Tom Bell, a professor at Chapman University School of Law, rejected the bill as "technical ignorance and moral hypocrisy." The bill violates the right of persons to "peaceably dispose of their income," Bell told *Congress Daily*.

As Congress debates the merits of criminal laws for online gambling, online gambling thrives. The online gambling industry, which handled approximately $1 billion in bets in 1998, continues to operate through internet web sites. The online gambling industry even expanded into Web TV in May 1999. That month, GalaxiWorld Limited announced that it was opening the first internet casino on Web TV.

Internet gambling is fraught with perils not only for the gambler but for credit card companies. Much of the online betting that is done is accomplished with credit cards. In 1998, Cynthia Haines of Marin County, California, who lost approximately $70,000 in online betting, filed a suit against online gambling operators and credit card companies, accusing them of engaging in illegal business practices by facilitating online betting. Haines argued that, with few exceptions, gambling is illegal and that she is not liable for her gambling debts. Haines is not the only person who is attacking the online gambling interests in court. Ari Jubelirer, a student at the University of Madison at Wisconsin, organized a CLASS ACTION suit against credit card companies in 1999 after he lost $20 playing blackjack on the Internet.

Internet Filters

In response to concerns by parents, educators, and employers, software companies have developed Internet filter programs that prevent persons from gaining access to certain types of user-defined Internet sites. For example, a computer administrator might instruct the program not to let a user visit a site where the word "sex" is found. Many public schools have used filtering technology to prevent students from accessing pornographic web sites. Traditionally, the courts have granted public schools much more latitude when it comes to making decisions about the materials that they use in the classroom and in the school library.

Some public libraries have also installed filters on their public computers, which has invited political and legal action on the part of people who believe filtering in this context infringes on an adult's FIRST AMENDMENT rights. Library administrators who have installed the filters have argued that libraries have always made judgments about what materials go on their shelves. Placing a filter on a public computer to prevent the user from accessing pornography is no different than the library declining to subscribe to magazines such as *Penthouse* or *Hustler*.

Nevertheless, the American Civil Liberties Union (ACLU) and other groups interested in the First Amendment in cyberspace have been outspoken in their opposition to filtering technology in public libraries. The first reported court case involving libraries and Internet filters occurred in *Mainstream Loudon v. Board of Trustees of the Loudon County Library*, 24 F.Supp. 2d 552 (E.D. Va.1998). A Virginia federal court judge ruled that the use of screening software was unconstitutional, as it restricted adults to materials that the software found suitable for children.

In October 1997, the Loudon County, Virginia, library board passed a "Policy on Internet Sexual Harassment." The policy stated that the library would provide Internet access to it patrons, but all library computers would be equipped with site-blocking software that would block all sites displaying child pornography and obscene materials and material deemed harmful to juveniles. In addition, the computers would be installed near and in full view of the library staff and patrons would not be permitted to access pornography. If they did so and refused to stop, library staff would call the police to intervene.

The site-blocking restriction raised the ire of a number of Loudon County residents. Mainstream Loudon, a nonprofit organization, and individual citizens filed suit in federal court alleging that the site-blocking policy violated the First Amendment rights of library patrons. They contended that the policy impermissibly discriminated against protected speech based on content and it constituted an unconstitutional PRIOR RESTRAINT on speech. The library board defended the policy as both reasonable and least restrictive means of achieving compelling government interests.

Judge Leonie M. Brinkema, herself a former librarian, ruled that the site blocking was unconstitutional. She rejected outright the board's contention that the policy should be construed as a "library acquisition decision" to which the First Amendment did not apply. Instead, she concluded that the policy implicated the First Amendment. Therefore, the county had to show that site blocking was the least restrictive means of achieving two compelling governmental interests: minimizing access to illegal pornography and avoiding the creation of a sexually hostile environment.

Judge Brinkema found that the two governmental interests were compelling, thereby focusing her analysis on whether the policy furthered these interests and whether the policy was narrowly tailored. She found that the county had failed to prove that there was a need for the policy. The library had never received a complaint about Internet use. Instead, the board described a few isolated incidents in other Virginia libraries. The board's expert named only three libraries in the United States that had experienced the problems that the Loudon County board sought to control. Even so, Judge Brinkema discounted the expert testimony as failing to show that anyone had been sexually harassed in a library as the result of Internet access.

The court noted that even if there was a necessity for the policy, it had to be narrowly tailored to restrict the least amount of speech. The library argued that the policy was the least restrictive means. The only other alternative was to have librarians directly monitor what their patrons view. The plaintiffs contended that other less restrictive means were available. These included designing an acceptable use policy, using privacy screens, using filters that can be turned off for adult use, changing the location of Internet computers, educating patrons on Internet use, placing time limits on use, and enforcing criminal laws when violations occur.

The court agreed with the plaintiffs that the policy was not narrowly tailored because less restrictive means were available. In addition, Brinkema concluded that the policy was overinclusive, restricting what adults may read to "a level appropriate for minors." The Supreme Court, in ruling portions of the Communications Decency Act unconstitutional, had found that suppressing "a large amount of speech that adults have a constitutional right to receive" could not be justified on the grounds that minors needed to be protected. *Reno v. American Civil Liberties Union*, 521 U.S. 844, 117 S. Ct. 2329, 138 L. Ed. 2d 874 (1997). Judge Brinkema echoed this ruling, finding the policy violated the First Amendment.

Following the decision, the board placed filters on some of the terminals, so parents could choose which computers to allow their children to use.

Despite the ruling's reaffirmation of the First Amendment, members of Congress continued to advocate mandatory filtering for schools and libraries. Senator JOHN MCCAIN (R-AZ) and other senators introduced in 1998 the Internet School Filtering Act. It would require schools and libraries receiving federal funding for Internet access to employ filtering technology. The bill does not specify what type of filtering must be used, leaving that decision in the hands of individual institutions.

The debate over Internet filtering is likely to continue. The American Library Association has issued a policy opposing filtering in libraries. Other commentators, including civil libertarians, have advocated using filters, but they draw a distinction between private and public use. Finally, some critics of filtering software argue that it is too unsophisticated and excludes access to legitimate sites merely because certain "bad" words are found on the sites.

Melissa Virus

The Internet has produced forms of terrorism that threaten the security of business, government, and private computers. Computer "hackers" have defeated computer network "firewalls" and vandalized or stolen electronic data. Another form of terrorism is the propagation and distribution over the Internet of computer viruses that can corrupt computer software, hardware, and data files. Many companies now produce virus-checking software that seeks to screen and disable viruses when they arrive in the form of an e-mail or e-mail attachment. However, computer hackers are constantly inventing new viruses, giving the viruses a window of time to wreak havoc before the virus checkers are updated. Moreover, the fear of viruses has led to hoaxes and panics.

The history of the Melissa virus demonstrated how easily a sophisticated virus can be created and how quickly it can spread around the world. On Friday, March 26, 1999, a file attachment called "Passcodes 3–26–99" appeared on alt.sex, a Usenet newsgroup dedicated to erotica. When the Usenet reader opened the file, it appeared to contain only a list of passwords to commercial pornographic sites on the World Wide Web. However, within a few hours a virus detector spotted a new virus, code-name Melissa.

The attachment to the e-mail arrived in the form of a Microsoft Word document entitled "list.doc". If, for example, recipient's name is Joe Smith, the e-mail bore the title "Important Message from Joe Smith," and Joe Smith was listed as the sender. If the user deleted the document without opening it, the computer was safe. Once opened, however, Melissa sent out e-mail using Microsoft's Outlook e-mail program. Melissa accessed all of the e-mail addresses stored in Outlook's address book and sent the messages to those recipients, making the e-mail look even more like a piece of innocuous, friendly correspondence. Meanwhile, the recipient of the virus did not know that the computer was transmitting these messages.

Melissa spread faster than any other computer virus. Within a few days, the virus had caused worldwide problems. Over three hundred computer networks shut down from the heavy loads of e-mail that Melissa generated. Other computer hackers used Melissa's code to make copycat viruses, further debilitating the Internet. Companies quickly updated their virus-checkers but the virus continued to appear on computers.

In the past law enforcement officials have had very little success in finding and prosecuting hackers. However, the Melissa virus demonstrated that computer technology and cybersleuthing has dramatically improved the chances of catching hackers. The automatic virus detector that first spotted Melissa recorded that the virus entered the e-mail system from an America Online (AOL) account. The Federal Bureau of Investigation (FBI) contacted AOL to find out who owned the e-mail address. They discovered that the account, listed to a man in Lynwood, Washington, had been "hijacked" by the Melissa hacker. It appeared that the hacker had used the account in the preceding fifteen months. The hacker had logged on from New Jersey and within a short time the FBI had traced the message to a specific telephone number.

While the FBI and AOL pursued their investigation, an informal network of virus hunters and writers began analyzing the virus. Richard M. Smith, president of Phar Lap Software, a Brookline, Massachusetts, company, looked at other viruses posted from the same e-mail account. In Stockholm, Sweden, a computer scientist surmised that Melissa's code resembled the work of a virus writer called Vicodin. Smith, who communicated with the other virus hunters through the Usenet alt.comp.virus newsgroup, visited Vicodin's web site and downloaded the virus tool kits he found there. Smith analyzed the files and found names embedded in the source code. The name David L. Smith appeared three times. As Smith pursued his investigation, he was aided by the inclusion of a "global user identification number," a serial number that current Microsoft applications like Outlook and Word embed in documents. Ironically, Richard Smith had gained international attention a few weeks before by publicizing this identification number and criticizing Microsoft for not informing its users of this hidden feature. He then contacted the FBI with his information about David L. Smith.

Meanwhile, the FBI had traced the telephone number to the Aberdeen, New Jersey, apartment of David L. Smith, a computer programmer. New Jersey state police arrested Smith on April 1, less than one week after he allegedly posted the Melissa virus. He was charged under New Jersey law with computer theft, wrongful access to a computer system, and disclosure of data from wrongful acts of a computer system. Prosecutors alleged that Smith had written the virus and named it after a topless dancer he had met in Florida. Officials stated that Smith was not the hacker Vicodin, even though the source code came from the hacker's site.

Smith was released after posting $100,000 bail. If convicted, he could face up to forty years in prison and a maximum fine of $48,000.

David Smith created the Melissa virus, which spread faster than any previous e-mail virus.

JEFF ZELEVANSKY/AP/WIDE WORLD PHOTOS

Although the Melissa virus caused worldwide problems, the quick investigation and successful apprehension of the virus writer put hackers on notice that things had changed. Law enforcement agencies have developed high-tech units to investigate "white-collar crime." These units can now be used to identify Internet terrorists, employing the same technology hackers use to catch them.

In April 1999, the U.S. House of Representatives Committee on Science held a hearing on the Melissa virus. Although the hearing was held to investigate security measures that might stop future episodes of Internet terrorism, the testimony revealed the tensions between the proposed security measures and the privacy of personal e-mail. Two forms of maintaining e-mail privacy, encryption and anonymous re-mailing, make it difficult to trace viruses. Encryption encodes e-mail messages so they can only be read by the holder of a key code, while anonymous re-mailers allow users to send e-mail messages to a party that strips out the identifying marks before sending it on to the recipients of the message. These techniques limit law enforcement efforts to stop e-mails that contain viruses.

CROSS REFERENCES

Abortion; Appendix: Child Online Protection Act; Appendix: Internet Tax Freedom Act; Computer Crime Computer Law; First Amendment; Gambling; Obscenity; Telecommunications

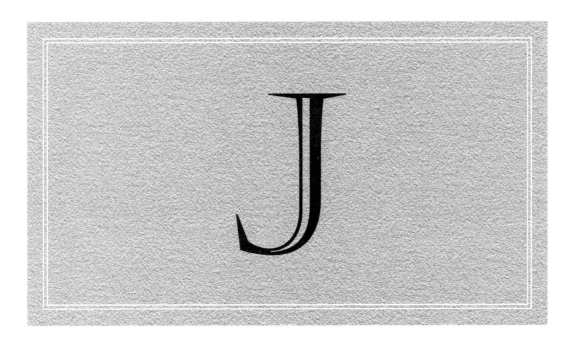

JUVENILE LAW

An area of the law that deals with the actions and well-being of persons who are not yet adults.

North Carolina v. T.D.R.

Since the 1970s, juveniles who commit serious crimes may be transferred from juvenile court to adult court for criminal prosecution as an adult. The various states have devised procedures for this transfer of jurisdiction. Critics of these transfer schemes contend that juveniles do not receive the due process rights they are guaranteed under the FOURTEENTH AMENDMENT. Instead, courts routinely transfer jurisdiction without requiring strong evidence.

The debate over prosecuting juveniles as adults is illustrated by the North Carolina Supreme Court's decision in *North Carolina v. T.D.R*, 347 N.C. 489, 495 S.E. 2d 700 (1998). The court overturned a lower court ruling that revoked the transfer of a juvenile to adult court. The lower court ruled that the juvenile had not been allowed to fully defend himself at the transfer hearing, but the supreme court found no deficiency.

In August 1996 T.D.R., then fifteen years old, was arrested in Durham County, North Carolina, for allegedly committing first-degree RAPE and first-degree BURGLARY. The prosecutor filed a delinquency petition in juvenile court but sought transfer of T.D.R. to adult criminal court to face the charges. Nothing happened over the next three months, as both the prosecutor and the defendant filed continuances. In December, the district court held a probable cause hearing. At the hearing, T.D.R. waived his right to a hearing on the probable cause and stip-ulated to a finding of probable cause. This meant that he admitted that the prosecutor had enough facts to justify bringing him to trial.

T.D.R.'s attorney then requested a two-week continuance of the hearing, at which time both sides would present to the judge their arguments on whether T.D.R. should be transferred to adult court. The attorney told the judge that he needed the continuance to obtain forensic psychological evaluations of T.D.R. and to collect evidence concerning treatment options if the judge decided to keep T.D.R. in the juvenile court system. The prosecutor objected and the judge denied the request and proceeded to hear evidence on the transfer of T.D.R. to adult court.

The prosecutor first put into evidence the facts of the case, including T.D.R.'s alleged use of a knife to attempt a sexual assault. Then the prosecutor called the county coordinator of an adolescent sex offender program as an expert witness. She testified that she had worked with violent sex offenders for twelve years and that based on the evidence she heard at the hearing, she concluded that T.D.R. had "committed a very sophisticated sexual crime based on the use of a weapon." She stated that the juvenile system "did not have the capacity to treat this serious an offense. The adult system does." Moreover, she believed that T.D.R. had a very high risk of re-offending. On cross-examination by T.D.R.'s lawyer, she admitted that sex offenders are given psychological tests to reveal depression and psychosis.

T.D.R.'s lawyer did not offer any evidence at the conclusion of the prosecutor's case. The court then ruled that because the juvenile system could not effectively treat T.D.R., he would transfer T.D.R. to the North Carolina Superior Court. Following transfer, a Durham County GRAND JURY indicted T.D.R. for the charged crimes. T.D.R. then asked the superior court to dismiss the indictments and return the case to the district court for a "full and meaningful transfer hearing." The superior court judge agreed, issuing an order that stated the district court had denied T.D.R. due process of law and "fundamental fairness" by refusing to hear or consider evidence regarding the appropriateness of retaining jurisdiction within the juvenile court.

The prosecutor appealed the dismissal to the North Carolina Court of Appeals. The court reversed the decision, which T.D.R. then appealed to the North Carolina Supreme Court. Chief Justice Burley B. Mitchell, writing for a unanimous court, ruled that the superior court's dismissal was improper.

Mitchell noted that the court of appeals had erred when it ruled that the superior court judge did not have the authority to review and to dismiss an indictment against a juvenile defendant. North Carolina law clearly gave the judge the right, but in this case there was no basis for the dismissal. The only finding made by the superior court judge related to whether T.D.R. had been denied the opportunity to present evidence contradicting the adolescent sex offender counselor. The finding was based on the district court judge's denial of the two-week continuance.

The state supreme court found nothing in the probable cause and transfer hearing that constituted a denial of DUE PROCESS. T.D.R. did not argue that the judge had "refused to hear or consider any evidence he sought to introduce." Thus, the sole issue was whether the denial of a continuance violated T.D.R.'s constitutional rights. The grant or denial of a continuance is "a matter ordinarily addressed to the sound discretion of the trial judge." The ruling was not reversible on appeal "absent an abuse of discretion." Under North Carolina case law, an abuse of discretion is established only upon showing that a court's actions "are manifestly unsupported by reason."

Justice Mitchell reviewed the transfer hearing and noted that T.D.R.'s attorney gave the court no reason why the three months from August to December had not proved sufficient to gather evidence. Part of the delay occurred because T.D.R. requested that his experts conduct DNA tests on the state's evidence before a determination of probable cause. Moreover,

T.D.R. did not make a written motion for a continuance before the hearing. The oral motion at the hearing was not accompanied by a supporting affidavit stating facts "that might be proved by any witness of if the continuance were granted." Taking all these circumstances together, the supreme court concluded that the district court judge had not abused his discretion in denying the continuance.

The court rejected T.D.R.'s argument that he did not know the transfer hearing would occur at the same time as the probable cause hearing. The record indicated his attorney knew both hearings would take place that day. Mitchell also rejected the superior court judge's conclusion that the evidence was not sufficient to justify the conclusion that the juvenile system could not provide rehabilitative service to T.D.R. The testimony of the sex offender counselor was not rebutted by T.D.R.

Based on this analysis, the supreme court returned the case to the superior court for reinstatement of the indictments against T.D.R. and prosecution of T.D.R. as an adult.

Trying Juveniles as Adults

Until the end of the nineteenth century, children accused of violating a criminal law were treated virtually the same as adults. They were tried in the same courts, subjected to the same penalties, and generally confined in the same prisons and jails. It was not until 1899 that a separate juvenile court was established in Illinois, which served as a model for the juvenile court system several decades later.

The focus on the juvenile justice system has traditionally been rehabilitative as opposed to punitive. The approach has been more holistic as the juvenile courts have been concerned primarily with the welfare of the children rather than the offenses that have brought them before the court. As stated by juvenile justice expert, J.C. Howell, "juvenile court [has] established a tradition of paying much less attention to the criminal act itself, instead looking at general circumstances lying behind the offender's misconduct. The goal [has been] to identify the cause of the behavior and then administer the appropriate rehabilitative measures."

During the last ten years, however, primarily as a consequence of increasing concern about the nature and amount of crime committed by children, juvenile justice laws have been amended to place a lower importance on rehabilitation and greater importance on public safety, punishment, and accountability. The

In October 1997, at age eleven, Nathaniel Abraham was the youngest person in Michigan history to be charged as an adult with murder.

CLARENCE TABB, JR./AP/WIDE WORLD PHOTOS

government has also reacted by reducing the jurisdiction of the juvenile court and expanding the role of the general criminal justice system in dealing with children.

One such example of a more punitive juvenile law is in effect in Michigan. With the enactment of the legislation known as the Juvenile Waiver Law, Michigan has became one of the toughest states on juveniles who commit crime. The statute was passed partially in response to cases where the community felt that judges were being too lenient in sentencing.

In 1990, Benjamin Gravel was returning home from the Bayview Yacht Club in Detroit when a group of young men, seeking transportation to a party, pulled a large tree log across the narrow road leading from the yacht club and carjacked Gravel's vehicle. In the process of stealing the car, Gravel was killed. Two of the teenage defendants were tried as adults and convicted of murder. The controversy began when the presiding judge sentenced them as juveniles, although the law in existence at the time gave him the discretion to sentence them as adults. The sentence was appealed to the Michigan Court of Appeals, which reversed the decision and ordered them sentenced as adults.

On January 7, 1997, the Michigan legislature enacted a law that lowered the age that juveniles could automatically be tried as adults and created a new process in which juveniles of any age could be charged, tried, and sentenced as adults in the juvenile system. The law has two significant provisions: the automatic waiver procedure and the juvenile designation provision (*MCL 712A.2d,4,9a,18,18b,18i,21; 762.15; 764.1f; 764.27; 766.14*).

The automatic waiver provision allows juveniles to be tried and sentenced as adults in the adult criminal court. This section of the law only applies to juveniles ages fourteen and older who are accused of one of the enumerated offenses. However, if convicted under this provision, the juvenile must be sentenced as an adult.

The other portion of the law, known as the juvenile designation provision, allows children younger than fourteen to be charged and sentenced as adults in juvenile court if they commit a crime known as a "life offense." A life offense is a serious crime, such a robbery, rape, or murder, for which a life sentence could be imposed if the defendant was an adult.

If a juvenile is convicted under this section of the statute, the judge has three options: adult prison or probation, juvenile rehabilitation until age twenty-one, or a delayed sentence. The third option allows initial suspension of the prison term to first attempt rehabilitation in the juvenile system. If this is unsuccessful, the adult sentence is reinstated and the juvenile may serve time in prison.

The effectiveness of the juvenile designation law has already been tested in Wayne County, Michigan. In March 1999, the Honorable Freddie G. Burton became the first judge in Michigan history to sentence through the juvenile system a juvenile to life in prison without parole.

Gregory Petty, sixteen years old, was convicted of first degree murder, armed robbery, and felony firearm in the robbery/murder of fifty-five-year-old Calvin Lee Whitaker outside a Detroit area delicatessen. After Judge Burton heard statements from the victim's family and testimony from counselors and psychologists describing Petty's character and social behavior, Judge Burton sentenced him as an adult offender. Although the judge could have sent him to a juvenile correctional facility, he determined that the boy was not amenable to treatment and instead imposed the mandatory adult sentence of life without parole for first degree murder.

Petty's accomplice, thirteen-year-old McKinley Moore, who was also tried as an adult, was spared the adult sentence and instead sentenced to at least six years in a high security juvenile facility with extensive therapy. Moore, who was actually the first juvenile in Michigan to be sentenced under the two-year-old law, was convicted of second degree murder. The testimony showed that Moore, who had a 55 IQ, had been influenced by Petty into committing the crime and was raised in an extremely neglectful home environment. Social workers testified that the boy and his mother lived with as many as twenty-two other people in their three bedroom home and that the mother exercised no supervision. Judge Burton was persuaded that boy could be rehabilitated in the juvenile system, with the option that if he did not benefit from juvenile detention, he could be transferred to adult prison.

The law has been applied to even younger defendants. In October 1997, at age eleven, special education student Nathaniel Jamar Abraham became the youngest person in Michigan history to be charged as an adult with murder. In statements given to police two days after the shooting, the boy said he was sitting on a berm near a Detroit area party store, aiming at trees and firing a stolen .22 caliber pistol, when he shot Ronnie Lee Green, eighteen years old, as he walked out of the store. Green died at the scene.

Although the boy's attorneys argued that he did not understand the consequences of his statements and the trial judge agreed, the Michigan Court of Appeals upheld the admission of the statements, which were made in the presence of the boy's mother. The statements can now be used at trial. During the summer of 1999 was Abraham detained at a juvenile detention center awaiting trial.

The Michigan Court of Appeals is being given several opportunities to review the juvenile waiver statute. Several other cases are on appeal that question the constitutionality of the automatic waiver provision. In cases where juveniles can be prosecuted as adults or children, county prosecutors decide whether a child under sixteen (over sixteen requires adult prosecution) will be tried as an adult or juvenile. Two trial judges have declared this provision unconstitutional, citing to the fact that this lets prosecutors decide the sentence as well, since a juvenile who is automatically waived must be sentenced as an adult.

The disparity in charging as adults or juveniles is also being reviewed, since there are no policies to provide consistency in uniform charging throughout the state. For instance, the Wayne County prosecutor charged a sixteen-year-old suburban Detroit girl, who was accused of solicitation and conspiracy to kill her grandmother and other crimes, as a juvenile. If charged as an adult, she would have faced the possibility of life in prison, but now if convicted at most will receive probation or placement in a juvenile detention facility. There have been similar cases, however, in which the juvenile has been charged as an adult requiring adult sentencing options. Some child advocates argue that the legislature has erred in allowing these discrepancies in the law.

CROSS REFERENCES
Criminal Law; Criminal Procedure; Due Process; Probable Cause

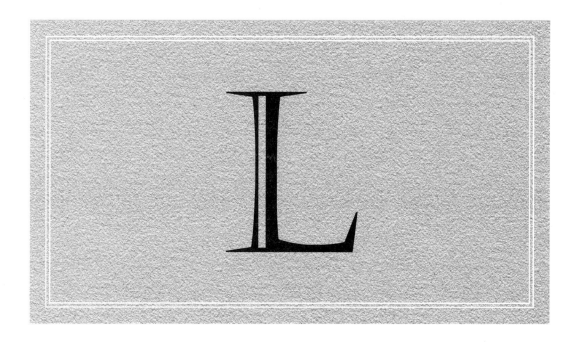

LABOR LAW

An area of law that deals with the rights of employers, employees, and labor organizations.

National Federation of Federal Employees, Local 1309 v. Department of the Interior

Federal government workers are governed by a system of federal labor laws different from those that regulate private employees. Private employees and employers are subject to the National Labor Relations Act (NLRA), 29 U.S.C.A. § 151 et seq., while federal employees and the government are governed by the Federal Service Labor-Management Relations Act (FSLMR), 5 U.S.C.A. § 7101 et seq. The main difference for employees is that those in the private sector may STRIKE, while federal workers must submit to compulsory ARBITRATION to resolve bargaining issues. The FSLMR established the Federal Labor Relations Authority (FLRA) to implement the law through the exercise of broad adjudicatory, policymaking, and rulemaking powers.

The Supreme Court examined the breadth of the FLRA's powers in *National Federation of Federal Employees, Local 1309 v. Department of the Interior*, __U.S.__, 119 S. Ct. 1003, 143 L. Ed. 2d 171 (1999). The Court was called upon to decide whether the FLRA could require agencies of the federal government and labor unions to engage in midterm bargaining of labor issues. Midterm bargaining refers to negotiations that occur, for example, in the third year of a five-year labor contract

The National Federation of Federal Employees, Local 1309, represented employees of the U.S. Geological Survey, an agency of the Department of the Interior. The union proposed that a midterm bargaining provision be included in the new basic labor contract that was under negotiation. The Department of the Interior refused to include the provision, citing a ruling by the Fourth Circuit Court of Appeals that prohibited midterm bargaining under the statute. *Social Security Administration v. FLRA*, 956 F. 2d 1280 (4ᵗʰ Cir. 1992).

The union then filed a complaint with the FLRA, arguing that the department had committed an unfair labor practice. The FLRA, which at one time had endorsed the Fourth Circuit's view, concluded that the statute imposed an obligation to engage in midterm bargaining. Therefore, it found that the department had committed an unfair labor practice and ordered it to bargain over the proposed clause. The department appealed the order to the Fourth Circuit, which set the ruling aside. 132 F. 3d 157 (4ᵗʰ Cir. 1997). The court reaffirmed its previous ruling about midterm bargaining.

The Supreme Court, on a 5–4 vote, reversed the Fourth Circuit and declared that it must follow the FLRA's judgment that federal law requires midterm bargaining. Justice STEPHEN BREYER, in his majority opinion, acknowledged that there was great confusion about this issue. The Fourth Circuit ruled that midterm bargaining was not permissible, while the Circuit Court of Appeals for the District of Columbia held that it was. *National Treasury Employees Union v. FLRA*, 810 F. 2d 295 (D.C. Dir. 1987).

Justice Breyer examined several arguments offered by the department concerning the text of the statute on this issue. He concluded that these "linguistic arguments" were unpersuasive, as nothing in § 7114(a)'s good faith bargaining requirement conclusively proved that midterm bargaining was prohibited. Moreover, he found that he could easily turn around these linguistic interpretations to support the union position. In short, the statutory language produced "ambiguity, not certainty."

The department also asserted that the FSLMR's policies required a reading of the statutory language that would have excluded midterm bargaining from the definition of collective bargaining. With midterm bargaining, a union could withhold certain subjects from the ordinary labor negotiations on a long-term contract and then raise them during the term. The department argued that unions would find midterm negotiations more advantageous, resulting in piecemeal bargaining that would undermine the basic COLLECTIVE BARGAINING process. Justice Breyer was not persuaded, noting other policy concerns called for a different reading of the statute. Without midterm bargaining it would be more difficult to find solutions to workplace problems, such as health and safety. This would undercut the statute's goal of promoting the "effective conduct of public business."

The department also argued that the history of the federal employee labor act and prior administrative practices supported its position. However, Justice Breyer found no more than a 1976 administrative decision in the record. He concluded that where the Fourth Circuit and the department found clear statutory denial of midterm bargaining, the Court found "ambiguity created by the Statute's use of language that might, or might not, encompass various forms of midterm bargaining."

However, this ambiguity was "perfectly consistent" with the conclusion that Congress delegated to the FLRA the power to determine, within appropriate legal bounds, "whether, when, where, and what sort of midterm bargaining is required." Breyer pointed out that the statute gave the FLRA broad powers to implement the act. The FLRA was analogous to the private-sector role of the National Labor Relations Board, which exerts national control over labor-management relations. In addition, the FLRA's function was to develop expertise in the labor relations and use that expertise "to give content to the principles and goals" set forth in the statute. Therefore, the Court concluded that Congress had left specific labor relations issues to the FLRA for definition and resolution.

In light of this interpretation, Justice Breyer ruled that the midterm bargaining issue must be remanded to the FLRA for a fresh consideration of the issues discussed by the Court. The Court clearly indicated it would defer to the FLRA's decision.

Justice SANDRA DAY O'CONNOR, in a dissenting opinion joined by Chief Justice WILLIAM H. REHNQUIST, and Justices ANTONIN SCALIA and CLARENCE THOMAS, argued that the majority had ignored the plain meaning of the statute. Unlike Justice Breyer, Justice O'Connor did not find the statute ambiguous. One provision of the law specified "a few instances where midterm bargaining is required." However, the remainder of the act did not contain language that "expressly or implicitly imposes a general duty on agencies to bargain during the term of the collective bargaining agreement." O'Connor also contended that the Court did not have to defer to the FLRA's interpretation of the statute, especially when was inconsistant in the issue.

Sweatshops

In early 1999, lawsuits about sweatshop labor involved major U.S. garment manufacturers and clothing stores. At the center of the storm were factories in Saipan, a tiny Pacific island. Activists alleged that Saipan factories grotesquely exploited Asian workers, who were underpaid, mistreated, and kept in virtual slavery while the island's factory owners enjoyed special tax breaks in the U.S. commonwealth. Three CLASS ACTION lawsuits sought nearly $1 billion from the factories and their clients, eighteen well-known manufacturers and retailers ranging from the Gap, J.Crew and Tommy Hilfiger to the Limited, Wal-Mart and Sears. Marking the biggest civil actions ever brought against U.S. sweatshops, the lawsuits, which came only months after a much-ballyhooed agreement over monitoring sweatshops, were filed by human rights groups and an apparel workers' union. The garment industry denied the allegations, and some critics suggested that the lawsuits had exaggerated the problem. But as hundreds of activists marched outside trendy clothing stores in January and March, the issue galvanized young people.

Part of the chain of Northern Marianas Islands, Saipan is situated in the Pacific ocean to the north of the Philippines and east of China. The island became a U.S. commonwealth after being liberated from Japanese occupation during World War II. During the mid-1980s, the fledgling garment industry on Saipan began to explode. It had sales of $5.4 million in 1985, but those numbers skyrocketed to $124 million three years later, and kept on increasing as Chinese entrepreneurs built numerous factories. By 1998, sales topped $1 billion. Fueling this meteoric rise was the island's special legal status: as a U.S. commonwealth, as goods produced in Saipan and shipped into the United States are not subject to duties—import taxes—thus allowing manufacturers to save some $200 million annually. Also influential was the island's proximity to mainland China, which provides a vast supply of labor.

While contributing to growth, the suits allege conditions also made Saipan ripe for corruption. Workers on Saipan are kept in involuntary servitude, according to the plaintiffs, who include apparel workers on Saipan, the human rights group Global Exchange and Sweatshop Watch, and the Union of Needletrades, Industrial and Textile Employees (UNITE). Largely Chinese laborers, they must often pay large fees to recruiters before being allowed to work on the island—amounts as high as $7,000—and often these are loans that must be worked off. Once on Saipan, the suits claimed, they are kept in cramped, vermin-infested barracks surrounded by barbed wire, paid only $3.05 an hour, worked twelve hours a day for seven days a week, physically abused, and even sometimes forced to undergo abortions. Sometimes, the suits contended, workers who failed to meet their quotas were punished by being locked inside factories and forced to work unpaid overtime. The lawsuits alleged that the defendants engaged in a racketeering conspiracy with factory owners to underpay up to 50,000 workers over a period of ten years, while also denying them basic human rights.

Some defendants denied the allegations. The Gap asserted that it "does not tolerate this type of conduct," and Wal Mart denied doing business with Saipan-based manufacturers at all. Denying that slavery conditions existed in Saipan, a lobbyist for the Marianas island chain told reporters that the greed of big law firms was behind the lawsuits. Nonetheless, in March, protesters from San Francisco to Manhattan gathered by the hundreds, protesting outside Gap stores in five different cities carrying signs with slogans like "Gap Gone Bad." The suits followed on the heels of other protests in January at Duke and Georgetown Universities, where students claimed the schools had failed to ensure that apparel bearing their schools' names was not produced in sweatshops.

Princeton University students protest against sweatshops.

DANIEL HULSHIZER/AP/WIDE WORLD PHOTOS

In April, an upsurge in protests brought a backlash. *Time* magazine reported that "many in the education community are questioning whether the wave of anti-sweatshop protest is an indigenous resurgence of campus activism or the handiwork of a powerful outside agitator—organized labor." The magazine quoted professors and administrators who speculated that UNITE, the garment union, was using students to advance its goal of relocating garment jobs in the United States. Student and union leaders denied the charges.

But skepticism came from other quarters, too. In February, an investigation by the *New York Times* expressed doubts about the class action litigation. The newspaper reported that factory conditions did not appear to be as awful as the litigants claimed. And in interviews with workers, another portrait of work on Saipan emerged in which the cultural expectations of Chinese laborers seemed to be met by their experience on the island: laborers told the paper that they came to the island voluntarily, wanted to work hard, and were banking thousands of dollars. While noting stories of abuse, the article charged that "lawyers in the class-action suit seem to exaggerate conditions, citing a few worst-case examples as typical." It noted that the lawsuit claimed Chinese women had to pay recruiting fees averaging $7,000, whereas the newspaper reported that the figure was generally between $1,000 and $3,000.

In Washington, response to the issue varied. In late 1998, American companies such as Nike and Liz Claiborne had agreed with human rights organizations to a program designed to curtail sweatshops. The agreement was praised by President BILL CLINTON and others as a groundbreaking blow against the exploitation of labor. Coming only two months later, the lawsuits implied that the issue was far from being put to rest.

As for Saipan, the Labor Department had for years been taking a dim view of practices on Saipan, issuing more than 1,000 safety citations and compelling manufacturers to reimburse workers for millions of dollars in unpaid wages. For some federal officials, the island appeared to be an embarrassment. Allen Stayman, a Department of the Interior official charged with overseeing the commonwealth, told the *New York Times* that it was a "dubious privilege" for the United States to lose $200 million annually in duties and tariffs while having to put up with the islands' human rights record. The island, meanwhile, lobbied passionately to preserve its duty-free status by flying lawmakers to Saipan and arguing that import duties would harm its economy. After several Saipan government-funded golf trips, some lawmakers, such as House Whip Tom DeLay (R-Tex.), were convinced that they should take a hands-off approach and trust to the free market.

CROSS REFERENCES
Labor Department; Labor Union; Wagner Act

LIABILITY

A comprehensive legal term that describes the condition of being actually or potentially subject to a legal obligation.

Jenny Jones Show Found Guilty

On May 7, 1999 after deliberating for less than seven hours, a Michigan jury found the Jenny Jones Show, its parent company, Warner Brothers and the production company Telepictures, negligent in the murder of Scott Amedure, a guest on the *Jenny Jones Show*. Although the Amedure's family asked for over $70 million in DAMAGES, the jury awarded over $25 million to the family.

In early March of 1995, Jonathon Schmitz and Scott Amedure appeared on a taping of the *Jenny Jones Show*. The topic of the show was "secret crushes." Jonathon Schmitz, a heterosexual, agreed to be a guest on the *Jenny Jones Show* and find out who had a secret crush on him. At the taping Scott Amedure, a one-time friend of Schmitz, professed that he had a crush on Schmitz and gave a complete description of his sexual fantasies involving Schmitz. Three days later, Schmitz shot his one-time friend to death.

In November 1996, Schmitz was tried and convicted of second degree MURDER for the death of Amedure. He was sentenced to twenty to twenty-five years in prison. A Michigan Court of Appeals, however, overturned the conviction due to an error in the jury selection process. Schmitz's second trial is scheduled for August 1999.

The episode about the same-sex secret crushes never aired, but the Jenny Jones Show was implicated when during the 911 call, Schmitz told the operator that Amedure had humiliated him on public television. The Amedure family filed a suit in a Michigan court alleging that the Jenny Jones Show, Warner Brothers and Telepictures were negligent in the events that led to the cause of Scott Amedure's death. Specifically, the complaint alleged that as a direct and proximate result of the NEGLIGENCE of the defendants, Scott Amedure was shot twice, at close range, to death with a newly purchased shotgun.

The legal definition of negligence is "the failure to use such care as a reasonably prudent and careful person would use under similar circumstances." In other words, it is the doing of an act, which a person of ordinary prudence would not have done under the same or similar circumstances. In order for a person to be found negligent, a plaintiff must prove that the defendant owed a duty to the plaintiff, the defendant breached that duty, the plaintiff suffered damages, and the defendant's breach of DUTY, or his or her negligence, was a PROXIMATE CAUSE of plaintiff's damages.

In this case the Amedure family argued that the defendants did everything that led to the murder of their son, except for actually pulling the trigger. They alleged that the show and its producers acted negligently in their screening process, and as a result subjected Scott Amedure to an unreasonable risk of harm from Jonathon Schmitz. They further argued that the harm was foreseeable in that a reasonable person could or should have foreseen that the situation created by the defendants was likely to humiliate, and embarrass Schmitz to such an extent as to incite violence against Amedure.

At trial the plaintiff's attorney presented evidence that the show's producers never explicitly told Schmitz that his admirer was a man. Rather, the show's producers allegedly misled Schmitz into appearing on the show, by failing to tell him that the subject of the show was same-sex crushes. The plaintiff further argued that the show deceived Schmitz even after he told them that he did not wish to appear on the show if his crush was a man. The plaintiff emphasized that it was this deceit and ambush that led Schmitz into the madness, which ended in the shooting of Amedure. Plaintiff also presented evidence that experts had previously warned the show's producers, that someone would be killed if they continued to produce ambush shows. The plaintiff argued that the episode with Schmitz and Amedure was one of this nature, as the producers of the show used deceptive tactics to lure Schmitz onto the program, and then they surprised him during the actual taping.

The plaintiff also argued to the jury that the *Jenny Jones Show* had poor screening tactics. They asserted that Schmitz should have been asked whether he suffered from a mental illness before he was allowed to appear on the show. Schmitz had a history of mental illness and suffered from a substance abuse problem. As a result the producers of the show should foreseen that the humiliation of being surprised by a gay crush could result in an emotionally unstable person having a violent reaction. Consequently, plaintiffs argued that a better, or more in depth screening process of potential guests would have detected this.

The defendants, on the other hand, argued that the show was not responsible for Schmitz's actions and suggested that something else happened between the men that triggered Amedure's murder. The producers denied misleading Schmitz before the show and insisted that they had no reason to suspect that Schmitz would have a violent reaction to learning about the crush his one-time friend had on him. Defendants argued to the jury that Schmitz had suspected Amedure's crush on him several months before the taping of the show. Further, they contended that when Schmitz was contacted by the show, the producers told him that his admirer could be a man, woman or transvestite. Schmitz accepted the offer to appear on the show approximately twenty minutes after he was first contacted. In addition, they argued that Schmitz consented to being surprised, because he knew the identity of the person would not be revealed until he or she walked out on stage. Therefore, the producers were not negligent in having Schmitz appear as a guest, as he knew the potential for embarrassment on the show.

The defendants further acknowledged that they did conduct a pre-show interview with Schmitz. During that interview, the defendants argued, that Schmitz assured the producers that he would be able to handle the secret crush regardless if it was a man. He indicated that he would be disappointed if it was a man, but that he would handle it okay.

Testimony was also presented that Schmitz was able to hide his mental illness from his closest friends. The defense argued that it was unreasonable for the producers of the show to have known that Schmitz had a mental illness, as even his close friends had no reason to suspect that Schmitz would react to the surprise in the manner that he did. Nothing was apparent in his background to indicate that he was homophobic. The defense presented additional evidence that Schmitz's actions did not reveal that he was upset or humiliated. Specifically he was partying with Amedure and a mutual friend after the taping of the show, and they had also made plans to go shopping.

The defense also emphasized to the jury that Schmitz admitted in his confession that he did not decide to kill Amedure until after he received a love note from him two days after the taping of the show. He further suggested that Schmitz's family's reaction to the taping of the show may have played a significant role in Schmitz's thinking and behavior. Consequently, he argued that the producers of the *Jenny Jones Show* could not have foreseen such a reaction from Jonathon Schmitz upon learning of the surprise same-sex crush.

Jenny Jones testifies during the trial which found her show partially liable for the death of Scott Amedure.

CHARLES V. TINES/AP/WIDE WORLD PHOTOS

The defendants maintained that they were not negligent and did not cause the death of Scott Amedure. The jury, however, in an eight to one verdict found in favor of the plaintiffs. They awarded the Amedure family $6,500 in funeral and burial expenses, $5 million for Scott Amedure's pain and suffering, and an additional $10 million each for the loss of companionship.

The defendants indicated that they would file an appeal, noting that the jury's decision would result in stifling the FREEDOM OF SPEECH of talk shows and affect the entertainment industry as a whole.

Mental Health Professionals Held Accountable for Their Patients

Psychiatrists, psychologists, and other mental health professionals must fulfill numerous educational and licensing requirements to work in the field. In the 1970s, the job of the mental health care professional became even more complicated when courts began to hold doctors liable for the dangerous criminal acts of their patients. The seminal case was the California Supreme Court's decision in *Tarasoff v. Regents of the University of California*, 529 P. 2d 553 (Cal. 1974), modified 551 P. 2d 334 (Cal. 1976).

In *Tarasoff* a psychiatric patient killed a young woman, and the killer's psychotherapists were sued in civil court. The plaintiffs argued that the psychotherapists knew that the patient was dangerous to the victim but did nothing to warn the victim, which constituted NEGLIGENCE. The psychotherapists argued, in part, that they were protecting the patient's confidentiality by keeping the therapy sessions secret, which is an important aspect of therapy. If a patient in therapy knows that the sessions are not confidential, the patient may feel reluctant to open up, which thwarts the whole object of therapy.

The *Tarasoff* court ruled that the psychotherapists could be sued for failing to notify others of the danger presented by their patient. The ruling put mental health therapists in a tenuous position: they needed complete truthfulness from their patients to help their patients make progress, yet they had to break a patient's confidentiality and notify others if the patient seemed to present a serious danger to another person. Two cases emerged in the late 1990s that transformed the notification requirement to a higher requirement.

In 1994, Wendell Williamson, a law student at the University of North Carolina, disrupted a class when he insisted that he had telepathic powers. At the suggestion of a dean at the law school, Williamson began to see Dr. Myron B. Liptzin, a psychiatrist at the university's health service. Dr. Liptzin, the director of psychiatric services, conducted six sessions with Williamson and learned of Williamson's history of mental instability. Williamson's mental health seemed to have taken a turn for the worse two years earlier, when he screamed at students at a campus gathering and began hitting himself in the face until he started to cry. Campus police picked up Williamson and took him to the hospital, where he told doctors that "the thing" was speaking to him and tormenting him with grotesque images. Williamson was hospitalized briefly and then released after doctors concluded that he did not pose a threat to anyone's safety, despite knowing that Williamson kept a gun in his apartment.

With the help of antipsychotic medication prescribed by Dr. Liptzin, Williamson was able to finish the school year. When summer came, Williamson moved to his parents' home in western North Carolina. Dr. Liptzin, who was retiring that summer, told Williamson to seek out a doctor and to continue to take his medication. Dr. Liptzin did not give Williamson a specific referral to another doctor, and he told Williamson to tell someone if he was going to stop taking his medication.

Williamson stopped taking the drugs and returned to law school in Chapel Hill in fall of 1994. In January 1995, Williamson took hundred of rounds of ammunition and rope and other hostage-taking gear, walked to Henderson Street in Chapel Hill and opened fire with his rifle.

Williamson killed two persons and wounded another. At his criminal trial for murder, Williamson argued that he was not guilty by reason of insanity. Williamson claimed that he suffered from paranoid schizophrenia, and that he believed he was saving the world by randomly killing people. A jury in North Carolina found Williamson not guilty by reason of insanity, and Williamson was committed to a secure state hospital. After the verdict, Williamson sued Dr. Liptzin in civil court, asking for monetary damages. Williamson alleged that Dr. Liptzin had caused him pain and suffering because Dr. Liptzin had misdiagnosed him as suffering from "delusional disorder grandiose," and not paranoid schizophrenia. Williamson further alleged that Dr. Liptzin was negligent because he had failed to follow up on Williamson's progress in summer 1994.

On September 21, 1998, a jury in North Carolina returned a verdict in favor of Williamson and ordered Dr. Liptzin to pay Williamson $500,000. Dr. Liptzin's lawyer, Bruce W. Berger, said the verdict was "part of the attempt to shift responsibility in our society." Many mental health professionals criticized the verdict. Itimar Salamon, an associate clinical professor of psychiatry at Albert Einstein College of Medicine, called the verdict a "miscarriage of justice." Williamson had "tried to soothe his own conscience," Salamon said "by placing all responsibility for what happened onto his former psychiatrist." Other mental health professionals were more accepting of the verdict. "The jury heard more than the public and concluded Dr. Liptzin was negligent," mental health advocate Beth Melcher told Gianelli.

In October 1998, another jury, this one in Connecticut, found a psychiatrist liable for his patient's sexual assault on a child. Dr. Douglas H. Ingram, a psychiatrist in the New York City borough of Manhattan, was treating Dr. Joseph DeMasi, a medical resident who intended to work as a child psychiatrist. In his therapy sessions, DeMasi informed Dr. Ingram that he was having sexual fantasies about children. DeMasi also opined in the sessions that children were not hurt by having sexual experiences with adults. Dr. Ingram did not notify anyone of DeMasi's tendencies, and DeMasi eventually molested a ten year-old boy at a hospital in Danbury, Connecticut. DeMasi was convicted of child sexual assault and was released in 1992. His victim, Denny Almonte, did not recover. Almonte became frustrated and full of rage as the years went on, and Almonte eventually landed in prison for assault. Almonte then sued Dr. Ingram for failing to notify others about the danger that DeMasi presented to children.

Dr. Ingram argued that he was ethically duty-bound to keep his sessions with DeMasi a secret. A federal jury in Connecticut disagreed, and in October 1998, the jury found Dr. Ingram negligent for failing to warn others about DeMasi. The night before the jury would hear arguments on the amount of DAMAGES for Almonte, Dr. Ingram settled with Almonte for an unspecified sum.

CROSS REFERENCES

Entertainment Law; Healthcare Law; Negligence

LIBEL AND SLANDER

Two TORTS that involve the communication of false information about an individual, group, or entity that can be seen, such as a writing, printing, effigy, movie, or statue.

Khawar v. Globe International, Inc.

The California Supreme Court issued a significant ruling on libel when it held in *Khawar v. Globe International, Inc.*, 19 Cal. 4th 254, 965 P. 2d 696 (1998), that the news media can be liable for reporting someone else's libelous statement about a private figure. In so ruling, the court rejected the media's argument that a "neutral reportage" defense that applies to public figures in some jurisdictions should also apply to private figures.

The controversy began in 1989 when the tabloid newspaper *Globe* presented an uncritical report about a little-known book in which the author claimed that Sirhan Sirhan had not been the assassin of ROBERT F. KENNEDY in 1968. Robert Morrow, the author of *The Senator Must Die* asserted that the real murderer was Khalid Khawar, a Pakistani reporter who was covering Kennedy's victory rally that night in a Los Angeles hotel for a newspaper in Pakistan. Morrow said Khawar had been an Iranian secret agent who had also worked with the Mafia. The book contained a photo of Khawar with Kennedy at the hotel that night.

The *Globe* article did not name Khawar but it contained the photograph with a circle and arrow pointing him out. The *Globe* did not contact Khawar before printing the story nor did it investigate Morrow's claims. Khawar claimed that people recognized his photograph and that he and his children received death threats. He also alleged that his house and his son's car were vandalized. By 1989, Khawar was a farmer in Bakersfield, California.

Khawar filed a libel suit against Morrow, his book publisher and Globe International, the publisher of the tabloid. Morrow defaulted and the publisher settled out of court, but Globe International fought the case all the way to trial. However, a jury awarded Khawar $1.175 million dollars for the damage done to his reputation by the article. This award included $500,000 in PUNITIVE DAMAGES. The Globe appealed to the California Court of Appeals, which affirmed the verdict. It then appealed to the California Supreme Court.

A unanimous court upheld the award. Justice Joyce L. Kennard, writing for the court, noted that the *Globe* believed it should not be held liable for any damages because it was merely reporting the contents of a newsworthy book about a controversial issue. It cited the "neutral reportage" libel defense as justifying its position. In addition, it contended that Khawar was a public figure. Justice Kennard pointed out that the California Supreme Court had never addressed the question whether the neutral reportage defense should be recognized.

In jurisdictions that recognize this defense, the news media entity must be neutral, merely reporting charges made by other persons without taking a position itself. In addition, the charges must be reported in a substantially accurate way. The news media argued that such a defense is necessary for them to report the news without the fear of unwarranted libel suits.

Justice Kennard declined to apply the neutral reportage defense, finding that Khawar was a private figure, not a public one. Kennard noted that the U.S. Supreme Court has described two types of public figures. All-purpose public figures place themselves in the forefront of a wide range of public controversies in order to influence the outcome of issues. They invite attention and comment. Limited-purpose public figures, on the other hand, are drawn into a particular public controversy and become public figures for a limited range of issues.

In contrast, a private individual has not accepted public office or assumed an influential role in society. Unlike public figures, who give up part of their interest in protecting their good name, private individuals do not. Therefore, private individuals are more vulnerable to injury than public officials and public figures.

The *Globe* claimed that Khawar was a involuntary, limited-purpose public figure relating to a particular public controversy. He was drawn into the controversy over the Kennedy assassination and became an involuntary public figure for the limited purpose of a report on Morrow's book. The court rejected this claim. In Kennard's view, an involuntary public figure must have access to the media to effectively defend his reputation in the public arena. Khawar did not acquire this type of media access, even after the publication of the book. The book sold poorly, less than 500 copies, suggesting again that Khawar had not become a public figure. In addition, his few interviews and comments after the tabloid article was published did not move him from private individual to public figure.

The supreme court said reports such as this one rarely benefit the public when the allegations are against a private individual. Kennard also noted that private persons rarely have sufficient media access to counter false accusations against them. She stated that "republications of accusations made against private figures are never protected by the neutral reportage privi-

Trent Lott
AP/WIDE WORLD PHOTOS

lege." However, she stopped short of recognizing such a privilege when public officials and figures are involved.

Moreover, the source for the article was a book that made undocumented charges—charges that were never verified by authorities who investigated the crime. Kennard concluded that the *Globe's* reporters and editors had "obvious reasons to doubt the accuracy" of the book's claims, yet they published it anyway. The tabloid did not attempt to balance the story or to contact Khawar for a rebuttal.

Several mainstream media, including the *Los Angeles Times*, the *New York Times*, CBS, NBC and ABC, supported the *Globe's* appeal. The major media argued that they often must report newsworthy charges and countercharges concerning controversial issues—charges that cannot always be verified. Some media attorneys said the case would make the media more reluctant to cover controversies involving private persons, thereby limiting freedom of the press in California.

On the other hand, Khawar's attorney said the court's ruling had "driven a stake through the heart of the neutral reportage concept." He commented that "neutral reportage is neither neutral nor legitimate reporting but simply an excuse to titillate by knowing repetition of falsehoods."

CROSS REFERENCES
First Amendment; *New York Times v. Sullivan*

LOTT, TRENT

Trent Lott has served in the U.S. government for over three decades. He was elected to both houses of the U.S. Congress and served subsequent terms as a member from the state of Mississippi.

A U.S. Senator from Mississippi, Trent Lott is a major political figure in the nation's capitol. He first came to Washington as a Democratic congressional aide in the early 1960s. Lott is best-known for his conservative views, having served as a Republican in both the House of Representatives and the U.S. Senate. Lott was recognized for his leadership skills in Congress and was able to organize support for important issues among both Republicans and Democrats. Paul Weyrich, a radio news commentator, once described Lott "as a wily Southerner. He likes to make deals, but sometimes, when he feels a great principle is at stake, he can be tough as nails." A skillful politician, he was elected by fellow senators as Senate majority leader on December 3, 1996.

Born on October 9, 1941, in Grenada County, Mississippi, Chester Trent Lott, moved with his family to the costal town of Pascagoula. As an only child, Trent received the full attention and love of his parents. His father, Chester, worked as a shipyard worker who later tried his hand in the furniture business. In a *U.S. News & World Report* interview with Gloria Borger, Lott described his father as "handsome and outgoing, and I always thought he might actually run for office someday."

Lott entered the University of Mississippi (Ole Miss) in the fall of 1959. While at Ole Miss, Lott had his first real experience at politics. His freshman year, he pledged the Sigma Nu social fraternity. While he participated in Sigma Nu activities, Lott also made many friends among members of other fraternities and independent student groups. Eventually, he was elected as president of both Sigma Nu and the university's interfraternity council. Cheerleaders at Ole Miss were also elected positions, and running for cheerleader provided Lott another opportunity to gain political skills in forming political blocks, cutting deals and doing door-to-door precinct work.

No African American students attended the University of Mississippi when Lott first entered the school. During Lott's senior year, on September 30, 1962, Air Force veteran James Meredith, protected by armed U.S. marshals, enrolled at Ole Miss. The small group was confronted by rock-throwing students and nonstudent protestors in violent demonstrations. By the time the violence ended, two people were dead and many others injured and arrested. Lott worked to keep Sigma Nu fraternity members from taking part. At the same time, he used his campus influence to call for peaceful campus integration.

Graduating with a bachelor's degree in public administration in the spring of 1963, Lott enrolled in the Ole Miss law school. He subsidized his graduate education with a federal student loan and also obtained a job with the university's recruitment office. Later, he was able to work for the alumni association as a fund raiser, a position that enabled him to make valuable political connections throughout his native state.

While Lott attended law school, the Vietnam War was expanding in scope and troop commitments. Like other college students Lott received a student deferment from the draft.

By the time he graduated from law school in 1967 Lott had married Patricia (Tricia) Thompson of Pascagoula and, under Selective Service rules, obtained a hardship exemption due to the birth of their first child, also named Chester.

After graduating from the Ole Miss law school, Lott and his family returned to Pascagoula. For a brief period Lott worked in a private law firm, leaving after less than a year when he was offered a top staff job by Congressman William M. Colmer, a Mississippi Democrat. The Lott family moved to Washington, D.C., in 1968. Political skills learned at Ole Miss in organizing and influencing people earned Lott a reputation as an effective and able congressional aide. When Congressman Colmer announced his retirement from the House of Representatives in 1972, Lott announced his candidacy as a Republican to seek the vacant office. Lott was able to win Colmer's endorsement and support. Lott had a well-organized and tireless campaign. With the aid of the landslide re-election of President RICHARD NIXON, he was able to win the House seat with a vote margin of 55 percent.

Arriving in Washington as a freshman Representative, Lott was appointed to membership on the House Judiciary Committee. As the youngest member of the committee, Lott became involved in the 1974 hearings to impeach President Nixon. The president had been implicated in the break-in of the Democratic National Committee headquarters at an office complex called Watergate. After the president released tape recordings and transcripts indicat-

TRENT LOTT

1941	Born in Grenada County, Mississippi
1963	Graduated from University of Mississippi
1972	Elected to U.S. House of Representatives
1981	Elected House minority whip
1988	Elected to U.S. Senate
1996	Elected as Senate majority leader

ing his involvement and a cover-up of the crime, Lott reversed his position as a staunch supporter and joined others in the call for the president's resignation, which occurred less than a week later.

Though Lott had vowed to fight against increased government controls from his seat in the House, he actually supported more federal spending for entitlement programs, farm subsidies, public works projects, and the military. During his sixteen-year tenure in the U.S. House of Representatives, Lott was never credited with authoring any major legislation. However, he won praise for his work on tax and budget reform. He was an active member of the House, and served on the powerful House Rules Committee from 1975–89. With the support of his fellow Representatives, Lott was elected and served as minority whip from 1981–89. As minority whip, he was the second ranking Republican in the House of Representatives. He was also named chair of the Republican National Convention's platform committees in 1980 and 1989. Lott, however, did not always support the legislative agenda of his political party. When President RONALD REAGAN proposed a tax reform bill in 1985, Lott used his political power as minority whip to oppose the measure. Two years later, Lott joined with Democrats to override a presidential veto of a highway spending bill which included several highway projects in his home district.

When the Mississippi Democratic Senator, John Stennis, retired in 1988, Lott announced that he would seek the vacant Senate seat. He won the Senate position with a 54 percent majority. As a Senator, Lott continued to focus his political talents on building coalitions and was appointed as a member of the Ethics Committee. He was later appointed as a member of the powerful Senate Budget Committee. Continuing his climb through the ranks of the Senate, Lott was elected as the secretary of the Senate Republican Conference in 1992. In 1994 he won the election for Senate majority whip by a one vote margin, making him the first person to be elected whip in both houses of Congress.

Lott's experiences as House minority whip helped him to establish a highly-organized whip system in the Senate. Individual members of Congress were drafted to organize and track colleagues on a regional basis. These regional whips provided daily briefing to Lott on crucial votes. One of the regional whips was also tasked to be on the Senate floor at all times. Lott's ability to work with both parties helped to end what was described in the popular press as budget gridlock. When the Senate majority leader, Bob Dole, announced his plans to retire from the Senate in order to run for president, Lott used his well-controlled whip organization to campaign for the vacant majority leader position. His organizational and political skills were rewarded, and he was elected Senate majority leader on June 13, 1996.

The Senator's stance on other major issues facing the nation were widely known. He articulated his views on numerous radio and television interview shows. He also took advantage of the electronic media and maintained an internet home page stating his position on key political and national issues. In regards to a balanced national budget, Lott declared, "I understand the concerns regarding the Balanced Budget Amendment and want to assure you that I do not take amending our Constitution lightly. However, having watched many futile attempts to reduce the deficit through legislation, I am convinced that an amendment to our Constitution is necessary." Lott also described his position concerning prayer in public schools on this site: "I have consistently advocated strong legislative action in support of the rights of students who wish to participate in voluntary prayer in their schools."

Lott's personal beliefs reflect those of his constituency, and his election to both houses of Congress show his successful representation of the people in his home district and home state. In Congress, his ability to mobilize his fellow Representatives and Senators in support of key legislation was recognized with prominent positions in both houses as minority whip in the House of Representatives, and in the Senate as majority whip and later Senate majority leader. Lott has the distinction of being the first Southerner to be House minority whip and the first person to be elected whip in both houses of Congress.

McCAIN, JOHN

Senator John S. McCain spent twenty-two years in the U.S. Navy before becoming a Republican congressman, then a senator, from Arizona. He did not however, have a typical military career. McCain endured five-and-a-half years as a prisoner of war (POW) in Vietnam. However, he prefers to be known for what he has accomplished as an elected official. In 1998, he won credit as the anti-tobacco crusader. McCain's name became synonymous with the drive to sharply decrease smoking in America by raising taxes and halting tobacco companies' ability to shield themselves from lawsuits. The bill eventually lost support, and the senator redirected his energy into other issues, such as campaign finance reform and telecommunications legislation. A respected Republican with admirers in both parties, McCain is running as a presidential candidate in the 2000 election.

John Sidney McCain was born on August 29, 1936, in the Panama Canal Zone to John Sidney McCain, Jr., and Roberta (Wright) McCain. He grew up on naval bases in the United States and overseas. The elder McCain was an admiral who served as commander of American forces in the Pacific during the Vietnam War. In fact, the family has a long lineage in the military. McCain's paternal grandfather, John S. McCain, Sr., was also an admiral, as well as commander of all aircraft carriers in the Pacific during World War II. He and McCain's father were the first father and son admirals in the history of the navy.

McCain graduated from Episcopal High School in Alexandria, Virginia, in 1954 and then attended the U.S. Naval Academy in Annapolis, Maryland, where he took courses in electrical engineering. There he was known as a rowdy and insubordinate student whose demerits for his antics dragged down his otherwise decent grades. He graduated in 1958 toward the bottom of his class (790 out of 795), but was nevertheless accepted to train as a naval aviator.

On October 26, 1967, the lieutenant commander lifted off from the carrier Oriskany in an A-4E Skyhawk on a mission over the Vietnamese capital, Hanoi. Above the city, an anti-aircraft missile sliced off the plane's right wing, forcing McCain to eject. With both arms broken, a shattered knee, and a broken shoulder, he landed in a lake where a Vietnamese man extracted him, then a crowd beat him, stabbed him with a bayonet, and took him into custody. He did not receive care for his wounds for nine days. When officials learned of his father's high rank, they admitted him to a hospital and later placed him with an American cell mate who helped nurse him back to health. Because of his father's status, McCain was offered an early release after just seven months. He denied it, insisting on following the U.S. prisoner of war code of conduct which states that prisoners should only accept release in the order in which they were captured.

After five-and-a-half years as a prisoner of war in Vietnam, McCain and the rest of the men in Hanoi were released on March 17, 1973. McCain was given a hero's welcome upon his return to the United States, meeting President RICHARD NIXON and California Governor RONALD REAGAN and receiving the Silver Star, Bronze Star, Legion of Merit, Purple Heart, and Distinguished Flying Cross. He went to the Na-

John McCain
AP/WIDE WORLD PHOTOS

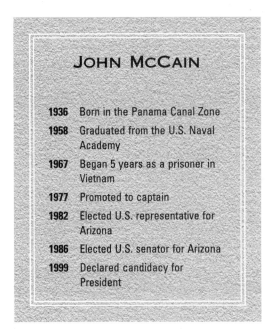

JOHN MCCAIN

1936 Born in the Panama Canal Zone

1958 Graduated from the U.S. Naval Academy

1967 Began 5 years as a prisoner in Vietnam

1977 Promoted to captain

1982 Elected U.S. representative for Arizona

1986 Elected U.S. senator for Arizona

1999 Declared candidacy for President

tional War College in Washington, D.C., in 1973 and 1974, but missed flying. After going back into a plane as a training squadron commander, he was promoted to captain in 1977.

In 1977 the navy named him its liaison to the U.S. Senate, marking the beginning of his political aspirations. He retired from the navy in 1981 and moved to Phoenix to work for his wife's father, a beer distributor. In 1982, despite his newcomer status in the state, he ran for the House of Representatives from Arizona's First Congressional District—a Republican-dominated area taking up much of Phoenix—and won. Unopposed in the 1984 primary, he was re-elected by a large majority over his Democratic contender. His conservative voting record followed the party line rather faithfully during the Reagan years. He supported prayer in public schools, the Gramm-Rudman deficit reduction bill, the use of lie-detector tests in certain forms of employment, and the reintroduction of certain handgun sales. He voted against the EQUAL RIGHTS AMENDMENT for women and extra money for the Clean Air Act. Understandably hawkish in his views on the military, he opposed the 1983 nuclear freeze resolution and supported more funding for MX missile development and other programs.

However, McCain showed in many ways that he was not afraid to voice his own opinion. He approved of sanctions in the apartheid-era South Africa, voting to override President Reagan's veto, and also spoke out against a maneuver to cut millions from a program providing food to the poverty-stricken in order to give raises to administrators. He also stood against direct U.S. intervention in Central America.

In 1986, McCain ran unopposed in the primary for the U.S. Senate seat vacated when Arizona's political icon BARRY GOLDWATER retired. He won the general election and was appointed to the Armed Services Committee and its subcommittees on readiness, personnel, and seapower; the Indian Affairs Committee; and the Senate Commerce, Science, and Transportation Committee. Of course, he has also lobbied for the rights of veterans and pushed to normalize relations with Vietnam, a goal he realized on July 11, 1995. His early record was punctuated by the passage of the line-item veto, a power given to the president to erase certain elements of a bill, usually inserted by congresspersons trying to add special interest or narrow constituent issues on to a larger, unrelated bill (called "pork barrel" politics). Though the federal courts eventually struck down the law in 1997, McCain became known as the champion fighting against pork, even hiring a staff member to sit in the Senate and spot any instances of such dealings at all hours.

McCain also rankled fellow Republicans when he took up the issue of campaign finance reform. Wanting to make sweeping changes to the way fund raising is handled, he joined forces with Democrat Russell Feingold around 1995. They sought to hammer out a bill to limit private donations to public office, as well as to even out the balance between lushly funded incumbents and their opponents. The unpopular measure was not taken seriously at first. "We were like the guys who introduced the metric system," McCain told Michael Lewis in the *New York Times* Magazine. Though Democrats have come out heavily in support of the idea, Lewis observed, "Their enthusiasm derives from their certainty that Republicans will find a way to kill it." The bill's most lofty intention was to close the loophole that allows parties to accept general donations then re-route them to specific candidates; these funds are called "soft money." The House of Representatives passed a version of the bill in August of 1998, but the Senate blocked it.

The lowest point in McCain's career was in 1989. He was counted as one of the notorious "Keating Five," along with Senators John Glenn, Donald Riegle, Dennis DeConcini, and Alan Cranston. They were implicated in a scandal to protect Charles Keating, the owner of Lincoln Savings and Loan. Keating gave generously to the senators and in return expected them to shelter him from federal bank regulators after his dealings ruined his financial institution and cost taxpayers more than $3 billion to bail out. The Senate Ethics Committee investigated and found that although McCain exercised "poor judgment," according to Lewis, he was not guilty of any wrongdoing. The affair hurt his reputation in the short term, but not fatally, and he was re-elected in 1992. McCain's later efforts, in addition to campaign reform, included an attention-getting $516 billion proposed bill that made tobacco companies more vulnerable to lawsuits filed by smokers and their families. He further proposed to sharply increase taxes on the substance. It made headlines for much of the first half of 1998, until it was voted down, basically due to its emphasis on raising taxes to those who buy tobacco products. In addition, McCain was also involved in a telecommunications reform measure, pushing to install Internet connections in schools, cut satellite and cable television costs, and introduce local telephone competition.

McCain married his first wife, Carol, in 1965 and adopted her two sons, Doug and Andrew. They also had a daughter together, Sidney Ann. After McCain's much-publicized affair with another woman, they divorced in 1980, and he married Cindy Hensley. They have four children, Meghan, Jack, Jimmy, and Bridget. McCain lives about two hours outside of Phoenix, Arizona.

McCARTHY, EUGENE J.

Obituary notice

Born on March 29, 1916, in Watkins, Minnesota; died Nov 24, 1997, in Washington, D.C. Eugene Joseph McCarthy had a long and influential career in American politics. As a member of the U.S. House of Representatives he stood up to the Communist-hunting Senator Joseph McCarthy. In the late 1950s he chaired the Senate Special Committee on Unemployment, part of an effort to investigate the causes of and solutions to unemployment. He also opposed incumbent President Lyndon Johnson for the Democratic presidential nomination in 1967 in an effort to force debate on Vietnam. Since leaving politics, McCarthy enjoyed a second career as a prolific writer.

McDONALD, GABRIELLE KIRK

Gabrielle Kirk was born on April 12, 1942, in St. Paul, Minnesota. As a young child she moved with her mother and brother to Man-

hattan and then to Teaneck, New Jersey. Mc-Donald was a child of divorced parents, and her mother, her grandparents, and her aunt Beverly Kirk Gayton were her guiding forces during her childhood.

McDonald studied at Boston University for three semesters before transferring to Hunter College in New York but never did receive an undergraduate degree. However, she went on to graduate cum laude and first in her class at Howard University Law School in 1966.

Since she was a teenager, McDonald wanted to be a civil rights lawyer. After graduating from Howard, she accepted a position as staff attorney with the NAACP Legal Defense and Educational Fund Inc. in New York. For three years McDonald canvassed Alabama, Mississippi, and Georgia to assist local residents and lawyers with issues involving school desegregation, equal employment, housing, and voting rights. Moreover, she worked on some of the first plaintiff employment discrimination cases based on Title VII of the Civil Rights Act of 1964.

In 1969 she joined her then-husband Mark McDonald, himself a lawyer who cooperated on NAACP cases, in solo practice in Houston. The Civil Rights Act of 1964 paved the way for lawsuits based on racial discrimination, and together the McDonalds built a reputation for pursuing plaintiff discrimination cases against labor unions and major corporations with significant operations in Texas, including Union Carbide Corporation, Monsanto Company, and Diamond Shamrock, Inc. McDonald's largest success came in 1976 when they negotiated a settlement with the Lone Star Steel Company on behalf of 400 black workers for $1.2 million in back wages. McDonald was one of the few African American lawyers to appear regularly in federal courts in Texas in the early 1970s.

In 1978, when a federal judgeship position opened, Texas Senator Lloyd Bentsen nominated her for the bench. In 1979 Jimmy Carter appointed McDonald as a federal district judge in Houston, only the third African American woman to be appointed to the federal bench. While on the bench, McDonald ruled on a wide variety of cases. For instance, she upheld as constitutional key sections of a Houston ordinance regulating the location of topless bars, finding that the ordinance did not interfere with the right of free speech.

In 1988 McDonald resigned from the bench. She opened the Austin office of Matthews and Branscomb and for the next two years handled

Gabrielle Kirk McDonald
FRED ERNST/ARCHIVE PHOTOS, INC.

Eugene McCarthy
THE LIBRARY OF CONGRESS

management-side employment discrimination defense work. She stayed with the firm for two years but did not enjoy the administrative aspects of running of her own practice.

In 1991 she left Matthews and Branscomb and joined the small Austin firm of Walker, Bright & Whittenton as of counsel. In 1970 she had taught an administrative law course at Texas Southern University Law School, and concurrent with joining the practice she resumed her teaching responsibilities, this time at St. Mary's University School of Law in San Antonio. In 1993 the dean at St. Mary's offered her a one-year teaching post to begin that fall. She accepted the position, but just before the semester began she was asked to consider a judgeship on the International Criminal Tribunal for the former Yugoslavia. After several days of persuasive conversations, though, she agreed to stand as the U.S. candidate for the position.

During the selection process, the United Nations general assembly considered twenty-two candidates for eleven positions. McDonald's broad experience as a civil rights lawyer, judge, and academic, as well as effective lobbying on her behalf by the U.S. State Department, made her a favorite, and she received the highest number of votes. She would be the sole American on the court and one of only two women. McDonald then spent September and October of

1993 drafting a proposed set of rules of procedure and evidence for the tribunal—all while still teaching full-time at St. Mary's. She was sworn into the tribunal in November and began to create a procedural code.

McDonald first served as presiding judge in the tribunal's Trial Chamber II. The tribunal has no autonomous police powers. Rather, the mission of the tribunal itself is to seek justice for the horrors of ethnic and religious persecution inflicted primarily in Bosnia and Croatia. The judges hear evidence, question witnesses, make rulings, and render the verdict and sentence. In the role of presiding judge, she not only conducted evidence and deferral hearings in a number of cases, but she also heard the historic case of one of Bosnia's most notorious criminals, Dusan Tadic, in the first war crimes trial since Nuremberg. On May 20, 1997, McDonald was re-elected for a second term on the tribunal and on November 19, 1997, was nominated and endorsed by the judges on the court as the president and presiding judge for the next two years. She thus heads the appeals chamber, the tribunal's highest judicial body. In essence, she is a world spokesperson for curbing human rights abuses.

CROSS REFERENCES
United Nations

MILITARY LAW

The body of laws, rules, and regulations developed to meet the needs of the military. It encompasses service in the military, the constitutional rights of service members, the military criminal justice system, and the INTERNATIONAL LAW of armed conflict.

Court-Martial in Ski Gondola Incident

An accident in Italy involving U.S. military personnel spawned a trial that attracted international interest. The accident occurred on February 3, 1998, when a Marine crew flew an U.S. military jet over a ski resort in the Italian Alps at such a low altitude that the plane's wing and tail severed the cables of a ski lift gondola, causing all twenty skier-passengers to plunge to their deaths. Captains Richard Ashby and Joseph Schweitzer, respective pilot and flight officer of the EA–6B Prowler electronic warfare jet, were both charged with twenty counts of INVOLUNTARY MANSLAUGHTER, CONSPIRACY, and OBSTRUCTION OF JUSTICE for having removed and destroyed an in-flight video film ostensibly showing the plane's maneuvers up until the time of the disaster. The officers were also charged with several lesser offenses, including conduct unbecoming an officer, dereliction of duty, and destruction of property. Charges were dropped against the remaining two crew members, also Marine captains.

On the day in question, Ashby and Schweitzer, along with the two other officers, were flying the Prowler on a routine training mission from the nearby NATO air base in Aviano, Italy. This was supposed to be their last such mission before returning to North Carolina following a six-month Bosnian tour. Undisputed facts showed that as the Prowler swooped down over a ski resort near Cavalese under a clear sky severed two ski lift cables suspended at 360 feet, causing the yellow gondola to plunge to the ground below, killing all aboard.

Under provisions of the Uniform Code of Military Justice (UCMJ), the men formally appeared before the military equivalent of a grand jury and were subsequently court-martialed. (NATO provisions denied Italy any jurisdiction over the accused men and allowed them to be tried in the United States.) They were free to retain their own private-sector counsel or choose military lawyers. Although the jury in a formal COURT-MARTIAL is comprised of military officers/peers, the conduct of the trial parallels that of a civilian-sector trial, in that elements of an offense or defense must be similarly proved, and evidentiary rules are also similar. Thus, as in private-sector criminal cases, the officers could be found guilty of the lesser crime of negligent homicide if the jury was not convinced that all elements of involuntary manslaughter had been proven. However, military juries require only a two-thirds vote to convict an accused.

The trial did not commence until the following February 1999, in Camp Lejeune, North Carolina. Ashby was tried first. The prosecution team, headed by Lieutenant Colonel Carol K. Joyce, ultimately alleged that on February 3, 1998, pilot Ashby breached rules and regulations regarding altitude and speed, which proximately caused the resulting tragedy. Characterizing Ashby as either "overconfident...or just plain cocky" in her opening statement, Joyce told the eight-member jury that another crew member would testify that Ashby "barrel-rolled" the jet prior to its hitting the cables. The prosecution's ploy was to piece together the evidence so as to create an overall picture of Ashby engaging in conduct akin to reckless joyriding ("flat-hatting") and wanton and wilful risk-taking. This could

support a finding of culpable negligence, a necessary element for involuntary manslaughter.

The prosecution went on to produce evidence showing that the cable was located at 360 feet, that the jet was required to fly no lower than 2000 feet in northern Italy (1000 feet otherwise), that the jet actually flew as low as 300 feet, and that the jet was traveling at a speed as great as 550 knots. However, prosecution was unable to proffer strong evidence that Ashby had been told of speed and altitude restrictions for that flight.

The defense countered that, although Ashby admitted flying the jet below 1000 feet, he had no knowledge of the 2000-foot minimum in northern Italy, a change which had become effective the previous year. Even more damaging to the prosecution was evidence showing that the outdated military maps provided to Ashby and his crew did not show the ski cable, notwithstanding that the cable had been there for more than thirty years. Moreover, the plane's radar altimeter, set to emit a warning buzzer if altitude fell below 800 feet, apparently did not work. Still, defense counsel presented testimony that flying low and fast was essential training for Prowler pilots. Cumulatively, defense evidence tended to show that the men were poorly trained and equipped, lacked crucial information for their flights, and that they may have been optically confused about their true altitude. Defense further argued that the men were set up as "scapegoats" for deficiencies higher up in the Marine Corps chain of command.

Captian Richard Ashby was found not guilty in severing the cables of a ski lift gondola with his jet.

MARY ANN CHASTAIN/AP/WIDE WORLD PHOTOS

After three weeks of proofs and seven hours of deliberation, the military jury acquitted Ashby of all charges on March 4, 1999. The outraged Italian government verbally protested that the Marines were protecting their own, and families of the victims were stunned by the verdict. Following this acquittal, manslaughter and homicide charges were dropped against Schweitzer, and the court-martial proceeded to the next phase, trying both men on charges of obstruction of justice and conspiracy.

On the day prior to the beginning of his court martial, Schweitzer pleaded guilty to both counts in a PLEA-BARGAIN agreement which assured him of a meted sentence of something less than prison. Under UMCJ rules, Schweitzer elected to have a military jury rather than judge sentence him, and evidence was taken. During these sentencing deliberations, Schweitzer testified that after they had safely returned to Aviano, Ashby removed the videotape from the cockpit and replaced it with blank film. Schweitzer further testified that he and Ashby had discussed the incident and the pending investigations, and Ashby gave the tape to Schweitzer after he agreed to destroy it. Schweitzer stated that he threw the tape into a bonfire because he feared that some of the maneuvers caught on film might have been misconstrued by Italians as reckless flying, and he feared that his smiling face, also part of the videotape, might be juxtaposed by the Italian press with film footage of the tragic wreck.

Following this testimony, Schweitzer's attorneys petitioned for his IMMUNITY if called to testify in Ashby's trial on the same charges. Fearing that any reversal of his plea-bargained conviction could expose him to full prosecution, defense counsel argued that his being called to testify in Ashby's case would cause him to incriminate himself. Prosecutors countered that Schweitzer had already waived his FIFTH AMENDMENT rights by pleading guilty, and that further, the plea bargain did not include any immunity provision. Ultimately, the judge gave prosecutors the option of granting immunity to Schweitzer in return for his testimony at Ashby's trial. He also ruled that Schweitzer could invoke his Fifth Amendment self-incrimination rights at any time.

In the middle of the prosecution's opening arguments at Ashby's trial for obstruction of justice, the defense requested a MISTRIAL, based on the prosecution's comments to the jury that Ashby had failed to tell authorities about the tape and had remained silent before an Italian magistrate. The defense charged that such statements to the jury were intended to imply that Ashby's silence was also an obstruction of justice and tantamount to an admission of guilt. The judge agreed, reminding counsel that it was improper to comment on an accused's exercise of constitutional rights. But the judge denied a mistrial, finding the requested remedy was not warranted, as the error could be cured with a simple jury instruction to disregard the prosecution's improper statement.

Ashby's failure to tell authorities about the tape, as well as his act of removing the tape and replacing it with blank tape, ultimately went against him. This evidence was coupled with the testimony of an assistant fire chief at the Aviano NATO base, who told the court-martial that Ashby twice tried to gain access to the jet's cockpit after the crash, claiming he needed to get a map and some other equipment. Added to this was Schweitzer's testimony about his discussions with Ashby which resulted in Ashby giving him the videotape to destroy. Finally, prosecution called one of the other two crewman on board the jet that day, who testified that Ashby and Schweitzer had told him they had switched tapes, and that he had advised them to destroy it.

On May 7, 1999, Ashby was convicted of obstruction of justice and conspiring to obstruct justice. The following Monday, May 10, 1999, he was sentenced to six months in prison and dismissal from the service.

In related matters, Italy's public and private outrage over the manslaughter acquittal raised new concerns that Americans might be banned from NATO air bases in Italy, a very strategically-desirable location. Also, under a 1951 NATO treaty provision, families of the gondola victims were allowed to file wrongful-death cases in Italy, but not the United States. The U.S. government previously had set aside $20 million for property damage in the incident, and in May 1999 Congress prepared to consider a $40 million appropriation to settle damage claims with victims' families.

Clinton v. Goldsmith

The Supreme Court resolved a major jurisdictional question involving the military courts in *Clinton v. Goldsmith*, __U.S.__, 119 S. Ct. 1538, __ L. Ed. 2d __ (1999). The Court ruled that the Court of Appeals for the Armed Forces (CAAF), the military's highest court, did not have the authority to issue an INJUNCTION preventing the U.S. Air Force from dropping a convicted officer from its rolls. The decision made clear that the president has the power to fire military personnel for the same offenses that resulted in their courts-martial and convictions.

James T. Goldsmith, a major in the U.S. Air Force, was ordered by his superior to inform his sexual partners that he was HIV-positive and to use condoms or other measures to prevent their infection. Goldsmith violated this order twice, by having unprotected sex once with a fellow officer and once with a civilian. He did not inform them of his HIV-positive status. Goldsmith was convicted by general COURT-MARTIAL in 1994 of willful disobedience of an order from a superior officer and two other related charges. The Court sentenced him to six years imprisonment and forfeiture of his salary each month. Nevertheless, he remained a member of the Air Force. The Air Force Court of Criminal Appeals affirmed Goldsmith's conviction and he declined to appeal to the CAAF, making his conviction final.

In 1996, Congress passed legislation that expanded the president's authority over the military. The president was empowered to drop from the rolls of the armed forces any officer who had been sentenced by a court-martial to more than six months' confinement and who had served at least six months. When a service member is dropped from the rolls, the member loses, among other things, military pay and health insurance coverage. The Air Force used this new power by notifying Goldsmith that it would act to drop him from the rolls.

Goldsmith challenged this proposed action by petitioning the Air Force Court of Criminal Appeals for an injunction to prevent from being dropped from the rolls. When the court ruled it had no jurisdiction to act, Goldsmith appealed to the CAAF. He argued that the proposed action was unconstitutional, violating both the EX POST FACTO Clause of the Constitution (Art. I, § cl. 3) and the DOUBLE JEOPARDY Clause of the FIFTH AMENDMENT. Goldsmith argued that the 1996 statute was enacted after his conviction, thus making it a prohibited ex post facto law. He also argued that dropping him from the Air Force rolls inflicted additional punishment based on the same conduct underlying his conviction. In his view, this constituted double jeopardy. The CAAF, on a 3–2 vote, agreed with Goldsmith. The court used the All Writs Act, 28 U.S.C.A. § 1651(a), for authority to issue an injunction preventing the president and other executive branch agencies from dropping Goldsmith from the Air Force's rolls. 48 M.J. 84 (1997).

The Supreme Court unanimously overturned the CAAF's decision. Justice DAVID H. SOUTER, writing for the Court, ruled that the CAAF did not have jurisdiction under the All Writs Act to issue the injunction. He noted that when Congress established the CAAF, it limited its jurisdiction to the review of sentences imposed by courts-martial and appellate decisions by the Court of Criminal Appeals. The CAAF had asserted that Congress intended it to have "broad responsibility with respect to administration of military justice."

Justice Souter rejected this interpretation. The All Writs Act gives all courts established by Congress the authority to issue WRITS "necessary or appropriate in aid of their respective jurisdictions and agreeable to the usages and principles of law." Although military courts could issue writs—injunctions and other types of court orders—they could do so only "in aid of" their existing statutory jurisdiction. The CAAF's "independent statutory jurisdiction" was "narrowly circumscribed," dealing with the criminal appeals. The Air Force's action to drop Goldsmith was an executive action, not a finding or a sentence that was imposed in a court-martial proceeding. The dropping of Goldsmith was beyond the jurisdiction of the CAAF, and therefore, was beyond the jurisdiction of the All Writs Act.

Goldsmith argued that the CAAF did have jurisdiction under the All Writs Act because "it protected and effectuated" the sentence handed down by the court-martial. Goldsmith noted that the court-martial could have dismissed him from the service rather than imposing imprisonment. Justice Souter rejected this argument for two reasons. First, Goldsmith's court-martial sentence had not been changed. Rather, another military agency had taken "independent action." Second, the CAAF has not been given authority to oversee "all matters arguably related to military justice." Moreover, the CAAF has no continuing jurisdiction to oversee the administration of sentences it "one time had the power to review."

Justice Souter ruled that even if the CAAF had jurisdiction in Goldsmith's situation, the All Writs Act would still be "out of bounds" as either necessary or appropriate because Goldsmith had alternative remedies. Courts can only use the residual authority of the act if there is not legal remedy available. In this case, Goldsmith had administrative and judicial remedies available.

Goldsmith had responded to the notice he was being dropped from the rolls by filing a claim with the secretary of the Air Force. If the secretary did drop Goldsmith, he would be entitled to appeal to the Air Force Board of Correction for Military Records (BCMR). The BCMR is a civilian body within the military service that has broad authority to review a service member's discharge or dismissal, other than those based on the sentence of a general court-martial. The board also has the power to correct an error or "remove an injustice" in a military record.

Justice Souter pointed out that if Goldsmith was not satisfied with the BCMR's decision, he could file an action in federal district court. BCMR decisions can be set aside if they are "arbitrary, capricious, or not based on substantial evidence." Therefore, Goldsmith had alternative remedies that prevented the application of the All Writs Act.

CROSS REFERENCES
Double Jeopardy; Ex Post Facto; Health Care Law; International Law; Negligence; Obstruction of Justice

MILLS, CHERYL

Cheryl Mills, a deputy White House counsel, gained fame for her representation of President BILL CLINTON during the January 1999 Senate IMPEACHMENT trial. Thirty-four-year-old Mills is one of the youngest attorneys in the White House.

Mills was born into an itinerant military family. Despite her nomadic childhood, Mills found that other black military families constituted a "community where support, grounding and nurturing" were emphasized. Mills went to

Cheryl Mills
JAMAL WILSON/ARCHIVE PHOTOS

CHERYL MILLS

1965	Born
1987	Graduated from University of Virginia
1990	Graduated from Stanford law school
1990	Hired by Hogan & Hartson law firm
1997	Appointed deputy counsel to the president

college at the University of Virginia. She graduated with honors in 1987, and then attended Stanford Law School, where she graduated in 1990. Mills then joined Hogan and Hartson, a prominent law firm in Washington D.C. In 1992 she left the firm to join the presidential campaign of Arkansas Governor William Jefferson Clinton.

When President Clinton was elected, Mills was tapped to join the office of White House counsel. Mills quickly gained a reputation for her candor and her willingness to challenge conventional thinking, especially on racial issues. Mills reportedly was asked by White House political operatives to tone down her inflammatory rhetoric during the Senate impeachment hearings.

Mills' presentation came on the heels of four-and-a-half days of speeches by congressmen. Following these pedantic and dry speeches, the appearance of the young—and some would say beautiful—Mills attracted attention. Mills proceeded to deliver a point-by-point rebuttal to charges that President Clinton had obstructed justice. The White House reportedly sent out notice that no phone calls would be received while Mills made her arguments.

Mills argued the facts, and she also addressed the wisdom of impeaching a president for the charges that had been levied. The Republican prosecutors from the House of Representatives had argued that a failure to impeach President Clinton for obstructing the civil rights case of Paula Jones could cause harm to the cause of CIVIL RIGHTS, and Mills mocked the claim. "I'm not worried about civil rights because this President's record on civil rights, on women's rights, on all of our rights is unimpeachable." Mills noted that minor transgressions by presidents were not uncommon and rarely caused sufficient harm to warrant impeachment. "We've had imperfect leaders in the past," Mills said, referring to THOMAS JEFFERSON, FREDERICK DOUGLASS, ABRAHAM LINCOLN, JOHN F. KENNEDY, and MARTIN LUTHER KING, JR., "and we'll have imperfect leaders in the future, but their imperfections did not roll back nor did they stop the march for civil rights." The Republican managers from the House argued that President Clinton should not receive special treatment under the law, but Mills argued that the circumstances of Clinton's transgressions trivialized the concept of equal treatment under the law. "Many have struggled and died for the right to be equal before the law, without regard to race, gender, privilege or station in life. If applied equally, the rule of law exonerates Bill Clinton."

Senators, Republican and Democrat alike, were impressed with Mills' presentation. "She put it in terms I could understand," said Robert Bennett (R-UT). Robert Torricelli (D-NJ) proclaimed that the day was a turning point. "When the final chapter is written," said Torricelli, "this day will be remembered as the beginning of the end." Byron Dorgan (D-ND) said that "[t]he presentation of Ms. Mills was one of the most remarkable that I've heard in the Senate or in my political career." Dawn Chirwa, another black female lawyer who Mills recruited to work at the White House, applauded her colleague. "She seizes the opportunity to reach out to those who may not have the networks and access white males have," Chirwa told *Essence* magazine.

Mills has had previous encounters with Congress. In 1997, she was accused by Representative David McIntosh (R-IN) of failing to turn over documents that had been SUBPOE-NAED by a congressional committee investigating the alleged misuse of a taxpayer-funded White House database system. According to McIntosh, the database, containing a list of the Clintons' friends and financial supporters, was improperly shared with the Democratic National Committee. In September 1998, McIntosh asked the U.S. DEPARTMENT OF JUSTICE to open up a criminal investigation of Mills, but the matter was dismissed as political.

Mills is a successful young black woman who has not forgotten her roots. When she was preparing herself for her Senate-floor defense of President Clinton, she calmed herself by repeating the words of educator Ann Julie Cooper, a black woman: "When and where I enter...the whole race enters with me."

CROSS REFERENCES
Appendix: Articles of Impeachment; Impeachment

MURDER

The unlawful killing of another human being without justification or excuse.

Charles Ng

In early 1999, one of the costliest criminal trials in California history ended with the conviction of serial killer Charles Ng. The case, with its shocking elements of RAPE, torture, and the murder of twelve people, dated to the mid-

1980s. Since that time, Ng, a thirty-eight-year old Hong Kong native and former U.S. Marine, had won numerous delays in bringing his case to trial. Fourteen years and over $10 million in state expenses later, the case concluded with a jury in Orange County, California, finding Ng guilty of multiple murders in a trial that featured intimate testimony by his parents as well as videotaped footage of him and his accomplice tormenting their victims.

Ng was a fugitive with a checkered past. He came to the United States in the 1970s on a student visa, but failed college. He falsified papers and joined the U.S. Marines in 1979, but in 1981 was arrested and charged with stealing weapons from a military base. He escaped, was recaptured, and in 1984 was once again on the lam with his friend, Leonard Lake, a Vietnam veteran and survivalist. Lake was impressed by John Fowles' best-selling 1963 novel, *The Collector*, in which a butterfly collector kidnaps a young woman named Miranda, but not as much by the novel's literary graces as by the fiendish possibility that it suggested: Lake wanted to imprison women as sex slaves in his cabin in the foothills of the Sierra Nevada. He called the idea his own "Miranda Project."

Over a nine-month period in 1984 and 1985, the two men captured, raped, and tortured three women. Ultimately these victims were slain, their corpses burned, and buried in shallow graves. Mingled with their remains lie those of the men and babies whom Ng and Lake also killed—the men for their money, vehicles, and identification; the babies simply to get rid of them. In all, twelve people died.

The crime spree ended on June 2, 1985, when police arrested Lake during a shoplifting attempt and discovered that he was driving a missing man's car and in possession of another man's driver's license. Under questioning, Lake confessed to his crimes and implicated Ng in the murders, but then committed suicide by swallowing a hidden cyanide capsule. On the next day, officers discovered the horrors at the cabin. Ng, meanwhile, had escaped and fled to Canada. His flight was brief; one month later, he was arrested in Calgary for robbing a department store, and later convicted and sent to prison.

From his Canadian jail cell, Ng successfully fought attempts by U.S. authorities to extradite him to California to stand trial. And even after his EXTRADITION in 1991, the case did not come to trial for another eight years. Numerous motions, extensive pre-trial media coverage that forced a change of trial VENUE, and problems

Charles Ng was convicted in one of the most expensive trials in California history.

FBI/AP/WIDE WORLD PHOTOS

with Ng's legal representation kept him out of court for an unusually long time. Ng sought additional delays in 1998. California Superior Court Judge John J. Ryan refused to postpone the trial any further and assigned public defenders to represent him.

At trial in October 1998, Ng maintained his innocence of murder. Although he admitted to engaging in rape and torture, he blamed all of the killings on Lake. His defense team characterized the prosecution's evidence as circumstantial: Ng had long absences at work at the time of certain killings, he was in possession of some of the victims' belongings, and he had drawn cartoons depicting the rapes and corpse burnings. Other evidence was even less tangible, such as the statements by his former Canadian prison cell mates that he admitted to participating in the killings. Even the physical evidence yielded few clues, as police had chiefly managed to unearth thousands of charred bone fragments.

But in a highly compelling move, prosecutors played graphic video tapes that Lake and Ng had made of their crimes. The tapes depicted the men tormenting women victims, whom they had shackled. Lake could be heard telling the women that they would become sex slaves or be killed. Hoping to counter this damaging evidence, Ng surprised the court at the close of the three-month long trial by taking the stand himself, professing his innocence and accusing Lake of influencing him. The gambit failed. On Feb-

ruary 24, 1999, jurors convicted him of eleven murders, although they were deadlocked on, and dropped, a twelfth murder count.

At a dramatic sentencing hearing in early May 1999, Ng's parents traveled from Hong Kong to plead for clemency. In tearful testimony, they admitted to abusing him as a child with harsh punishments. Also seeking to have Ng's life spared, the defense team focused on his damaged psyche, portraying him as a weak personality who had fallen under the control of strong personalities all his life. Unmoved by these arguments, the jury recommended the death sentence.

Samuel Bowers Convicted

After thirty-two years, a former imperial wizard of the White Knights of the KU KLUX KLAN was convicted of the racially-motivated ARSON and MURDER of a civil rights activist. Samuel Holloway Bowers was tried four times for the murder of Vernon Dahmer before the August 21, 1998, VERDICT, but each time the case ended in a HUNG JURY. Bowers once bragged that a jury would never convict a white man for killing a black man in Mississippi. Of the four previous trials for Bowers, at least two were before all-white juries. Klan experts estimate that Bowers orchestrated over three hundred bombings, assaults and arsons, in addition to nine murders. Bowers served six years in prison on conspiracy charges for the deaths of three civil rights workers—Andrew Goodman, Michael Schwerner and James Chaney—whose murders were depicted in the movie *Mississippi Burning.*

Bowers ordered the murder due to his outrage at Dahmer's efforts to assist blacks in voting. Dahmer was a NAACP branch president and store owner. The day before his murder, Dahmer announced his plan to allow blacks to pay the $2 poll tax at his grocery store. The poll tax was designed to limit the number of black voters. In 1960, less than 100 of the 8,000 voting-age blacks in Forrest County were registered to vote. Anyone who paid the poll tax was granted suffrage.

On January 10, 1966, while Dahmer's family slept, two cars of Klansmen firebombed the Dahmer home in Hattiesburg, Mississippi. Dahmer stalled for time and fended off the attackers as his family escaped. Although successful in warding off the Klansmen, Dahmer's lungs were seared by the flames. He died several hours later.

Fourteen men were initially indicted for the attack on the Dahmer home. Thirteen were eventually brought to trial, eight on charges of arson and murder. Four of the Klansmen were convicted. Three were sentenced to life terms, but each served less than ten years. Another was sentenced to ten years for arson but served two. One Klansman, Billy Roy Pitts, entered a guilty plea. He served four years on federal CONSPIRACY charges but was never sent back to Mississippi to serve his life term for murder. Billy Roy Pitts testified against the others in separate trials. He would later testify against Samuel Bowers.

Mike Moore, Mississippi's attorney general, reopened the investigation in 1991 when new evidence was discovered. Bob Stringer, Bowers' errand boy at the time of the murder, provided the state with crucial evidence. Stringer overheard Bowers give the "Code 4" for Dahmer, which in Klansmen terminology means murder. As imperial wizard, Bowers was the only person with authority to order murder. Newly discovered evidence also indicated jury tampering in Bowers' earlier trials. On June 17, 1968, one month after Bowers' arson trial, an informant provided critical information. Notes from the FBI files reveal that the informant admitted that Klansmen had contacted three jurors. According to the notes, "one juror said no, the other said...doubtful and the third said yes to fixing the trial." Once the case was reopened, the state released 132,000 pages of documents from the Mississippi Sovereignty Commission. The commission was created by the state legislature in 1956 to prevent civil rights activists from changing the segregationist way of life in Mississippi. When the commission closed in 1973, it contained files on 87,000 people. Vernon Dahmer's name appears more than eighty times in those documents. The commission has been dubbed the largest state-level spying effort in U.S. history.

In May 1998, three men were indicted for Dahmer's 1966 murder—Samuel Bowers, Charles Noble, and Deavours Nix. Charles Noble claimed that he was denied a speedy trial. Nonetheless, a circuit court refused to dismiss the murder and arson charges. Noble had a short trial—beginning June 14, 1999, and ending June 15, 1999,— when Judge Richard McKenzie (the same judge who presided over Bowers' trial) declared a MISTRIAL. At Noble's trial, Billy Roy Pitts testified that he was being watched by a Klansman and felt threatened by testifying. Noble's attorney argued that his client's rights had been trampled upon. Apparently agreeing that the information was highly prejudicial, the

In 1998 Sam Bowers was brought to trial for the 1966 murder of Vernon Dahmer.

ROGELIO SOLIS/AP/WIDE WORLD PHOTOS

judge declared a mistrial. Deavours Nix testified in Bowers' trial but died before standing his own trial.

Judge Richard McKenzie presided over Bower's murder trial that began August 17, 1998. Dahmer's widow, Ellie, was the first person to testify at the trial. She recounted the events of that 1966 night in vivid detail. The youngest two Dahmer children also recounted the tragedy. They were ten and twelve at the time of the incident. Former Klansman, Billy Roy Pitts, also testified against Bowers in exchange for IMMUNITY from prosecution. Several other Klansmen testified. Some attempted to discredit Bowers while others testified that he was a good citizen and neighbor. All of the Klansmen testified to Bowers' unfettered authority as the leader of Mississippi's Klan. It took less than three hours for the jury—comprised of five blacks, six whites, and one Asian—to convict Bowers. The murder conviction carries an automatic life imprisonment in the state of Mississippi.

There was no immediate indication whether Bowers, seventy-three years old at time of conviction, would appeal. If Bowers does appeal, his possible defenses are "double jeopardy" and "speedy trial." Double jeopardy is the protection against a second prosecution for the same offense after acquittal or conviction. It is guaranteed by the FIFTH AMENDMENT of the CONSTITUTION and is enforceable against states through the FOURTEENTH AMEND-

MENT. A speedy trial is the right of an accused granted under the Sixth Amendment. The trial must be had as quickly as possible to avoid prejudicial delays. When a significant period of time elapses, several factors must be considered in determining whether the delay was unreasonable. However, the final determination depends on the circumstances in each case.

CROSS REFERENCES
Civil Rights; Extradition

NATIVE AMERICAN RIGHTS

Hunting and Fishing Rights

In a case watched closely by Native American tribes and state officials across the nation, the Supreme Court ended a decade-old legal battle over Indian fishing and hunting rights. On March 24, 1999, the Court ruled in favor of the Chippewa Indians' right to fish and hunt in northern Minnesota without state regulation (*Minnesota v. Mille Lacs Band of Chippewa Indians*, __ U.S. __, 119 S. Ct.1187, 143 L. Ed. 2d 270 [1999]). By a 5–4 vote, the Court upheld an appeals court decision finding that the tribe's rights under an 1837 treaty were still valid. The ruling marked a final victory for the tribe in its long fight to assert its treaty rights and defend its cultural traditions. Brought by the band in 1990, the lawsuit proved highly controversial in Minnesota, which regarded it as a threat to the $54 million in tourism revenue generated by the Mille Lacs Lake resort industry. But like two lower courts before it, the Supreme Court rejected the state's arguments that the 162-year old treaty had been invalidated by presidential order, later treaties, and even by Minnesota's gaining of statehood.

In 1990, angered by state regulations, the Mille Lacs Band of Chippewa Indians asserted that the regulations did not affect its right to hunt and fish outside reservation lands. State regulations applied only to non-Indians, said the band, pointing to an 1837 treaty between several Chippewa bands and the federal government. Under the TREATY, the bands ceded control of millions of acres of land in present-day Wisconsin and Minnesota, and in return, the federal government guaranteed them hunting, fishing, and gathering rights on that land. The Mille Lacs Band claimed that the state violated the treaty by holding it to the same regulatory limits as non-Indian hunters and fishermen. Moreover, the band said that the survival of its cultural history—in which hunting and fishing assume significant roles—was threatened by the state regulations. Joined by several other Chippewa bands and the U.S. Department of Justice, the band filed suit for enforcement of the treaty.

In Minnesota, the claims ignited controversy. State lawmakers, counties, and landowners in northern Minnesota viewed the lawsuit as a direct threat to the state's lucrative tourism industry. The area encompassed by the Indians' treaty claims included Mille Lacs, a lake dotted with popular resorts and renowned for its walleye fishing that generates approximately $54 million annually in tourism revenue. Fishing became the focus of these opponents' protests. They objected to the Indians' desire to fish out of season, exceed limits imposed on sports fishermen, and to fish using traditional spears. Arguing that the Chippewa would deplete fishing stocks on the lake, opponents, led by the former Minnesota Vikings football team coach Bud Grant, pressured state lawmakers to reject a proposed settlement in 1993 between tribal officials and the state Department of Natural Resources. As a result, the suit proceeded to trial.

In 1994, the U.S. district court ruled that state had to respect the tribe's rights under the treaty. Three years later, the court approved a plan for several bands to hunt and fish according to their methods and during their own seasons. Although the state appealed, the Eighth

Circuit Court of Appeals upheld the decision in *Minnesota v. Mille Lacs Band of Chippewa Indians* (124 F. 3d 904 [8th 1997]).

On appeal to the Supreme Court, the state and nine counties and landowners maintained that the treaty was no longer in force for three reasons. First, they contended that an 1850 Executive Order by President Zachary Taylor, which required the removal of Chippewa from the land, had invalidated the treaty. Second, they argued that in another treaty with the United States, signed in 1855, the Chippewa had given up all their legal interests in the land. And third, the plaintiffs said that the treaty was extinguished when Minnesota was admitted into the Union as a state in 1858.

By a 5–4 vote, the Supreme Court rejected each of these arguments. Justice SANDRA DAY O'CONNOR's majority opinion ranged widely over U.S.-Indian history and gave a highly nuanced reading to the treaties and orders in question. President Taylor's Executive Order of 1850, she wrote, was ineffective to terminate the treaty rights because it lacked the key requirements of such presidential orders: it did not stem either from an act of Congress or from the Constitution itself. Indeed, some provisions in the order revoked Indian hunting and fishing rights. But these provisions could not stand on their own because the primary purpose of the order had been to remove the Chippewa from the land, O'Connor explained.

The Court also ruled that the 1855 treaty did not relinquish the hunting and fishing rights secured in the earlier treaty. The 1855 treaty contained a sentence relinquishing the tribes' "right, title and interest" to all of the land, but the sentence did not mention the 1837 treaty. That was significant, O'Connor observed, given the "sophistication" of federal treaty drafters in other historical instances where they wished to take away Indian treaty rights. The historical record, purpose, and context of the 1855 negotiations all pointed to one conclusion, she wrote: the federal government wanted to transfer Chippewa land to the United States, not terminate the earlier treaty rights.

Finally, the Court swept aside the statehood argument. The majority held that treaty rights could be revoked only when Congress clearly intended to do so. Admission of a state to the Union by itself "is insufficient to extinguish Indian treaty rights to hunt, fish and gather on land within state boundaries," O'Connor wrote. Thus Minnesota's acquisition of statehood some twenty-one years later had no bearing on the 1837 treaty.

Three justices joined a dissent written by Chief Justice WILLIAM H. REHNQUIST. The lengthy dissent, which covered the same historical ground as the majority opinion, contested the majority's reasoning in several respects, from its view of the validity of the Executive Order to the role of Minnesota's statehood, which Chief Justice Rehnquist particularly emphasized as having extinguished the treaty.

Predictably, the decision drew a mixed reaction in Minnesota. The Mille Lacs Band of Chippewa hailed the Court's respect for treaty rights. "Today the United States has kept a promise," Marge Anderson, the band's chief executive, said at a press conference, "a promise that our rights are not just words on paper." Representatives of the attorney general's office, land owners and counties expressed their sharp disappointment. Governor Jesse Ventura, an outspoken opponent of the tribe's position, nonetheless urged Minnesotans to abide by the Court's decision.

Tribal Sovereignty and Taxes

In two separate decisions, the U.S. Supreme Court dealt setbacks to tax claims by Native Americans. Both cases dealt with novel situations involving reservations, where there is no taxation by the federal government and little by state or local governments. In each case, Native American parties said that taxation would violate their national sovereignty, but a unanimous Supreme Court disagreed on both occasions. In *Arizona Department of Revenue v. Blaze Construction Co., Inc.*, ___U.S.___, 119 S. Ct. 957, 143 L. Ed. 2d. 27 (1999), the Court held that states may tax businesses that build federally-owned roads on reservations. And in *Cass County, Minnesota v. Leech Lake Band of Chippewa Indians*, ___U.S.___, 118 S. Ct. 1904, 141 L. Ed. 2d. 90 (1998), the Court ruled on the tax status of reservation land that had been taken from Indian use in the late nineteenth century, sold to non-Indians, and repurchased by a Native American tribe in the twentieth century. Rejecting a claim of tax exempt status by the tribe, the Court held that state and local governments may tax this reacquired reservation land.

Both cases shared in common their focus on the unique legal status of Native American reservations. Since the early nineteenth century, the U.S. Supreme Court has explicitly recognized the sovereignty of Indian tribes—their right to self-governance as distinct nations.

States are largely prevented from applying their laws and regulations to reservations. However, Native American sovereignty is far from total. As a consequence of the long, complex and controversial relationship between Washington and the tribes, Congress retains far-reaching power over tribal affairs. Moreover, as part of its so-called trust relationship with Native Americans, the federal government is the legal titleholder to much Indian land.

Taxation is also a matter of sovereignty. The federal government does not tax reservations, and states are generally prevented from doing so, too, under what is known as Indian law pre-emption analysis. In 1980, the Supreme Court announced the modern formulation of this analysis in *White Mountain Apache Tribe v. Bracker*, 448 U.S. 136, 100 S.Ct. 2578, 65 L.Ed.2d. 665 (1980): state law is generally inapplicable to conduct on reservations that involves only Indians, as the state's regulatory interest is likely to be small and the federal interest in encouraging tribal self-government is at its strongest. But this exemption does not cover all cases. When the conduct of non-Indians on the reservation is at issue, the Court has shown greater openness to permitting state taxation—for example, allowing a state to tax cigarettes sold on a reservation to non-members of a tribe.

The first case involved the issue of taxing a federal contractor that worked on reservations. Between 1986–90, the Bureau of Indian Affairs (BIA) contracted with Blaze Construction Company, an Indian-owned contractor, for repairs and improvements to federal roads on six reservations within the state of Arizona. The projects were funded by the Federal Highway Administration. After conducting a tax audit, the Arizona Department of Revenue concluded in 1993 that Blaze Construction owed approximately $1.2 million in delinquent state taxes. In general, states can tax the earnings that private companies make from federal contracts, and as such, Arizona wanted to tax Blaze's federal earnings. Blaze Construction contended that it owed nothing to the state, arguing that Indian law exempted it from state taxation. In 1997, the Arizona Court of Appeals ruled for the company after weighing the respective state, federal and tribal interests according to Indian law pre-emption analysis (*Arizona Department of Revenue v. Blaze Construction Co.*, 947 P.2d 836 [Ariz.App. 1997]).

But in a unanimous verdict on March 2, 1999, the U.S. Supreme Court overturned that decision. Justice CLARENCE THOMAS' opinion cited *United States v. New Mexico*, 455 U.S. 720, 102 S. Ct. 1373, 71 L. Ed. 2d 580 (1982), which established as a "clear rule" that states have the right to tax federal contractors—and that only the federal government and its agencies were exempt from such taxation. The Court had concluded that the principles of that decision alone controlled the case.

Blaze's legal status as a business guided the Court's refusal to apply the preemption analysis to Indian law. Though the business is incorporated under the laws of the Blackfeet Tribe of Montana and owned by a member of that tribe, the work it performed did not occur on the Blackfeet Reservation. Hence, for purposes of the case, Blaze was regarded as a non-Indian contractor. For that reason, the Supreme Court refused to perform the complex balancing test undertaken by the appeals court. Such a test would "only cloud the clear rule established…in *New Mexico*, " wrote Justice Thomas. The state was free to tax non-Indian companies that took federal contracts to do work on reservations. One consequence of the ruling might be a large tax windfall for states: between fiscal 1998 and 2003, the federal government will spend approximately $1.6 billion nationwide for federal roads on reservations, much of which could be taxable under the decision.

In the second case, the Supreme Court took up the question of taxation on reacquired reservation land. In *Cass County, Minnesota v. Leech Lake Band of Chippewa Indians*, the Court considered whether cities and counties can tax parcels of reservation land that had been sold to non-Indians and later reacquired by the tribe. In a unanimous verdict on June 18, 1998, the Court announced ruled such parcel taxable.

The roots of the case stretched to the late nineteenth century, when the federal government pursued a radical new policy toward reservation land. Until this time, it had set aside reservation lands for exclusive use by Indian tribes under federal supervision or "protection." In legal terms, the government held the land in trust for the tribes—it held the legal title to the land, but had an obligation to see that the tribes benefitted from use of the land. Wishing to forcibly assimilate Native Americans into U.S. society as well as to allow non-Indians to buy reservation land, lawmakers allotted parcels of reservations to individual Indians and put much of the rest up for sale.

As part of this agenda, the federal government began carving up the reservation lands of the Leech Lake Band of Chippewa Indians in Minnesota in 1889. Some parcels were allotted to individual Indians, others were sold at public auction to non-Indians for farming and lumbering, and yet more parcels were sold to non-Indian settlers as homesteads. Nationally, this so-called allotment policy ended in the 1930s, when Congress realized its forty-year experiment had been a mistake. But by 1977, the band owned less than 5 percent of the original 600,000-acre reservation.

After the Leech Lake Band began purchasing back former reservation land from private owners, it came into conflict with Cass County. The county had been assessing taxes on the land's non-Indian owners, and it continued to assess these taxes on the tribe. Bringing suit against the county, the tribe contended that the land should not be taxable as the tribe's tax immunity had merely lay dormant during the period when the land was held by other owners, it argued, but was revived once it repurchased the land. The Eighth U.S. Circuit Court of Appeals issued a mixed decision: it ruled that Cass County could tax the land purchased from individual Indians, but could not tax the land bought from non-Indians.

Unanimously rejecting this mixed approach, the Supreme Court held that all the reacquired land was taxable. Justice Thomas's opinion noted the Court's traditional approach toward the issue: state and local governments may not tax reservation land except when Congress made its intent "unmistakably clear" to allow such taxation. In decisions in both 1902 and 1992, the Court twice concluded that Congress expressed this clear intent when it withdrew reservation lands from federal protection and allotted them to individual Indians, in *Goudy v. Meath*, 203 U.S. 146, 27 S. Ct. 48, 51 L. Ed.130 (1906) and *County of Yakima v. Confederated Tribes and Bands of Yakima Nation*, 502 U.S. 251, 112 S. Ct. 683, 116 L. Ed2d. 687 (1992), respectively. Yet the appeals court had mistakenly "attributed to Congress the odd intent that parcels conveyed to Indians are to assume taxable status," wrote Justice Thomas, "while parcels sold to the general public are to remain tax-exempt." This was clearly not so. The act of removing the lands from federal protection—regardless of who later owned them—showed that Congress had clearly intended to make the land subject to state and local taxation.

Ultimately, noted Justice Thomas, the land's reacquisition by the tribe had no bearing on its taxable status. Justice Thomas observed, however, that another recourse lay open to the plaintiffs. The Indian Reorganization Act (48 Stat. 984, 25 U.S.C. § 461 et seq.) explicitly allows tribes to petition the U.S. secretary of the interior to place reservation lands in federal trust and thus make them non-taxable. Mere repurchase did not automatically trigger such protection, a petition was necessary. The Leech Lake Band "apparently realizes this," Justice Thomas wrote, noting that the band successfully petitioned in 1995 to restore federal trust status to seven parcels of land.

CROSS REFERENCES
Executive Order; Fish and Fishing; Taxation; Treaty

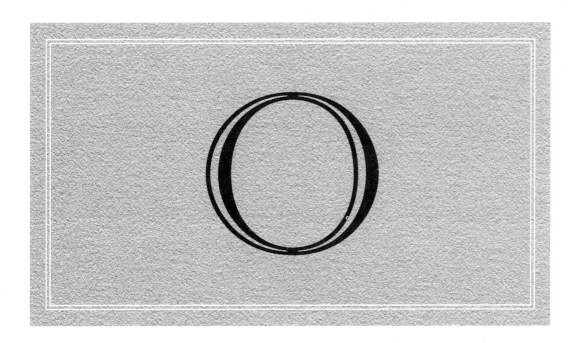

ORGAN DONATION LAW

Organ Procurement and Transplantation Network Final Rule

In 1984, Congress passed the National Organ Transplant Act (NOTA) (Pub. L. 98–507, Oct. 19, 1984, 98 Stat. 2339 [Title 42, §273 et seq.]). This law established the nationwide Organ Procurement and Transplantation Network (OPTN) to help in distributing donated organs to those in need of transplants. Five years later, the Department of HEALTH AND HUMAN SERVICES (HHS) set up the United Network for Organ Sharing (UNOS) to oversee the routine operation of NOTA. UNOS established a procedure in which the United States was divided into sixty-three local areas. When a donated organ became available, UNOS would look first for a patient in the donor's area, then in the surrounding region, and finally would make the organ available anywhere in the country.

By the late 1990s, the UNOS procedure had caused a raging controversy. As of 1996, an estimated 55,000 patients were on the national waiting list for transplants of various types (heart, lung, liver, kidney, and pancreas), but only 20,000 transplants were annually performed because of a shortage of donated organs. As a result, 4,000 people died that year while awaiting a transplant. There was a huge difference in the waiting time for a transplant in different parts of the country. For instance, a patient awaiting a kidney transplant could expect to be on a waiting list only 107 days in Oregon, but as long as 1,680 days in New York. A severely ill patient in one state could die while waiting, even though a patient in another state could receive a transplant before he or she was even sick enough to be hospitalized.

Because of this disparity, in early 1998 HHS released a proposed new regulation for public comment, which would require organ distributions to be based on medical need, not just geography. HHS Secretary Donna Shalala announced the proposed regulation, the Organ Procurement and Transplantation Network Final Rule (Fed. Reg. 16295, April 2, 1998 [to be codified at 42 CFR Part 121]). As she was quoted in the *HHS News*, "Patients who need an organ transplant should not have to gamble that an organ will become available in their local area, nor should they have to travel to transplant centers far from home simply to improve their chances of getting an organ." The regulation would require development of new criteria that allocated organs to the most seriously ill patients first. It also would require medically objective criteria that all transplant centers would use in placing patients on waiting lists and in prioritizing patients on the list, rather than allowing each center to set up its own standards.

Almost immediately after the proposed regulation was announced, opponents began to protest its adoption. Hearings were quickly scheduled jointly before the U.S. Senate Labor and Human Resources Committee and the House Commerce Committee (June 18, 1998), and before the U.S. Senate Committee on Appropriations' Subcommittee on Labor, HHS, and Education (September 10, 1998). Many small transplant centers, which often cared for less seriously ill patients, were concerned that they would be driven out of business by the larger centers that catered to sicker patients.

UNOS itself questioned the rule, arguing that people would not get transplants unless they were very ill, and so were less likely to survive the surgery. HHS insisted that it was not requiring a single national list, but instead was leaving the development of the new system largely in the hands of the transplant network. However, as the controversy mounted HHS was forced by a last-minute piece of legislation (Public Law 105–174) to extend the public comment period until August 31, 1998, and to postpone the adoption of the regulation until October 1, 1998.

Four states (Louisiana, Oklahoma, South Carolina, and Wisconsin) quickly passed laws that required keeping a donated organ within the state if a patient there could benefit from a transplant. (By early 1999, Florida had joined these states.) Nancy Kay, executive director of the South Carolina Organ Procurement Agency, illustrated the reasoning behind these laws: "Our work is based on the giving of South Carolinians…We like to take care of our neighbors here." On October 1, 1998, HHS was forced to again postpone the regulation when a federal district court judge in Louisiana, Judge Ralph Tyson, temporarily blocked the HHS regulation. Louisiana Attorney General Richard Ieyoub had argued that a federal regulation could not preempt Louisiana's new law that gave Louisiana residents a "first right of refusal" for organs donated within the state.

Meanwhile, Representative Bob Livingston (R-LA) attached a rider to the HHS federal appropriation bill, blocking implementation of the regulation for a year and the Senate version of the bill adopted this rider as well. The Health and Human Services portion of the Omnibus Consolidated and Emergency Supplemental Appropriations Act of 1999 (P.L. 105–277, §213(a)) provided that the Organ Procurement and Transplantation Network Final Rule could not become effective before October 21, 1999. This act also required a study of current organ allocation policies and the new rule, to be conducted by the Institute of Medicine within the National Academy of Sciences. The study was ordered to address issues such as access to transplants and cost of transplantation services.

As the Organ Procurement and Transplantation Network Final Rule remained in limbo, several states threatened to sue the federal government if the rule went into effect in October 1999. The Louisiana lawsuit had been placed on hold after the one-year delay of the rule, but could be revived. In South Carolina, Attorney General Charlie Condon vowed to do "everything possible" to keep his state's current procedure in place. As he told *Transplant Weekly*, the federal government already got tax money from South Carolina and, "Now they want our body parts." The three other states with similar laws (Florida, Oklahoma, and Wisconsin) could conceivably join South Carolina and Louisiana in court. The U.S. Congress also could step in once again, and permanently block the adoption of the regulation.

CROSS REFERENCES
Administrative Law; Federal Preemption; Health Care Law

ORIGINAL JURISDICTION

The authority of a tribunal to entertain a lawsuit, try it, and set forth a JUDGMENT on the law and facts.

New York and New Jersey Fight For Ellis Island

In May 1998 the Supreme Court handed down a decision in the case of *New Jersey v. New York*, 523 U.S. 767, 118 S. Ct. 1726, 140 L. Ed. 2d 993 (1998), which was brought before the Court nearly five years ago. In 1993, the state of New Jersey asked the Supreme Court to recognize it as having dominant control over Ellis Island. The island is located in Upper New York Bay just offshore from Jersey City, New Jersey, but a mile from the shoreline of Manhattan. New Jersey and New York have disputed their borders for nearly four centuries.

The U.S. JUSTICE DEPARTMENT encouraged the Supreme Court in 1993 not to hear the case because the outcome would have little practical impact. The federal government controls the land and the National Park Service oversees its preservation. The state of New York donated the island to the federal government for use as a port of entry in 1880. From 1892–1954 Ellis Island operated as the nation's primary arrival point for more than twelve million immigrants. Nearly one-third of all Americans today can trace one of their ancestors back to the island.

When the federal government opened the immigration facilities on Ellis Island in January 1892 the island only consisted of 3 acres. Between 1891 and 1933 landfill operations were conducted that added another 24.5 acres to the island. In 1904 New Jersey signed over the rights to 38 acres of submerged land and landfill around Ellis Island. That acreage was the land primarily in question. For more than a century New York has claimed sovereign authority

The Supreme Court divided Ellis Island between New York and New Jersey following the terms of an 1834 compact.

MARTY LEDERHANDLER/AP/WIDE WORLD PHOTOS

over the entire island and New Jersey did little to challenge that authority.

Groups such as the National Trust for Historic Preservation were concerned about the outcome of the case because ownership of Ellis Island will ultimately influence redevelopment activities. The main concerns are accessibility to the public, preservation, and possible redevelopment of more than two dozen abandoned buildings on the south side of the island.

The National Park Service began restoration efforts on Ellis Island in 1976. The main immigration building in the center of the island was restored in 1990 and turned into a museum which is visited by nearly two million tourists a year. Hospitals and other buildings constructed on the landfill have yet to be restored. Plans have been proposed to restore some of these structures and there is some potential for future development on the island as well. However, none of these plans have enough funds to start in the near future.

Ellis Island is an icon of U.S. history and has been listed as one of the nations' most endangered landmarks by the National Trust for Historic Preservation. The island was the site of the founding of the U.S. Health Service and played a major role in the tale of U.S. immigration. It is often referred to as the "historic gateway to America." Thus, New York and New Jersey both stand to gain from being able to claim authority over the island.

New Jersey v. New York was not heard in any lower court so the Supreme Court was placed in the somewhat unusual position of having to gather evidence. This is known as "original jurisdiction." The Supreme Court appointed Paul R. Verkuil as a special master to gather evidence relating to the case. Verkuil, a former law professor and Dean of the Benjamin Cardozo Law School at Yeshiva University, accepted historical records during the summer of 1996 which he used to make a recommendation to the Supreme Court.

Evidence submitted to Verkuil included documents dating back to pre-Revolution days. New Jersey presented tax rolls and maps noting Ellis Island, New Jersey. However, steamship packets regularly showed the destination as Ellis Island, New York. Moreover, births, deaths and marriages on the island were all recorded in New York.

In addition to the evidence presented, Verkuil relied on an 1834 compact signed between New Jersey and New York. This compact determined the boundary between the two states. It also specified that New York had the rights to the above water portion of Ellis Island and New Jersey had the rights to all of the surrounding waters and submerged land. New York argued that potential growth of the island was foreseeable through the use of landfill. New Jersey argued that the compact did not provide for the island multiplying in size several times.

After reviewing all the evidence, Verkuil made a recommendation to the Supreme Court on April 1, 1997. He suggested that the 1834 compact should serve as the basis for the Court's decision with a few minor adjustments. Verkuil recommended that the original three acres remain under the control of New York plus an additional two acres which would provide New York with access to the center of the island as well as prevent historic structures from being split between the two states. Verkuil advised that the remaining 22.5 acres be turned over to New Jersey.

The Supreme Court justices resolved that the Court had no authority to change the boundary set forth in the 1834 compact. Furthermore, any change in the boundary would have to be negotiated between the two states. Following that determination, the Supreme Court began to hear arguments on January 12, 1998.

The Supreme Court handed down its decision in May 1998 with a 6–3 vote. Following the terms of the 1834 compact, Ellis Island was divided between New York and New Jersey. New York received control of the original three acres that sit in the center of the island today. This includes the museum building. New Jersey received the other 24.5 acres and the buildings on it. However, some of the buildings, which straddle the boundary line, have been divided. This could prove to be problematic if those buildings are restored in a manner that ends up generating revenue. The Supreme Court also determined that tax revenues from the existing concessions, all on New York's portion of the island, must be split.

Both New Jersey and New York will have a say in preservation of this historic site as well as restoration of abandoned buildings on the island. They will also share any future revenue generated. Despite the decision, little will change and the federal government will retain control of Ellis Island.

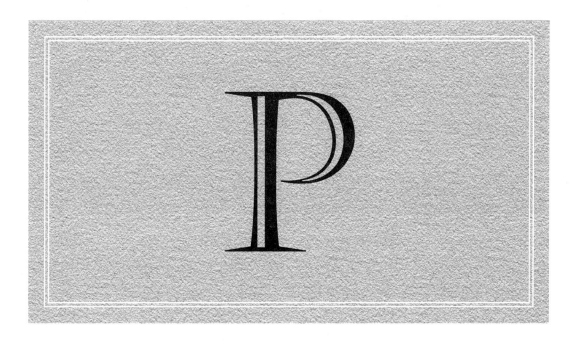

PEREMPTORY CHALLENGE

The right to challenge a juror without assigning, or being required to assign, a reason for the challenge.

Striking Prospective Jurors For Religious Affiliation Violates Equal Protection Clause

In April 1999, the Supreme Court of Connecticut ruled that the Equal Protection Clause prohibits states from striking prospective jurors from jury service based on their religious affiliation. The court also ruled, however, that states may strike prospective jurors whose religious beliefs would prevent them from performing their duties as jurors. *State v. Hodge*, 726 A. 2d 531 (Conn. 1999).

Hodge extends prior U.S. Supreme Court decisions concerning the use of peremptory challenges during jury selection. Historically, attorneys were allowed to use peremptory challenges to strike prospective jurors for any reason or no reason at all. However, the Equal Protection Clause of the FOURTEENTH AMENDMENT of the U.S. Constitution says no state may "deny to any person within its jurisdiction the equal protection of the laws." Ratified in the aftermath of the Civil War, it has been America's constitutional device for eradicating discrimination. Applying the equal protection clause, the U.S. Supreme Court previously ruled that state prosecutors may not use peremptory challenges to strike prospective jurors because of their race or gender. *Batson v. Kentucky*, 476 U.S. 79, 106 S. Ct. 1712, 90 L. Ed. 2d 69 (1986) (race); *J.E.B. v. Alabama*, 511 U.S. 127, 114 S. Ct. 1419, 128 L. Ed. 2d 89 (1994) (gender).

In *Batson*, the prosecutor struck four African American jurors to seat an all white jury in a burglary trial against an African American defendant. The trial court overruled defendant's objection, and did not require the prosecutor to give a race-neutral explanation for his conduct. The Supreme Court reversed the defendant's conviction, explaining that racially motivated peremptory challenges harm the defendant, the prospective juror, and society: "Discrimination within the judicial system is most pernicious because it is 'a stimulant to that race prejudice which is an impediment to securing to [black citizens] that equal justice which the law aims to secure to all others.'"

In *J.E.B.*, the Supreme Court extended that reasoning to gender motivated peremptory challenges: "Intentional discrimination on the basis of gender by state actors violates the Equal Protection Clause, particularly where, as here, the discrimination serves to ratify and perpetuate invidious, archaic, and overbroad stereotypes about the relative abilities of men and women." Writing for the majority, Justice HARRY A. BLACKMUN explained that eliminating such discrimination was essential to providing the equal protection of the laws guaranteed by the Fourteenth Amendment.

> Equal opportunity to participate in the fair administration of justice is fundamental to our democratic system. It not only furthers the goals of the jury system. It reaffirms the promise of equality under the law—that all citizens, regardless of race, ethnicity, or gender, have the chance to take part directly in our democracy....When

persons are excluded from participation in our democratic processes solely because of race or gender, this promise of equality dims, and the integrity of our judicial system is jeopardized.

The same year it decided *J.E.B.*, the U.S. Supreme Court declined to review a case in which the prosecutor excluded a Jehovah's Witness from the jury because in her experience Jehovah's Witnesses were "reluctant to exercise authority over their fellow human beings." *Davis v. Minnesota*, 511 U.S. 1115 (1994) (Justice Clarence Thomas, dissenting). While three state appellate courts have ruled that excluding a prospective juror because of his religious affiliation does not violate the equal protection clause, and eight have ruled that it violates their state constitutions, no state appellate court ruled that the practice violates the equal protection clause until *Hodge*.

Hodge began on May 4, 1992, when defendant Dennis Hodge, an African American, murdered two Jewish insurance adjusters for paying less than Hodge expected for his mother's kitchen fire losses. During jury selection at Hodge's murder trial, the attorneys learned that prospective juror M.F. was an African American man of the Islamic faith. Upon further questioning, M.F. said that if the law the judge instructed him to apply conflicted with Islamic law, he would consult his religious advisor about what to do. The prosecutor used a peremptory challenge to strike M.F. from the jury, which ultimately convicted Hodge of murder, manslaughter, and carrying a pistol without a permit.

On appeal, Hodge argued that the prosecutor excluded M.F. from the jury because of his religious affiliation in violation of the equal protection clause. The Supreme Court of Connecticut analyzed the decisions in *Batson* and *J.E.B.* and decided there was no principled reason not apply them to cases involving a prospective juror's religious affiliation. Writing for the majority, Justice Richard Palmer said:

> Although one's religious *beliefs* may render a prospective juror unsuitable for service in a particular case, one's religious *affiliation*, like one's race or gender, bears no relation to that person's ability to serve as a juror....Moreover, to allow the exclusion of an otherwise qualified venireperson simply on account of that person's religious affiliation would amount to permitting jury selection procedures that promote

'state-sponsored group stereotypes rooted in, and reflective of, historical prejudice.'

Applying this principle, however, the Supreme Court of Connecticut decided that the prosecutor properly question M.F about, and struck him because of, his religious beliefs, not his religious affiliation. The prosecutor asked about M.F.'s Islamic sect to determine if it was affiliated with Louis Farrakhan, who embraces anti-Semitism, or Elijah Muhammed, whom the prosecutor considered to be an extremist. The prosecutor also asked M.F. whether he shared the Nation of Islam's general belief that women are inferior to men, which may have affected M.F.'s ability to serve on a jury with women. Finally, when M.F. indicated he would consult his spiritual advisor if the law applicable to the case conflicted with Islamic law, the prosecutor had justifiable concerns about whether M.F. would follow the law as instructed by the judge, including the instruction not to discuss the case with anyone until its conclusion.

In a concurring opinion joined by Chief Justice Robert J. Callahan, Justice Francis M. McDonald disagreed with extending *Batson* and *J.E.B.* to cases where a juror is struck because of his religious affiliation. He suggested that discrimination on the basis of religious affiliation is less likely to occur because race and gender are obvious, while religion is not. He also suggested that such discrimination is less harmful because religion is a matter of choice, while race and gender are not. Justice McDonald also warned that proving that a peremptory strike is based on religious affiliation will require religious questioning that is impermissible under the First Amendment of the U.S. Constitution, which protects freedom of religion. (Such questioning was not prohibited in *Hodge* because the judge revealed the issue by asking M.F. why he was wearing a hat, which happened to be an Islamic custom. Questioning then was proper because it related to M.F.'s religious beliefs, not his religious affiliation, as they might affect his performance as a juror.)

Justice McDonald's greatest concern, however, was that the majority's decision would eliminate peremptory challenges entirely:

> The expansion of *Batson* to religious beliefs or affiliation would lead to its application to national origin, political affiliation and philosophy as well as other things that may distinguish potential jurors....Trial lawyers have found these challenges necessary for

centuries because peremptory challenges allow them to act on their intuition that a potential juror would not be sympathetic to their case….I see no reason to take from Connecticut trial lawyers that time-honored privilege.

Hodge only applies in the state of Connecticut. In *Davis*, which the U.S. Supreme Court declined to review in 1994, the Supreme Court of Minnesota held that striking jurors based on religious affiliation does not violate the U.S. Constitution. *Davis v. Minnesota*, 504 N.W.2d 767 (Minn. 1993).

CROSS REFERENCES
Equal Protection; Jury

PLEA BARGAINING

The process whereby a criminal defendant and PROSECUTOR reach a mutually satisfactory disposition of a criminal case, subject to court approval.

Immunity for Testimony Challenged

Since the colonial period, prosecutors in the United States have offered bargains to certain criminal suspects and defendants in exchange for their help in catching other criminals. In such "leniency" deals, a prosecutor may promise to lower or drop criminal charges against a person if the person testifies against, or gives information on, other criminal suspects or defendants. Although the deals seem like bribes, the practice was commonplace and tacitly sanctioned by the courts.

That year, Sonya E. Singleton faced FELONY charges of conspiring to distribute drugs and money laundering. The source of the charges was Napoleon Douglas, a Wichita, Kansas, drug dealer, who was facing prosecution for his own felonies. Douglas agreed with prosecutors to testify truthfully against Singleton in exchange for a reduction in the charges against him.

Singleton denied being part of a drug CONSPIRACY and money laundering ring. Before trial, Singleton moved the court to keep Douglas' TESTIMONY out of the trial, but the court refused. John V. Wachtel, Singleton's attorney, argued inventively that the agreement between the prosecution and Douglas was BRIBERY, but the trial court judge rejected the argument. Douglas testified against Singleton, and Singleton was convicted of money laundering and conspiring to distribute cocaine.

Singleton appealed to the U.S. Court of Appeals for the Tenth Circuit. Wachtel decided to argue again that the prosecutor's agreement with Douglas constituted bribery. Under 18 U.S.C.A. § 201(c)(2), "[w]hoever…directly or indirectly, gives, offers, or promises anything of value to any person, for or because of the testimony under oath or affirmation given or to be given by such person as a witness upon a trial…before any court…shall be fined under this title or imprisoned for not more than two years, or both." Douglas was offered something of value—his freedom—in exchange for his testimony. According to Singleton, the so-called "anti-gratuity" statute applied to prosecutors and clearly forbid such a transaction.

In a surprise ruling, a three-judge panel of the Tenth Circuit appeals court agreed with Singleton. "The judicial process is tainted and justice is cheapened when factual testimony is purchased, whether with leniency or money," wrote the panel. The U.S. Department of Justice called the decision "absurd" and noted that it made "a criminal out of nearly every Federal prosecutor." The ruling sent the entire federal criminal justice system into a state of panic and adversely affected important, ongoing prosecutions.

In the days following the decision, defense attorneys in criminal courts across the country filed motions asking for a ruling on the propriety of allowing witnesses who have plea bargained with the prosecution to testify for the prosecution. Lawyers for Singleton applauded the verdict.

Just days after the panel's decision, the full compliment of twelve judges convened and nullified the ruling. The Tenth Circuit Court of Appeals then decided to review the case EN BANC (with all the judges present). The United States argued that including prosecutors in the definition of "whoever" in the anti-gratuity statute would criminalize an ingrained practice of the criminal justice system. The United States further insisted that Congress could not have intended to include prosecutors' leniency deals in the statute because such a reading would make prosecutions much more difficult. Singleton countered that the anti-gratuity statute was enacted precisely to deter the kinds of deals struck by the prosecutors with Douglas. In January 1999, the appeals court announced that it had reversed the panel's decision by a vote of 9–3. *United States v. Singleton*, 165 F. 3d 1297 (10th Cir. 1999).

According to the majority of the appeals court, Congress did not intend to include prosecutors in the anti-gratuity statute. Singleton's argument, the majority felt, ignored "a fundamental fact: the capacity in which the government's lawyer appears in the courts." The prosecutors for the federal government are agents of the government and the "alter ego" of the government, and the argument that "whoever" could include the government in its sovereign prosecutorial capacity was "patently absurd." On a more fundamental level, the plain meaning of the word "whoever" contemplated persons, not inanimate objects like a government. Finally, the majority decided that Singleton's reading would rob the government of a "recognized or established prerogative, title, or interest." The majority agreed with Singleton that the government is not above the law, but it believed that the anti-gratuity statute did "not exist for the government."

Two judges wrote concurring opinions. Judge Lucero, joined by Judge Henry, believed that the majority's construction of the anti-gratuity statute "would permit the conclusion that consistent with the provisions of § 201, a United States Attorney may pay a prosecution witness for false testimony." There were plenty of statutes that guided prosecutors in fashioning plea bargains with criminal defendants, and those statutes were exceptions to the anti-gratuity statute. Judge Lucero insisted that the anti-gratuity statute applies to a United States attorney if the attorney "does not act within the provisions of those specific statutes that conflict with § 201."

Three judges dissented. Writing for the dissent, Judge Kelly dismissed concerns that a holding for Singleton would be "the death knell for the criminal justice system as we know it." Such claims were made when the U.S. Supreme Court created the *Miranda* rights and other rules that regulated law enforcement, but the country experienced no apocalypse because of them. Furthermore, the dissent opined, "whoever" included inanimate entities as well as actual persons.

Finally, the dissent noted that the practice of giving freedom for testimony was not as long-standing and traditional as the United States claimed. "Constitutional law manifests another vital legal tradition which the government's position undercuts—the policy of ensuring a level playing field between the government and defendant in a criminal case."

CROSS REFERENCES
Bribery; Criminal Law; Immunity

POLICE BRUTALITY
The use of excessive force or deliberately brutal treatment by police officers.

Shooting of Amadou Diallo
Concern over police brutality in New York City escalated with the February 1999 shooting death of Guinean immigrant Amadou Diallo in front of his Bronx apartment house. The killing set off a firestorm of protest and ultimately resulted in the indictment on murder charges of the four officers involved. Critics alleged that the police had acted without restraint and with insufficient concern for the life of a poor black peddler. In response, police officials defended their methods as necessary and proper in the fight against crime. New York's mayor, RUDOLPH GIULIANI, became the focus of a series of massive CIVIL RIGHTS rallies designed to highlight the issue of police brutality. The case attracted national attention and prompted the federal government to launch an inquiry into New York City's police practices.

Police brutality had long been a cause of concern in New York City, particularly within the black and Latino communities. The choking death of Anthony Baez in a confrontation with a police officer in 1994 prompted a lawsuit that cost the city $3 million—the largest settlement ever recovered in a police brutality case. The brutal torture of Haitian immigrant Abner Louima in a Brooklyn station house in 1997 caused many to question that tactics and methods being employed by New York's police in the fight against crime.

The issue of excessive police force came to the fore again on the night of February 4, 1999. Amadou Diallo, a street peddler who had emigrated to New York from Guinea in 1997, was returning to his Bronx apartment building when an unmarked car pulled up and four plainclothes policemen got out. The men attempted to question Diallo who, they later said, declined to respond to their inquiries and reached for something in his back pocket. The four officers immediately began firing their weapons. In all, forty-one shots were discharged. Nineteen of those bullets hit their target. Diallo collapsed against the door of his building and died instantly. He was unarmed and had no criminal record.

The four officers involved—Sean Carroll, Edward McMellon, Richard Murphy, and Kenneth Boss—were all members of New York City's "'Aggressive Street Crimes Unit,'" a force of some four hundred plainclothes police offi-

Demonstrators protest against the death of Amadou Diallo, who was unarmed when the New York police killed him.

MARK LENNIHAN/AP/WIDE WORLD PHOTOS

cers charged with patrolling high-crime areas. At the time of Diallo's killing, the men were investigating a series of RAPES and robberies in the area. They believed the unarmed peddler resembled a suspect in the crime spree.

Within days of Diallo's killing, a number of official steps were taken. The four officers were immediately placed on administrative leave pending an inquiry into the circumstances of the shooting. On February 5, the U.S. attorney in Manhattan, Mary Jo White, announced that her office would work closely with the Bronx district attorney's office to investigate the case. The aggressive federal response, considered highly unusual by many legal experts, was seen as an effort to assuage public fears about police brutality. Mayor Giuliani said he welcomed federal involvement and appealed to city residents to remain calm until all the facts came to light.

These official actions did little to stem a rising tide of public outrage, however. Civil rights leaders and human rights organizations joined forces with Diallo's parents to call for an independent commission to investigate police brutality. Just three days after the killing, protestors staged a massive rally outside Diallo's building. In early March, Reverend Al Sharpton, moved the civil disobedience campaign outside police headquarters in downtown Manhattan. Crowds continued to grow throughout the month. In just over two weeks of daily protests, more than one thousand people were arrested. Celebrities like Susan Sarandon, Ossie Davis, and former New York Mayor David Dinkins soon joined the effort to draw attention to the cause. As the case against the officers moved to the indictment stage, the rallies migrated to the steps of the Bronx courthouse where the GRAND JURY was being empanelled. The climate of public discontent with police practices prompted U.S. Attorney Mary Jo White to broaden her federal inquiry to focus more closely on the "stop and frisk" tactics of the Street Crimes Unit.

In presenting his case to the grand jury, Bronx District Attorney Robert T. Johnson faced a difficult choice. He could seek indictment against the officers solely on the charges of second-degree murder—defined as the intentional killing of a person or a killing resulting from depraved indifference to life—or he could include a series of lesser charges—such as MANSLAUGHTER—that he could fall back on later if the murder charge proved untenable. In the end, Johnson opted to charge each of the officers with one count of second-degree murder "with intent to cause the death of a person" and one count of second-degree murder for "evincing a depraved indifference to human life." Each of these charges carried a maximum sentence of twenty-five years to life in prison. In so framing his case to the grand jury, Johnson gave it the simplest possible context and signaled his confidence that the evidence would support his argument. Each of the officers was also charged with a separate count of recklessly endangering bystanders.

On March 25, 1999, the grand jury completed its inquiry as a large crowd of protestors rallied outside the Bronx courthouse. The INDICTMENTS remained sealed for five days in accordance with New York State law. On March 31, the indictments were unsealed and the four officers were arraigned on charges of second-degree murder. They were accordingly suspended from the police force and had their weapons and badges taken away. In their first public statements since Diallo's death, each of the four defendants pleaded "not guilty" to the charges leveled against them.

As the case proceeded to the trial stage, the four defendants faced the difficult task of escaping conviction in a highly-charged political climate. The first of the murder charges leveled against them required proof that some or all of the officers intended to kill Diallo at the time of the shooting. Prosecutors did not have to show proof of pre-meditation. On the other charge, prosecutors could win conviction merely by proving that the officers "recklessly" caused Diallo's death, whether or not they intended to kill him. Defense lawyers for the four accused cops gave indications that they intended to persuade the court to acquit on the grounds that the officers simply made a mistake in the line of duty. Under New York State law, police officers may use deadly force only if they have a reasonable belief that their lives or the lives of other people are in danger. The officers' suspicion that Diallo was reaching for a weapon before they fired seemed likely to become a major point at issue in the trial.

Even if prosecutors failed to prove their murder case beyond a reasonable doubt, however, the defendants still faced an uncertain fate. Under New York State law, prosecutors could ask the judge in the case to allow the jury to consider lesser charges than second-degree murder. The officers, for example, might be found guilty of the next most serious charge, manslaughter, if the jury determined that they intended to cause Diallo serious injury when they killed him.

CROSS REFERENCES

Civil Rights; Due Process of Law; King, Rodney

PORNOGRAPHY

The representation in books, magazines, photographs, films, and other media of scenes of sexual behavior that are erotic or lewd and are designed to arouse sexual interest.

Clampdown in New York City

New York City is famous for offering a rich tapestry of life. Traditionally, New York City has been less concerned with promoting good manners and wholesome values than with promoting its myriad assortment of entertainment. This approach began to change in the 1990s with the 1992 election of RUDOLPH GIULIANI to the mayor's office. In 1995, Mayor Giuliani pushed through a strict city ZONING ordinance that was designed to rid Manhattan of sex shops and strip clubs. In 1998, Mayor Giuliani began to wage a "civility campaign" that stressed the enforcement of such crimes as jaywalking. Some in New York City have applauded Mayor Giuliani's efforts, but others compared the measures to authoritarianism.

The zoning ordinance, passed in 1995, forbids "adult establishments" from operating within five hundred feet of homes, houses of worship, schools, or other sex-oriented businesses. In effect, the ordinance forces sex-oriented businesses to move to outlying areas of town if they want to stay in business. City lawmakers have consistently contended that they do not want to suppress free expression, and that the purpose of the ordinance to reduce the crime, noise, traffic, and other unpleasantries that pervade neighborhoods that are dominated by adult-oriented businesses. The ordinance was challenged by the sex shop owners after it went into effect, but the city has won the court battles on the state and federal level. In March 1998, a federal appeals court affirmed a federal trial court's dismissal of the legal challenge. Judge Pierre N. Leval, writing for a three-judge panel, opined that the ordinance did not violate the FIRST AMENDMENT right to free speech because it did not "represent an attempt by the City of New York to disfavor the viewpoint of female eroticism." Nor did the ordinance violate the FOURTEENTH AMENDMENT's guarantee of EQUAL PROTECTION of the laws by prohibiting only women from baring their breasts. "Rightly or wrongly," Judge Leval explained, "our society continues to recognize a fundamental difference between the male and female breast." *Buzzetti v. City of New York*, 140 F. 3d 134 (2nd Cir. 1998).

In 1998, the sex-shop owners lost their bid to stop enforcement of the ordinance while it was being appealed to the U.S. Supreme Court. The city of New York began to enforce the ordinance in July 1998. In January 1999, the U.S. Supreme Court refused to hear the appeal of the sex-shop owners.

Mayor Giuliani hailed the Supreme Court's non-decision. The crackdown on the sex shops was, Giuliani told *CNN*, "one of the prime reasons for the revival of the city in the sense that the city is a more decent place and a nicer place for people to visit." Beth Haroules of the New York Civil Liberties Union, was less upbeat about the High Court's refusal to hear the case. Haroules argued that the operation of adult-oriented businesses, while distasteful to many persons, was protected by the First Amendment. "You may not like it, I may not like it," Haroules told *CNN*, "but it's protected."

Despite the passage of the anti-pornography zoning ordinance and its subsequent judicial approval, sex shops in New York City are finding ways to stay in business. A strip club called "Ten's" stayed open by allowing minors to enter, which set the club apart from the "adults-only" definition of banned businesses under the ordinance. Under the ordinance, an adult establishment is one that does not allow minors to enter. Another club, the VIP, tried the same thing, but lost its court battle. According to Judge Stephen G. Crane, the same judge who had let Ten's remain open, the VIP had not allowed minors to enter long enough to qualify as an exception to the ordinance. Stores that sell pornographic videos and other materials have stayed open by stocking enough non-pornographic material to take the stores out of the ordinance's reach.

In July 1998, the ordinance affected 146 of the 164 sex-oriented businesses then in existence in New York City. As of January 1999, New York City had succeeded in closing only 26 of the 61 sex shops that it had targeted. Eighteen other adult businesses had closed voluntarily. Herald Price Fahringer, an attorney for more than 100 adult businesses in New York City, told David Rohde of *New York Times* that the city "expected everyone to pack up and go out of business…[b]ut they're standing their ground, and they're succeeding."

The legislative assault on pornography had not been confined to New York City. In February 1999, the Richmond Virginia City Council passed an ordinance that made it illegal for persons to give a pornographic performance at a show where minors are present. The ordinance defines a pornographic performance as any performance containing an enactment of any sex act, a display of genitalia, or the display of an excretory function. On the federal level, Congress passed a law in 1998 called the Child Online Protection Act, which makes it a federal crime to possess computer images that look like children are engaged in sex. In March 1998, a federal district court ruled that the law was too vague and was therefore unconstitutional, but in January 1999, the U.S. Court of Appeals for the First Circuit reversed that decision and upheld the law. Supporters of the law praise it as bringing child pornography laws "into the computer age," while opponents focus on the murky definitions in the law that could ensnare an innocent computer user. Judge Hugh Brownes, writing for the appeals court, explained that it was up to a jury to decide, "based on the totality of the circumstances, whether a reasonable unsuspecting viewer would consider the depiction to be of an actual individual less than 18 engaged in sexual activity."

CROSS REFERENCES
First Amendment; Internet; Pornography

POWELL, LEWIS F., JR.

Obituary notice

Born on September 19, 1907, in Suffolk, Virginia; died August 25, 1998 in Richmond, Virginia. Powell was a corporate lawyer who became a U.S. Supreme Court justice. He became the intellectual leader of the Court's moderate center until his 1987 retirement. Powell's best known opinion was in *California Board of Regents v. Bakke* (1978), where he cast the deciding vote and wrote the authoritative individual opinion.

Lewis F. Powell, Jr.
ARCHIVE PHOTOS, INC.

PRIVACY

The constitutional law, the right of people to make personal decisions regarding intimate matters; under the COMMON law, the right of people to lead their lives in a manner that is reasonable secluded from public scrutiny, whether such scrutiny comes from a neighbor's prying eyes, an investigator's eavesdropping ears, or a news photographer's intrusive camera; and in statutory law, the right of people to be free from unwarranted drug testing and ELECTRONIC SURVEILLANCE.

Employees' Genes Tested Without Their Knowledge

Genetics is the study of genes, which are the physical properties that determine a person's biological makeup. Genes are usually found on chromosomes and in deoxyribonucleic acid DNA, and they can be studied by extracting a sample of blood, saliva, sweat, or tissue from a

DO DNA DATABASES
VIOLATE PRIVACY?

All fifty states and the federal government maintain DNA databases of certain convicted criminals. DNA, or deoxyribonucleic acid, is the chemical that reveals a persons genetic makeup. A database containing the DNA of convicted criminals helps law enforcement find and identify repeat criminal offenders. Prior to 1998, the federal DNA database and the state databases were not completely integrated, so sharing DNA information between the states was not an easy task.

In October 1998, the Federal Bureau of Investigation (FBI) began operating a nationwide DNA database called the National DNA Index System. The national database consists of the DNA databases from all fifty states and the FBI's own DNA database. The national database makes it possible for law enforcement officials in one state to compare DNA found at a crime scene with DNA samples that exist in the DNA databases of other states. When the national DNA database was installed, FBI director Louis Freeh predicted that it would "be of great value to city, county, state and federal law enforcement agencies if they work together to apprehend violent criminals."

The national DNA database in the United States is similar to the one that has been used in England since 1995. In Great Britain, the empire-wide DNA database includes DNA samples from crime scenes, from anyone convicted of a crime, and from persons who are suspects in unsolved cases. The Police Superintendents Association in England has even proposed obtaining DNA samples from every person in England. Personal privacy is a stronger political value in the United States than in England, so the plans for the national database in the United States do not involve such widespread DNA gathering.

One issue that has plagued the use of DNA databases is the question of who should be required to give a DNA sample. Dr. Eric Juengst, a bioethicist at Case Western Reserve University in Cleveland, told the *New York Times* that the national DNA database would be "suitable only for our most serious category of criminals." Juengst, a member of the FBI's DNA Advisory Board, also said that "as a society we have to learn how to control powerful tools...I don't see it as endless slippery slope." However, M. Dawn Herkenham, chief of the FBI's Forensic Science Systems Unit, believes that "the trend is that 10 years from now all felonies will be covered." Herkenham recommends that DNA samples be taken from persons who commit "violent felonies, burglaries, [and from] juveniles." Herkenham also recommends that persons on parole be retroactively required to give a DNA sample.

On the state level, the use of DNA databases varies from state to state. Almost all states require that persons convicted of serious sex offenses give a DNA sample upon their conviction.

IN FOCUS

person's body. Genetic testing and research began to increase in the 1980s after Congress passed laws giving universities and researchers the right to apply for patents on government-supported genetic testing and laws encouraging partnerships between government researchers and private companies. A 1980 U.S. Supreme Court decision allowing a patent on a bacterial life-form also opened the way for increased genetic research.

Genetic testing and research is helpful to humans in many ways. The information about human bodies that is gained through genetics helps researchers develop cures for diseases. Genetics also help doctors identify who is at risk for particular diseases, making it easier to anticipate and prevent disease and illness. This predictive aspect of genetics is, however, a double-edged sword. Genetic research and testing, when used as a method of predicting or determining a person's health, raises serious issues related to personal privacy.

Genetic research raises issues of privacy because of what it reveals about a person. Genetic testing and research can determine a person's susceptibility to certain diseases and, according to some researchers, genetic testing can also reveal information about a person's behavioral traits, a person's ethnic origin, and a person's sexual orientation. To many people, genetic testing also violates a person's privacy because it violates the integrity of a person's body. Genetic testing of a person can be done only by extracting matter from a person or collecting liquid or matter deposited by a person.

The privacy issues associated with genetics have led to various legal disputes. The lawsuits over genetic research and testing concern matters such as: the taking of the blood or tissue; the use of the blood or tissue; the distribution of the blood or tissue; the use of previously acquired samples of blood or tissue to conduct new tests; and whether a gene can receive patent protection. One of the more emotional issues associated with genetic testing is the testing of persons without their consent. In one recent case, *Norman-Bloodsaw v. Lawrence Berkeley Lab-*

However, the states differ on whether to mandate DNA profiling of all violent felons, persons paroled from jail, and juvenile offenders. In Louisiana, for example, every person who is arrested must submit a DNA sample to the state. In other states, such as Virginia, Wyoming, New Mexico, and Alabama, all convicted felons must submit to DNA sampling. New Jersey takes DNA samples only from persons convicted of a serious sex offense, and New York extracts DNA samples from persons convicted of one of twenty-one different offenses. However, New York is considering taking DNA samples from all criminal suspects, as is North Carolina. The legal challenges to state DNA databases have been thwarted in all states except for Massachusetts.

The national DNA database may be a boon for law enforcement personnel, but it raises privacy concerns. In the *New York Times*, Philip L. Bereano, a professor of technology and public policy at the University of Washington in Seattle, observed that "[t]he DNA database started out with pariahs—the sex offenders—but has already been enlarged to include other felons and will probably be extended to include everyone, giving elites the power to control 'unruly' citizens."

In response to privacy concerns about the national DNA database, the FBI has set up a secure system to maintain privacy and has required all database users to undergo background checks. In March 1999, U.S. Attorney General JANET RENO requested that a federal commission look into the possibility of requiring that all arrested persons give a DNA sample. The notion that a person may be required under federal law to give a DNA sample based on the mere suspicion of criminal activity is chilling to civil libertarians. "[I]f you're found innocent," Barry Steinhardt of the American Civil Liberties Union told *U.S. News & World Report*, "your DNA sample…will still be on file." According to Steinhardt, "that has tremendous potential for abuse." John Bentivoglio, an attorney in the U.S. JUSTICE DEPARTMENT, said that Reno wanted to ensure that the privacy issues were "fully vetted as people consider expanding DNA testing."

Many persons herald the coming of a national DNA database for its exculpatory potential. A person may easily be eliminated as a suspect through DNA evidence and, in some cases, DNA evidence can prove a convicted defendant's innocence, which results in freedom and true, albeit tardy, justice. Opponents of a comprehensive national DNA database concede that DNA evidence can be exculpatory, but groups such as the American Civil Liberties Union are gearing up for a legal battle that will almost certainly reach the U.S. Supreme Court.

Several other questions spring from the issue of who should have to give a sample. For example, if a state or federal law requires DNA sampling of all violent felons, what is the law's definition of a "violent felon?" Will that definition merely include persons who have injured, attempted to injure, or threatened to injure another person, or will it also include persons convicted of drug offenses and persons convicted of crimes against property? Is a person a "violent felon" is he or she has been arrested for a third drunk driving offense, which constitutes a felony in some states? These questions may become mere bumps in the road toward a national DNA database of all persons, regardless of their criminal records.

---

oratory, a research lab under the U.S. Department of Energy was sued for secretly testing certain employees.

Norman-Bloodsaw began in 1994, when Marya Norman-Bloodsaw, a forty-one-year-old clerk in the accounting department of Lawrence Berkeley Laboratory, asked to see her medical records. When she inspected her records, Norman-Bloodsaw recognized the code for syphilis testing. Norman-Bloodsaw did not recall being told that she was being tested for syphilis, nor did she recall requesting such testing. At Norman-Bloodsaw's urging, several other employees consulted their own medical files and found that they too had been tested for genetic defects and other medical conditions without their knowledge or consent.

The secret testing seemed to establish a pattern of discrimination. Although the lab had tested all new employees for syphilis, African Americans and Latinos were re-tested for the disease. The lab also tested and re-tested its African American employees for sickle cell anemia, and women were tested regularly for pregnancy. White men were not re-tested for any diseases, except for white men who were married to black women who secretly tested for syphilis.

The lab testing by Lawrence Berkeley Laboratory allegedly constituted illegal discrimination and the violation of privacy rights. Vertis Ellis, a forty-seven-year-old African-American woman, for example, had been tested for sickle cell anemia and for pregnancy, but she had never requested the tests, authorized the tests, or received results from the tests. "I felt so violated," Ellis told *U.S. News & World Report*. "I thought, 'Oh, my God. Do they think all black women are nasty and sleep around?'" Norman-Bloodsaw, Ellis, and five other employees of Lawrence Berkeley Laboratories filed a CLASS ACTION suit against the lab, alleging violations of privacy and CIVIL RIGHTS.

Lawrence Berkeley Laboratory, the oldest research lab in the country, argued that it was not liable because the employees had all agreed to receive comprehensive physical examinations.

A defendant in the case, Thomas Budinger, a former medical director of the lab, defended the testing of African-Americans for syphilis. "[T]hat's where the prevalence of the disease is," Budinger explained to Hawkins. "How come only people over a certain age would get an EKG? See the logic?" The laboratory also denied that the testing was done in secret. According to attorney Douglas Barton, the lab posted test results on a wall in the exam room. The plaintiffs in the case disputed that assertion and they argued that they had not agreed to repeated testing without their consent, but the federal district court in San Francisco dismissed the case. According to Judge Vaughn Walker of the federal trial court in San Francisco, the tests "were administered as part of a comprehensive medical examination to which [the employees] had consented."

The plaintiffs appealed the dismissal of the case to the Ninth Circuit Court of Appeals. In February 1998, the federal appeals court reversed the ruling and remanded the case for trial. *Norman-Bloodsaw v. Lawrence Berkeley Laboratory*, 135 F.3d 1260 (9th Cir. 1998). According to the appeals court, the testing violated constitutional privacy rights if the employees had not given their consent and there were no reasonable medical or public health needs that justified the testing. The testing also violated Title VII of the CIVIL RIGHTS ACT OF 1964 if the testing was conducted based on race- and gender-specific traits. The appeals court put a stop to the testing and ordered the lab to delete all of the secret test results from the personnel files of the employees.

Norman-Bloodsaw is important because it places some limits on the use of genetic testing of employees. Every year, genetic researchers are discovering new genetic predictors for diseases, and insurance companies may begin to base eligibility for their medical and life insurance policies on a person's genetic predisposition to diseases. If, for example, a person seeking insurance is genetically tested and found to have a predisposition for a fatal disease, the insurance company may wish to deny coverage.

Wilson v. Layne

Police and the news media have a long history of collaborating on crime stories. Under this arrangement police garner favorable publicity for their crime-fighting efforts, while the news media obtains dramatic photographs, film, or videotape. In the 1990s police aggressively promoted "media ride along" programs and several television networks produced popular shows that were edited videotapes of police raids. The most dramatic footage in these programs involved breaking into houses, rousting the occupants, and arresting the suspects.

The Supreme Court, in *Wilson v. Layne*, __ U.S. __, 119 S. Ct.1692, __ L. Ed. 2d __ (1999), announced an end to the media ride along in homes, ruling that they violate the FOURTH AMENDMENT. The Court made clear that there was no compelling reason to allow the violation of personal privacy. In the future, police officers will be LIABLE for DAMAGES if they bring the news media into a home that they are searching.

In 1992, the U.S. Marshals Service began working with state and local police to apprehend dangerous criminals who were wanted for serious drug and violent felonies. "Operation Gunsmoke," as the program was called, proved effective, resulting in over 3,000 arrests in forty metropolitan areas. As part of the program, federal and county law officers in Rockville, Maryland, went with an arrest WARRANT to the supposed residence of Dominic Wilson. Wilson, who had violated his probation on previous felony charges of robbery, theft, and assault, was believed to be armed and dangerous.

In the early morning hours of an April morning, the Gunsmoke team assembled for a raid on the residence. Accompanying them were a reporter and a photographer from the *Washington Post* newspaper. They had been invited on the mission as part of the marshal's ride-along program. Police entered the dwelling with the media representatives just before 7:00 A.M. Charles and Geraldine Wilson, Dominic's parents, were in bed when they heard the officers enter the home. Charles Wilson, clad only in briefs, ran to the living room and angrily confronted the intruders, who had their guns drawn. The police believed he was Dominic and quickly wrestled him to the floor and subdued him. Geraldine Wilson then entered the room, wearing only a nightgown, and observed her husband being restrained.

The police soon discovered that Dominic Wilson was not in the house and then left the house. During the course of the raid, the photographer had taken many pictures and the reporter had observed the altercation between Charles Wilson and the police. The newspaper never published any photographs of the incident.

The Wilson's sued both the federal and county law officers for damages, alleging that the officers' actions in bringing members of the news media to observe and record the attempted execution of the arrest warrant violated their Fourth Amendment rights. The federal district court denied the officers' motion to dismiss the case based on their qualified IMMUNITY, but the Fourth Circuit Court of Appeals reversed. 141 F. 3d 111 (4th Cir. 1998). The appeals court found that no court had held at the time of the raid that the presence of media during a police entry into a residence violated the Fourth Amendment. Therefore, the right allegedly violated was not clearly established and the officers were entitled to qualified immunity. The court made no ruling on whether media presence violated the Fourth Amendment.

The Supreme Court, in a unanimous decision, ruled that the media ride-along violated the Fourth Amendment. Chief Justice WILLIAM H. REHNQUIST, writing for the Court, recognized the long-held tradition of in England and the United States that a "man's home is his castle." The Fourth Amendment embodied this "centuries-old principle of respect for the privacy of the home." The amendment stated that persons have a right to be secure in their "houses," and prior Court decisions had declared that physical entry of the home was the chief evil addressed by the provision.

Rehnquist acknowledged that the officers had a valid warrant and that they had a legitimate right to enter the Wilson's home. However, this right did not extend to inviting a reporter and photographer to accompany them. The Fourth Amendment requires that "police actions in execution of a warrant be related to the objectives of the authorized intrusion." Rehnquist concluded that the presence of the media in the house was not related to the objectives of the intrusion. The media did not assist the police in executing the warrant, which was the main objective of the raid.

The officers asserted several reasons that justified the presence of the reporters. They argued that officers should be able to exercise reasonable discretion about when it would further "the law enforcement mission" to invite members of the news media to accompany them in executing a warrant. Rehnquist rejected this argument because it "ignores the importance of the right of residential privacy at the core of the Fourth Amendment." The ride-along program may serve generalized law enforcement purposes but they were insufficient to "trump" the Fourth Amendment.

The officers also asserted that the presence of third parties could aid government efforts to combat crime and facilitate accurate news re-

porting on law enforcement activities. While acknowledging these goals and the importance of the FIRST AMENDMENT, Rehnquist noted that the Fourth Amendment "also protects a very important right." Good public relations were not enough "to justify the ride-along intrusion into a private home."

Finally, the officers claimed that the presence of third parties served in some situations to minimize police abuses and to protect suspects. Rehnquist saw no merit in this claim. If police videotaped their raids as a "quality control measure," that was one thing. It was another thing for media representatives, who were working on a story for their private purposes, to report and photograph the raid. Rehnquist noted that the newspaper retained the photographs.

Therefore, the Court ruled that the officers had no justification for their actions. However, the Court, on an 8–1 vote, agreed with the Fourth Circuit that the officers could not be held liable. The Court ruled that because it had just articulated this Fourth Amendment right, it could not have been clearly established in 1992. It would be unfair to hold the officers liable for a rule of law that did not exist when they made their entry into the Wilson's home.

Justice JOHN PAUL STEVENS dissented as to the grant of qualified immunity to the officers. He contended that "it should have been perfectly obvious to the officers" that their invitation to the media violated the Fourth Amendment.

CROSS REFERENCES
Civil Rights; Criminal Law; DNA Evidence; Fourth Amendment; Genetic Screening; Immunity

PROPERTY LAW

Sightseeing Tours of the Titanic

Most persons are familiar with the story of the Titanic, the enormous, "unsinkable" ship that was launched in 1912 as the "largest and finest steamship ever built." On its maiden voyage, the Titanic ran into an iceberg en route from Southampton, England, to New York City and sank approximately three hours later. The event was memorialized in two Hollywood films and is etched in the world's collective consciousness, but few are as familiar with the struggles behind the property rights to the Titanic.

In 1985, divers discovered the wreck of the Titanic at the bottom of the North Atlantic Ocean, approximately four hundred miles from the coast of Newfoundland. The ship was rest-

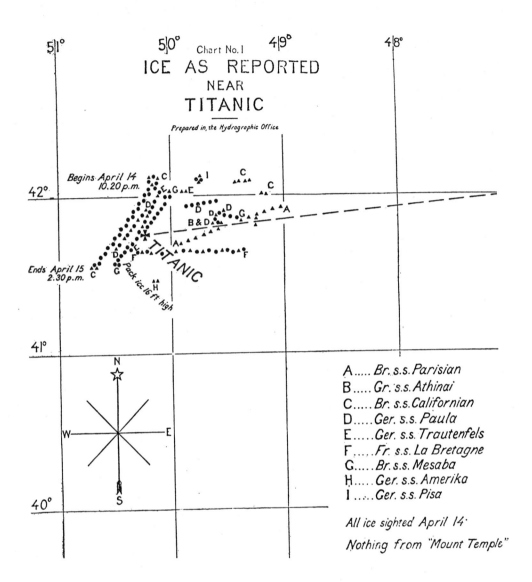

ing under 12,500 feet of water. Companies began to vie for the right to salvage the remains of the ship. Titanic Ventures, a Connecticut company working with the Institute of France for the Research and Exploration of the Sea, began to salvage the wreck. The group conducted thirty-two dives over the course of sixty days and recovered approximately 1,800 artifacts. Titanic Ventures and the Institute later sold its interest in the salvage operation and the artifacts to R.M.S. Titanic. R.M.S. Titanic then conducted its own expedition and brought up 800 more artifacts in 1993.

In 1994, the district court in the Eastern District of Virginia awarded exclusive salvage rights and ownership of the recovered artifacts to R.M.S. Titanic, Inc., a Florida-based corporation. Two years later, the court turned back challenges to the exclusive rights of R.M.S. Titanic. The court then issued an INJUNCTION to

protect the rights of R.M.S. Titanic. Specifically, all persons, except those associated with R.M.S. Titanic, were prohibited from "conducting search, survey, or salvage operations, or obtaining any image, photographing or recovering any objects, entering, or causing to enter" the area around the Titanic.

Some salvage companies were reluctant to comply with the order. R.M.S. Titanic went back to court and in June 1998 the court specifically enjoined Christopher S. Haver and Deep Ocean Expeditions, a British Virgin Islands corporation, from interfering with the salvage rights of R.M.S. Titanic. Deep Oceans Expeditions was planning a sightseeing tour of the Titanic in late summer of 1998, and Haver, a Phoenix, Arizona-based businessman, planned to go on the trip.

Haver and Deep Oceans Expeditions appealed the ruling to the U.S. Court of Appeals for the Fourth Circuit. According to Haver and Deep Oceans Expeditions, the district court in Virginia lacked jurisdiction over the matter and the scope of the court's injunction was too broad. The zone that around the Titanic that could not be pierced was 175 miles around the wreck. The appeals court agreed and reversed parts of the district court's rulings. In a unanimous decision written by Judge Paul V. Niemeyer, the court decided that "a property right does not normally include the right to exclude viewing and photographing of the property when it is located in a public place." The appeals court decided to allow expeditions to get near the wreck, look at it, and take pictures or videotape of it, so long as the divers did not interfere with the work of R.M.S. Titanic. The appeals court also ruled that the federal district court in Virginia could exercise jurisdiction over the far-away wreck. The attorney for R.M.S. Titanic had presented to the district court a wine decanter from the Titanic, which gave the court the power to rule in the case. The appeals court noted the difficulty in determining the rights to property that lies in international waters, and concluded that any court with the parties and at least some of the property could hear the case. Any court in the world "would have reached the same conclusions," the appeals court opined. The appeals court further ruled that the exclusive rights to the ship lay with R.M.S. Titanic.

R.M.S. Titanic was disappointed that it had lost exclusive photographic rights to the Titanic, but it was pleased that it had retained the rights to the ship itself. "That was a big threshold question," noted Mark S. Davis, R.M.S. Titanic's attorney, as reported in the *Knight-Ridder/Tribune Business News*. "The 4th Circuit has never come out and said that." Haver and Deep Ocean also were pleased. Alex Blanton, an attorney for Haver and Deep Ocean, announced that Haver and Deep Ocean's positions were "completely vindicated."

CROSS REFERENCES
Admiralty Law; International Law

REAL ESTATE

Land, buildings, and things permanently attached to land and buildings. Also called realty and REAL PROPERTY.

Real Estate Settlement Procedures Act

The Real Estate Settlement Procedures Act of 1974 (RESPA) is a set of federal laws which mandates that mortgage lenders make various disclosures to consumers. Enacted in 1974, RESPA has been modified multiple times since its inception. RESPA is administered by the U.S. Department of Housing and Urban Development (HUD). The Truth-in-Lending Act, administered by the Federal Reserve System, and RESPA are the two main laws covering the practice of mortgage lending.

In 1996, Congress and HUD made several changes to RESPA. Many of the amendments made the business of home mortgages a little easier for the mortgage companies. One of the major issues surrounding RESPA was the treatment of MORTGAGE companies that own other companies that work on other aspects of home sales. These other companies are called "affiliated businesses," and they cannot do business with the mortgage company without strict adherence to certain guidelines. Generally, a mortgage company must disclose to the consumer the company's connection to affiliated businesses in the mortgage transaction. Under § 8 of the act, RESPA also bars certain types of payments to and from affiliated businesses to prevent kickbacks. There are exemptions to the anti-kickback provisions. The 1996 amendments eliminated an exemption in § 8 and replaced it with two more narrow exemptions. Prior to the 1996 amendments, a mortgage company could make payments to its employees for referring customers to affiliated businesses. Under the new provisions in § 8: a mortgage company may make payments to a managerial employee for referring business to affiliated businesses when the bonuses are not calculated according to the number or value of the referrals made by the employee. In addition, a mortgage company may make payments to a non-managerial employee for referring business if the employee does not perform services associated with settlement of the mortgage.

In June 1998, HUD and the Federal Reserve System proposed more changes to RESPA. One measure was intended to require that the mortgage company disclose to the consumer, early in the mortgage settlement process, the price of "bundled" closing costs of a mortgage. A "bundled" closing cost is one that figures all mortgage-related costs into the calculation. Another measure was intended to require that mortgage companies disclose the annual percentage rate of the mortgage at an earlier point in the transaction. A third measure was proposed to determine precisely how binding an annual percentage rate is on rates that are fixed before the closing of the mortgage deal.

HUD and the Federal Reserve System also proposed to combine RESPA with the Truth-in-Lending Act. The proposal made it unclear which agency would administer such a combined set of laws. HUD and the Federal Reserve System considered requiring mortgage companies to give customers a guaranteed closing cost for bundled mortgage services. Such a measure was not expected to pass because some banks, especially those in rural areas, do not engage in enough mortgage transactions to accurately estimate the cost of the entire transaction.

Also in 1998, HUD and the Federal Reserve System created a sensation in Washington in a report to Congress. Officials from both agencies told Congress that important parts of RESPA are unenforceable. According to the agencies, protections for consumers against misrepresentations and fraud by loan officers, realty agents, title companies, escrow companies, and settlement companies have no provisions for enforcement. In other words, there are no penalties for misrepresentation and FRAUD in certain parts of the mortgage transaction. A lender suffers no penalty for the tardy return of ESCROW funds when home owners refinance the mortgage with a different lender. Servicers of mortgages suffer no penalties if they make late payments to the lender, even if the servicer incurs penalties that are passed on to the consumer. Furthermore, there is nothing to stop lenders from forcing consumers to buy high-cost hazard insurance from a specific company if the consumer allows the original policy to lapse.

CROSS REFERENCES
Housing and Urban Development Department

RELIGION

International Religious Freedom Act

In an effort to oppose religious persecution worldwide, Congress passed and President BILL CLINTON signed the International Religious Freedom Act (IRFA) in October 1998. (22 U.S.C. § 6401–6481.)

IRFA's enactment coincides with a worldwide increase of religious persecution, particularly of Christians in African and Asian countries. In November 1998, a Nigerian lay preacher told a Presbyterian congregation in Colorado of how Muslims back home tied him to a tree and stoned him for insulting the Islamic prophet Mohammed by preaching the Gospel of Jesus. Christians are imprisoned and tortured in China, Pakistan, and Sudan. In Russia, Greece, and Central and South America, dominant Christian churches are the aggressors, persecuting members of other sects who they believe threaten their supremacy.

Worldwide religious persecution, however, is not limited to Christianity. In July 1998, Iran hanged a man of the Bahai faith for trying to convert a Muslim. In Chinese occupied Tibet, Buddhist monks are tortured, and Buddhists who display pictures of the Dalai Lama, their religious leader, are imprisoned. The Islamic government in Sudan massacres people of African faiths as well as Christians.

Backed by groups as diverse as the National Council of Catholic Bishops, the ANTI-DEFAMATION LEAGUE, the Episcopal Church, the International Campaign for Tibet, the National Jewish Coalition, and the Religious Action Center of Reform Judaism, IRFA opposes religious persecution of all kinds in all countries. The act begins by noting that "freedom of religious belief and practice," one of the reasons for the existence of the United States, is "a universal human right and fundamental freedom." After describing worldwide religious persecution in general, IRFA announces the United States's policy "to condemn violations of religious freedom" and "to use and implement appropriate tools in the United States foreign policy apparatus, including diplomatic, political, commercial, charitable, educational, and cultural channels, to promote respect for religious freedom by all governments and peoples." (22 U.S.C. § 6401.)

To implement its policy, IRFA established the position of Ambassador at Large for International Religious Freedom, who will operate under the president in the Department of State. (22 U.S.C. § 6411.) The ambassador will help the secretary of state compile an annual report concerning worldwide religious persecution. The report will identify countries engaging in or permitting two levels of persecution. The first level, called "violations of religious freedom," includes virtually any type of restriction on religious freedom or punishment of religious conduct. The second level, called "particularly severe violations of religious freedom," is reserved for countries engaging in or allowing "systematic, ongoing, egregious violations of religious freedom," including torture, detention, abduction, "or other flagrant denial[s] of the right to life, liberty, or the security of persons." (22 U.S.C. § 6402.) The secretary of state may classify information in the report if necessary for national security, the safety of individuals, or to otherwise serve IRFA's purposes. (22 U.S.C. § 6412.)

IRFA also created the Commission on International Religious Freedom to work independently of the state department. The commission will be staffed by the ambassador and nine members appointed by the president, the president pro tempore of the Senate, and the Speaker of the House of Representatives. (22 U.S.C. § 6431.) The commission's primary responsibilities are to review the annual report prepared by the ambassador and secretary of state, make general policy recommendations concerning international religious freedom, and recommend specific sanctions against countries engaging in or permitting violations of religious freedom. (22 U.S.C. § 6432.)

After reviewing the reports and recommendations from the state department and the commission, the president must choose from a list of sanctions to punish offending countries. For those allowing violations of religious freedom, there are sixteen possible sanctions, including private or public condemnation, delay or cancellation of scientific or cultural exchanges, denial, delay or cancellation of working, official, or state visits, and seven financial and economic penalties. For countries guilty of particularly severe violations of religious freedom, the president only may choose from the list of financial and economic penalties, which includes withholding financial assistance, export licenses, and procurement contracts. (22 U.S.C. § 6441, 6442, 6445.)

Critics of IRFA say the bill lacks teeth. Security classification allows the State Department, commission, and president to hide the identities of countries who are engaging in religious persecution. Loopholes then allow the president to forego sanctions against such countries. For example, a loosely worded paragraph allows the president to take "commensurate" action against violating countries instead of one of the sixteen specific sanctions. (22 U.S.C. § 6445(b).) The president may waive financial sanctions against countries guilty of particularly severe violations of religious freedom if waiver is in the national interest. (22 U.S.C. § 6447.) Finally, the act states that no one may challenge the president's or the state department's actions in court. (22 U.S.C. § 6450.)

The Clinton administration claimed that such flexibility was necessary to prevent the act from damaging relations with important foreign countries who happen to violate the act. Indeed, inflexibility was the reason the administration opposed the Freedom from Religious Persecution Act (FRPA), which the House of Representatives passed earlier in 1998. FRPA automatically would have cut financial aid to countries guilty of severe violations of religious freedom. Trade and industry groups complained that FRPA would have interfered with their foreign operations. Opponents of FRPA also claimed that the act defined religious persecution too narrowly, limiting it to threats to life and limb. IRFA expanded the definition of religious persecution while giving the president flexibility when punishing violators.

September 1, 1999, was the first deadline for presidential action against offending countries. Meanwhile, the Clinton administration has acted on its own to oppose worldwide religious persecution. Speaking before a trip to China in June 1998, Clinton declared, "We in the United States believe that all governments everywhere should ensure fundamental rights, including the right of people to worship when and where they choose." During that speech Clinton and Secretary of State MADELEINE ALBRIGHT announced the creation of a new state department position, Senior Advisor for International Religious Freedom, to which they appointed Dr. Robert Seiple.

The Clinton administration's military actions also reflected its concern for worldwide religious persecution. On August 21, 1998, the United States bombed a factory in Sudan that was manufacturing chemicals used in nerve gas production. President Clinton said the factory was associated with Osama bin Laden, a Saudi businessman who was accused of bombing the U.S. embassies in Kenya and Tanzania two weeks earlier. The United States generally accuses the Islamic government of Sudan with harboring anti-Israeli terrorists and massacring the primarily Christian and Animist rebels in southern Sudan who say they are fighting for religious freedom.

On March 25, 1999, American led NATO forces opened a cruise missile attack on the Yugoslavian government of President Slobodon Milosevic. Over the prior year, Milosevic's Serbian forces increasingly bombed, torched, and massacred Albanian civilians in their villages in Kosovo, which Serbians regard as their birthplace. President Clinton accused Milosevic of feeding the "flames of ethnic and religious division" in Kosovo.

Public School Teacher Fired for Leading Students in Prayer

Mildred Rosario, a bilingual public school teacher in the Bronx, New York, was fired in June 1998 for praying with her students. The incident fueled an ongoing public debate over the issue of school prayer, making Rosario a hero to some and a villain to others.

The dispute began on June 8, 1998, as Rosario's sixth grade students gathered in her class at Intermediate School 74 waiting for her to take attendance. Over the school intercom, the principal asked for a moment of silence for

Christopher Lee, a fifth grade student who had drowned. Luisa Corporan, age eleven, followed the silence by asking, "Where is Christopher Lee?"

"In heaven," answered Rosario. Rosario's students followed with questions about God and heaven. Before proceeding, Rosario told her students that those who did not want to participate could read in the back of the room. Then Rosario, a member of a Pentecostal church in East Harlem, answered her students' questions. She explained, "God sent Jesus, our savior, to die for us, and he came to save all the human race." Rosario ultimately asked her students if they wanted to be saved. When they all raised their hands, Rosario put her hand on each of their foreheads and asked Jesus to take care of them and their families.

One of Rosario's students, a Jehovah's Witness, was so frightened by Rosario's conduct that she called home immediately after class. Soon several parents called the principal for an explanation of what Rosario had done. That led to an investigation of whether Rosario had violated the school's policy against proselytizing, or religious conversion. After Rosario submitted a written account of the incident, she appeared at a disciplinary hearing before the New York City Board of Education on June 12. There the district administrator asked Rosario if she could refrain from "preaching" in the future. When Rosario said she could not make such a promise, the school board fired her.

For opponents of school prayer, Rosario's conduct clearly violated the ESTABLISHMENT CLAUSE of the FIRST AMENDMENT of the U.S. Constitution, which says, "Congress shall make no law respecting an establishment of religion." By operation of the FOURTEENTH AMENDMENT, the Establishment Clause also prohibits similar conduct by the states and, therefore, by public schools. In *Engle v. Vitale*, 370 U.S. 421, 82 S. Ct. 1261, 8 L. Ed. 2d 601 (1962), the U.S. Supreme Court ruled that the Establishment Clause prohibits public schools from requiring or permitting their teachers to pray with their students. According to the Supreme Court, the Establishment Clause created a "constitutional wall of separation between Church and State." The purpose of the wall is to protect the sanctity of religion and to prevent the religious persecution that historically comes when government favors one religion over others.

Rosario's opponents say she clearly violated *Engle* by promoting her Pentecostal faith to students in a state-funded school. The fact that she allowed students to avoid the discussion does not matter. In *Engle*, the Supreme Court said the Establishment Clause creates no exceptions for non-coercive prayers. Some also claim Rosario's conduct resulted in persecution, because the Jehovah's Witness who initially complained has been harassed by angry students for getting Rosario fired. According to an account in the *New York Post*, students cursed at the girl and blocked her from trying to escape from the classroom. In tears, the girl packed her school bag and said she would not return to the school.

Rosario's supporters claim she was the victim of a school system and government that are abusing the Establishment Clause. The language "wall of separation between church and state" appears nowhere in the U.S. Constitution or the First Amendment. In fact, U.S. courts adopted that language from a letter written in 1802 by President THOMAS JEFFERSON to the Danbury Baptist Association. In 1998, Library of Congress scholar James H. Hutson released an analysis of the letter claiming that Jefferson meant it to be a tool to win support from New England constituents, not a foundation for First Amendment law.

On a more practical level, Rosario's supporters say her treatment by the school board reflects the sad state of affairs in America's public schools. Teachers accused of sexually abusing their students receive better treatment, going on paid administrative leave pending a long review process. This led House Majority Whip Tom Delay (R-Tex.) to quip, "pedophiles have more access to our children than teachers who have a deep commitment to faith." Michael Scanlon, one of Delay's aides, added:

> Our public school systems are overrun with drugs, crime and guns, and several undesirable influences. And

while these children are offered condoms and needles, they are denied the opportunity to reach out to their teachers in times of grief and confusion because it might strike up a conversation that deals with faith and morality.

Even one of Rosario's students reportedly observed, "We talk about guns and condoms—and they give us condoms to have safe-sex on the streets. But we can't talk about the one who made us."

In June 1998, such concerns led the U.S. House of Representatives to consider the Religious Freedom Amendment, a constitutional amendment to allow organized prayer in public schools. The proposed amendment failed by a vote of 224–203, 61 votes short of the two-thirds majority necessary to pass an amendment. Representative Delay still called Rosario's firing unconstitutional and asked New York Republican Governor George Pataki to get Rosario's job back. Meanwhile, New York City Mayor RUDOLPH GIULIANI said that Rosario should have received a warning, but should not have been fired.

Rosario filed a grievance with her union, the United Federation of Teachers, and considered filing a lawsuit. Her opponents, however, said that as a temporary teacher, Rosario was not entitled to a formal hearing prior to termination. The school board claimed, moreover, that before the incident, Rosario was scheduled to be fired at the end of the school year. Her personnel file reportedly contained ten memoranda concerning poor performance, inadequate teaching methods, and absenteeism.

CROSS REFERENCES
First Amendment

REPARATION

COMPENSATION for an injury; REDRESS for a wrong inflicted.

Holocaust Survivors Sue Swiss Banks

On August 12, 1998, a $1.2 billion settlement was reached between Jewish Holocaust survivors and Swiss banks, including Credit Suisse Group and UBS. This settlement was reached after a CLASS ACTION suit was brought against the Swiss banks for taking assets from Holocaust victims' bank accounts. Credit Suisse and UBS announced that the settlement would satisfy all claims on Swiss banks involving dor-

Ruth Abraham and Michael Schonberger are plaintiffs in an $18 million lawsuit against two German banks.

mant accounts and the banks' activities during World War II. In exchange, the plaintiffs agreed to drop all claims against the Swiss state and Swiss companies. They did not, however, agree to drop any claims against Swiss insurance companies which are involved in a separate class-action lawsuit along with several other European insurance companies.

This $1.2 billion settlement will be distributed to those who offer valid claims. The distribution of the money poses additional issues. The first portion must go to the actual heirs of the Jewish victims that had assets in Swiss bank accounts. However, that still leaves a remainder of $1 billion. Jewish humanitarian groups contend that they deserve a bulk of the remaining distribution so they may continue and grow. However, the Holocaust survivors and their lawyers believe the remaining funds should go directly to the survivors. The World Jewish Restitution Organization met in November 1998 to discuss distribution of the $1 billion. Its proposal was that 80 percent of the funds should go to needy survivors and the other 20 percent should go to promote Holocaust related educational programs. As time passes, there will be even fewer Holocaust survivors to receive compensation. Estimates show that there are only 350,000 Holocaust survivors and their average age is 80 years.

In addition to the lawsuit against the Swiss banks, legal actions are being brought against Barclays Bank, Chase Manhattan, Deutsche Bank, Dresdner Bank and Commerzbank, among others, for holding onto assets belonging to the Jewish victims who lost their lives during the Holocaust. Deutsche Bank has also been accused of providing funding for the construction of Auschwitz concentration camp. In speaking about the increasing number of such suits, Whittier Law School Professor Michael J. Bazyler stated in the *New York Times* that the number of lawsuits for Holocaust claims have tripled since 1996, when fewer than a dozen of these types of suits had been filed.

Holocaust survivors have also brought claims against many European and U.S. manufacturers who profited from slave labor during the Holocaust. The plaintiffs are seeking both compensatory and punitive damages for inhumane treatment, forced labor and lost compensation. The defendant corporations in these suits include BMW, Daimler Benz, Audi, Volkswagen, Krupp, and Fords. A class action suit was filed in a federal court in New Jersey against Ford Motor Company contending that a Ford subsidiary in Cologne, Germany, profited during the war from prisoners' work. Ford claims that it had little or no control over this subsidiary.

Lawsuits have also been brought against European and U.S. companies for their financial support in the German war and Holocaust effort. A class-action suit has been brought against Degussa, a German corporation, and its U.S. subsidiary, Degussa Corp., for supplying bomb technology for Nazi troops and Zyklon-b gas used in the gas chambers in the concentration camps. They are also accused of aiding in the efforts to launder gold and other metals stolen by the Nazis. Although an actual suit has not been brought against General Motors Corporation, reports from the National Archives show that one of General Motors's subsidiaries, Adam Opel, supplied approximately 6,500 trucks annually to the German Nazis during World War II. General Motors contends that this subsidiary was wholly-owned by the Germans.

Insurance companies are also being held responsible for policies filed by concentration camp victims before the war. After World War II ended, most survivors were denied claims because they did not have death certificates or that those monies covering their policies were seized during the war. In order to address these claims, the International Commission was established by the National Association of Insurance Commissioners, six European Insurers and several Jewish organizations. A conference was held in late 1998, where the commission agreed to establish a $90 million humanitarian fund to aid Holocaust survivors and to open up offices in London and Washington. Elan Steinburg, Executive Director of the World Jewish Congress in New York called this pledge a "gesture of good faith, but not the final amount." Additionally, many of the insurance companies have paid out settlements in class action lawsuits.

Unlike the war itself, many of the class action lawsuits listed above are being fought on U.S. soil. Moreover, there are many individual suits now being filed in the United States against responsible United States and European corporations. In May 1998, California passed a law allowing Holocaust victims and their survivors to file claims in the California courts against European-based insurers doing business in California. In the beginning of 1999, a Los Angeles Superior Court judge denied a motion brought by Assicurazioni Generali to either dismiss a lawsuit filed by Holocaust survivors and their heirs based on lack of jurisdiction, or to have it transferred to the Czech Republic. The Superior Court judge sustained the lawsuit against the Italian insurance company that was licensed to sell insurance in California.

In addition to the compensation that has been awarded to Holocaust survivors and their heirs by the courts, relief is also being offered by the U.S. government. In March 1999, the U.S. announced that it was going to allocate $4 million from 1998 economic support funds to the Conference on Jewish Material Claims Against Germany to go to Holocaust survivors in Eastern Europe and the former Soviet Union. Moreover, on January 15, 1999, the United States and Germany announced a tentative agreement in which the German government agreed to compensate approximately 240 Americans, which include mostly Jewish persons and some captured U.S. soldiers, taken into Nazi concentration camps. Although the exact terms of the agreement have not been made public, it is speculated that a total sum of $24 million will be paid. This would give each victim $100,000.

Many are now wondering if this movement for restitution has lost it original purpose and is now all about money. In August 1999, some of the plaintiffs in the $1.2 million settlement with the Swiss banks withdrew from the suit. They claimed that the lawyers were going to keep too much of the money for fees. This will give them the option to pursue their claims at a future date. Roman Kent, Chairman of the American Gathering of Jewish Holocaust Survivors told *Time*, "This is not how the survivors want the Holocaust to be remembered. The image and the memory of those killed have been put in the background and all I hear about now is the glitter of gold." Others wonder if the suits are being brought against those not responsible. Alan Dershowitz, Harvard University law professor, pointed out to *Time* that, "When you're taking money from Volkswagen today, it's coming not from the Nazis, but from a thirty-year-old German." However, Michael Haysfeld, a class action lawyer from Washington argued, "These lawsuits will complete a picture of the Holocaust that has never before been fully developed about the willing accomplices and companies that stood behind the direct participants."

Many institutions, such as Deutsche Bank, Siemens, Volkswagen and Daimler-Chrysler, and nations, such as France and Poland, have made verbal apologies for the horrors committed by the Nazi regime, accepting their share of the responsibility.

REPRODUCTION

Legal rights associated with human conception, including birth control, abortion, artificial insemination, and in vitro fertilization.

Kass v. Kass

Advances in medical procedures have provided new opportunities for conceiving children. The most promising development has been in vitro fertilization. This technique involves the retrieval of the egg from the woman and the fertilization of the egg outside the womb. The embryo is then transferred to a woman's uterus. Because these embryos can be frozen and stored indefinitely, legal disputes now arise over the rights to this genetic material when a husband and wife divorce.

The New York Court of Appeals, that state's highest court, confronted this type of dispute in *Kass v. Kass*, 91 N.Y. 2d 554, 696 N.E. 2d 174 (1998). The court ruled that the custody of five frozen embryos should be determined by the terms of the contract the couple signed before the in vitro fertilization process began.

Steven and Maureen Kass were married in 1988, and almost immediately began trying to conceive a child. When Maureen Kass failed to become pregnant, the couple turned to a Long Island, New York, hospital. After artificial insemination failed, they turned to in vitro fertilization. Beginning in March 1990, Kass underwent the egg retrieval process five times and doctors transferred fertilized eggs to her nine times. She became pregnant twice in 1991, but Kass first had a miscarriage and a few months later an ectopic pregnancy had to be surgically terminated.

In May 1993, the couple signed four consent forms provided by the hospital before the freezing of additional embryos. The forms consisted of twelve single-spaced typewritten pages explaining the procedure, its risks and benefits, and the need for the Kasses to make informed decisions regarding disposition of the fertilized eggs. They signed an addendum to the consent forms that stated if they "no longer wish to initiate a pregnancy or are unable to make a decision" regarding the frozen embryos, the hospital would have the right to use the embryos for research purposes. After several more attempts at pregnancy failed, the couple agreed to divorce. However, five frozen embryos still remained.

The couple first wrote and unsigned an uncontested DIVORCE agreement, in which they agreed to allow the disposition of the embryos according to the terms of the consent agreement. Later, however, Maureen Kass changed her mind and demanded custody of the embryos, as she still wanted to become pregnant. Steven Kass objected to this and the matter entered the New York courts.

The trial court awarded custody to Maureen Kass. The judge concluded that a woman had the right to make all decisions about pregnancy. On appeal, the New York Appellate Division reversed the decision, finding that the consent agreements were valid contracts that must be enforced.

The New York Court of Appeals affirmed this decision. The court noted that "tens of thousands of frozen embryos annually are stored in liquid nitrogen canisters, some having been in that state for more than ten years with no instructions for their use or disposal." A few states have enacted laws that deal with the disposition of stored embryos, but New York did not have such a law. Therefore, the court looked at case law from other states.

In *Davis v. Davis*, 842 S.W. 2d 588 (Tenn. 1992), the court recognized the "procreative autonomy" of both the egg and sperm provider. This includes an interest in avoiding genetic parenthood as well as an interest in becoming a genetic parent. In the absence of any prior written agreement between the parties which should be presumed valid, and implemented according to *Davis*, courts must balance these competing interests, each deserving of judicial respect. In *Davis* that balance weighed in favor of the husband's interest in avoiding genetic parenthood, which was found to be more significant than the wife's desire to donate the embryos to a childless couple.

The court also reviewed legal commentary on the issue of embryo disposition. Some commentators argue that one of the two providers should be given control. Other commentators believe that participation in an in vitro fertilization program implied a contract to procreate. Finally, some thinkers regard the two providers as holding a "bundle of rights" in relation to the embryos that could be exercised through a joint disposition agreement.

The court cited a New York State Task Force on Life and Law that no embryo should be implanted, destroyed, or used in research over the objection of an individual with decision-making authority. The court concluded that there was a need for "clear, consistent principles to guide parties in protecting their interests and resolving their disputes." In addition, there was the need for "particular care in fashioning such principles as issues are better defined and appreciated."

Turning to the dispute, the court found that the key question was who had the authority to dispose of the embryos. In this case, the answer was found in the consent agreements signed by the couple. The court held that agreements between donors regarding the disposition of their embryos "should generally be presumed valid and binding, and enforced in any dispute between them." The court urged future participants in this method of fertilization to "think through possible contingencies and carefully specify their wishes in writing."

The court noted that Steven and Maureen Kass did not contest the legality of the consent agreements nor did they dispute that they were an expression of their intent regarding disposition. The only issue in dispute was whether the consent agreements clearly expressed their intent regarding disposition of the embryos in case of divorce. Maureen Kass contended that the agreements were ambiguous in this respect, while Steven Kass contended that the agreements mandated transfer to the hospital's research program.

The appeals court applied basic principles of contract law to determine whether the agreements were ambiguous. After reviewing the provisions of the agreements, the court concluded that the contracts were not ambiguous. The informed consents signed by the couple "unequivocally manifest their mutual intention that in the present circumstances" the embryos should be donated for research. Moreover, the consents revealed that what the couple "above all did not want was a stranger taking that decision out of their hands. Even in unforeseen circumstances, even if they were unavailable, even if they were dead, the consents jointly specified the disposition that would be made." Therefore, the court ruled that embryos must be donated to the hospital for approved research purposes.

CROSS REFERENCES

Contract Law; Fetal Rights; Husband and Wife; Women's Rights

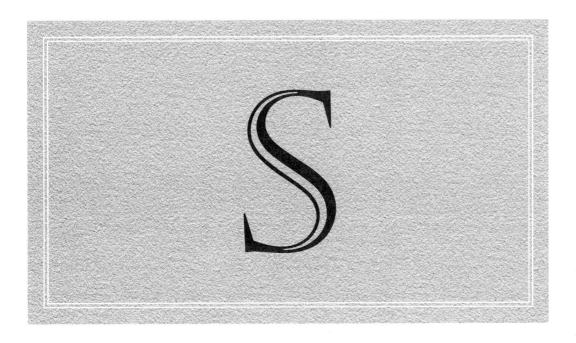

SCHOOL DESEGREGATION

Desegregation in San Francisco

In early 1999, the public school district of San Francisco, California, settled the five-year-old class action law suit filed in federal district court by Chinese-American students angered by with AFFIRMATIVE ACTION quotas based on racial and ethnic criteria. (*San Francisco Unified School District v. Ho Ho*, 147 F. 3d 854 [1998]). The quotas had been in force for the previous fifteen years. Originally set up as a desegregation effort for the district's 62,000 students, it involved assigning students to certain schools, classes or programs based upon their race or ethnicity. The quota policy began in 1983 when the California Department of Education and the San Francisco school district agreed to a consent decree ending a long court battle with the National Association for the Advancement of Colored People (NAACP). In that case, the NAACP had charged that the district's schools were segregated and that the system as a whole discriminated against black children. The 1983 consent decree was pursuant to the settlement with the NAACP and was the subject of litigation in the CLASS ACTION suit.

The at-issue quota policy under the consent decree required the division of all 62,000 students into nine ethnic and racial categories: American Indian, black, Chinese, Filipino, Japanese, Korean, Spanish-surnamed, other white, and non-white. None of the nine groups could exceed 45 percent of the total student population at any one school, and at least four of the nine groups had to be represented in each of the district's schools. Since the original consent decree went into effect, California has spent

an extra $300 million in thirty-seven schools to ensure its provisions.

Historically, the U.S. Supreme Court has continued to strike down most affirmative action quotas (excepting, e.g., in court-ordered circumstances), busing, and other forms of forced preferential treatment which may result in the viable concept of "reverse discrimination." (See *Regents of the University of California v. Bakke*, 438 U.S. 265, 98 S. Ct. 2733, 57 L. Ed. 2d 750 [1978]. Such reverse discrimination challenges are often predicated upon FOURTEENTH AMENDMENT EQUAL PROTECTION.)

In the present class action suit, Chinese American students alleged that they were turned away from their choice of schools because those schools had already reached their quota of Chinese American students. For the same reason, two other plaintiffs were refused attendance at their neighborhood elementary schools and forced to enroll elsewhere. In one claim, a fourteen-year-old Chinese American was refused admission to a top-ranked high school because Chinese Americans needed higher scores on admissions exams than those of other races, to keep quotas in order.

The school district had to prove that the district still discriminated, and therefore, needed the quota and busing policies to stay intact to win the suit. The case was scheduled to begin trial in February 1999, but a settlement was reached at that time.

Under the terms of the settlement, a ban on racial and ethnic admissions was drafted, and will become effective for the 1999–2000 school year for new students entering kindergarten, as well as sixth and ninth grade students. The following school year it will become effective for all grades. The district's other efforts at desegregation will remain in effect under court supervision for three years. This will allow the district to continue to receive $37 million annually from the state for remedial, enrichment and other programs having objectives directed toward eliminating effects of segregation. Moreover, under the settlement plan, the NAACP retains its right to return to court seeking REMEDY if schools again become segregated. However, it is clear that emphasis under the new policy will be on economic status and the expansion of opportunity for the underprivileged.

Once the quotas were eliminated, the district planned to implement other replacement or alternative measures to maintain desegregation. Some of the proposed measures involve the geographic reconstituting of school boundaries as well as the drafting of preferential programs for low-income and other underprivileged children. By this plan, the school district hopes to not only end discrimination against Chinese Americans, but it also helps to bring disadvantaged children into many schools and programs who would otherwise not be enrolled. Many educators and researchers have long believed that the disparity in both opportunity and educational ability is related to economics, not race or ethnicity.

Other cities or school districts which had lifted prior quota or preferential programs included Denver, Oklahoma City, Cleveland, Houston, Buffalo, and the Boston Latin School. The settlement in the San Francisco case contains language emphasizing that while race cannot be a "predominant consideration," the city may still seek racial diversity and preferential treatment for disadvantaged children. Additionally, the new plan prohibits the district from requiring identification of race or ethnicity on school enrollment forms (although the schools will still need to track the composition of each school's student body). The settlement was praised by the federal district judge as a "successful and peaceful solution" to a court battle which could have been protracted and divisive for the community.

Meanwhile, in January 1999, another class action suit was filed by the NAACP and a coalition of civil rights groups in Florida state court, alleging that the state violated the rights of thousands of minorities by failing to provide them with an adequate education. Similar suits have been filed in Alabama, North Carolina, Ohio,

and Connecticut. The Florida case differs only in that the focus is less on allegations of racial inequality and more on allegations of educational inadequacy. As federal desegregation cases have dropped off, there is instead a growing trend for minority plaintiffs to allege inadequate education rather than discriminatory education. More than one-third of the state's 1.4 million students have failed the state exams providing minimum functional literacy scales. Most of the affected schools had high enrollments of Hispanic and black students.

SCHOOLS AND SCHOOL DISTRICTS

Vouchers Allowed

Article I of the Bill of Rights under the U.S. Constitution (the FIRST AMENDMENT) states that Congress "shall make no law respecting an establishment of religion, or prohibiting the free exercise thereof." Most often referred to as the ESTABLISHMENT CLAUSE of the CONSTITUTION, this provision has undergone considerable refinement by the U.S. Supreme Court in the last three decades, particularly in the context of public education. Separation of church and state under the Constitution has historically prohibited the use or application of any public funds, grants or other monies toward "establishing," supporting, enriching, or otherwise conferring benefit upon, religion, religious causes, or religious entities.

But other clauses in the Constitution, including the rights of equal protection and due process, often work to prohibit the denial of benefits to persons (irrespective of religious beliefs) which are, in fact, bestowed upon or granted to others. The manifestation of these competing interests and protections has been unusually pronounced in the issue of school "voucher" programs, a system where individual credit vouchers given to parents by local, state or federal government entities, are used to send children to a school of the parents' choosing. Most of the school vouchers have been used to send children to private, parochial schools.

In November 1998, the U.S. Supreme Court, by an 8–1 vote, denied CERTIORARI on a decision by the Wisconsin Supreme Court, *Jackson v. Benson*, 218 Wis. 2d 835, 578 N.W. 2d 602 (1998), that upheld the constitutionality of the Milwaukee school voucher program. While the Court's action set no national legal precedent, similar voucher programs elsewhere may be able to withstand constitutional muster by ensuring that funding to private schools is the result of designations by individuals and not the government.

Wisconsin had been using a voucher system since 1989, but in 1995 the Wisconsin legislature amended the law. The original voucher plan allowed up to 1.5 percent of Milwaukee public school students to attend any private non-sectarian school of their choice. The plan succeeded in overcoming several court challenges, and in 1995 the program was expanded. The new program allowed use of the vouchers for enrollment in sectarian private schools, and it increased the student enrollment to 15 percent of the public school enrollment. But most significant was its mandate that monies would no longer be paid directly to the chosen schools. Instead, the state's check would be paid to the student's parent or guardian, who would endorse the check and forward it to the school of choice.

The Milwaukee Teachers' Association and others joined in suit to challenge the constitutionality of the program under both the Wisconsin State Constitution and the Establishment Clause of the First Amendment to the U.S. Constitution. The trial court found that the voucher program violated the Wisconsin constitution under its "religious benefits and compelling support" clauses. This decision was upheld by the Wisconsin Court of Appeals. But in June 1998, the Wisconsin Supreme Court went beyond the state constitution and reversed the lower court's decision based on the U.S. Constitution.

After generally reviewing the U.S. Supreme Court's previous decisions of church-state controversies, the Wisconsin Court focused on the three-pronged standard which was articulated in *Lemon v. Kurtzman*, 403 U.S. 602, 91 S. Ct. 2105, 29 L. Ed. 2d 745 (1971). In that case, the U.S. Supreme Court held that a statute would not violate the establishment clause if "(1) it has a secular legislative purpose; (2) its principal or primary effect neither advances nor inhibits religion; and (3) it does not create excessive entanglement between government and religion."

The Wisconsin Supreme Court, in evaluating the Wisconsin voucher-program law, concluded that the purpose of the program was to provide low-income parents with an opportunity to have their children educated somewhere other than the poorly-rated Milwaukee public system. This being a "secular legislative purpose," it passed the first part of the test articulated in *Lemon*. In assessing whether the voucher program's principal effect offered assurance that

it "neither advanced nor inhibited religion," (the second prong), the Wisconsin Court drew from the U.S. Supreme Court 1993 decision of *Zobrest v. Catalina Foothills School District*, 509 U.S. 1, 113 S. Ct. 2462, 125 L. Ed. 2d 1 (1993). In *Zobrest*, the Court ruled that since a deaf student was entitled by law to an interpreter/education assistant at government expense, he was still entitled to the interpreter's services even if he attended a Catholic rather than public school. The Court held that:

> We have consistently held that government programs that neutrally provide benefits to a broad class of citizens defined without reference to religion are not readily subject to an establishment clause challenge just because sectarian institutions may also receive an attenuated financial benefit.

The Wisconsin Court accordingly concluded that the Milwaukee voucher program provided parents with "a religious-neutral benefit—the opportunity to choose the educational opportunities that they deem best for their children." The Court went on to say that because the parents' choices included public school, a different public school within the district, a specialized public school, a private non-sectarian school, or a private sectarian school, "the amended program is in no way skewed towards religion." Therefore the Court concluded that the voucher program could constitutionally provide public aid to both sectarian and nonsectarian institutions as long as the aid was provided "on the basis of neutral, secular criteria that neither favor nor disfavor religion; and, only as a result of numerous private choices of the individual parents..." The Court also held that the state's overseeing of the program required no more oversight than already existing, so that there would be no "excessive entanglement."

Thus, school voucher programs which emphasize "private choice" are now able to survive constitutional challenge under the ESTABLISHMENT CLAUSE. In previous cases where the law or the proposed aid/assistance survived challenge, a private individual, not the government, made the decision to apply public funds to a particular school, even a religious school.

On a national level, voucher programs have enjoyed broad support. The biggest opposition is from teachers' unions, including the National Educational Association and the American Federation of Teachers, whose membership could experience loss of jobs if public school enrollments continue to decline in favor of vouchers going out to private schools. The Milwaukee program provides approximately $5,000 to any child whose family income is near the poverty level. The parents of the child may apply this money to any school of their choosing, secular or nonsecular.

CROSS REFERENCES
Affirmative Action; Equal Protection

SEARCH AND SEIZURE

A hunt by law enforcement officials for property or communications believed to evidence of crime, and the act of taking possession of this property.

Student Drug-testing Policy Struck Down

In *Trinidad School District No. 1 v. Lopez*, 963 P. 2d 1095 (Colo. 1998), the Colorado Supreme Court reversed a trial court's decision and held that the Trinidad School District's student drug-testing policy was unconstitutional under the U.S. and Colorado Constitutions as an unreasonable search and seizure. (U.S. Constitution, amend. 4; Colorado Constitution, art. 2, § 7.) Although the U.S. Supreme Court in 1995 had found that an Oregon school's drug-testing policy for all student-athletes (as a condition of participation) was constitutionally permissible, the Colorado Supreme Court struck down Trinidad's policy as unconstitutional, distinguishing its scope and implementation from the Oregon case.

In 1994, the Trinidad school board authorized an attitudinal and behavioral study, conducted by the Search Institute of Minneapolis, of its students enrolled in grades six through twelve. The survey disclosed a high level of illicit drug use by the Trinidad students that was above the national average. Based on the results of this survey, the school board developed and implemented a drug-testing policy for all students in grades six through twelve who desired to participate in any extracurricular activity to commence in the 1996–97 school year. Under the policy, each student was required to submit a urine sample for testing of illicit drugs by an outside company. The student and one parent were required to sign a consent and authorization form for the testing. The policy also allowed school officials to test any student participating in an extracurricular activity if they had a reasonable suspicion that the student was under the influence of illicit drugs. For any positive result, the school scheduled a hearing with the student and parent, and the student was re-

quired to complete a drug assistance program or be suspended from participation in the activity.

Carlos Lopez was a senior in the high school during the 1996–97 school year and had enrolled in two band classes to earn credit toward graduation. Lopez, a gifted musician, was also a member of the high school marching band. It was necessary for Lopez to enroll in two band classes to be allowed to participate in the marching band. Because the marching band was considered an extracurricular activity, he was also subject to the drug-testing policy that had been implemented by the school board. Lopez refused to take the mandatory drug test and was suspended from the band classes and the marching band. Lopez, through his parents, filed a lawsuit and requested an injunction against the implementation of the policy on the grounds that it was unconstitutional. After conducting a two-day trial, the district court decided that Trinidad's drug-testing policy was constitutional. The Colorado Supreme Court granted the parties' request for an expedited review.

In a 4–2 decision (one justice did not participate in the case), the state supreme court reversed the trial court's determination that the policy of "suspicionless" testing was constitutional. In delivering the majority opinion for the court, Justice Mary J. Mullarkey examined Trinidad's drug-testing policy under the framework established by the U.S. Supreme Court in *Vernonia School District 47J v. Acton* 515 U. S. 646, 115 S. Ct. 2386, 132 L. Ed. 2d 564 (1995). First, the policy must be based on a "special need" that overrides the probable cause requirement under the U.S. Constitution. If the policy is based on a legitimate special need, then the court must examine the nature of the privacy interest upon which the search intrudes, the character of the intrusion, and, finally, the nature and immediacy of the governmental concern at issue.

Mullarkey began the court's analysis by first recognizing that "students within the school environment have a lesser expectation of privacy than members of the population generally." This is due to the unique supervisory role that school officials have when students are in school. In analyzing the factors established in *Veronia*, Mullarkey drew several significant distinctions between the application of Trinidad's policy to its students and the policy in *Veronia*. While Mullarkey agreed with the trial court that a drug problem did exist in the Trinidad schools, there was not enough evidence to indicate that those students (particularly band members) who participated in extracurricular activities had a higher incidence of drug use than the general student population, as was the case with the student-athletes in *Veronia*. Mullarkey stated that the safety concerns relied upon in *Veronia* (sports-related injuries due to drug use) were not a legitimate concern for band members. Mullarkey also pointed out that Lopez was enrolled in a class linked directly to the marching band and had not volunteered to give up his privacy rights to participate in an extracurricular activity. In essence, the policy "swept within its reach students participating in an extracurricular activity who were not demonstrated to play a role in promoting drugs and for whom there was no demonstrated risk of physical injury." Mullarkey concluded that, based on these distinctions, the policy was too broad and therefore unconstitutional.

Justice Gregory Kellam Scott, in a dissenting opinion, admitted that the question before the court was a close and difficult one, but the distinctions relied upon by the majority were not persuasive in supporting an outcome different than the one in *Veronia*. Scott was extremely critical of the majority's distinction regarding the issue of class credit seeing "no distinction of legal significance to be drawn because a student engaged in Band as an extracurricular activity or co-curricular activity is also awarded academic credit for their participation." Scott noted that Lopez could have elected to take other band classes offered by the school to earn credit that were not linked to the extracurricular marching band. In effect, the same level of "volunteerness" existed in this case as it did in *Veronia*. Therefore, applying the same legal framework as the majority, Scott found the application of Trinidad's drug-testing policy to be substantially similar and consistent with the policy found constitutional in *Veronia*.

United States v. Ramirez

The U.S. Supreme Court reexamined police standards for "no-knock" searches in *United States v. Ramirez*, 523 U.S. 65, 118 S. Ct. 992, 140 L. Ed. 2d 191 (1998). The Court held that the FOURTH AMENDMENT does not hold officers to a higher standard when a "no-knock" entry results in the destruction of property. In so ruling, the Court overturned Ninth Circuit Court of Appeals precedent and created a "no-knock" exception to the federal statute 18 U.S.C.A. § 3109.

The police actions in question came in response to the escape of Alan Shelby from the Oregon state prison system. Shelby, who had allegedly made threats to kill witnesses and police officers, was thought to have access to large supplies of weapons. A reliable police informant told a federal agent that Shelby was staying at Hernan Ramirez's home in Boring, Oregon. The informant and the agent drove to an area near Ramirez's house, where the agent observed a man working outside who resembled Shelby.

Based on this information, a deputy U.S. Marshal received a no-knock WARRANT granting permission to enter and search Ramirez's house. By this time, the confidential informant had told authorities that Ramirez might have guns and drugs hidden in his garage.

In the early morning, forty-five officers stormed Ramirez's house. They broke a window in his garage and pointed a gun through the opening in hopes of preventing an occupant from rushing to the weapons the officers believed might be in the garage. Ramirez and his family were asleep inside. Awakened by the noise, Ramirez thought his home was being burglarized. He grabbed a pistol and fired it into the ceiling of his garage. The officers fired back and shouted "police." Ramirez, realizing it was the police entering his home, ran to his living room, threw his gun away, and threw himself on the floor. He admitted to police that he had fired the gun and that he owned both that weapon and another that was inside the house. He also admitted he was a convicted felon. Officers then obtained a search warrant, which they used to retrieve the two guns. Alan Shelby, the object of the no-knock search, was not found.

Ramirez was indicted for being a felon in possession of a firearm. However, the federal district court suppressed the two weapons as evidence because the police officers had violated the Fourth Amendment and 18 U.S.C.A. § 3109, which permits federal law enforcement officers to damage property in certain instances. The court ruled that there were "insufficient exigent circumstances" to justify the police officers' destruction of property in their execution of the warrant.

The Ninth Circuit Court of Appeals affirmed, 91 F. 3d 1297 (9rd. Cir. 1996). The court, applying Ninth Circuit precedent, found that while a "mild exigency" is sufficient to justify a no-knock entry that can be accomplished without the destruction of property, "more specific inferences of exigency are necessary" when property is destroyed. In Ramirez's case, this heightened standard had not been met.

The U.S. Supreme Court unanimously rejected the Ninth Circuit's conclusions and reasoning. Chief Justice WILLIAM H. REHNQUIST, writing for the Court, relied on *Richards v. Wisconsin*, 520 U.S. 385, 117 S. Ct. 1404, 137 L. Ed. 2d 615 (1997), which set out the Court's opinion on no-knock entries. The Court in *Richards* held that the Fourth Amendment does not permit a blanket exception to the knock-and-announce requirement for FELONY drug investigations. While the requirement can give way under circumstances presenting a threat of physical violence or where officers believe that evidence would be destroyed if advance notice were given, this did not mean that police in felony drug investigations could routinely ignore the need to apply to a court for a no-knock warrant that contained specific information about the need for such a warrant.

The Court in *Richards* was concerned about creating exceptions to the requirement based on the culture surrounding a general category of criminal behavior. The proposed exception contained considerable over-generalization that would prevent judicial review in cases in which a drug investigation does not pose special risks. In addition, creating an exception in one category could lead to its application in other categories. If an automatic exception were allowed for each criminal activity category that included a considerable risk of danger to officers or destruction of evidence, the knock-and-announce requirement would be meaningless. The Court concluded that a "no-knock" entry is justified when the police have a reasonable suspicion that knocking and announcing their presence, under the particular circumstances, would be "dangerous or futile," or that it would inhibit the effective investigation of the crime. It believed that this standard struck the appropriate balance between the legitimate law enforcement concerns at issue in the execution of search warrants and the individual privacy interests affected by no-knock entries.

Chief Justice Rehnquist found nothing in *Richards* or prior rulings that addressed the question of whether the lawfulness of a no-knock entry depended on whether property is damaged in the course of entry. Excessive or unnecessary destruction of property during a search may violate the Fourth Amendment, "even though the entry itself is lawful and the fruits of the search not subject to suppression."

Turning to the facts of the case, Rehnquist found that the police actions were "clearly reasonable" because of the information provided by the informant. The manner in which the entry was accomplished was also reasonable, as the police wished to discourage Shelby from seeking out weapons in the garage. Therefore, the no-knock entry did not violate the Fourth Amendment.

As to 18 U.S.C.A. § 3109, Ramirez contended that the evidence should be suppressed because the statute gave police permission to break a window to execute a search warrant only if the police first give notice and are refused admittance into the house. Therefore, all other property-damaging entries are forbidden under the law. Justice Rehnquist rejected this argument, stating that the provisions of § 3109 prohibit nothing. The statute "merely authorizes officers to damage property in certain instances." The court settled the issue by holding that § 3109 must be interpreted using the reasonableness standard articulated in prior rulings to include "an exigent circumstances exception." The police met that reasonableness standard in Ramirez's case, so § 3109 was not violated. The Court sent the case back to the district court for a trial on the weapons charge.

CROSS REFERENCES
Automobile Searches

SELF-INCRIMINATION

Giving TESTIMONY in a trial or other legal proceeding that could subject one to criminal prosecution.

Mitchell v. United States

The FIFTH AMENDMENT states in part that no person "shall be compelled in any criminal case to be a witness against himself." The right to remain silent is one of the cornerstones of U.S. criminal law and the courts have consistently enforced this provision. However, once a person testifies voluntarily, she gives up her right against self-incrimination and must answer all questions truthfully. The Supreme Court, in *Mitchell v. United States*, ___ U.S. ___, 119 S. Ct. 1307, 143 L. Ed. 2d 424 (1998), examined the self-incrimination clause from another aspect. It held that a person who pleads guilty to a crime does not waive the self-incrimination privilege at sentencing.

Amanda Mitchell was charged in federal court with one count of conspiring to distribute five or more kilograms of cocaine and with three counts of distributing cocaine within one thousand feet of a school or playground. Mitchell pleaded guilty to all four counts and did so without any plea agreement as to her sentence. She reserved the right to contest the drug quantity attributable to her under the conspiracy count, and the district court judge advised her that the drug quantity would be determined at her sentencing hearing.

Before accepting the plea, the judge informed her of the consequences of her guilty plea, including the penalties for her offenses. The judge told petitioner she faced a mandatory minimum of one year in prison under for distributing cocaine near a school or playground. She also faced punishment depending on the quantity involved for the conspiracy, with a mandatory minimum of ten years in prison if she could be held responsible for at least 5 kilograms but less than 15 kilograms of cocaine. The judge advised her that by pleading guilty, Mitchell would waive various rights, including the right at trial to remain silent under the Fifth Amendment. Mitchell told the court she understood some of what the judge had said but indicated she had not delivered any cocaine. Nevertheless, Mitchell again confirmed her intention to plead guilty and the court accepted the plea.

At her sentencing hearing, other members of the drug conspiracy testified that Mitchell had been an active trafficker of large amounts of cocaine. Mitchell presented no evidence at sentencing, nor did she testify to rebut the evidence about drug quantity. The court ruled that because of her guilty plea, Mitchell had no right to remain silent with respect to the details of her crimes. The court found credible the testimony indicating Mitchell had been a drug courier on a regular basis. The judge, noting that he "held it against" Mitchell that she claimed her Fifth Amendment right against self-incrimination, sentenced her to the statutory minimum of ten years of imprisonment.

Mitchell appealed but the Court of Appeals for the Third Circuit affirmed the sentence. 122 F.3d 185 (3rd Cir. 1997). It acknowledged that other circuit courts had held that a witness can remain silent if the witness's testimony might be used to enhance the witness's sentence. The Third Circuit declared that it would be illogical to "fragment the sentencing process," retaining the privilege against self-incrimination as to one or more components of the crime while waiving it as to others.

The Supreme Court agreed to hear Mitchell's appeal to resolve the conflict between the circuit courts of appeal on this issue. The Court, on a 5–4 vote, overruled the Third Circuit and held that a guilty plea does not waive the right against self-incrimination at a sentencing. Justice ANTHONY M. KENNEDY, writing for the majority, acknowledged that it is well established that a witness, in a single proceeding, may not testify voluntarily about a subject and then invoke the privilege against self-incrimination when questioned about the details. A witness may not "pick and choose what aspects of a particular subject to discuss without casting doubt on the trustworthiness of the statements and diminishing the integrity of the factual inquiry."

However, Justice Kennedy found a significant difference between the waiver of the right against self-incrimination in a trial and in a sentencing hearing. The concerns which justify the cross-examination when the defendant testifies are absent at a plea hearing. In his view, the purpose of a plea colloquy—the dialogue between the judge and the defendant—is to protect the defendant from an unintelligent or involuntary plea. He concluded that the Third Circuit's ruling would turn "this constitutional shield into a prosecutorial sword" by having the defendant give up all rights against compelled self-incrimination by pleading guilty, including the right to remain silent at sentencing.

Justice Kennedy also made clear that the purpose of plea colloquy is to inform the defendant of what she loses by not going to trial, not to elicit a waiver of constitutional privileges what would be a "grave encroachment" on a defendant's rights. Treating a guilty plea as a waiver of the self-incrimination clause would allow prosecutors to indict a person without specifying the quantity of drugs at issue, obtain a guilty plea, and then put the defendant on the witness stand to tell the court the quantity. Such a scenario would make the defendant "an instrument of his or her own condemnation." This would undermine constitutional criminal procedure, turning an adversarial system into an inquisition.

Justice Kennedy concluded that before sentencing a defendant might have a legitimate fear of adverse consequences if she testifies. Therefore, any attempt to compel testimony violated the Fifth Amendment, as it may be invoked in any part of a criminal case. It was "contrary to the Federal Rules of Criminal Procedure and to common sense" to argue that a sentencing proceeding was not part of a criminal case.

The Court also made clear that a sentencing court may not draw an adverse inference from the defendant's refusal to testify to facts relating to the circumstances and details of the crime. Therefore, the Court reversed the Third Circuit's decision and remanded the case so Mitchell could be resentenced.

Justice ANTONIN SCALIA, in a dissenting opinion joined by Chief Justice WILLIAM H. REHNQUIST, Justices SANDRA DAY O'CONNOR and CLARENCE THOMAS, agreed that Mitchell had the right to remain silent during the sentencing phase of her criminal case. However, Scalia argued that the judge was entitled to make the "adverse inferences that reasonably flow from her failure to testify." Based on his reading of the text and history of the Fifth Amendment, Scalia concluded that there is no constitutional prohibition against a judge drawing an adverse inference from the defendant's silence.

United States v. Dickerson

In *Miranda v. Arizona*, 384 U.S. 436, 86 S.Ct. 1602, 16 L.Ed. 694 (1966), the Supreme Court changed the way federal and state police officers conducted arrests and interrogations by requiring them to give persons in custody a series of *Miranda* warnings before attempting to interrogate them. Congress responded in 1968 by enacting 18 U.S.C.A. § 3501 (1985), seeking to restore voluntariness as the test for admitting confessions in federal court. However, the U.S. Department of Justice refused to enforce the provision, believing the law to be unconstitutional. In *United States v. Dickerson*, 166 F. 3d 667 (4th Cir. 1999), the Fourth Circuit Court of Appeals held that Congress, pursuant to its power to establish the rules of evidence and procedure in the federal courts, acted within its authority in enacting § 3501. Therefore, § 3501, rather than *Miranda* governs the admissibility of confessions in federal court.

Charles T. Dickerson confessed to robbing a series of banks in Maryland and Virginia and was indicted by a federal GRAND JURY on a variety of federal criminal charges. Before trial, however, Dickerson moved to suppress his confession. Although the district court specifically found that Dickerson's confession was voluntary for purposes of the FIFTH AMENDMENT, it nevertheless suppressed the confession because it believed that police had not read Dickerson his *Miranda* warnings before he confessed.

The federal prosecutor appealed this ruling to the Fourth Circuit, arguing that the confession was ADMISSIBLE because police had read Dickerson his rights before he began talking about the bank robberies. The prosecutor did not, however, claim that Dickerson's confession was admissible under § 3501. This law provides that "a confession... shall be admissible in evidence if it is voluntarily given."

The three-judge panel of the Fourth Circuit reacted negatively to the Department of Justice's refusal to argue that § 3501 was both constitutional and applicable in this case. In a rare display, the court on its own examined § 3501, concluding that Congress enacted § 3501 with the express purpose of legislatively overruling *Miranda* and restoring voluntariness as the test for admitting confessions in federal court. The court noted that the Department of Justice had taken the unusual step of actually prohibiting the federal prosecutor from briefing the issue, and had, during the 1990s, "affirmatively impeded" the enforcement of § 3501. With the Department of Justice unwilling to defend the constitutionality of § 3501, and no criminal defendant likely to press the issue, it concluded that "the question of whether that statute, rather than *Miranda*, governs the admission of confessions in federal court will most likely not be answered until a Court of Appeals exercises its discretion to consider the issue."

The court addressed two questions: (1) Does § 3501 purport to supersede *Miranda*? And (2) If so, did Congress have the legislative authority to overrule *Miranda*? The court answered both questions in the affirmative. It reviewed the legal history of confessions up to the *Miranda* decision and found that the Supreme Court deciding *Miranda* rejected the long held view that courts should on a case-by-case basis determine whether a confession was voluntary. Instead, the Court held that any statement stemming from the custodial interrogation of a suspect would be presumed involuntary, and therefore inadmissible, unless the police first provided the suspect with four warnings: 1) that the suspect has the right to remain silent; (2) that any statements he makes can be used against him; (3) that he has the right to the presence of an attorney during questioning; and (4) that an attorney will be appointed for him if he cannot afford one.

The court then turned to the legislative history of § 3501. Based on the legislative history, the court concluded that Congress enacted § 3501 with the express purpose of restoring voluntariness as the test for admitting confessions in federal court. The court noted, however, that Congress did not completely abandon *Miranda's* four warnings that are designed to protect the Fifth Amendment privilege against self-incrimination. Section 3501 specifically lists the *Miranda* warnings as factors that a district court should consider when determining whether a confession was given voluntarily. The appellate court found that "Congress simply provided that the failure to administer the warnings to a suspect would no longer create an irrebuttable presumption that a subsequent confession was involuntarily given."

The court then addressed the most important question: did Congress have the constitutional authority to overrule *Miranda*? The law's constitutionality turned on whether the rule set forth by the Supreme Court in *Miranda* is required by the Constitution. If it is, Congress lacked the authority to enact § 3501, and *Miranda* would continue to control the admissibility of confessions in federal court. If it is not required by the Constitution, then Congress possessed the authority to supersede *Miranda* legislatively, and § 3501 would control the admissibility of confessions in federal court.

After closely reviewing the *Miranda* decision, the appellate court found that "Surprisingly, the sixty-page opinion does not specifically state the basis for its holding that a statement obtained from a suspect without the warnings would be presumed involuntary." The *Miranda* decision does not refer to the warnings as constitutional rights and the Court acknowledged that the Constitution did not require the warnings, disclaimed any intent to create a "constitutional straightjacket," repeatedly referred to the warnings as "procedural safeguards," and invited Congress and the states "to develop their own safeguards for [protecting] the privilege." The Fourth Circuit panel concluded from these statements that the Supreme Court had no illusions that it was creating a constitutional right that Congress could not overrule.

The appeals court put great weight in the fact that the Supreme Court in *Miranda* had acted in an absence of a relevant act of Congress. It is well established that the Court's power to prescribe nonconstitutional rules of procedure and evidence for the federal courts exists only in the absence of a relevant act of Congress. Therefore, the appeals court concluded, "just as the Court was free to create an irrebuttable presumption that statements obtained without certain procedural safeguards are involuntary, Congress was free to overrule that judicially created rule." Therefore, Congress did have the authority to overrule *Miranda* and return to a case-by-case determination of whether the confession was voluntary.

Despite this ruling, the appeals court did not overrule *Miranda* completely. It stated that "nothing in today's opinion provides those in law enforcement with an incentive to stop giving the now familiar *Miranda* warnings." It advised district courts to consider the four warnings as fac-

tors when determining whether a confession was voluntarily given. Moreover, from a practical point of view for law enforcement, "providing the four *Miranda* warnings is still the best way to guarantee a finding of voluntariness."

Having concluded that § 3501 should be used to assess Dickerson's confession, the appeals court noted that the trial judge had found that Dickerson had made it voluntarily, even though he had not been given his *Miranda* warnings. Therefore, the court ruled that the court could admit the confession into evidence at Dickerson's trial.

CROSS REFERENCES
Confession; Fifth Amendment; Miranda Warning

SEX DISCRIMINATION

Discrimination on the basis of gender.

Father Denied Parental Leave

In the fall of 1994, Kevin Knussman and his wife Kimberly, were expecting a baby. Knussman, a Maryland state trooper working as a paramedic, asked for a leave of absence from work in October 1994. Under the Family and Medical Leave Act, Knussman had the right to take time off to care for his newborn child. The federal law required that companies with fifty or more workers give employees twelve weeks of unpaid family leave to care for a new baby, or for a family member who is seriously ill. Under the federal law, a worker who has accumulated enough sick time or vacation time may take a paid leave for the period of paid time that has been accumulated.

Knussman, who had more than 1,200 hours of sick leave and 250 hours of annual and personal leave, requested a paid leave of absence under the federal law. His supervisors turned down his request of four to eight weeks of paid leave. In November 1994, Kimberly Knussman was hospitalized with complications associated with her pregnancy. On December 2, 1994, a personnel manager with the Maryland state trooper's office informed Knussman of a new state law that gave thirty days of paid parental leave to the primary caregiver of a newborn baby. Secondary caregivers were given only ten days for a paid leave of absence. Knussman, who could not afford to take an unpaid leave of absence, asked his supervisors again for a paid leave under the state law. Again his supervisors refused. According to one female supervisor, "God decided only women can give birth," and "unless your wife is in a coma or dead" Knussman

Kevin Knussman was denied parental leave.

Jr., the jury returned with a verdict in favor of Knussman. The jury awarded Knussman $375,000 for the emotional suffering caused by the supervisors' decisions. Deborah A. Jeon, an attorney for the American Civil Liberties Union of Maryland representing Knussman, declared that "Knussman truly showed himself to be one of 'Maryland's finest' by standing up for the Constitution through a long and difficult legal fight." Sara Mandelbaum, Knussman's lead attorney, rejoiced that the verdict delivered "a strong message to employers that it is illegal sex discrimination to deny the rights of fathers who want to be with their children." Mandelbaum noted that "the culture hasn't caught up with the law" in the area of family leave. "[M]en are still discouraged from taking time off to take care of babies," Mandelbaum lamented. Knussman announced that he had no regrets. "It would have been worth it even if we hadn't won," Knussman said after the verdict. "This was illegal discrimination against fathers."

Approximately two years before the jury reached a verdict in the case, the Knussmans had another baby girl. This time, Knussman was allowed twelve weeks of paid leave.

Female Students with Children Denied Entry to National Honor Society

Admission into the National Honor Society (NHS) is a goal for many high school students. The NHS is a group that recognizes and awards the top students from high schools across the country. Each year, local chapters of the NHS and local school boards must determine which students merit such recognition. The boards generally base their decisions on academic performance, character, community service, and leadership qualities.

In 1998, two female students at Grant County High School in Kentucky alleged that they were wrongfully denied admission to the NHS based on their sexual activity. The students, Somer Chipman and Chasity Glass, had high grade point averages, but also had become pregnant. Chipman was pregnant during her junior year, and Glass gave birth in her sophomore year. Out of all the students who qualified for NHS consideration, Chipman and Glass were the only ones who were denied entry by the board. When Chipman and Glass asked the Grant County Board of Education why they had been rejected, they were told that they had not met the criteria for admission.

Chipman and Glass suspected that they had been rejected because of their status as mothers

could not be deemed the primary caregiver. Another reason for Knussman's secondary status cited by the supervisor was that "only women have the capacity to breast feed a baby."

Kimberly Knussman eventually gave birth, prematurely, to a daughter on December 9, 1994. Knussman took ten days off from work, but during that time he made repeated requests to his supervisors for more paid leave, arguing that his wife was not well and that he was the primary caregiver. Knussman's supervisors consistently claimed that, under the state law, women were considered the primary caregivers. Knussman returned to work after he was told that his job would be jeopardized if he did not return.

Knussman filed suit in federal court in April 1995, alleging that the Maryland state police had violated the federal Family and Medical Leave Act and the state law on family leave and Knussman's FOURTEENTH AMENDMENT right to EQUAL PROTECTION under the law. The Maryland state police argued that Knussman's supervisors had not discriminated against Knussman, and that they had simply been confused by the new statute. According to Betty Sconion, a lawyer for the state police, Knussman's supervisors "acted reasonably based on the information available to them. What they knew was that they had a statute in front of them that nobody knew how to apply."

On February 2, 1999, after many delays and a jury trial conducted by Judge Walter E. Black,

and their unconcealable sexual activity. Both were honors students who had taken accelerated courses, and both had won academic awards on the local and state levels. Under NHS guidelines, "pregnancy—whether within or without wedlock—cannot be the basis for automatic denial of the right to participate in any public school activities." "It may properly be considered, however, like any other circumstance, as a factor to be assessed in determining character as it applies to the National Honor Society." Importantly, the rules also state that "pregnancy may be taken into account in determining character only if evidence of paternity is similarly regarded." In other words, girls could be denied entry to NHS based on their sexual activity only if boys also were denied entry for having sex.

Donald J. Ruberg, a lawyer for the school board, admitted before trial that the school board based its decision on the fact that the girls were pregnant. Williamstown, Kentucky, is a resolutely Christian, conservative area that bans the sale of alcohol. "[T]he admissions committee," Ruberg told the *New York Times*, "did not feel that someone who had engaged in premarital sex should be held up as a role model for the rest of the students to emulate, whether male or female."

Seeing no male students denied entry to NHS because of sexual activity, Chipman and Glass decided to sue in federal court for membership in the NHS. With the assistance of the American Civil Liberties Union (ACLU), Chipman and Glass filed suit against the Grant County Board of Education, seeking an injunction from the court ordering the school board to admit them to the NHS. On December 30, 1998, Chief Judge William O. Bertelsman, presiding over the U.S. District Court for the Eastern District of Kentucky, ruled in favor of Chipman and Glass. The school board had argued at trial that it had not base its decision on pregnancy but on the fact that Chipman and Glass had engaged in non-marital sex. However, several students who had been admitted to NHS had submitted affidavits to the court testifying that they were never asked about their sex lives. "[T]he disparate impact," wrote Judge Bertelsman, "on young women such as [Chipman and Glass] is apparent." Bertelsman ruled that the denial of girls based on sexual activity, without the same standards for boys, was a violation of Title IX of the Education Amendments of 1972 and the FOUTEENTH AMENDMENT's guarantee of EQUAL PROTECTION under the laws.

Judge Bertelsman issued only a PRELIMINARY INJUNCTION in the case. Sara L. Mandelbaum, Senior Staff Attorney for the ACLU's Women's Rights Project and attorney, vowed to push for a permanent injunction. Glass was upbeat about the positive message in the court's decision. "Times are changing," she told Bronner. "Not all teen mothers are stereotypes."

Sex Discrimination in College Athletics

Colleges and universities are required to afford opportunities in their intercollegiate athletic programs to both men and women in a nondiscriminatory manner. The main reason for this requirement is the application of federal law known as Title IX of the Education Amendments of 1972. Specifically, Title IX prohibits sex discrimination in "any educational program or activity receiving Federal financial assistance." (20 U.S.C. §1681[a]). The U.S. Supreme Court has held that Title IX applies to colleges and universities because they receive federal financial assistance that is given to their students to pay for educational expenses. The question, however, of whether Title IX applies to the National Collegiate Athletic Association (NCAA), the private association that regulates collegiate athletics, had not been determined until the U.S. Supreme Court handed down its decision in *National Collegiate Athletic Association v. Smith*, 525 U.S. __, 119 S. Ct. 924, 142 L. Ed. 2d 929 (1999). Justice RUTH BADER GINSBURG delivered the opinion of a unanimous Supreme Court holding that the NCAA does not receive federal financial assistance and therefore could not be sued in a private action under Title IX.

In 1991, Renee Smith entered St. Bonaventure University, a member of the NCAA, as a freshman on an academic scholarship. Smith was an outstanding volleyball player in high school and, shortly after enrolling, tried out and earned a spot on the women's volleyball team. Smith played for the team in the 1991–92 and 1992–93 athletic seasons. Also an excellent student, Smith graduated from St. Bonaventure in two-and-one-half-years and elected not to play on the university's volleyball team during the 1993–94 athletic season. After earning her bachelor's degree, Smith enrolled in a graduate school program at Hofstra University, also an NCAA member, for the 1994–95 academic year. Smith then enrolled in law school at the University of Pittsburgh, another NCAA member, beginning in the 1995–96 academic year. Because Smith was graduated early from St. Bonaventure, she still had two years of athletic eligibility remaining under NCAA rules and desired to play intercollegiate volleyball at both Hofstra and Pittsburgh. However, the NCAA denied her

Renee Smith and her lawyer, Carter Phillips, lost their claim under Title IX.

eligibility to participate based on its rule that does not allow a student-athlete to participate in intercollegiate athletics at a member institution other than the one where he or she earned an undergraduate degree. Both Hofstra and the Pittsburgh petitioned the NCAA for a waiver of the rule on behalf of Smith, but the waivers were denied.

This denial led Smith to file a lawsuit in federal district court (she drafted the complaint while she was a student in law school) alleging that the NCAA's denial of the waivers caused her to be excluded from participating in intercollegiate athletics based upon her sex, in violation of Title IX. Smith did not attack the rule itself as being unfair, rather that the NCAA granted more waivers to male student-athletes than to female student-athletes.

In district court, the NCAA filed a motion for dismissal of Smith's case based on her failure to claim that the NCAA received federal financial assistance. Smith responded by arguing that the NCAA benefitted economically by virtue of its role of regulating the federally funded athletic programs of its 1200 member schools. The question of whether the athletic programs are an educational activity as defined in Title IX was not in dispute. The district court concluded that any connection between the NCAA and federal funds received by its member institutions was too weak to sustain a claim against the NCAA under Title IX and dismissed Smith's case (978 F. Supp. 213 [W.D. Pa. 1997]). Smith then petitioned the district court to allow her to amend her complaint to add Hofstra University and the University of Pittsburgh as defendants, and to also allege that

the NCAA receives federal financial assistance through another recipient and operates an educational program or activity which receives or benefits from such assistance. The district court denied Smith's motion to amend and Smith appealed to the Third Circuit Court of Appeals.

Although the court of appeals agreed with the district court that Smith's original complaint failed to state a claim under Title IX, it reversed the district court's ruling on whether to allow Smith to amend her complaint (139 F. 3d 180 [3rd Cir. 1998]). The court of appeals held that Smith's proposed amended complaint, alleging that the NCAA (through the receipt of dues from its member schools) was a recipient of federal funds, was enough to satisfy and proceed with a claim under Title IX. The U.S. Supreme Court agreed to hear the NCAA's appeal of the circuit court's decision on the narrow issue of whether a private organization that does not receive federal financial assistance is subject to Title IX because it receives payments form entities that receive assistance.

Justice RUTH BADER GINSBURG on sex-based discrimination began the Court's analysis by examining the definition of a "recipient" of federal funds from the Court's previous decisions. Ginsburg noted that the Court previously held that colleges and universities do receive federal financial assistance, albeit indirectly, when they enroll students who receive federal funds to pay for their education. In another case, the Court found that those who only benefit from federal financial assistance cannot be considered "recipients." If beneficiaries of federal aid were subject to the law, the Court stated, it would result in "limitless coverage."

Ginsburg also reviewed a regulation issued by the Department of Education regarding the definition of "recipient" under Title IX. This regulation defines "recipient" as any entity "to whom Federal financial assistance is extended directly or through another recipient and which operates an education program or activity which receives benefits from such assistance (34 C.F.R. § 106.2(h) [1997]). Ginsburg stated that the court of appeals misinterpreted this regulation when it found that beneficiaries of federal funding are also subject to Title IX. Ginsburg concluded that the language of this regulation was clear: that only recipients and not beneficiaries of federal funds must comply with Title IX—which is consistent with the Court's prior decisions.

After reviewing the Court's prior decisions and the applicable regulations, Ginsburg concluded that the NCAA, by virtue of its receipt of dues from its members, cannot be subject to a claim under Title IX. Ginsburg stated "... there is no allegation that the NCAA members paid their dues with federal funds earmarked for that purpose. At most, the Association's receipt of dues demonstrates that it indirectly benefits from the federal assistance afforded its members." Finally, Smith presented two alternative theories to the Court to show that the NCAA was subject to a Title IX claim. Smith argued that the NCAA received federal funds directly for its administration of the National Youth Sports Program. Smith also argued that when a recipient gives up control over a federally funded program to another entity, the controlling entity becomes subject to Title IX. Ginsburg dismissed both arguments, not on their merits, but because these issues were not decided by the lower courts first. This leaves open the possibility that a future decision may hold the NCAA subject to Title IX.

CROSS REFERENCES
Colleges and Universitites; Education; Equal Protection; Family Leave; Title IX

SEXUAL HARASSMENT

Unwelcome sexual advances, requests for sexual favors, and other verbal or physical conduct of a sexual nature that tends to create a hostile or offensive work environment.

Burlington Industries, Inc. v. Ellerth

The Supreme Court released its decision in *Burlington Industries, Inc. v. Ellerth*, 524 U.S. 742, 118 S. Ct. 2257, 141 L. Ed. 2d 633 (1998) on the same day that it issued *Faragher v. City of Boca Raton*. In *Burlington*, the Court ruled that an employee could sue for DAMAGES for sexual harassment under Title VII even if the employee did not suffer any adverse job consequences, such as demotion or termination. However, the Court also gave employers the ability to limit their liability by establishing a sexual harassment policy and making the policy available to employees. If an employee failed to take advantage of this policy, the employer would not be liable at all.

Kimberly Ellerth resigned fifteen months after she went to work as a salesperson for a division of Burlington Industries. She alleged that she left the job because one of her supervisors, Ted Slowik, subjected her to constant sexual harassment. The alleged harassment began during the hiring process, when Slowik asked questions during an interview that Ellerth considered strange. He also stared at her body in a way she felt inappropriate, yet she accepted the job when it was offered to her a week later.

Ellerth worked out of Chicago, while Slowik worked at the corporate headquarters in New York. However, she was required to talk and work with Slowik on a regular basis. Over the course of her employment, Ellerth alleged that Slowik had made sexual comments and had engaged in inappropriate touching. In one alleged incident, Slowik commented on Ellerth's breasts and legs. He told her to "loosen up" and later said he could make her job "very hard or very easy." Ellerth contended in her lawsuit that she repeatedly told Slowik that his advances were unwelcome.

One year after being hired, Ellerth applied for a promotion. Slowik, who had final approval on the promotion, interviewed Ellerth, at which time he allegedly rubbed her knee and told her he was hesitant to promote her because she had rejected his advances. Despite these comments, Ellerth received the promotion. Slowik's harassment, however, continued.

Burlington Industries had a policy against sexual harassment, which Ellerth was aware existed. The policy encouraged employees to report harassing conduct to their "supervisor or human resources representative or use the grievance procedure promptly." Nevertheless, she did not report Slowik's conduct. Ellerth later claimed that she was unsure whether the company enforced the policy and feared Slowik would retaliate. In May 1994 Ellerth resigned her position but did not tell her immediate supervisor of the harassment. However, she did send a letter that detailed Slowik's offensive conduct and stated that his conduct caused her to resign. Ellerth then sued Burlington, alleging that the company was liable for Slowik's conduct under Title VII.

The federal district court dismissed Ellerth's lawsuit, ruling that Burlington was not liable for Slowik's actions. The Seventh Circuit Court of Appeals reversed the lower court, ruling that Ellerth had presented sufficient evidence to pursue her claim against the company. The appeals court also found that because the company invested Slowik with authority over Ellerth's work assignment and promotion opportunities, it could be held liable for Slowik's conduct, even though Ellerth had not suffered any adverse employment actions. 123 F.3d 490 (7th Cir. 1997).

The Supreme Court, on a 7–2 vote, upheld the court of appeals decision, but presented a more focused holding that sought to clarify a confusing area of sexual harassment litigation. Justice ANTHONY M. KENNEDY, writing for the majority, stated that under Title VII, an employee who refuses "unwelcome and threatening sexual advances of supervisor, yet suffers no adverse, tangible job consequences" may recover damages from an employer. The employee does not have to show that the employer was NEGLIGENT or at fault for the supervisor's actions to recover damages. However, the employer may offer an AFFIRMATIVE DEFENSE.

Justice Kennedy acknowledged that Slowik had not carried out his threats against Ellerth. If he had, Ellerth would have been able to sue under Title VII under a QUID PRO QUO theory of sexual harassment. This theory applies when a victim's hire, job security, pay, receipt of benefits, or status depends on her or his response to a superiors sexual overtures, comments, or actions. The quid pro quo may be direct, as when a superior explicitly demands sexual favors and threatens firing if the demands are not met, or it may be indirect, as when a superior suggests that employment success depends on "personality" or "friendship" rather than competence. The Court, in *Meritor Savings, FSB v. Vinson*, 477 U.S. 57, 106 S. Ct. 2399, 91 L. Ed. 2d 49 (1986), recognized that both quid pro quo and "hostile work environment" theories are actionable under Title VII.

Justice Kennedy noted that after *Meritor*, the circuit courts of appeal had held if a plaintiff established a quid pro quo claim, the employer was subject to liability for the harassing conduct of its employees. This rule encouraged Title VII plaintiffs to use the quid pro quo theory, which resulted in "expansive pressure on the definition." This had occurred in Ellerth's action, as the question presented to the Court asked whether she could state a quid pro quo claim, not whether the employer is vicariously liable. Because the threats were not carried out, however, the case was properly viewed as a hostile work environment claim. Therefore, Kennedy saw little value in trying to use the quid pro quo framework to address the issues in the case.

With confusion about these issues widespread in the lower courts, Justice Kennedy concluded that the Court must establish a "uniform and predictable standard" as matter of federal law. The Court based its new standard on principles of AGENCY LAW, as it did in *Faragher*. Agency law describes the responsibilities of employers and employees to each other and to third parties. Kennedy invoked the agency principle

that makes employers liable for the torts of employees who act or speak on behalf of the employer, and whose apparent authority the victimized employee relies upon. In Ellerth's case, Burlington conveyed supervisory authority to Slowik. Ellerth relied on his actual or apparent authority by first resisting the unwelcome advances and then by resigning from the company.

Although the Court gave employees like Ellerth more opportunity to make Title VII sexual harassment claims, the Court also gave employers a powerful defense to fight such actions. If a supervisor has harassed an employee, but no tangible employment action is taken against the employee, the employer may present an affirmative defense. This defense includes a showing that the employer exercised reasonable care to prevent and correct sexually harassing behavior. Burlington's policy against sexual harassment would be relevant to demonstrate reasonable care. The defense also allows the employer to show that the employee had unreasonably failed to take advantage of the employer's anti-harassment procedures, Here too, Ellerth's failure to use the company's anti-harassment policy could be used by the employer to escape or limit liability.

The Court remanded the case to the district court so Ellerth could apply the Court's ruling to the facts in her case.

Justice CLARENCE THOMAS filed a dissenting opinion, which Justice ANTONIN SCALIA joined. Thomas argued that the Court had "manufactured" a vicarious liability rule for sexual harassment. He found this troubling because employer liability under Title VII would now be "judged by different standards depending upon whether a sexually or racially hostile work environment is alleged. The standard of employer liability should be the same in both instances: An employer should be liable if, and only if, the plaintiff proves that the employer was negligent in permitting the supervisor's conduct to occur."

School Found Liable for Boy Harassing Girl

The Supreme Court, in a critical decision affecting every public school in the United States, ruled that parents may sue school officials for DAMAGES when one student is sexually harassed by another. The Court, in *Davis v. Monroe County Board of Education* __ U.S. __, 119 S. Ct.1661, __ L. Ed. 2d __ (1999), ruled that Title IX of the Education Amendments of 1972 (20 U.S.C.A. § 1681) permits recovery for

Attorney Verna Williams speaks to reporters while Aurelia and Leroy Davis look on.

student-on-student sexual harassment, but only where school officials have notice of the harassment and do nothing to correct it. Moreover, the Court made clear that the harassment must be so "severe, pervasive, and objectively offensive" that a student is deprived of educational benefits and opportunities. The 5–4 decision produced a long and bitter dissent by Justice ANTHONY M. KENNEDY, who argued that the decision will lead to more litigation and will involve the federal courts in local schools.

Aurelia Davis brought the lawsuit on behalf of her daughter LaShonda for actions that occurred when LaShonda attended fifth grade in a Monroe County, Georgia, public school. Davis alleged that the school ignored repeated acts of sexual harassment committed by a fifth-grade classmate, G.F. The alleged harassment began in December 1992, when G.F. attempted to touch LaShonda's breasts and genital area and

made vulgar statements such as "I want to get in bed with you." The harassing conduct continued through the winter and early spring of 1993, with LaShonda reporting each act to the appropriate teacher. Her mother contacted the principal about the incidents but she alleged that no disciplinary action was taken against G.F. Moreover, three months elapsed before LaShonda was permitted to change her classroom seat so that she was no longer seated next to G.F.

The harassment did not end until May 1993, when G.F. was charged with, and pleaded guilty to, sexual battery for his misconduct. The lawsuit alleged that LaShonda had suffered during the months of harassment. Her previously high grades allegedly dropped as she became unable to concentrate on her studies and in April 1993, her father discovered that she had written a suicide note. Davis asked for damages from the principal, the school superintendent, and the school board, based on Title IX's prohibition against discrimination based on sex.

The federal district court dismissed the lawsuit, ruling that school officials and the board were not liable under Title IX unless "the board or an employee of the board had any role in the harassment." The Eleventh Circuit Court of Appeals affirmed this decision, finding that Title IX applied to discriminatory conduct by school employees but not to sexual harassment by students. 120 F.3d 1390 (11ᵗʰ Cir. 1998). The Supreme Court agreed to hear the appeal because the circuit courts of appeal were divided over whether and under what circumstances a recipient of federal educational funds can be liable for student-on-student sexual harassment.

Justice SANDRA DAY O'CONNOR, writing for the majority, reversed the Eleventh Circuit. O'Connor acknowledged that an implied right of private action exists under Title IX, allowing parents to sue on behalf of their children for misconduct by school officials. She carefully noted that the school board, as a recipient of federal educational funds, was liable only for its misconduct, not G.F.'s. Davis sought to hold the board liable for "its *own* decision to remain idle in the face of known student-on-student harassment in its schools."

The Court relied on the standard set out in *Gebser v. Lago Vista Independent School District*, 524 U.S. 274, 118 S. Ct. 1989, 141 L. Ed. 2d 277, (1998), for determining the liability of school officials under Title IX. Justice O'Connor, who also wrote the *Gebser* opinion, stated that a school district will be liable for damages under Title XI when it is deliberately indifferent to known acts of harassment of students by either school employees or by students. Deliberate indifference "makes sense as a direct liability theory only where the recipient has the authority to take remedial action." If school employees do not engage in the harassment directly, the school board may not be liable unless its deliberate indifference causes students to undergo harassment or make them vulnerable to it. In addition, the harassment must take place "in a context subject to the school district's control."

O'Connor dismissed fears that this standard of liability would hobble school administrators. She concluded that "administrators will continue to enjoy the flexibility they require in making disciplinary decisions" because liability for student-on-student harassment will attach only where administrators' failure to respond "is clearly unreasonable in light of the known circumstances."

The Court also applied the *Gebser* decision's ruling that harassment qualifies as "discrimination" under the provisions of Title IX. In the context of student-on-student harassment, Davis did not have to prove that there was an "overt, physical deprivation of access to school resources" to make a claim. However, she did have to show that the harassment was

> so severe, pervasive, and objectively offensive, and that so undermines and detracts from the victims' educational experience, that the victims are effectively denied equal access to an institution's resources and opportunities.

O'Connor stated that there was no one formula to determine whether gender-oriented conduct is harassment. Instead, a court has to look at a "constellation of surrounding circumstances, expectations, relationships." She acknowledged that schoolchildren "may regularly interact in ways that would be unacceptable among adults." Therefore, the offensive behavior must be serious enough to "have the systemic effect of denying the victim equal access to an education program or activity." She emphasized that a single instance of severe student-on-student harassment would trigger liability. Moreover, student-on-student harassment that violated equal access to educational benefits would be harder to prove than harassment by a school employee.

Therefore, the Court sent the case back to the district court to give Davis a chance to prove her case under the standards announced in the ruling.

Justice Kennedy, in a dissenting opinion joined by Chief Justice WILLIAM H. REHNQUIST, and Justices ANTONIN SCALIA and CLARENCE THOMAS, argued that Congress had not intended Title IX to allow private lawsuits based on student-on-student harassment. He lamented the decision because it would divert "scarce resources" and would pressure school districts to "adopt whatever federal code of student conduct and discipline the Department of Education sees fit to impose upon them." Historically, states and local communities had governed the public schools. However, this decision meant by accepting federal funds, the states had ceded "to the federal government power over the day-to-day disciplinary decisions of schools."

Faragher v. City of Boca Raton

Sexual harassment in the workplace has emerged as one of the most serious forms of employment discrimination. Litigation has increased since the Supreme Court upheld the concept of a hostile work environment as actionable under Title VII of the Civil Rights Act of 1964 (42 U.S.C.A. § 2000e et seq.) in *Meritor Savings, FSB v. Vinson*, 477 U.S. 57, 106 S. Ct.2399, 91 L. Ed.49 (1986). Following *Meritor*, however, the Court has been called upon to further define the limits of liability for sexual harassment under Title VII.

In *Faragher v. City of Boca Raton*, 524 U.S. 775,118 S. Ct. 2275, 141 L. Ed. 2d 662 (1998), the Supreme Court addressed whether an employer may be vicariously liable for the sexual harassment of its supervisors. VICARIOUS LIABILITY is a TORT doctrine that imposes responsibility upon one person for the failure of another, with whom the person has a special relationship, such as employer and employee, to exercise such care as a reasonably prudent person would use under similar circumstances. The Court held that an employer is vicariously liable under Title VII for the discrimination caused by a supervisor. However, the Court also created an affirmative defense for the employer to raise that looks to both the reasonableness of both the employer's and the employee's conduct. Civil rights and employer groups hailed the decision, as it spells out a standard that courts can follow in the future.

Beth Ann Faragher worked for five years as a lifeguard for the city of Boca Raton, Florida, while attending college. Two years after she resigned from her job, she filed a Title VII lawsuit against her two immediate supervisors in the city recreation department and the city. Faragher alleged that the two male supervisors repeatedly subjected her and other female lifeguards to "uninvited and offensive touching," by making lewd remarks, and by speaking of women in offensive terms. Because of these actions, the men had created a sexually hostile work environment that violated Title VII. Faragher included the city in her lawsuit because the two supervisors were agents of the city, thus making the city vicariously liable for their illegal actions.

Following a BENCH TRIAL—a trial conducted by a judge without a jury—the federal district court judge ruled that the supervisors' conduct constituted sexual harassment and that the city could be held liable for this harassment because the conduct was pervasive enough that the city should have known about it. The court reasoned that the supervisors acted as the city's agents when they committed the harassment.

The Eleventh Circuit Court of Appeals reversed the trial court and ruled that the city was not liable. (111 F. 3d 1530 [11th Cir. 1997]). The appeals court, on a 7–5 vote, held that the *Meritor* decision and basic principles governing agency made clear that the city could not be liable. Because the supervisors were not acting within the scope of their employment when they harassed the female workers, the city was not liable under AGENCY principles. Moreover, knowledge of the offensive behavior could not be imputed to the city nor could the city be liable for negligence for failing to prevent the supervisors' conduct.

The Supreme Court, on a 7–2 vote, reversed the court of appeals. Justice DAVID H. SOUTER, writing for the majority, announced the rule that an employer is vicariously liable for prohibited discrimination caused by a supervisor. However, this LIABILITY is subject to an affirmative defense by the employer that assesses the reasonableness of the employer's and the employee's conduct. Souter acknowledged that in previous employment sexual harassment cases the Court had "established few definitive rules for determining when an employer will be liable for a discriminatory environment that is otherwise actionably abusive." *Meritor* was the only case that touched on these issues, yet the Court only stated that "traditional agency principles were relevant for determining employer liability."

Justice Souter surveyed the current state of the law and found confusion and conflict. With no guidance from the Supreme Court, the circuits typically ruled that Title VII supervisory sexual harassment fell outside the scope of employment. Therefore, under established principles of agency law, the employer was not liable for the torts of an employee. However, this line of cases conflicted with another line that held that employers are vicariously liable for employees' intentional torts, including sexual assault. Although these actions were not within the scope of employment, courts held that these actions were a foreseeable consequence of its business.

Faced with this conflict, Justice Souter rejected the idea that sexual harassment is one of the normal risks of doing business, which would make employers automatically liable for acts of sexual harassment by its employees. He based his rejection on two factors (1) Congress did not intend to create such a sharp break with common law agency principles and (2) the lower federal courts had used a negligence standard to judge employer liability, resulting in the conclusion that sexual harassment was outside the scope of employment.

Nevertheless, Justice Souter also found that the court of appeals had been mistaken in rejecting another agency principle. This principle provides that an employer is not subject to the torts of his employees acting outside their scope of employment unless the employee purported to act or speak on behalf of the employer and there was reliance on this authority by another person. Translated into the Title VII sphere, this meant that an employer is liable for the harassing conduct of a supervisor "made possible by use of his supervisory authority."

Souter noted that this did not mean an employer was "automatically" liable for harassment by a supervisor. To prevent the risk of this happening, the Court considered two alternatives. The first was to require the employee to prove that the supervisor invoked his authority in the course of his harassing activity. Justice Souter dismissed this alternative, believing its adoption would lead to "close judgment calls" and a wide of range of results that would appear contradictory. Employees would have a difficult meeting this proof requirement because it is often difficult to make a distinction between a direct invocation of authority and an implicit one.

Justice Souter preferred a second alternative, permiting the employer to present an affirmative defense that shows the employer's conduct was reasonable, even if the supervisor has created a hostile work environment. Evidence of reasonableness includes the development of policies against sexual harassment that permit a harassed employee to report the offensive conduct to the employer. Souter concluded that this alternative would provide employers with an incentive to prevent and eliminate harassment.

Therefore the Court held, as it did in *Burlington Industries, Inc. v. Ellerth*, 524 U.S. 742, 118 S. Ct. 2257, 141 L. Ed. 2d 633 (1998) that an employer is subject to vicarious liability to a victimized employee for the hostile work environment created by a supervisor with immediate or higher authority over the employee. But the employer may raise as a defense that the employee did not act at the time to report the offensive conduct. There are two necessary elements to the defense: (1) the employer exercised reasonable care to prevent and correct promptly any harassing conduct; and (2) the plaintiff employee "unreasonably failed to take advantage of any preventive or corrective opportunities provided by the employer or to avoid harm otherwise." Evidence of an employer anti-harassment policy will generally satisfy the first element,

while evidence of the employee's failure to use a complaint procedure will satisfy the second element. However, Justice Souter stated that this affirmative defense does not apply when the "supervisor's harassment culminates in a tangible employment action, such as discharge, demotion, or undesirable reassignment."

The Court applied this new standard to the facts of Faragher's case, finding that Boca Raton could not make an affirmative defense. The trial record disclosed that the city had not disseminated its sexual harassment policy to lifeguards and other beach employees, that it had made no attempt to keep track of the supervisors' conduct, and that the city's policy did not give employees the option of bypassing the harassing supervisor in registering complaints. Based on these circumstances the Court found it unnecessary to return the case to the trial court to determine whether the city had exercised reasonable care to prevent the supervisor's harassing conduct. Instead, the Court ruled as a matter of law that the city was liable to Faragher for damages for the conduct of her supervisors.

Justice CLARENCE THOMAS, joined by Justice ANTONIN SCALIA, filed a dissenting opinion. Thomas rejected the Court's reasoning, concluding that "absent an adverse employment consequence, an employer cannot be held vicariously liable if a supervisor creates a hostile work environment. Petitioner suffered no adverse employment consequence."

Fredette v. BVP Management Associates

Until the 1990s, federal courts confronted Title VII sexual harassment actions that involved parties of the opposite sex. Though most sexual harassment litigation has involved male harassers and female victims, cases began to appear in the 1990s that involved same-sex sexual harassment, usually involving two males. These were cases of first impression and not surprisingly, a number went to the federal circuit courts of appeal. The Fifth Circuit ruled that same-sex sexual harassment was not actionable under Title VII, but several other circuits found nothing in the law to prevent such claims. The Fifth's Circuit's holding was overturned by the Supreme Court in *Oncale v. Sundowner Offshore Services, Inc.*, 523 U.S. 75, 118 S. Ct. 998, 140 L. Ed. 2d 201 (1998), endorsing the decisions made by the Fourth, Sixth, and Eleventh Circuits.

The Eleventh Circuit's ruling in *Fredette v. BVP Management Associates*, 112 F. 3d 1503 (11th Cir.1997) examined in more detail than *Oncale* the various grounds for permitting a same-sex sexual harassment lawsuit under Title VII. The case involved Robert Fredette, who had been employed as a waiter in one of BVP's Florida restaurants. Fredette alleged that Dana Sunshine, a male restaurant manager, had repeatedly propositioned Fredette for sexual favors. Sunshine offered Fredette employment benefits in exchange for sex but Fredette refused his advances. After Fredette reported the offensive conduct to BVP management, Sunshine retaliated against him in various work-related ways. Fredette filed a Title VII lawsuit against BVP, seeking to hold the business responsible for the acts of one of its supervisors.

The federal district court dismissed Fredette's action, concluding that Fredette could not show the harassment occurred "because of sex." On appeal, the Eleventh Circuit reversed the trial judge's decision, finding that same-sex harassment claims were within the scope of Title VII. The court examined the language of the statute, the context of the statutory language, its legislative history, the Equal Employment Opportunity Commission's (EEOC) interpretation of the law, and the case law of the various circuits.

The court first reviewed the relevant provision of Title VII, which states that "It shall be an unlawful employment practice…to discriminate against any individual with respect to his compensation, terms, conditions, or privileges of employment, because of such individual's…sex…" 42 U.S.C.A. § 2000e-2(a)(1). It read the statute as prohibiting an "employer," whether male or female, from discriminating against "any individual," whether male or female. The plain meaning of the statute failed to show that a "cause of action is limited to opposite gender contexts."

As for the causation requirement, that the discrimination was based on sex, the appeals court concluded that harassment by a male against a female was "because of sex." Shifting the situation to a male against male situation changed nothing: Sunshine's offensive conduct towards Fredette was also because of sex. A harasser "makes advances towards the victim because the victim is a member of the gender the harasser prefers." Fredette had offered evidence to the trial court that Sunshine had not made advances towards women, only men.

The appeals court then examined Title VII's legislative history. It found no evidence that Congress intended to exclude same-sex harassment claims from the coverage of Title VII. Though Congress might have focused on the more visible problem of male harassment of fe-male employees, the court noted that the Supreme Court had extended the protection of other Title VII provisions to men. Because there was no evidence that Congress intended to exclude same-sex harassment, the courts were not precluded from holding that in some circumstances it was actionable.

The EEOC's interpretation of Title VII also supported the inclusion of same-sex harassment lawsuits. The EEOC Compliance Manual states that the victim "does not have to be of the opposite sex from the harasser." The manual characterizes the "crucial inquiry" as "whether the harasser treats a member or members of one sex differently from members of the other sex." The sexual harassment could, for example, be based on the victim's sex and not on the victim's sexual preference. § 615.2(b)(3) (1987).

The appeals court also looked at the case law surrounding same-sex harassment. It noted that the Sixth Circuit had found that Title VII encompassed same-sex harassment suits and had rejected the idea that only "traditional" forms of sex discrimination were actionable under the statute. *Yeary v. Goodwill Industries-Knoxville, Inc.*, 107 F. 3d 443 (6th Cir.1997). The Sixth Circuit characterized the facts before it as "about as traditional as they come, albeit with a twist." It made no difference that the male harasser happened to sexually proposition and physically assault a man rather than a woman.

The Fourth Circuit, like the Sixth Circuit and the *Fredette* court, relied on the statute's plain language, the EEOC manual, and case law to justify same-sex sexual harassment claims. *Wrightson v. Pizza Hut of America, Inc.*, 99 F. 3d 138 (4th Cir.1996). Other circuits, while not ruling on same-sex harassment claims, used language in their decisions to suggest that such claims might be actionable under Title VII.

The Fifth Circuit was the only appeals court that rejected Title VII's application to same-sex harassment. In the case the Supreme Court would eventually overturn, the court failed to provide any reasons for why same-sex harassment was barred. *Oncale v. Sundowner Offshore Services, Inc.*, 83 F. 3d 118 (5th Cir.1996). It merely invoked, what the *Fredette* court called a "cryptic" prior decision, which also failed to give a rationale for its ruling.

Having surveyed the circuit courts, the Eleventh Circuit rejected a federal district court case that held that a Title VII claim is viable only where the work environment is dominated by members of one gender and the workplace is hostile to the other gender. *Goluszek v. H.P. Smith*, 697 F.Supp. 1452 (N.D. Ill.1988). The circuit court found this reasoning flawed, as the courts have established that Title VII "protects men as well as women, without regard to whether the workplace is male-dominated."

The Eleventh Circuit also rejected BVP's claim that a decision in favor of Fredette would protect against discrimination based on sexual orientation. The court emphasized the narrowness of its holding and restated that discrimination because of sexual orientation is not actionable. It held that the facts presented by Fredette supported his right to bring a Title VII claim for gender discrimination. Therefore, the court remanded the case to the trial court so Fredette could pursue his claim.

Gebser v. Lago Vista Independent School District

The Supreme Court clarified the civil LIABILITY of school districts when a school teacher sexually harasses a student. The Court, in *Gebser v. Lago Vista Independent School District*, 524 U.S. 274, 118 S. Ct. 1989, 141 L. Ed. 2d 277 (1998), ruled that a school district cannot be LIABLE for DAMAGES unless a school official with authority to take corrective measures has actual notice of the teacher's misconduct and takes no action to correct the behavior. In so ruling, the Court closely examined a provision of Title IX of the Education Amendments of 1972, 20 U.S.C.A. § 1681(a), which forbids recipients of federal education aid from subjecting anyone to discrimination based on gender.

The case arose out of the actions of Frank Waldrop, a teacher at the Lago Vista Texas high school. Waldrop initiated a sexual relationship with fifteen-year-old Alida Gebser, who was one of his students. They had numerous sexual encounters, some of which took place during school time but off school property. The relationship ended when a police officer discovered them having sex and arrested Waldrop. The Lago Vista Independent School District fired Waldrop and the state of Texas revoked his teaching license. Gebser did not report the relationship to school officials because she was uncertain how to react and she wanted to continue having him as a teacher.

In the months before his arrest, parents of other students complained to Waldrop's principal about sexually suggestive remarks he had made to their children. The parents, the principal, and Waldrop met about the issue and though he denied making the remarks, he apologized and said it would not happen again. The principal did not forward this information to the school superintendent, who, under Title IX, was the person designated to receive information on discriminatory conduct.

Gebser and her mother sued the school district under Title IX for damages. The federal district court dismissed the suit, and the Fifth Circuit Court of Appeals sustained the dismissal. The appeals court held that school districts are not liable under Title IX for teacher-student sexual harassment unless a supervising school official knew of the abuse and did nothing to end it. In Gebser's case, school officials did not have knowledge of the relationship, therefore the lawsuit had to be dismissed. 106 F. 3d 1223 (5th Cir.1997).

The Supreme Court, on a 5–4 vote, upheld the appeals court. Justice SANDRA DAY O'CONNOR, writing for the majority, agreed that school officials must have actual notice of sexual harassment and do nothing before liability attaches to a school district under Title IX. Title IX's main prohibition provides that:

> No person in the United States shall, on the basis of sex, be excluded from participation in, be denied the benefit of, or be subjected to discrimination under any education program or activity receiving Federal financial assistance…20 U.S.C.A. § 1681(a),

However, the Supreme Court ruled in *Cannon v. University of Chicago*, 441 U.S. 677, 99 S. Ct. 1946, 60 L. Ed. 2d 560 (1979), that Title IX is also enforceable through an implied private right of action. This means that private citizens can sue an educational institution for damages for harassment and other forms of sexual discrimination. Gebser had argued that the standards developed by the Supreme Court in Title VII cases should be applied to lawsuits based on Title IX. Title VII makes an employer liable for the conduct of its employee if the employer has constructive notice of the conduct. Constructive notice is a legal determination that someone should have known something. Thus, if school official should have known about the sexual relationship but did not have actual notice, Title VII would allow Gebser to obtain damages.

Nevertheless, Justice O'Connor rejected the application of Title VII to Title IX litigation. Unlike Title IX, Title VII contains "an express cause of action for a damages remedy." Because Title IX's private action is a judicial rather than a legislative creation, the Court had to speculate how Congress would have addressed the issue of monetary damages under Title IX. O'Connor compared Title IX to Title VI and Title VII of the Civil Rights Act of 1964. Title VII is much different from Titles VI and IX. It contains an express private right of action, subject to a limit on the amount of damages that can be awarded in an individual case. In contrast, Title VI prohibits recipients of federal funds from practicing racial discrimination, while Title IX does the same for gender discrimination.

Justice O'Connor stated that the Court will "examine the propriety of private actions holding recipients liable in damages" for violating a condition of receiving federal money. Congress' intent about Title IX was best assessed by looking at the rules governing administrative enforcement of the act. Under Title IX, the federal agency must give actual notice to officials of the recipient so they have an opportunity to voluntarily comply with the law and correct the problem. Allowing recovery in a private action based on constructive notice "would be at odds" with the basic objective of Title IX administrative enforcement to prevent the cutoff of aid from an entity that is willing to institute "prompt corrective measures." Moreover, O'Connor believed it "unsound" to have Title IX's express enforcement system require actual notice while allowing the judicially implied system to permit "substantial liability" through the use of constructive notice.

The Court made clear that unless Congress amended Title IX, the implied damages remedy must be modeled on the express enforcement remedy. Therefore, a private damages remedy is not permitted under Title IX unless an official who has "authority to address the alleged discrimination" and to take corrective measures has "actual knowledge of discrimination" and fails adequately to respond. In addition, the official's response must amount to "deliberate indifference." This means that a school official would have to make a conscious choice not to do something.

The Court applied this ruling to the facts in the case and concluded that the action must be dismissed because the Lago Vista school district did not have actual notice of the affair until police arrested Waldrop.

Justice JOHN PAUL STEVENS, in a dissenting opinion joined by Justices DAVID H. SOUTER, RUTH BADER GINSBURG, and STEPHEN BREYER, contended that the Court could fashion a remedy different than that established by Congress for administrative en-forcement. He concluded that the "majority's policy judgment about the appropriate remedy in this case thwarts the purposes of Title IX."

Jones v. Clinton

Paula Jones and President BILL CLINTON agreed in November 1998 to settle Jones' sexual harassment lawsuit against the president. The settlement came after an Arkansas federal judge dismissed Jones' case but before the Eighth Circuit Court of Appeals ruled on her appeal. Although the alleged harassment occurred when Clinton was governor of Arkansas, the lawsuit and the information that resulted proved damaging to his presidency. In April 1999, the federal judge held Clinton in CONTEMPT for giving false TESTIMONY to Jones' lawyers in a January 1998 DEPOSITION about his relationship with Monica Lewinsky.

In her lawsuit, Jones alleged that on May 8, 1991, while Governor Clinton was still governor of Arkansas and she was an employee of the Arkansas Industrial Development Commission, she was persuaded by a member of the Arkansas state police to visit the governor in a business suite at the hotel, where he made sexual advances that she rejected. Jones also claimed that because she rejected Clinton's advances, her superiors dealt with her in a rude and hostile manner and changed her job duties. She charged that the state police officer who allegedly sent her to Clinton's suite had defamed her by stating that Jones had accepted the governor's overtures. In addition, she alleged that various persons authorized to speak for President Clinton had publicly called her a liar by denying that the incident took place.

Jones filed her lawsuit in 1994, alleging that Clinton's alleged actions violated her CIVIL RIGHTS. She sought compensatory damages of $75,000 and PUNITIVE DAMAGES of $100,000. U.S. District Court Judge SUSAN WEBBER WRIGHT denied Clinton's motion to dismiss the case based on presidential IMMUNITY, ruled that DISCOVERY could begin, but held that she would not conduct the trial until after Clinton left the presidency. Both Clinton and Jones appealed to the Eighth Circuit Court of Appeals. The Eighth Circuit held that the district court properly rejected the motion to dismiss but reversed the order to postpone the trial because it appeared to be the "functional equivalent" of a grant of temporary immunity. 72 F. 3d 1354 (8th Cir. 1996).

Clinton appealed this ruling to the Supreme Court. The Court, in *Clinton v. Jones*, 520 U.S. 681, 117 S. Ct. 1636, 137 L. Ed. 2d 945 (1997), rejected Clinton's position, ruling that Jones' lawsuit should be allowed to proceed. Justice John Paul Stevens, writing for the Court, rejected the president's contention that defending the lawsuit would impose unacceptable burdens on the president's time and energy. It seemed unlikely to the Court that Clinton would have to be occupied with the Jones lawsuit for any substantial amount of time.

Jones' attorneys then sought to obtain evidence for the trial. Clinton agreed to be deposed in Washington, D.C., on January 17, 1998, the first sitting president to do so. At the deposition, Jones' attorney asked him whether he been involved in a sexual relationship with former White House intern Monica Lewinsky. He denied that there had been such a relationship and made other denials to questions about his conduct with Lewinsky. In written responses to interrogatories, Clinton made similar denials. Within days the news media reported about allegations of a sexual affair between the president and the intern, beginning a process that would culminate with Clinton's acquittal at a Senate impeachment trail in February 1999.

Clinton's legal problems during this thirteen-month period intensified after he changed his answers about his involvement with Lewinsky during his Whitewater GRAND JURY appearance on August 17, 1998. In response to questions from independent counsel KENNETH W. STARR's attorneys, Clinton admitted he had been alone with Lewinsky and that they had engaged in "inappropriate intimate contact." Much of Clinton's grand jury testimony contradicted the sworn testimony he gave at the Jones deposition.

On April 1, 1998, Judge Wright dismissed the Jones lawsuit. She ruled that assuming the harassing conduct occurred, it did not constitute a sexual assault and that there was no proof that Jones was emotionally injured or punished in the workplace for rejecting Clinton's advances. Jones appealed the ruling, but both parties began a round of settlement talks.

On November 13, 1998, Jones agreed to drop her lawsuit in return for $850,000. Jones dropped her previous demand that Clinton apologize or make an admission of guilt. On January 12, 1999, Clinton sent a check for the agreed amount to Jones' attorneys. An insurance company paid $475,000 of the amount to buy out the president's personal LIABILITY policy. The other $375,000 came from a blind trust that managed the investments for the president and HILLARY RODHAM CLINTON. The first lady had made most of the money in the trust from

Kenneth W. Starr

her work as a lawyer. President Clinton had agreed to the settlement after his advisors stated that the money would be raised independently for him. However, these advisors discovered that they could not use Clinton's legal defense fund because it was restricted to paying attorney fees and expenses.

After Clinton's impeachment acquittal it appeared his legal woes might be finally over. However, on April 12, 1999, Judge Wright found him in contempt of court for giving intentionally false testimony about his relationship with Lewinsky during the January 1998 deposition. Judge Wright, in reviewing Clinton's "misleading statements," stated that "[t]he record demonstrates by clear and convincing evidence that the president [gave] false, misleading and evasive answers that were designed to obstruct the judicial process." She also found that the president had "undermined the integrity of the judicial system." The judge felt compelled to cite him with contempt to deter others from "emulating the president of the United States by willfully violating...orders of this and other courts."

Judge Wright ordered Clinton to compensate Jones and her attorneys, as well as the judge and her law clerk, for any expenses related to his "willful failure to obey this court." In addition, the judge forwarded her order to the Arkansas Supreme Court's Committee on Professional Conduct for review and possible discipline. The committee could suspend or disbar Clinton from the practice of law.

Jones's lawyers asked the court to award them almost $500,000 in legal reimbursements based on the contempt. In late May 1999, Clinton's attorneys called the claim "excessive and unreasonable," proposing that Jones was entitled to approximately $34,000. Judge Wright must determine the appropriate amount.

CROSS REFERENCES
Civil Rights; Contempt; Employment Law; Schools and School Districts; Whitewater; Womens' Rights

STARR, KENNETH W.

Kenneth Starr has served as a judge on the court of appeals, as U.S. SOLICITOR GENERAL, and is most prominently as INDEPENDENT COUNSEL investigating President BILL CLINTON and his administration. Appointed as independent counsel in 1994, Starr has garnered both vilification and praise for his investigation into the Arkansas land deal known as WHITE-

WATER and the investigation into the president's affair with Monica Lewinsky, a young White House intern.

Starr was born in Vernon, Texas, on July 21, 1946, to Willie and Vannie Starr. His father was a minister for the Church of Christ in Thalia, Texas; he also barbered and sold milk from the family cow. The children had a strict upbringing commensurate with their father's calling. When Starr was young, the family moved to San Antonio, where he was elected as class president of Sam Houston High during his junior and senior years. He was first interested by the political process during the 1960 presidential election between JOHN F. KENNEDY and RICHARD M.NIXON.

After high school graduation, Starr attended Harding College, a school affiliated with the Church of Christ and located in Searcy, Arkansas. To help defray his expenses, he sold Bibles door-to-door. According to one of his roommates, Starr did not deviate from his conservative upbringing. Nevertheless, he reportedly defended the rights of VIETNAM WAR protesters as an editor of the college newspaper, although he supported the war. To better pursue his interest in politics, he transferred to George Washington University in Washington, D.C., graduating in 1968. He obtained a master's from Brown University in Providence, Rhode Island, then attended Duke University Law School. At Duke, he served as an editor of the *Duke Law Journal*. After graduation in 1973, he clerked for a federal appellate judge in the District of Columbia, worked briefly as an associate in a law firm, then was selected to clerk for Supreme Court Chief Justice WARREN E. BURGER.

In private practice after his clerkship, Starr became acquainted with William French Smith. When Ronald Reagan appointed Smith to be attorney general in 1981, Starr joined the JUSTICE DEPARTMENT. Starr's typically conservative opinions generally meshed extremely well with the Reagan administration. He did not, however, evince an unswerving devotion; he disagreed with the administration when it supported a Christian evangelical college's efforts to retain certain tax benefits after it was disclosed that the institution had discriminated against minorities.

Reagan rewarded Starr with an appointment to the U.S. Court of Appeals for the District of Columbia, which is considered the most prestigious federal appellate court. In 1983, at age thirty-seven, Starr was the youngest person ever to be appointed to the court of appeals.

KENNETH W. STARR

1946 Born in Vernon, Texas

1973 Graduated Duke University Law School

1983 Appointed U.S. Court of Appeals

1989 Appointed solicitor general

1994 Appointed independent counsel

During his six-year tenure, Starr consistently displayed his conservative ideology, but inspired respect, both from conservatives and liberals, for his judicial integrity.

Starr accepted the position of solicitor general offered him by President George Bush in 1989. His duties as solicitor general included arguing cases on behalf of the United States in the Supreme Court and deciding which government cases merited appeal. He returned to private practice when President Clinton took office. On August 5, 1994, a three-judge panel selected Starr to replace Robert B. Fiske, Jr., as independent counsel for the inquiry into the Whitewater affair clouding the Clinton administration.

Although Fiske had already done so, Starr investigated President and Mrs. Clinton's connection to the failure of the Madison Guaranty Savings & Loan, a bank in Little Rock, Arkansas, owned by James and Susan McDougal, business partners of the Clintons. Susan McDougal refused to testify before Starr's grand jury, and consequently served about eighteen months in prison on CONTEMPT charges. Starr also reopened an investigation into the 1993 death of White House counsel Vincent W. Foster, Jr. Fiske had concluded that Foster had committed suicide, but conspiracy theories abounded that the death had been murder. Starr's July 1997 report concluded that the death was a suicide. At the request of Attorney General Janet Reno, Starr also investigated the 1993 firing of White House travel employees at a time when friends of the Clintons were getting into the travel business, and the misappropriation of FBI files on Republicans by White House staffers.

Starr took an unprecedented step when he called HILLARY CLINTON to testify before a

GRAND JURY in 1996. Starr had earlier SUB-POENAED from Hillary Clinton's Little Rock law firm billing records relating to her work for the failed Madison Guaranty. Some of the records were missing until early 1996, when they were discovered in the Clintons' private living quarters of the White House. Starr sought the First Lady's testimony to determine whether the Clintons or others in the administration had hidden evidence or otherwise tried to obstruct justice.

Starr faced significant criticism from the beginning of his tenure for the perceived partisan nature of his investigation, as well as for the cost of the investigation, estimated at $40 million through 1998. Starr has been criticized for a paucity of results. Former Arkansas governor Jim Guy Tucker was convicted of conspiracy for actions in a real estate scheme from his days as a lawyer in public practice, and Susan and Jim McDougal also were found guilty of criminal charges. Webster Hubbell, Hillary Clinton's former law partner and high-ranking Justice official, pleaded guilty in 1994 to two counts of TAX EVASION and MAIL FRAUD. David Hale, a former municipal judge and businessman, was convicted on fraud and conspiracy charges and has claimed that he was pressured by Clinton to make an illegal loan, but these charges are unsubstantiated. Starr failed to obtain convictions in a 1996 trial involving bank officers accused of misappropriating funds, which Starr tried to link to Clinton's 1986 campaign for governor.

In early 1998 revelations involving President Clinton and White House intern Monica Lewinsky began to surface, and Starr's office was immediately in the midst of controversy. Starr sanctioned the wiring of Pentagon employee Linda R. Tripp, a confidant of Lewinsky, in order to learn more about the alleged affair between the president and Lewinsky, and to discover any attempts to conceal the affair. Under significant criticism that his investigation had gone too far, Starr continued investigating the president to determine whether he had committed perjury or attempted to obstruct justice in connection with the SEXUAL HARASSMENT case brought against Clinton by former Arkansas state employee, Paula Corbin Jones. In early January 1998, Lewinsky offered an affidavit in the Jones case denying that she had had a sexual relationship with the president. On January 17, 1998, Clinton made the same denial in a deposition in the *Jones* case. Starr's investigation was further complicated in April 1998 when Federal District Judge SUSAN WEBBER WRIGHT dis-

missed the Jones lawsuit before trial. Dismissal of the lawsuit engendered further criticism for Starr when he refused to drop his perjury and obstruction of justice investigation.

In July 1998, Starr subpoenaed Clinton to testify before the grand jury. The subpoena was later withdrawn when Clinton agreed to testify voluntarily. President Clinton also voluntarily provided to the office of independent counsel a vial of blood to determine whether a dress of Lewinsky's was stained with his semen. The president testified via videotape to the grand jury on August 17, 1998. Later that day, he admitted in a televised speech that he had had an "inappropriate" relationship with Lewinsky, but he steadfastly maintained that he had not committed PERJURY or obstructed justice. In the speech, Clinton severely castigated Starr's investigation, a move that angered many of the president's supporters. However, the investigator became the investigated on October 30, 1998, when a federal judge approved a special investigator to inquire whether Starr's office had leaked secret grand jury information.

In September 1998 Starr delivered his report and thirty-six boxes of accompanying evidence to Capitol Hill, detailing the president's sexual conduct and setting out possible grounds for impeachment. Although Clinton continued to enjoy significant support from the public, the Starr Report prompted the House Judiciary Committee to open an investigation into Clinton's actions in October 1998. Starr testified before the House Judiciary Committee for twelve hours in November 1998, and the next month the committee sent four articles of impeachment to the full House. The four articles were pared to two by the full House in December—one article for perjury before a grand jury, and another for obstruction of justice in the Jones lawsuit. Clinton was acquitted in February 1999.

Prosecutions by the office of independent counsel continued in the first half of 1999, but showed signs of slowing down. Susan McDougal was acquitted in late April on an obstruction of justice charge, and the jury failed to reach a verdict on two counts of criminal contempt. In May 1999, a mistrial was declared when the jury failed to reach a verdict in the case of Julie Hiatt Steele, whom Starr charged had obstructed justice and made false statements regarding the investigation of alleged misconduct by the president toward Kathleen Willey. Starr later announced that he would not retry either McDougal or Steele. Webster Hubbell faces trial on charges that he lied to bank regulators to conceal work by himself and Hillary Clinton on an Arkansas land development project when they were partners in Little Rock. On June 1, 1999, a federal appeals court reinstated a count against Hubbell that had previously been dismissed by a federal district judge. Finally, Starr scored a victory when federal judge Susan Webber Wright held President Clinton in civil contempt for lying in his deposition in the Jones sexual harassment lawsuit.

Senate hearings began in February 1999 to determine whether the Independent Counsel Act, enacted in 1974 in the wake of the Watergate scandal, should be allowed to expire. Kenneth Starr testified against extension of the law.

CROSS REFERENCES
Appendix: Articles of Impeachment; Impeachment; Independent Counsel; White, Susan Webber; Whitewater

SUICIDE

The deliberate taking of one's own life.

Dr. Jack Kevorkian Convicted of Second-Degree Murder

After four victories in cases where he was charged with assisted suicide earlier in the decade, Dr. Jack Kevorkian was convicted of second-degree murder by a jury in Pontiac, Michigan, in March 1999. (*Michigan v. Kevorkian*, 98–163675–FC). Kevorkian administered a lethal injection in September 1998 to Thomas Youk, a fifty-two-year-old man who suffered from amyotrophic lateral sclerosis, or Lou Gehrig's disease, a fatal neurological disorder that slowly disables its victims. Kevorkian will serve a sentence of ten to twenty-five years and will not be eligible for parole for six years.

Kevorkian has been on a campaign to legalize euthanasia and assisted suicide since 1990, when he helped Janet Adkins, a fifty-four-year-old woman with Alzheimer's disease, commit suicide in his Volkswagen van. Kevorkian believes that every person has a fundamental right to choose the time and manner of his death. (In 1997, however, the U.S. Supreme Court said there is no constitutional right to physician-assisted suicide. *Washington v. Glucksberg*, 521 U.S. 702, 117 S. Ct. 2258, 138 L. Ed. 2d 772 [1997]; *Vacco v. Quill*, 521 U.S. 743, 117 S. Ct. 2293, 138 L. Ed. 2d 834 [1997]). Prior to Youk's death, Kevorkian helped over 130 people to self-administer lethal medication through a device he constructed. The state of Michigan prosecuted Kevorkian once in 1994, twice in 1996, and once in 1997 for assisted suicide deaths. Each time Kevorkian presented powerful evidence of his patients' illnesses and suffering. Three trials ended in acquittal and one ended in a MISTRIAL.

Then in September 1998, Thomas Youk approached Kevorkian to end his suffering. Once an amateur race car driver, Youk was confined to a wheelchair without use of his left arm or either of his legs. Difficulty swallowing forced Youk to eat through a tube and frequently caused him to choke on his own saliva. Youk, who almost could not speak, told Kevorkian that although he did not want to die, he did not want to continue living with his disease. Unlike Kevorkian's previous patients, Youk agreed to have Kevorkian kill him with a lethal injection. Kevorkian planned to use Youk's case to get national attention for his campaign to legalize active euthanasia.

On September 16, 1998, Kevorkian went to Youk's home to videotape Youk's decision. On camera, Youk signed a form saying his goal was "to end with certainty my intolerable and hopelessly incurable suffering." The next day, Kevorkian returned to Youk's home and videotaped his administration of muscle relaxants and then potassium chloride to end Youk's life. Kevorkian gave the tapes to the CBS television program *60 Minutes*, which aired them amidst great controversy on November 23, 1998. Kevorkian told *The Oakland Press* of Michigan, "I want to be prosecuted for euthanasia. I am going to prove that this is not a crime, ever, regardless of what words are written on paper."

After reviewing the tapes and conducting an independent investigation, Michigan prosecutors indicted Kevorkian for first-degree MURDER, assisted suicide, and delivery of a controlled substance. (Michigan revoked Kevorkian's medical license in 1991, making his administration of drugs to Youk illegal). Although he was represented by an attorney at his previous trials, Kevorkian decided to represent himself, insisting that only he could explain to the jury that he did not intend to kill Youk, but to end his suffering.

A pretrial hearing focused on whether Kevorkian could present evidence of Youk's disease and suffering. Such evidence had persuaded jurors in previous cases to acquit Kevorkian of charges of assisted suicide. Judge Jessica Cooper ruled that such evidence would be relevant to the charge of assisted suicide, because it would prove why Youk killed himself with Kevorkian's assistance. However, under first-degree murder,

the issue would be whether Kevorkian intended to, and did, kill Thomas Youk, not why he did so. Youk's suffering and consent would be irrelevant to that charge. To take advantage of the ruling, prosecutors withdrew the charge of assisted suicide, and Kevorkian stool trial on the charges of first-degree murder and delivery of a controlled substance.

The trial began on March 22, 1999. In opening statements, Kevorkian said that as a doctor he has a duty to end suffering, and that by killing Youk he was only carrying out that duty, just as an executioner carries out his duty when he executes an inmate on death row. Prosecutor John Skrzynski described Kevorkian as a medical hit man. Skrzynski then presented evidence that consisted of the tapes made by Kevorkian and testimony from investigators on the case. After the prosecution rested, Kevorkian tried to call Youk's wife, Melody, and brother, Terry, as witnesses to testify that Kevorkian's intent was not to kill, but to end Youk's suffering. Terry said his brother once described feeling like "a body plugged into an electrical socket." Judge Cooper, however, refused to allow the witnesses to testify because of her ruling that Youk's suffering was irrelevant to the charges. Kevorkian then rested without testifying or otherwise presenting evidence for his defense.

In closing arguments Kevorkian compared himself to the Reverend Dr. Martin Luther King, Jr., and Rosa Parks, civil rights activists who broke laws they believed to be unjust in a civilized society. Kevorkian warned the jurors that if they convicted his act of merciful euthanasia, they would have to "take the harsh judgement of history, and the harsher judgment of your children and grandchildren in they ever come to need that precious choice." In an allusion to the Holocaust, Prosecutor Skrzynski remarked, "There are 11 million souls buried in Europe that can tell you that when you make euthanasia a state policy, some catastrophic things can evolve from that." Skrzynski, however, reminded the jury that the case was not about whether euthanasia should be legal, but whether Kevorkian murdered Thomas Youk. After deliberating for thirteen hours, the jury found Kevorkian guilty of second-degree murder (which does not require premeditation) and delivery of a controlled substance.

At the sentencing hearing, Judge Cooper had harsh words for Kevorkian. "You had the audacity to go on national television, show the world what you did, and dare the legal system to stop you. Well, sir, consider yourself stopped." Although she could have given Kevorkian life in prison, Judge Cooper used sentencing guidelines to give him ten to twenty-five years for the murder conviction and three to seven years for delivery of a controlled substance.

Kevorkian, who has threatened to starve himself to death if sent to prison, has appealed his conviction. His lawyers have identified at least two grounds for appeal. One is that the judge should have permitted Youk's wife and brother to testify that Kevorkian's intent was not to kill, but to end Youk's suffering. Another is that during Kevorkian's closing argument, Skrzynski interrupted with an improper objection by saying "He can't testify now. He could have…," at which point Judge Cooper stopped him. Under the U.S. Constitution's FIFTH AMENDMENT right against self-incrimination, defendants do not have to testify, and prosecutors are prohibited from commenting to the jury about that decision. However, in May 1999, Kevorkian surprised many, including his former lawyers, by filing an appeal on the grounds of ineffective legal counsel—even though he chose to represent himself at his trial.

Oregon's Death With Dignity Act

In 1998, at least fifteen terminally ill patients in Oregon committed suicide under that state's Death with Dignity Act (DWDA). DWDA allows physicians to prescribe lethal medication to Oregon residents who request it if they are eighteen years of age or older, are able to make and communicate health care decisions, and have been diagnosed with a terminal illness that likely will result in death within six months. While physicians may make the prescription, patients must self-administer it—DWDA specifically prohibits "lethal injection, mercy killing, or active euthanasia." The act makes Oregon the only jurisdiction in the world that has legalized physician-assisted suicide.

The Oregon legislature enacted DWDA after residents voted in favor of the law twice, 51 percent in favor in 1994, then 60 percent in favor in 1997. The law originally went into effect in 1994, but immediately was suspended by court INJUNCTIONS pending legal challenges. In unrelated cases in June 1997, the U.S. Supreme Court ruled that there is no constitutional right to physician-assisted suicide, but that the states are free to allow it. (*Washington v. Glucksberg*, 521 U.S. 702, 117 S. Ct. 2258, 138 L. Ed. 2d 772 [1997]; *Vacco v. Quill*, 521 U.S. 793, 117 S. Ct. 2293, 138 L. Ed. 2d 834 [1997]). When the U.S. Supreme Court refused to hear a case concerning DWDA, the Ninth Circuit Court of Appeals lifted an injunction and the law went into effect on October 27, 1997.

DWDA has strict requirements that are designed to prevent abuse of the act. Patients must make two verbal requests for lethal medication separated by at least fifteen days, plus a written request. Two physicians must independently confirm that the patient has a terminal illness likely to result in death within six months, and that the patient is capable to make and communicate health care decisions. If either physician believes the patient suffers from depression or any other psychiatric or psychological disorder, she must refer the patient for counseling. The prescribing physician must request, but not require, the patient to inform her next of kin of the suicide decision. The prescribing physician also must inform the patient of alternatives to suicide, including hospice care and pain control, and give the patient the opportunity to change her mind after the fifteen day waiting period.

DWDA's strict requirements have not silenced its critics. Opponents in the medical community, including Physicians for Compassionate Care, believe that physician-assisted suicide is contrary to the profession's very purpose—to promote health. Religious opponents, including the Roman Catholic Church, Mormons, and Christian fundamentalists, feel that suicide of any kind devalues life. Not Dead Yet, an organization of disabled persons, believes that states should instead enact legislation to improve access to health and hospice care, and the overall quality of life, for terminally ill patients. Many opponents are concerned that poor or uneducated patients will be pressured by family members or the health insurance industry to chose death over life with its medically expensive consequences.

To DWDA's supporters, however, physician-assisted suicide is a matter of personal autonomy and control. The Hemlock Society, an organization that supports physician-assisted suicide, claims that terminally ill patients must be allowed to end their lives voluntarily rather than suffer through the painful and disabling effects of a terminal illness.

Al Sinnard, one of the orginal sponsers of Oregon's Death with Dignity Act, holds a photo of his wife who ended her life.

JACK SMITH/AP/WIDE WORLD PHOTOS

In February 1999, the Oregon Health Division (OHD) released a mandatory annual report of physician-assisted suicides under DWDA during 1998. (Although DWDA went into effect in October 1997, no prescriptions were written until 1998). Of the twenty-three patients who received prescriptions for lethal medication, fifteen died after taking their medication, six died from their illnesses, and two were alive as of January 1, 1999. The OHD report compared the fifteen patients who died from their medication with statistics on all deaths in Oregon in 1996 (the most recent year with available data) and with the 1998 deaths of forty-three Oregonians who suffered from similar terminal illnesses. OHD's conclusions were encouraging: "Patients who chose physician-assisted suicide in 1998 were similar to all Oregonians who died of similar underlying illnesses with respect to age, race, sex, and Portland residence. Patients who chose physician-assisted suicide were not disproportionately poor (as measured by Medicaid status), less educated, lacking in insurance coverage, or lacking in access to hospice care." Relying on these findings and the relatively low number of physician-assisted suicides under DWDA in 1998, supporters called the act a success.

DWDA's opponents, however, were not satisfied. They said the statistics do not reflect the number of unreported physician-assisted suicides. OHD's report acknowledged that an anonymous survey in 1995 found that seven percent of surveyed physicians prescribed lethal medications before the law legalized physician-assisted suicide. Opponents also frequently point to the Netherlands, where physician-assisted suicide is technically illegal but is widely practiced and rarely prosecuted. Physician-assisted suicides there were low when the practice began in the 1970s. The latest official Dutch report, however, says that annual physician-assisted suicides have reached almost 5,000. Furthermore, a study by the Dutch government found that in 1990, 1,040 people died from involuntary euthanasia, meaning they were killed without their knowledge or consent.

DWDA's opponents fear that it too will become a tool for active euthanasia, eventually blurring the line between mercy killing and murder. For example, when Oregon resident Patrick Matheny began to take his legally prescribed lethal medication in March 1999, he had trouble and had to be helped by his brother-in-law, Joe Hayes. (Hayes has not explained how he helped Matheny, and Matheny's body was unavailable for an autopsy because it was cremated.) Eventually, disabled persons who are unable to self-administer lethal medication are likely to challenge the DWDA's prohibition of active euthanasia under the Oregon state constitution and the federal Americans with Disabilities Act.

The debate over assisted suicide thus continues. While Attorney General JANET RENO said in June 1998 that physicians acting under DWDA will not be prosecuted under the federal Controlled Substances Act, the Clinton administration officially is opposed to assisted suicide. A federal law that would have doomed DWDA, however, failed to pass Congress late in 1998. Meanwhile, voters in Michigan defeated a referendum for a law similar to DWDA in November 1998, and the Hawaii legislature voted against a similar law in February 1999. Legislatures in Arizona, Connecticut, Louisiana, and New Hampshire are considering legislation to legalize physician-assisted suicide, and the Supreme Court of Alaska is considering a case that could legalize the practice there.

CROSS REFERENCES
Appendix: Death With Dignity Act; Death and Dying; Patients' Rights; Physicians and Surgeons

SUPREME COURT OF THE UNITED STATES

Protest of Low Minority Representation in U.S. Supreme Court Law Clerks

The *USA Today* published an article in March 1998, which showed a surprisingly low representation of minorities working as law clerks to the justices of the U.S. Supreme Court. According to the article, of the 394 clerks hired by the justices during their combined tenures, only seven (or 1.8 percent) had been African American, along with approximately 1 percent Hispanic, 4 percent Asian, and no Native American hirees. The article further indicated that about 40 percent of candidates selected for clerkships came from the law schools of Harvard and Yale.

Soon thereafter, the Coalition of Bar Associations of Color (including the National Bar, the Hispanic National Bar, the Native American Bar, and the Asian Pacific Bar Associations), met in Washington, D.C. to pool resources. Their invitation to Chief Justice WILLIAM H. REHNQUIST for a meeting on the subject was declined, but Rehnquist replied in correspondence that he did not believe the meeting would

Kweisi Mfume is arrested for protesting the low number of minority Supreme Court law clerks.

KHUE BUI/AP/WIDE WORLD PHOTOS

serve any useful purpose, inviting them instead to make recommendations to him in support of particular applicants.

A few weeks later, at the Atlanta meeting of the National Association for the Advancement of Colored People (NAACP), president Kweisi Mfume referred to the Supreme Court justices as "hypocrites" in matters of diversity or affirmative action. The matter escalated when hiring results for the October 1998-October 1999 session were made known, showing that only one minority, an Hispanic female, was hired to fill any of the thirty-four available law clerk positions.

On October 5, 1998, the opening day of the Court's new term, a group of approximately 1000 civil rights activists protested the hiring practices in front of the U.S. Supreme Court building in Washington. Police barricades were soon compromised, and nineteen protesters were arrested for crossing the police barricade in a united act of civil disobedience, ostensibly to hand resumes of available clerks to the justices. Among the group of protesters was Mfume, along with Thom White Wolf Fassett, general secretary of the United Methodist Board of Church and Society, and U.S. Congressmen Gregory W. Meeks (D-NY) and Albert Wynn (D-MD). The NAACP also asked its members to write letters of protest to the Court.

Within days, Congressman Jesse Jackson, Jr., (D-IL) introduced a House bill which he referred to as the Judicial Branch Employment Nondiscrimination Act of 1998, subjecting all employment practices of the federal judiciary to the CIVIL RIGHTS ACT OF 1964. Three other House members, Danny K. Davis (D-IL), Elijah E. Commings (D-MD), and Gregory W. Meeks (D-NY) wrote letters to each justice individually, urging the Court to meet with minority bar groups about the hiring process for clerkships.

By letter dated November 17, 1998, Rehnquist responded to the three black congressmen. While acknowledging the low number of minorities hired for law clerk positions, he rejected the appropriateness of any justice seeking guidance "from special constituencies." Speaking on behalf of all the justices, Rehnquist further made it clear that the statistics were not the result of any discrimination. "...[Y]ou must realize that many factors entirely unrelated to the hiring of law clerks are responsible for this situation," he wrote, "...As the demographic makeup of this [applicant] pool changes, it seems entirely likely that the underrepresentation of minorities to which you refer in your letter will also change." The correspondence was made public the following Monday.

During the March 1999 presentation of the Court's budget request to Congress and the subsequent House Appropriations subcommittee meeting, Democratic Representatives Julian C. Dixon (D-CA) and Jose E. Serrano (D-NY) took the opportunity to query Justices DAVID H. SOUTER and CLARENCE THOMAS on the Court's hiring practices. The congressmen further implied that House members would likely raise the issue on the floor when considering the Court-related appropriations and legislation. Both justices staunchly defended the hiring practices, reiterating to the subcommittee that their selections were based on the applicant pool supplied to them by law schools and other courts. Both justices stated that there were correlative low numbers of minorities in the top ranks of major law schools and in lower-court clerkships.

The issue reached national television and the Internet during "The NewsHour" with Jim Lehrer. The show's Elizabeth Farnsworth interviewed five former law clerks to justices of the Supreme Court: Sheryll Cashin, who clerked for Justice THURGOOD MARSHALL; John Yoo, for Justice Thomas; Neal Katyal, for Justice STEPHEN BREYER; Kathryn Bradley, for Justice BYRON WHITE, and Ted Cruz, for Chief Jus-

tice Rehnquist. Each qualified as a "minority" for purposes of the diversity issue.

Four of the five guests agreed that diversity among the law clerks would be a worthwhile goal. John Yoo qualifiedly agreed, stating that if diversity were the natural result of the election process it would be positive. But he pointed out that placing diversity above academic excellence or success at school, in order to make the judiciary "representative of the people," could be dangerous. If "everybody has a piece or a quota or a setaside for clerks," he added, it would compromise the notion of a neutral, impartial judiciary, separated from society. Yoo then supported his contention with an hypothetical argument, that if in 1954, segregationists from the South had a quota of Supreme Court clerks would *Brown v. Board of Education* have been decided the way it was?

Yoo felt that the whole idea behind creating diversity was premised upon flawed assumptions: that the selected minorities would reflect some presumedly common opinion among members of the minority class they represented (or that there would even be a dominant opinion among that class) and that the selected law clerk would or could successfully impose that opinion upon the justice he or she worked for.

Cashin was quick to point out that no one was asking for a quota, just an expanded pool of applicants. She also felt that the notion of a diverse membership among clerks somehow influencing judicial decisions was insulting to the justices. Notwithstanding, Cashin, Cruz, Bradley and Katyal all went on to admit that their own respective backgrounds (as minorities) did, in fact, influence the way they viewed cases, and in many instances, the way they presented the cases to the justices.

Ultimately, and importantly, none blamed the High Court for discriminatory practices or attitudes. Neal Katyal added that the High Court's numbers paralleled those found at top law firms and in judges' ranks. All felt that the problem was in the low minority representation of the applicant pool, not the selection pool.

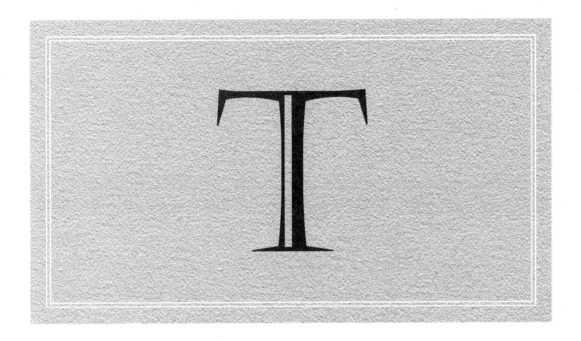

TAXATION

The process whereby charges are imposed on persons or property by the legislative branch of the federal government and by many state and local governments to raise funds for public purposes.

South Central Bell Telephone Co. v. Alabama; United States v. Estate of Romani

Tax law can be a vague area of the law, as federal and state tax codes and court decisions grow more complex over time. When tax cases reach the Supreme Court they typically appear in two varieties: disputes over the interpretation of a particular tax law or regulation, or disputes over the fairness of a particular tax scheme. These two varieties are illustrated by *United States v. Estate of Romani*, 523 U.S. 517, 118 S. Ct. 1478, 140 L. Ed. 2d 710 (1998) and *South Central Bell Telephone Co. v. Alabama*, __ U.S. __, 119 S. Ct. 1180, 143 L. Ed. 2d 258 (1999).

In *Romani*, the Supreme Court examined whether a federal tax LIEN—a right created by law in favor of certain creditor—takes priority over all creditors who are owed money by a deceased taxpayer. In 1985, a Pennsylvania court entered a judgment for $400,000 in favor of Romani Industries, Inc., and against Francis J. Romani. The judgment was recorded in the clerk's office and became a lien on all of Romani's real property in the county where he resided. In the years that followed, the Internal Revenue Service (IRS) filed a series of notices of tax liens on Romani's property. The claims for unpaid taxes, interest and penalties amounted to approximately $490,000.

When Romani died in 1992, his entire estate consisted of real estate worth only $53,000. Because both the judgment lien and the federal tax liens encumbered the property, the administrator of Romani's estate sought permission from a Pennsylvania court to transfer the property to the judgment creditor, Romani Industries. The federal government admitted that its tax liens were not valid against the earlier judgment lien. However, it opposed the transfer on the ground that a federal priority statute, 31 U.S.C.A. § 3713(a), gave it the right to be paid first.

The Pennsylvania courts rejected the federal claim. The Supreme Court of Pennsylvania determined that there was a "plain inconsistency" between § 3713(a), which appears to give the United States "absolute priority" over all competing claims, and the Tax Lien Act of 1966, 26 U.S.C.A. § 6323(a), which provides that the federal tax lien "shall not be valid" against judgment lien creditors until a prescribed notice has been given. The court concluded that the 1966 Act had the effect of limiting the operation of § 37139(a) as to tax debts. (547 Pa. 41, 688 A.2d 703 [1997]).

The Supreme Court agreed with the state supreme court. Justice JOHN PAUL STEVENS, writing for the Court, held that § 3713(a) does not require that a federal tax claim be given preference over a judgment creditor's perfected lien on real property. The judgment creditor had a valid lien on Romani's property before the IRS served notice of its tax liens. A review of the Tax Lien Act's legislative history revealed that Congress had repeatedly amended the act to ameliorate "harsh consequences for the delinquent taxpayer's other secured creditors."

Justice Stevens concluded that the Court needed to "harmonize" the impact of the two federal statutes on the government's power to collect delinquent taxes. He concluded that the Tax Lien Act governed the interpretation, as it was "the later statute, the more specific statute, and its provisions are comprehensive." Therefore, it would be "anomalous to conclude that Congress intended the priority statute to impose greater burdens on the citizen than those specifically crafted for tax collection purposes."

In *South Central Bell Telephone Co. v. Alabama*, the Supreme Court looked at a much different issue. The state of Alabama imposed a corporate FRANCHISE tax on all corporations. Those corporations headquartered in Alabama paid the tax based on a valuation of the firm's stock that was well below book or market value. However, out-of-state firms paid the tax based on the value of the actual amount of capital the firms employed in the state. A group of out-of-state corporations sued in Alabama state court, asking for a tax refund on the franchise taxes they had paid in. They alleged that the tax discriminated against foreign corporations in violation of the COMMERCE CLAUSE and the FOURTEENTH AMENDMENT's Due Process Clause. The Alabama Supreme Court rejected their claims, ruling that the special burden placed on foreign corporations offset a different burden placed on Alabama corporations in the form of domestic shares tax. *White v. Reynolds Metals Co.*, 558 So. 2d 373 (Ala. 1989).

While the Alabama courts were considering *Reynolds Metals*, different foreign corporations, including South Central Bell Telephone Company, brought a lawsuit that asserted the same Commerce Clause and Equal Protection Clause claims as had Reynolds Metals. The only difference was that South Central Bell sought tax refunds for different tax years. By the time the case came to trial, the Alabama Supreme Court had issued its decision in *Reynolds Metals*. Based on this ruling, the trial court dismissed the Bell lawsuit. The Alabama Supreme Court affirmed this decision without an opinion. (711 So. 2d 1005 [Ala. 1998].)

The U.S. Supreme Court, in a unanimous decision, struck down the foreign corporation tax. Nevertheless, before the Court could make that ruling, it first had to dispose of procedural objections offered by the state. Alabama believed that Bell was prohibited from raising its claims based on the rule of RES JUDICATA. Courts use res judicata to prevent a dissatisfied party from trying to litigate the issue a second time. A fi-

nal judgment on the merits is conclusive between the parties to a suit as to all matters that were litigated or that could have been litigated in that suit. Alabama contended that Bell was aware of the other lawsuit and that one of the lawyers in that case represented Bell.

Justice STEPHEN G. BREYER, writing for the Court, rejected the res judicata argument. *Reynolds Metals* involved different plaintiffs and tax years, making the Bell plaintiffs "strangers" to the earlier judgment. Therefore, they were not bound by that judgment. Breyer attached no importance to the fact that the two lawsuits had a lawyer in common.

Turning to the substance of the case, Justice Breyer concluded that the franchise tax on foreign corporations "impermissibly discriminates against commerce, in violation of the Commerce Clause." Alabama gave domestic corporations the ability to reduce their tax by reducing the value of their stock, but did not give foreign corporations the ability to do the same. He ruled that Alabama could not justify this discrimination on the grounds that it was a compensatory tax that offset the tax burden that another tax imposed on Alabama corporations. The "relevant tax burdens" were not "roughly approximate," nor were they "similar in substance." Therefore, the tax was unconstitutional.

CROSS REFERENCES
Commerce Clause; Res Judicata

TELECOMMUNICATIONS

The transmission of words, sounds, images, or data in the form of electronic or electromagnetic signals or impulses.

AT&T Corporation v. Iowa Utilities Board

The telecommunications industry has undergone dramatic changes since American Telephone and Telegraph's (AT&T) MONOPOLY over virtually all aspects of the telephone business was broken in the early 1980s. AT&T settled an ANTITRUST lawsuit in 1982 by divesting itself of its local operating companies, while retaining control of its long distance activities. Seven regional telephone companies, known as Baby Bells, were given responsibility for local telephone service. Other companies then entered the long-distance service market to compete with AT&T.

Congress enacted the Telecommunications Act of 1996, (Pub. L. No. 104–104), to increase competition within the industry and end state-sanctioned monopolies. The act allowed the Baby Bells to compete in the long-distance telephone market but more importantly, it permitted AT&T and other long-distance carriers, as well as cable companies, to sell local telephone service. It required the local exchange carriers (LEC), such as the Baby Bells, to share their networks with their competitors. The act also gave the FEDERAL COMMUNICATIONS COMMISSION the authority to issue regulations that would implement the local-competition provisions of the act. This new authority, however, led to disputes with state utility commissions that regulate local telephone rates. These commissions asserted that local telephone service was intrastate commerce, and therefore it was not subject to federal regulation.

Several of the commissions, with the support of the LECs, filed lawsuits in federal court challenging the authority of the FCC to issue regulations regarding pricing, local access, and other services. AT&T and other long-distance carriers supported the FCC's position. These lawsuits were ultimately consolidated into one action.

The Supreme Court resolved the dispute in *AT&T Corporation v. Iowa Utilities Board*, __U.S.__, 119 S. Ct. 721, 142 L. Ed. 2d 835 (1999). The Court ruled that the FCC has the authority to implement the 1996 act and that all but one of its rules was consistent with the act. In so ruling, the Court overruled the Eighth Circuit Court of Appeals. 124 F. 3d 934 (8th Cir. 1997).

Justice ANTONIN SCALIA, writing for the Court, addressed three main issues: (1) whether the FCC has the authority to adopt rules to set prices for services and network elements that local telephone companies are required to provide to new entrants; (2) whether the FCC's regulation, Rule 319, allowing new entrants in the local phone market to obtain and use existing combinations of network elements from LECs was valid; and (3) whether the FCC's "pick and choose" rule, Rule 315(b), which allows new entrants to select provisions of other negotiated agreements to establish their own service, was valid.

Justice Scalia found that the FCC had general jurisdiction to implement all of the 1996 act's local competition provisions. Congress had expressly made these provisions part of the Communications Act of 1934, (47 U.S.C.A. § 151 et seq.), which authorizes the FCC to prescribe rules and regulations to carry out the law's provisions. Therefore, the FCC's rulemaking authority extended to implementation of the new provisions. Although § 152(b) of the 1934 act generally preserves the states' authority over intrastate matters, Justice Scalia concluded that it was inapplicable because the 1996 act "clearly applies to intrastate matters."

Scalia also found unpersuasive the attempt by the LECs and state commissions to invoke "states' rights." "The question is not whether states will be allowed to do their own thing, but whether it will be the FCC or the federal courts that draw the lines to which [the states] must hew." He added that "a federal program administered by 50 independent state agencies," without oversight and guidance from a federal agency, "is surpassing[ly] strange."

Justice Scalia reversed the Eighth Circuit's ruling that the FCC had no jurisdiction to adopt rules to implement the act's dialing parity for intrastate calls. Dialing parity gives customers the ability to pre-subscribe to a carrier such as AT&T for local and long-distance calls without having to dial additional digits.

Justice Scalia then turned to Rule 319, which allows new entrants in the local telephone market to obtain and use existing combinations of network elements from LECs. Network elements include the local loop, the network interface device, switching capability, interoffice transmission facilities, signaling networks and call-related databases, operations support systems, and operator services and directory assistance. The Court vacated the rule, finding that the FCC did not adequately consider § 251(d)(2). This section requires the FCC to consider (1) whether access to a particular new entrant is "necessary" for LECs to provide service and (2) whether providing service would "impair" the LECs' ability to compete. Justice Scalia concluded that the FCC ignored these standards by requiring LECs to make available any network elements upon a showing of technical feasibility. In redrafting the rules, the FCC must consider the availability of elements outside the LEC's network, and cannot regard any increased cost or decreased service quality to the new entrant as justifying access to the LEC's service.

The Court then examined the "pick and choose" rule, Rule 315(b), which prohibits LECs from separating already combined network elements, except at a new entrant's request. Justice Scalia found that the rule was supported by the act's nondiscrimination requirements, which according to the FCC prohibited LECs from "sabotaging" their network elements to "impose wasteful costs" on their competitors. Scalia concluded that the FCC made a reasonable decision "to opt in favor of ensuring against an anticompetitive practice." He agreed with the FCC that "unbundled" did not mean "physically separate." It meant the ability to establish separate prices in order to provide additional options. Therefore, new entrants could "pick and choose" the network services they wanted from the LECs.

The decision was a significant victory for long-distance carriers such as AT&T, as the FCC's views on competition have tended to be more favorable to long distance companies than the state utility boards. Long-distance companies now have the ability to compete with LECs for local telephone service by purchasing access and services they want from the same LECs.

Slamming

In the competitive telecommunications industry, "slamming" is the switching of a customer's service provider. In practice, slamming a customer usually means changing a customer's long-distance telephone carrier from the customer's chosen carrier to another carrier that charges exorbitant prices. In recent years, slamming has branched out to affect the charges for systems that merge voice services with computer and data services.

Popular opinion is strongly opposed to the practice of slamming. Many people pay their monthly utility bills without scrutinizing the charges, and the unauthorized overcharges can continue for months or years. In response to a flood of consumer complaints, public service commissions and other government agencies at the state and federal level are scrambling to regulate the practice of telecommunications slamming.

Michael Jewell, a senior attorney for AT&T, speaks before a Senate committee in Austin, Texas.

HARRY CABLUCK/AP/WIDE WORLD PHOTOS

In October 1998, the Alabama Public Service Commission fined Business Options Inc. of Indiana a sum of $28,000 for replacing their long-distance carrier service without the consent of their customers. The commission used Alabama's anti-slamming law, passed in 1997, to fine the company after receiving approximately 200 complaints about the slamming. The commission also ordered the company to issue refunds or long-distance credits to customers who had valid complaints.

Also in October 1998, a New Jersey-based telephone firm agreed to pay a fine of $1 million to 20 different states. In a settlement with the states, Minimum Rate Pricing also agreed to stop slamming customers in those states.

Congress passed some anti-slamming provisions in § 258 of the Telecommunications Act of 1996, but the measures failed to put a stop to the practice. The most controversial measure forced the slamming company to pay the customer revenues gained by the slam to the original carrier. In 1998, additional legislation on slamming had been proposed by the House of Representatives, but the legislation never made it out of the Senate. In December 1998, several members of Congress, led by House Commerce Committee Chairman Thomas Bliley (R-VA) and Senate Majority Leader TRENT LOTT (R-MS), crafted an "honor code" proposal on the topic of slamming and presented it to the Federal Communications Commission (FCC). The honor code recommended to the FCC that it give long distance carriers two alternatives: 1) comply with a "rigorous code of subscriber protection policies, which the [FCC] would be required to adopt with input from the Federal Trade Commission, consumer groups and industry," or 2) refrain from subscribing to the rigorous code and risk larger fines and penalties. If a company subscribed to the code, it could still be fined and penalized, but the fines and penalties would be lower for those who made the honor code pledge.

The FCC was not required to adopt the proposed honor code, but·it did begin to take action in December 1998. On December 17, 1998, the FCC announced that it would rewrite the rules on slamming to favor the consumer more and long distance carriers less. By a vote of 4–1, the FCC board decided that slammed consumers would not have to pay for charges incurred on their long distances bills for a period of up to thirty days after the slam is discovered. The FCC also would reinforce verification rules to ensure that telecommunications customers know what they are getting and are getting what they ordered. The FCC also decided to institute a "preferred carrier freeze" that would prevent the switching of phone companies without the explicit oral or written consent of the customer.

The FCC reported that it had received approximately 20,000 complaints about slamming in 1998 alone. FCC Chairman William E. Kennard announced that "[l]iterally hundreds of people have come up to me and complained about slamming...I think it's fair to say that this Commission has sent a very clear message to anyone out there who is involved in slamming that there are cops on the beat." At the same meeting, the FCC announced that it was fining Business Discount Plan of Long Beach, California, and Long Distance Direct of Pearl River, New York, a total of $4.4 million for slamming, illegal billing, and misrepresentation of prices.

Many telecommunications companies viewed the reforms as unjust. After the commission's December 17, 1998, meeting, the companies weighed in with their concerns and convinced the FCC to keep the matter open for additional comments. Specifically, the telecommunications companies were worried about false claims of slamming. In some cases, consumers may forget that they changed phone companies, or they may not know that another member of the household changed the service, or they may not have noticed that a form they were signing authorized the change. The telecommunications companies also felt that the thirty days of free phone service for slamming victims was unnecessary and excessive, especially if a slamming victim has been reimbursed for the overcharged amount. Under the rules, both companies would lose the revenue from thirty days of phone use.

Despite the outcry from some telecommunications companies, the FCC anti-slamming rules began to go into effect in March 1999. The companies did win one small battle by gaining the right to be the first to handle slamming disputes. Rather than taking a slamming case straight to a government agency, customers must first attempt to resolve the problem with the carrier.

The federal rules are only effective on the federal level, and states are struggling to keep up with the problem of slamming. In January 1999, Senator Susan Collins (R-ME) proposed a bill called the Telephone Services Fraud Prevention and Enforcement Act on the topic of slamming. The act, according to Sen. Collins, would let states set rules to protect telecommunications consumers from unscrupulous telecommunications companies.

Slamming continues to inspire the filing of lawsuits and he imposition of fines. In February 1999, three companies agreed to pay $1.3 million to the state of Florida and agreed not to do business there again. In March 1999, US West filed five lawsuits in federal court against companies that were pretending to be US West to lure customers. In April 1999, on the day that the long-distance "preferred carrier freeze" became available to consumers, AT&T, identified by some states as the biggest slammer in the telecommunications business, began a public relations campaign designed to steer consumers away from choosing to freeze their long-distance accounts with a particular carrier.

CROSS REFERENCES
Federal Communications Commission

TOBACCO

FDA Lacks Authority to Regulate Tobacco Products

In the midst of growing challenges to the tobacco industry, the U.S. Fourth Circuit Court of Appeals ruled that the Food and Drug Administration (FDA) lacked jurisdiction to restrict the distribution and sale of tobacco products. On August 14, 1998, in *Brown & Williamson Tobacco Corp. v. FDA*, 153 F. 3d 155 (4th Cir. 1998), a three-judge panel held (by a 2–1 vote) that the FDA's 1996 regulations, restricting the sale and distribution of cigarettes and smokeless tobacco to children and adolescents, went beyond the agency's statutory authority. These regulations were known as the "Regulations Restricting the Sale and Distribution of Cigarettes and Smokeless Tobacco to Protect Children and Adolescents" (61 Fed. Reg. 44,396 [1996]).

The roots of this decision lay in a series of individual lawsuits filed by North Carolina tobacco manufacturers shortly after the FDA approved the regulations, its first attempt to regulate tobacco products. Key provisions of the regulations that the FDA had already begun to enforce set a national minimum age for buying tobacco products at eighteen, and required stores to ask for photo identification if a customer looked younger than twenty-seven. Other provisions, scheduled to take effect in the future, would have further restricted tobacco product advertising and sales on the federal level. In particular, they would have banned many cigarette machines and sales of sportswear bearing cigarette brand names, as well as prohibiting tobacco advertising near school property.

Much of the momentum for the regulations came from top secret tobacco company documents that were released in 1994 and 1995, under terms of settlements reached with several state attorneys general. These documents revealed that the tobacco industry had known about the dangers of cigarette smoking even before the government was aware of them, and that it had directly targeted sales to teenagers. The FDA (under activist commissioner David Kessler) had originally considered banning sales of cigarettes altogether, but decided that it would be too difficult to ban a product to which millions of people were addicted.

The individual lawsuits in North Carolina were eventually consolidated into a single case, *Brown & Williamson Tobacco Corp. v. FDA.* Brown & Williamson, the country's third largest cigarette manufacturer and seller, distributes several well-known brands including Lucky Strike and Kool. However, at the district court level the key opinion was *Coyne Beahm Inc. v. FDA,* 966 F. Supp. 1374 (M.D.N.C. 1997). On April 25, 1997, District Court Judge William Osteen found that the federal Food, Drug, and Cosmetic Act (21 U.S.C.A. § 321) gave the FDA jurisdiction over cigarettes and smokeless tobacco as "drug-delivering devices." He upheld the minimum-age and photo-ID provisions of the regulations; however, he also ruled that the FDA had overstepped its authority by trying to restrict tobacco advertising. Given this mixed ruling, both the FDA and the tobacco companies appealed to the Fourth Circuit panel, which rejected the lower court opinion.

In overturning Judge Osteen's opinion, the three-judge circuit panel concluded that Congress had never intended tobacco products to come under the jurisdiction of the FDA, whether or not they were considered "drug-delivering devices." Speaking for the 2–1 majority, Circuit Judge H. Emory Widener, Jr., gave several reasons why he thought the FDA lacked jurisdiction and also why Congress had meant to reserve jurisdiction over the tobacco industry for itself. The reasons included that the FDA, on many occasions prior to 1996 (in more tobacco-friendly times), had said that it did not have the authority to regulate tobacco products, unless the manufacturers claimed that smoking provided health benefits. The majority opinion also relied on congressional rejection of several pieces of proposed legislation that would have specifically granted the FDA this authority, the

rejection of some bills that would have regulated the sale or advertising of cigarettes, and the passage of others (such as the ban on radio and television advertising of cigarettes and cigarette warning labels). The U.S. JUSTICE DEPARTMENT, on behalf of the FDA, appealed this judgment to the full panel of judges on the Fourth Circuit, but on November 10, 1998, that group refused to rehear the case. Of its thirteen judges, six voted not to rehear and three to rehear; four judges abstained from voting, ensuring that the case would not be reheard.

The Justice Department also appealed this opinion, asking the U.S. Supreme Court to overrule the circuit. On April 26, 1999, the Supreme Court agreed to review the case, now labeled *FDA v. Brown & Williamson,* __ U.S. __, 119 S. Ct. 1495, 143 L. Ed 2d 650 (1990). The appeal was supported by the attorneys general of thirty-nine states. According to ex-FDA commissioner David Kessler, now dean of Yale University Medical School (as quoted by ABC News), "It will be the most important public health case the Supreme Court hears in decades. The goal is certainly to reduce the number of people who smoke and the best way to do that is to reduce the number of young people who start." Lawyers for the tobacco industry in turn argued that the FDA had overreached its authority, and that most of the limits it wanted were already being carried out under the "global tobacco settlement" the industry had reached with forty-six states.

The FDA case must be seen as part of a growing movement by both government bodies and individuals to either seek damages from the tobacco industry for its past actions, or to restrict the industry's actions in the future. One of the key provisions of the FDA regulations, banning of the sale of tobacco products to anyone under eighteen, already has been adopted by every state. The "global tobacco settlement" reached between tobacco companies and individual states requires tobacco companies to pay the states almost $250 billion to offset the costs of treatment for illnesses caused by tobacco products. Many states also have filed actions against tobacco companies to recover MEDICAID funds spent to treat tobacco-related illnesses.

And lawsuits filed by individual smokers or their families have sought huge damage awards against tobacco companies, alleging that the companies knew their products could cause cancer and other serious illnesses. In February 1999, a jury in California awarded a Marlboro smoker with inoperable lung cancer over $50 million in damages against Philip Morris. The following month, an Oregon jury ordered Philip Morris to pay an even larger award to the family of a Marlboro smoker who had died of lung cancer. The Oregon award of $81 million was the largest ever made to an individual in a tobacco case. Similar large awards of damages have been overturned or reduced on appeal, but these cases are noteworthy for finding that there is a direct link between smoking and cancer, and making the companies responsible for any harm.

However, advocates for restrictions on tobacco products are hoping for action that goes beyond the state and individual levels. The FDA regulations would serve as an important federal statement that tobacco products are addictive and harmful, and so should be regulated nationwide. An attempt in 1998 to pass federal tobacco legislation, sponsored by Senator JOHN MCCAIN (R-AZ), failed to clear the Senate. (Former surgeon general, CHARLES EVERETT KOOP angrily called the defeat of the bill "public health malpractice.") At the same time, the Department of HEALTH AND HUMAN SERVICES was considering whether to file its own Medicaid-recovery suit, and the Justice Department was investigating the possibility of criminal FRAUD charges against industry executives.

Tobacco Litigation

The tobacco industry experienced its worst legal year ever in the twelve months preceding April 1999. In the aftermath of a $206 billion settlement reached in 1998 with forty-six states (and five U.S. territories) which had sued the industry, the tobacco companies' were still on the defensive. As of March 1999, more than five hundred lawsuits were still pending against Philip Morris alone, including at least sixty class action suits.

While many of the suits involved individual plaintiff claims, it was the clearly the class-action suits that caused the most concern. In a growing legal enterprise of mass tort litigation, over sixty-five major law firms around the country had joined forces after 1994 to coordinate claims against the industry for DAMAGES to individuals caused by nicotine addiction, and the first big wave of cases were just coming to trial. Over fifty law firms had been recruited to coordinate suits filed by state attorneys general to recoup MEDICAID and health care costs shelled out for tobacco-related illness and disease. In addition, an onslaught of suits from health-care providers and insurers in general, all wanting their money back for medical bills and benefits paid on behalf of insured's suffering from tobacco-related diseases were filed. Thousands of union employees were in CLASS ACTION suits representing millions of workers around the country. Class action suits represented non-smokers who claimed to have been harmed by second-hand smoke, including flight attendants and casino workers. Suits were also filed on behalf of the future smokers of tomorrow, who might still become addicted as a result of the tobacco companies' targeted advertising.

It has been estimated by the U.S. Center for Disease Control (CDC) that 400,000 deaths per year are caused by tobacco use. In the past, individual lawsuits had been successfully defended by placing responsibility for tobacco use upon the individual user, emphasizing that in the 1950s and 1960s, lessons on the dangers of smoking were part of the nation's schools' curricula, and by 1965, Congress required warning labels on cigarette packs. By 1971, radio and television commercials had been banned. In response to allegations of "addiction," the industry pointed out the more than 50 million smokers who have successfully quit.

But once mass litigation came into the picture, the industry's success abated. It was the lawyers for the first four states to settle (Mississippi, Texas, Florida and Minnesota) who exposed the alleged concealment of information and deceit in advertising that provoked a strong response. The response resulted in the mobilization of both resources and persons, joining in litigation by common complaints and gaining bargaining clout by pure strength in numbers.

The massive 1998, $206 billion settlement with the states provided no protection for the tobacco industry against individual or class action lawsuits. Such protection had been proposed in an earlier $368 billion plan, but the final plan agreed upon and entered on the record afforded no such insulation. Other provisions of the final plan were that the industry would not be penalized if youth smoking did not decrease, and cigarette producers could raise the price of a pack of cigarettes by 35 cents. On the other hand, the tobacco companies agreed to remove all advertising from outdoor billboards around the nation, with the remaining lease fees for the advertising (estimated at near $100 million) turned over to the states to post anti-tobacco messages, particularly targeting youth. (The total settlement value was closer to $246 billion, including the value of the nearly $40 billion settlement with the four original states.)

Union health funds and benefit providers became the largest group of new players in the class-action milieu. Their suits specified numerous allegations of concealment and deceit in promoting to blue-collar workers such advertising campaign heroes as the Marlboro Man and Joe Camel. Many of the class-action suits filed in federal district courts also alleged federal ANTITRUST and RICO claims along with the state claims of FRAUD and concealment. Indeed, while these suits were being filed, the U.S. JUSTICE DEPARTMENT was investigating "possible anticompetitive practices" in a preliminary antitrust inquiry involving the possible exclusionary contract deals with tobacco middlemen during the leaf-buying stages of tobacco products manufacturing. Additionally, two separate federal grand juries, in Washington and New York respectively, were also investigating evidence of whether industry officials had lied to Congress or concealed other evidence about their knowledge of tobacco dangers and addictions. Still yet another inquiry continued through 1998 involving allegations of price-fixing in Latin America by two of three of the nation's largest tobacco companies, Philip Morris, and Brown & Williamson. Bolivia, Panama and Nicaragua filed their own claims in the United States against the tobacco companies. The crowning blow was the Clinton administration's characterization of tobacco as the national enemy, and its announcement that it had directed the U.S. Justice Department to pursue litigation against the industry to recover an estimated $150–200 billion in tobacco-related Medicare costs and other related federal fund expenditures.

The tobacco industry was not ready to give up, and in fact, rallied behind several major victories involving the class actions suits, particularly those brought by labor union funds. First, in March 1999, a federal jury in Akron, Ohio, ruled in favor of the tobacco companies in a class-action suit involving more than 100 union health plans representing several blue-collar building trades who sued for reimbursement for the costs of treating smoking-related illnesses. Also in March and April 1999, both the Third and the Second U.S. Circuit Courts of Appeals ordered, in two separate appellate cases, the dismissal of union fund class actions. These followed no less than twelve separate federal district court dismissals of similar claims.

Another important case collapsed in April 1999, when a superior court in New Jersey denied class certification to a group of non-smoking casino workers, finding that there were "simply too many variations in products and people to permit class certification," including the predominance of individual issues over common issues of law and fact.

In March 1999, the state of Florida's Third District Court of Appeals upheld a $349 million class-action settlement filed on behalf of 60,000 non-smoking flight attendants who sued for illnesses related to secondhand cigarette smoke in airplane cabins during flights. A major forum for pending class-actions was California, where, by April 1999, no less than forty trials filed by various health plans were moved to San Diego Superior Court, where one judge would preside over all.

In the area of individual private suits, two separate state cases in California and Oregon, tried within weeks of one another in March 1999, were remarkable for the huge jury verdicts awarded to both plaintiffs, $51 million and $81 million respectively. Most disturbing to the tobacco company defendants was the fact that actual COMPENSATORY DAMAGES amounted to only $1.5 million and $1.6 million respectively. The remainder of both awards was in the form of PUNITIVE DAMAGES.

CROSS REFERENCES
Administrative Law; Class Action; Federal Regulation

UDALL, MORRIS

Former Democratic Congressman Morris King Udall, who died on December 12, 1998, at the age of seventy-six, won high regard as an environmentalist during his three decades as a federal lawmaker. As a representative of Arizona from 1961 to 1999, "Mo" Udall frequently defied his conservative constituency with his liberal politics yet always won reelection on his strong environmental record, affable personality, and self-deprecating humor. "I'm a one-eyed Mormon Democrat from conservative Arizona," he was famous for saying, "and you can't have a higher handicap than that." Udall championed the preservation of federal wild lands, expanded the national park system, and promoted campaign reform and anti-tobacco measures years before these became popular issues. Yet despite earning a national reputation, his presidential aspirations were never fulfilled. A few years after a disastrous showing in the 1976 Democratic primaries, he was diagnosed as having Parkinson's disease, which ultimately forced his resignation from Congress in 1991.

Born on June 15, 1922, Udall came from a Mormon family with deep legal and political roots. His father, Levi Stewart Udall, served as justice of the Arizona Supreme Court. His mother, Louise Lee Udall, worked as a Democratic party activist. Both he and his brother Stewart planned to follow their father into law. In fact, Stewart became a politician first, serving as an Arizona congressman until his appointment as secretary of the interior in 1961.

As a child Udall learned to overcome the first of many physical hardships. At the age of

seven he injured his right eye in an accident playing with a knife. The mistake of an alcoholic surgeon caused an infection that cost him the eye. Two years later, he contracted spinal meningitis. Yet Udall, a keen student and gifted athlete, did more than cope. He became quarterback of his high school football team, served as student body president and valedictorian, later won a basketball scholarship to the University of Arizona, and even briefly played professional basketball for the Denver Nuggets.

World War II interrupted Udall's college study for three years. He served as commander of an all-black squadron, which he said sensitized him to discrimination. Later he withdrew from the Mormon Church when it refused to ordain black priests. Despite only two years' training in pre-law, he provided legal defense in military court for an African-American airman accused of killing a white guard. However, the man was sentenced to death by six white officers. Udall professed to be haunted by the case his entire life.

Earning his bachelor of law degree from the University of Arizona in 1949, Udall passed the state bar exam that year with the highest score in his field. After he and his brother formed a law practice, he quickly made a name for himself in Arizona legal circles. In 1950, he was named chief deputy attorney for Pima County, an appointment that set the stage for his election two years later as county attorney. Although he failed in a bid for superior court judge in 1954, Udall wrote his first book, *Arizona Law of Evidence*, in 1960, and it became the standard text on the subject.

Stewart first got into politics and won election to Congress. Now, in 1961, his appoint-

Morris Udall

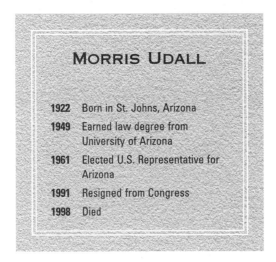

MORRIS UDALL

1922   Born in St. Johns, Arizona

1949   Earned law degree from University of Arizona

1961   Elected U.S. Representative for Arizona

1991   Resigned from Congress

1998   Died

ment as interior secretary led to a special election to fill his seat. Morris ran, and narrowly edged out a Republican opponent.

From the start, Udall appeared to be at odds with the politics of his staunchly conservative state. Arizona's best-known politician was Republican Senator Barry Goldwater, famous for his hawkish militarism and hard line on social issues. Udall was different—an outspoken and unapologetic liberal with reformist views that were ahead of his time. In his first term, he proposed that the Food and Drug Administration have control over cigarettes and tobacco products. An early leader in disclosing his campaign finances and opposing lobbyists, he became an avid reformer of federal campaign and election law, and his efforts led to passage of the Federal Election Campaign Act of 1971—the first major revision of federal election law in half a century. He also advocated a strong national health care system that guaranteed decent health care regardless of a person's ability to pay.

In a 1967 speech that received national attention, Udall became one of the first politicians in Congress to speak out against the VIETNAM WAR, retracting his early support for U.S. involvement there. And in 1969, he opened a congressional investigation into the massacre of hundreds of civilians by American troops in the Vietnam village of My Lai.

Udall's most lasting contributions came in the area of environmental legislation. As chairman of the Interior Committee, he succeeded in setting aside millions of acres of federal land for conservation while also nearly doubling the total size of federal park land. A tireless opponent of industry, he fought for years to place federal limits on strip mining before his efforts came to fruition in 1977. A similar lengthy campaign

against oil drilling in the Arctic National Wildlife Refuge in Alaska was also successful. Though these positions sometimes earned him powerful enemies, they played well year after year with environmentally-minded voters in his home state, where he established the huge water system known as the Central Arizona Project.

Udall's political aspirations were dealt a crushing defeat in 1976, when JIMMY CARTER trounced him in twenty-two separate Democratic party presidential primaries. Unbowed, he promptly published *Too Funny to Be President*, a collection of witticisms. Yet in his personal life, mishaps and tragedies followed. That year he fell off a ladder and broke both arms. In 1979, he was diagnosed with the incurable degenerative nerve disorder, Parkinson's disease, which led him to reject the idea of another presidential bid in 1984. In 1988, his wife committed suicide. After a fall in his home in 1991 accelerated the progress of his disease, his family announced his resignation from office.

Leaders of both political parties fondly remembered Udall in eulogies, and President BILL CLINTON praised his "uncommon wisdom, wit and dedication." Udall's legacy of environmental concern is carried forth in the Morris K. Udall Foundation, which Congress established in 1992, and he has been followed into politics by his son, Mark, and nephew, Tom, elected to Congress from Colorado and New Mexico, respectively.

CROSS REFERENCES
Goldwater, Barry; Environmental Protection Agency

UNAUTHORIZED PRACTICE

The performance of professional services, such as the rendering of medical treatment or legal assistance, by a person who is not licensed by the state to do so.

Nolo Press

Suspicion of law books and computer software led the state of Texas to allege these materials were illegally trying to replace human lawyers. As an official state body pursued this unique line of reasoning, the accusation provoked controversy in the legal profession. Attorneys often mobilize against the unauthorized practice of law (UPL), which is banned in every state. The dispute led to passionate debate over the nature of legal professionalism, the merits of self-lawyering, and the limits of FIRST AMENDMENT protection for self-help materials. Stand-

ing on one side was a state legal establishment with little patience for interlopers, whether on the page or CD-ROM. Opposing it were publishers, libraries, and legal observers who argued that in an age of technological progress, Texas was standing in the way of the future.

The controversy originated with actions by the Texas Unauthorized Practice of Law (UPL) Committee, an official subcommittee of the Texas Supreme Court. It consists of lawyers who meet to enforce § 81.101 of the Texas Government Code, which broadly defines UPL violations as "any service requiring the use of legal skill or knowledge" by any person not barred and licensed to practice law in the state. Anyone may file a complaint with the subcommittee, including its members. Most complaints fall against paralegals—legal assistants—who have been caught dispensing legal advice. The law empowers the committee to file a civil lawsuit against violators.

In 1998, the UPL subcommittee took aim against two publishers who sell products in Texas. First, the committee brought suit against Iowa-based Parson's Technology, Inc., a division of Mattel, to halt sales in Texas of its software program Quicken Family Lawyer. Advertised as a replacement for a lawyer, the software can prepare more than 100 legal documents in such areas as estate planning, sales, health care and business. To the UPL subcommittee, the software constituted a "cyberlawyer"—an artificially-intelligent imposter that was practicing il-

legally in Texas. Subcommittee attorney Mark A. Ticer, who brought the case against Parson's, compared the software to "somebody sitting on the other side of the desk and drafting the document for you."

The committee also named Berkeley, California, publisher Nolo Press in its complaint. One of the largest self-help legal publishers in the nation, Nolo, founded in 1971, earned over $7 million in sales in 1998 on books such as "How to Win Your Personal Injury Claim" and computer software like its Living Trust Maker. But the subcommittee believed that the publisher's materials posed a danger to Texas consumers, especially because they appear to have a certain official legitimacy. Subcommittee member Ticer advanced this public policy reason for clamping down on books and software, asking rhetorically, "Now what happens to the person who uses that and uses the will form and discovers that the I.R.S. has come in and taken more than they've got?" He said that Texas was proactively moving to head off damage before it happened.

Officials at Nolo Press scoffed at that argument. The press claimed it had never received any complaints from consumers. Associate publisher Stephen R. Elias believed another reason explained the investigation—the Texas attorneys were simply trying to protect against incursions onto their high-priced turf, where Dallas lawyers can charge $400 an hour. Nolo Press, in fact, was founded to do just that. The publisher, whose logo depicts a lawyer as a shark with a necktie and briefcase and which even publishes collections of lawyer jokes, was the brainchild of former Legal Aid attorneys who took an activist position on legal knowledge. "Nolo's products express a definite and politically-charged viewpoint—that legal consumers have a constitutional right to handle their own legal tasks with the help of plain English self-help law materials," the company's website proclaims. The publisher filed suit in 1998 to force the secretive UPL subcommittee to open its records and procedures to public scrutiny.

But the subcommittee distinguished between a consumer's access to information and the type of material Nolo publishes. Ticer noted that citizens can easily get legal information from libraries or via the Internet, but, despite Nolo's claims, he said there was no constitutional right to practice law in the state of Texas. Indeed, in another sense, the subcommittee appeared to be defending the state legal profession's traditional ability to set its own standards for admission and practice. As subcommittee member Jeffrey A. Lehman asked in the *New York Times*, would consumers simply allow anyone to perform brain surgery upon them?

That viewpoint has drawn several knocks from within the legal profession. Advocates of Nolo and Parson's right to sell cyber-materials claim that, in certain instances, technology can easily do what lawyers were formally required to accomplish. New York University law professor Steven Gillers characterizes this position when he calls some legal services, such as drafting wills and divorce papers, "cookie-cutter tasks." Gillers told *Time* magazine that the routine nature of much legal work makes it "easy…to substitute a computer for a lawyer." Other attorneys and media commentators took potshots at Texas for an anachronistic attempt to stop the free flow of information. "There's no way to police this," Stanford Law School professor Deborah Rhode told *Forbes*. "This is Custer's last stand."

The controversy continued in 1999 with two contrasting developments. First, in February, the UPL Committee won its case against Parson's. Dallas U.S. Senior District Judge Barefoot Sanders ruled that one feature of the Quicken program—an interactive question-and-answer segment with video footage of a law professor—violated the state law because it "adapts the content of the form to the responses given by the user." (*Unauthorized Practice of Law Committee v. Parsons Technology, Inc.*No. 07–CV–2859–H). Judge Sanders rejected the publisher's First Amendment arguments, holding that its program was "content-neutral"—a category of speech that expresses no opinion and to which courts generally afford less protection. Parsons appealed the decision.

Second, Nolo won an early round in its battle against the Texas legal establishment. On April 15, the Texas Supreme Court, by vacating one of its earlier rulings, took away the subcommittee's power to operate in strict secrecy. At the same time, Nolo filed a separate lawsuit seeking a judgment that its books and software do not practice law. Also asserting general First Amendment protection for its right to publish, that lawsuit was joined by the Texas Library Association and the American Association of Law Libraries.

CROSS REFERENCES
First Amendment

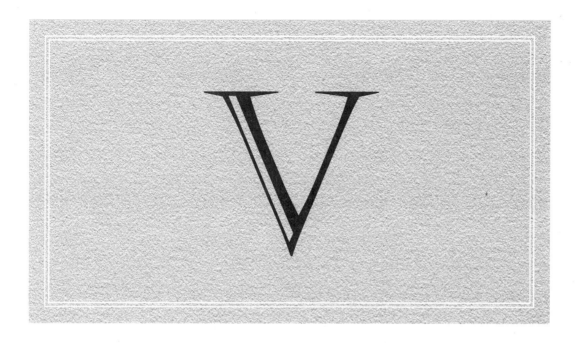

VENUE

A place, such as the territory from which residents are selected to serve as jurors.

A proper place, such as the correct COURT to hear a case because it has authority over events that have occurred within a certain geographical area.

United States v. Rodriguez-Moreno

On April 12, 1999, the Supreme Court gave the government wide berth to choose where to prosecute cases involving gun use in violent interstate crimes. *United States v. Rodriguez-Moreno*, __ U.S. __, 119 S. Ct. 1239 143 L. Ed. 2d 388 (1999), concerned the federal offense of using a gun "during and in relation to any crime of violence or drug trafficking" as specified under 18 U.S.C.A. § 924(c)(1), popularly known as the Federal Firearms Statute and intended to deter the use of guns in felonies. Jacinto Rodriguez-Moreno, the defendant, was convicted of KIDNAPPING. For threatening the victim with a gun, he also was convicted under the Federal Firearms Statute. But an appeals court overturned the gun conviction, ruling that he should not have been convicted in New Jersey for his use of a gun in Maryland. By a 7–2 margin, the Supreme Court disagreed. The majority held that the firearms offense can be prosecuted anywhere that the main violent crime took place, not merely where the gun was used.

The kidnapping grew out of a drug deal that went bad in October 1994, when a New York drug dealer cheated a Texas distributor out of half a million dollars in cocaine. Furious, the distributor hired Rodriguez-Moreno and four others to find the missing dealer. They kidnapped Ephrain Avendano, a middleman in the soured deal, and used him to lead them to their target. The kidnappers took Avendano from Houston to New Jersey, where they also held his wife and children captive, and from there to New York and Maryland. But in Maryland, the hunt turned more ugly. As it became obvious that the devious dealer had escaped, Rodriguez-Moreno put a .357 magnum revolver to the back of Avendano's neck and threatened to kill him, but the others calmed him down. Later, the victim escaped, ran to a nearby house, and found help. Maryland police arrested Rodriguez-Moreno and the others.

Subsequently, a federal district court jury in New Jersey convicted all six men of multiple felonies. Rodriguez-Moreno was convicted of kidnapping and conspiring to kidnap Avendano and his wife. In addition, his use of the handgun led to his conviction under 18 U.S.C.A. § 924(c)(1), which reads: "Whoever, during and in relation to any crime of violence or drug trafficking crime…for which he may be prosecuted in a court of the United States, uses or carries a firearm, shall, in addition to the punishment provided for such crime of violence or drug trafficking crime, be sentenced to imprisonment for five years." This statute, dating to the late 1960s, has long been used to add additional punishment to such convictions and the drug trafficking provision was added in the 1980s. It involves two elements. First, the defendant must have been convicted of a crime of violence or drug trafficking—known as the underlying crime. Second, the defendant must have used or carried a gun "during and in relation to" the underlying crime. Thus for his use of a handgun during the kidnapping, Rodriguez-Moreno received an additional five year prison sentence beyond the sentences imposed for his kidnapping and conspiracy convictions.

In *United States v. Palma-Ruedas* (121 F. 3d 841 [3rd Cir. 1997]), a case that consolidated the appeals of all six defendants, a three-judge panel of the Third U.S. Circuit Court of Appeals upheld all but one of the convictions. The single exception was Rodriguez-Moreno's firearm conviction, which it overturned on the ground that the conviction was obtained in the wrong venue—a court in the wrong jurisdiction. Rodriguez-Moreno had held Avendano and his wife in New Jersey, so it was appropriate for the kidnapping count to be tried there, the appeals court ruled. But New Jersey was the wrong venue for trying the firearm offense, it said, because Rodriguez-Moreno had threatened Avendano with the gun in Maryland.

By a 2–1 vote, the appeals panel reached its conclusion by considering both the issue of venue and the federal firearms statute itself. The court noted that "proper venue is not just a mere formal requirement but, rather, a right of constitutional dimension," observing that Article 3 of the Constitution declares that trials shall be held in the state where the crimes were allegedly committed, and that this guarantee is reinforced by the SIXTH AMENDMENT. To analyze the Federal Firearms Statute, the majority put it under a kind of linguistic microscope. The Court applied the so-called "verb test," a methodology dating from the early twentieth century that reduces the complex language of statutes to their most important verbs in order to determine where an offense is committed. The statute "unambiguously designates the criminal conduct that is prohibited as 'using' or 'carrying' a firearm," the majority opinion concluded. "It follows that one 'commits' a violation of § 924(c)(1) in the district where one 'uses' or 'carries' a firearm." In dissent, one judge on the panel argued that the majority relied too much on grammar and should have spent more effort considering the substance of the firearms statute.

The 7–2 majority on the Supreme Court thought similarly. Although conceding that the verb test has some value as an interpretive tool, the majority opinion by Justice CLARENCE THOMAS said the test was insufficient to decide this case. Moreover, the nature of the multi-state kidnapping itself was relevant. "Kidnapping, once begun, does not end until the victim is free," wrote Justice Thomas. "It does not make sense, then, to speak of it in discrete geograph-

ical fragments...It does not matter that [Rodriguez-Moreno] used the .357 magnum revolver...only in Maryland because he did so 'during and in relation to' a kidnapping that was begun in Texas and continued in New York, New Jersey, and Maryland." Turning to precedents that are eight decades old, Justice Thomas cited *United States v. Lombardo* 241 U.S. 73, 36 S. Ct. 508, 60 L. Ed. 897 (1916) and *Hyde v. United States* 225 U.S. 347, 32 S. Ct. 793, 56 L. Ed. 114 (1912) as cases that illustrate how a crime with distinct parts may be properly tried in a venue other than where the crime was committed. The kidnapping "was committed in all of the places that any part of it took place, and venue for the kidnapping charge against respondent was appropriate in any of them," the opinion stated, just as it was for the gun charge.

While reinstating Rodriguez-Moreno's conviction on the gun crime, the broader significance of the decision lay in giving flexibility to federal prosecutors. They had argued in the appeal for the power to bring firearms charges in any state where the underlying crime occurred, and the Court delivered this option. But the outcome troubled two justices on the Court. In dissent, Justices ANTONIN SCALIA and JOHN PAUL STEVENS argued that the decision violated the defendant's constitutional rights under Article 3 and the Sixth Amendment. They also suggested that the majority's reasoning had been illogical. Scalia, who wrote the dissent, scoffed that the defendant had been convicted "for using a gun during a kidnapping in a state and district where all agree he did not use a gun during a kidnapping."

CROSS REFERENCES
Drugs and Narcotics; Gun Control

VETO

The refusal of an executive officer to assent to a BILL that has been created and approved by the LEGISLATURE, thereby depriving the bill of any legally binding effect.

Clinton v. City of New York

The Supreme Court struck down the Line Item Veto Act (2 U.S.C.A. § 691 et seq.) in *Clinton v. City of New York*, 524 U.S. 417, 118 S. Ct. 2091, 141 L. Ed. 2d 393 (1998), ruling that the law was unconstitutional because it violated the Constitution's PRESENTMENT CLAUSE. The Court indicated that a constitutional amendment would be needed in order to grant the president a line item veto.

In 1996, Congress enacted the Line Item Veto Act, giving the president the authority to selectively delete certain types of items from appropriation and budget bills, many of which are hundreds of pages long. The popularity of the line item veto (forty-three states give their governor this power) is based on the desire to eliminate "pork"—appropriations or programs included by a legislator as a political gift to constituents—and other vote-influencing expenditures.

The day after President BILL CLINTON signed the act into law, Sen. Robert C. Byrd (D-W.Va.), joined by five other senators and congressmen who had voted against the bill, filed suit in federal district court, asking that the court strike down the law as unconstitutional. Congress had anticipated the court challenge by authorizing any member "adversely affected" by the act to bring an action.

Byrd alleged that the line item veto disrupted the historic balance of powers between the legislative and executive branches and that it violated Article I, § 7. The district court agreed with Byrd, finding that the law was an unconstitutional delegation of legislative power to the president. The government then appealed to the Supreme Court.

In *Raines v. Byrd*, 521 U.S. 811, 117 S. Ct. 2312, 138 L. Ed. 2d 849 (1997), the Court refused to rule on the merits of the issue. Instead, the Court held that Byrd and his fellow legislators lacked legal STANDING to file suit because they could show no personal injury from the new power.

In August 1997 President Clinton exercised his power under the act by vetoing selected provisions of a budget bill and a tax relief bill. Two groups of plaintiffs who had been affected by the vetoing of these legislative provisions filed suit in federal court. The first group included New York City, two New York associations, one hospital and two unions that represented health care employees. The other group was the Snake River Potato Growers, Inc., which consisted of approximately thirty potato growers located throughout Idaho.

In *City of New York v. Clinton*, 985 F.Supp. 168 (D.D.C. 1998), Judge Thomas F. Hogan found that the plaintiffs had standing to sue and ruled that the Line Item Veto Act was unconstitutional because it violated the procedural requirements of Article I of the Constitution and upset the balance of powers prescribed by the Constitution's Framers. An expedited appeal was then taken to the Supreme Court.

The Supreme Court, on a 6–3 vote, ruled that the Line Item Veto Act was unconstitutional. Justice JOHN PAUL STEVENS, writing for the majority, noted that the act empowered the president to cancel an "item of new direct spending," specifying that such cancellation prevents a provision "from having legal force or effect." Therefore, in both legal and practical effect, the president's use of the line item veto had amended two acts of Congress by repealing a portion of each. Justice Stevens concluded that there was no constitutional authorization for the president to amend or repeal. Under the Presentment Clause (Article I, § 7), after a bill has passed both Houses, but "before it become[s] a Law," it must be presented to the president, who "shall sign it" if he approves it, but "return it," if he does not.

Justice Stevens held that there are important differences between such a "return" and cancellation under the Line Item Veto Act. The constitutional return is of the entire bill and takes place before it becomes law, whereas the statutory cancellation occurs after the bill becomes law and affects it only in part. The Article I procedures governing statutory enactment were the product of the debates and compromises that produced the Constitution. A review of historical materials led Stevens to conclude that the power to enact statutes may only "be exercised in accord with a single, finely wrought and exhaustively considered, procedure." The procedures contained in the Line Item Veto Act were not the product of the "finely wrought" procedure, but truncated versions of two bills that passed both houses.

Justice Stevens rejected the government's contention that the cancellations were "merely exercises of the President's discretionary authority" contained in the budget and tax relief bills, read in light of the previously enacted Line Item Veto Act. He agreed that the Court had upheld laws that gave the president the power to suspend import duty exemptions. But a suspension was contingent on a condition that did not predate the statute and the president had an absolute duty to suspend once it was determined that the contingency had arisen. Moreover, the suspension executed congressional policy. Stevens found the Line Item Veto Act was much different. It authorized the president to effect the repeal of laws, for his own policy reasons, without observing Article I, § 7 procedures.

Justice Stevens also rejected the government's contention that the cancellation powers contained in the act were no different than the president's traditional statutory authority to decline to spend appropriated funds or to implement specified tax measures. The Line Item Veto Act, unlike earlier laws, gave the president the unilateral power to change the text of a properly enacted statute.

The Supreme Court was aware of the importance of its decision. Justice Stevens emphasized that the Court expressed no opinion about the "wisdom" of the act's procedures; its decision was based on the underlying lack of congressional authority under the Constitution to make such a law. If there is to be a new procedure in which the president plays a different role, Justice Stevens concluded that the Constitution must be amended.

Justice STEPHEN BREYER, in a dissent joined by Justices SANDRA DAY O'CONNOR and ANTONIN SCALIA, argued that the Line Item Veto Act did not violate any specific textual constitutional command, nor did it violate any implicit separation of powers principle. Therefore, he concluded that the act was constitutional.

CROSS REFERENCES
Congress; Presidential Powers

VOTING RIGHTS ACT OF 1965

An enactment by Congress in 1965 (42 U.S.C.A. § 1973 et seq.) that prohibits the states and their political subdivisions from imposing voting qualifications or prerequisites to voting or standards, practices, or procedures that deny or curtail the right of a U.S. citizen to vote because of race, color, or membership in a language minority group.

Lopez v. Monterey County

Section 5 of the Voting Rights Act of 1965 requires states or political subdivisions that have a history of racial discrimination ("covered jurisdictions") in voting to obtain "preclearance" from the Department of Justice or the U.S. District Court for the District of Columbia before making changes in their electoral systems. A covered jurisdiction has the burden of proving that the proposed changes do not have the purpose or "effect of denying or abridging the right to vote on account of race or color." This section of the act has proved to be the broadest part of the law for covered jurisdictions, applying to any change that alters the state's voting or election law in even a minor way.

The Supreme Court, in *Lopez v. Monterey County*, __U.S.__, 119 S. Ct. 693, 142 L. Ed. 2d 728 (1999), reaffirmed its tradition of requiring preclearance, ruling that a county attempting to change the way local judges are elected must submit its plan for approval under § 5. The Court was unmoved by Monterey County's claim that it did not have to seek preclearance because the state of California, which itself was not a covered jurisdiction, mandated the election change.

In 1971, Monterey County was designated a covered jurisdiction based on findings that the county maintained California's statewide literacy test as a prerequisite to voting and less than 50 percent of the county's voting age population participated in the November 1968 presidential election. Therefore, Monterey County was required to obtain federal preclearance for any change in the voting scheme that was in place on November 1, 1968.

Hispanic voters in Monterey County filed suit in 1991, claiming that the county had failed to fulfill its § 5 obligation to preclear a series of ordinances passed between 1972 and 1983 that changed the way municipal judges were elected. Under the ordinances, three municipal judge election districts were consolidated into one district, with Hispanic voters arguing that the plan diluted their ability to elect Hispanic judges. A three-judge federal district court panel ruled that the ordinances were voting changes requiring preclearance under § 5 and that the ordinances were unenforceable until they were precleared. The county and the plaintiffs then sought to negotiate an alternative judicial election scheme, but the efforts were ultimately unsuccessful. The controversy continued in the federal courts throughout most of the 1990s.

In 1997, a federal district court ruled that Monterey County's judicial election plans did not have to be precleared. It based its decision on the fact that a 1979 California law had consolidated the three existing municipal courts and mandated that there be one municipal court district in the county. This statute did not require preclearance because it was the product of a noncovered jurisdiction.

The Supreme Court, on an 8–1 vote, reversed the district court's decision. Justice SANDRA DAY O'CONNOR, writing for the majority, concluded that Monterey County was required to seek preclearance before implementing California laws that affect voting changes in the county. Justice O'Connor noted that § 5, on its face requires preclearance whenever a covered jurisdiction "shall enact or seek to administer any voting" changes. The plain language of the statute supported the conclusion that the preclearance requirement applied to the county, even though the county was required to act at the direction of a state law. The Supreme Court found no evidence that the phrase "seek to administer" was limited to only the discretionary acts of the county. Justice O'Connor concluded that the word "administer" encompassed both discretionary and nondiscretionary acts under § 5.

Justice O'Connor pointed out that the Court's prior decisions "reveal a clear assumption" that preclearance is required where a "noncovered State affects voting changes in covered counties." Additional evidence supporting this assumption were the more than 1,300 submissions to the Department of Justice seeking to preclear state laws from the seven states that are currently partially covered: California, Florida, Michigan, New Hampshire, New York, North Carolina, and South Dakota. The fact that courts and parties routinely assumed a need for preclearance under circumstances similar to Monterey County reinforced O'Connor's conclusion that preclearance was required.

Another source of support for the Court's view was the fact that the attorney general consistently construed § 5 to require preclearance when a covered political subdivision "seek[s] to administer" an enactment of a partially covered state. Justice O'Connor acknowledged that the Court had traditionally given substantial deference to the attorney general's interpretation of § 5 in light of the central role the attorney general plays in formulating and implementing that section.

The state of California had argued that requiring preclearance would intrude on rights constitutionally reserved to the states. It contended that because it had not been designated as a covered jurisdiction, its voting laws were not subject to § 5 preclearance. Justice O'Connor acknowledged that the Voting Rights Act of 1965 did alter the balance between state and federal power on voting issues, but concluded that there was constitutional authority for doing so. The FIFTEENTH AMENDMENT, which was passed after the CIVIL WAR, states that a person cannot be denied the right to vote because of his race. Congress based the Voting Rights Act on this amendment, which, like the THIRTEENTH and FOURTEENTH AMENDMENTS, was a deliberate intrusion on the powers of the states. Moreover, legislation that deters or remedies constitutional violations can fall within Congress' enforcement power, even if it prohibits conduct that is not itself unconstitutional.

Justice O'Connor also pointed out that over thirty years before the Court had upheld the constitutionality of § 5 against arguments that it usurped powers reserved to the states. *South Carolina v. Katzenbach*, 383 U.S. 301, 86 S. Ct. 803, 15 L. Ed. 2d 769 (1966). The Court in *Katzenbach* had made clear that once a jurisdiction has been designated as covered, the act may guard against both discriminatory intent and the potential harmful effect of neutral laws in that jurisdiction. Therefore, the Court ruled that Monterey County must seek preclearance before implementing the voting changes required by state law.

Justice CLARENCE THOMAS, in a dissenting opinion, read § 5 to "require preclearance only of those voting changes that are the direct product of a covered jurisdiction's policy choices." Because Monterey County did not make the policy but only sought to implement it, it should not be subject to the preclearance requirement.

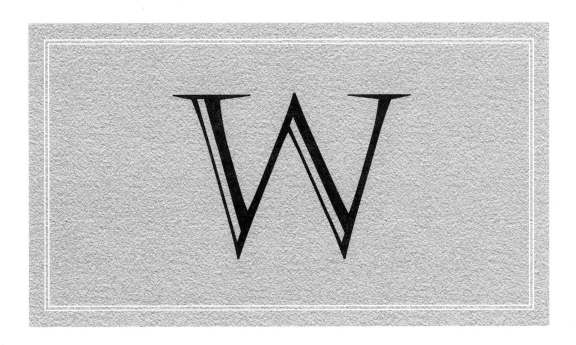

WALLACE, GEORGE

Obituary notice

Born on August 25, 1919 in Clio, Alabama; died September 13, 1998 in Montgomery, Alabama. Wallace received his law degree from the University of Alabama and was admitted to the bar in 1942. Between 1942 and 1945 Wallace served in the U.S. Army Air Force. After the war, he became assistant attorney general of Alabama. In 1947 he entered the Alabama legislature, representing Barbour County, and remained until 1953. He served as judge of the Third Judicial District of Alabama between 1953 and 1958, after which he returned to private law practice in Clayton. Wallace's experiences in Alabama politics prepared him for his election to governor in 1962. An outspoken critic of federal-government interference in southern schools and an ardent segregationist, Wallace entered a number of presidential primary races in 1964, largely to channel opposition to the civil rights bill.

WELFARE

Government benefits distributed to impoverished persons to enable them to maintain a minimum standard of well-being.

New-Resident Limits on Welfare Rejected

Welfare reform dominated much of the 1990s as state and federal governments explored ways of changing government assistance programs that appeared to foster dependence rather than personal responsibility. Many states lowered their maximum benefits to discourage becoming "welfare magnets" while fifteen states placed residency restrictions on welfare recipients. In 1992, California enacted a law that limited new residents to the benefits they would have received in the state of their prior residence. The law was immediately challenged, with the state announcing that it would not try to enforce the limitations on benefits. However, after Congress enacted a sweeping welfare reform in 1996 which encouraged states to experiment with welfare programs, California announced it would enforce the law.

In May 1999 the Supreme Court, in *Saenz v. Doe*, __ U.S. __, 119 S. Ct. 1518, 143 L. Ed. 2d 689 (1999), struck down the California law as an infringement on the right to travel. The Court also employed the FOURTEENTH AMENDMENT's Privileges and Immunities Clause, which has been used sparingly since the 1870s, to justify its decision. The decision made it more difficult for states to place any restrictions on newly arrived welfare recipients.

California has the sixth highest welfare benefit levels in the United States. When it enacted the limitation on benefits for persons residing in California less than one year, it hoped to save 11 million dollars a year in its Aid to Families with Dependent Children program. California officials estimated that each year more than 50,000 people applying for benefits in the state had lived in another state during the previous twelve months. Many of these people came from states that had much lower benefit levels. For example, a family of four who arrived from Mississippi would have received $144 in that state. In comparison, but for the one-year residency limitation, they would receive $673 from California.

George Wallace
AP/WIDE WORLD PHOTOS

A 1992 federal lawsuit by three California residents who were eligible for AFDC benefits led to a district court INJUNCTION against California's enforcement of the law. While the state appealed this decision to the Supreme Court, the U.S. secretary of HEALTH AND HUMAN SERVICES revoked approval of the plan, which depended on federal funds for AFDC. The Supreme Court then dismissed the lawsuit and the limitation of benefits scheme appeared dead.

However, California decided to implement the law again after Congress enacted the Personal Responsibility and Work Opportunity Reconciliation Act of 1996 (PRWORA). This law replaced the AFDC program with a new one, Temporary Assistance to Needy Families (TANF). Congress expressly authorized states that receive a block grant under TANF to "apply to a family the rules (including benefit amounts) of the [TANF] program…of another State if the family has moved to the State from the other State and has resided in the State for less than 12 months." 42 U.S.C.A. § 604(c). The law in effect removed the need for California to receive approval from Health and Human Services.

After California announced that it would implement the law, two persons sued in federal court, challenging the residency requirement. The judge issued a RESTRAINING ORDER against the state, prohibiting the law's implementation. He noted that California's higher benefits were somewhat offset by higher housing costs and that residents coming from forty-three states would face higher costs of living in California. Moreover, the judge questioned the assumption that people moved to the state to obtain higher welfare benefits. The Ninth Circuit Court of Appeals upheld the restraining order, leading to the Supreme Court challenge.

The Court, on a 7–2 vote, ruled that the law was unconstitutional. In addition, it found that Congress had no authority to allow the states to carry out such plans. Justice JOHN PAUL STEVENS, writing for the majority, acknowledged that the word "travel" is not found in the Constitution, yet the constitutional right to travel from one state to another "is firmly embedded in our jurisprudence."

The Court, in *Shapiro v. Thompson*, 394 U.S. 618, 89 S. Ct. 1322, 22 L. Ed. 2d 600 (1969), struck down the laws of three states that denied all welfare benefits to persons who had resided in their states less than one year. In that case the Court ruled that it was "constitutionally impermissible" for a state to enact residency requirements that sought to inhibit the migration of needy persons into the state. These laws restricted a person's right to travel. California argued that its law had not been enacted for the purpose of inhibiting the migration of poor people and that it merely reduced the level of benefits rather denying benefits.

Justice Stevens stated that the right to travel has three components:

It protects the right of a citizen of one State to enter and to leave another State, the right to be treated as a welcome visitor rather than an unfriendly alien when temporarily present in the second State, and, for those travelers who elect to become permanent residents, the right to be treated like other citizens of that State.

In the present case, the third component of the right to travel was present. The Privileges and Immunities Clause of the Fourteenth Amendment safeguarded this component, as it states that "[t]he Citizens of each State shall be entitled to all Privileges and Immunities of Citizens in the several States." Stevens found that the right to travel is protected "not only by the new arrival's status as a state citizen, but also by her status as citizen of the United States." He admitted that the clause had been severely limited in the *Slaughterhouse Cases*, 83 U.S. 36, 21 L. Ed. 394 (1873), yet even in that case the Court had acknowledged the right of a citizen to "become a citizen of any State of the Union."

Justice Stevens then applied the right to travel to the California law. He held that there was no compelling government interest to justify the limitation on benefits to new citizens of the state. He concluded that "the state's legitimate interest in saving money provides no justification for its decision to discriminate among equally eligible citizens." Citizens, regardless of their incomes, have the right to choose to be citizens of state in which they reside. The states, however, "do not have any right to select their citizens."

The congressional approval of residency requirements contained in the welfare reform law of 1996 did not, in Steven's words, "resuscitate" the constitutionality of the California law. He emphasized that the Court had consistently ruled that Congress may not authorize the states to violate the Fourteenth Amendment.

Chief Justice WILLIAM H. REHNQUIST filed a dissenting opinion, which Justice CLARENCE THOMAS joined. Rehnquist said he would uphold the law because Congress decided that it made good welfare policy to give states "the authority and flexibility to ensure" that their programs were not exploited. He noted that if states can require individuals to comply with one-year residency requirements before paying lower rates of college tuition, or before terminating a marriage, "then states may surely do the same for welfare benefits."

Justice Thomas, in a separate dissent that Chief Justice Rehnquist joined, expressed concern about the Court's use of the Privileges and Immunities Clause. He expressed concern that "it might become yet another convenient tool for inventing new rights, limited solely by the predilections of those who happen at the time to be members of this court."

CROSS REFERENCES
Fourteenth Amendment

WHITEWATER

Susan McDougal Acquitted of Obstruction of Justice

In April 1999, a federal jury in Little Rock, Arkansas, acquitted Susan McDougal of one charge of obstruction of justice and deadlocked on two charges of criminal contempt, leading U.S. District Court Judge George Howard, Jr., to declare a mistrial on the contempt charges. McDougal was a business partner with her former husband, the late James B. McDougal, President BILL CLINTON, and First Lady HILLARY RODHAM CLINTON in a complex series of land and loan transactions that has become known as Whitewater. McDougal was on trial for refusing to answer questions posed by GRAND JURY prosecutors working under Independent Counsel KENNETH STARR. Starr has been investigating the Whitewater scandal and related matters since August 1994.

The Whitewater scandal dates back to 1978, when the Clintons and the McDougals purchased 230 acres of land along the White River in the Ozarks in Arkansas. As they financed the entire purchase with loans, neither the Clintons nor the McDougals paid any money down for the property. In 1979 they transferred the land into the Whitewater Development Corporation, the source for the scandal's name. When lot sales failed to generate enough money to cover mortgage loan payments in the ensuing years, the Clintons and the McDougals executed a series of complex transactions to extend some mortgage loans and to pay others.

In the meantime, in 1982, the McDougals purchased stock in the Woodruff County Savings and Loan Association, which they renamed Madison Guaranty Savings & Loan Association. In 1983 they purchased more stock to acquire exclusive control of the S & L. According to a report issued by the U.S. Senate's Special Committee to Investigate Whitewater Development Corporation and Related Matters, James McDougal "viewed Madison Guaranty as a personal 'candy store.'" The report says Mr. McDougal improperly used funds from Madison Guaranty to finance personal real estate investments, including Whitewater loan payments.

Susan McDougal's contempt trial stemmed from a portion of the Whitewater scandal that led to the 1996 FRAUD trial and conviction of the McDougals and former Arkansas Governor Jim Guy Tucker. The star witness at the 1996 trial was David Hale, former president of Capital Management Services, Inc. (CMS), a company that was licensed by the Small Business Administration (SBA) to make federally backed loans to small businesses that were economically or socially disadvantaged. Hale testified that in 1985 he conspired with Tucker and James McDougal to defraud the SBA by making an illegal $300,000 loan from CMS. According to Hale, at a meeting in early 1986 with McDougal and then Governor Clinton, McDougal proposed that CMS make the illegal loan to Susan McDougal as president of Master Marketing, purportedly an advertising company. Also according to Hale, Clinton offered to provide security for the loan, but said to Hale, "be sure— my name cannot show up on this." Hale also

Susan McDougal was found not guilty on charges of obstruction of justice.

JIM YATES/AP/WIDE WORLD PHOTOS

claimed that Clinton urged Hale to make the loan to "help my friends." (Report of the Special Committee, part 3, part IV.) According to testimony by an FBI agent, after CMS made the loan, the McDougals used some of the $300,000 to pay off most of a $27,600 Whitewater loan from Madison Guaranty to Clinton.

In videotaped testimony at the 1996 trial, President Clinton said he was unaware of the $300,000 loan or its use by McDougal for Whitewater expenses. He also denied being at a meeting with Hale, offering security for the loan, asking that his name not appear on loan papers, or generally urging Hale to make the loan.

After the jury convicted the McDougals and Tucker of fraud, Starr organized a grand jury investigation of whether President Clinton committed any crimes in connection with the loan or lied in his videotaped testimony. On September 3, 1996, Starr got an order from U.S. District Court Judge SUSAN WEBBER WRIGHT granting Susan McDougal IMMUNITY for her grand jury testimony. The order compelled Mc-Dougal to testify by preventing her from invoking her FIFTH AMENDMENT privilege against self-incrimination in exchange for guaranteeing that her testimony would not be used to convict her of a crime.

On September 4, 1996, when McDougal appeared before the grand jury, prosecutors asked her whether she ever discussed the $300,000 loan with then Governor Clinton, and whether Clinton lied during his videotaped testimony at her 1996 trial. McDougal, however, refused to answer any questions until after she read a prepared statement. Prosecutors and the grand jury would not allow McDougal to read the statement until after she answered their questions, which she refused to do. Judge Wright held McDougal in civil contempt and sent her to jail for eighteen months for disobeying the September 3 order.

On April 23, 1998, prosecutors called Mc-Dougal before the grand jury again to explain the notation "Payoff Clinton" that appeared in the memo section of a check that McDougal signed in August 1983. Judge Wright confirmed that McDougal was still compelled to testify under the September 3 immunity order. McDougal refused to answer the prosecutors' questions, however, saying they were "conflicted" from handling the investigation because they were determined to convict President Clinton at any cost. McDougal said she would answer questions before the grand jury only after Starr and his

team resigned and were replaced by truly independent counsel.

On May 4, 1998, Starr indicted McDougal on two charges of criminal contempt and one charge of obstruction of justice for twice refusing to obey Judge Wright's September 3 order. The federal criminal contempt statute defines CONTEMPT of court as "Disobedience or resistance to its lawful … order." (18 U.S.C. § 401(3).) The obstruction of justice statute seeks to punish anyone who "corruptly … endeavors to … impede any grand or petit juror … in the discharge of his duty." (18 U.S.C. § 1503(a).) At McDougal's trial, which began on March 10, 1999, prosecutors presented a straightforward case to the jury, arguing that McDougal's willful refusal to obey Judge Wright's order amounted to contempt of court and obstruction of justice.

In McDougal's defense, attorney Mark Geragos attacked Starr and his Whitewater investigation. In opening statements, Geragos told that jury that McDougal refused to testify before the grand jury because Starr wanted her to lie to implicate President Clinton in criminal conduct. To prove this, Geragos presented testimony by Claudia Riley, a longtime friend of the McDougals. Riley testified that James McDougal once grabbed Susan's arm and threatened never to speak to her again if she did not cooperate with Starr. Riley also said Starr's office told McDougal they could get her out of an unrelated EMBEZZLEMENT trial and tax investigation if she cooperated.

Testifying in her own defense, McDougal told the jury that her late husband once said prosecutor W. Hickman Ewing wanted her to lie about having an affair with Clinton. McDougal also said that prosecutor W. Ray Jahn threatened her with an income tax investigation if she did not cooperate with Starr's team, and that Starr offered to make the unrelated embezzlement case against her disappear if she did cooperate.

While testifying, McDougal answered the questions put to her before the grand jury in 1996 and 1998. McDougal said she never discussed the $300,000 loan with President Clinton and she did not think he lied during his videotaped testimony at her 1996 fraud trial. She explained that the notation "Payoff Clinton" in the 1983 check referred to a land deal in Clinton, Arkansas, not to Bill Clinton. When asked why she did not present this evidence to the grand jury, McDougal explained that she was afraid Starr would indict her for PERJURY if she did not give testimony that implicated Clinton in a crime.

To support this story, attorney Geragos presented testimony by Julie Hiatt Steele. Steele once reported to the press that former White House volunteer Kathleen Willey said President Clinton sexually harassed her in the Oval Office in 1993. After Steele refused to repeat this story before a grand jury, saying it had been a lie, Starr indicted her for obstruction of justice and making false statements. McDougal explained to the jury that she feared the same treatment by Starr.

After both sides rested, Judge Howard told the jury they could consider McDougal's evidence of Starr's alleged prosecutorial misconduct only when deliberating the charge of obstruction of justice. Judge Howard emphasized that such evidence was irrelevant to the two charges of criminal contempt, where the sole issue was whether McDougal willfully violated Judge Wright's order to testify before Starr's grand jury. After heated deliberations, the jury returned with a verdict of not guilty on obstruction of justice, but reported a deadlock on the charges of contempt. After nine of the twelve jurors told Judge Howard that further deliberations would not break the deadlock, he declared a mistrial on the contempt charges and entered the verdict of not guilty on obstruction of justice.

In interviews after the trial, jury foreman Donald Thomas, who wanted to acquit McDougal on all counts, said Starr's team was arrogant, and the testimony of Starr's deputy, W. Hickman Ewing, was evasive. Juror Charles Adams, however, who wanted to convict McDougal on all charges, said it appeared that Starr was on trial, and some jurors "were just not going to give any ammunition to them to help get the President."

Weeks later, in May 1999, the jury in the Steele trial also became deadlocked, resulting in a mistrial on all charges against her. Starr reported that he would not seek to retry McDougal or Steele on the mistried charges.

In June 1999, just before the demise of the special counsel law that allowed Starr to pursue the Whitewater investigation, the case of Webster Hubbell, another alleged Whitewater partner, was resolved. Hubbell, a former Justice Department leader and friend of the Clintons, admitted one of the fifteen charges against him in a plea deal. As a result, Hubbell was sentenced to probation and the other charges were dropped. Hubbell pled guilty to lying to regulators in the investigation, though he insisted that his admission had nothing to do with Hillary Rodham Clinton. He continued to maintain that Mrs. Clinton had done nothing wrong.

CROSS REFERENCES
Clinton, Hillary Rodham; Clinton, William Jefferson; Independent Counsel; Starr, Kenneth W.

WISDOM, JOHN MINOR

Obituary notice

Born on May 17, 1905, in New Orleans, Louisiana; died May 15, 1999, in New Orleans, Louisiana. Wisdom served as a judge of the U.S. Court of Appeals for the Fifth Circuit beginning in 1957. As a judge, he was known for making civil rights rulings that were often unpopular with his southern constituents. Among the decisions were *Meredith v. Fair* (1962), which desegregated the University of Mississippi, *Local 189, United Papermakers and Paperworkers v. United States* (1976), which prohibited promotion based on racially-based seniority systems, and his enforcement of the *Brown v. Board of Education* (1954) Supreme Court decision.

WORKERS' COMPENSATION

A system whereby an employer must pay, or provide INSURANCE to pay, the lost wages and medical expenses of an employee who is injured on the job.

American Manufacturers Mutual Insurance Co. v. Sullivan

The U.S. Supreme Court upheld a Pennsylvania workers' compensation law permitting private insurers and self-insured employers to withhold payments for disputed medical treatment pending independent reviews by private health care providers. *American Manufacturers Mutual Insurance Co. v. Sullivan*, __ U.S. __, 119 S. Ct. 977, 143 L. Ed. 2d 130 (1999). The Court rejected the plaintiff's argument and a decision by the Third Circuit Court of Appeals that by withholding payments for medical care, insurers violated the due process rights of injured workers by depriving them of property without notice or the opportunity to be heard.

In Pennsylvania, once an employer accepts liability or is deemed liable for providing workers' compensation benefits to an injured worker, that employer or its workers' compensation insurer must provide medical treatment that is reasonable and necessary to cure or relieve the effects of the injury. The state law mandates that insurers pay for such treatment within thirty days of receiving the medical bill. Whether medical treatment is reasonable or necessary is often disputed.

In an effort to control workers' compensation costs and make certain that injured workers receive only those medical benefits that are reasonable and necessary, in 1993 Pennsylvania revised its workers compensation laws. Among the amendments was the creation of medical peer review procedure 77 Pa. Stat. Ann. § 531(6) (Purdon Supp. 1998). Under this procedure, insurers can, within the thirty day time period for paying medical bills, request that the reasonableness and necessity of the medical treatment be determined by a "utilization review organization" (URO). These private organizations have as members doctors and other licensed health care providers who specialize in the area of medical treatment under review. Members of a URO are responsible for reviewing medical records regarding the injured worker, allowing the treating provider an opportunity to discuss the treatment under review, and then determining the reasonableness and necessity of the treatment.

When a determination is made in favor of an employee, the insurer must pay the disputed medical bill, along with interest, and must also pay for the cost of the utilization review. When a determination is made in favor of the employer or insurer, the employee may appeal the decision to a workers' compensation judge, but the insurer is not responsible for paying for the disputed treatment unless and until a judge overturns the decision of the URO.

Ten individual employees and two organizations representing employees filed a lawsuit under the CIVIL RIGHTS ACT OF 1964, 42 U.S.C. § 1983, alleging that the defendants, acting under color of state law, were withholding workers' compensation benefits without notice and an opportunity to be heard, depriving the plaintiffs of property in violation of due process. The defendants included state officials who administer the Pennsylvania act, the director of the state's worker insurance fund, the self-insured School District of Pennsylvania, and several private workers' compensation insurance companies.

The trial court dismissed the lawsuit on the grounds that private insurers are not state actors, and that the law in dispute did not violate due process. The U.S. Third Circuit Court of Appeals, however, held that private insurers do act under color of state law because they provide public benefits that honor state entitlements. The Third Circuit further found no dispute that the plaintiffs had a protected property interest in receiving workers' compensation medical benefits. Based on that rationale, the appellate court struck from the statute language permitting the non-payment of medical benefits during the utilization review process.

The U.S. Supreme Court granted CERTIORARI to resolve the issues of whether private insurers that provide workers' compensation insurance under the regulation of state laws are state actors, and whether withholding payments for medical treatment pending a review procedure violated due process.

Chief Justice WILLIAM H. REHNQUIST wrote the opinion, with Justice JOHN PAUL STEVENS partially dissenting. Rejecting the argument that the defendants constituted "state actors" for purposes of determining a FOURTEENTH AMENDMENT due process violation, the Court emphasized that a state action requires 1) an allegation of constitutional deprivation caused by acts taken pursuant to state law, and 2) that the conduct alleged to be unconstitutional be fairly attributable to the state. The Court found that the plaintiffs failed to meet the second prong of the two-prong requirement.

The Court conceded that the business of workers' compensation insurance, although private, is heavily regulated by the state. Nevertheless, it found that actions taken by private insurers cannot be held to constitutional standards without a sufficiently close nexus between the state and the challenged action. One factor in determining whether such a nexus exists is the degree of overt or covert encouragement that the state provides the private player. In this case, the Court found that although the state participated in the dispute process by requiring the submission of a form and performing other related functions, it did not encourage or authorize the insurers' decisions to dispute and withhold the payment of medical benefits. Nor did the state delegate to private insurers traditional state powers. The Court found nothing in Pennsylvania's history, constitution, or statutes obligating the state to provide benefits to injured workers; rather, the state legislated the provision of such benefits to be made by private insurers. Even private businesses that are heavily regulated by the state, such as insurance companies, are not joint participants for purposes of state action, according to the Court.

The justices similarly rejected the plaintiffs' argument that the Pennsylvania act deprived them of property in violation of the DUE PROCESS CLAUSE of the Fourteenth Amendment. Such a holding would require a finding that the plaintiffs had been deprived of a protected property interest; namely, their workers' compensation medical benefits. The Court instead found that insurers and employers in Pennsylvania are not required to provide injured workers with any and all medical treatment, but rather only medical treatment that is both reasonable and necessary. Thus an injured worker has no protected property interest in unreasonable or unnecessary medical benefits. Since the question of whether the medical benefits were reasonable and necessary caused the dispute in the first place, the plaintiffs could not show that they were deprived of a protected property interest.

The *Sullivan* decision may impact more than just employers and workers' compensation insurers in Pennsylvania. The significance of the decision, which for the first time explicitly stated that private industries do not become agents of the government merely because the government strongly regulates them, may be far reaching. Health insurers and automobile insurers also are heavily regulated by federal and state laws.

CROSS REFERENCES
Employment Law; Insurance; State Action

WRIGHT, SUSAN WEBBER

In the early 1970s, Susan Webber Wright was a law student at the University of Arkansas, and BILL CLINTON was her law professor for an admiralty law class. The future president lost a batch of final exams, including Webber's. Clinton offered her a B+ for the course, but she convinced him to let her retake the exam, and she earned an A. Over two decades later, Wright, now a federal judge in her home state of Arkansas, was assigned the case of *Jones v. Clinton*, a lawsuit alleging that the president had sexually harassed a state employee while he was governor of Arkansas. On April 12, 1999, Judge Susan Webber Wright made an unprecedented ruling when she held the president of the United States, in CONTEMPT of court in *Jones v. Clinton*.

Wright was born in Texarkana, Arkansas, on August 22, 1948, to Thomas Edward and Betty Jane Webber. Her father died when she was a teenager. The resulting financial strain made scholarships and waitress jobs crucial to funding her college education at Randolph-Macon Woman's College in Virginia. After graduating in 1970, Wright obtained a master of public administration from the University of Arkansas at Fayetteville in 1972. Her father, grandfather, and an uncle were all attorneys (her younger sister also became one), and Wright then entered law school, earning a J.D. with high honors in 1975 from the University of Arkansas law school. She had the distinction of

---

SUSAN WEBBER WRIGHT

1948	Born in Texarkana, Arkansas
1972	Earned an M.P.A. from University of Arkansas
1975	J.D. from University of Arkansas
1990	Appointed federal district court judge
1994	Assigned *Jones v. Clinton*
1998	Dismissed *Jones v. Clinton*
1999	Held President Clinton in contempt

---

being the law review's first female editor. Following graduation, Wright accepted a clerkship with the Eighth Circuit Court of Appeals, then embarked on a career in academia, teaching law at Ohio State College of Law and Louisiana State University, and eventually landing at the University of Arkansas law school teaching courses in gas, oil, and mineral rights. She married a colleague, professor Robert Wright, in 1983 and has one daughter.

Despite Wright's lack of experience as a trial lawyer, President GEORGE BUSH appointed her as a federal district court judge in 1990. During her years on the bench she has generally received high marks for her competence, and has gained a reputation as an independent jurist. She has developed a reputation for being tough-minded and fair. She has been the principal judge assigned to prosecutions stemming from independent counsel KENNETH STARR's investigations. Perhaps one measure of Wright's evenhandedness comes from the fact that she has in turn been criticized by Republicans for being too easy on Clinton, and by Democrats for favoring the independent counsel's office.

Wright's rulings in the *Jones* and WHITEWATER cases have infuriated Clintonites with Susan McDougal's eighteen month prison stint for contempt, when McDougal refused to testify about her Whitewater dealings with Clinton while he was governor of Arkansas. On the other hand, she ruled in 1994 that the Paula Jones lawsuit could be held in abeyance until after the president finished his tenure in office (although she denied his motion to dismiss on the

Susan Webber Wright

DANNY JOHNSTON/AP/WIDE WORLD PHOTOS

grounds that he was immune from the suit). In May 1997, the U.S. Supreme Court ruled that Wright had abused her discretion in postponing the trial, and ordered the case to go forward.

In a January 7, 1998, AFFIDAVIT in the *Jones* case, former White House intern Monica Lewinsky denied having had a sexual relationship with President Clinton. Ten days later, Clinton also denied having had a relationship with Lewinsky in a DEPOSITION. In the days following Clinton's deposition, numerous allegations of the Clinton and Lewinsky affair surfaced in the media, but Clinton publicly denied the allegations, once stating "I did not have sex with that woman, Ms. Lewinsky." On April 1, 1998, Judge Wright dismissed the lawsuit against the president, ruling that his behavior, if true, may have been "boorish," but that it did not rise to a level constituting sexual harassment under Arkansas law, nor did Jones suffer from a "hostile work environment" after her alleged encounter with Clinton. Jones appealed Wright's decision, but reached a settlement with Clinton in November 1998 before a ruling was made on her appeal. Jones settled the suit for $850,000. In a September 1998 ruling in the case, Judge Wright expressed her concerns over Clinton's deposition, but deferred a contempt decision to a later date.

The president's testimony and actions in the *Jones* case with respect to Lewinsky ultimately resulted in his IMPEACHMENT. On February 12, 1999, the Senate acquitted the president on the two articles of impeachment. With the impeachment trial over, Judge Wright ruled on April 12, 1999 that President Clinton was in contempt of court, the first time a sitting president has ever been cited for contempt. Judge Wright forcefully rejected Clinton's claim that his characterization of his affair with Monica Lewinsky had been legally accurate. She ruled that Clinton had given "false, misleading, and evasive answers that were designed to obstruct the judicial process" in the Jones sexual harassment lawsuit. She called the president's testimony "intentionally false, notwithstanding tortured definitions and interpretations of the term 'sexual relations.'" She also ruled that Clinton had "undermined the integrity of the judicial system" and noted that "[i]t is difficult to construe the president's sworn statements in this civil lawsuit concerning his relationship with Ms. Lewinsky as anything other than a willful refusal to obey this court's discovery orders."

The ruling was a finding of civil contempt, not criminal contempt, and as such only subjects the president to the possibility of civil fines. In addition, Clinton also faces the possibility of losing his law license, a matter the judge referred to the Arkansas Supreme Court Committee on Professional Conduct for determination. Clinton did not appeal the 32-page decision, nor did he ask for a hearing, as Judge Wright indicated he could. She ordered Clinton to pay $1,202 for her court expenses incurred when she traveled to oversee Clinton's January 17, 1998 deposition in Washington, D.C.

As a result of the contempt citation, Clinton's lawyers and Jones's lawyers are haggling over fees and expenses to be paid. Jones's lawyers asked Judge Wright to order Clinton to pay attorney fees of nearly $500,000. Clinton's attorneys argued that the president should be liable for less than $35,000 in legal fees and costs.

CROSS REFERENCES
Clinton, William J.; Contempt; Sexual Harassment; Starr, Kenneth W.

CHILD ONLINE PROTECTION ACT

47 U.S.C.A. § 231

§ 231. Restriction of access by minors to materials commercially distributed by means of world wide web that are harmful to minors

(a) Requirement to restrict access

(1) Prohibited conduct

Whoever knowingly and with knowledge of the character of the material, in interstate or foreign commerce by means of the World Wide Web, makes any communication for commercial purposes that is available to any minor and that includes any material that is harmful to minors shall be fined not more than $50,000, imprisoned not more than 6 months, or both.

(2) Intentional violations

In addition to the penalties under paragraph (1), whoever intentionally violates such paragraph shall be subject to a fine of not more than $50,000 for each violation. For purposes of this paragraph, each day of violation shall constitute a separate violation.

(3) Civil penalty

In addition to the penalties under paragraphs (1) and (2), whoever violates paragraph (1) shall be subject to a civil penalty of not more than $50,000 for each violation. For purposes of this paragraph, each day of violation shall constitute a separate violation.

(b) Inapplicability of carriers and other service providers

For purposes of subsection (a), a person shall not be considered to make any communication for commercial purposes to the extent that such person is—

(1) a telecommunications carrier engaged in the provision of a telecommunications service;

(2) a person engaged in the business of providing an Internet access service;

(3) a person engaged in the business of providing an Internet information location tool; or

(4) similarly engaged in the transmission, storage, retrieval, hosting, formatting, or translation (or any combination thereof) of a communication made by another person, without selection or alteration of the content of the communication, except that such person's deletion of a particular communication or material made by another person in a manner consistent with subsection (c) or section 230 shall not constitute such selection or alteration of the content of the communication.

(c) Affirmative defense

(1) Defense

It is an affirmative defense to prosecution under this section that the defendant, in good faith, has restricted access by minors to material that is harmful to minors—

(A) by requiring use of a credit card, debit account, adult access code, or adult personal identification number;

(B) by accepting a digital certificate that verifies age; or

(C) by any other reasonable measures that are feasible under available technology.

(2) Protection for use of defenses

No cause of action may be brought in any court or administrative agency against any person on account of any activity that is not in violation of any law punishable by criminal or civil penalty, and that the person has taken in good faith to implement a defense authorized under this subsection or otherwise to restrict or prevent the transmission of, or access to, a communication specified in this section.

(d) Privacy protection requirements

(1) Disclosure of information limited

A person making a communication described in subsection (a)—

(A) shall not disclose any information collected for the purposes of restricting access to such communications to individuals 17 years of age or older without the prior written or electronic consent of—

(i) the individual concerned, if the individual is an adult; or

(ii) the individual's parent or guardian, if the individual is under 17 years of age; and

(B) shall take such actions as are necessary to prevent unauthorized access to such information by a person other than the person making such communication and the recipient of such communication.

(2) Exceptions

A person making a communication described in subsection (a) may disclose such information if the disclosure is—

(A) necessary to make the communication or conduct a legitimate business activity related to making the communication; or

(B) made pursuant to a court order authorizing such disclosure.

(e) Definitions

For purposes of this subsection, the following definitions shall apply:

(1) By means of the world wide web

The term "by means of the World Wide Web" means by placement of material in a computer server-based file archive so that it is publicly accessible, over the Internet, using hypertext transfer protocol or any successor protocol.

(2) Commercial purposes; engaged in the business

(A) Commercial purposes

A person shall be considered to make a communication for commercial purposes only if such person is engaged in the business of making such communications.

(B) Engaged in the business

The term "engaged in the business" means that the person who makes a communication, or offers to make a communication, by means of the World Wide Web, that includes any material that is harmful to minors, devotes time, attention, or labor to such activities, as a regular course of such person's trade or business, with the objective of earning a profit as a result of such activities (although it is not necessary that the person make a profit or that the making or offering to make such communications be the person's sole or principal business or source of income). A person may be considered to be engaged in the business of making, by means of the World Wide Web, communications for commercial purposes that include material that is harmful to minors, only if the person knowingly causes the material that is harmful to minors to be posted on the World Wide Web or knowingly solicits such material to be posted on the World Wide Web.

(3) Internet

The term "Internet" means the combination of computer facilities and electromagnetic transmission media, and related equipment and software, comprising the interconnected worldwide network of computer networks that employ the Transmission Control Protocol/Internet Protocol or any successor protocol to transmit information.

(4) Internet access service

The term "Internet access service" means a service that enables users to access content, information, electronic mail, or other services offered over the Internet, and may also include access to proprietary content, information, and other services as part of a package of services offered to consumers. Such term does not include telecommunications services.

(5) Internet information location tool

The term "Internet information location tool" means a service that refers or links users to an online location on the World Wide Web. Such term includes directories, indices, references, pointers, and hypertext links.

(6) Material that is harmful to minors

The term "material that is harmful to minors" means any communication, picture, image, graphic image file, article, recording, writing, or other matter of any kind that is obscene or that—

(A) the average person, applying contemporary community standards, would find, taking the material as a whole and with respect to minors, is designed to appeal to, or is designed to pander to, the prurient interest

(B) depicts, describes, or represents, in a manner patently offensive with respect to minors, an actual or simulated sexual act or sexual contact, an actual or simulated normal or perverted sexual act, or a lewd exhibition of the genitals or post-pubescent female breast; and

(C) taken as a whole, lacks serious literary, artistic, political, or scientific value for minors.

(7) Minor

The term "minor" means any person under 17 years of age.

THE OREGON DEATH WITH DIGNITY ACT

Section I GENERAL PROVISIONS

1.01 Definitions The following words and phrases, whenever used in this Act, shall have the following meanings:

(1) "Adult" means an individual who is 18 years of age or older.

(2) "Attending physician" means the physician who has primary responsibility for the care of the patient and treatment of the patient's disease.

(3) "Consulting physician" means the physician who is qualified by specialty or experience to make a professional diagnosis and prognosis regarding the patient's disease.

(4) "Counseling" means a consultation between a state licensed psychiatrist or psychologist and a patient for the purpose of determining whether the patient is suffering from a psychiatric or psychological disorder, or depression causing impaired judgment.

(5) "Health care provider" means a person licensed, certified, or otherwise authorized or permitted by the law of this State to administer health care in the ordinary course of business or practice of a profession, and includes a health care facility.

(6) "Incapable" means that in the opinion of a court or in the opinion of the patient's at-

tending physician or consulting physician, a patient lacks the ability to make and communicate health care decisions to health care providers, including communication through persons familiar with the patient's manner of communicating if those persons are available. Capable means not incapable.

(7) "Informed decision" means a decision by a qualified patient, to request and obtain a prescription to end his or her life in a humane and dignified manner, that is based on an appreciation of the relevant facts and after being fully informed by the attending physician of:

(a) his or her medical diagnosis;

(b) his or her prognosis:

(c) the potential risks associated with taking the medication to be prescribed;

(d) the probable result of taking the medication to be prescribed;

(e) the feasible alternatives, including, but not limited to, comfort care, hospice care and pain control.

(8) "Medically confirmed" means the medical opinion of the attending physician has been confirmed by a consulting physician who has examined the patient and the patient's relevant medical records.

(9) "Patient" means a person who is under the care of a physician.

(10) "Physician" means a doctor of medicine or osteopathy licensed to practice medicine by the Board of Medical Examiners for the State of Oregon.

(11) "Qualified patient" means a capable adult who is a resident of Oregon and has satisfied the requirements of this Act in order to obtain a prescription for medication to end his or her life in a humane and dignified manner.

(12) "Terminal disease" means an incurable and irreversible disease that has been medically confirmed and will, within reasonable medical judgment, produce death within six (6) months.

Section 2 WRITTEN REQUEST FOR MEDICATION TO END ONE'S LIFE IN A HUMANE AND DIGNIFIED MANNER

2.01 Who may initiate a written request for medication

An adult who is capable, is a resident of Oregon, and has been determined by the attending physician and consulting physician to be suffering from a terminal disease, and who has voluntarily expressed his or her wish to die, may make a written request for medication for the purpose of ending his or her life in a humane and dignified manner in accordance with this Act.

2.02 Form of the written request

(1) A valid request for medication under this Act shall be in substantially the form described in Section 6 of this Act, signed and dated by the patient and witnessed by at least two individuals who, in the presence of the patient, attest that to the best of their knowledge and belief the patient is capable, acting voluntarily, and is not being coerced to sign the request.

(2) One of the witnesses shall be a person who is not:

(a) A relative of the patient by blood, marriage or adoption;

(b) A person who at the time the request is signed would be entitled to any portion of the estate of the qualified patient upon death under any will or by operation of law; or

(c) An owner, operator or employee of a health care facility where the qualified patient is receiving medical treatment or is a resident.

(3) The patient's attending physician at the time the request is signed shall not be a witness.

(4) If the patient is a patient in a long term care facility at the time the written request is made, one of the witnesses shall be an individual designated by the facility and having the qualifications specified by the Department of Human Resources by rule.

Section 3 SAFEGUARDS

3.01 attending physician responsibilities

The attending physician shall:

(1) Make the initial determination of whether a patient has a terminal disease, is capable, and has made the request voluntarily;

(2) Inform the patient of;

(a) his or her medical diagnosis;

(b) his or her prognosis;

(c) the potential risks associated with taking the medication to be prescribed;

(d) the probable result of taking the medication to be prescribed;

(e) the feasible alternatives, including, but not limited to, comfort care, hospice care and pain control.

(3) Refer the patient to a consulting physician for medical confirmation of the diagnosis, and for determination that the patient is capable and acting voluntarily;

(4) Refer the patient for counseling if appropriate pursuant to Section 3.03;

(5) Request that the patient notify next of kin;

(6) Inform the patient that he or she has an opportunity to rescind the request at any time and in any manner, and offer the patient an opportunity to rescind at the end of the 15 day waiting period pursuant to Section 3.06;

(7) Verify, immediately prior to writing the prescription for medication under this Act, that the patient is making an informed decision;

(8) Fulfill the medical record documentation requirements of Section 3.09;

(9) Ensure that all appropriate steps are carried out in accordance with this Act prior to writing a prescription for medication to enable a qualified patient to end his or her life in a humane and dignified manner.

3.02 Consulting Physician Confirmation

Before a patient is qualified under this Act, a consulting physician shall examine the patient and his or her relevant medical records and confirm, in writing, the attending physician's diagnosis that the patient is suffering from a terminal disease, and verify that the patient is capable, is acting voluntarily and has made an informed decision.

3.03 Counseling Referral

If in the opinion of the attending physician or the consulting physician a patient may be suffering from a psychiatric or psychological disorder, or depression causing impaired judgment, either physician shall refer the patient for counseling. No medication to end a patient's life in a humane and dignified manner shall be prescribed until the person performing the counseling determines that the person is not suffering from a psychiatric or psychological disorder, or depression causing impaired judgment.

3.04 Informed decision

No person shall receive a prescription for medication to end his or her life in a humane and dignified manner unless he or she has made an informed decision as defined in Section 1.01(7). Immediately prior to writing a prescription for medication under this Act, the attending physician shall verify that the patient is making an informed decision.

3.05 Family notification

The attending physician shall ask the patient to notify next of kin of his or her request for medication pursuant to this Act. A patient who declines or is unable to notify next of kin shall not have his or her request denied for that reason.

3.06 Written and oral requests

In order to receive a prescription for medication to end his or her life in a humane and dignified manner, a qualified patient shall have made an oral request and a written request, and reiterate the oral request to his or her attending physician no less than fifteen (15) days after making the initial oral request. At the time the qualified patient makes his or her second oral request, the attending physician shall offer the patient an opportunity to rescind the request.

3.07 Right to rescind request

A patient may rescind his or her request at any time and in any manner without regard to his or her mental state. No prescription for medication under this Act may be written without the attending physician offering the qualified patient an opportunity to rescind the request.

3.08 Waiting periods

No less than fifteen (15) days shall elapse between the patient's initial and oral request and the writing of a prescription under this Act. No less than 48 hours shall elapse between the patient's written request and the writing of a prescription under this Act.

3.09 Medical record documentation requirements

The following shall be documented or filed in the patient's medical record:

(1) All oral requests by a patient for medication to end his or her life in a humane and dignified manner;

(2) All written requests by a patient for medication to end his or her life in a humane and dignified manner;

(3) The attending physician's diagnosis and prognosis, determination that the patient is capable, acting voluntarily and has made an informed decision.

(4) The consulting physician's diagnosis and prognosis, and verification that the patient is capable, acting voluntarily and has made an informed decision;

(5) A report of the outcome and determinations made during counseling, of performed;

(6) The attending physician's offer to the patient to rescind his or her request at the time of the patient's second oral request pursuant to Section 3.06; and

(7) A note by the attending physician indicating that all requirements under this Act have been met and indicating the steps taken to carry out the request, including a notation of the medication prescribed.

3.10 Residency requirements

Only requests made by Oregon residents, under this Act, shall be granted.

3.11 Reporting requirements

(1) The Health Division shall annually review a sample of records maintained pursuant to this Act.

(2) The Health Division shall make rules to facilitate the collection of information regarding compliance with this Act. The information collected shall not be a public record and may not be made available for inspection by the public.

(3) The Health Division shall generate and make available to the public an annual statistical report of information collected under Section 3.11(2) of this Act.

3.12 Effect on construction of wills, contracts and statutes

(1) No provision in a contract, will or other agreement, whether written or oral, to the extent the provision would affect whether a person may make or rescind a request for medication to end his or her life in a humane and dignified manner, shall be valid.

(2) No obligation owing under any currently existing contract shall be conditioned or affected by the making or rescinding of a request, by a person, for medication to end his or her life in a humane and dignified manner.

3.13 Insurance or annuity policies

The sale, procurement, or issuance of any life, health, or accident insurance or annuity policy or the rate charged for any policy shall not be conditioned upon or affected by the making or rescinding of a request, by a person, for medication to end his or her life in a humane and dignified manner. Neither shall a qualified patient's act of ingesting medication to end his or her life in a humane and dignified manner have an effect upon a life, health, or accident insurance or annuity policy.

3.14 Construction of act

Nothing in this Act shall be construed to authorize a physician or any other person to end a patient's life by lethal injection, mercy killing or active euthanasia. Actions taken in accordance with this Act shall not, for any purpose, constitute suicide, assisted suicide, mercy killing or homicide, under the law.

Section 4 IMMUNITIES AND LIABILITIES

4.01 Immunities

Except as provided in Section 4.02:

(1) No person shall be subject to civil or criminal liability or professional disciplinary action for participating in good faith compliance with this Act. This includes being present when a qualified patient takes the prescribed medication to end his or her life in a humane and dignified manner.

(2) No professional organization or association, or health care provider, may subject a person to censure, discipline, suspension, loss of license, loss of privileges, loss of membership or other penalty for participating or refusing to participate in good faith compliance with this Act.

(3) No request by a patient for or provision by an attending physician of medication in good faith compliance with the provisions of this Act shall constitute neglect for any purpose of law or provide the sole basis for the appointment of a guardian or conservator.

(4) No health care provider shall be under any duty, whether by contract, by statute or by any other legal requirement to participate in the provision to a qualified patient of medication to end his or her life in a humane and dignified manner. If a health care provider is unable or unwilling to carry out a patient's health care provider shall transfer, upon request, a copy of the patient's relevant medical records to the new health care provider.

4.02 Liabilities

(1) A person who without authorization of the patient willfully alters or forges a request for medication or conceals or destroys a rescission of that request with the intent or effect of causing the patient's death shall be guilty of a Class A felony.

(2) person who coerces or exerts undue influence on a patient to request medication for the purpose of ending the patient's life, or to destroy a rescission of such a request, shall be guilty of a Class A felony.

(3) Nothing in this Act limits further liability for civil damages resulting from other negligent conduct or intentional misconduct by any persons.

(4) The penalties in this Act do not preclude criminal penalties applicable under other law for conduct which is inconsistent with the provisions of this Act.

Section 5 SEVERABILITY

5.01 Severability

Any section of this Act being held invalid as to any person or circumstance shall not affect the application of any other section of this Act which can be given full effect without the invalid section or application.

Section 6 FORM OF THE REQUEST

6.01 Form of the request

A request for a medication as authorized by this Act shall be in substantially the following form:

REQUEST FOR MEDICATION TO END MY LIFE IN A HUMANE AND DIGNIFIED MANNER

I, _____, am an adult of sound mind.

I am suffering from _____ _____, which by my attending physician has determined is a terminal disease and which has been medically formed by a consulting physician.

I have been fully informed of my diagnosis, prognosis, the nature of medication to be prescribed and potential associated risks, the expected result, and the feasible alternatives, including comfort care, hospice care and pain control.

I request that my attending physician prescribe medication that will end my life in a humane and dignified manner.

INITIAL ONE:

_____ I have informed my family of my decision and taken their opinions into consideration.

_____ I have decided not to inform my family of my decision.

_____ I have no family to inform of my decision.

I understand that I have the right to rescind this request at any time.

I understand the full import of this request and I expect to die when I take the medication to be prescribed.

I make this request voluntarily and without reservation, and I accept full moral responsibility for my actions.

Signed: _____

Dated: _____

DECLARATION OF WITNESSES

We declare that the person signing this request:

(a) Is personally known to us or has provided proof of identity;

(b) Signed this request in our presence;

(c) Appears to be of sound mind and not under duress, fraud or undue influence;

(d) Is not a patient for whom either of us is attending physician.

_____
Witness 1/__ Date

_____
Witness 2/__ Date

Note: One witness shall not be a relative (by blood, marriage or adoption) of the person signing this request, shall not be entitled to any portion of the person's estate upon death and shall not own, operate or be employed at a health care facility where the person is a patient or resident. If the patient is an inpatient at a health care facility, one of the witnesses shall be an individual designated by the facility.

ARTICLES OF IMPEACHMENT: WILLIAM JEFFERSON CLINTON

The House Judiciary Committee Republicans proposed four articles of impeachment against President William Jefferson Clinton. Here is the final version of Article I, preceded by the Impeachment Resolution. On December 11, 1998, the House Judiciary Committee voted 21-16 to approve this Article, and recommend the impeachment of President Clinton.

RESOLUTION

Impeaching William Jefferson Clinton, President of the United States, for high crimes and misdemeanors.

Resolved. That William Jefferson Clinton, President of the United States, is impeached for high crimes and misdemeanors, and that the following articles impeachment be exhibited to the United States Senate:

Articles of impeachment exhibited by the House of Representatives of the United States of America in the name of itself and of the people of the United States of America, against William Jefferson Clinton, President of the United States of America, in maintenance and support of its impeachment against him for high crimes and misdemeanors.

ARTICLE I

In his conduct while President of the United States, William Jefferson Clinton, in violation of his constitutional oath faithfully to execute the office of President of the United States and, to the best of his ability, preserve, protect, and defend the Constitution of the United States, and in violation of his constitutional duty to take care that the laws be faithfully executed, has willfully corrupted and manipulated the judicial process of the United States for his personal gain and exoneration, impeding the administration of justice, in that:

On August 17, 1998, William Jefferson Clinton swore to tell the truth, the whole truth, and nothing but the truth before a Federal grand jury of the United States. Contrary to that oath, William Jefferson Clinton willfully provided perjurious, false and misleading testimony to the grand jury concerning one or more of the following:

(1) the nature and details of his relationship with a subordinate Government employee;

(2) prior perjurious, false and misleading testimony he gave in a Federal civil rights action brought against him;

(3) prior false and misleading statements he allowed his attorney to make to a Federal judge in that civil rights action; and

(4) his corrupt efforts to influence the testimony of witnesses and to impede the discovery of evidence in that civil rights action.

In doing this, William Jefferson Clinton has undermined the integrity of his office, has brought disrepute on the Presidency, has betrayed his trust as President, and has acted in a manner subversive of the rule of law and justice, to the manifest injury of the people of the United States.

Wherefore, William Jefferson Clinton, by such conduct, warrants impeachment and trial, and removal from office and disqualification to hold and enjoy any office of honor, trust or profit under the United States.

ARTICLE II

In his conduct while President of the United States, William Jefferson Clinton, in violation of his constitutional oath faithfully to execute the office of President of the United States and, to the best of his ability, preserve, protect, and defend the Constitution of the United States, and in violation of his constitutional duty to take care that the laws be faithfully executed, has willfully corrupted and manipulated the judicial process of the United States for his personal gain and exoneration, impending the administration of justice, in that:

(1) On December 23, 1997, William Jefferson Clinton, in sworn answers to written questions asked as part of a Federal civil rights action brought against him, willfully provided perjurious, false and misleading testimony in response to questions deemed relevant by a Federal judge concerning conduct and proposed conduct with subordinate employees.

(2) On January 17, 1988, William Jefferson Clinton swore under oath to tell the truth, the whole truth, and nothing but the truth in a deposition given as part of a Federal civil rights action brought against him. Contrary to that oath, William Jefferson Clinton willfully provided perjurious, false and misleading testimony in repose to questions deemed relevant by a Federal judge concerning the nature and details of his relationship with a subordinate government employee and his corrupt efforts to influence the testimony of that employee.

In all of this, William Jefferson Clinton has undermined the integrity of his office, has brought disrepute on the Presidency, has betrayed his trust as President, and has acted in a manner subversive of the rule of law and justice, to the manifest injury of the people of the United States.

Wherefore, William Jefferson Clinton, by such conduct, warrants impeachment and trial, and removal from office and disqualification to hold and enjoy any office of honor, trust or profit under the United States.

ARTICLE III

In his conduct while President of the United States, William Jefferson Clinton, in violation of his constitutional oath faithfully to execute the office of President of the United States and, to the best of his ability, preserve, protect, and defend the Constitution of the United States, and in violation of his constitutional duty to take care that the laws be faithfully executed, has prevented, obstructed, and impeded the administration of justice, and has to that end engaged personally, and through his subordinates and agents, in a course of conduct or scheme designed to delay, impede, cover up, and conceal the existence of evidence and testimony related to a Federal civil rights action brought against him in a duly instituted judicial proceeding.

The means used to implement this course of conduct or scheme included one or more of the following acts:

(1) On or about December 17, 1997, William Jefferson Clinton corruptly encouraged a witness in a Federal civil rights action brought against him to execute a sworn affidavit in that proceeding that he knew to be perjurious, false and misleading.

(2) On or about December 17, 1997, William Jefferson Clinton corruptly encouraged a witness in a Federal civil rights action brought against him to give perjurious, false and misleading testimony if and when called to testify personally in that proceeding.

(3) On or about December 28, 1997, William Jefferson Clinton corruptly engaged in, encouraged, or supported a scheme to conceal evidence that had been subpoenaed in a Federal civil rights action brought against him.

(4) Beginning on or about December 7, 1997, and continuing through and including January 14, 1998, William Jefferson Clinton intensified and succeeded in an effort to secure job assistance to a witness in a Federal civil rights action brought against him in order to corruptly prevent the truthful testimony of that witness in that proceeding at a time when the truthful tes-

timony of that witness would have been harmful to him.

(5) On January 17, 1998, at his deposition in a Federal civil rights action brought against him, William Jefferson Clinton corruptly allowed his attorney to make false and misleading statements to a Federal judge characterizing an affidavit, in order to prevent questioning deemed relevant by the judge. Such false and misleading statements were subsequently acknowledged by his attorney in a communication to that judge.

(6) On or about January 18 and January 20–21, 1998, William Jefferson Clinton related a false and misleading account of events relevant to a Federal civil rights action brought against him to a potential witness in that proceeding, in order to corruptly influence the testimony of that witness.

(7) On or about January 21, 23 and 26, 1998, William Jefferson Clinton made false and misleading statements to potential witnesses in a Federal grand jury proceeding in order to corruptly influence the testimony of those witnesses. The false and misleading statements made by William Jefferson Clinton were repeated by the witnesses to the grand jury, causing the grand jury to receive false and misleading information.

In all of this, William Jefferson Clinton has undermined the integrity of his office, has brought disrepute on the Presidency, has betrayed his trust as President, and has acted in a manner subversive of the rule of law and justice, to the manifest injury of the people of the United States.

Wherefore, William Jefferson Clinton, by such conduct, warrants impeachment and trial, and removal from office and disqualification to hold and enjoy any office of honor, trust or profit under the United States.

ARTICLE IV

Using the powers and influence of the office of President of the United States, William Jefferson Clinton, in violation of his constitutional oath faithfully to execute the office of President of the United States and, to the best of his ability, preserve, protect, and defend the Constitution of the United States, and in disregard of his constitutional duty to take care that the laws be faithfully executed, has engaged in conduct that resulted in misuse and abuse of his high office, impaired the due and proper administration of justice and the conduct of lawful inquiries, and contravened the authority of the legislative branch and the truth-seeking purpose of a coordinate investigative proceeding in that, as President, William Jefferson Clinton, refused and failed to respond to certain written requests for admission and willfully made perjurious, false and misleading sworn statements in response to certain written requests for admission propounded to him as part of the impeachment inquiry authorized by the House of Representatives of the Congress of the United States.

William Jefferson Clinton, in refusing and failing to respond, and in making perjurious, false and misleading statements, assumed to himself functions and judgments necessary to the exercise of the sole power of impeachment vested by the Constitution in the House of Representatives and exhibited contempt for the inquiry.

In doing this, William Jefferson Clinton has undermined the integrity of his office, has brought disrepute on the Presidency, has betrayed his trust as President, and has acted in a manner subversive of the rule of law and justice, to the manifest injury of the people of the United States.

Wherefore, William Jefferson Clinton, by such conduct, warrants impeachment and trial, and removal from office and disqualification to hold and enjoy any office of honor, trust or profit under the United States.

INTERNET TAX FREEDOM ACT

Internet Tax Freedom Act (Introduced in the House)

HR 1054 IH

105th CONGRESS

1st Session

H. R. 1054

To amend the Communications Act of 1934 to establish a national policy against State and local interference with interstate commerce on the Internet or interactive computer services, and to exercise congressional jurisdiction over interstate commerce by establishing a moratorium on the imposition of exactions that would interfere with the free flow of commerce via the Internet, and for other purposes.

IN THE HOUSE OF REPRESENTATIVES

March 13, 1997

Mr. COX of California (for himself and Mr. WHITE) introduced the following bill; which was referred to the Committee on Commerce, and in addition to the Committee on the Judiciary, for a period to be subsequently determined by the Speaker, in each case for consideration of such provisions as fall within the jurisdiction of the committee concerned

A BILL

To amend the Communications Act of 1934 to establish a national policy against State and local interference with interstate commerce on the Internet or interactive computer services, and to exercise congressional jurisdiction over interstate commerce by establishing a moratorium on the imposition of exactions that would interfere with the free flow of commerce via the Internet, and for other purposes.

Be it enacted by the Senate and House of Representatives of the United States of America in Congress assembled,

Section 1. SHORT TITLE.

This Act may be cited as the 'Internet Tax Freedom Act'.

Section 2. FINDINGS.

The Congress finds the following:

(1) As a massive global network spanning not only State but international borders, the Internet is inherently a matter of interstate and foreign commerce within the jurisdiction of the United States Congress under Article I, Section 8 of the United States Constitution.

(2) Even within the United States, the Internet does not respect State lines and operates independently of State boundaries. Addresses on the Internet are designed to be geographically indifferent. Internet transmissions are insensitive to physical distance and can have multiple geographical addresses.

(3) Because transmissions over the Internet are made through packet-switching, it is impossible to determine with any degree of certainty the precise geographic route or endpoints of specific Internet transmissions, and infeasible to separate intrastate from interstate, and domestic from foreign, Internet transmissions.

(4) Inconsistent and unadministrable taxes imposed on Internet activity by State and local governments threaten not only to subject consumers, businesses, and other users engaged in interstate and foreign commerce to multiple, confusing, and burdensome taxation, but also to restrict the growth and continued technological maturation of the Internet itself, and to call into question the continued viability of this dynamic medium.

(5) Because the tax laws and regulations of so many jurisdictions were established before the Internet or interactive computer services, their application to this new medium in unintended and unpredictable ways threatens every Internet user, access provider, vendor, and interactive computer service provider.

(6) The electronic marketplace of services, products, and ideas available through the Internet or interactive computer services can be especially beneficial to senior citizens, the physically challenged, citizens in rural areas, and small businesses. It also offers a variety of uses and benefits for educational institutions and charitable organizations.

(7) Consumers, businesses, and others engaging in interstate and foreign commerce through the Internet or interactive computer services could become subject to more than 30,000 separate taxing jurisdictions in the United States alone.

(8) The consistent and coherent national policy regarding taxation of Internet activity that is needed to avoid burdening this evolving form of interstate and foreign commerce can best be achieved by the United States exercising its authority under Article I, Section 8, Clause 3 of the United States Constitution.

Section 3. MORATORIUM ON IMPOSITION OF TAXES ON INTERNET OR INTERACTIVE COMPUTER SERVICES.

(a) MORATORIUM- Except as otherwise provided in this section, no State or local government (including any political subdivision) may impose, assess, or attempt to collect any tax or fee directly or indirectly on—

(1) the Internet or interactive computer services; or

(2) the use of the Internet or interactive computer services.

(b) PRESERVATION OF STATE AND LOCAL TAXING AUTHORITY- Subsection (a)—

(1) does not apply to taxes imposed on and measured by net income derived from the Internet or interactive computer services;

(2) does not apply to fairly apportioned business license taxes applied to businesses that have a business location in the taxing jurisdiction, and

(3) does not affect the authority of a State, or political subdivision thereof, to impose a sales or use tax on sales or other transactions effected by use of the Internet or interactive computer services if—

(A) the tax is the same as the tax imposed and collected by that State, or political subdivision thereof, on sales or interstate transactions effected by mail order, telephone, or other remote means within its taxing jurisdiction; and

(B) the obligation to collect the tax from sales or other transactions effected by use of the Internet or interactive computer services is imposed on the same person or entity as in the case of sales or transactions effected by mail order, telephone, or other remote means.

Section 4. ADMINISTRATION POLICY RECOMMENDATIONS TO CONGRESS.

(a) CONSULTATIVE GROUP- The Secretaries of the Treasury, Commerce, or State, in consultation with appropriate committees of the Congress, consumer and business groups, States and political subdivisions thereof, and other appropriate groups, shall—

(1) undertake an examination of United States domestic and international taxation of the Internet and interactive computer services, as well as commerce conducted thereon; and

(2) jointly submit appropriate policy recommendations concerning United States domestic and foreign policies toward taxation of the Internet and interactive computer services, if any, to the President within 18 months after the date of enactment of this Act.

(b) PRESIDENT- Not later than 2 years after the date of enactment of this Act, the President shall transmit to the appropriate committees of Congress policy recommendations on the taxation of sales and other transactions effected on the Internet or through interactive computer services.

(c) RECOMMENDATIONS TO BE CONSISTENT WITH TELECOMMUNICATIONS ACT OF 1996 POLICY STATEMENT—The Secretaries and the President shall take care to ensure that any such policy recommendations are fully consistent with the policy set forth in paragraphs (1) and (2) of section 230(b) of the Communications Act of 1934 (47 U.S.C. 230(b)).

Section 5. BAN ON REGULATION OF INTERNET PRICES BY THE FEDERAL COMMUNICATIONS COMMISSION.

(a) PROHIBITION ON COMMISSION REGULATION OF COMPUTER SERVICES— Section 230 of the Communications Act of 1934 (47 U.S.C. 230) is amended—

(1) by redesignating subsections (d) and (e) as subsections (e) and (f), respectively; and

(2) by inserting after subsection (c) the following new subsection:

(d) PROHIBITION ON COMMISSION REGULATION OF COMPUTER SERVICES- The Commission shall have no authority or jurisdiction under this Act, nor shall any State commission have any authority or jurisdiction, to regulate the prices or charges paid by subscribers for interactive computer services, or information services transmitted through the Internet, except for the requirement in section 254(h) that such services be provided at affordable rates to rural health care providers, schools, and libraries.'

(b) CONFORMING AMENDMENT- Section 223(h)(2) of the Communications Act of 1934 (47 U.S.C. 223(h)(2)) is amended by striking '230(e)(2)' and inserting '230(f)(2)'.

Section 6. DECLARATION THAT THE INTERNET BE FREE OF FOREIGN TARIFFS, TRADE BARRIERS, AND OTHER RESTRICTIONS.

It is the sense of the Congress that the President should seek bilateral and multilateral agreements through the World Trade Organization, the Organization for Economic Cooperation and Development, the Asia Pacific Economic Cooperation Council, or other appropriate international fora to establish activity on the Internet and interactive computer services is free from tariff and taxation.

Section 7. DEFINITIONS.

For purposes of this Act—

(1) INTERNET; INTERACTIVE COMPUTER SERVICE—The terms 'Internet' and 'interactive computer service' have the meaning given such terms by paragraphs (1) and (2), respectively, of section 230(e) of the Communications Act of 1934 (47 U.S.C. 230 (e)).

(2) TAX— The term 'tax' includes any tax, license, or fee that is imposed by any governmental entity and the imposition on the seller of an obligation to collect and remit a tax imposed on the buyer.

A.	Atlantic Reporter
A. 2d	Atlantic Reporter, Second Series
AA	Alcoholics Anonymous
AAA	American Arbitration Association; Agricultural Adjustment Act of 1933
AALS	Association of American Law Schools
AAPRP	All African People's Revolutionary Party
AARP	American Association of Retired Persons
AAS	American Anti-Slavery Society
ABA	American Bar Association; Architectural Barriers Act, 1968; American Bankers Association
ABM Treaty	Anti-Ballistic Missile Treaty of 1972; antiballistic missile
ABVP	Anti-Biased Violence Project
A/C	account
AC.	appeal cases
ACAA	Air Carrier Access Act
ACF	Administration for Children and Families
ACLU	American Civil Liberties Union
ACRS	Accelerated Cost Recovery System
ACS	Agricultural Cooperative Service
ACT	American College Test
Act'g Legal Adv.	Acting Legal Advisor
ACUS	Administrative Conference of the United States
ACYF	Administration on Children, Youth, and Families
A.D. 2d	Appellate Division, Second Series, N.Y.
ADA	Americans with Disabilities Act of 1990
ADAMHA	Alcohol, Drug Abuse, and Mental Health Administration
ADC	Aid to Dependent Children
ADD	Administration on Developmental Disabilities
ADEA	Age Discrimination in Employment Act of 1967
ADL	Anti-Defamation League
ADR	alternative dispute resolution
AEC	Atomic Energy Commission
AECB	Arms Export Control Board
AEDPA	Antiterrorism and Effective Death Penalty Act
A.E.R.	All England Law Reports
AFA	American Family Association; Alabama Freethought Association

AFB	American Farm Bureau
AFBF	American Farm Bureau Federation
AFDC	Aid to Families with Dependent Children
aff'd per cur.	affirmed by the court
AFIS	automated fingerprint identification system
AFL	American Federation of Labor
AFL-CIO	American Federation of Labor and Congress of Industrial Organizations
AFRes	Air Force Reserve
AFSC	American Friends Service Committee
AFSCME	American Federation of State, County, and Municipal Employees
AGRICOLA	Agricultural Online Access
AIA	Association of Insurance Attorneys
AIB	American Institute for Banking
AID	artificial insemination using a third-party donor's sperm; Agency for International Development
AIDS	acquired immune deficiency syndrome
AIH	artificial insemination using the husband's sperm
AIM	American Indian Movement
AIPAC	American Israel Public Affairs Committee
AIUSA	Amnesty International, U.S.A. Affiliate
AJS	American Judicature Society
Alcoa	Aluminum Company of America
ALEC	American Legislative Exchange Council
ALF	Animal Liberation Front
ALI	American Law Institute
ALJ	administrative law judge
All E.R.	All England Law Reports
ALO	Agency Liaison
A.L.R.	American Law Reports
AMA	American Medical Association
AMAA	Agricultural Marketing Agreement Act
Am. Dec.	American Decisions
amdt.	amendment
Amer. St. Papers, For. Rels.	American State Papers, Legislative and Executive Documents of the Congress of the U.S., Class I, Foreign Relations, 1832-1859
AMS	Agricultural Marketing Service
AMVETS	American Veterans of World War II
ANA	Administration for Native Americans
Ann. Dig.	Annual Digest of Public International Law Cases
ANRA	American Newspaper Publishers Association
ANSCA	Alaska Native Claims Act
ANZUS	Australia-New Zealand-United States Security Treaty Organization
AOA	Administration on Aging
AOE	Arizonans for Official English
AOL	America Online
APA	Administrative Procedure Act of 1946
APHIS	Animal and Plant Health Inspection Service
App. Div.	Appellate Division Reports, N.Y. Supreme Court
Arb. Trib., U.S.-British	Arbitration Tribunal, Claim Convention of 1853, United States and Great Britain Convention of 1853
Ardcor	American Roller Die Corporation
ARPA	Advanced Research Projects Agency
ARPANET	Advanced Research Projects Agency Network
ARS	Advanced Record System
Art.	article
ARU	American Railway Union

ASCME	American Federation of State, County, and Municipal Employees
ASCS	Agriculture Stabilization and Conservation Service
ASM	Available Seatmile
ASPCA	American Society for the Prevention of Cruelty to Animals
Asst. Att. Gen.	Assistant Attorney General
AT&T	American Telephone and Telegraph
ATFD	Alcohol, Tobacco and Firearms Division
ATLA	Association of Trial Lawyers of America
ATO	Alpha Tau Omega
ATTD	Alcohol and Tobacco Tax Division
ATU	Alcohol Tax Unit
AUAM	American Union against Militarism
AUM	Animal Unit Month
AZT	azidothymidine
BALSA	Black-American Law Student Association
BATF	Bureau of Alcohol, Tobacco and Firearms
BBS	Bulletin Board System
BCCI	Bank of Credit and Commerce International
BEA	Bureau of Economic Analysis
Bell's Cr. C.	Bell's English Crown Cases
Bevans	United States Treaties, etc. *Treaties and Other International Agreements of the United States of America, 1776-1949* (compiled under the direction of Charles I. Bevans, 1968-76)
BFOQ	bona fide occupational qualification
BI	Bureau of Investigation
BIA	Bureau of Indian Affairs; Board of Immigration Appeals
BJS	Bureau of Justice Statistics
Black.	Black's United States Supreme Court Reports
Blatchf.	Blatchford's United States Circuit Court Reports
BLM	Bureau of Land Management
BLS	Bureau of Labor Statistics
BMD	ballistic missile defense
BNA	Bureau of National Affairs
BOCA	Building Officials and Code Administrators International
BOP	Bureau of Prisons
BPP	Black Panther Party for Self-defense
Brit. and For.	British and Foreign State Papers
BSA	Boy Scouts of America
BTP	Beta Theta Pi
Burr.	James Burrows, *Report of Cases Argued and Determined in the Court of King's Bench during the Time of Lord Mansfield* (1766-1780)
BVA	Board of Veterans Appeals
c.	chapter
C³I	Command, Control, Communications, and Intelligence
C.A.	Court of Appeals
CAA	Clean Air Act
CAB	Civil Aeronautics Board; Corporation for American Banking
CAFE	corporate average fuel economy
Cal. 2d	California Reports, Second Series
Cal. 3d	California Reports, Third Series
CALR	computer-assisted legal research
Cal. Rptr.	California Reporter
CAP	Common Agricultural Policy
CARA	Classification and Ratings Administration
CATV	community antenna television
CBO	Congressional Budget Office
CCC	Commodity Credit Corporation

CCDBG	Child Care and Development Block Grant of 1990
C.C.D. Pa.	Circuit Court Decisions, Pennsylvania
C.C.D. Va.	Circuit Court Decisions, Virginia
CCEA	Cabinet Council on Economic Affairs
CCP	Chinese Communist Party
CCR	Center for Constitutional Rights
C.C.R.I.	Circuit Court, Rhode Island
CD	certificate of deposit; compact disc
CDA	Communications Decency Act
CDBG	Community Development Block Grant Program
CDC	Centers for Disease Control and Prevention; Community Development Corporation
CDF	Children's Defense Fund
CDL	Citizens for Decency through Law
CD-ROM	compact disc read-only memory
CDS	Community Dispute Services
CDW	collision damage waiver
CENTO	Central Treaty Organization
CEQ	Council on Environmental Quality
CERCLA	Comprehensive Environmental Response, Compensation, and Liability Act of 1980
cert.	*certiorari*
CETA	Comprehensive Employment and Training Act
C & F	cost and freight
CFC	chlorofluorocarbon
CFE Treaty	Conventional Forces in Europe Treaty of 1990
C.F. & I.	Cost, Freight, and Insurance
CI NP	Community Food and Nutrition Program
C.F.R.	Code of Federal Regulations
CFTA	Canadian Free Trade Agreement
CFTC	Commodity Futures Trading Commission
Ch.	Chancery Division, English Law Reports
CHAMPVA	Civilian Health and Medical Program at the Veterans Administration
CHEP	Cuban/Haitian Entrant Program
CHINS	children in need of supervision
CHIPS	child in need of protective services
Ch N.Y.	Chancery Reports, New York
Chr. Rob.	Christopher Robinson, *Reports of Cases Argued and Determined in the High Court of Admiralty* (1801-1808)
CIA	Central Intelligence Agency
CID	Commercial Item Descriptions
C.I.F.	cost, insurance, and freight
CINCNORAD	Commander in Chief, North American Air Defense Command
CIO	Committee for Industrial Organizations; Congress of Industrial Organizations
CIPE	Center for International Private Enterprise
CJ	chief justice
CJIS	Criminal Justice Information Services
CJ.S.	Corpus Juris Secundum
Claims Arb. under Spec. Conv., Nielsen's Rept.	Frederick Kenelm Melsen, *American and British Claims Arbitration under the Special Agreement Concluded between the United States and Great Britain, August 18, 1910* (1926)
CLASP	Center for Law and Social Policy
CLE	Center for Law and Education; Continuing Legal Education
CLEO	Council on Legal Education Opportunity; Chief Law Enforcement Officer
CLP	Communist Labor Party of America

CLS	Christian Legal Society; critical legal studies (movement), Critical Legal Studies (membership organization)
C.M.A.	Court of Military Appeals
CMEA	Council for Mutual Economic Assistance
CMHS	Center for Mental Health Services
C.M.R.	Court of Military Review
CNN	Cable News Network
CNO	Chief of Naval Operations
CNR	Chicago and Northwestern Railway
CO	Conscientious Objector
C.O.D.	cash on delivery
COGP	Commission on Government Procurement
COINTELPRO	Counterintelligence Program
Coke Rep.	Coke's English King's Bench Reports
COLA	cost-of-living adjustment
COMCEN	Federal Communications Center
Comp.	Compilation
Conn.	Connecticut Reports
CONTU	National Commission on New Technological Uses of Copyrighted Works
Conv.	Convention
COPA	Child Online Protection Act (1998)
COPS	Community Oriented Policing Services
Corbin	Arthur L. Corbin, *Corbin on Contracts: A Comprehensive Treatise on the Rules of Contract Law* (1950)
CORE	Congress on Racial Equality
Cox's Crim. Cases	Cox's Criminal Cases (England)
COYOTE	Call Off Your Old Tired Ethics
CPA	certified public accountant
CPB	Corporation for Public Broadcasting, the
CPI	Consumer Price Index
CPPA	Child Pornography Prevention Act
CPSC	Consumer Product Safety Commission
Cranch	Cranch's United States Supreme Court Reports
CRF	Constitutional Rights Foundation
CRR	Center for Constitutional Rights
CRS	Congressional Research Service; Community Relations Service
CRT	critical race theory
CSA	Community Services Administration
CSAP	Center for Substance Abuse Prevention
CSAT	Center for Substance Abuse Treatment
CSC	Civil Service Commission
CSCE	Conference on Security and Cooperation in Europe
CSG	Council of State Governments
CSO	Community Service Organization
CSP	Center for the Study of the Presidency
C-SPAN	Cable-Satellite Public Affairs Network
CSRS	Cooperative State Research Service
CSWPL	Center on Social Welfare Policy and Law
CTA	*cum testamento annexo* (with the will attached)
Ct. Ap. D.C.	Court of Appeals, District of Columbia
Ct. App. No. Ireland	Court of Appeals, Northern Ireland
Ct. Cl.	Court of Claims, United States
Ct. Crim. Apps.	Court of Criminal Appeals (England)
Ct. of Sess., Scot.	Court of Sessions, Scotland
CU	credit union
CUNY	City University of New York

Cush.	Cushing's Massachusetts Reports
CWA	Civil Works Administration; Clean Water Act
DACORB	Department of the Army Conscientious Objector Review Board
Dall.	Dallas' Pennsylvania and United States Reports
DAR	Daughters of the American Revolution
DARPA	Defense Advanced Research Projects Agency
DAVA	Defense Audiovisual Agency
D.C.	United States District Court; District of Columbia
D.C. Del.	United States District Court, Delaware
D.C. Mass.	United States District Court, Massachusetts
D.C. Md.	United States District Court, Maryland
D.C.N.D.Cal.	United States District Court, Northern District, California
D.C.N.Y.	United States District Court, New York
D.C.Pa.	United States District Court, Pennsylvania
DC-S	Deputy Chiefs of Staff
DCZ	District of the Canal Zone
DDT	dichlorodiphenyltricloroethane
DEA	Drug Enforcement Administration
Decl. Lond.	Declaration of London, February 26, 1909
Dev. & B.	Devereux & Battle's North Carolina Reports
DFL	Minnesota Democratic-Farmer-Labor
DFTA	Department for the Aging
Dig. U.S. Practice in Intl. Law	Digest of U.S. Practice in International Law
Dist. Ct. D.C.	United States District Court, District of Columbia
D.L.R.	Dominion Law Reports (Canada)
DMCA	Digital Millennium Copyright Act
DNA	deoxyribonucleic acid
Dnase	deoxyribonuclease
DNC	Democratic National Committee
DOC	Department of Commerce
DOD	Department of Defense
DODEA	Department of Defense Education Activity
Dodson	Dodson's Reports, English Admiralty Courts
DOE	Department of Energy
DOER	Department of Employee Relations
DOJ	Department of Justice
DOL	Department of Labor
DOMA	Defense of Marriage Act, 1996
DOS	disk operating system
DOT	Department of Transportation
DPT	diphtheria, pertussis, and tetanus
DRI	Defense Research Institute
DSAA	Defense Security Assistance Agency
DUI	driving under the influence; driving under intoxication
DWI	driving while intoxicated
EAHCA	Education for All Handicapped Children Act of 1975
EBT	examination before trial
E.coli	Escherichia coli
ECPA	Electronic Communications Privacy Act of 1986
ECSC	Treaty of the European Coal and Steel Community
EDA	Economic Development Administration
EDF	Environmental Defense Fund
E.D.N.Y.	Eastern District, New York
EDP	electronic data processing
E.D.	Pa. Eastern-District, Pennsylvania
EDSC	Eastern District, South Carolina

E.D.	Va. Eastern District, Virginia
EEC	European Economic Community; European Economic Community Treaty
EEOC	Equal Employment Opportunity Commission
EFF	Electronic Frontier Foundation
EFT	electronic funds transfer
Eliz.	Queen Elizabeth (Great Britain)
Em. App.	Temporary Emergency Court of Appeals
ENE	early neutral evaluation
Eng. Rep.	English Reports
EOP	Executive Office of the President
EPA	Environmental Protection Agency; Equal Pay Act of 1963
ERA	Equal Rights Amendment
ERDC	Energy Research and Development Commission
ERISA	Employee Retirement Income Security Act of 1974
ERS	Economic Research Service
ERTA	Economic Recovery Tax Act, 1981
ESA	Endangered Species Act of 1973
ESF	emergency support function; Economic Support Fund
ESRD	End-Stage Renal Disease Program
ETA	Employment and Training Administration
ETS	environmental tobacco smoke
et seq.	*et sequentes* or *et sequentia* (and the following)
EU	European Union
Euratom	European Atomic Energy Community
Eur. Ct. H.R.	European Court of Human Rights
Ex.	English Exchequer Reports, Welsby, Hurlstone & Gordon
Exch.	Exchequer Reports (Welsby, Hurlstone & Gordon)
Ex Com	Executive Committee of the National Security Council
Eximbank	Export-Import Bank of the United States
F.	Federal Reporter
F. 2d	Federal Reporter, Second Series
FAA	Federal Aviation Administration; Federal Arbitration Act
FAAA	Federal Alcohol Administration Act
FACE	Freedom of Access to Clinic Entrances Act of 1994
FACT	Feminist Anti-Censorship Task Force
FAMLA	Family and Medical Leave Act of 1993
Fannie Mae	Federal National Mortgage Association
FAO	Food and Agriculture Organization of the United Nations
FAR	Federal Acquisition Regulations
FAS	Foreign Agricultural Service
FBA	Federal Bar Association
FBI	Federal Bureau of Investigation
FCA	Farm Credit Administration
F. Cas.	Federal Cases
FCC	Federal Communications Commission
FCIA	Foreign Credit Insurance Association
FCIC	Federal Crop Insurance Corporation
FCRA	Fair Credit Reporting Act
FCU	federal credit unions
FCUA	Federal Credit Union Act
FCZ	Fishery Conservation Zone
FDA	Food and Drug Administration
FDIC	Federal Deposit Insurance Corporation
FDPC	Federal Data Processing Center
FEC	Federal Election Commission
FECA	Federal Election Campaign Act of 1971

Fed. Cas.	Federal Cases
FEMA	Federal Emergency Management Agency
FFB	Federal Financing Bank
FFDC	Federal Food, Drug, and Cosmetics Act
FGIS	Federal Grain Inspection Service
FHA	Federal Housing Administration
FHWA	Federal Highway Administration
FIA	Federal Insurance Administration
FIC	Federal Information Centers; Federation of Insurance Counsel
FICA	Federal Insurance Contributions Act
FIFRA	Federal Insecticide, Fungicide, and Rodenticide Act
FIP	Forestry Incentives Program
FIRREA	Financial Institutions Reform, Recovery, and Enforcement Act of 1989
FISA	Foreign Intelligence Surveillance Act of 1978
FJC	Federal Judicial Center
FLSA	Fair Labor Standards Act
FMC	Federal Maritime Commission
FMCS	Federal Mediation and Conciliation Service
FmHA	Farmers Home Administration
FMLA	Family and Medical Leave Act of 1993
FNMA	Federal National Mortgage Association, "Fannie Mae"
F.O.B.	free on board
FOIA	Freedom of Information Act
FOMC	Federal Open Market Committee
FPC	Federal Power Commission
FPMR	Federal Property Management Regulations
FPRS	Federal Property Resources Service
FR	Federal Register
FRA	Federal Railroad Administration
FRB	Federal Reserve Board
FRC	Federal Radio Commission
F.R.D.	Federal Rules Decisions
FSA	Family Support Act
FSLIC	Federal Savings and Loan Insurance Corporation
FSQS	Food Safety and Quality Service
FSS	Federal Supply Service
F. Supp.	Federal Supplement
FTA	U.S.-Canada Free Trade Agreement, 1988
FTC	Federal Trade Commission
FTCA	Federal Tort Claims Act
FTS	Federal Telecommunications System
FTS2000	Federal Telecommunications System 2000
FUCA	Federal Unemployment Compensation Act of 1988
FUTA	Federal Unemployment Tax Act
FWPCA	Federal Water Pollution Control Act of 1948
FWS	Fish and Wildlife Service
GAL	guardian ad litem
GAO	General Accounting Office; Governmental Affairs Office
GAOR	General Assembly Official Records, United Nations
GA Res.	General Assembly Resolution (United Nations)
GATT	General Agreement on Tariffs and Trade
GCA	Gun Control Act
Gen. Cls. Comm.	General Claims Commission, United States and Panama; General Claims United States and Mexico
Geo. II	King George II (Great Britain)
Geo. III	King George III (Great Britain)

GI	Government Issue
GID	General Intelligence Division
GM	General Motors
GNMA	Government National Mortgage Association, "Ginnie Mae"
GNP	gross national product
GOP	Grand Old Party (Republican)
GOPAC	Grand Old Party Action Committee
GPA	Office of Governmental and Public Affairs
GPO	Government Printing Office
GRAS	generally recognized as safe
Gr. Br., Crim. Ct. App.	Great Britain, Court of Criminal Appeals
GRNL	Gay Rights-National Lobby
GSA	General Services Administration
Hackworth	Green Haywood Hackworth, *Digest of International Law* (1940-44)
Hay and Marriott	Great Britain. High Court of Admiralty, *Decisions in the High Court of Admiralty during the Time of Sir George Hay and of Sir James Marriott, Late Judges of That Court* (1801)
HBO	Home Box Office
HCFA	Health Care Financing Administration
H.Ct.	High Court
HDS	Office of Human Development Services
Hen. & M.	Hening & Munford's Virginia Reports
HEW	Department of Health, Education, and Welfare
HFCA	Health Care Financing Administration
HGI	Handgun Control, Incorporated
HHS	Department of Health and Human Services
Hill	Hill's New York Reports
HIRE	Help through Industry Retraining and Employment
HIV	human immunodeficiency virus
H.L.	House of Lords Cases (England)
H. Lords	House of Lords (England)
HNIS	Human Nutrition Information Service
Hong Kong L.R.	Hong Kong Law Reports
How.	Howard's United States Supreme Court Reports
How. St. Trials	Howell's English State Trials
HUAC	House Un-American Activities Committee
HUD	Department of Housing and Urban Development
Hudson, Internatl. Legis.	Manley O. Hudson, ed., *International Legislation: A Collection of the Texts of Multipartite International Instruments of General Interest Beginning with the Covenant of the League of Nations* (1931)
Hudson, World Court Reps.	Manley Ottmer Hudson, ea., *World Court Reports* (1934-)
Hun	Hun's New York Supreme Court Reports
Hunt's Rept.	Bert L. Hunt, *Report of the American and Panamanian General Claims Arbitration* (1934)
IAEA	International Atomic Energy Agency
IALL	International Association of Law Libraries
IBA	International Bar Association
IBM	International Business Machines
ICBM	intercontinental ballistic missile
ICC	Interstate Commerce Commission
ICJ	International Court of Justice
ICM	Institute for Court Management
IDEA	Individuals with Disabilities Education Act, 1975
IDOP	International Dolphin Conservation Program
IEP	individualized educational program
IFC	International Finance Corporation

IGRA	Indian Gaming Regulatory Act, 1988
IJA	Institute of Judicial Administration
IJC	International Joint Commission
ILC	International Law Commission
ILD	International Labor Defense
Ill. Dec.	Illinois Decisions
ILO	International Labor Organization
IMF	International Monetary Fund
INA	Immigration and Nationality Act
IND	investigational new drug
INF Treaty	Intermediate-Range Nuclear Forces Treaty of 1987
INS	Immigration and Naturalization Service
INTELSAT	International Telecommunications Satellite Organization
Interpol	International Criminal Police Organization
Int'l. Law Reps.	International Law Reports
Intl. Legal Mats.	International Legal Materials
IPDC	International Program for the Development of Communication
IPO	Intellectual Property Owners
IPP	independent power producer
IQ	intelligence quotient
I.R.	Irish Reports
IRA	individual retirement account; Irish Republican Army
IRCA	Immigration Reform and Control Act of 1986
IRS	Internal Revenue Service
ISO	independent service organization
ISP	Internet service provider
ISSN	International Standard Serial Numbers
ITA	International Trade Administration
ITI	Information Technology Integration
ITO	International Trade Organization
ITS	Information Technology Service
ITT	International Telephone and Telegraph Corporation
ITU	International Telecommunication Union
IUD	intrauterine device
IWC	International Whaling Commission
IWW	Industrial Workers of the World
JAGC	Judge Advocate General's Corps
JCS	Joint Chiefs of Staff
JDL	Jewish Defense League
JNOV	Judgment *non obstante veredicto* (judgment "nothing to recommend it") or (judgment "notwithstanding the verdict")
JOBS	Jobs Opportunity and Basic Skills
John. Ch.	Johnson's New York Chancery Reports
Johns.	Johnson's Reports (New York)
JP	justice of the peace
K.B.	King's Bench Reports (England)
KGB	Komitet Gosudarstvennoi Bezopasnosti (the State Security Committee for countries in the former Soviet Union)
KKK	Ku Klux Klan
KMT	Kuomintang
LAD	Law Against Discrimination
LAPD	Los Angeles Police Department
LC	Library of Congress
LCHA	Longshoremen's and Harbor Workers Compensation Act of 1927
LD50	lethal dose 50
LDEF	Legal Defense and Education Fund (NOW)

LDF	Legal Defense Fund, Legal Defense and Educational Fund of the NAACP
LEAA	Law Enforcement Assistance Administration
L.Ed.	Lawyers' Edition Supreme Court Reports
LLC	Limited Liability Company
LLP	Limited Liability Partnership
LMSA	Labor-Management Services Administration
LNTS	League of Nations Treaty Series
Lofft's Rep.	Lofft's English King's Bench Reports
L.R.	Law Reports (English)
LSAC	Law School Admission Council
LSAS	Law School Admission Service
LSAT	Law School Aptitude Test
LSC	Legal Services Corporation; Legal Services for Children
LSD	lysergic acid diethylamide
LSDAS	Law School Data Assembly Service
LTBT	Limited Test Ban Treaty
LTC	Long Term Care
MAD	mutual assured destruction
MADD	Mothers against Drunk Driving
MALDEF	Mexican American Legal Defense and Educational Fund
Malloy	William M. Malloy, ed., *Treaties, Conventions International Acts, Protocols, and Agreements between the United States of America and Other Powers* (1910-38)
Martens	Georg Friedrich von Martens, ea., *Noveau recueil ge'neral de traites et autres act es relatifs azlx rapports de droit international* (Series I, 20 vols. [1843-75]; Series II, 35 vols. [1876-1908]; Series III [1909-])
Mass.	Massachusetts Reports
MCC	Metropolitan Correctional Center
MCH	Maternal and Child Health Bureau
Md. App.	Maryland, Appeal Cases
M.D. Ga.	Middle District, Georgia
Mercy	Movement Ensuring the Right to Choose for Yourself
Metc.	Metcalf's Massachusetts Reports
MFDP	Mississippi Freedom Democratic party
MGT	management
MHSS	Military Health Services System
Miller	David Hunter Miller, ea., *Treaties and Other International Acts of the United States America* (1931-1948)
Minn.	Minnesota Reports
MINS	minors in need of supervision
MIRV	multiple independently targetable reentry vehicle
MIRVed ICBM	Multiple Independently Targetable Reentry Vehicled Intercontinental Ballistic Missile
Misc.	Miscellaneous Reports, New York
Mixed Claims Comm., Report of Decs	Mixed Claims Commission, United States and Germany, Report of Decisions
MJ.	Military Justice Reporter
MLAP	Migrant Legal Action Program
MLB	Major League Baseball
MLDP	Mississippi Loyalist Democratic party
MMI	Moslem Mosque, Incorporated
MMPA	Marine Mammal Protection Act of 1972
Mo.	Missouri Reports
MOD	Masters of Deception
Mod.	Modern Reports, English King's Bench, etc.
Moore, Dig. Intl. Law	John Bassett Moore, *A Digest of International Law*, 8 vols. (1906)

Moore, Intl. Arbs.	John Bassett Moore, *History and Digest of the International Arbitrations to Which United States Has Been a Party*, 6 vols. (1898)
Morison	William Maxwell Morison, *The Scots Revised Report: Morison's Dictionary of Decisions* (1908-09)
M.P.	member of Parliament
MPAA	Motion Picture Association of America
MPAS	Michigan Protection and Advocacy Service
mpg	miles per gallon
MPPDA	Motion Picture Producers and Distributors of America
MPRSA	Marine Protection, Research, and Sanctuaries Act of 1972
M.R.	Master of the Rolls
MS-DOS	Microsoft Disk Operating System
MSHA	Mine Safety and Health Administration
MSSA	Military Selective Service Act
N/A	Not Available
NAACP	National Association for the Advancement of Colored People
NAAQS	National Ambient Air Quality Standards
NAB	National Association of Broadcasters
NABSW	National Association of Black Social Workers
NAFTA	North American Free Trade Agreement, 1993
NALA	National Association of Legal Assistants
NAM	National Association of Manufacturers
NAR	National Association of Realtors
NARAL	National Abortion and Reproductive Rights Action League
NARF	Native American Rights Fund
NARS	National Archives and Record Service
NASA	National Aeronautics and Space Administration
NASD	National Association of Securities Dealers
NATO	North Atlantic Treaty Organization
NAVINFO	Navy Information Offices
NAWSA	National American Woman's Suffrage Association
NBA	National Bar Association; National Basketball Association
NBC	National Broadcasting Company
NBLSA	National Black Law Student Association
NBS	National Bureau of Standards
NCA	Noise Control Act; National Command Authorities
NCAA	National Collegiate Athletic Association
NCAC	National Coalition against Censorship
NCCB	National Consumer Cooperative Bank
NCE	Northwest Community Exchange
NCF	National Chamber Foundation
NCIP	National Crime Insurance Program
NCJA	National Criminal Justice Association
NCLB	National Civil Liberties Bureau
NCP	national contingency plan
NCSC	National Center for State Courts
NCUA	National Credit Union Administration
NDA	new drug application
N.D. Ill.	Northern District, Illinois
NDU	National Defense University
N.D. Wash.	Northern District, Washington
N.E.	North Eastern Reporter
N.E. 2d	North Eastern Reporter, Second Series
NEA	National Endowment for the Arts; National Education Association
NEH	National Endowment for the Humanities
NEPA	National Environmental Protection Act; National Endowment Policy Act

NET Act	No Electronic Theft Act
NFIB	National Federation of Independent Businesses
NFIP	National Flood Insurance Program
NFPA	National Federation of Paralegal Associations
NGLTF	National Gay and Lesbian Task Force
NHRA	Nursing Home Reform Act, 1987
NHTSA	National Highway Traffic Safety Administration
Nielsen's Rept.	Frederick Kenelm Melsen, *American and British Claims Arbitration under the Special Agreement Concluded between the United States and Great Britain, August 18, 1910* (1926)
NIEO	New International Economic Order
NIGC	National Indian Gaming Commission
NIH	National Institutes of Health
NIJ	National Institute of Justice
NIRA	National Industrial Recovery Act of 1933; National Industrial Recovery Administration
NIST	National Institute of Standards and Technology
NITA	National Telecommunications and Information Administration
NJ.	New Jersey Reports
N.J. Super.	New Jersey Superior Court Reports
NLRA	National Labor Relations Act
NLRB	National Labor Relations Board
NMFS	National Marine Fisheries Service
No.	Number
NOAA	National Oceanic and Atmospheric Administration
NOI	Nation of Islam
NORML	National Organization for the Reform of Marijuana Laws
North Carolina A&T	North Carolina Agricultural and Technical College
NOW	National Organization for Women
NOW LDEF	National Organization for Women Legal Defense and Education Fund
NOW/PAC	National Organization for Women Political Action Committee
NPDES	National Pollutant Discharge Elimination System
NPL	national priorities list
NPR	National Public Radio
NPT	Nuclear Non-Proliferation Treaty of 1970
NRA	National Rifle Association; National Recovery Act
NRC	Nuclear Regulatory Commission
NRLC	National Right to Life Committee
NRTA	National Retired Teachers Association
NSI	Network Solutions, Inc.
NSC	National Security Council
NSCLC	National Senior Citizens Law Center
NSF	National Science Foundation
NSFNET	National Science Foundation Network
NTIA	National Telecommunications and Information Administration
NTID	National Technical Institute for the Deaf
NTIS	National Technical Information Service
NTS	Naval Telecommunications System
NTSB	National Transportation Safety Board
NVRA	National Voter Registration Act
N.W.	North Western Reporter
N.W. 2d	North Western Reporter, Second Series
NWSA	National Woman Suffrage Association
N.Y.	New York Court of Appeals Reports
N.Y. 2d	New York Court of Appeals Reports, Second Series
N.Y.S.	New York Supplement Reporter

N.Y.S. 2d	New York Supplement Reporter, Second Series
NYSE	New York Stock Exchange
NYSLA	New York State Liquor Authority
N.Y. Sup.	New York Supreme Court Reports
NYU	New York University
OAAU	Organization of Afro American Unity
OAP	Office of Administrative Procedure
OAS	Organization of American States
OASDI	Old-age, Survivors, and Disability Insurance Benefits
OASHDS	Office of the Assistant Secretary for Human Development Services
OCC	Office of Comptroller of the Currency
OCED	Office of Comprehensive Employment Development
OCHAMPUS	Office of Civilian Health and Medical Program of the Uniformed Services
OCSE	Office of Child Support Enforcement
OEA	Organizaci&acuteo;n de los Estados Americanos
OEM	Original Equipment Manufacturer
OFCCP	Office of Federal Contract Compliance Programs
OFPP	Office of Federal Procurement Policy
OICD	Office of International Cooperation and Development
OIG	Office of the Inspector General
OJARS	Office of Justice Assistance, Research, and Statistics
OMB	Office of Management and Budget
OMPC	Office of Management, Planning, and Communications
ONP	Office of National Programs
OPD	Office of Policy Development
OPEC	Organization of Petroleum Exporting Countries
OPIC	Overseas Private Investment Corporation
Ops. Atts. Gen.	Opinions of the Attorneys-General of the United States
Ops. Comms.	Opinions of the Commissioners
OPSP	Office of Product Standards Policy
O.R.	Ontario Reports
OR	Official Records
OSHA	Occupational Safety and Health Act
OSHRC	Occupational Safety and Health Review Commission
OSM	Office of Surface Mining
OSS	Office of Strategic Services
OST	Office of the Secretary
OT	Office of Transportation
OTA	Office of Technology Assessment
OTC	over-the-counter
OTS	Office of Thrift Supervisors
OUI	operating under the influence
OWBPA	Older Workers Benefit Protection Act
OWRT	Office of Water Research and Technology
P.	Pacific Reporter
P. 2d	Pacific Reporter, Second Series
PAC	political action committee
Pa. Oyer and Terminer	Pennsylvania Oyer and Terminer Reports
PATCO	Professional Air Traffic Controllers Organization
PBGC	Pension Benefit Guaranty Corporation
PBS	Public Broadcasting Service; Public Buildings Service
P.C.	Privy Council (English Law Reports)
PC	personal computer; politically correct
PCBs	polychlorinated biphenyls
PCIJ	Permanent Court of International Justice Series A-Judgments and Orders (1922-30)

Series B-Advisory Opinions (1922-30)

Series A/B-Judgments, Orders, and Advisory Opinions (1931-40)

Series C-Pleadings, Oral Statements, and Documents relating to Judgments and Advisory Opinions (1923-42)

Series D-Acts and Documents concerning the Organization of the World Court (1922 -47)

Series E-Annual Reports (1925-45)

PCP	Phencyclidine
P.D.	Probate Division, English Law Reports (1876-1890)
PDA	Pregnancy Discrimination Act of 1978
PD & R	Policy Development and Research
Pepco	Potomac Electric Power Company
Perm. Ct. of Arb.	Permanent Court of Arbitration
PES	Post-Enumeration Survey
Pet.	Peters' United States Supreme Court Reports
PETA	People for the Ethical Treatment of Animals
PGA	Professional Golfers Association
PGM	Program
PHA	Public Housing Agency
Phila. Ct. of Oyer and Terminer	Philadelphia Court of Oyer and Terminer
PHS	Public Health Service
PIC	Private Industry Council
PICJ	Permanent International Court of Justice
Pick.	Pickering's Massachusetts Reports
PIK	Payment in Kind
PINS	persons in need of supervision
PIRG	Public Interest Research Group
P.L.	Public Laws
PLAN	Pro-Life Action Network
PLI	Practicing Law Institute
PLLP	Professional Limited Liability Partnership
PLO	Palestine Liberation Organization
PLRA	Prison Litigation Reform Act of 1995
PNET	Peaceful Nuclear Explosions Treaty
PONY	Prostitutes of New York
POW-MIA	prisoner of war-missing in action
Pratt	Frederic Thomas Pratt, *Law of Contraband of War, with a Selection of Cases from Papers of the Right Honourable Sir George Lee* (1856)
PRIDE	Prostitution to Independence, Dignity, and Equality
Proc.	Proceedings
PRP	potentially responsible party
PSRO	Professional Standards Review Organization
PTO	Patents and Trademark Office
PURPA	Public Utilities Regulatory Policies Act
PUSH	People United to Serve Humanity
PUSH-Excel	PUSH for Excellence
PWA	Public Works Administration
PWSA	Ports and Waterways Safety Act of 1972
Q.B.	Queen's Bench (England)
QTIP	Qualified Terminable Interest Property
Ralston's Rept.	Jackson Harvey Ralston, ed., *Venezuelan Arbitrations of 1903* (1904)
RC	Regional Commissioner
RCRA	Resource Conservation and Recovery Act
RCWP	Rural Clean Water Program
RDA	Rural Development Administration
REA	Rural Electrification Administration

Rec. des Decs. des Trib. Arb.Mixtes	G. Gidel, ed., *Recueil des decisions des tribunaux arbitraux mixtes, institués par les traités de paix* (1922-30)
Redmond	Vol. 3 of Charles I. Bevans, *Treaties and Other International Agreements of the United States of America, 1776-1949* (compiled by C. F. Redmond) (1969)
RESPA	Real Estate Settlement Procedure Act of 1974
RFC	Reconstruction Finance Corporation
RFRA	Religious Freedom Restoration Act of 1993
RICO	Racketeer Influenced and Corrupt Organizations
RNC	Republican National Committee
Roscoe	Edward Stanley Roscoe, ed., *Reports of Prize Cases Determined in the High Court Admiralty before the Lords Commissioners of Appeals in Prize Causes and before the judicial Committee of the Privy Council from 1745 to 1859* (1905)
ROTC	Reserve Officers' Training Corps
RPP	Representative Payee Program
R.S.	Revised Statutes
RTC	Resolution Trust Corp.
RUDs	reservations, understandings, and declarations
Ryan White CARE Act	Ryan White Comprehensive AIDS Research Emergency Act of 1990
SAC	Strategic Air Command
SACB	Subversive Activities Control Board
SADD	Students against Drunk Driving
SAF	Student Activities Fund
SAIF	Savings Association Insurance Fund
SALT	Strategic Arms Limitation Talks
SALT I	Strategic Arms Limitation Talks of 1969-72
SAMHSA	Substance Abuse and Mental Health Services Administration
Sandf.	Sandford's New York Superior Court Reports
S and L	savings and loan
SARA	Superfund Amendment and Reauthorization Act
SAT	Scholastic Aptitude Test
Sawy.	Sawyer's United States Circuit Court Reports
SBA	Small Business Administration
SBI	Small Business Institute
SCCC	South Central Correctional Center
SCLC	Southern Christian Leadership Conference
Scott's Repts.	James Brown Scott, ed., *The Hague Court Reports*, 2 vols. (1916-32)
SCS	Soil Conservation Service; Social Conservative Service
SCSEP	Senior Community Service Employment Program
S.Ct.	Supreme Court Reporter
S.D. Cal.	Southern District, California
S.D. Fla.	Southern District, Florida
S.D. Ga.	Southern District, Georgia
SDI	Strategic Defense Initiative
S.D. Me.	Southern District, Maine
S.D.N.Y.	Southern District, New York
SDS	Students for a Democratic Society
S.E.	South Eastern Reporter
S.E. 2d	South Eastern Reporter, Second Series
SEA	Science and Education Administration
SEATO	Southeast Asia Treaty Organization
SEC	Securities and Exchange Commission
Sec.	Section
SEEK	Search for Elevation, Education and Knowledge
SEOO	State Economic Opportunity Office
SEP	simplified employee pension plan

Ser.	Series
Sess.	Session
SGLI	Servicemen's Group Life Insurance
SIP	state implementation plan
SLA	Symbionese Liberation Army
SLAPPs	Strategic Lawsuits Against Public Participation
SLBM	submarine-launched ballistic missile
SNCC	Student Nonviolent Coordinating Committee
So.	Southern Reporter
So. 2d	Southern Reporter, Second Series
SPA	Software Publisher's Association
Spec. Sess.	Special Session
SRA	Sentencing Reform Act of 1984
SS	Schutzstaffel (German for Protection Echelon)
SSA	Social Security Administration
SSI	Supplemental Security Income
START I	Strategic Arms Reduction Treaty of 1991
START II	Strategic Arms Reduction Treaty of 1993
Seat.	United States Statutes at Large
STS	Space Transportation Systems
St. Tr.	State Trials, English
STURAA	Surface Transportation and Uniform Relocation Assistance Act of 1987
Sup. Ct. of Justice, Mexico	Supreme Court of Justice, Mexico
Supp.	Supplement
S.W.	South Western Reporter
S.W.	2d South Western Reporter, Second Series
SWAPO	South-West Africa People's Organization
SWAT	Special Weapons and Tactics
SWP	Socialist Workers party
TDP	Trade and Development Program
Tex. Sup.	Texas Supreme Court Reports
THAAD	Theater High-Altitude Area Defense System
THC	tetrahydrocannabinol
TI	Tobacco Institute
TIA	Trust Indenture Act of 1939
TIAS	Treaties and Other International Acts Series (United States)
TNT	trinitrotoluene
TOP	Targeted Outreach Program
TPUS	Transportation and Public Utilities Service
TQM	Total Quality Management
Tripartite Claims Comm., Decs. And Ops.	Tripartite Claims Commission (United States, Austria, and Hungary), Decisions and Opinions
TRI-TAC	Joint Tactical Communications
TRO	temporary restraining order
TS	Treaty Series, United States
TSCA	Toxic Substance Control Act
TSDs	transporters, storers, and disposers
TSU	Texas Southern University
TTBT	Threshold Test Ban Treaty
TV	Television
TVA	Tennessee Valley Authority
TWA	Trans World Airlines
UAW	United Auto Workers; United Automobile, Aerospace, and Agricultural Implements Workers of America
U.C.C.	Uniform Commercial Code; Universal Copyright Convention

U.C.C.C.	Uniform Consumer Credit Code
UCCJA	Uniform Child Custody Jurisdiction Act
UCMJ	Uniform Code of Military Justice
UCPP	Urban Crime Prevention Program
UCS	United Counseling Service
UDC	United Daughters of the Confederacy
UFW	United Farm Workers
UHF	ultrahigh frequency
UIFSA	Uniform Interstate Family Support Act
UIS	Unemployment Insurance Service
UMDA	Uniform Marriage and Divorce Act
UMTA	Urban Mass Transportation Administration
U.N.	United Nations
UNCITRAL	United Nations Commission on International Trade Law
UNCTAD	United Nations Conference on Trade and Development
UN Doc.	United Nations Documents
UNDP	United Nations Development Program
UNEF	United Nations Emergency Force
UNESCO	United Nations Educational, Scientific, and Cultural Organization
UNICEF	United Nations Children's Fund
UNIDO	United Nations Industrial and Development Organization
Unif. L. Ann.	Uniform Laws Annotated
UN Repts. Intl. Arb. Awards	United Nations Reports of International Arbitral Awards
UNTS	United Nations Treaty Series
UPI	United Press International
URESA	Uniform Reciprocal Enforcement of Support Act
U.S.A.	United States of America
USAF	United States Air Force
USF	U.S. Forestry Service
U.S. App. D.C.	United States Court of Appeals for the District of Columbia
U.S.C.	United States Code; University of Southern California
U.S.C.A.	United States Code Annotated
U.S.C.C.A.N.	United States Code Congressional and Administrative News
USCMA	United States Court of Military Appeals
USDA	U.S. Department of Agriculture
USES	United States Employment Service
USFA	United States Fire Administration
USICA	International Communication Agency, United States
USMS	U.S. Marshals Service
USSC	U.S. Sentencing Commission
U.S.S.R.	Union of Soviet Socialist Republics
UST	United States Treaties
USTS	United States Travel Service
v.	versus
VA	Veterans Administration
VAR	Veterans Affairs and Rehabilitation Commission
VAWA	Violence Against Women Act
VFW	Veterans of Foreign Wars
VGLI	Veterans Group Life Insurance
Vict.	Queen Victoria (Great Britain)
VIN	vehicle identification number
VISTA	Volunteers in Service to America
VJRA	Veterans Judicial Review Act of 1988
V.L.A.	Volunteer Lawyers for the Arts
VMI	Virginia Military Institute
VMLI	Veterans Mortgage Life Insurance

VOCAL	Victims of Child Abuse Laws
VRA	Voting Rights Act
WAC	Women's Army Corps
Wall.	Wallace's United States Supreme Court Reports
Wash. 2d	Washington Reports, Second Series
WAVES	Women Accepted for Volunteer Service
WCTU	Women's Christian Temperance Union
W.D. Wash.	Western District, Washington
W.D. Wis.	Western District, Wisconsin
WEAL	West's Encyclopedia of American Law, Women's Equity Action League
Wend.	Wendell's New York Reports
WFSE	Washington Federation of State Employees
Wheat.	Wheaton's United States Supreme Court Reports
Wheel. Cr. Cases	Wheeler's New York Criminal Cases
WHISPER	Women Hurt in Systems of Prostitution Engaged in Revolt
Whiteman	Marjorie Millace Whiteman, *Digest of International Law*, 15 vols. (1963-73)
WHO	World Health Organization
WIC	Women, Infants, and Children program
Will. and Mar.	King William and Queen Mary (Great Britain)
WIN	WESTLAW Is Natural; Whip Inflation Now; Work Incentive Program
WIPO	World Intellectual Property Organization
WIU	Workers' Industrial Union
W.L.R.	Weekly Law Reports, England
WPA	Works Progress Administration
WPPDA	Welfare and Pension Plans Disclosure Act
WTO	World Trade Organization
WWI	World War I
WWII	World War II
Yates Sel. Cas.	Yates' New York Select Cases
YWCA	Young Women's Christian Association

INDEX